Little Lulu®

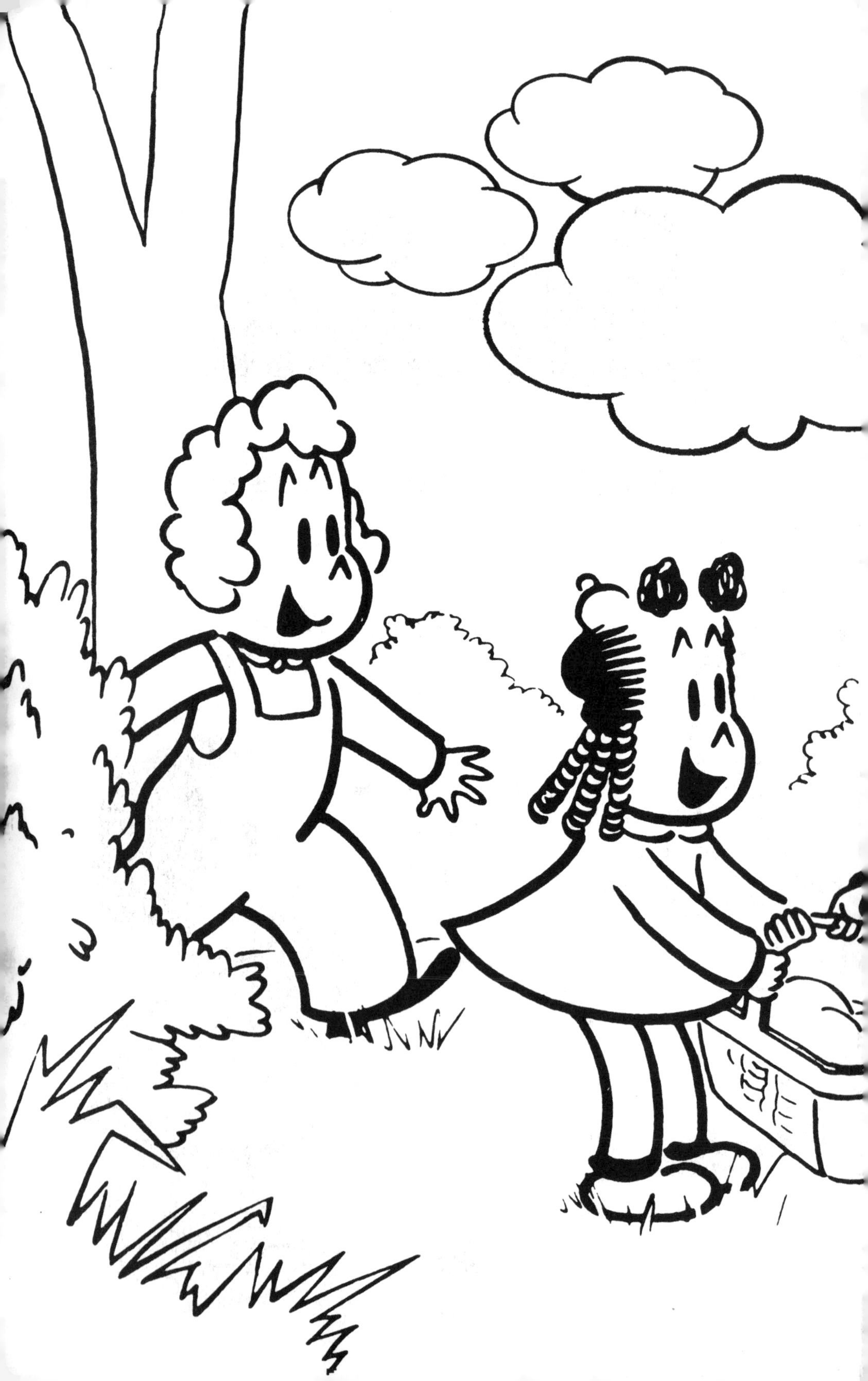

Little Lulu®

My Dinner with Lulu

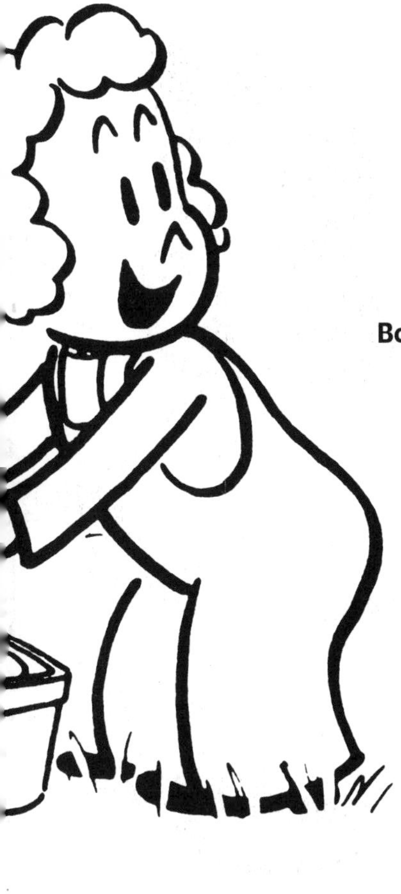

Story and Art
John Stanley
and
Irving Tripp

Based on the character
created by
Marge Buell

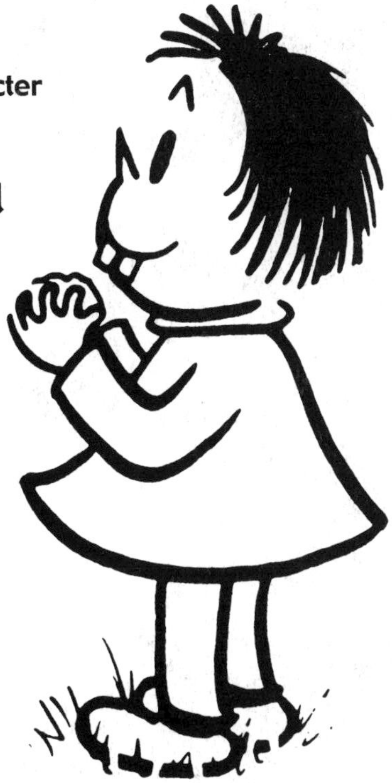

DARK HORSE BOOKS™

Publisher
Mike Richardson

Editor
Shawna Gore

Editorial Assistant
Gina Gagliano

Collection Designer
Debra Bailey

Art Director
Lia Ribacchi

Published by
Dark Horse Books
A division of Dark Horse Comics, Inc.
10956 SE Main Street
Milwaukie, OR 97222

First edition: April 2005
ISBN: 1-59307-318-6

1 3 5 7 9 10 8 6 4 2
Printed in Canada

A note about Lulu

Little Lulu came into the world through the pen of cartoonist Marjorie "Marge" Henderson Buell in 1935. Originally commissioned as a series of single-panel cartoons by *The Saturday Evening Post*, Lulu took the world by storm with her charm, smarts, and sass. Within ten years, she not only was the star of her own cartoon series, but a celebrity spokesgirl for a variety of high-profile commercial products.

Little Lulu truly hit her stride as America's sweetheart in the comic books published by Dell Comics starting in 1945. While Buell was solely responsible for Lulu's original single-panel shenanigans, the comic-book stories were put into the able hands of comics legend John Stanley. Stanley wrote and laid out the comics while artist Irving Tripp provided the finished drawings. After a number of trial appearances in Dell Comics, Lulu's appeal was undeniable, and she was granted her very own comic-book series, called *Marge's Little Lulu*, which was published regularly through 1984.

This volume contains every comics story from Dell Comics issues 74, 97, 110, 115, and 120.

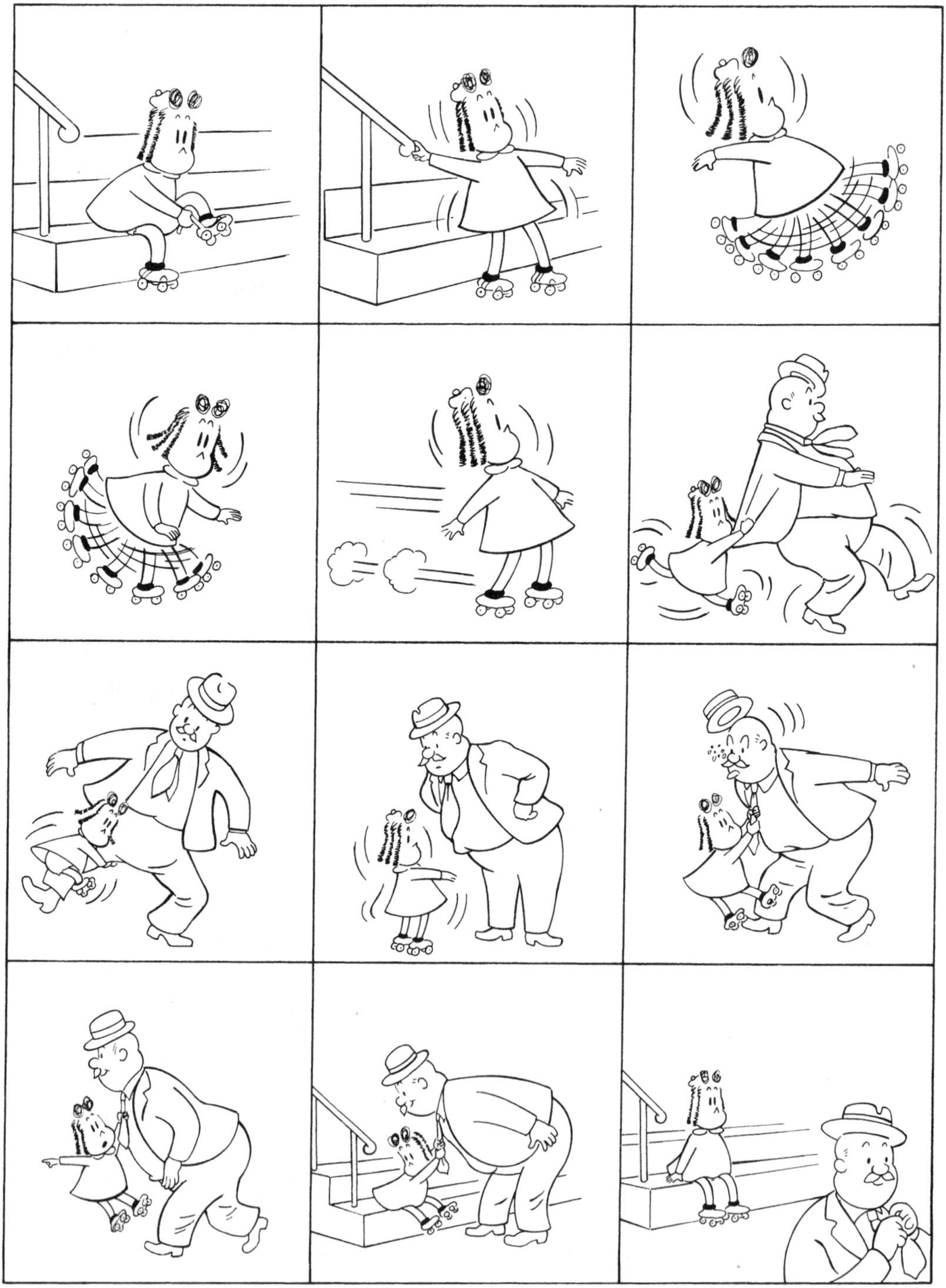

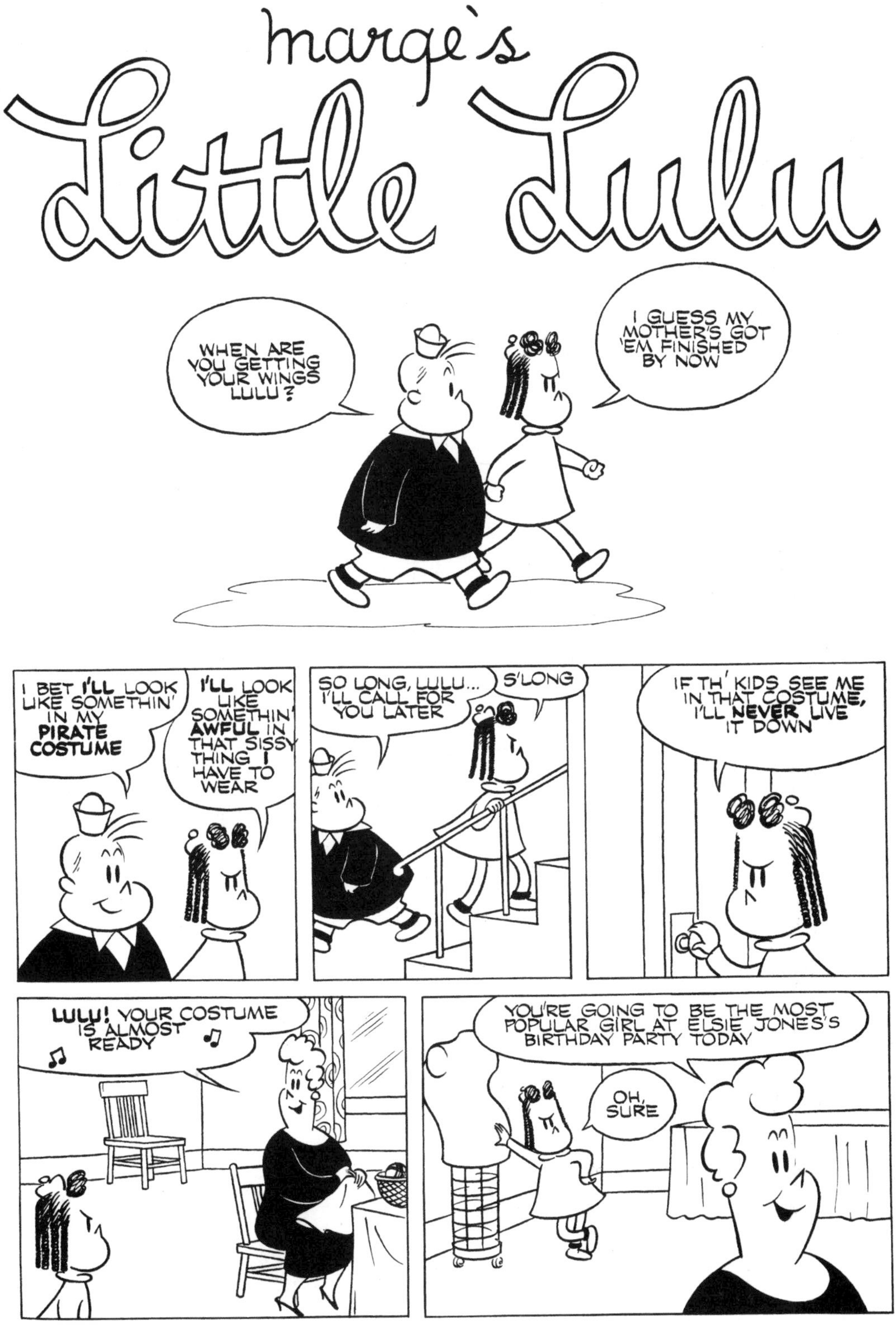
marge's
Little Lulu
WHEN ARE YOU GETTING YOUR WINGS LULU?
I GUESS MY MOTHER'S GOT 'EM FINISHED BY NOW
I BET I'LL LOOK LIKE SOMETHIN' IN MY PIRATE COSTUME
I'LL LOOK LIKE SOMETHIN' AWFUL IN THAT SISSY THING I HAVE TO WEAR
SO LONG, LULU... I'LL CALL FOR YOU LATER
S'LONG
IF TH' KIDS SEE ME IN THAT COSTUME, I'LL NEVER LIVE IT DOWN
LULU! YOUR COSTUME IS ALMOST READY
YOU'RE GOING TO BE THE MOST POPULAR GIRL AT ELSIE JONES'S BIRTHDAY PARTY TODAY
OH, SURE

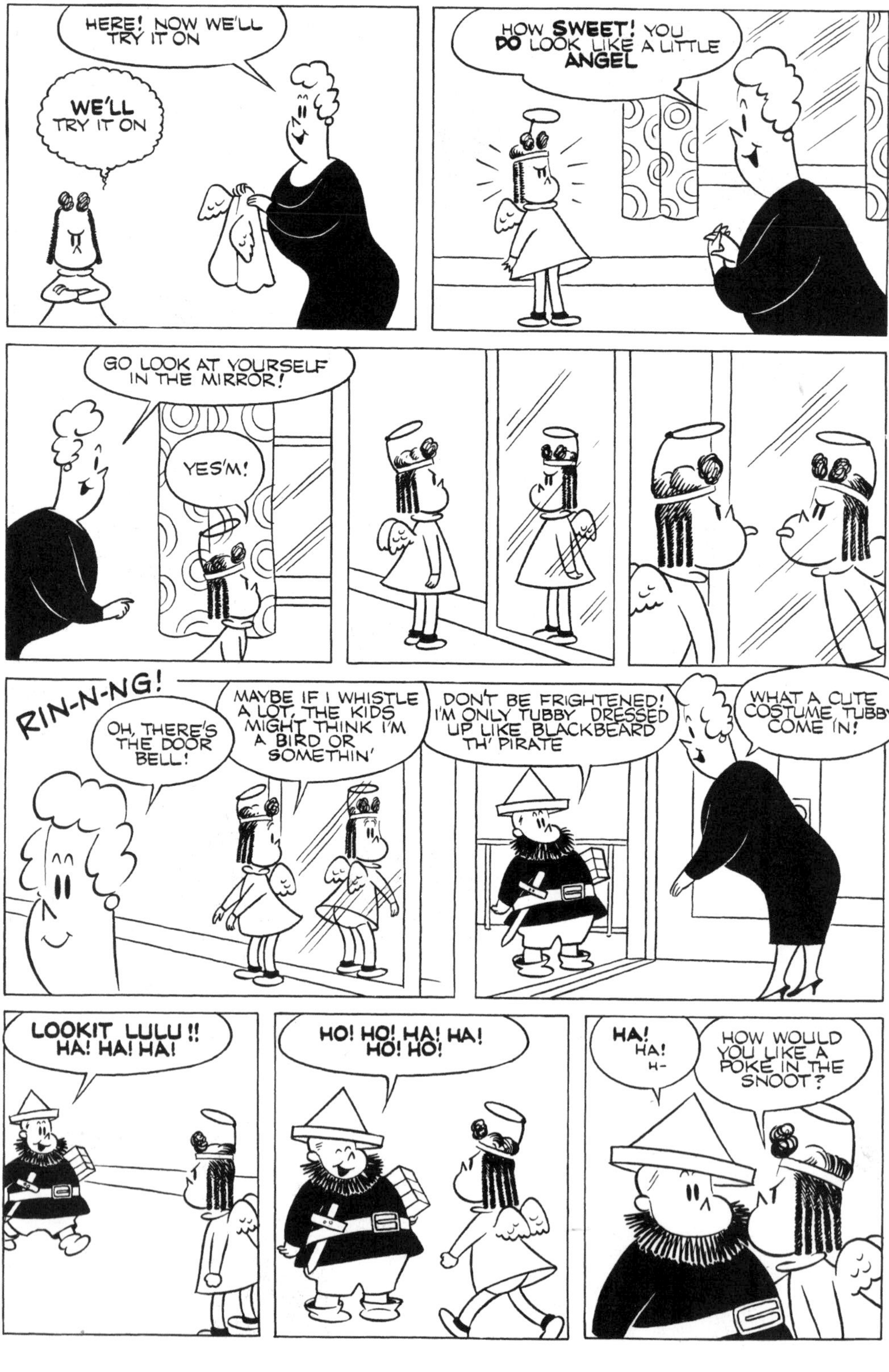

WE'LL TRY IT ON
HERE! NOW WE'LL TRY IT ON
HOW SWEET! YOU DO LOOK LIKE A LITTLE ANGEL
GO LOOK AT YOURSELF IN THE MIRROR!
YES'M!
RIN-N-NG!
OH, THERE'S THE DOOR BELL!
MAYBE IF I WHISTLE A LOT, THE KIDS MIGHT THINK I'M A BIRD OR SOMETHIN'
DON'T BE FRIGHTENED! I'M ONLY TUBBY DRESSED UP LIKE BLACKBEARD TH' PIRATE
WHAT A CUTE COSTUME, TUBBY... COME IN!
LOOKIT LULU !! HA! HA! HA!
HO! HO! HA! HA! HO! HO!
HA! HA! H-
HOW WOULD YOU LIKE A POKE IN THE SNOOT?

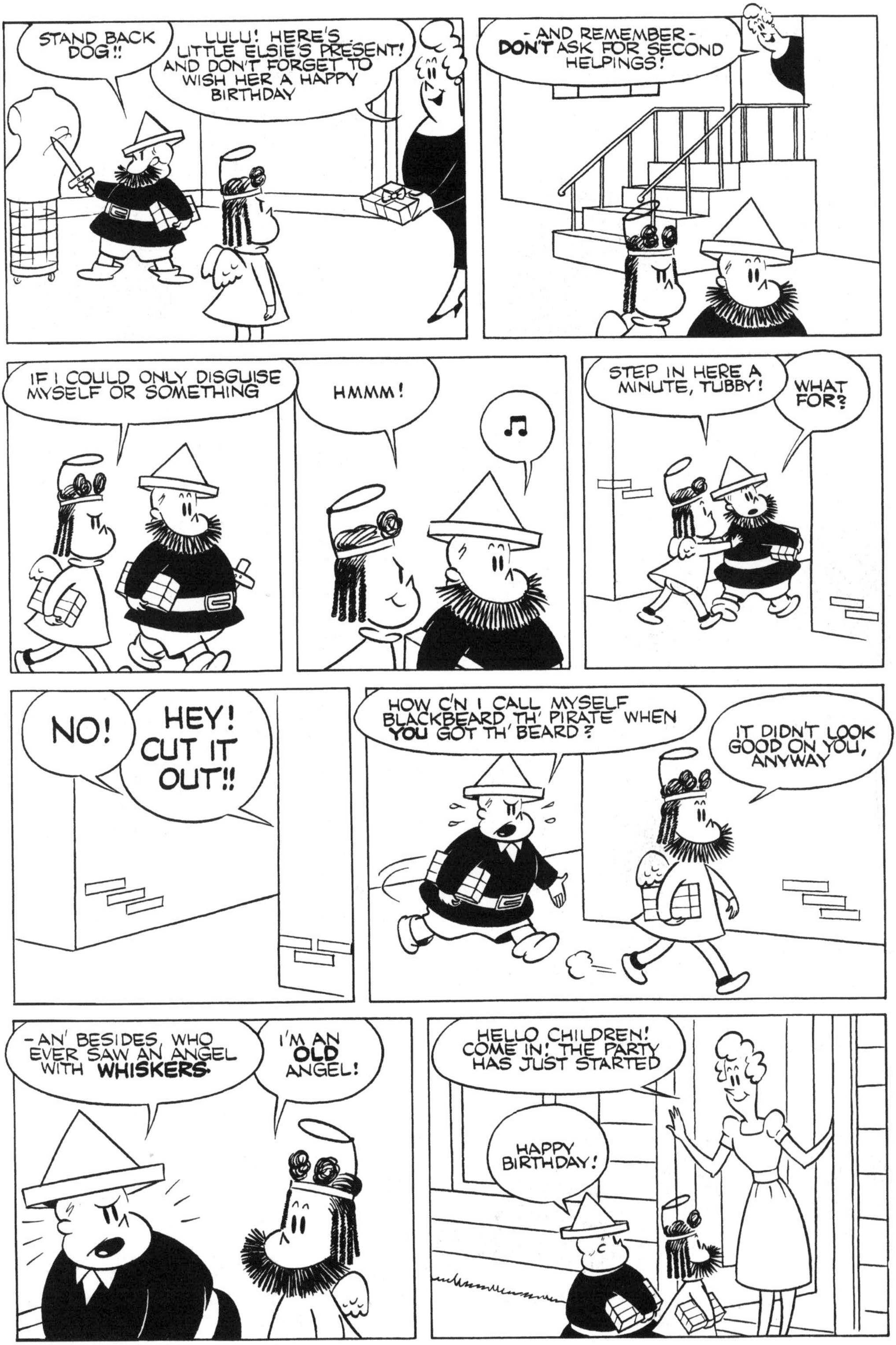
STAND BACK DOG!!
LULU! HERE'S LITTLE ELSIE'S PRESENT! AND DON'T FORGET TO WISH HER A HAPPY BIRTHDAY
- AND REMEMBER - **DON'T** ASK FOR SECOND HELPINGS!
IF I COULD ONLY DISGUISE MYSELF OR SOMETHING
HMMM!
♫
STEP IN HERE A MINUTE, TUBBY!
WHAT FOR?
NO!
HEY! CUT IT OUT!!
HOW C'N I CALL MYSELF BLACKBEARD TH' PIRATE WHEN **YOU** GOT TH' BEARD?
IT DIDN'T LOOK GOOD ON YOU, ANYWAY
- AN' BESIDES, WHO EVER SAW AN ANGEL WITH **WHISKERS**.
I'M AN **OLD** ANGEL!
HELLO CHILDREN! COME IN! THE PARTY HAS JUST STARTED
HAPPY BIRTHDAY!

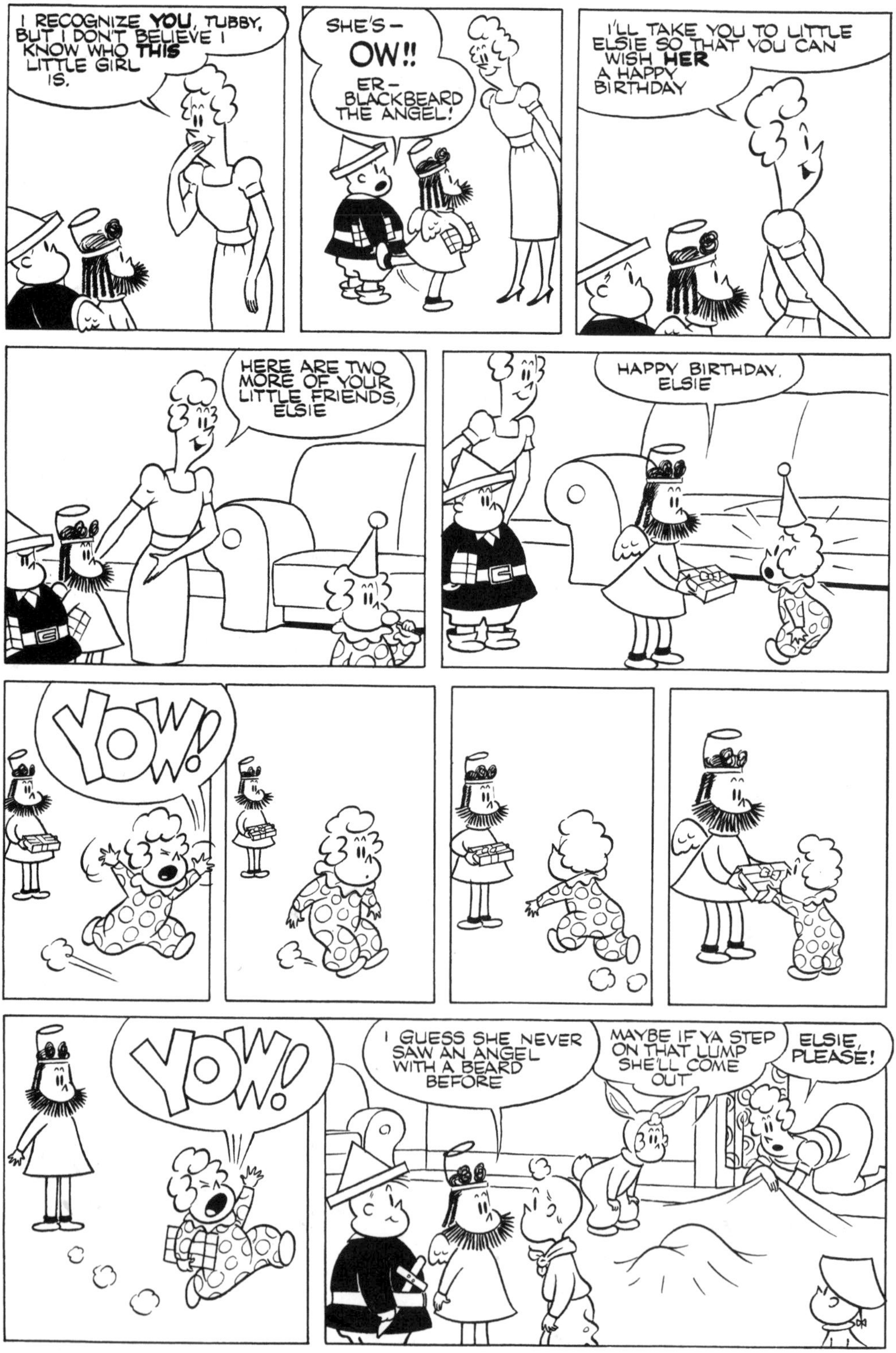
I RECOGNIZE **YOU**, TUBBY, BUT I DON'T BELIEVE I KNOW WHO **THIS** LITTLE GIRL IS.
SHE'S – OW!! ER– BLACKBEARD THE ANGEL!
I'LL TAKE YOU TO LITTLE ELSIE SO THAT YOU CAN WISH **HER** A HAPPY BIRTHDAY
HERE ARE TWO MORE OF YOUR LITTLE FRIENDS, ELSIE
HAPPY BIRTHDAY, ELSIE
YOW!
YOW!
I GUESS SHE NEVER SAW AN ANGEL WITH A BEARD BEFORE
MAYBE IF YA STEP ON THAT LUMP SHE'LL COME OUT
ELSIE, PLEASE!

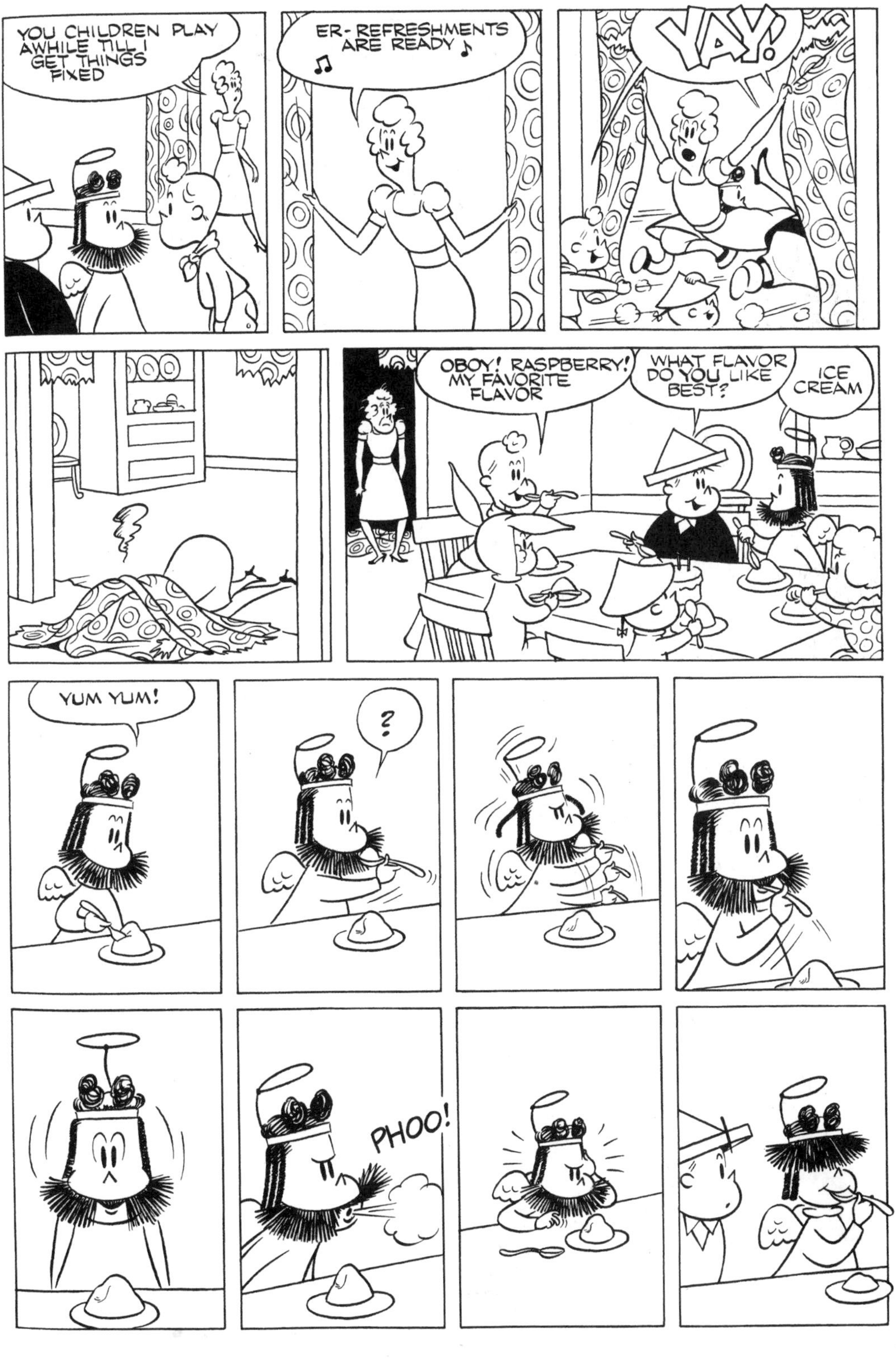
YOU CHILDREN PLAY AWHILE TILL I GET THINGS FIXED
ER-REFRESHMENTS ARE READY
YAY!
OBOY! RASPBERRY! MY FAVORITE FLAVOR
WHAT FLAVOR DO YOU LIKE BEST?
ICE CREAM
YUM YUM!
?
PHOO!

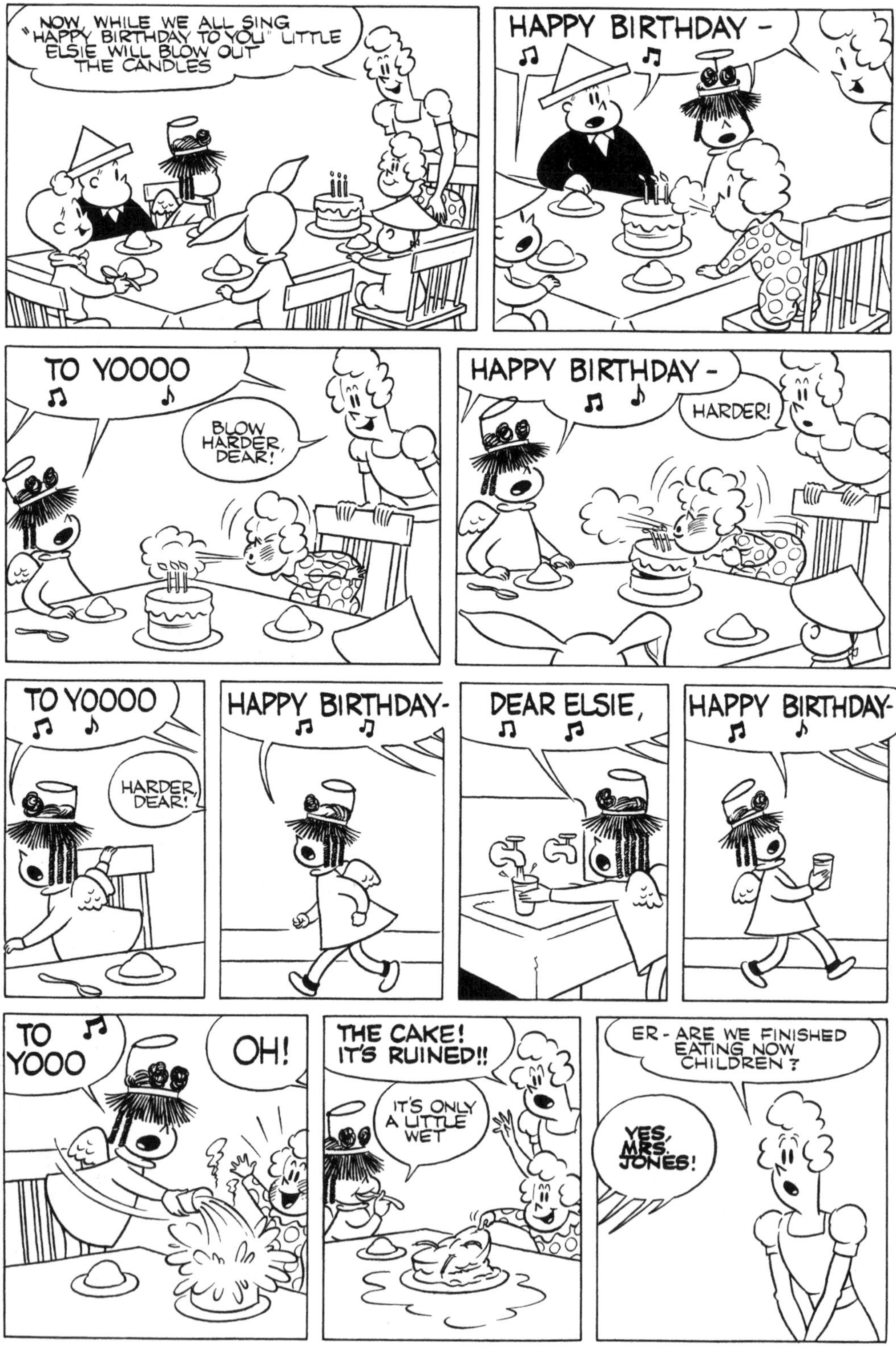
NOW, WHILE WE ALL SING "HAPPY BIRTHDAY TO YOU" LITTLE ELSIE WILL BLOW OUT THE CANDLES
HAPPY BIRTHDAY -
TO YOOOO
BLOW HARDER, DEAR!
HAPPY BIRTHDAY -
HARDER!
TO YOOOO
HARDER, DEAR!
HAPPY BIRTHDAY-
DEAR ELSIE,
HAPPY BIRTHDAY-
TO YOOO
OH!
THE CAKE! IT'S RUINED!!
IT'S ONLY A LITTLE WET
ER - ARE WE FINISHED EATING NOW CHILDREN ?
YES, MRS. JONES!

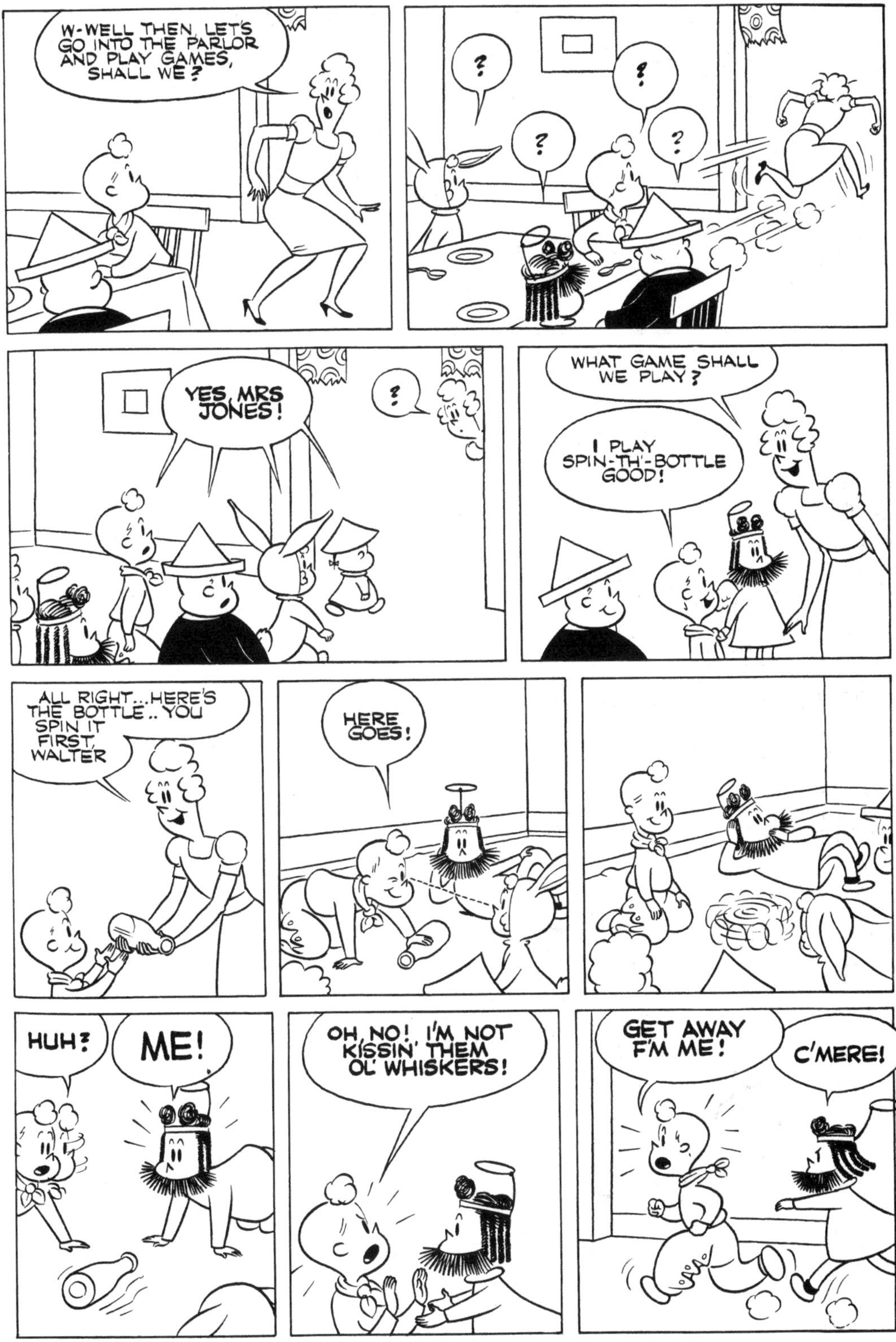
W-WELL THEN, LET'S GO INTO THE PARLOR AND PLAY GAMES, SHALL WE?
?
?
?
?
YES, MRS JONES!
?
WHAT GAME SHALL WE PLAY?
I PLAY SPIN-TH'-BOTTLE GOOD!
ALL RIGHT... HERE'S THE BOTTLE.. YOU SPIN IT FIRST, WALTER
HERE GOES!
HUH?
ME!
OH, NO! I'M NOT KISSIN' THEM OL' WHISKERS!
GET AWAY F'M ME!
C'MERE!

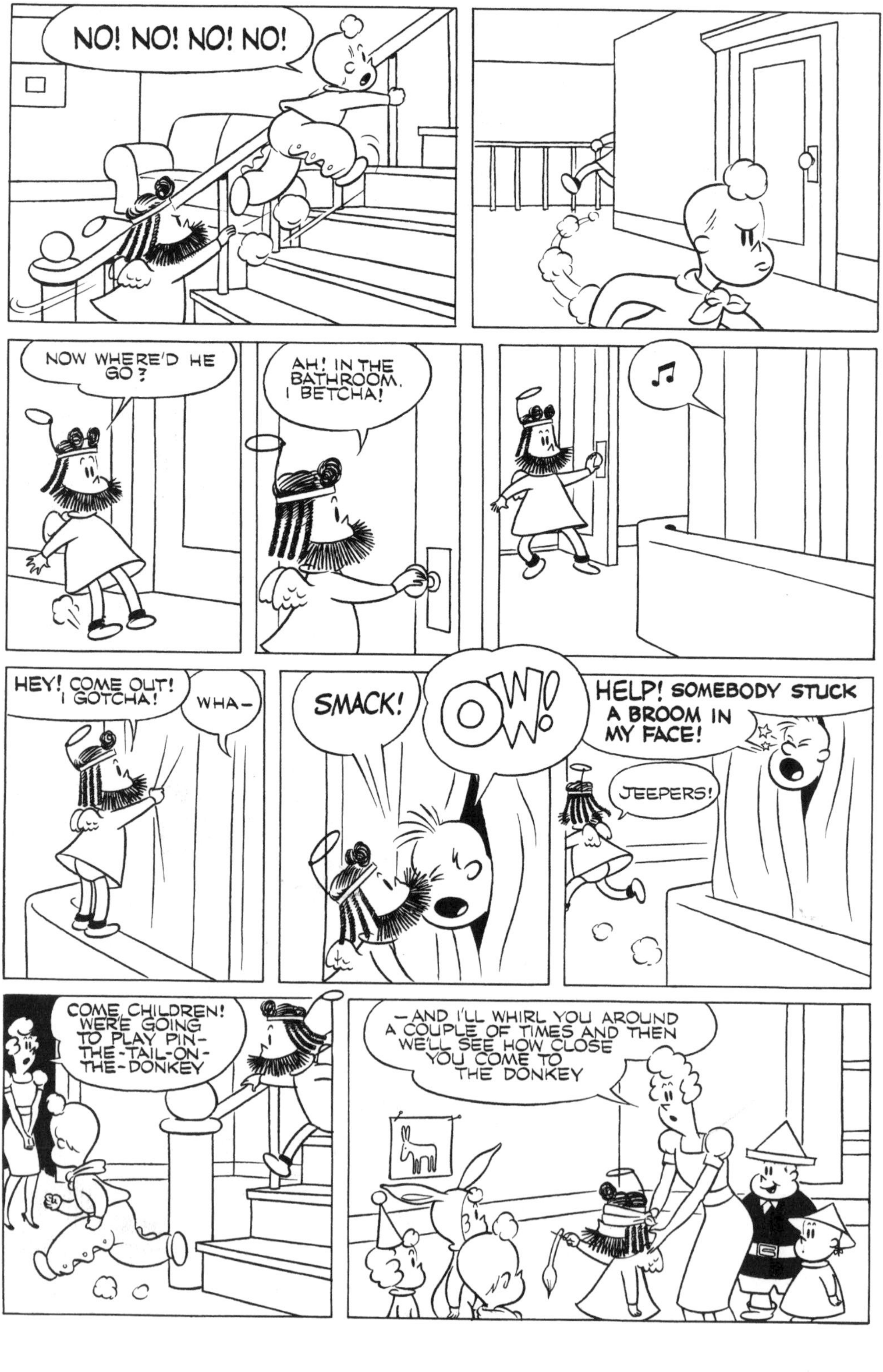
NO! NO! NO! NO!
NOW WHERE'D HE GO?
AH! IN THE BATHROOM, I BETCHA!
♪
HEY! COME OUT! I GOTCHA!
WHA—
SMACK!
OW!
HELP! SOMEBODY STUCK A BROOM IN MY FACE!
JEEPERS!
COME CHILDREN! WE'RE GOING TO PLAY PIN-THE-TAIL-ON-THE-DONKEY
—AND I'LL WHIRL YOU AROUND A COUPLE OF TIMES AND THEN WE'LL SEE HOW CLOSE YOU COME TO THE DONKEY

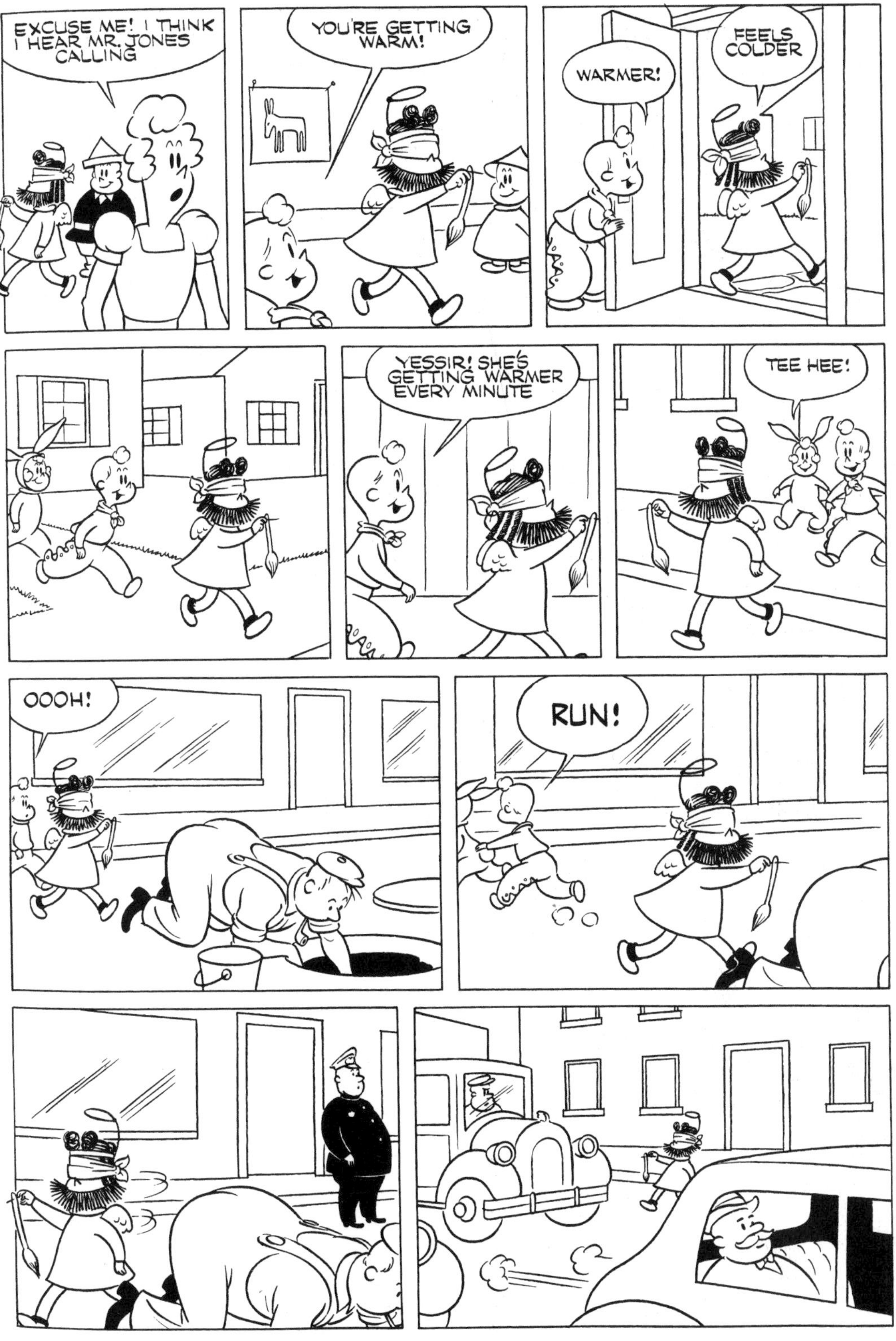
EXCUSE ME! I THINK I HEAR MR. JONES CALLING
YOU'RE GETTING WARM!
WARMER!
FEELS COLDER
YESSIR! SHE'S GETTING WARMER EVERY MINUTE
TEE HEE!
OOOH!
RUN!

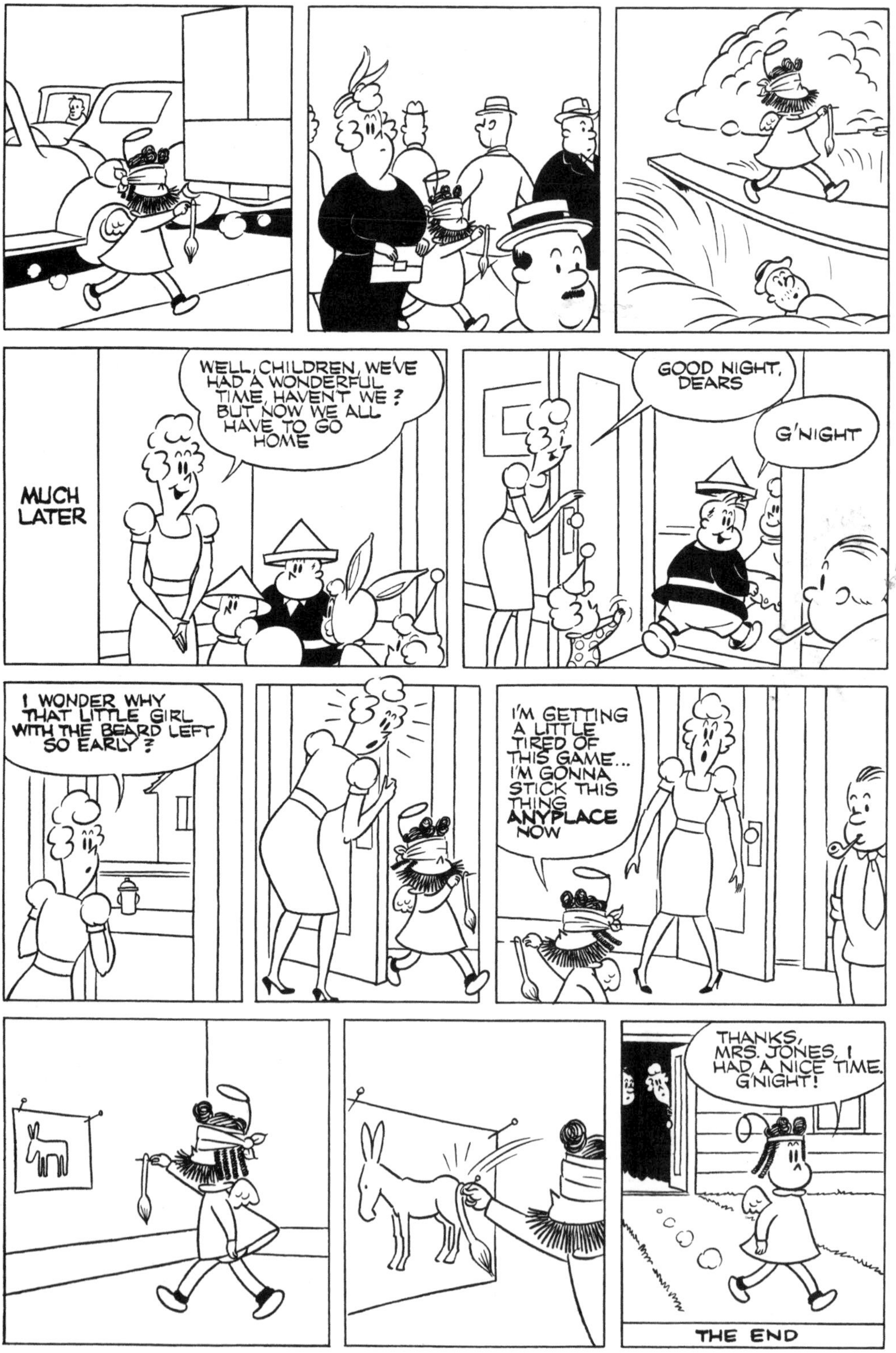
WELL, CHILDREN, WE'VE HAD A WONDERFUL TIME, HAVEN'T WE? BUT NOW WE ALL HAVE TO GO HOME
MUCH LATER
GOOD NIGHT, DEARS
G'NIGHT
I WONDER WHY THAT LITTLE GIRL WITH THE BEARD LEFT SO EARLY?
I'M GETTING A LITTLE TIRED OF THIS GAME... I'M GONNA STICK THIS THING ANYPLACE NOW
THANKS, MRS. JONES, I HAD A NICE TIME. G'NIGHT!
THE END

"A BONE TO PICK"

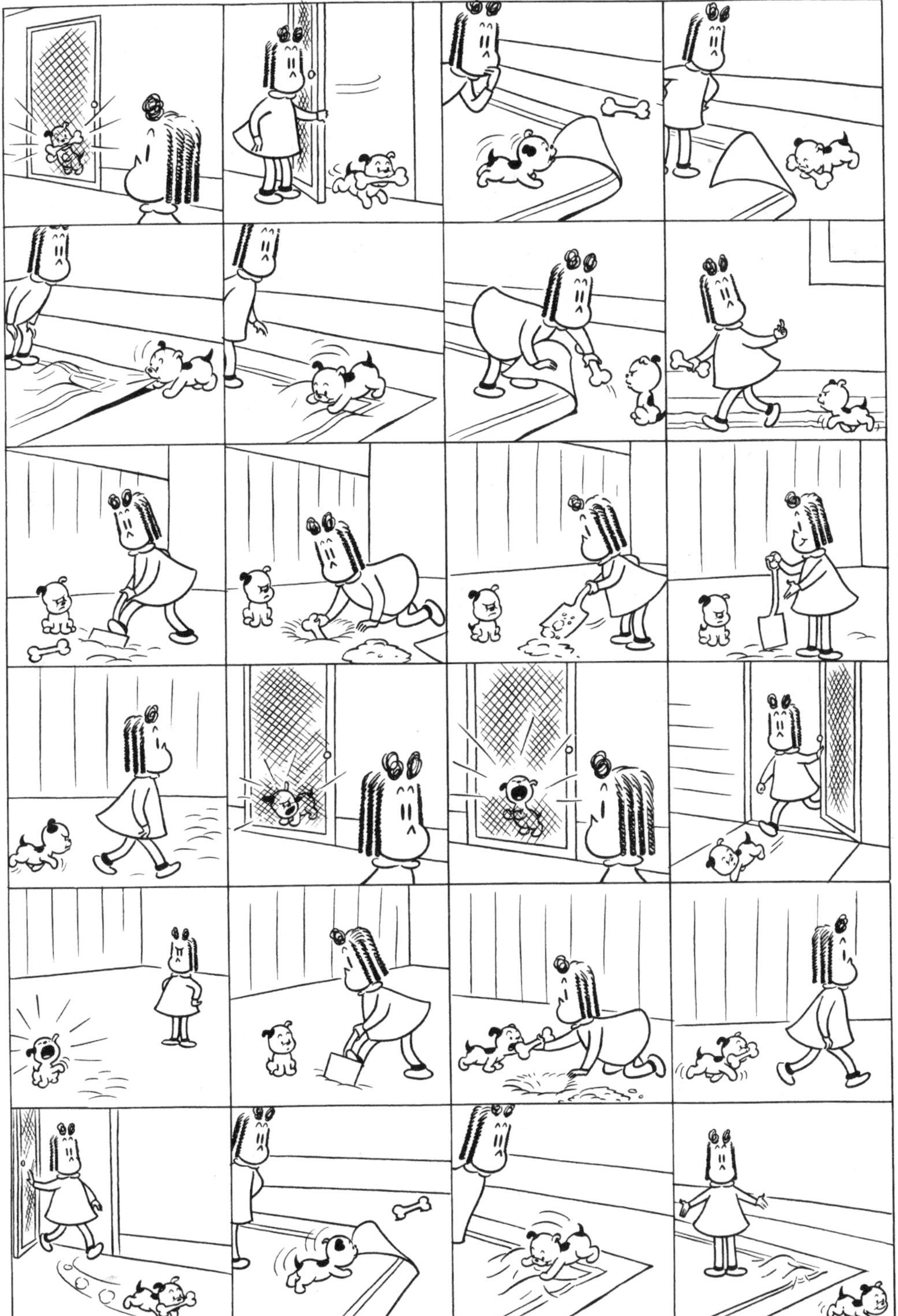

ONE, TWO, THREE, KICK!

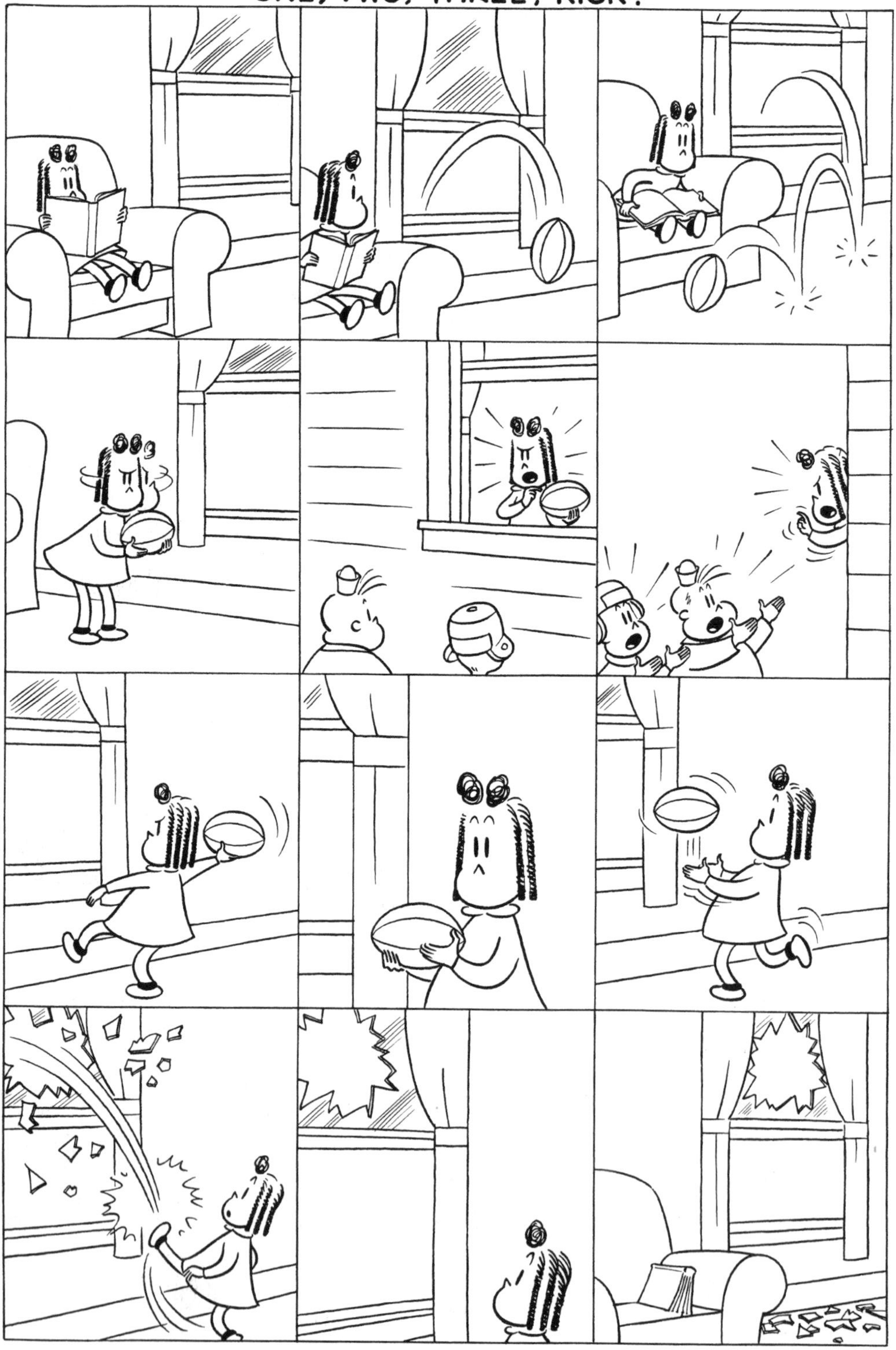

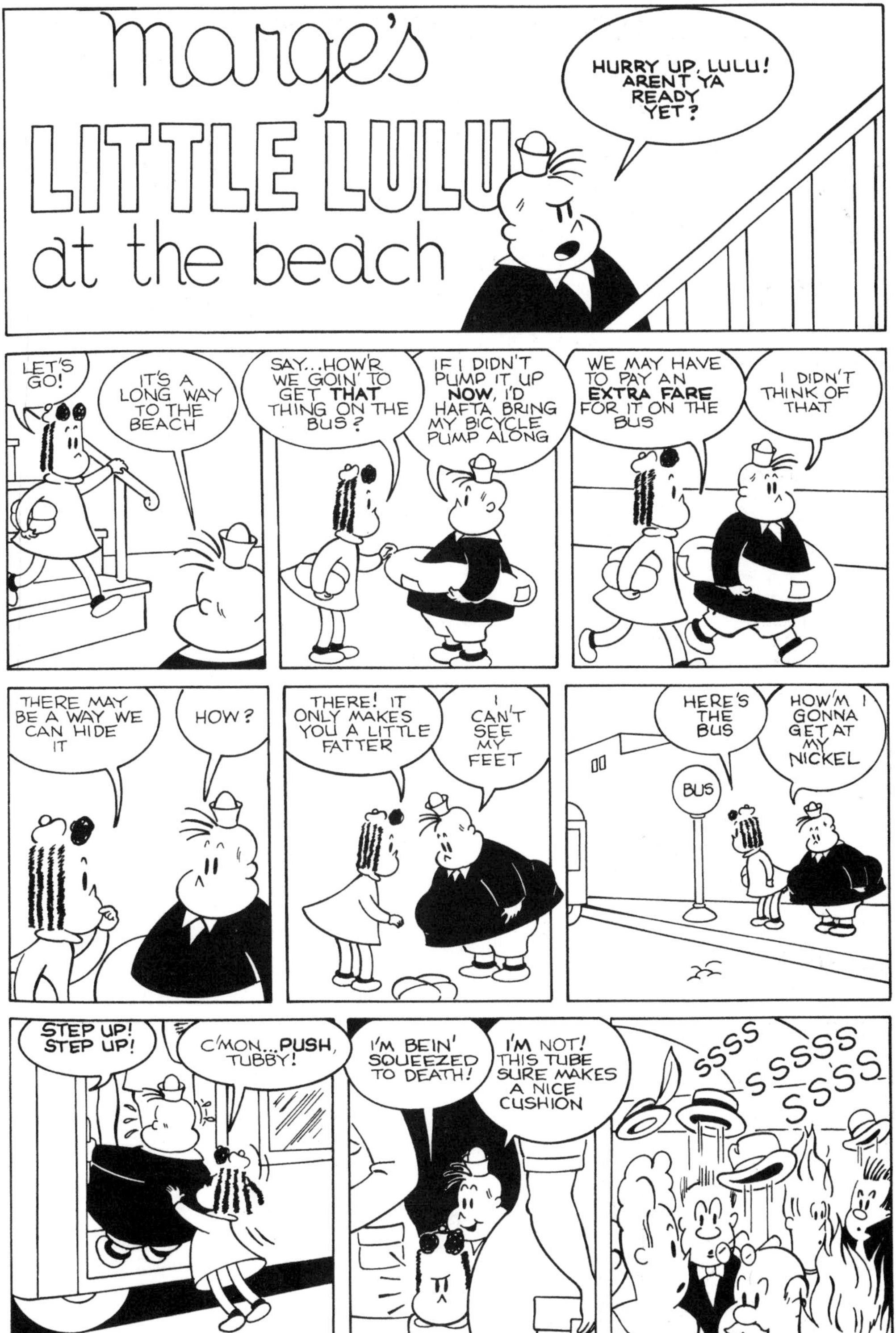
marge's
LITTLE LULU
at the beach
HURRY UP, LULU! AREN'T YA READY YET?
LET'S GO!
IT'S A LONG WAY TO THE BEACH
SAY...HOW'R WE GOIN' TO GET **THAT** THING ON THE BUS?
IF I DIDN'T PUMP IT UP **NOW**, I'D HAFTA BRING MY BICYCLE PUMP ALONG
WE MAY HAVE TO PAY AN **EXTRA FARE** FOR IT ON THE BUS
I DIDN'T THINK OF THAT
THERE MAY BE A WAY WE CAN HIDE IT
HOW?
THERE! IT ONLY MAKES YOU A LITTLE FATTER
I CAN'T SEE MY FEET
HERE'S THE BUS
HOW'M I GONNA GET AT MY NICKEL
BUS
STEP UP! STEP UP!
C'MON...**PUSH**, TUBBY!
I'M BEIN' SQUEEZED TO DEATH!
I'M NOT! THIS TUBE SURE MAKES A NICE CUSHION
SSSS SSSSS SSSS

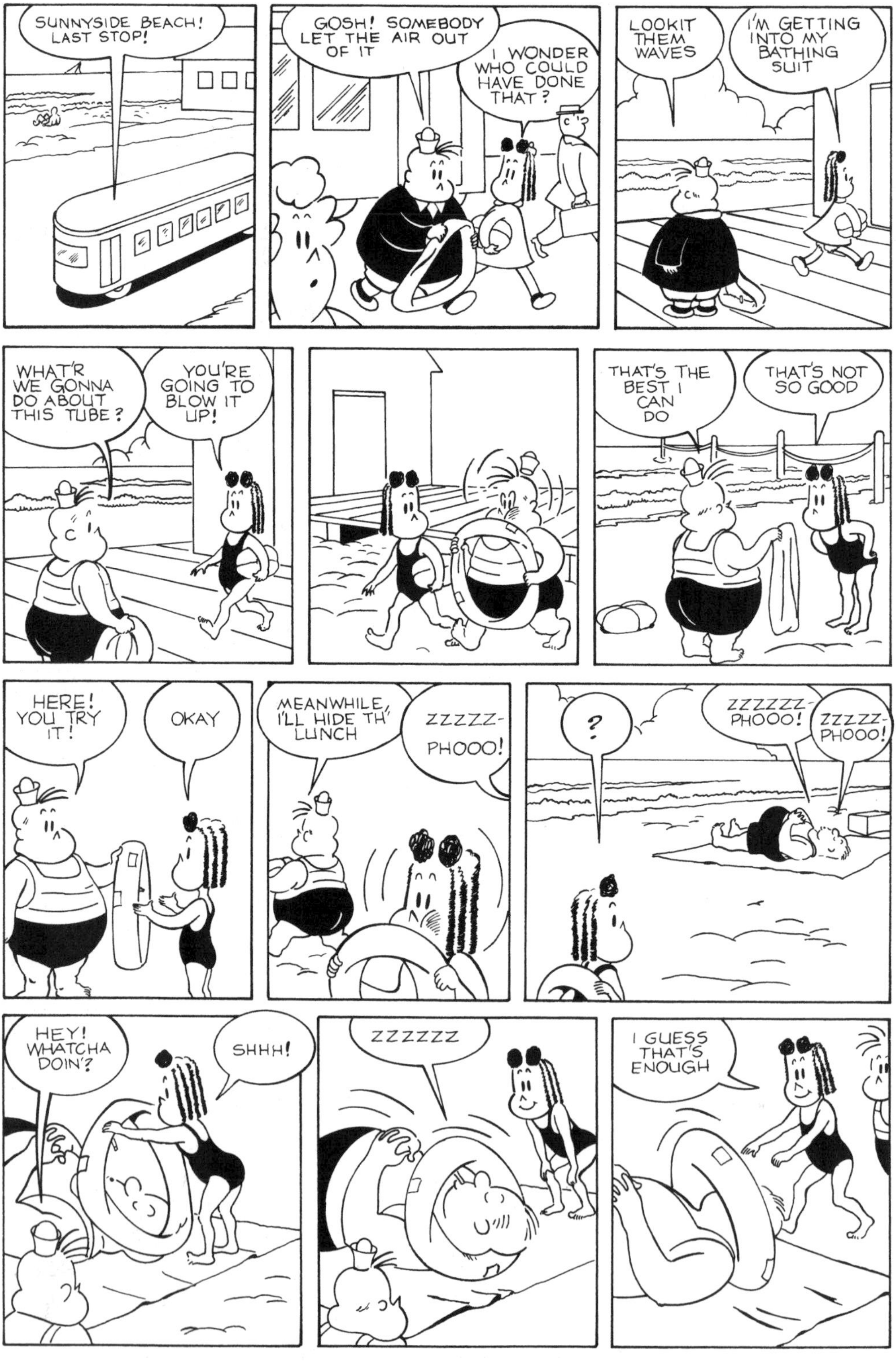
SUNNYSIDE BEACH! LAST STOP!
GOSH! SOMEBODY LET THE AIR OUT OF IT
I WONDER WHO COULD HAVE DONE THAT?
LOOKIT THEM WAVES
I'M GETTING INTO MY BATHING SUIT
WHAT'R WE GONNA DO ABOUT THIS TUBE?
YOU'RE GOING TO BLOW IT UP!
THAT'S THE BEST I CAN DO
THAT'S NOT SO GOOD
HERE! YOU TRY IT!
OKAY
MEANWHILE, I'LL HIDE TH' LUNCH
ZZZZZ-PHOOO!
?
ZZZZZZ-PHOOO!
ZZZZZ-PHOOO!
HEY! WHATCHA DOIN'?
SHHH!
ZZZZZZ
I GUESS THAT'S ENOUGH

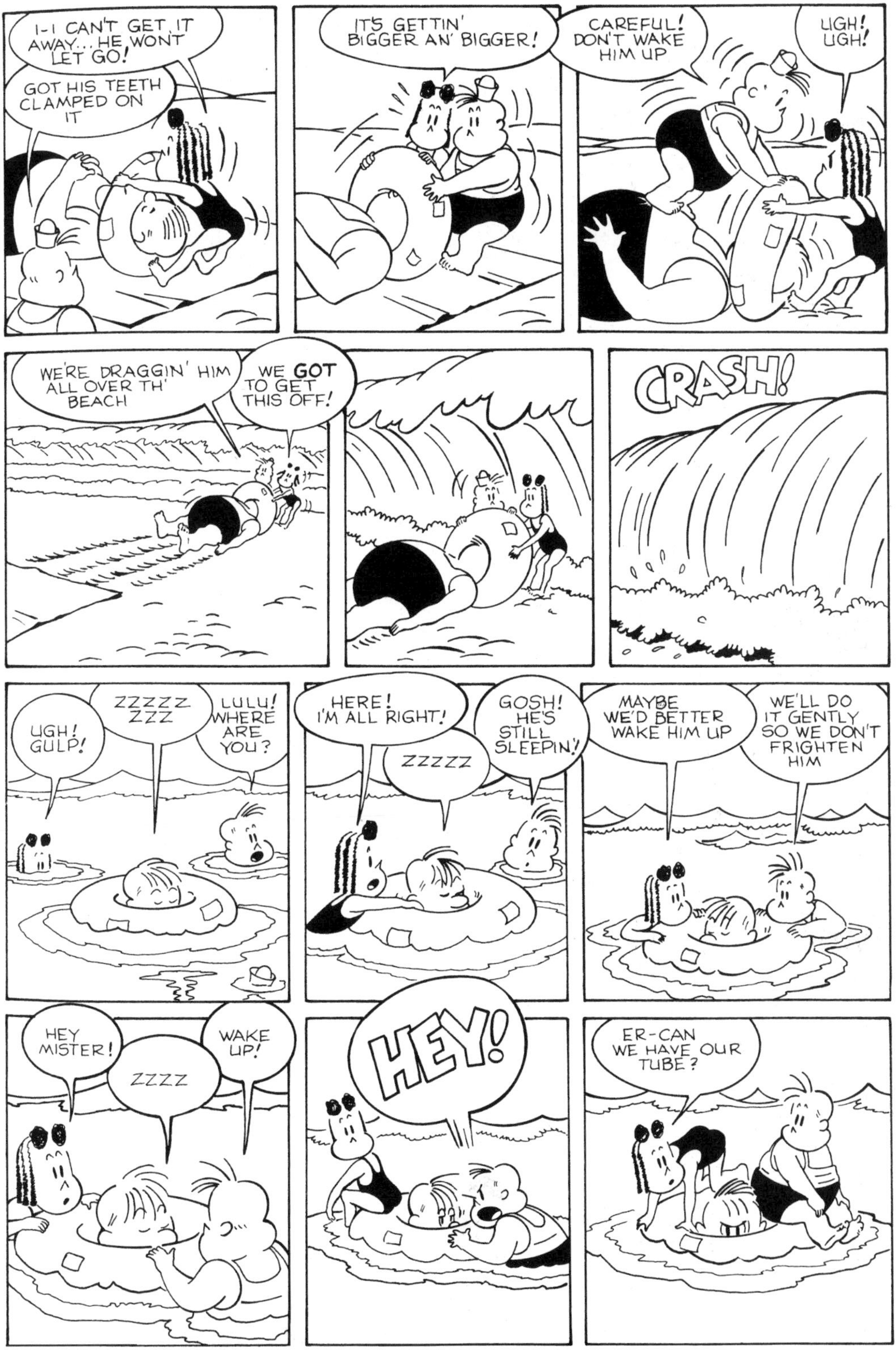
I-I CAN'T GET IT AWAY... HE WON'T LET GO!
GOT HIS TEETH CLAMPED ON IT
IT'S GETTIN' BIGGER AN' BIGGER!
CAREFUL! DON'T WAKE HIM UP
UGH! UGH!
WE'RE DRAGGIN' HIM ALL OVER TH' BEACH
WE GOT TO GET THIS OFF!
CRASH!
UGH! GULP!
ZZZZZ ZZZ
LULU! WHERE ARE YOU?
HERE! I'M ALL RIGHT!
ZZZZZ
GOSH! HE'S STILL SLEEPIN'!
MAYBE WE'D BETTER WAKE HIM UP
WE'LL DO IT GENTLY SO WE DON'T FRIGHTEN HIM
HEY MISTER!
ZZZZ
WAKE UP!
HEY!
ER-CAN WE HAVE OUR TUBE?

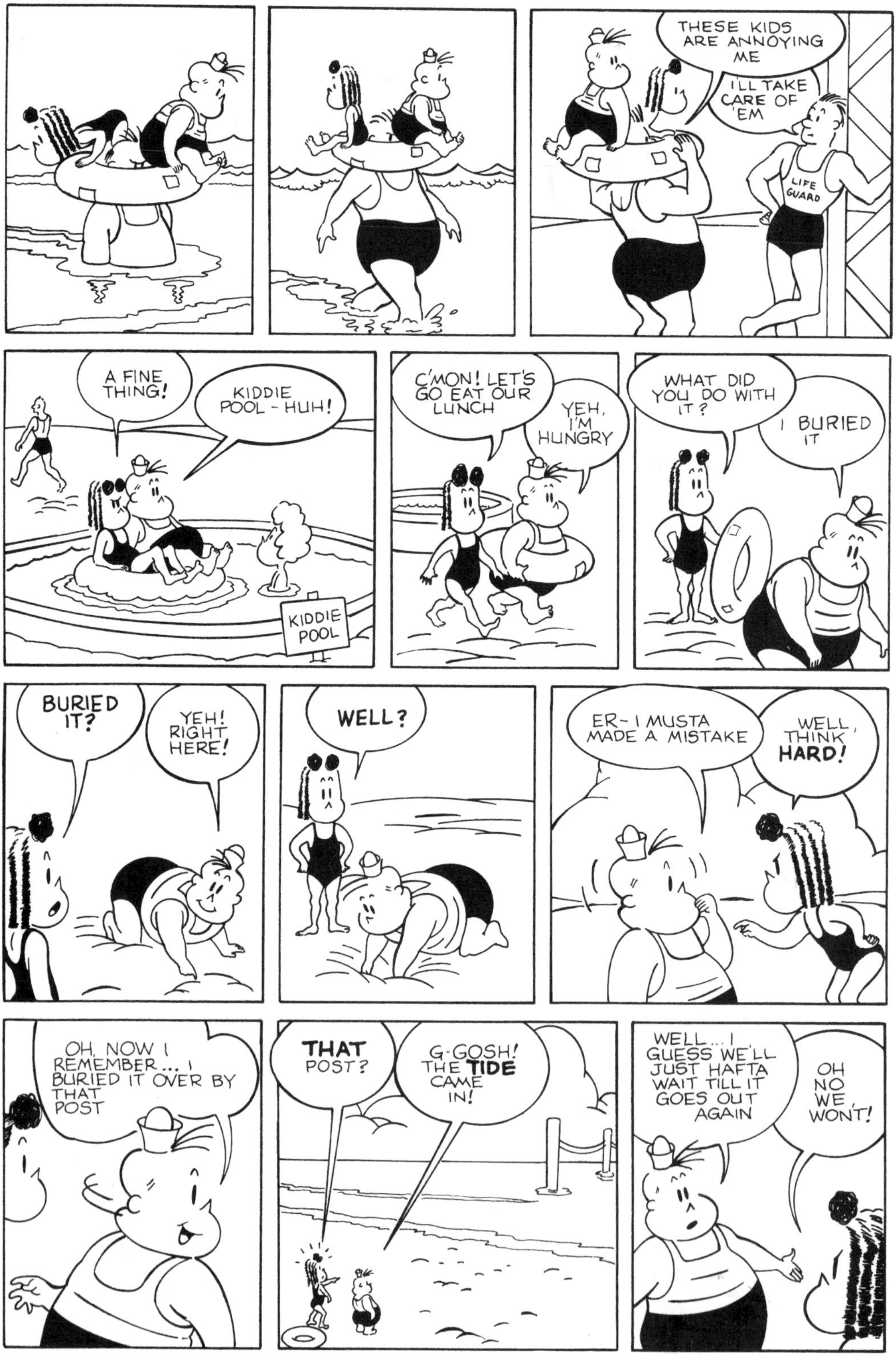
THESE KIDS ARE ANNOYING ME
I'LL TAKE CARE OF 'EM
LIFE GUARD
A FINE THING!
KIDDIE POOL - HUH!
KIDDIE POOL
C'MON! LET'S GO EAT OUR LUNCH
YEH, I'M HUNGRY
WHAT DID YOU DO WITH IT?
I BURIED IT
BURIED IT?
YEH! RIGHT HERE!
WELL?
ER- I MUSTA MADE A MISTAKE
WELL, THINK HARD!
OH, NOW I REMEMBER... I BURIED IT OVER BY THAT POST
THAT POST?
G-GOSH! THE TIDE CAME IN!
WELL... I GUESS WE'LL JUST HAFTA WAIT TILL IT GOES OUT AGAIN
OH NO WE WON'T!

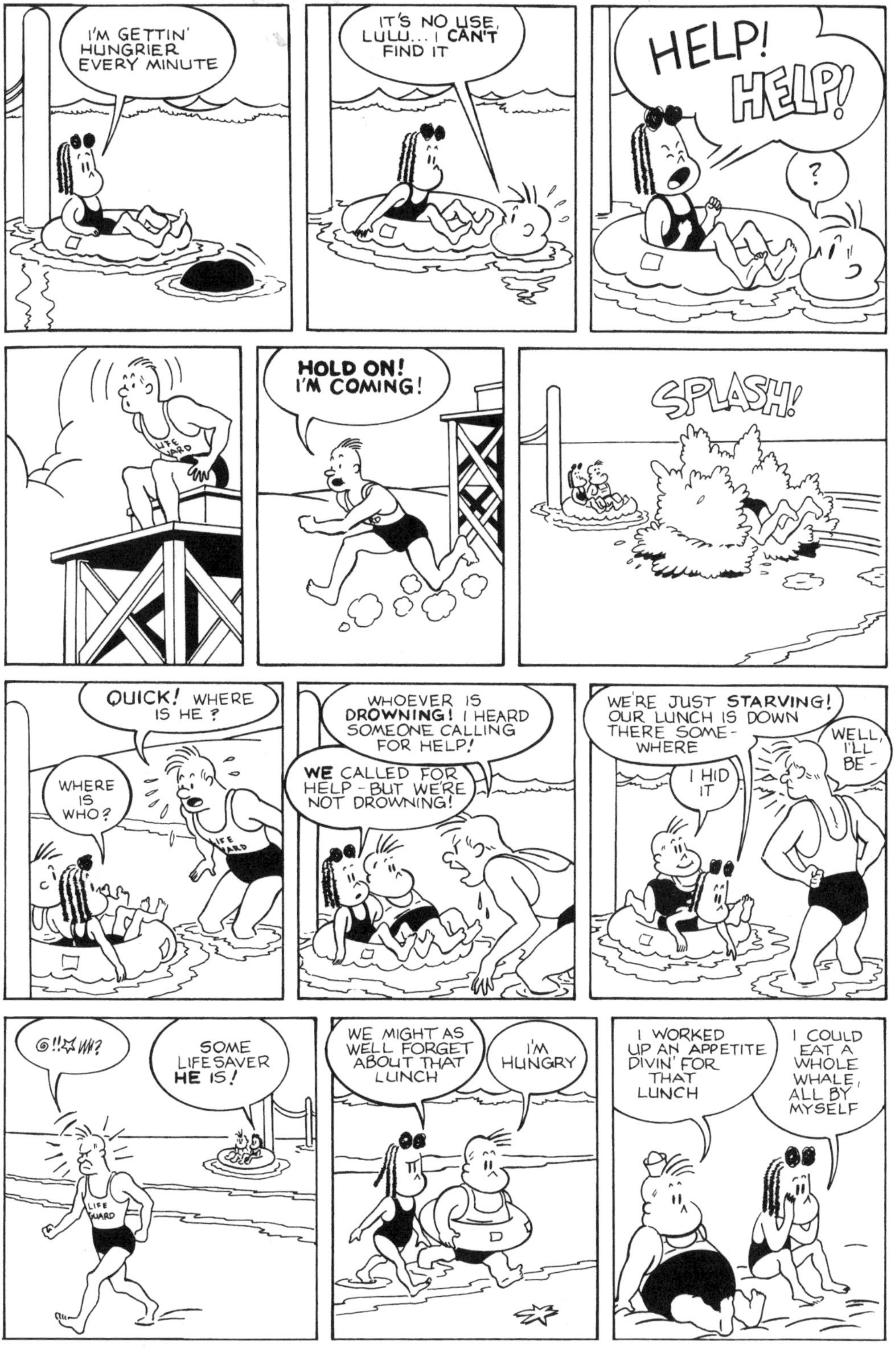
I'M GETTIN' HUNGRIER EVERY MINUTE
IT'S NO USE, LULU... I **CAN'T** FIND IT
HELP! HELP!
?
HOLD ON! I'M COMING!
SPLASH!
QUICK! WHERE IS HE?
WHERE IS WHO?
WHOEVER IS **DROWNING!** I HEARD SOMEONE CALLING FOR HELP!
WE CALLED FOR HELP - BUT WE'RE NOT DROWNING!
WE'RE JUST **STARVING!** OUR LUNCH IS DOWN THERE SOMEWHERE
I HID IT
WELL, I'LL BE-
SOME LIFESAVER **HE** IS!
WE MIGHT AS WELL FORGET ABOUT THAT LUNCH
I'M HUNGRY
I WORKED UP AN APPETITE DIVIN' FOR THAT LUNCH
I COULD EAT A WHOLE WHALE, ALL BY MYSELF

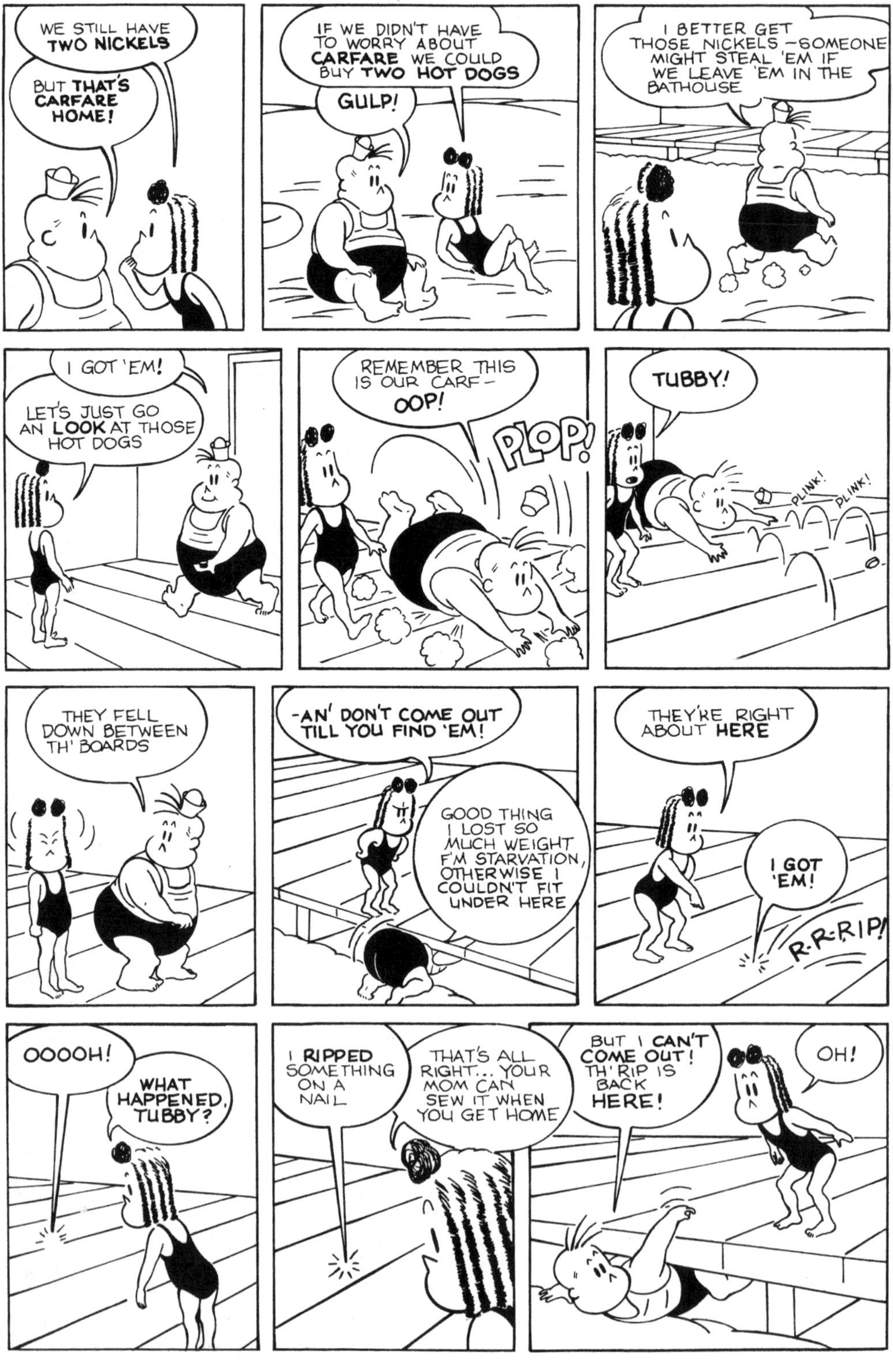
WE STILL HAVE TWO NICKELS
BUT THAT'S CARFARE HOME!
IF WE DIDN'T HAVE TO WORRY ABOUT CARFARE WE COULD BUY TWO HOT DOGS
GULP!
I BETTER GET THOSE NICKELS—SOMEONE MIGHT STEAL 'EM IF WE LEAVE 'EM IN THE BATHOUSE
I GOT 'EM!
LET'S JUST GO AN LOOK AT THOSE HOT DOGS
REMEMBER THIS IS OUR CARF— OOP!
PLOP!
TUBBY!
PLINK!
PLINK!
THEY FELL DOWN BETWEEN TH' BOARDS
-AN' DON'T COME OUT TILL YOU FIND 'EM!
GOOD THING I LOST SO MUCH WEIGHT F'M STARVATION, OTHERWISE I COULDN'T FIT UNDER HERE
THEY'RE RIGHT ABOUT HERE
I GOT 'EM!
R-R-RIP!
OOOOH!
WHAT HAPPENED, TUBBY?
I RIPPED SOMETHING ON A NAIL
THAT'S ALL RIGHT... YOUR MOM CAN SEW IT WHEN YOU GET HOME
BUT I CAN'T COME OUT! TH' RIP IS BACK HERE!
OH!

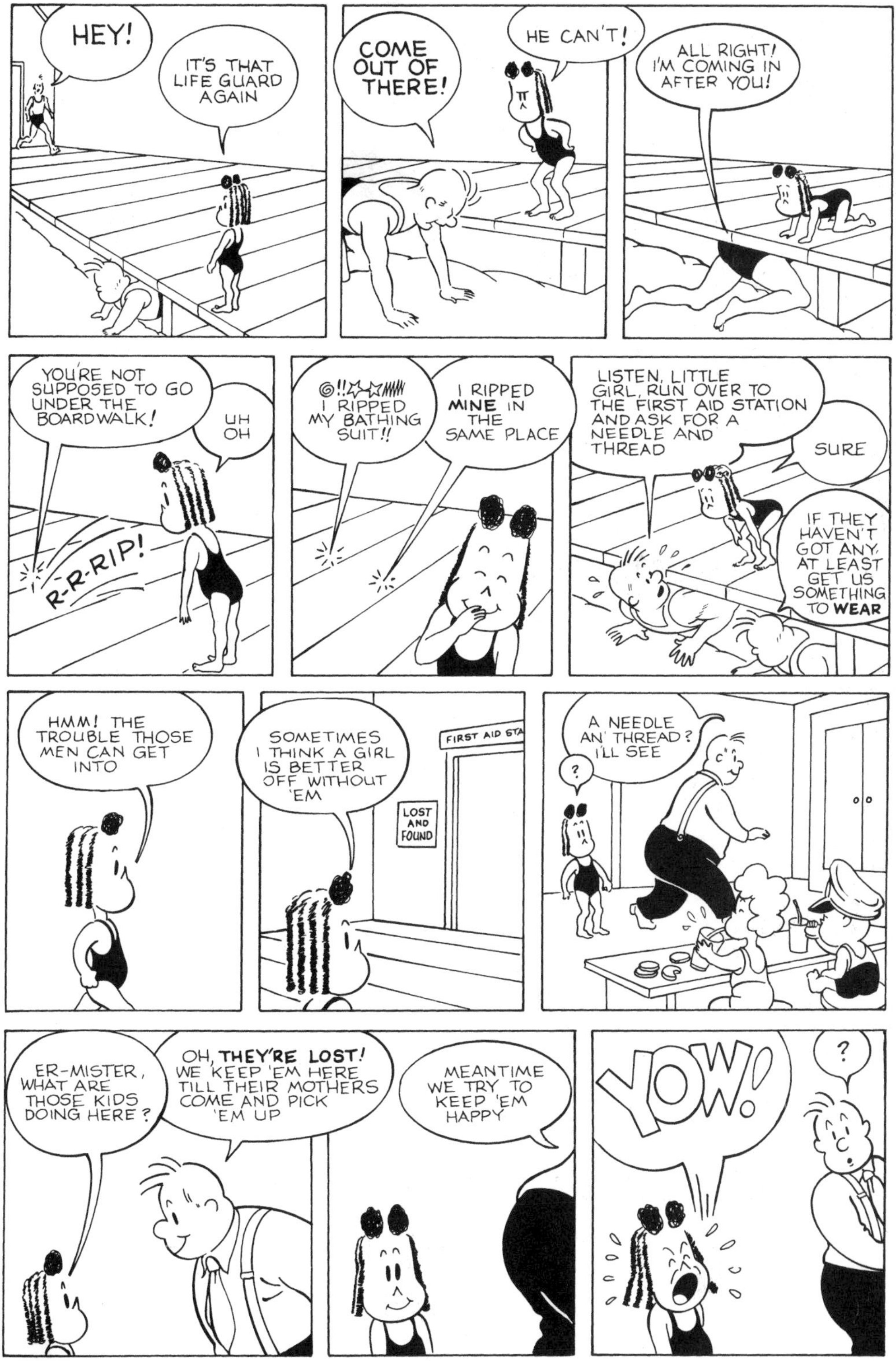
HEY!
IT'S THAT LIFE GUARD AGAIN
COME OUT OF THERE!
HE CAN'T!
ALL RIGHT! I'M COMING IN AFTER YOU!
YOU'RE NOT SUPPOSED TO GO UNDER THE BOARDWALK!
UH OH
R-R-RIP!
I RIPPED MY BATHING SUIT!!
I RIPPED MINE IN THE SAME PLACE
LISTEN, LITTLE GIRL, RUN OVER TO THE FIRST AID STATION AND ASK FOR A NEEDLE AND THREAD
SURE
IF THEY HAVEN'T GOT ANY, AT LEAST GET US SOMETHING TO WEAR
HMM! THE TROUBLE THOSE MEN CAN GET INTO
SOMETIMES I THINK A GIRL IS BETTER OFF WITHOUT 'EM
FIRST AID STA
LOST AND FOUND
A NEEDLE AN' THREAD? I'LL SEE
?
ER-MISTER, WHAT ARE THOSE KIDS DOING HERE?
OH, THEY'RE LOST! WE KEEP 'EM HERE TILL THEIR MOTHERS COME AND PICK 'EM UP
MEANTIME WE TRY TO KEEP 'EM HAPPY
YOW!
?

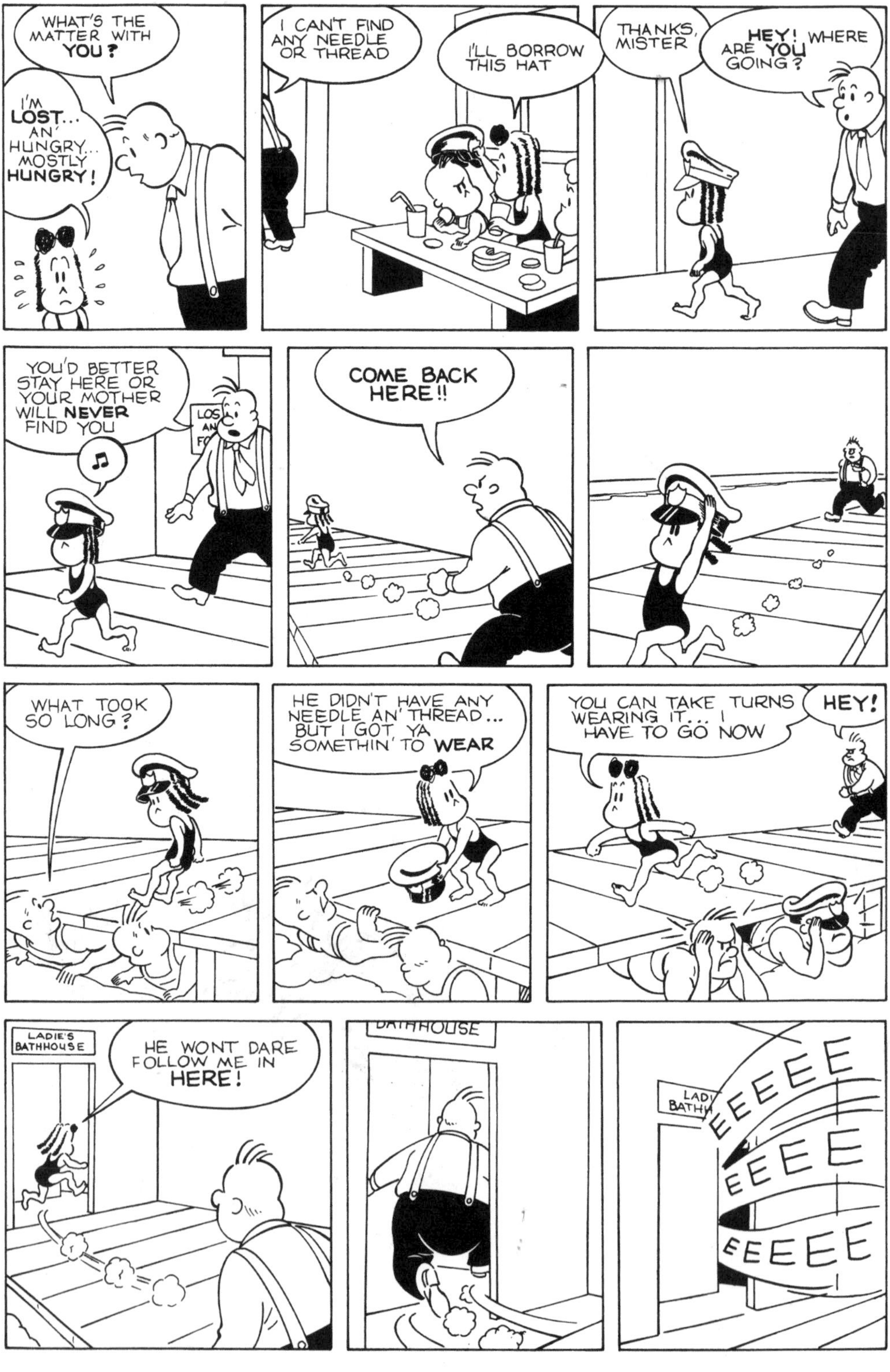
WHAT'S THE MATTER WITH **YOU?**
I'M **LOST**... AN' HUNGRY... MOSTLY **HUNGRY!**
I CAN'T FIND ANY NEEDLE OR THREAD
I'LL BORROW THIS HAT
THANKS, MISTER
HEY! WHERE ARE **YOU** GOING?
YOU'D BETTER STAY HERE OR YOUR MOTHER WILL **NEVER** FIND YOU
COME BACK HERE!!
WHAT TOOK SO LONG?
HE DIDN'T HAVE ANY NEEDLE AN' THREAD... BUT I GOT YA SOMETHIN' TO **WEAR**
YOU CAN TAKE TURNS WEARING IT... I HAVE TO GO NOW
HEY!
LADIE'S BATHHOUSE
HE WONT DARE FOLLOW ME IN **HERE!**
EEEEE EEEEE EEEEE

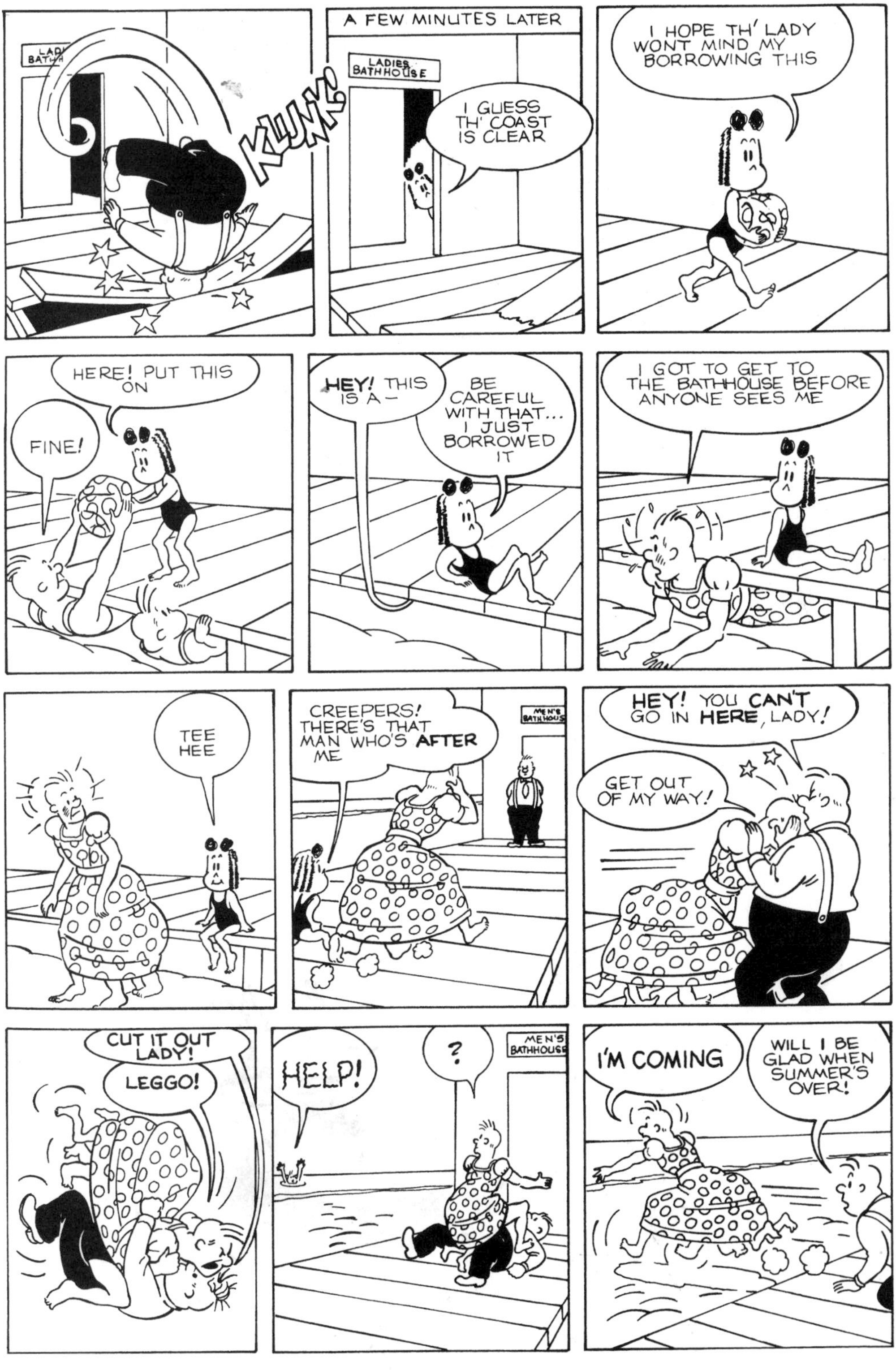

LADIES BATH...
KLUNK!
A FEW MINUTES LATER
LADIES BATHHOUSE
I GUESS TH' COAST IS CLEAR
I HOPE TH' LADY WONT MIND MY BORROWING THIS
HERE! PUT THIS ON
FINE!
HEY! THIS IS A —
BE CAREFUL WITH THAT... I JUST BORROWED IT
I GOT TO GET TO THE BATHHOUSE BEFORE ANYONE SEES ME
TEE HEE
CREEPERS! THERE'S THAT MAN WHO'S AFTER ME
MEN'S BATHHOUS
HEY! YOU CAN'T GO IN HERE, LADY!
GET OUT OF MY WAY!
CUT IT OUT LADY!
LEGGO!
HELP!
?
MEN'S BATHHOUSE
I'M COMING
WILL I BE GLAD WHEN SUMMER'S OVER!

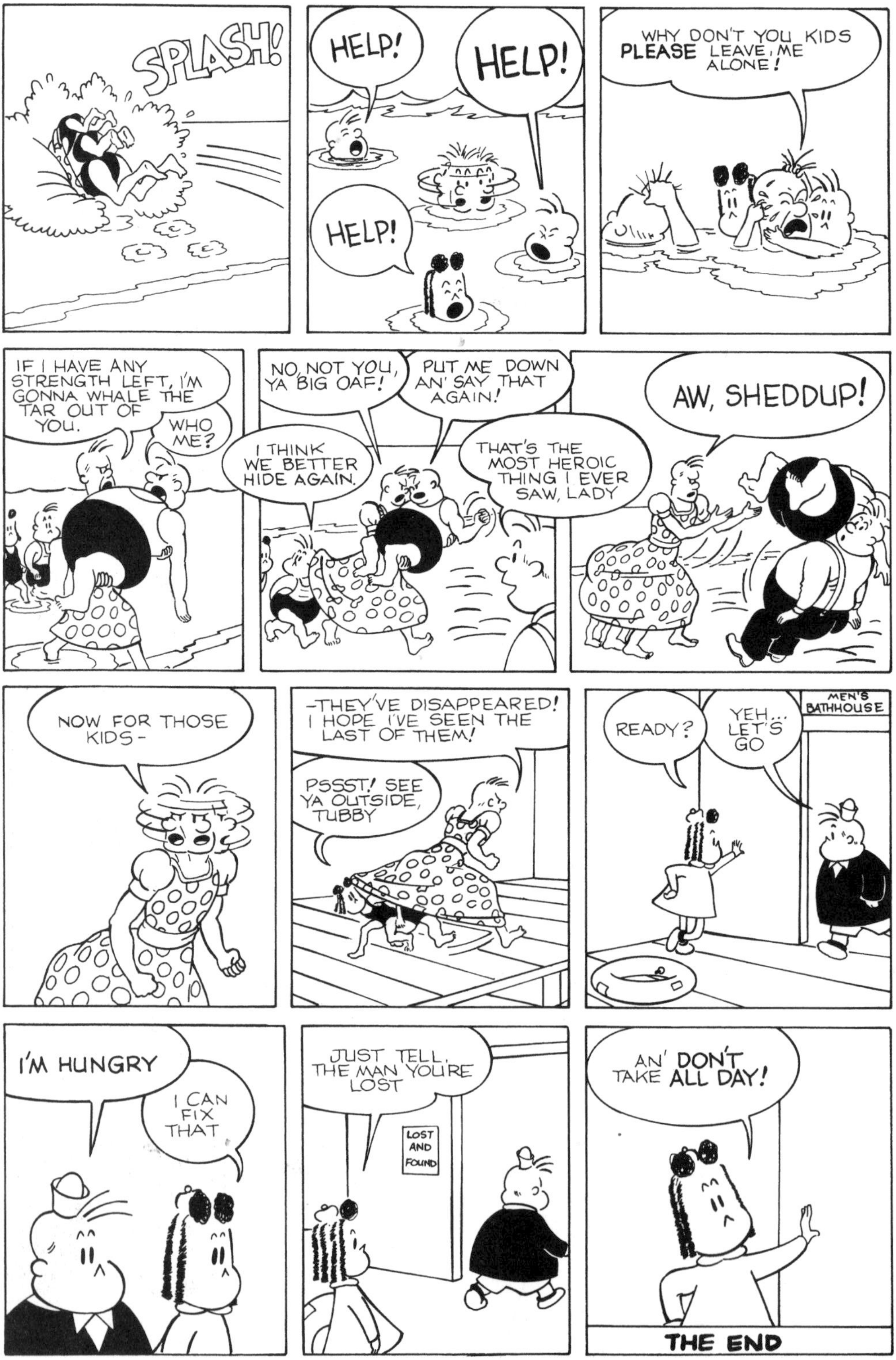
SPLASH!
HELP!
HELP!
HELP!
WHY DON'T YOU KIDS PLEASE LEAVE ME ALONE!
IF I HAVE ANY STRENGTH LEFT, I'M GONNA WHALE THE TAR OUT OF YOU.
WHO ME?
NO, NOT YOU, YA BIG OAF!
PUT ME DOWN AN' SAY THAT AGAIN!
I THINK WE BETTER HIDE AGAIN.
THAT'S THE MOST HEROIC THING I EVER SAW, LADY
AW, SHEDDUP!
NOW FOR THOSE KIDS -
-THEY'VE DISAPPEARED! I HOPE I'VE SEEN THE LAST OF THEM!
PSSST! SEE YA OUTSIDE, TUBBY
MEN'S BATHHOUSE
READY?
YEH... LET'S GO
I'M HUNGRY
I CAN FIX THAT
JUST TELL THE MAN YOU'RE LOST
LOST AND FOUND
AN' DON'T TAKE ALL DAY!
THE END

"JINGLE BELLS"

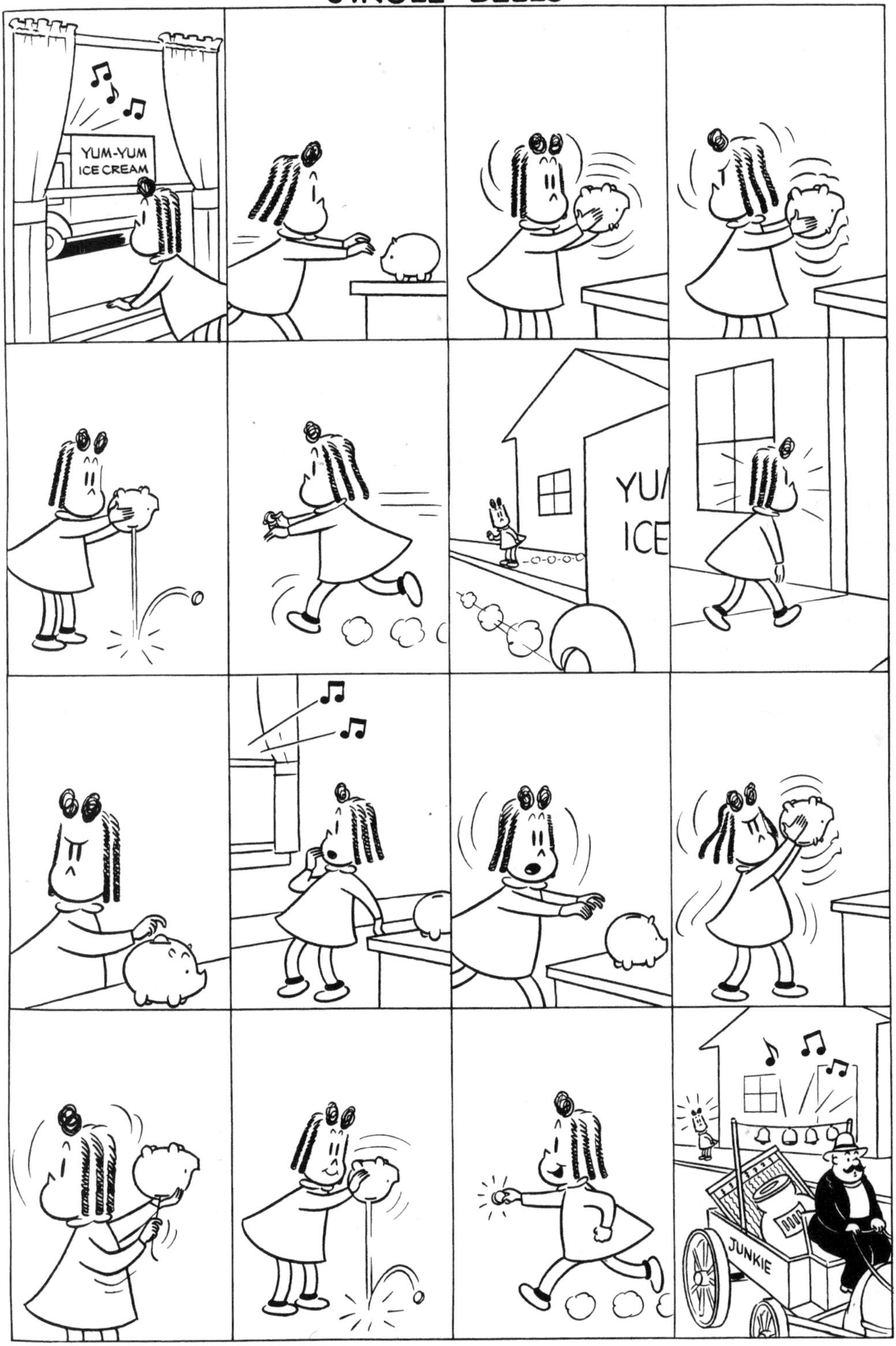
YUM-YUM
ICE CREAM
YU
ICE
JUNKIE

marge's LITTLE LULU minds Alvin

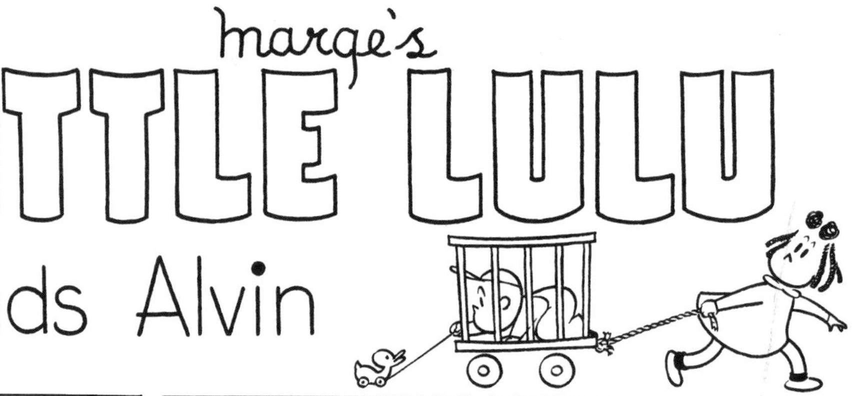

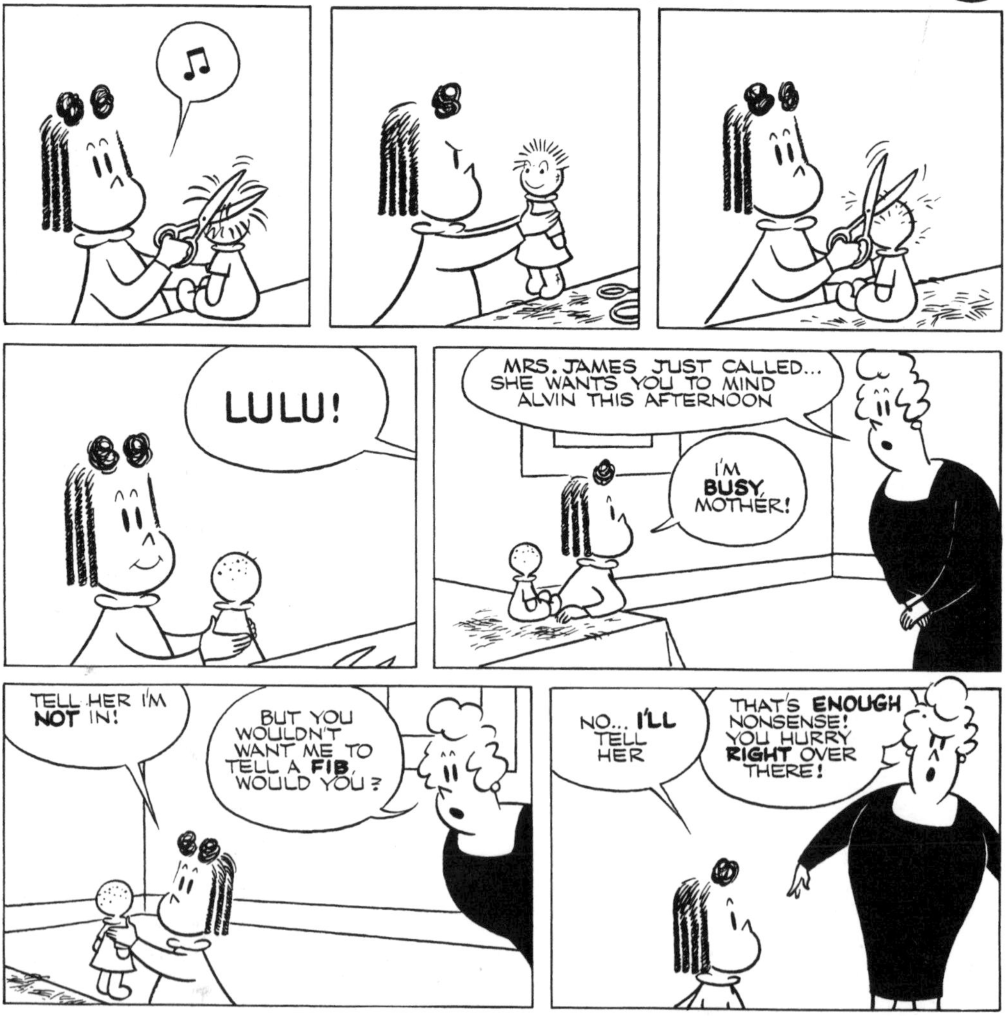

LULU!
MRS. JAMES JUST CALLED... SHE WANTS YOU TO MIND ALVIN THIS AFTERNOON
I'M **BUSY**, MOTHER!
TELL HER I'M **NOT** IN!
BUT YOU WOULDN'T WANT ME TO TELL A **FIB**, WOULD YOU?
NO... **I'LL** TELL HER
THAT'S **ENOUGH** NONSENSE! YOU HURRY **RIGHT** OVER THERE!

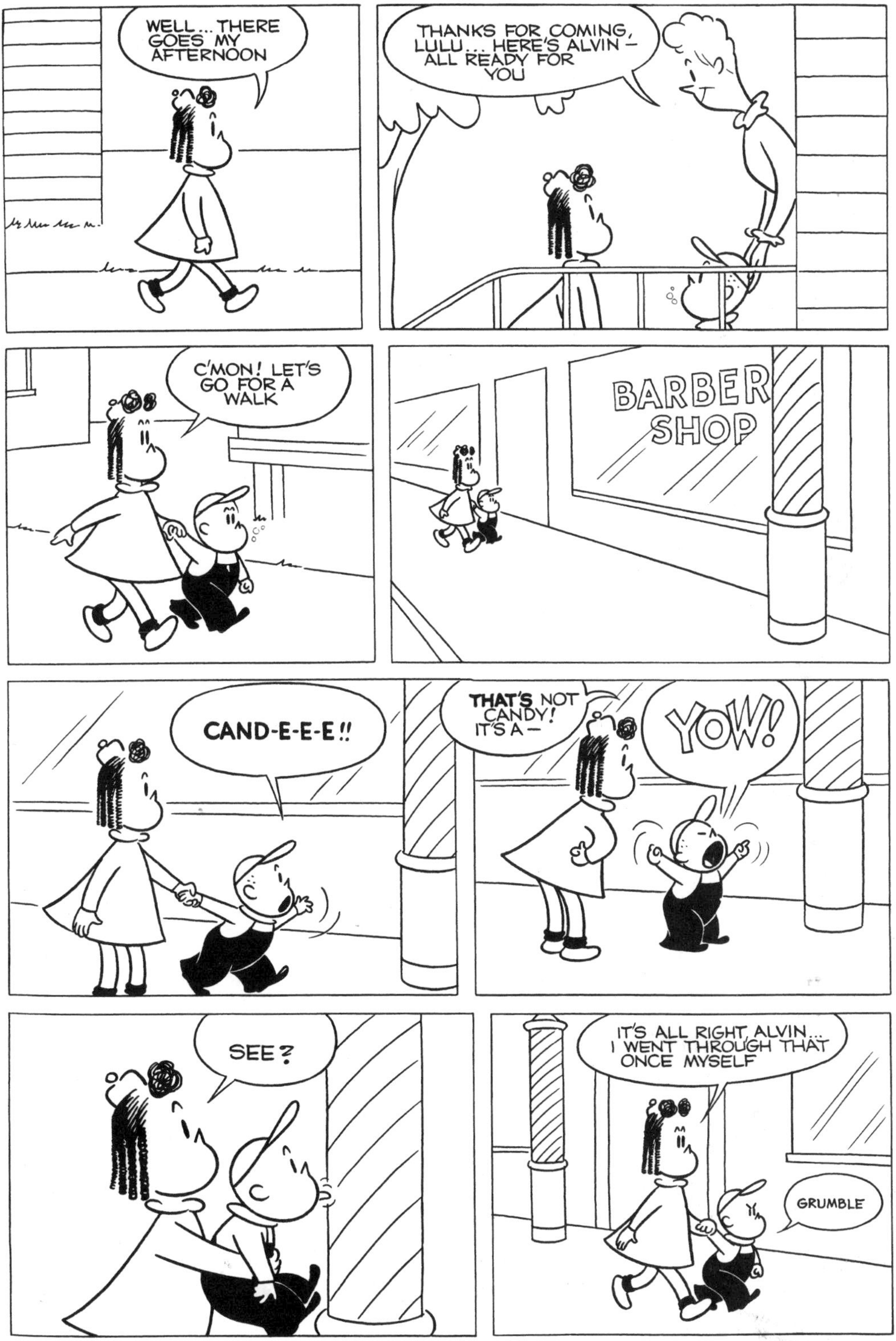
WELL... THERE GOES MY AFTERNOON
THANKS FOR COMING, LULU... HERE'S ALVIN — ALL READY FOR YOU
C'MON! LET'S GO FOR A WALK
BARBER SHOP
CAND-E-E-E!!
THAT'S NOT CANDY! IT'S A —
YOW!
SEE?
IT'S ALL RIGHT ALVIN... I WENT THROUGH THAT ONCE MYSELF
GRUMBLE

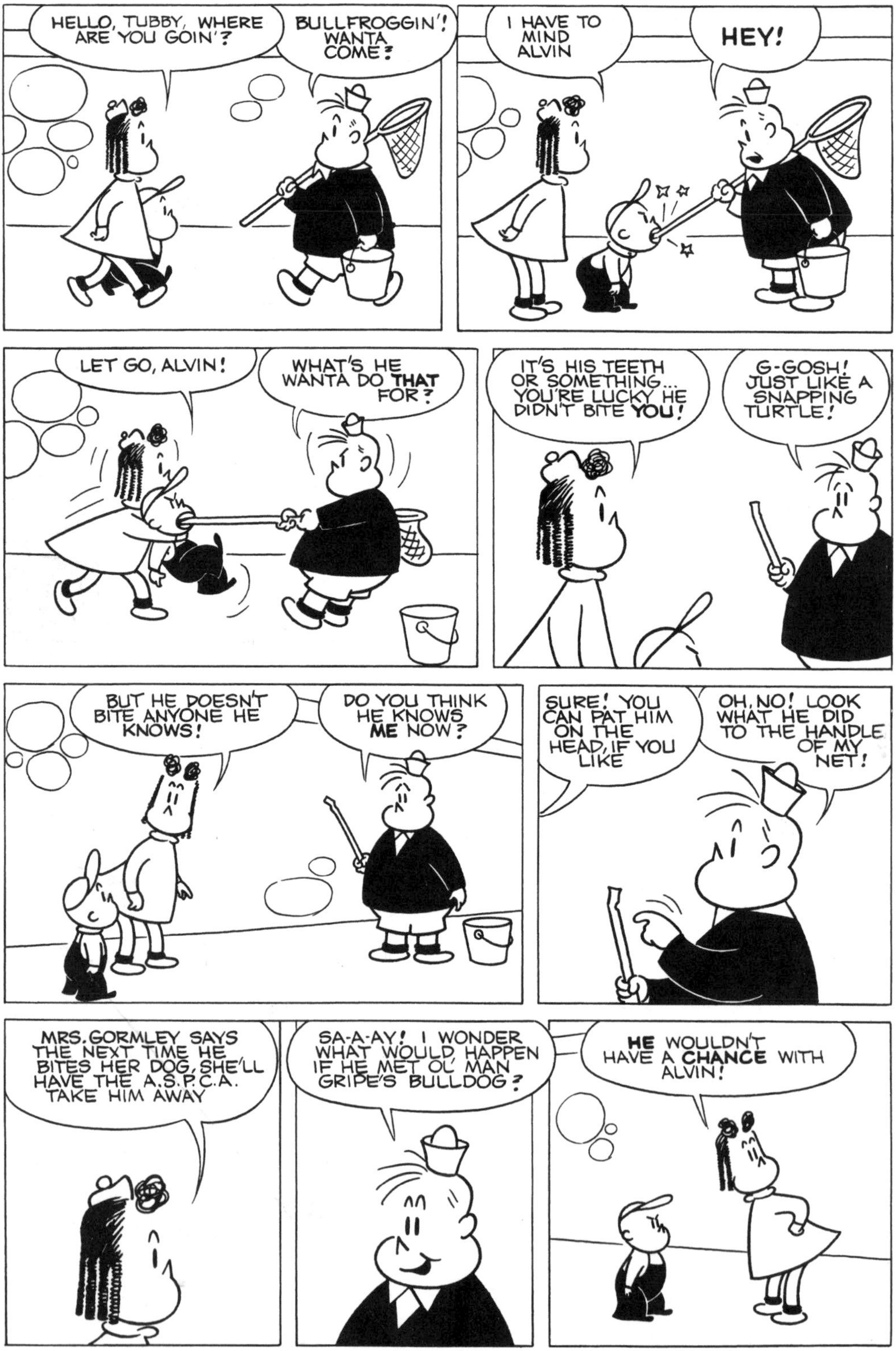
HELLO, TUBBY, WHERE ARE YOU GOIN'?
BULLFROGGIN'! WANTA COME?
I HAVE TO MIND ALVIN
HEY!
LET GO, ALVIN!
WHAT'S HE WANTA DO THAT FOR?
IT'S HIS TEETH OR SOMETHING... YOU'RE LUCKY HE DIDN'T BITE YOU!
G-GOSH! JUST LIKE A SNAPPING TURTLE!
BUT HE DOESN'T BITE ANYONE HE KNOWS!
DO YOU THINK HE KNOWS ME NOW?
SURE! YOU CAN PAT HIM ON THE HEAD, IF YOU LIKE
OH, NO! LOOK WHAT HE DID TO THE HANDLE OF MY NET!
MRS. GORMLEY SAYS THE NEXT TIME HE BITES HER DOG, SHE'LL HAVE THE A.S.P.C.A. TAKE HIM AWAY
SA-A-AY! I WONDER WHAT WOULD HAPPEN IF HE MET OL' MAN GRIPE'S BULLDOG?
HE WOULDN'T HAVE A CHANCE WITH ALVIN!

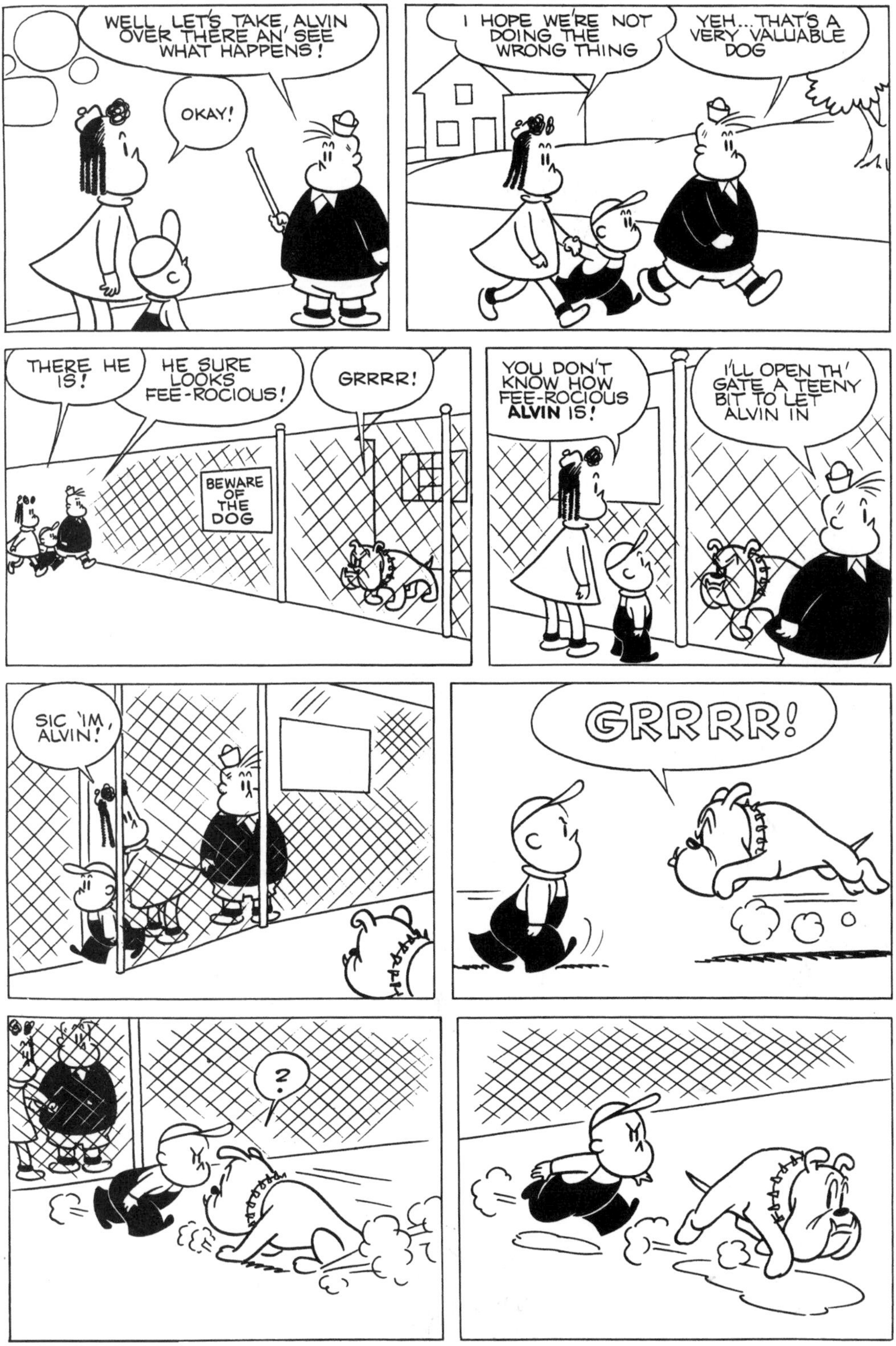
WELL, LET'S TAKE ALVIN OVER THERE AN' SEE WHAT HAPPENS!
OKAY!
I HOPE WE'RE NOT DOING THE WRONG THING
YEH... THAT'S A VERY VALUABLE DOG
THERE HE IS!
HE SURE LOOKS FEE-ROCIOUS!
GRRRR!
BEWARE OF THE DOG
YOU DON'T KNOW HOW FEE-ROCIOUS ALVIN IS!
I'LL OPEN TH' GATE A TEENY BIT TO LET ALVIN IN
SIC 'IM, ALVIN!
GRRRR!
?

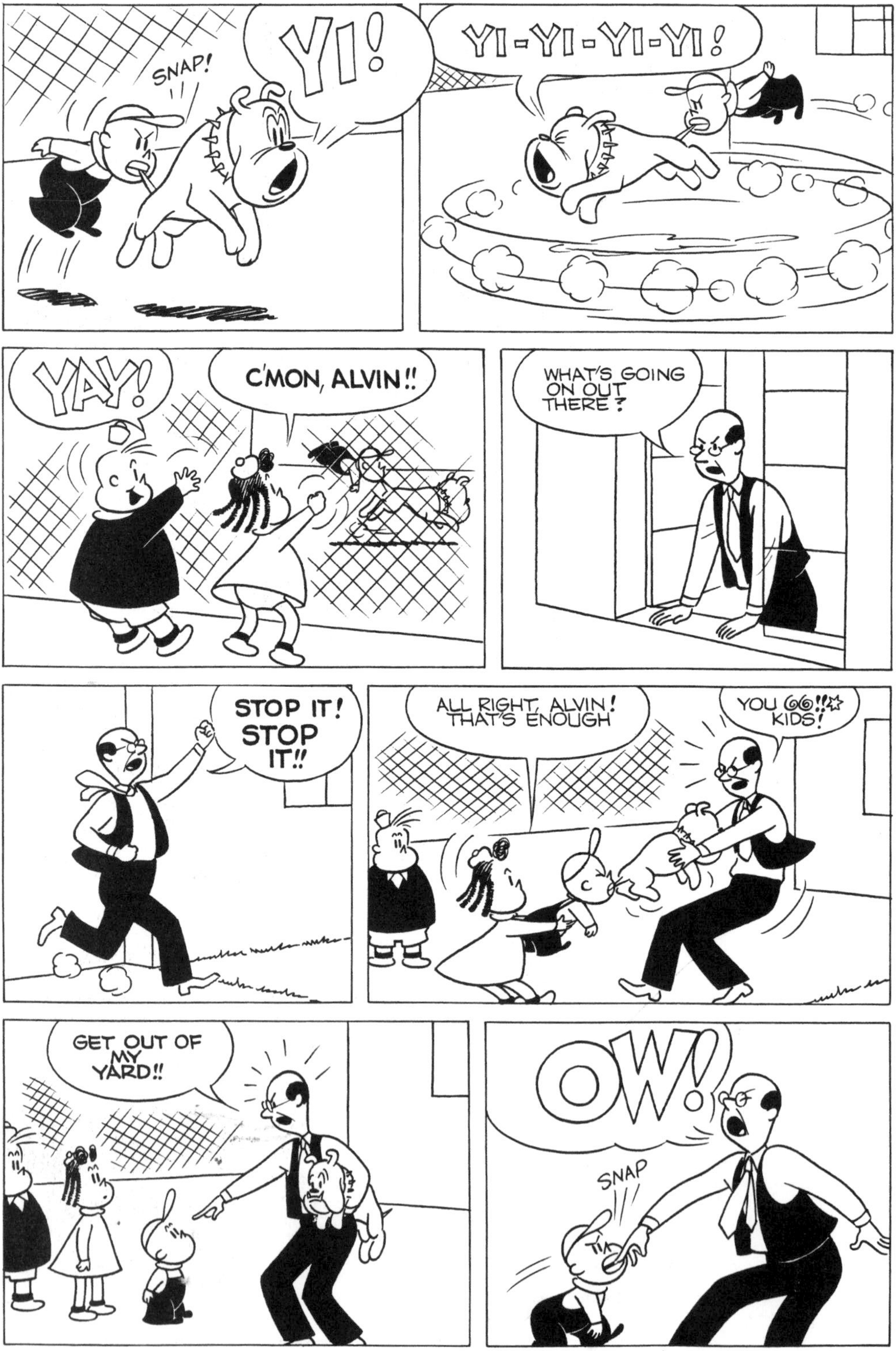
SNAP!
YI!
YI-YI-YI-YI!
YAY!
C'MON, ALVIN!!
WHAT'S GOING ON OUT THERE?
STOP IT! STOP IT!!
ALL RIGHT, ALVIN! THAT'S ENOUGH
YOU @@!!☆ KIDS!
GET OUT OF MY YARD!!
OW!
SNAP

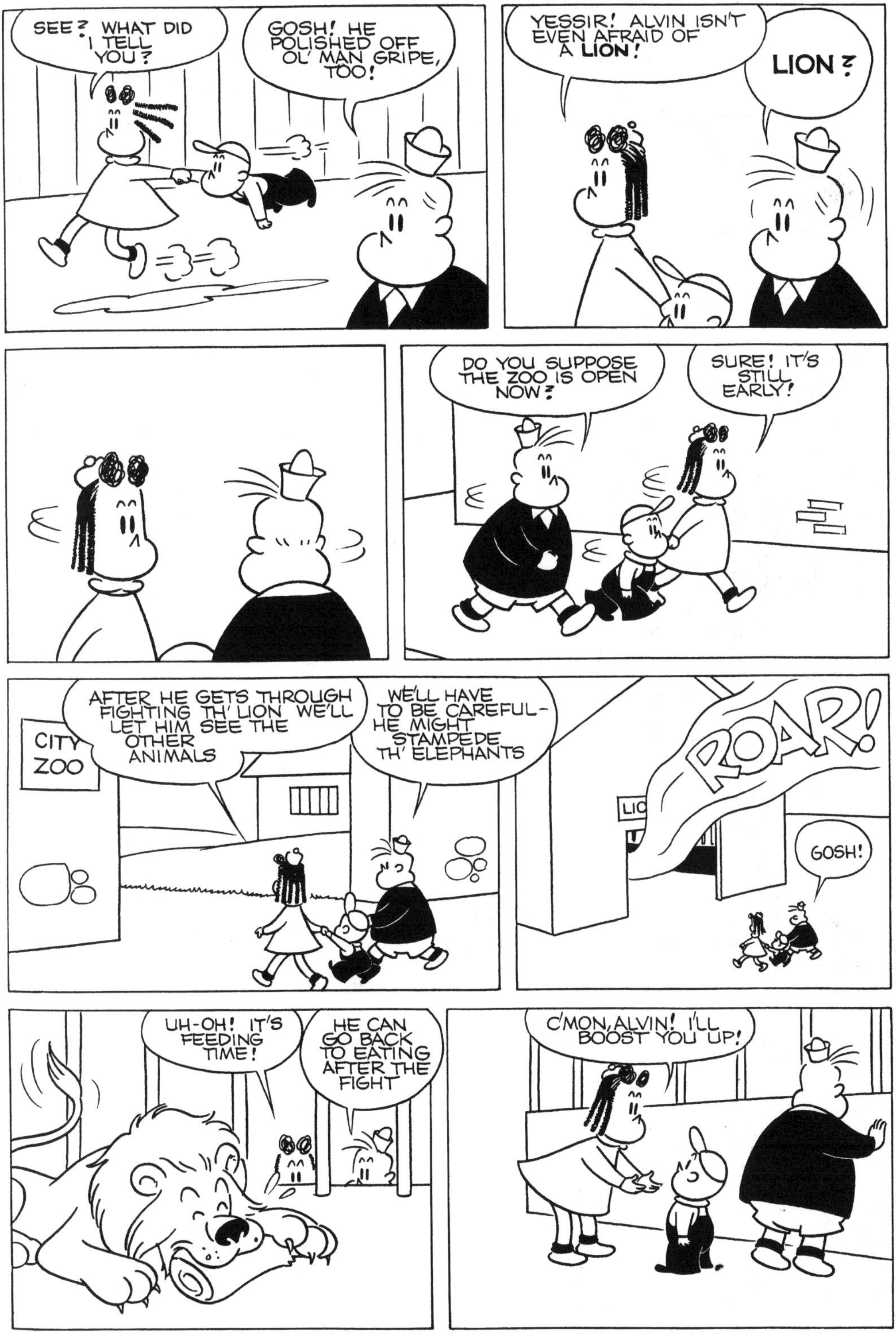
SEE? WHAT DID I TELL YOU?
GOSH! HE POLISHED OFF OL' MAN GRIPE, TOO!
YESSIR! ALVIN ISN'T EVEN AFRAID OF A **LION**!
LION?
DO YOU SUPPOSE THE ZOO IS OPEN NOW?
SURE! IT'S STILL EARLY!
CITY ZOO
AFTER HE GETS THROUGH FIGHTING TH' LION WE'LL LET HIM SEE THE OTHER ANIMALS
WE'LL HAVE TO BE CAREFUL- HE MIGHT STAMPEDE TH' ELEPHANTS
ROAR!
GOSH!
UH-OH! IT'S FEEDING TIME!
HE CAN GO BACK TO EATING AFTER THE FIGHT
C'MON, ALVIN! I'LL BOOST YOU UP!

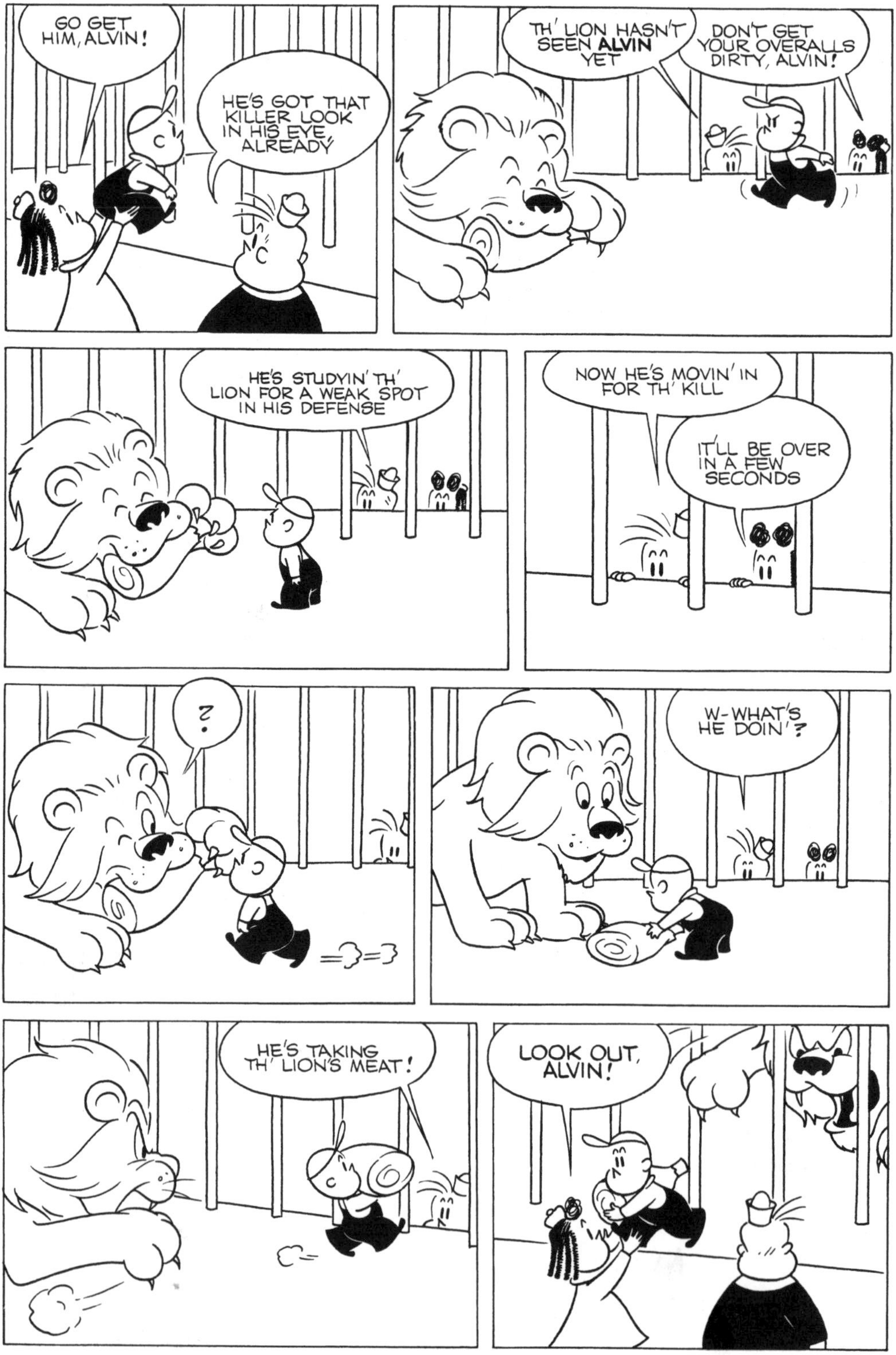
GO GET HIM, ALVIN!
HE'S GOT THAT KILLER LOOK IN HIS EYE ALREADY
TH' LION HASN'T SEEN **ALVIN** YET
DON'T GET YOUR OVERALLS DIRTY, ALVIN!
HE'S STUDYIN' TH' LION FOR A WEAK SPOT IN HIS DEFENSE
NOW HE'S MOVIN' IN FOR TH' KILL
IT'LL BE OVER IN A FEW SECONDS
?
W-WHAT'S HE DOIN'?
HE'S TAKING TH' LION'S MEAT!
LOOK OUT, ALVIN!

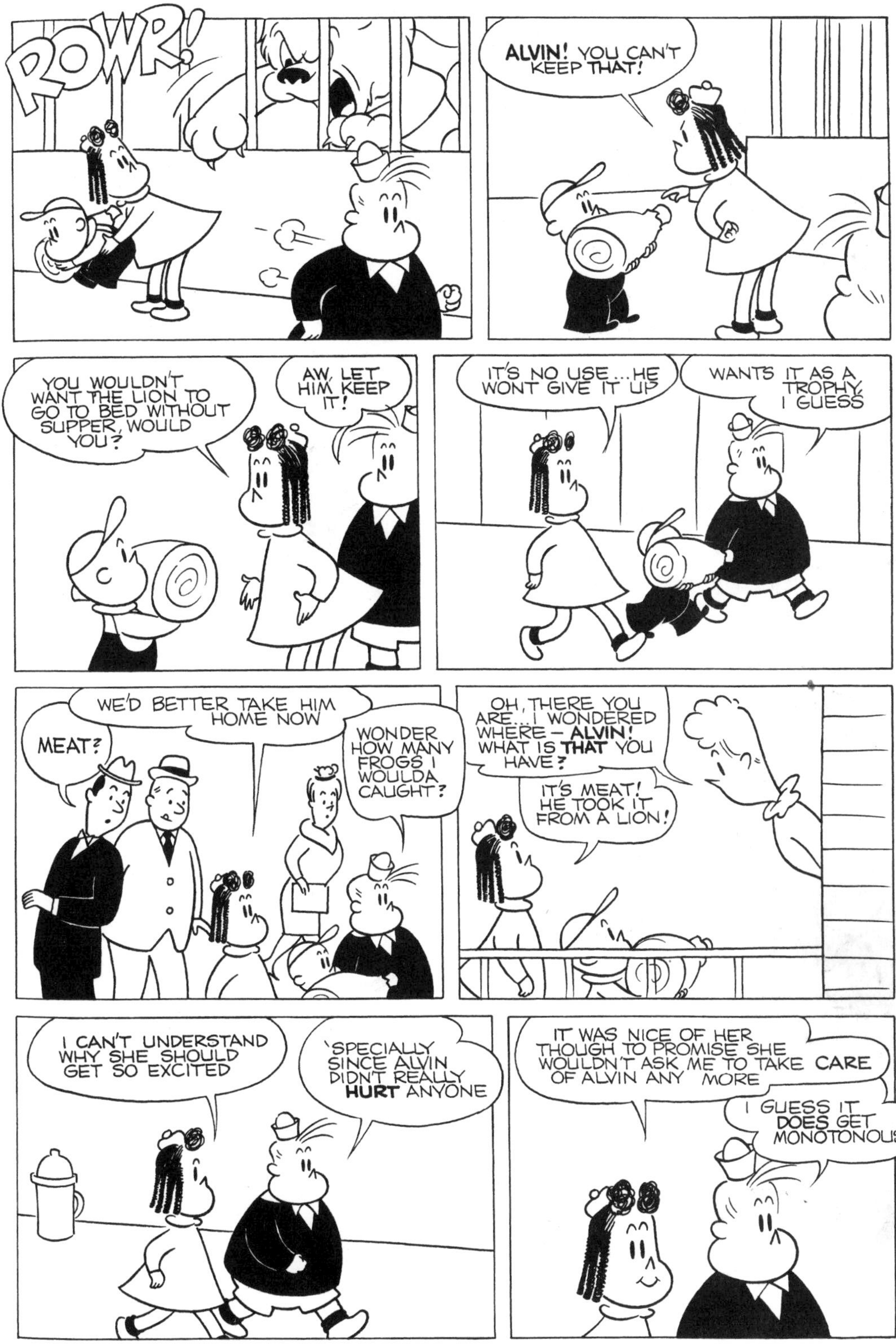
ROWR!
ALVIN! YOU CAN'T KEEP THAT!
YOU WOULDN'T WANT THE LION TO GO TO BED WITHOUT SUPPER, WOULD YOU?
AW, LET HIM KEEP IT!
IT'S NO USE... HE WONT GIVE IT UP
WANTS IT AS A TROPHY, I GUESS
MEAT?
WE'D BETTER TAKE HIM HOME NOW
WONDER HOW MANY FROGS I WOULDA CAUGHT?
OH, THERE YOU ARE... I WONDERED WHERE – ALVIN! WHAT IS THAT YOU HAVE?
IT'S MEAT! HE TOOK IT FROM A LION!
I CAN'T UNDERSTAND WHY SHE SHOULD GET SO EXCITED
'SPECIALLY SINCE ALVIN DIDN'T REALLY HURT ANYONE
IT WAS NICE OF HER THOUGH TO PROMISE SHE WOULDN'T ASK ME TO TAKE CARE OF ALVIN ANY MORE
I GUESS IT DOES GET MONOTONOUS

ROCKABYE BABY

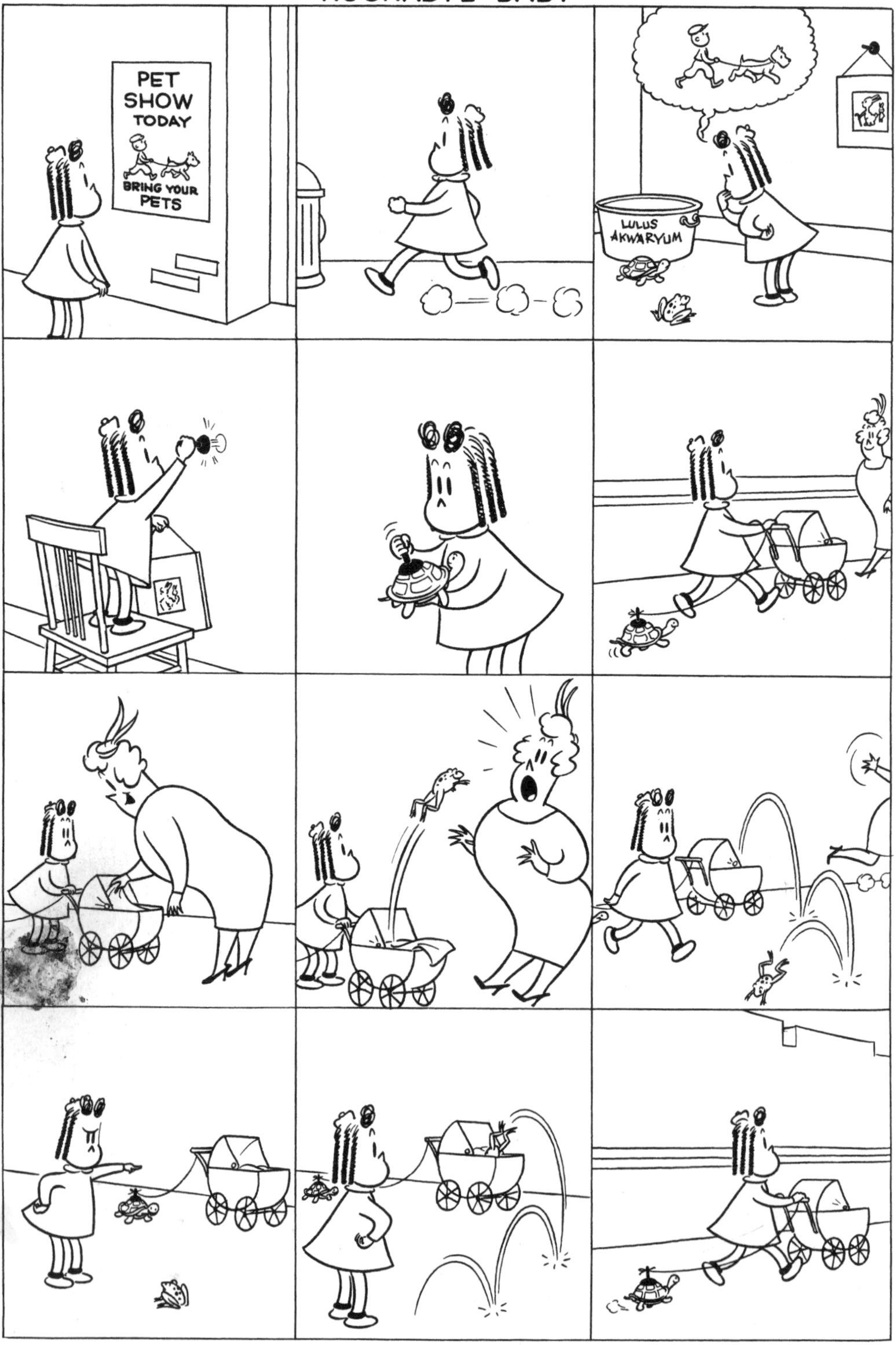

PET
SHOW
TODAY
BRING YOUR
PETS
LULUS
AKWARYUM

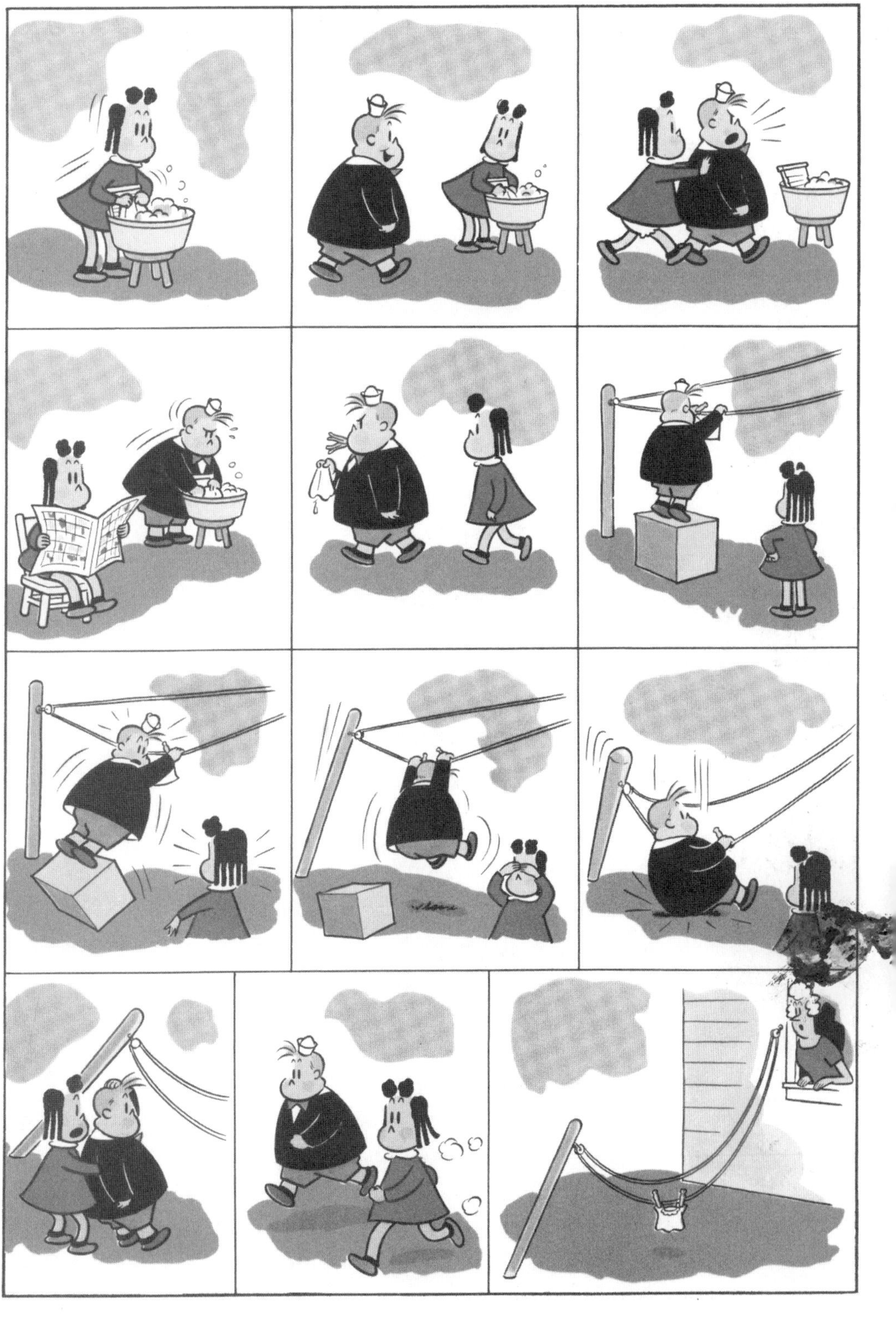

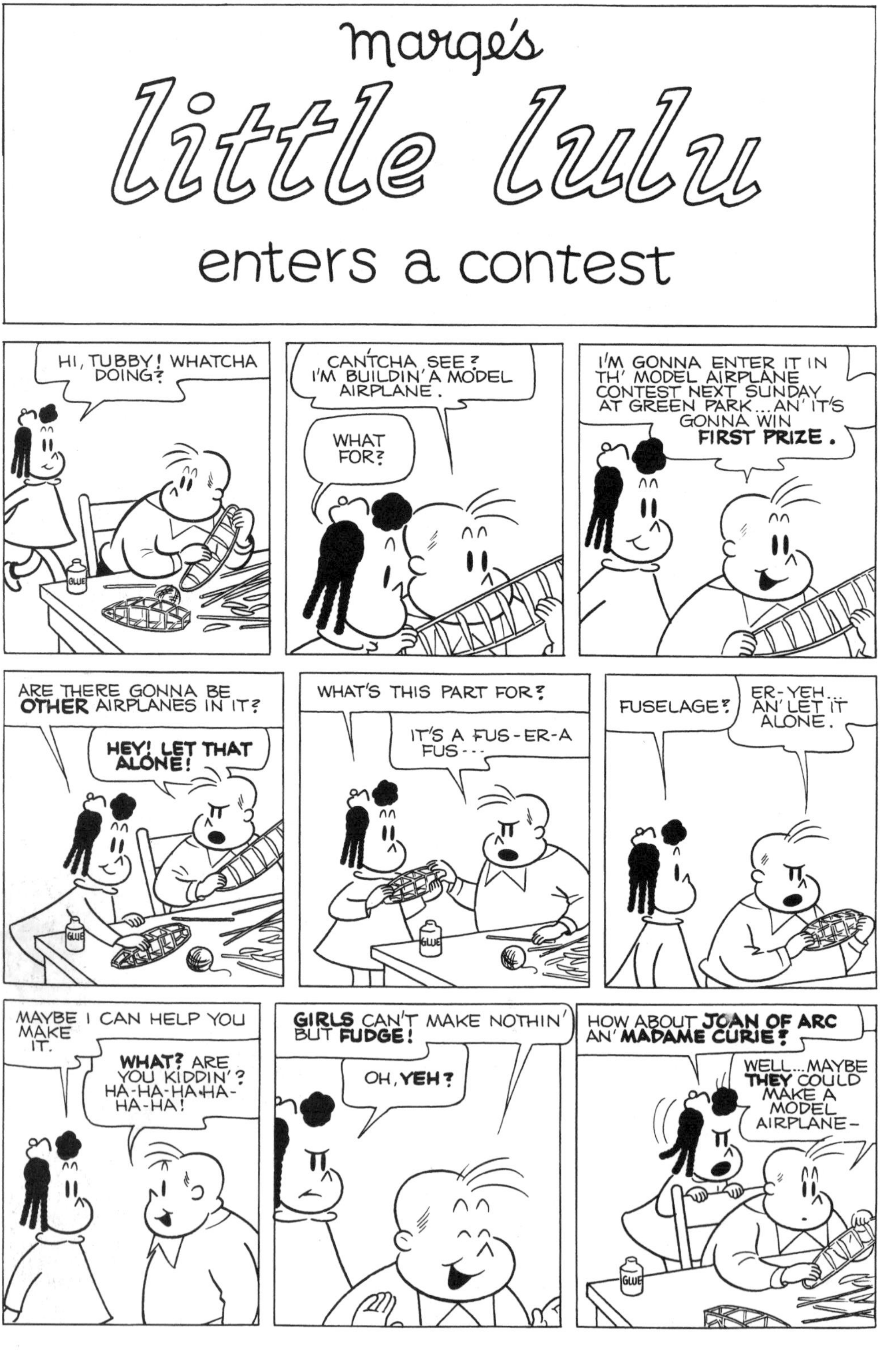
marge's
little lulu
enters a contest
HI, TUBBY! WHATCHA DOING?
CAN'TCHA SEE? I'M BUILDIN' A MODEL AIRPLANE.
WHAT FOR?
I'M GONNA ENTER IT IN TH' MODEL AIRPLANE CONTEST NEXT SUNDAY AT GREEN PARK... AN' IT'S GONNA WIN FIRST PRIZE.
GLUE
ARE THERE GONNA BE OTHER AIRPLANES IN IT?
HEY! LET THAT ALONE!
WHAT'S THIS PART FOR?
IT'S A FUS-ER-A FUS---
FUSELAGE?
ER-YEH... AN' LET IT ALONE.
MAYBE I CAN HELP YOU MAKE IT.
WHAT? ARE YOU KIDDIN'? HA-HA-HA-HA-HA-HA!
GIRLS CAN'T MAKE NOTHIN' BUT FUDGE!
OH, YEH?
HOW ABOUT JOAN OF ARC AN' MADAME CURIE?
WELL... MAYBE THEY COULD MAKE A MODEL AIRPLANE-

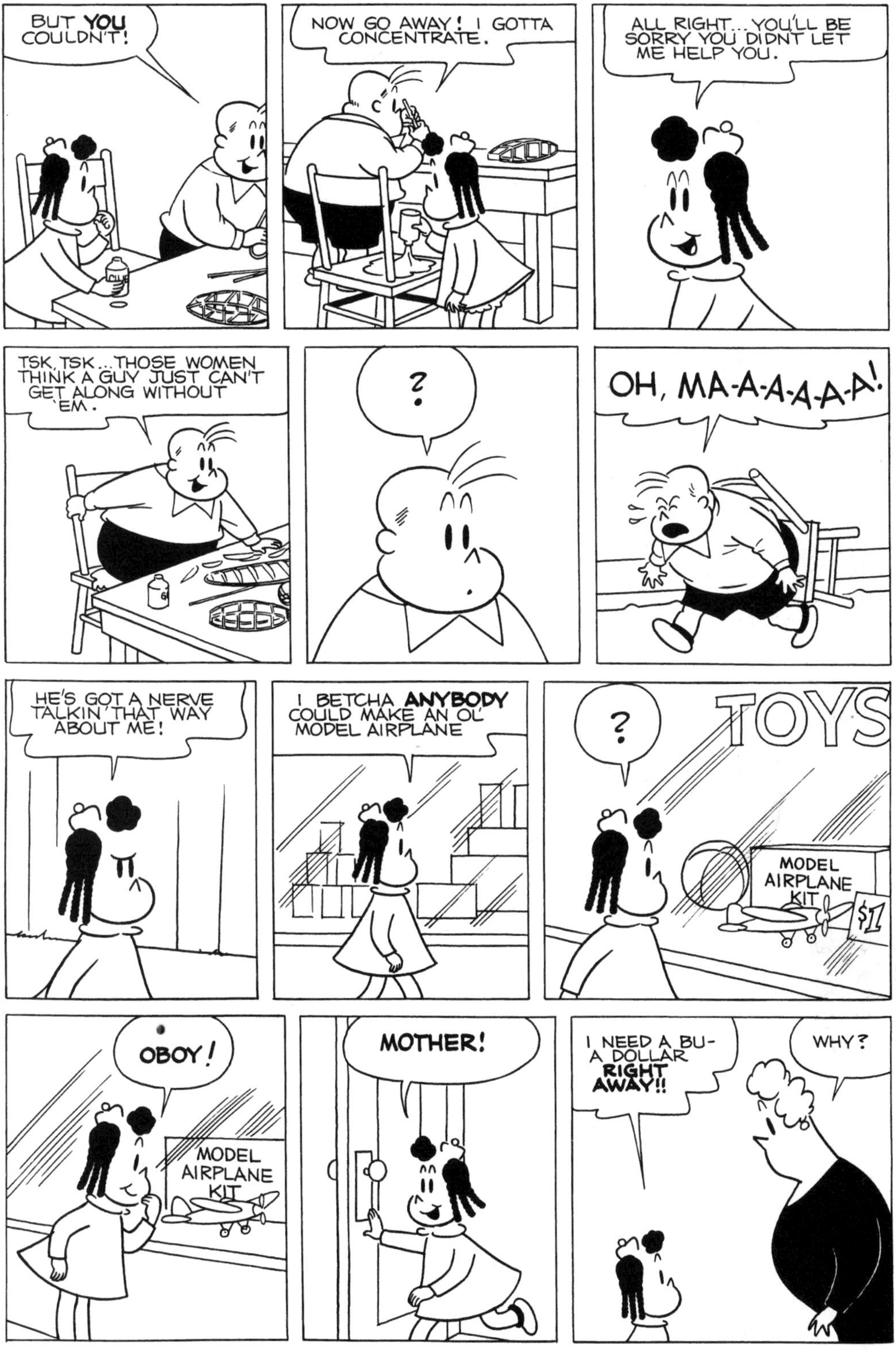

BUT YOU COULDN'T!
NOW GO AWAY! I GOTTA CONCENTRATE.
ALL RIGHT... YOU'LL BE SORRY YOU DIDN'T LET ME HELP YOU.
TSK, TSK... THOSE WOMEN THINK A GUY JUST CAN'T GET ALONG WITHOUT 'EM.
?
OH, MA-A-A-A-A-A!
HE'S GOT A NERVE TALKIN' THAT WAY ABOUT ME!
I BETCHA ANYBODY COULD MAKE AN OL' MODEL AIRPLANE
?
TOYS
MODEL AIRPLANE KIT
$1
OBOY!
MODEL AIRPLANE KIT
MOTHER!
I NEED A BU- A DOLLAR RIGHT AWAY!!
WHY?

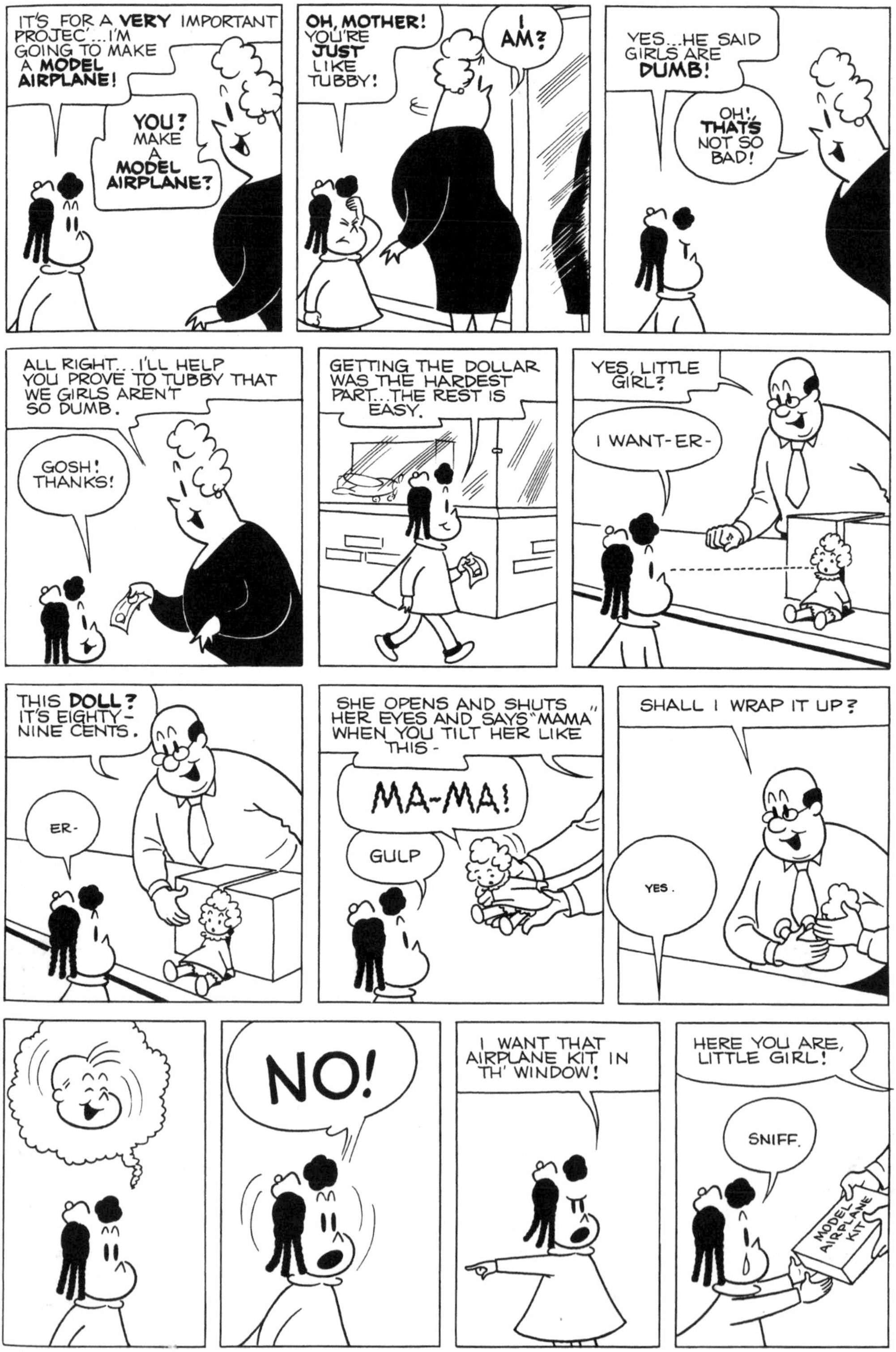
IT'S FOR A **VERY** IMPORTANT PROJEC'...I'M GOING TO MAKE A **MODEL AIRPLANE**!
YOU? MAKE A **MODEL AIRPLANE?**
OH, MOTHER! YOU'RE **JUST** LIKE TUBBY!
I **AM?**
YES...HE SAID GIRLS ARE **DUMB**!
OH! **THAT'S** NOT SO BAD!
ALL RIGHT...I'LL HELP YOU PROVE TO TUBBY THAT WE GIRLS AREN'T SO DUMB.
GOSH! THANKS!
GETTING THE DOLLAR WAS THE HARDEST PART...THE REST IS EASY.
YES, LITTLE GIRL?
I WANT-ER-
THIS **DOLL?** IT'S EIGHTY-NINE CENTS.
ER-
SHE OPENS AND SHUTS HER EYES AND SAYS "MAMA" WHEN YOU TILT HER LIKE THIS-
MA-MA!
GULP
SHALL I WRAP IT UP?
YES.
NO!
I WANT THAT AIRPLANE KIT IN TH' WINDOW!
HERE YOU ARE, LITTLE GIRL!
SNIFF.
MODEL AIRPLANE KIT

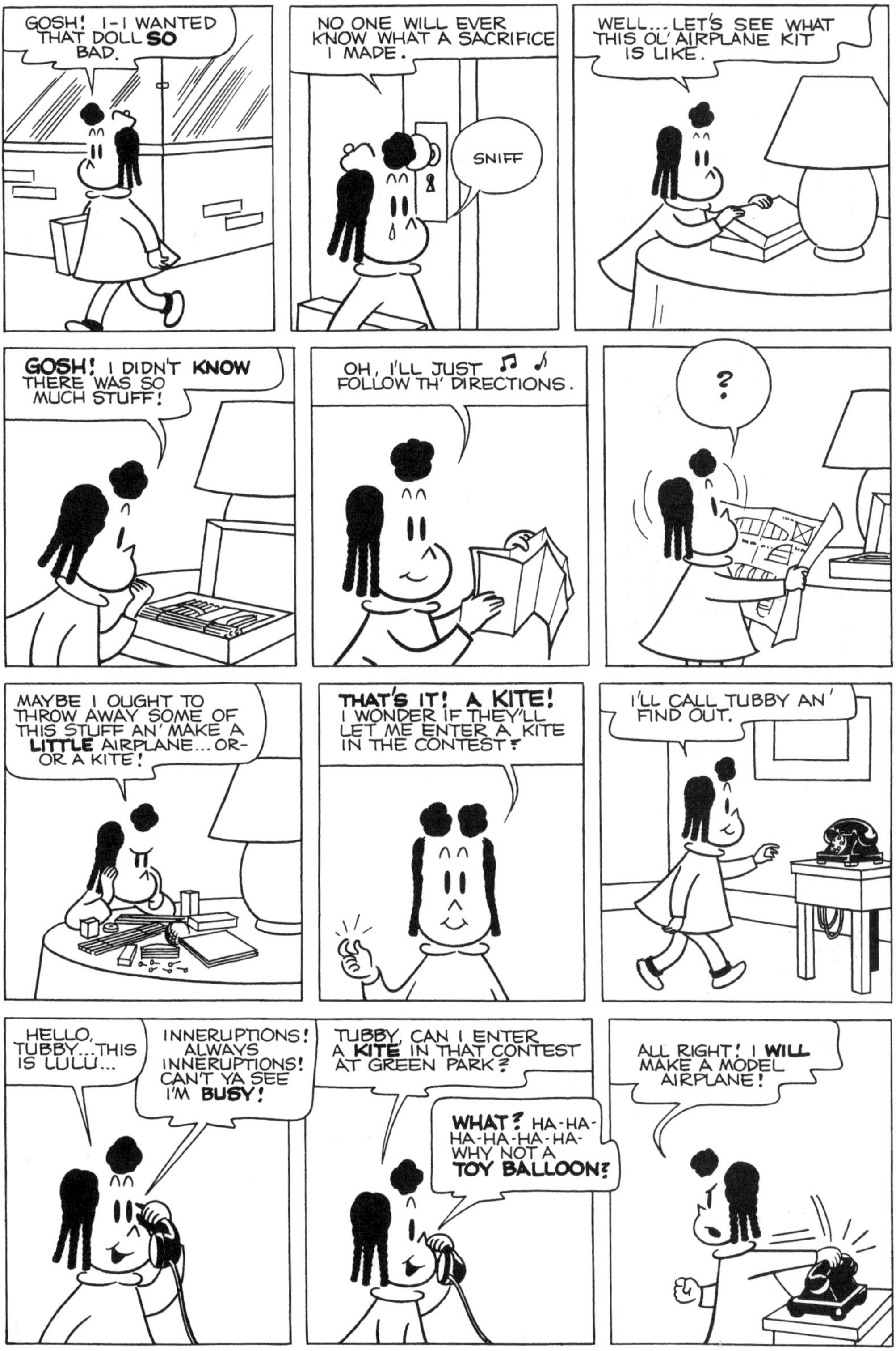
GOSH! I-I WANTED THAT DOLL **SO** BAD.
NO ONE WILL EVER KNOW WHAT A SACRIFICE I MADE.
SNIFF
WELL... LET'S SEE WHAT THIS OL' AIRPLANE KIT IS LIKE.
GOSH! I DIDN'T **KNOW** THERE WAS SO MUCH STUFF!
OH, I'LL JUST ♫ ♪ FOLLOW TH' DIRECTIONS.
?
MAYBE I OUGHT TO THROW AWAY SOME OF THIS STUFF AN' MAKE A **LITTLE** AIRPLANE... OR-OR A KITE!
THAT'S IT! A KITE! I WONDER IF THEY'LL LET ME ENTER A KITE IN THE CONTEST?
I'LL CALL TUBBY AN' FIND OUT.
HELLO, TUBBY...THIS IS LULU...
INNERUPTIONS! ALWAYS INNERUPTIONS! CAN'T YA SEE I'M **BUSY!**
TUBBY, CAN I ENTER A **KITE** IN THAT CONTEST AT GREEN PARK?
WHAT? HA-HA-HA-HA-HA-HA-WHY NOT A **TOY BALLOON?**
ALL RIGHT! I **WILL** MAKE A MODEL AIRPLANE!

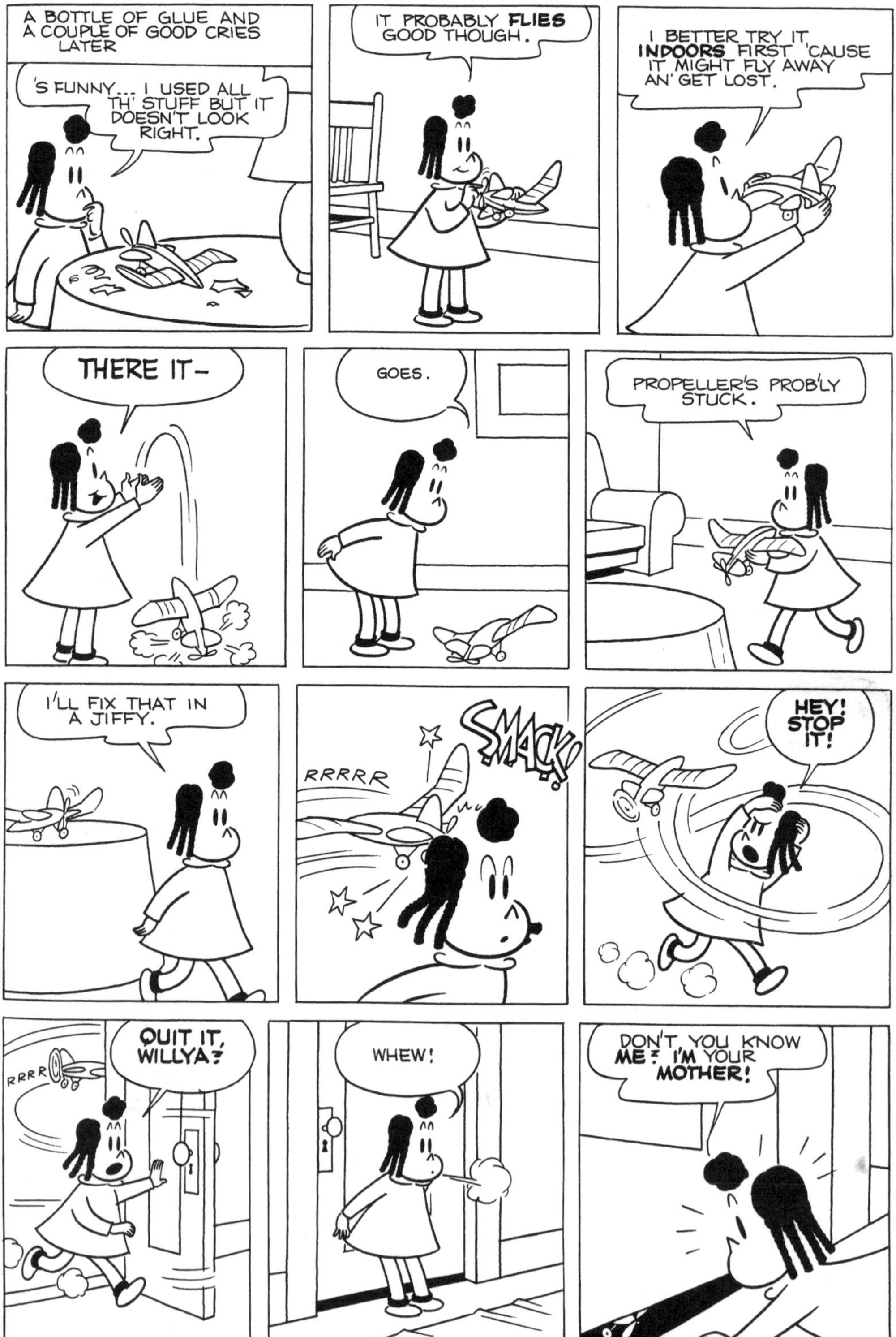
A BOTTLE OF GLUE AND A COUPLE OF GOOD CRIES LATER
'S FUNNY... I USED ALL TH' STUFF BUT IT DOESN'T LOOK RIGHT.
IT PROBABLY **FLIES** GOOD THOUGH.
I BETTER TRY IT **INDOORS** FIRST 'CAUSE IT MIGHT FLY AWAY AN' GET LOST.
THERE IT-
GOES.
PROPELLER'S PROB'LY STUCK.
I'LL FIX THAT IN A JIFFY.
RRRRR
SMACK!
HEY! STOP IT!
RRRR
QUIT IT, WILLYA?
WHEW!
DON'T YOU KNOW **ME**? **I'M** YOUR **MOTHER!**

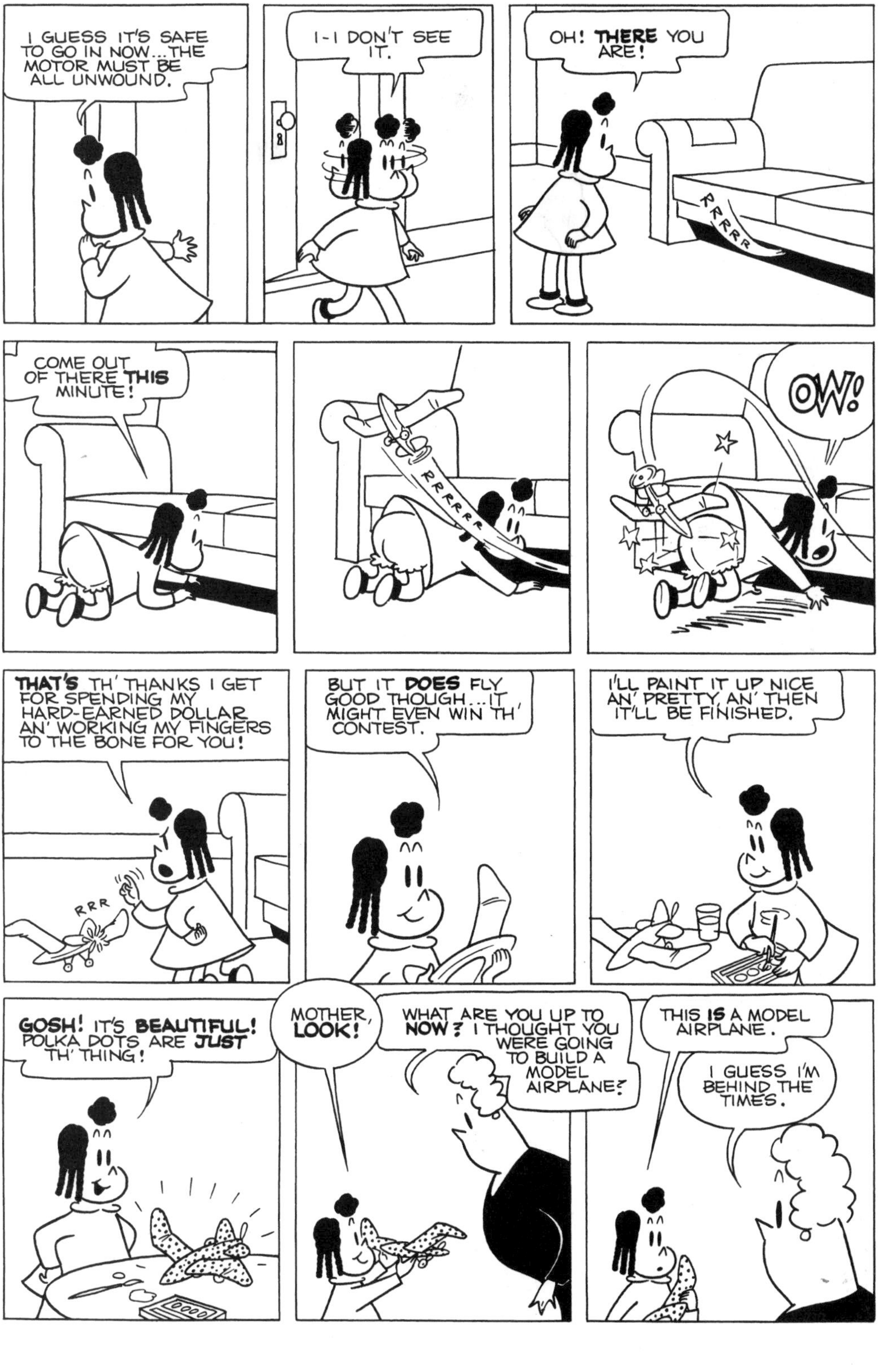
I GUESS IT'S SAFE TO GO IN NOW... THE MOTOR MUST BE ALL UNWOUND.
I-I DON'T SEE IT.
OH! THERE YOU ARE!
RRRRR
COME OUT OF THERE THIS MINUTE!
RRRRRR
OW!
THAT'S TH' THANKS I GET FOR SPENDING MY HARD-EARNED DOLLAR AN' WORKING MY FINGERS TO THE BONE FOR YOU!
RRR
BUT IT DOES FLY GOOD THOUGH... IT MIGHT EVEN WIN TH' CONTEST.
I'LL PAINT IT UP NICE AN' PRETTY, AN' THEN IT'LL BE FINISHED.
GOSH! IT'S BEAUTIFUL! POLKA DOTS ARE JUST TH' THING!
MOTHER, LOOK!
WHAT ARE YOU UP TO NOW? I THOUGHT YOU WERE GOING TO BUILD A MODEL AIRPLANE?
THIS IS A MODEL AIRPLANE.
I GUESS I'M BEHIND THE TIMES.

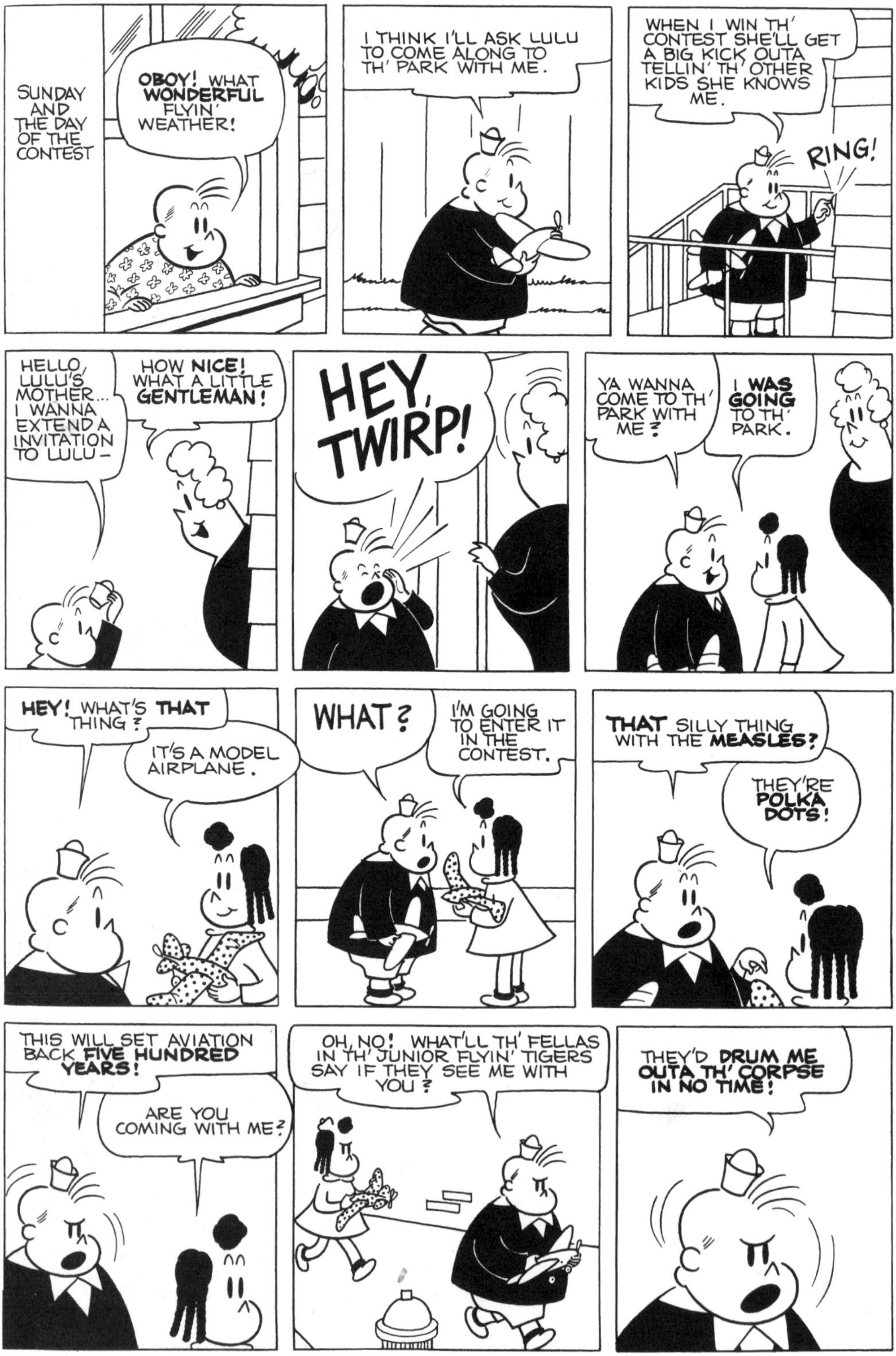
SUNDAY AND THE DAY OF THE CONTEST
OBOY! WHAT WONDERFUL FLYIN' WEATHER!
I THINK I'LL ASK LULU TO COME ALONG TO TH' PARK WITH ME.
WHEN I WIN TH' CONTEST SHE'LL GET A BIG KICK OUTA TELLIN' TH' OTHER KIDS SHE KNOWS ME.
RING!
HELLO, LULU'S MOTHER... I WANNA EXTEND A INVITATION TO LULU—
HOW NICE! WHAT A LITTLE GENTLEMAN!
HEY, TWIRP!
YA WANNA COME TO TH' PARK WITH ME?
I WAS GOING TO TH' PARK.
HEY! WHAT'S THAT THING?
IT'S A MODEL AIRPLANE.
WHAT?
I'M GOING TO ENTER IT IN THE CONTEST.
THAT SILLY THING WITH THE MEASLES?
THEY'RE POLKA DOTS!
THIS WILL SET AVIATION BACK FIVE HUNDRED YEARS!
ARE YOU COMING WITH ME?
OH, NO! WHAT'LL TH' FELLAS IN TH' JUNIOR FLYIN' TIGERS SAY IF THEY SEE ME WITH YOU?
THEY'D DRUM ME OUTA TH' CORPSE IN NO TIME!

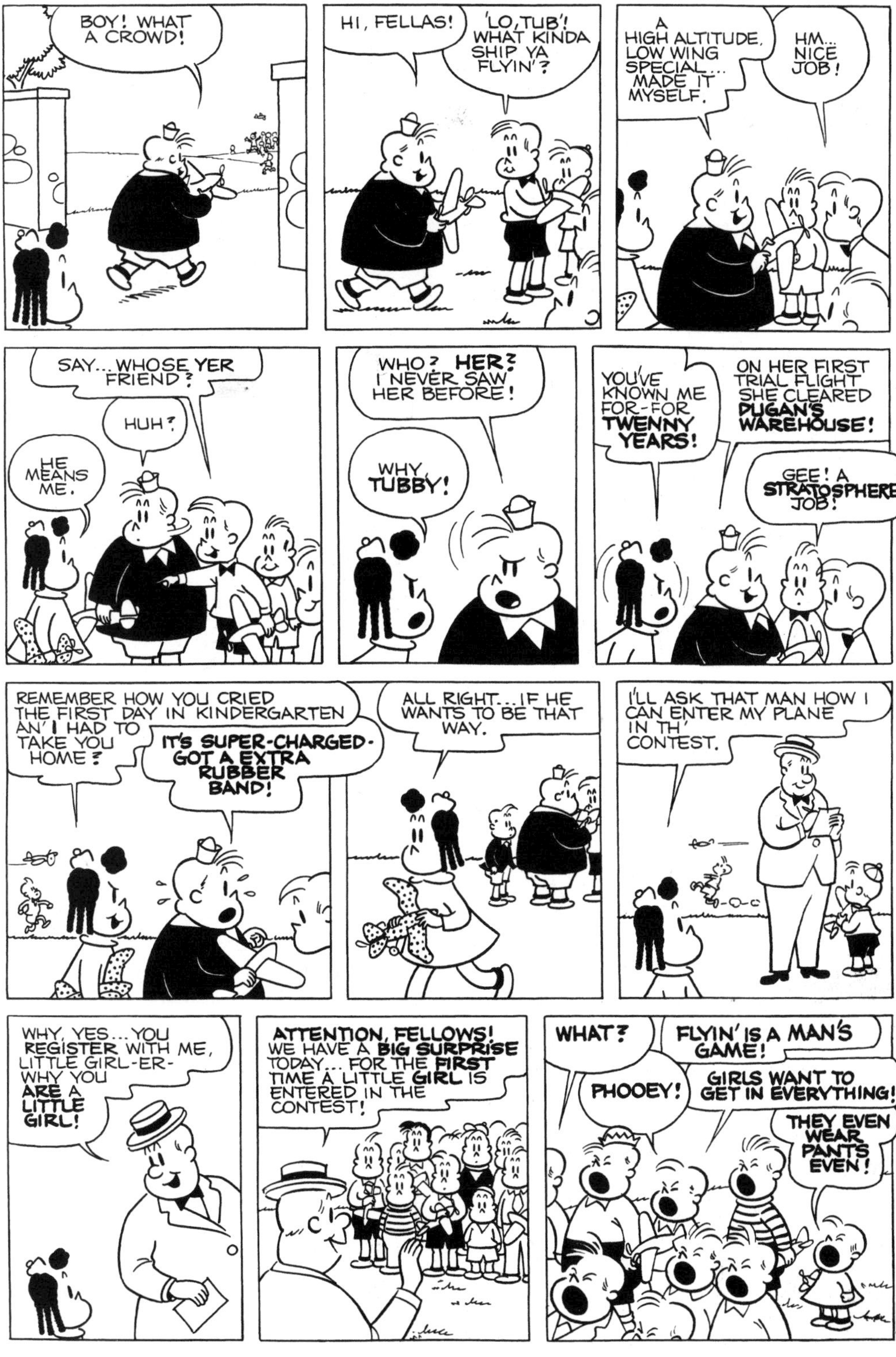
BOY! WHAT A CROWD!
HI, FELLAS!
'LO, TUB'! WHAT KINDA SHIP YA FLYIN'?
A HIGH ALTITUDE, LOW WING SPECIAL... MADE IT MYSELF.
HM... NICE JOB!
SAY... WHOSE YER FRIEND?
HUH?
HE MEANS ME.
WHO? HER? I NEVER SAW HER BEFORE!
WHY, TUBBY!
YOU'VE KNOWN ME FOR-FOR TWENNY YEARS!
ON HER FIRST TRIAL FLIGHT SHE CLEARED DUGAN'S WAREHOUSE!
GEE! A STRATOSPHERE JOB!
REMEMBER HOW YOU CRIED THE FIRST DAY IN KINDERGARTEN AN' I HAD TO TAKE YOU HOME?
IT'S SUPER-CHARGED-GOT A EXTRA RUBBER BAND!
ALL RIGHT... IF HE WANTS TO BE THAT WAY.
I'LL ASK THAT MAN HOW I CAN ENTER MY PLANE IN TH' CONTEST.
WHY, YES... YOU REGISTER WITH ME, LITTLE GIRL-ER-WHY YOU ARE A LITTLE GIRL!
ATTENTION, FELLOWS! WE HAVE A BIG SURPRISE TODAY... FOR THE FIRST TIME A LITTLE GIRL IS ENTERED IN THE CONTEST!
WHAT?
FLYIN' IS A MAN'S GAME!
PHOOEY!
GIRLS WANT TO GET IN EVERYTHING!
THEY EVEN WEAR PANTS EVEN!

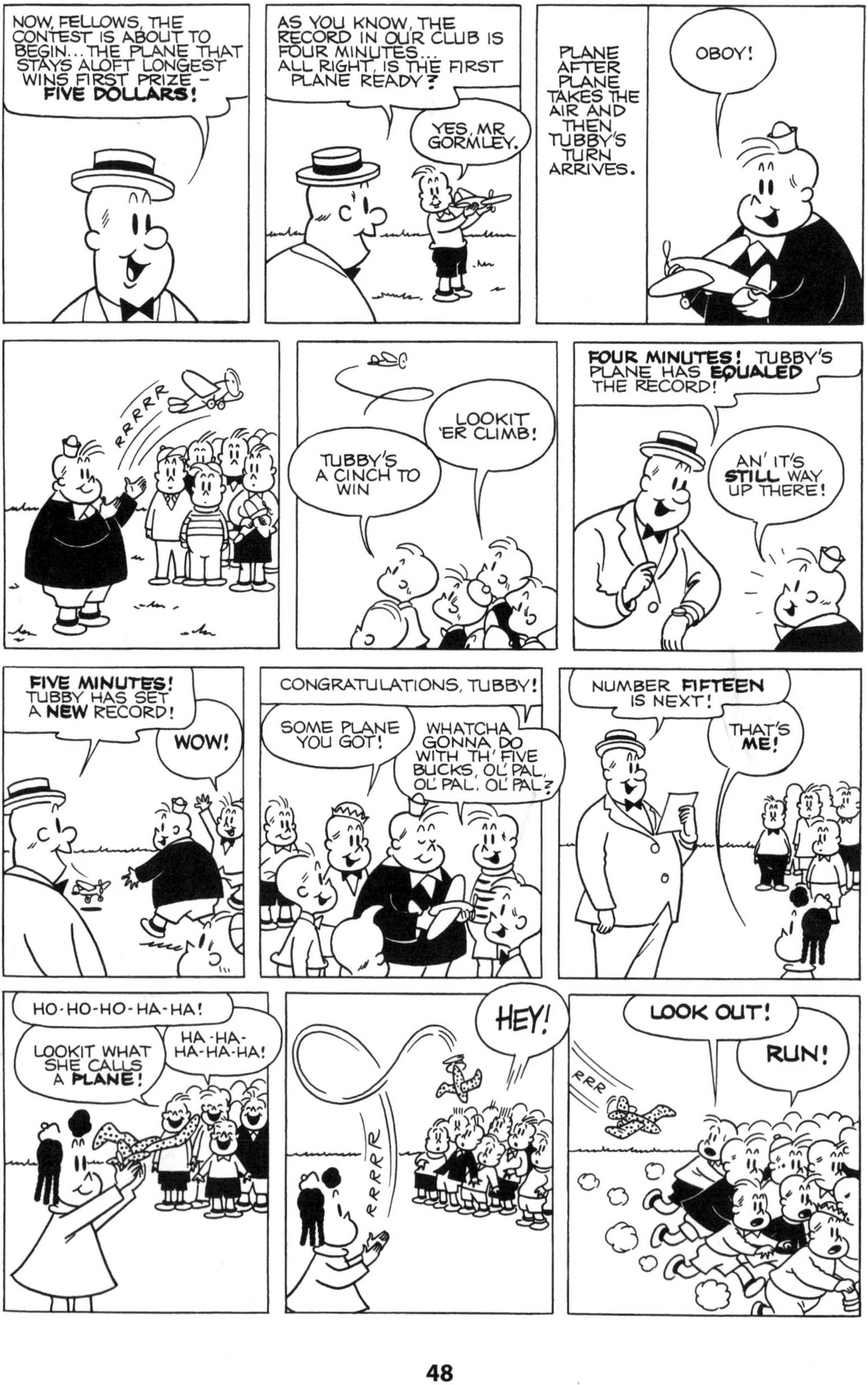
NOW, FELLOWS, THE CONTEST IS ABOUT TO BEGIN... THE PLANE THAT STAYS ALOFT LONGEST WINS FIRST PRIZE - **FIVE DOLLARS!**
AS YOU KNOW, THE RECORD IN OUR CLUB IS FOUR MINUTES... ALL RIGHT, IS THE FIRST PLANE READY?
YES, MR GORMLEY.
PLANE AFTER PLANE TAKES THE AIR AND THEN TUBBY'S TURN ARRIVES.
OBOY!
RRRRR
TUBBY'S A CINCH TO WIN
LOOKIT 'ER CLIMB!
FOUR MINUTES! TUBBY'S PLANE HAS **EQUALED** THE RECORD!
AN' IT'S **STILL** WAY UP THERE!
FIVE MINUTES! TUBBY HAS SET A **NEW** RECORD!
WOW!
CONGRATULATIONS, TUBBY!
SOME PLANE YOU GOT!
WHATCHA GONNA DO WITH TH' FIVE BUCKS, OL' PAL, OL' PAL, OL' PAL?
NUMBER **FIFTEEN** IS NEXT!
THAT'S **ME!**
HO-HO-HO-HA-HA!
LOOKIT WHAT SHE CALLS A **PLANE!**
HA-HA-HA-HA-HA!
HEY!
RRRRR
LOOK OUT!
RUN!
RRR

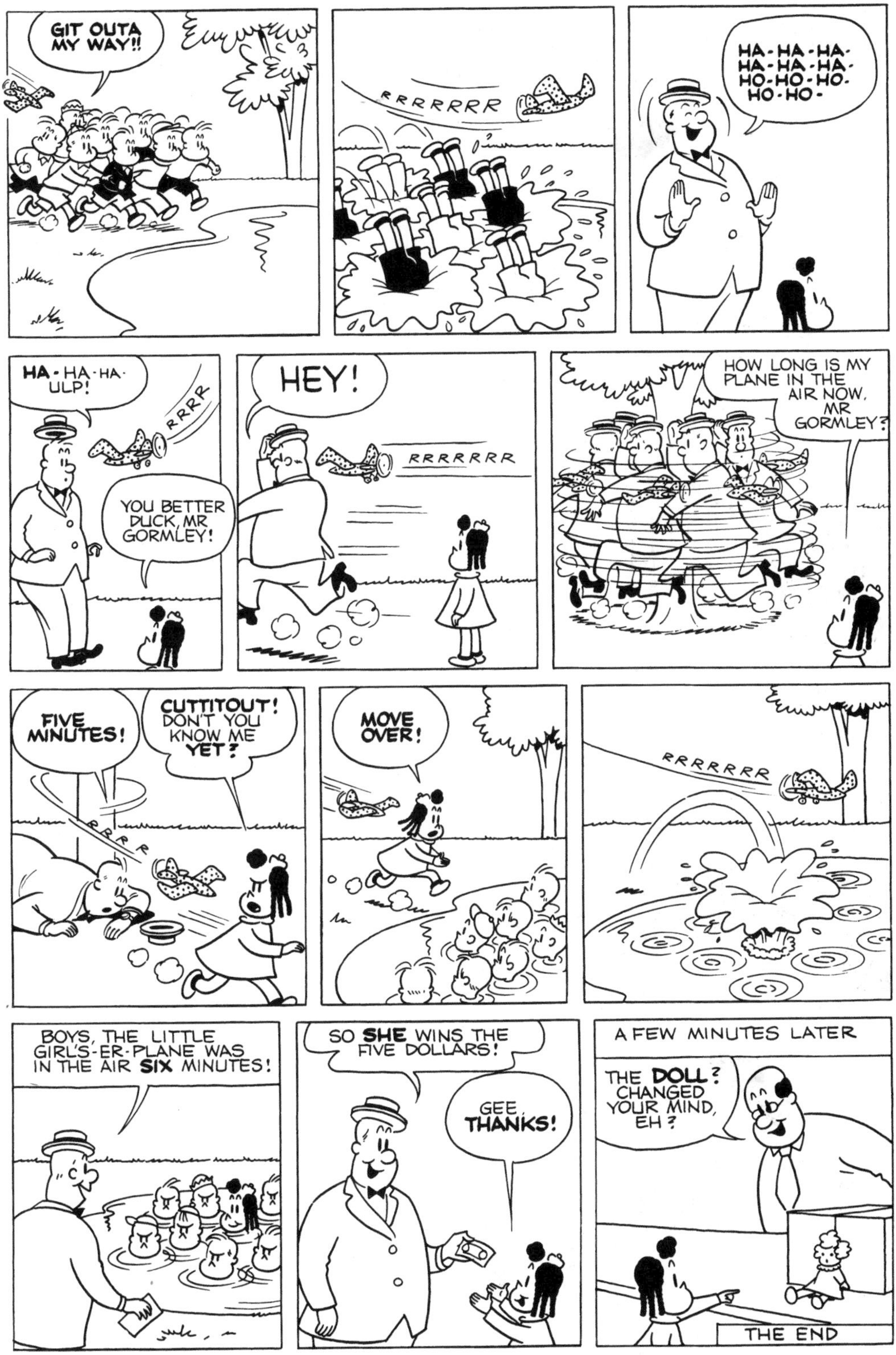
GIT OUTA MY WAY!!
RRRRRRR
HA-HA-HA-HA-HA-HA-HO-HO-HO-HO-HO-
HA-HA-HA-ULP!
RRRR
YOU BETTER DUCK, MR GORMLEY!
HEY!
RRRRRRR
HOW LONG IS MY PLANE IN THE AIR NOW, MR GORMLEY?
FIVE MINUTES!
CUTTITOUT! DON'T YOU KNOW ME YET?
RRRR
MOVE OVER!
RRRRRRR
BOYS, THE LITTLE GIRL'S-ER-PLANE WAS IN THE AIR SIX MINUTES!
SO SHE WINS THE FIVE DOLLARS!
GEE THANKS!
A FEW MINUTES LATER
THE DOLL? CHANGED YOUR MIND, EH?
THE END

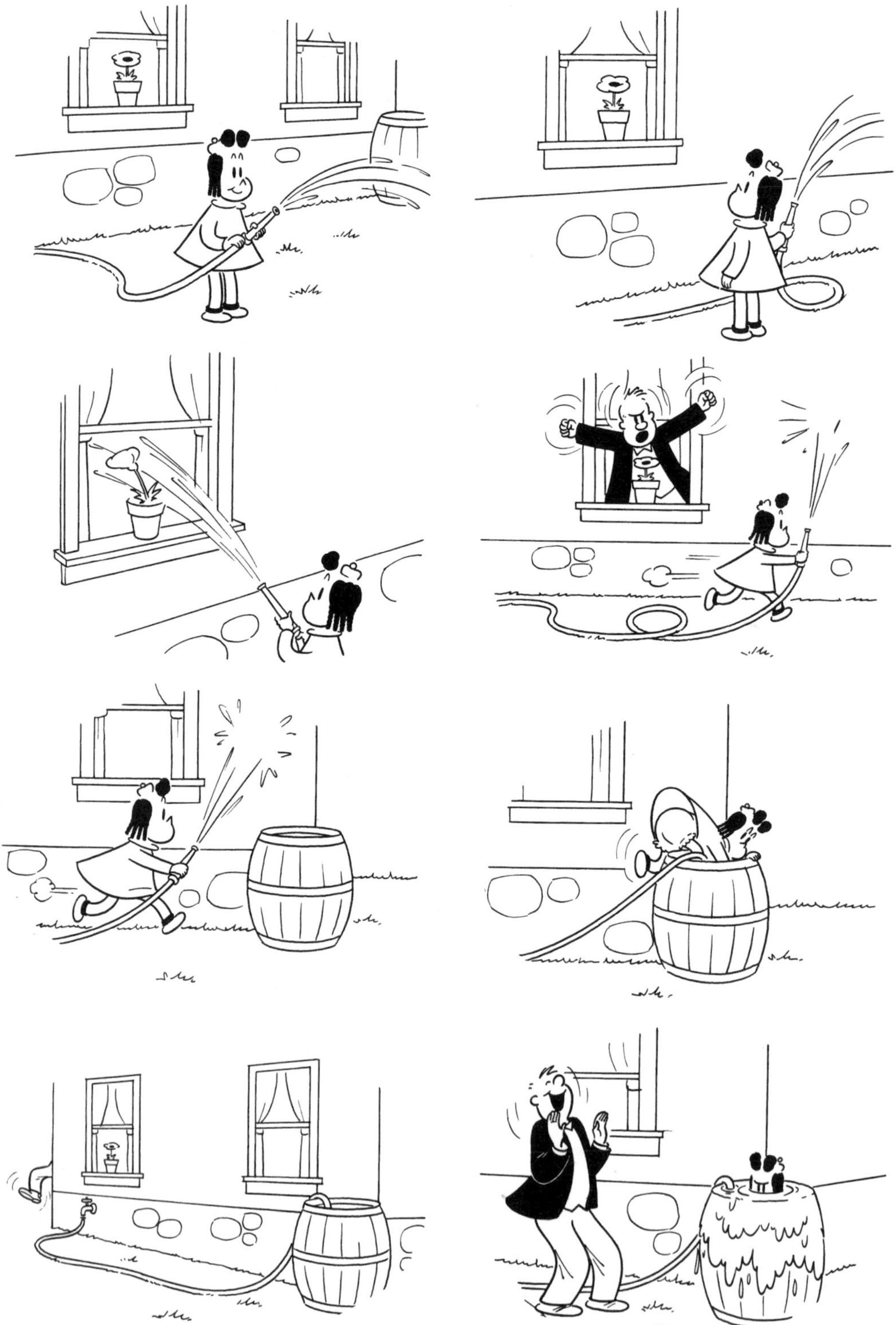

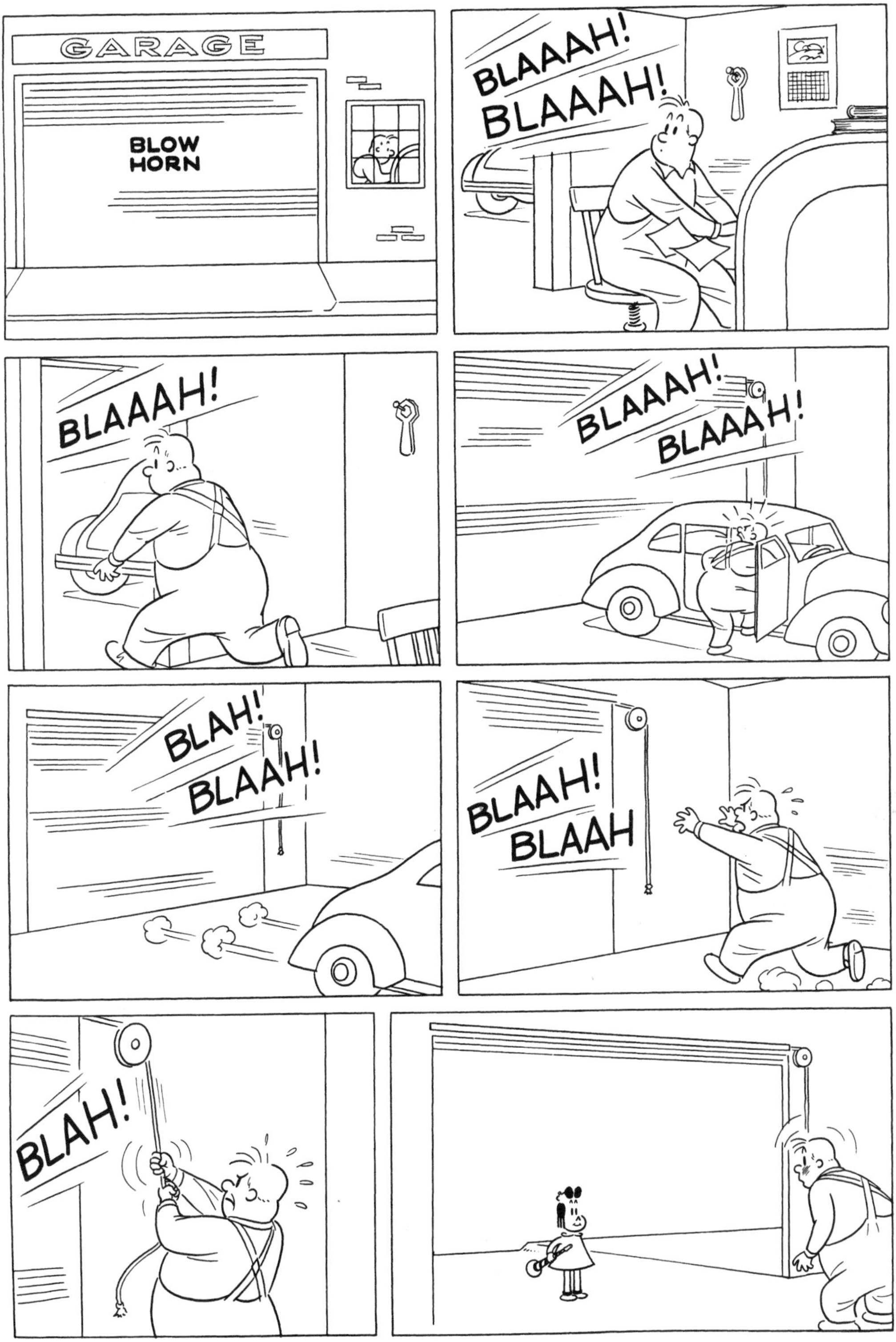
GARAGE
BLOW HORN
BLAAAH!
BLAAAH!
BLAAAH!
BLAAAH!
BLAAAH!
BLAH!
BLAAH!
BLAAH!
BLAAH
BLAH!

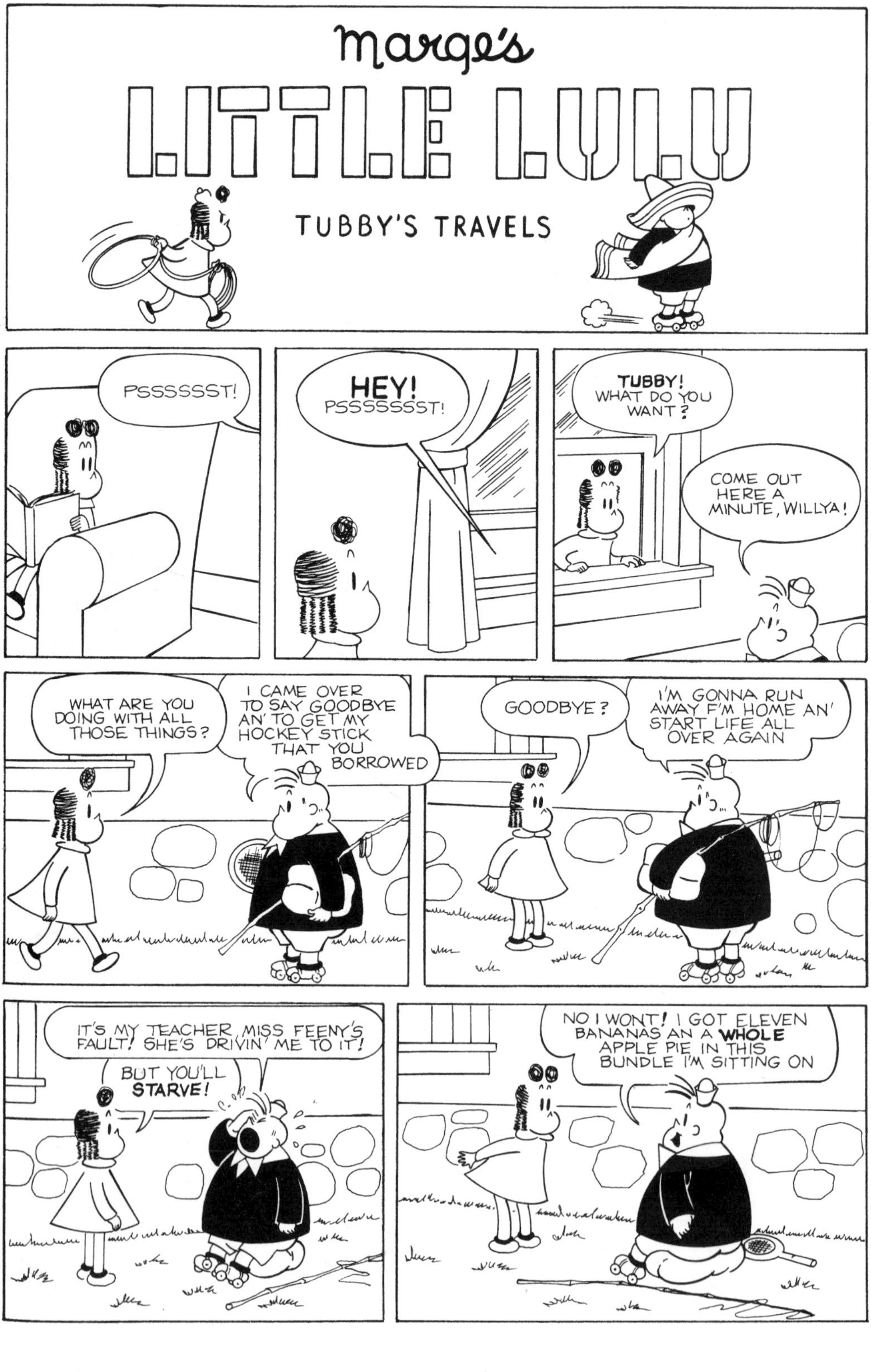
marge's
LITTLE LULU
TUBBY'S TRAVELS
PSSSSSST!
HEY!
PSSSSSSST!
TUBBY!
WHAT DO YOU WANT?
COME OUT HERE A MINUTE, WILLYA!
WHAT ARE YOU DOING WITH ALL THOSE THINGS?
I CAME OVER TO SAY GOODBYE AN' TO GET MY HOCKEY STICK THAT YOU BORROWED
GOODBYE?
I'M GONNA RUN AWAY F'M HOME AN' START LIFE ALL OVER AGAIN
IT'S MY TEACHER MISS FEENY'S FAULT! SHE'S DRIVIN' ME TO IT!
BUT YOU'LL STARVE!
NO I WONT! I GOT ELEVEN BANANAS AN A WHOLE APPLE PIE IN THIS BUNDLE I'M SITTING ON

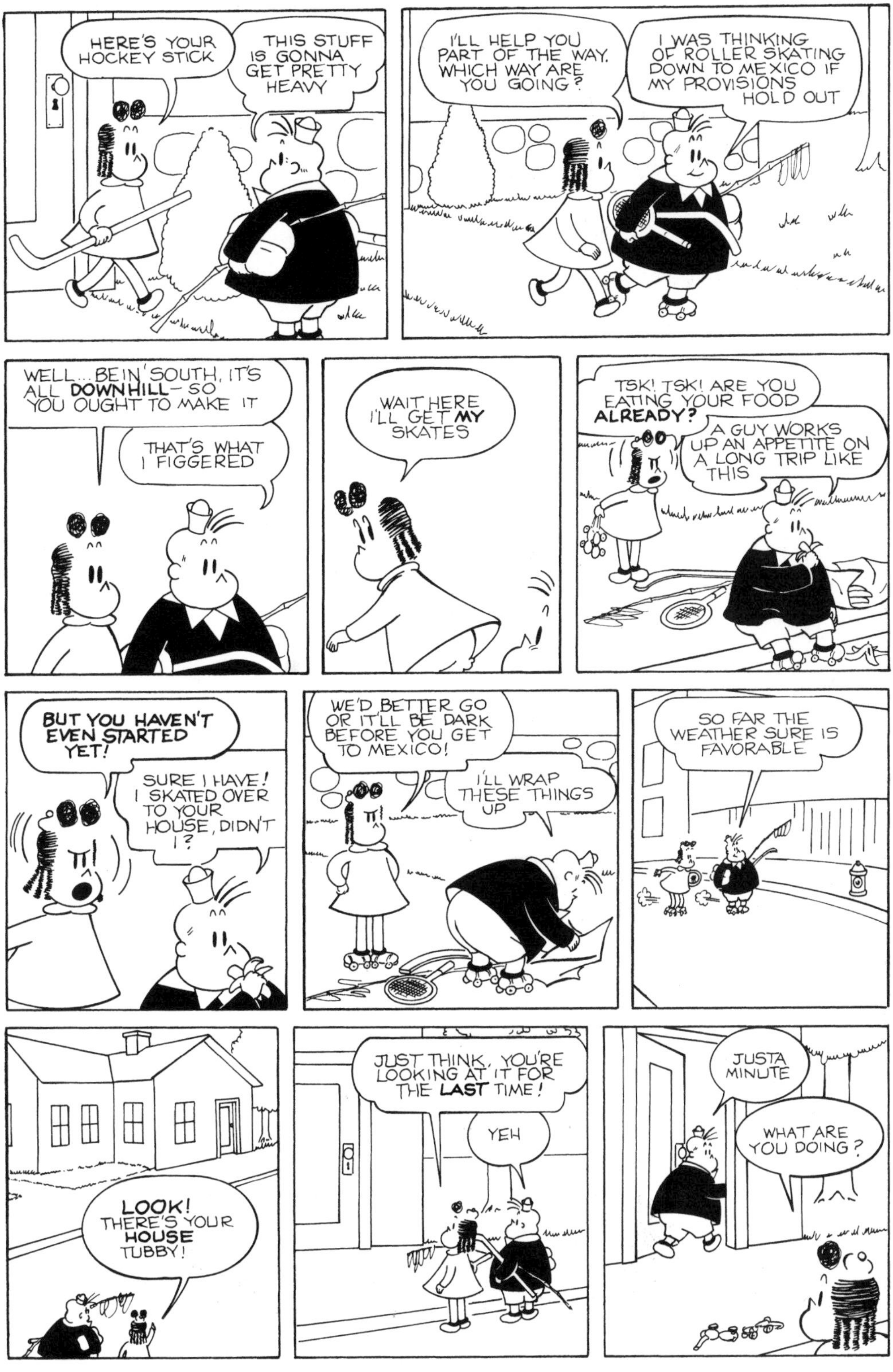
HERE'S YOUR HOCKEY STICK
THIS STUFF IS GONNA GET PRETTY HEAVY
I'LL HELP YOU PART OF THE WAY. WHICH WAY ARE YOU GOING?
I WAS THINKING OF ROLLER SKATING DOWN TO MEXICO IF MY PROVISIONS HOLD OUT
WELL... BEIN' SOUTH, IT'S ALL DOWNHILL—SO YOU OUGHT TO MAKE IT
THAT'S WHAT I FIGGERED
WAIT HERE I'LL GET MY SKATES
TSK! TSK! ARE YOU EATING YOUR FOOD ALREADY?
A GUY WORKS UP AN APPETITE ON A LONG TRIP LIKE THIS
BUT YOU HAVEN'T EVEN STARTED YET!
SURE I HAVE! I SKATED OVER TO YOUR HOUSE, DIDN'T I?
WE'D BETTER GO OR IT'LL BE DARK BEFORE YOU GET TO MEXICO!
I'LL WRAP THESE THINGS UP
SO FAR THE WEATHER SURE IS FAVORABLE
LOOK! THERE'S YOUR HOUSE TUBBY!
JUST THINK, YOU'RE LOOKING AT IT FOR THE LAST TIME!
YEH
JUSTA MINUTE
WHAT ARE YOU DOING?

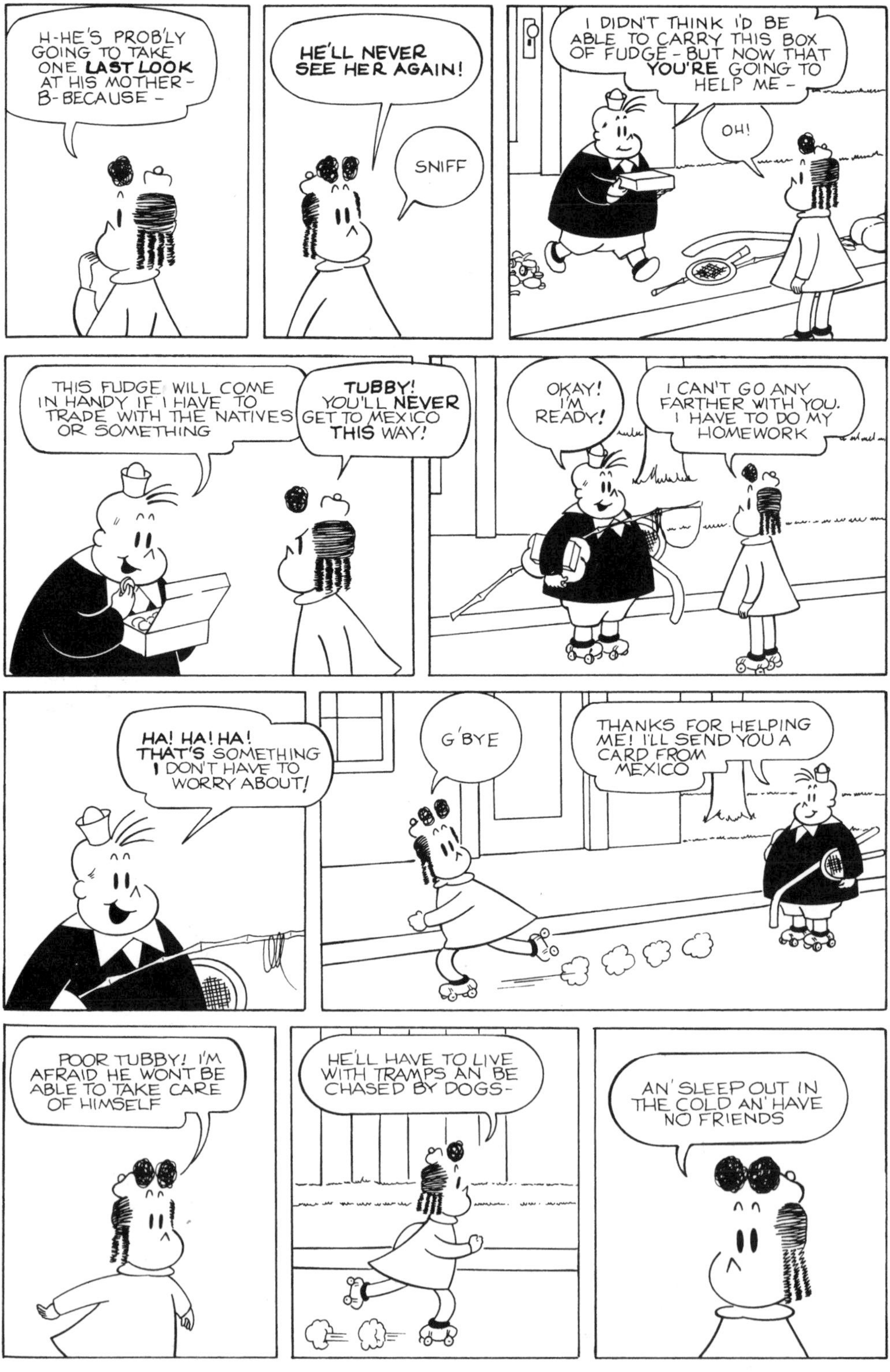
H-HE'S PROB'LY GOING TO TAKE ONE **LAST LOOK** AT HIS MOTHER- B-BECAUSE -
HE'LL NEVER SEE HER AGAIN!
SNIFF
I DIDN'T THINK I'D BE ABLE TO CARRY THIS BOX OF FUDGE - BUT NOW THAT **YOU'RE** GOING TO HELP ME -
OH!
THIS FUDGE WILL COME IN HANDY IF I HAVE TO TRADE WITH THE NATIVES OR SOMETHING
TUBBY! YOU'LL **NEVER** GET TO MEXICO **THIS** WAY!
OKAY! I'M READY!
I CAN'T GO ANY FARTHER WITH YOU. I HAVE TO DO MY HOMEWORK
HA! HA! HA! THAT'S SOMETHING **I** DON'T HAVE TO WORRY ABOUT!
G'BYE
THANKS FOR HELPING ME! I'LL SEND YOU A CARD FROM MEXICO
POOR TUBBY! I'M AFRAID HE WON'T BE ABLE TO TAKE CARE OF HIMSELF
HE'LL HAVE TO LIVE WITH TRAMPS AN' BE CHASED BY DOGS-
AN' SLEEP OUT IN THE COLD AN' HAVE NO FRIENDS

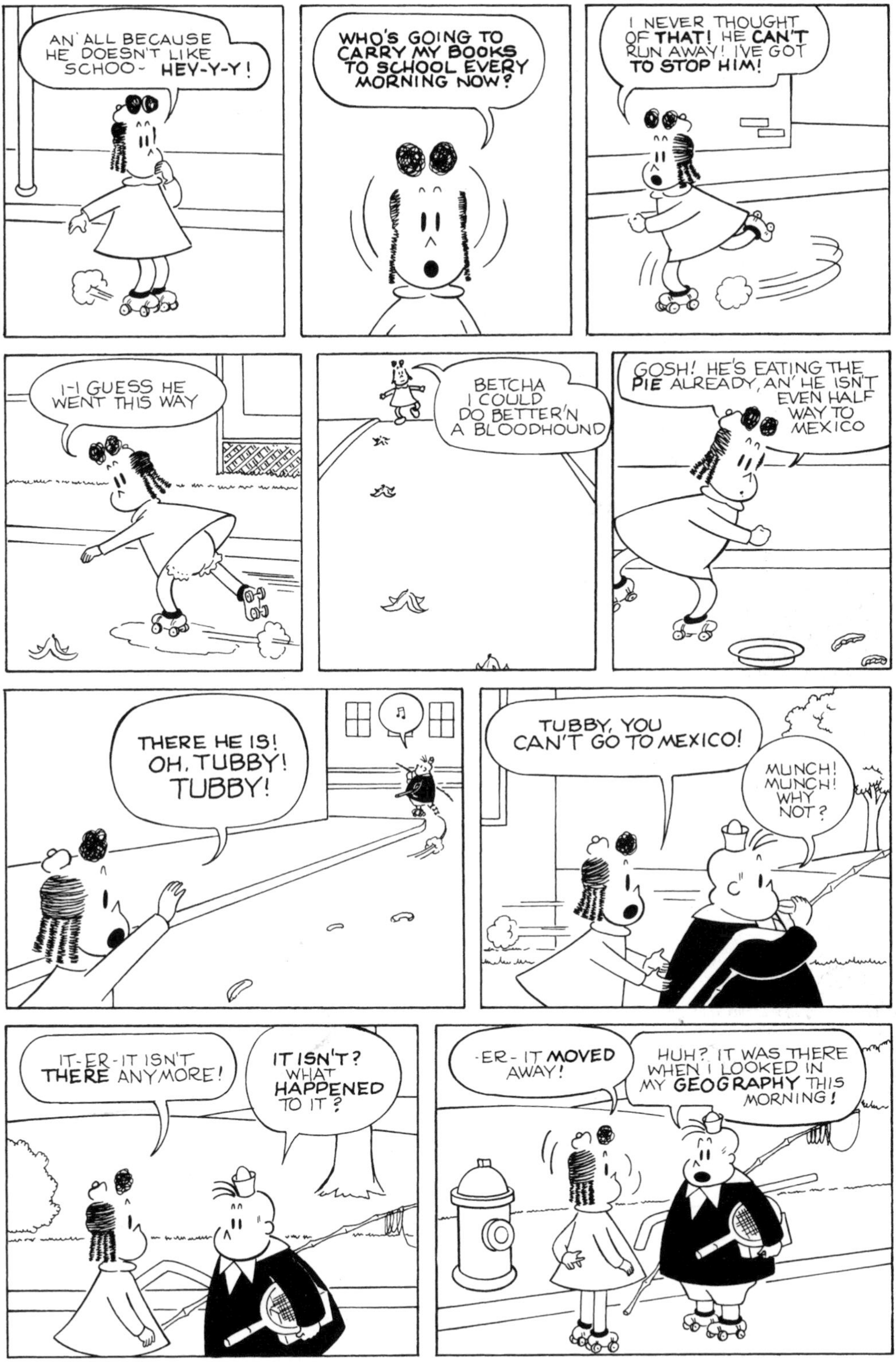
AN' ALL BECAUSE HE DOESN'T LIKE SCHOO- HEY-Y-Y!
WHO'S GOING TO CARRY MY BOOKS TO SCHOOL EVERY MORNING NOW?
I NEVER THOUGHT OF THAT! HE CAN'T RUN AWAY! I'VE GOT TO STOP HIM!
I-I GUESS HE WENT THIS WAY
BETCHA I COULD DO BETTER'N A BLOODHOUND
GOSH! HE'S EATING THE PIE ALREADY, AN' HE ISN'T EVEN HALF WAY TO MEXICO
THERE HE IS! OH, TUBBY! TUBBY!
TUBBY, YOU CAN'T GO TO MEXICO!
MUNCH! MUNCH! WHY NOT?
IT-ER-IT ISN'T THERE ANYMORE!
IT ISN'T? WHAT HAPPENED TO IT?
-ER- IT MOVED AWAY!
HUH? IT WAS THERE WHEN I LOOKED IN MY GEOGRAPHY THIS MORNING!

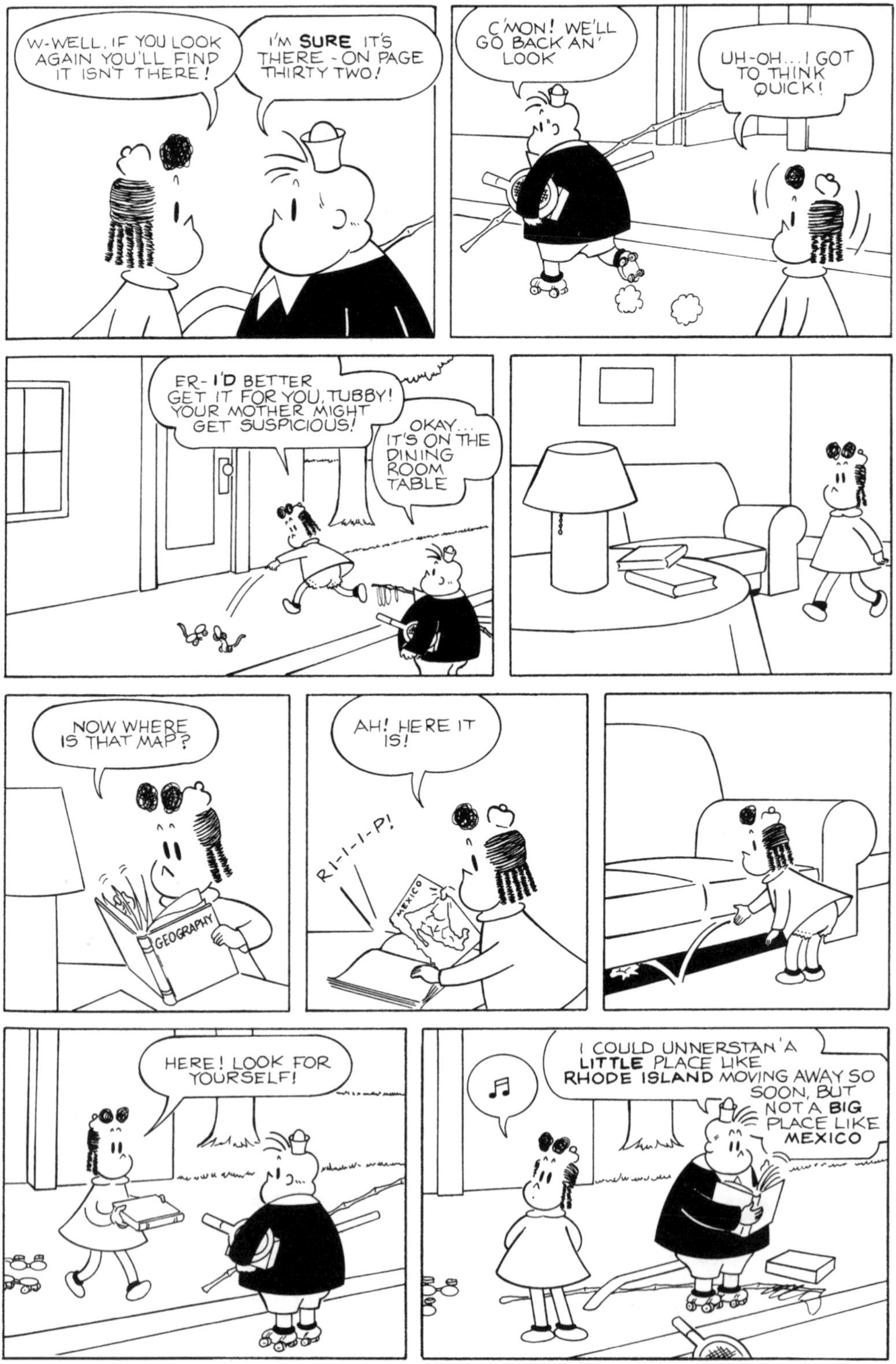
W-WELL, IF YOU LOOK AGAIN YOU'LL FIND IT ISN'T THERE!
I'M **SURE** IT'S THERE - ON PAGE THIRTY TWO!
C'MON! WE'LL GO BACK AN' LOOK
UH-OH... I GOT TO THINK QUICK!
ER- **I'D** BETTER GET IT FOR YOU, TUBBY! YOUR MOTHER MIGHT GET SUSPICIOUS!
OKAY... IT'S ON THE DINING ROOM TABLE
NOW WHERE IS THAT MAP?
GEOGRAPHY
AH! HERE IT IS!
RI-I-I-P!
MEXICO
HERE! LOOK FOR YOURSELF!
I COULD UNNERSTAN' A **LITTLE** PLACE LIKE **RHODE ISLAND** MOVING AWAY SO SOON, BUT NOT A **BIG** PLACE LIKE **MEXICO**

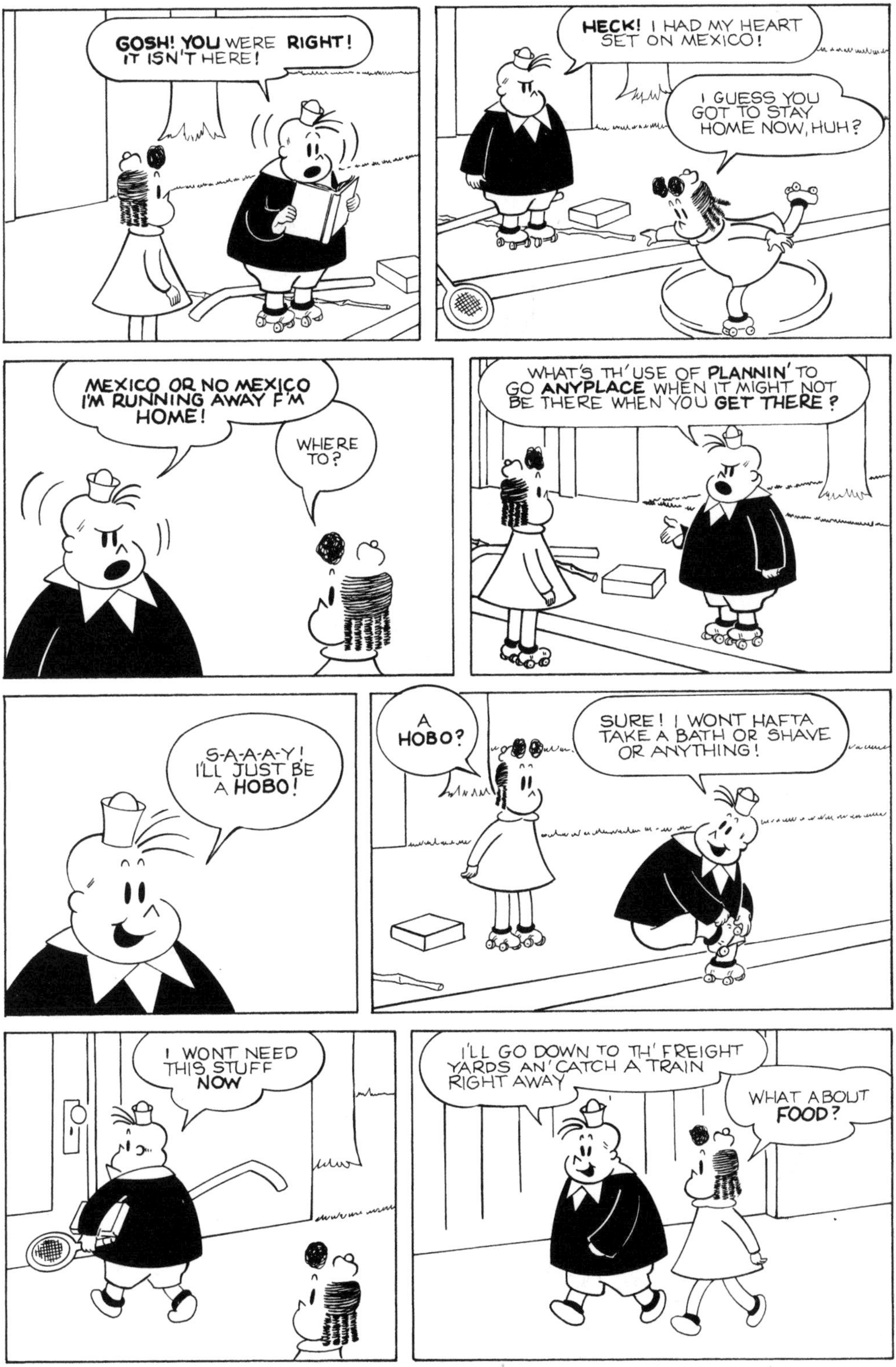
GOSH! YOU WERE RIGHT! IT ISN'T HERE!
HECK! I HAD MY HEART SET ON MEXICO!
I GUESS YOU GOT TO STAY HOME NOW, HUH?
MEXICO OR NO MEXICO I'M RUNNING AWAY F'M HOME!
WHERE TO?
WHAT'S TH' USE OF PLANNIN' TO GO ANYPLACE WHEN IT MIGHT NOT BE THERE WHEN YOU GET THERE?
S-A-A-A-Y! I'LL JUST BE A HOBO!
A HOBO?
SURE! I WONT HAFTA TAKE A BATH OR SHAVE OR ANYTHING!
I WONT NEED THIS STUFF NOW
I'LL GO DOWN TO TH' FREIGHT YARDS AN' CATCH A TRAIN RIGHT AWAY
WHAT ABOUT FOOD?

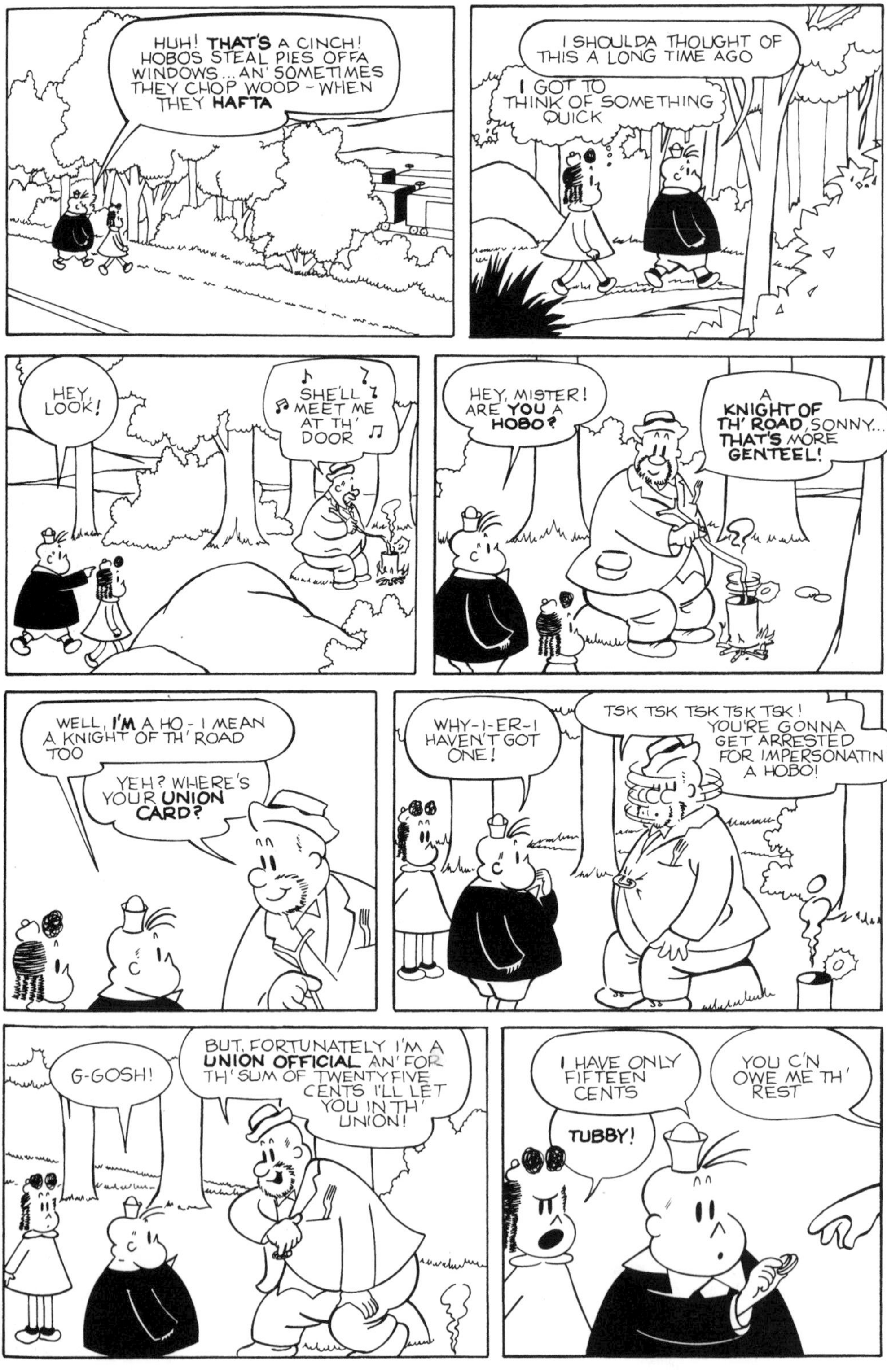
HUH! THAT'S A CINCH! HOBOS STEAL PIES OFFA WINDOWS... AN' SOMETIMES THEY CHOP WOOD - WHEN THEY HAFTA
I SHOULDA THOUGHT OF THIS A LONG TIME AGO
I GOT TO THINK OF SOMETHING QUICK
HEY, LOOK!
SHE'LL MEET ME AT TH' DOOR
HEY, MISTER! ARE YOU A HOBO?
A KNIGHT OF TH' ROAD, SONNY... THAT'S MORE GENTEEL!
WELL, I'M A HO - I MEAN A KNIGHT OF TH' ROAD TOO
YEH? WHERE'S YOUR UNION CARD?
WHY-I-ER-I HAVEN'T GOT ONE!
TSK TSK TSK TSK TSK! YOU'RE GONNA GET ARRESTED FOR IMPERSONATIN' A HOBO!
G-GOSH!
BUT, FORTUNATELY I'M A UNION OFFICIAL AN' FOR TH' SUM OF TWENTYFIVE CENTS I'LL LET YOU IN TH' UNION!
I HAVE ONLY FIFTEEN CENTS
TUBBY!
YOU C'N OWE ME TH' REST

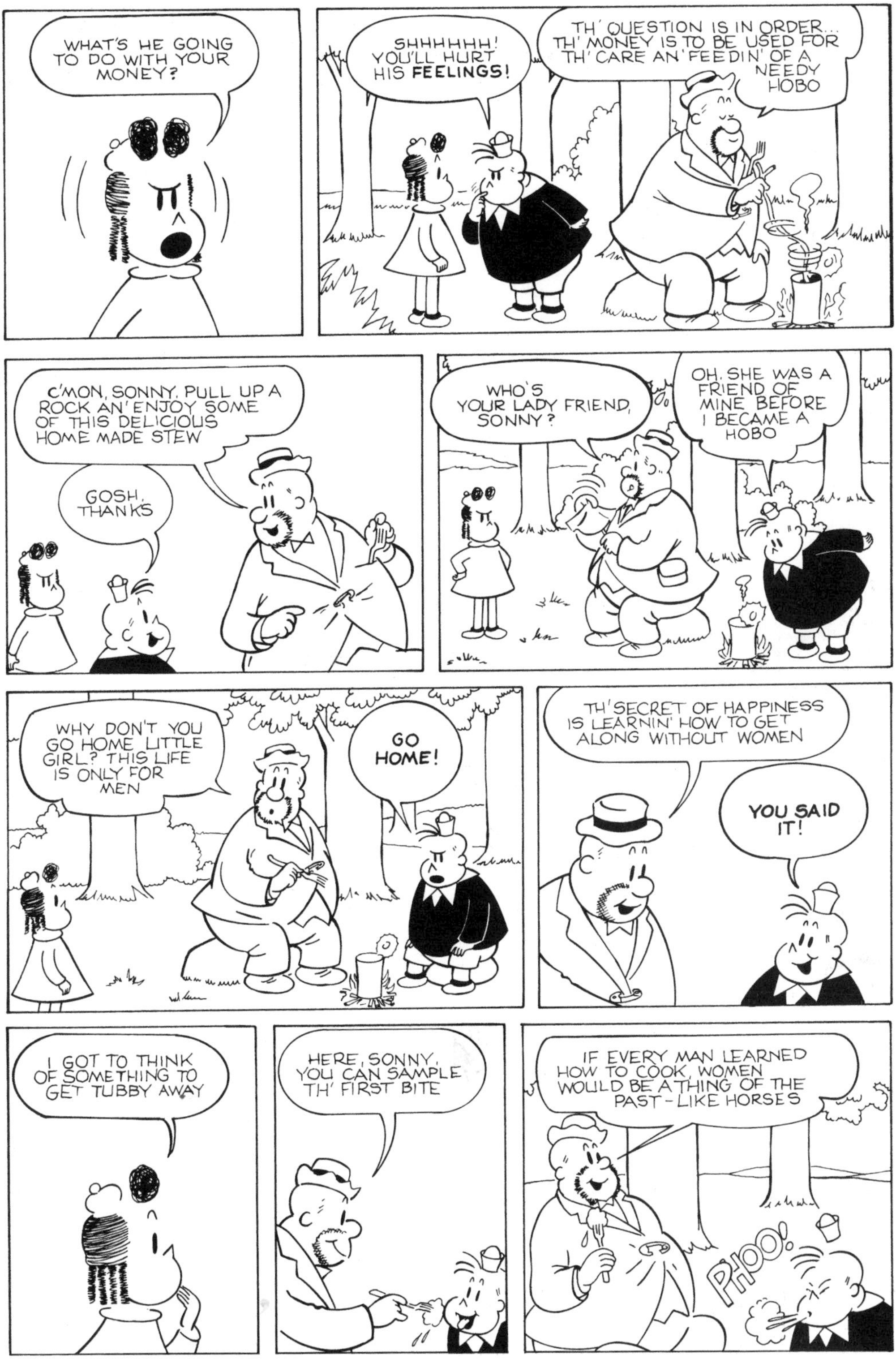
WHAT'S HE GOING TO DO WITH YOUR MONEY?
SHHHHHH! YOU'LL HURT HIS FEELINGS!
TH' QUESTION IS IN ORDER... TH' MONEY IS TO BE USED FOR TH' CARE AN' FEEDIN' OF A NEEDY HOBO
C'MON, SONNY, PULL UP A ROCK AN' ENJOY SOME OF THIS DELICIOUS HOME MADE STEW
GOSH, THANKS
WHO'S YOUR LADY FRIEND, SONNY?
OH, SHE WAS A FRIEND OF MINE BEFORE I BECAME A HOBO
WHY DON'T YOU GO HOME LITTLE GIRL? THIS LIFE IS ONLY FOR MEN
GO HOME!
TH' SECRET OF HAPPINESS IS LEARNIN' HOW TO GET ALONG WITHOUT WOMEN
YOU SAID IT!
I GOT TO THINK OF SOMETHING TO GET TUBBY AWAY
HERE, SONNY, YOU CAN SAMPLE TH' FIRST BITE
IF EVERY MAN LEARNED HOW TO COOK, WOMEN WOULD BE A THING OF THE PAST - LIKE HORSES
PHOO!

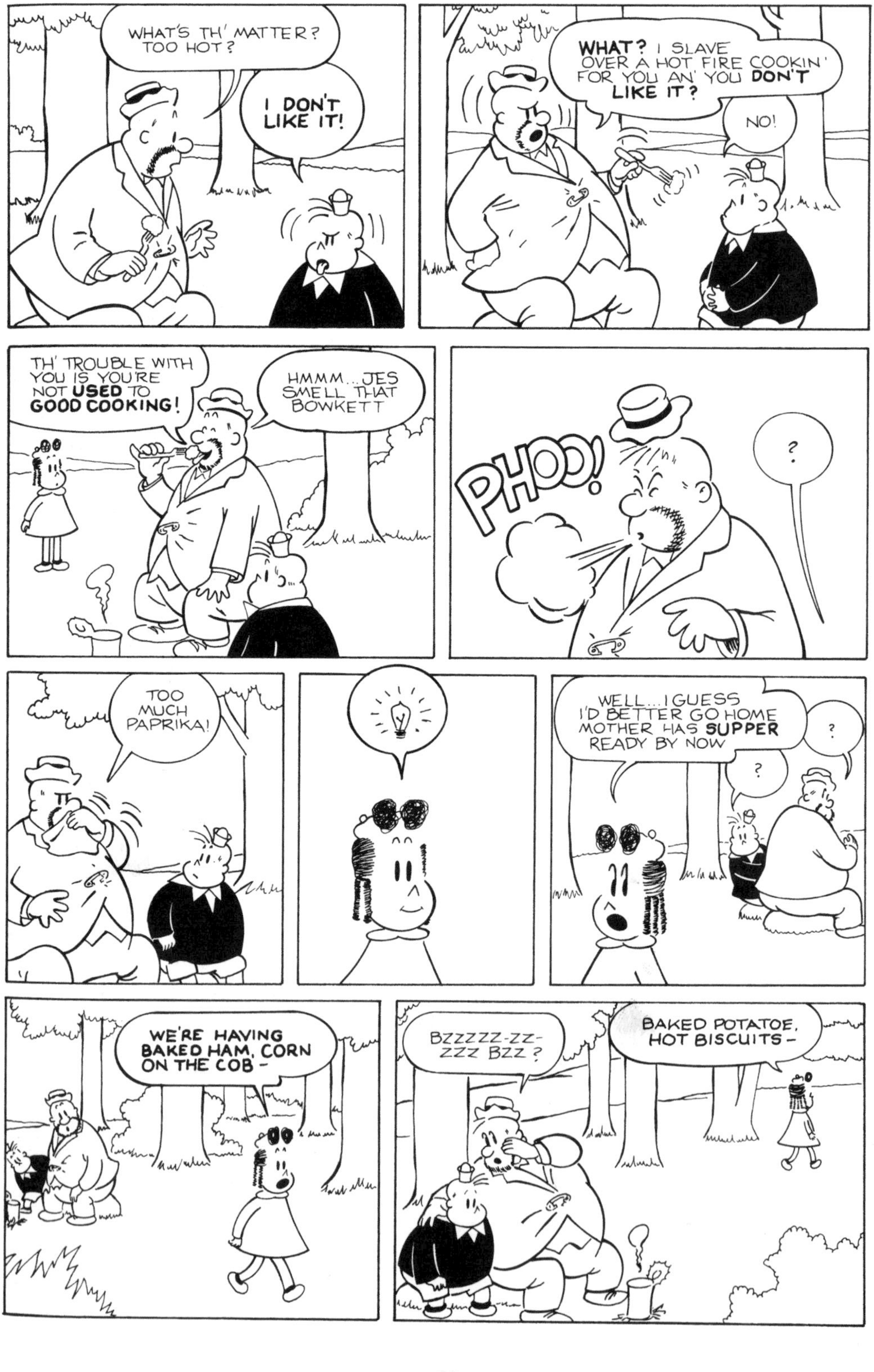
WHAT'S TH' MATTER? TOO HOT?
I DON'T LIKE IT!
WHAT? I SLAVE OVER A HOT FIRE COOKIN' FOR YOU AN' YOU DON'T LIKE IT?
NO!
TH' TROUBLE WITH YOU IS YOU'RE NOT USED TO GOOD COOKING!
HMMM...JES SMELL THAT BOWKETT
PHOO!
?
TOO MUCH PAPRIKA!
WELL...I GUESS I'D BETTER GO HOME MOTHER HAS SUPPER READY BY NOW
?
?
WE'RE HAVING BAKED HAM, CORN ON THE COB-
BZZZZZ-ZZ-ZZZ BZZ?
BAKED POTATOE, HOT BISCUITS-

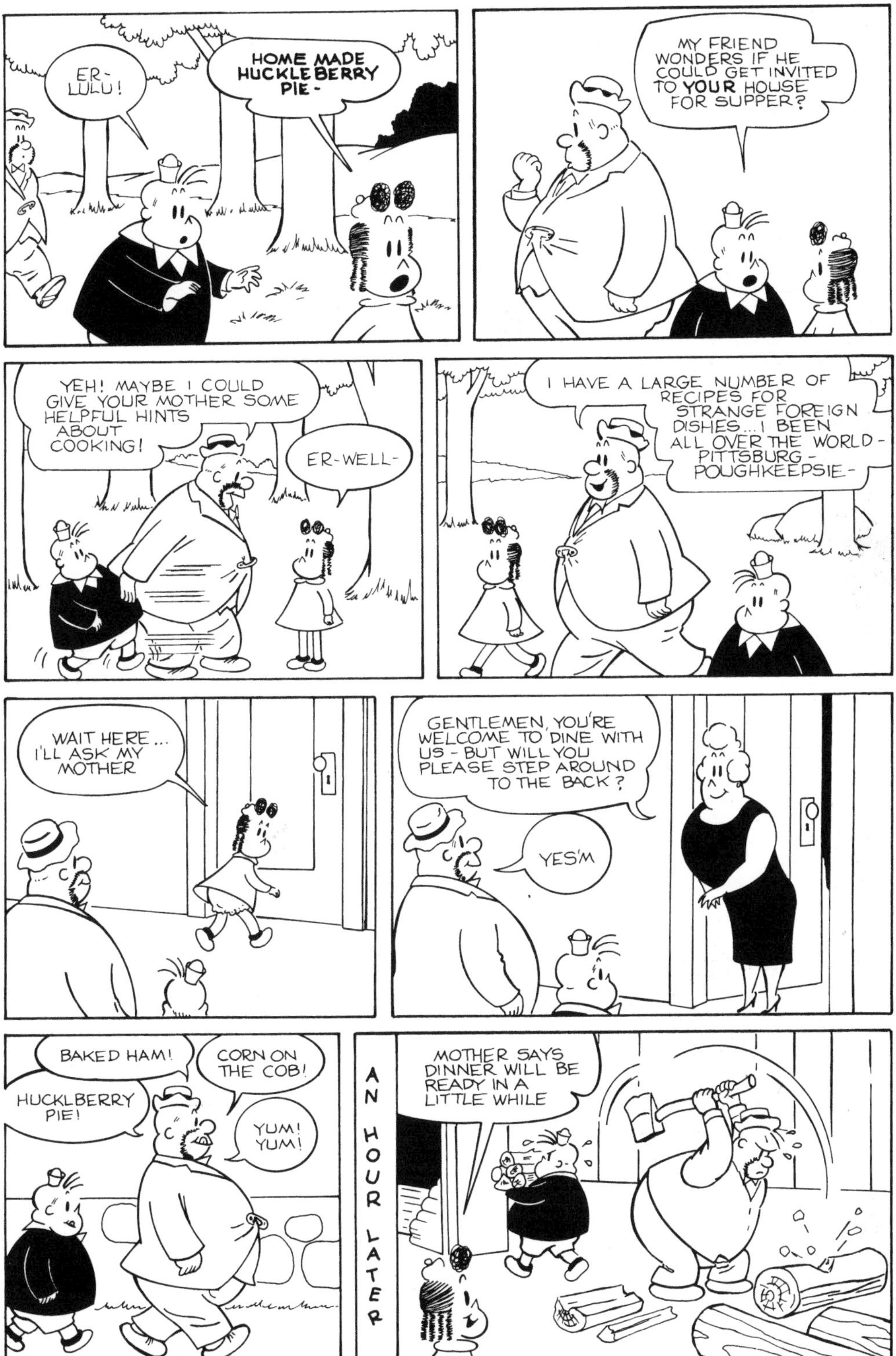
ER-LULU!
HOME MADE HUCKLEBERRY PIE-
MY FRIEND WONDERS IF HE COULD GET INVITED TO YOUR HOUSE FOR SUPPER?
YEH! MAYBE I COULD GIVE YOUR MOTHER SOME HELPFUL HINTS ABOUT COOKING!
ER-WELL-
I HAVE A LARGE NUMBER OF RECIPES FOR STRANGE FOREIGN DISHES...I BEEN ALL OVER THE WORLD-PITTSBURG-POUGHKEEPSIE-
WAIT HERE... I'LL ASK MY MOTHER
GENTLEMEN, YOU'RE WELCOME TO DINE WITH US - BUT WILL YOU PLEASE STEP AROUND TO THE BACK?
YES'M
BAKED HAM!
HUCKLBERRY PIE!
CORN ON THE COB!
YUM! YUM!
AN HOUR LATER
MOTHER SAYS DINNER WILL BE READY IN A LITTLE WHILE

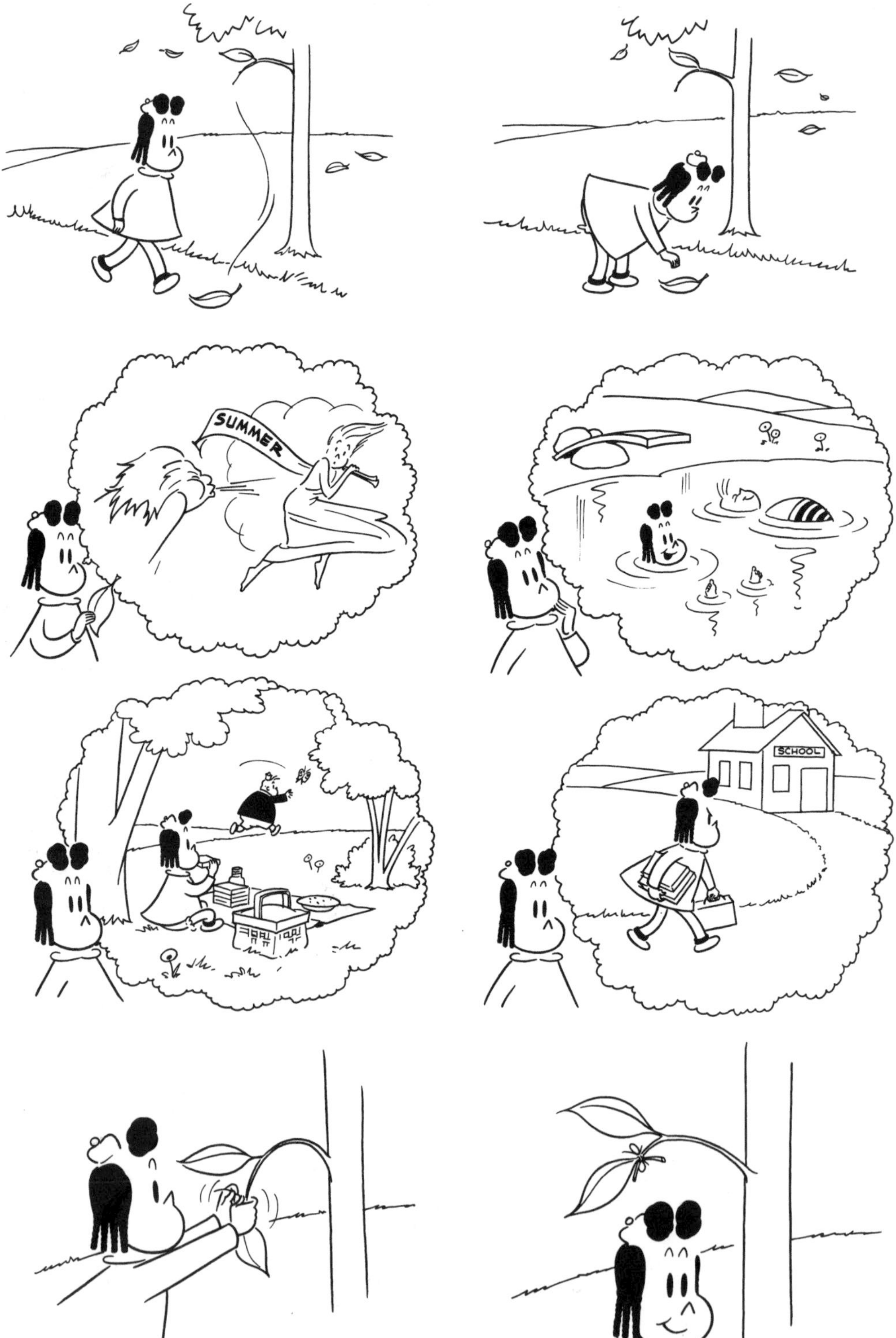
SUMMER
SCHOOL

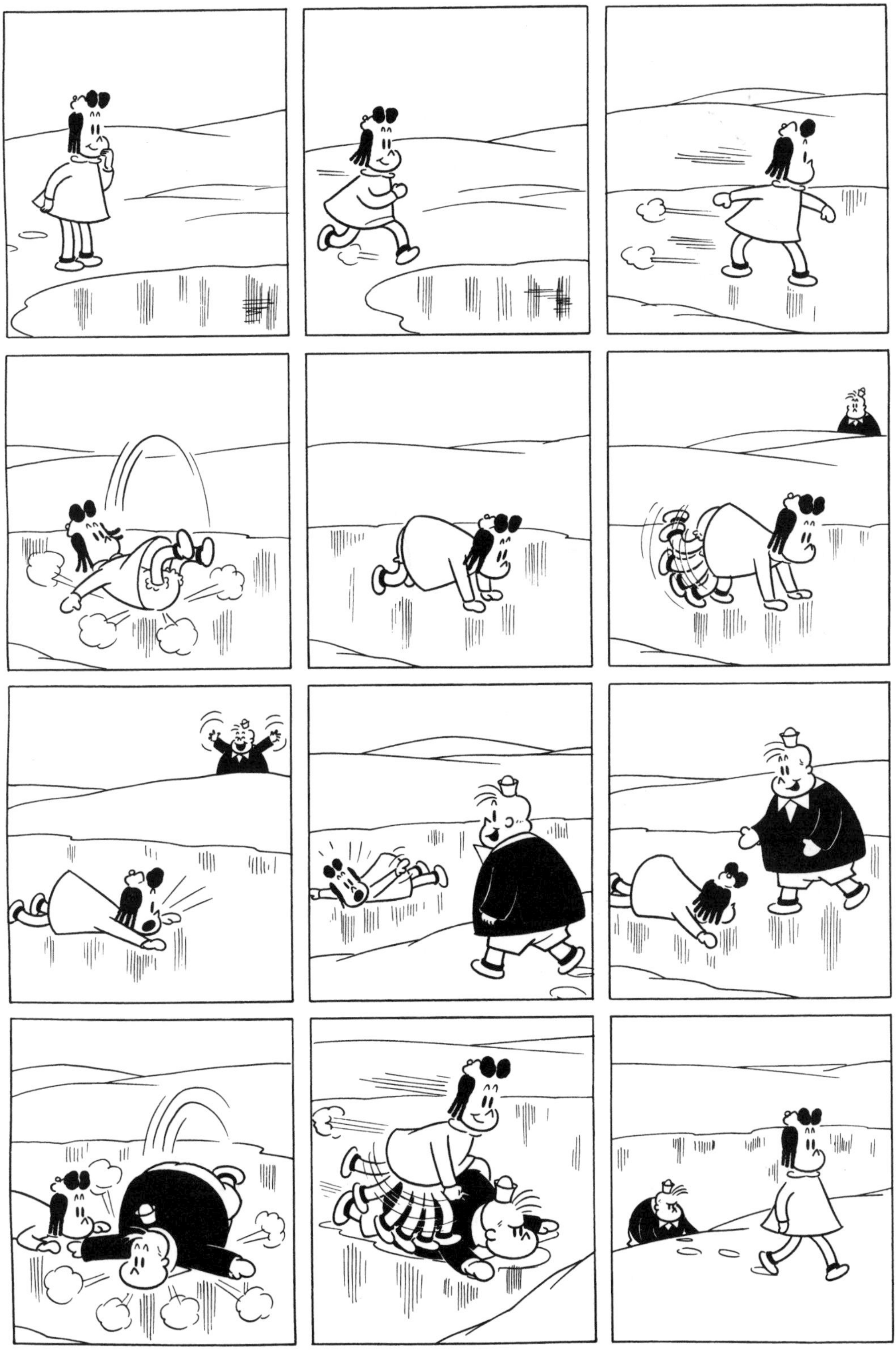

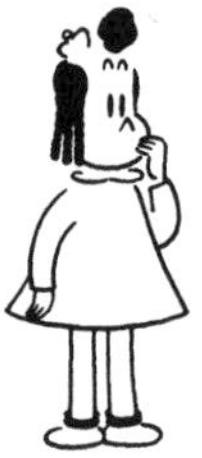

marge's Little Lulu

has family trouble

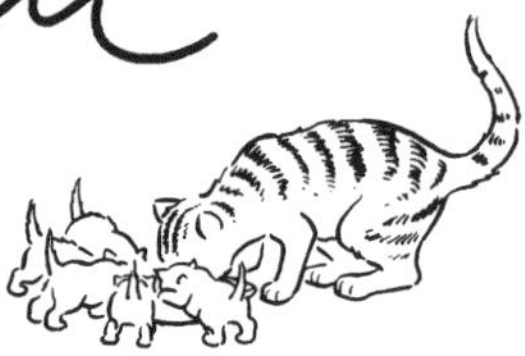

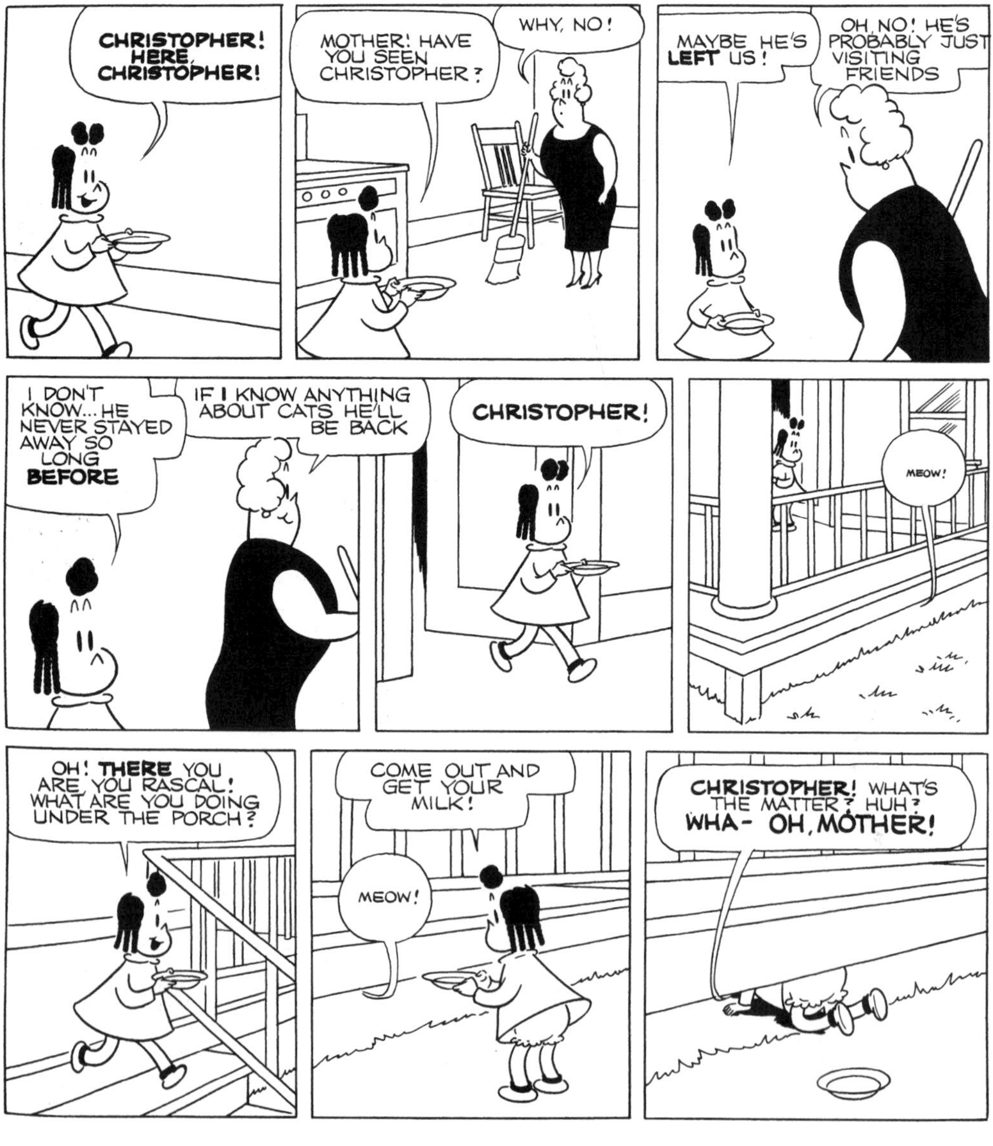

CHRISTOPHER! HERE, CHRISTOPHER!
MOTHER! HAVE YOU SEEN CHRISTOPHER?
WHY, NO!
MAYBE HE'S LEFT US!
OH, NO! HE'S PROBABLY JUST VISITING FRIENDS
I DON'T KNOW... HE NEVER STAYED AWAY SO LONG BEFORE
IF I KNOW ANYTHING ABOUT CATS HE'LL BE BACK
CHRISTOPHER!
MEOW!
OH! THERE YOU ARE, YOU RASCAL! WHAT ARE YOU DOING UNDER THE PORCH?
COME OUT AND GET YOUR MILK!
MEOW!
CHRISTOPHER! WHAT'S THE MATTER? HUH? WHA- OH, MOTHER!

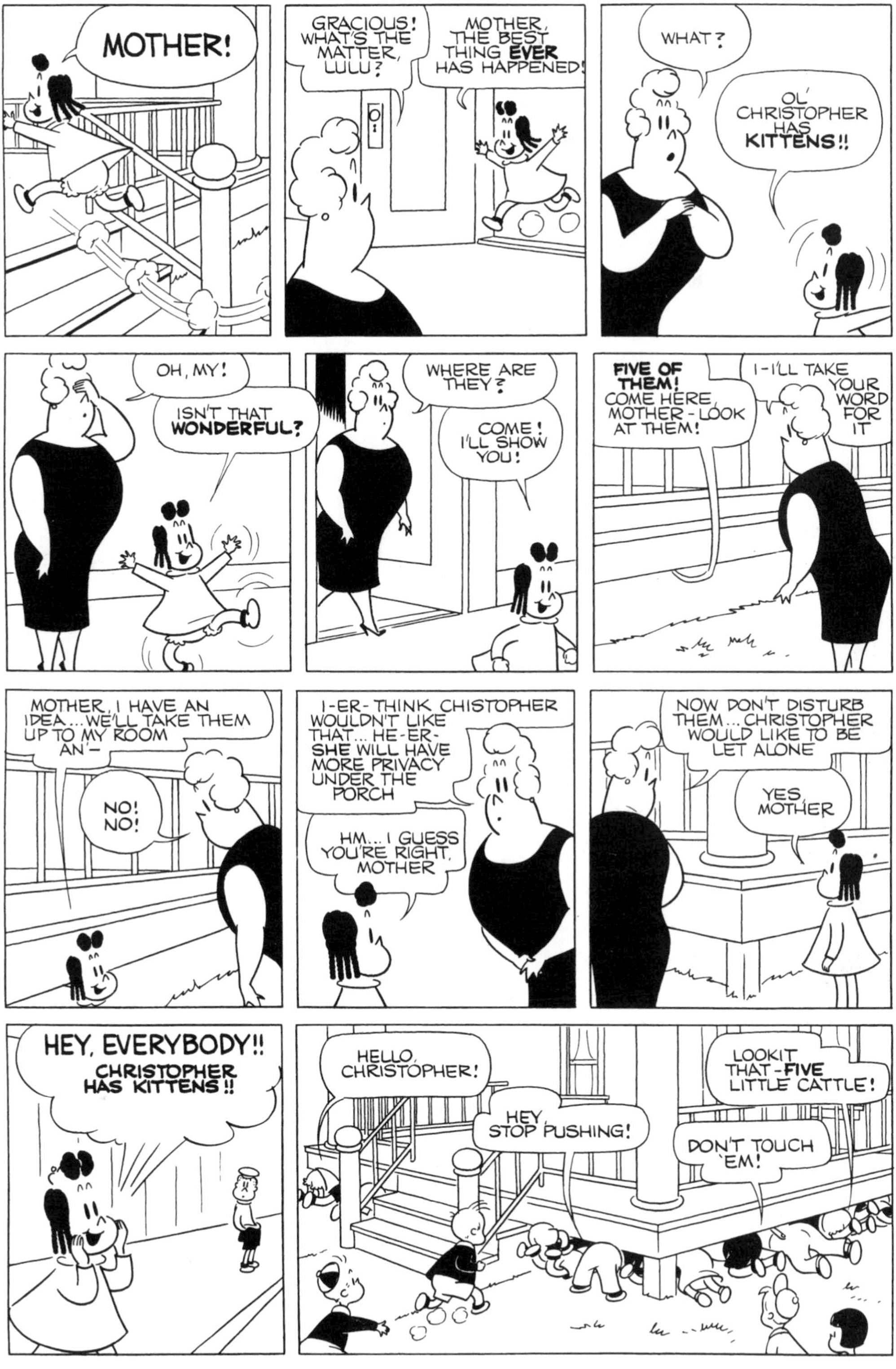
MOTHER!
GRACIOUS! WHAT'S THE MATTER, LULU?
MOTHER, THE BEST THING EVER HAS HAPPENED!
WHAT?
OL' CHRISTOPHER HAS KITTENS!!
OH, MY!
ISN'T THAT WONDERFUL?
WHERE ARE THEY?
COME! I'LL SHOW YOU!
FIVE OF THEM! COME HERE, MOTHER - LOOK AT THEM!
I-I'LL TAKE YOUR WORD FOR IT
MOTHER, I HAVE AN IDEA...WE'LL TAKE THEM UP TO MY ROOM AN'—
NO! NO!
I-ER- THINK CHISTOPHER WOULDN'T LIKE THAT... HE-ER- SHE WILL HAVE MORE PRIVACY UNDER THE PORCH
HM... I GUESS YOU'RE RIGHT, MOTHER
NOW DON'T DISTURB THEM... CHRISTOPHER WOULD LIKE TO BE LET ALONE
YES, MOTHER
HEY, EVERYBODY!! CHRISTOPHER HAS KITTENS!!
HELLO, CHRISTOPHER!
HEY, STOP PUSHING!
LOOKIT THAT - FIVE LITTLE CATTLE!
DON'T TOUCH 'EM!

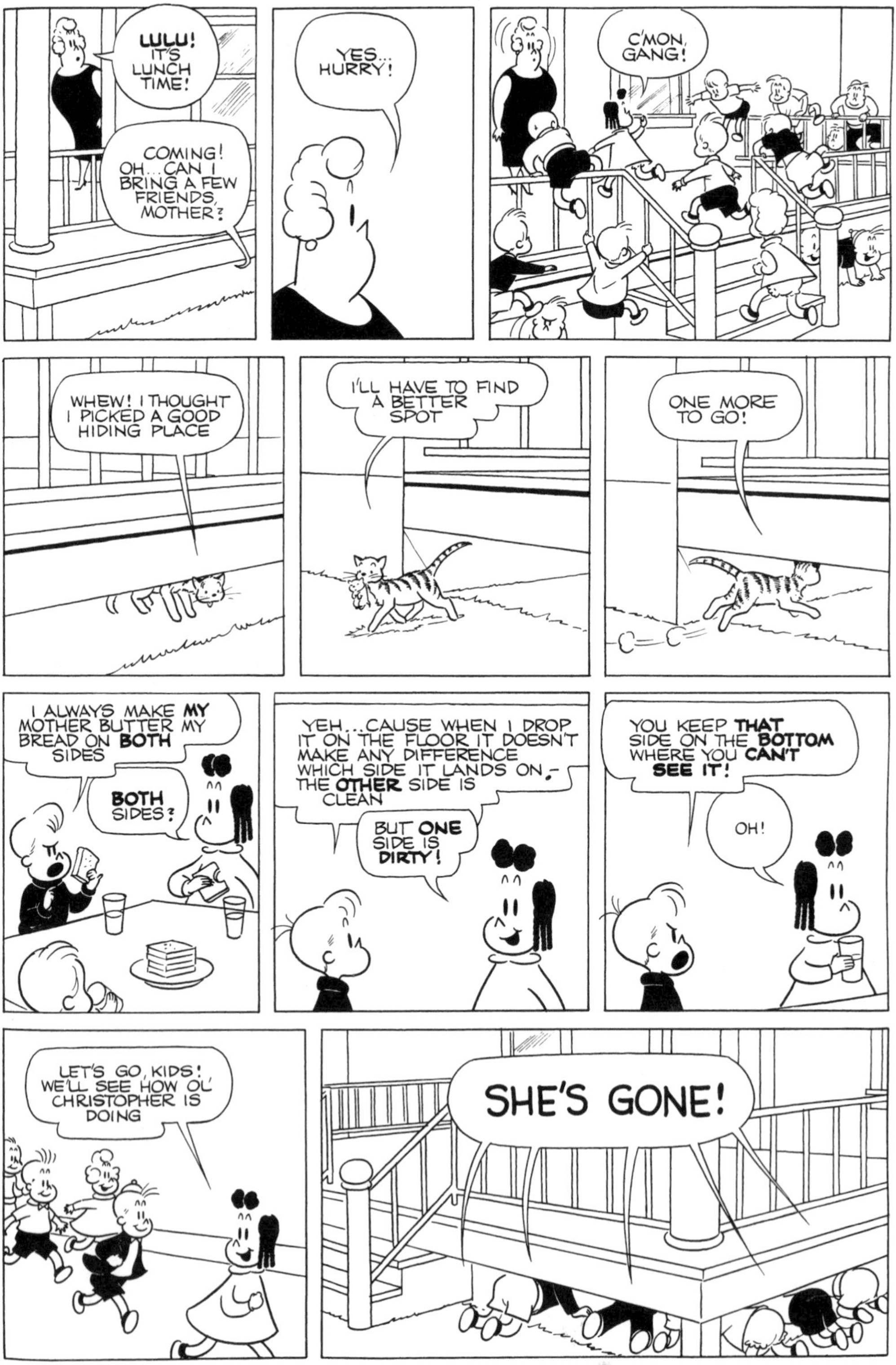
LULU! IT'S LUNCH TIME!
COMING! OH...CAN I BRING A FEW FRIENDS, MOTHER?
YES... HURRY!
C'MON, GANG!
WHEW! I THOUGHT I PICKED A GOOD HIDING PLACE
I'LL HAVE TO FIND A BETTER SPOT
ONE MORE TO GO!
I ALWAYS MAKE MY MOTHER BUTTER MY BREAD ON BOTH SIDES
BOTH SIDES?
YEH...CAUSE WHEN I DROP IT ON THE FLOOR IT DOESN'T MAKE ANY DIFFERENCE WHICH SIDE IT LANDS ON,- THE OTHER SIDE IS CLEAN
BUT ONE SIDE IS DIRTY!
YOU KEEP THAT SIDE ON THE BOTTOM WHERE YOU CAN'T SEE IT!
OH!
LET'S GO, KIDS! WE'LL SEE HOW OL' CHRISTOPHER IS DOING
SHE'S GONE!

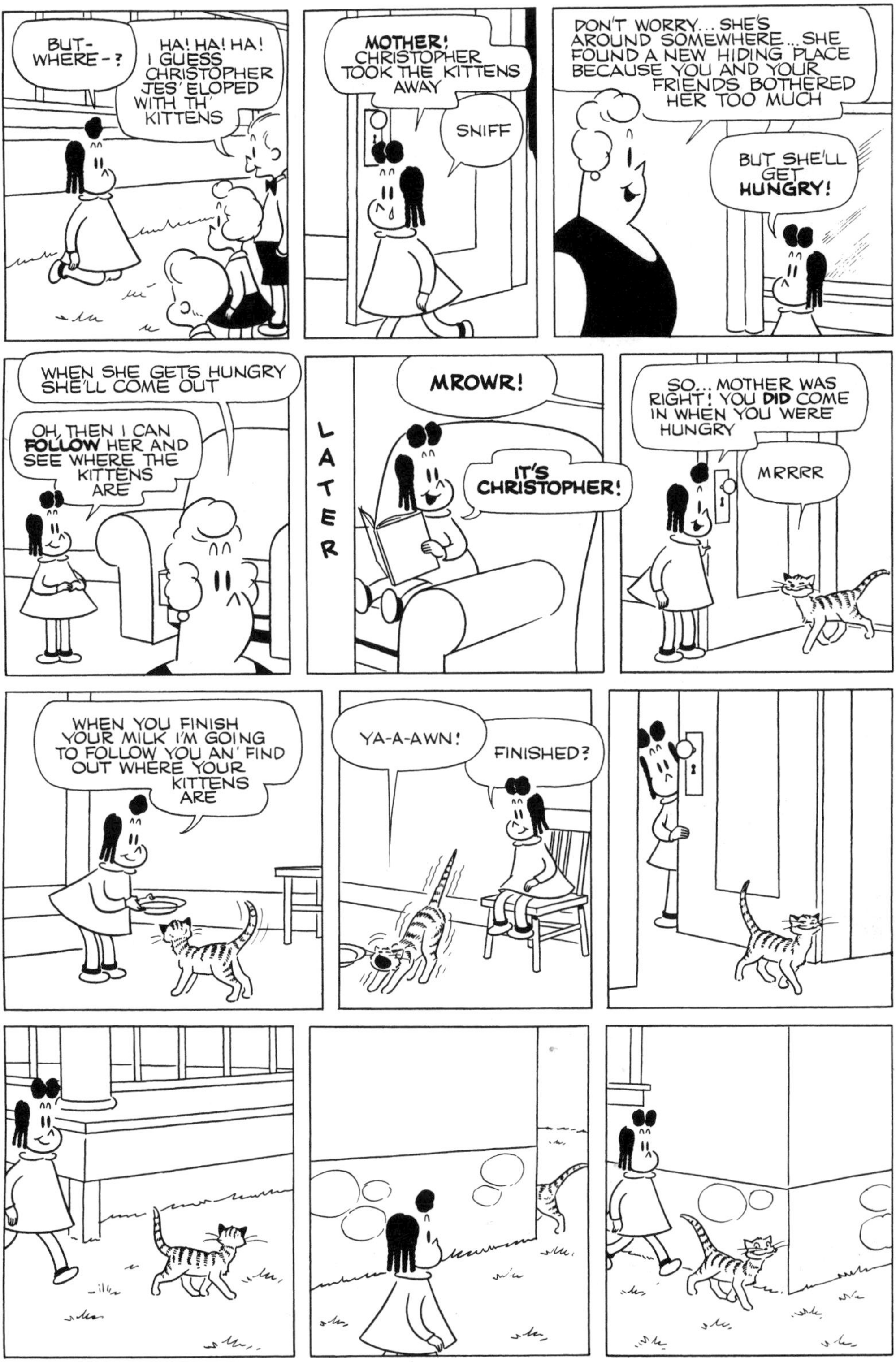
BUT- WHERE-?
HA! HA! HA! I GUESS CHRISTOPHER JES' ELOPED WITH TH' KITTENS
MOTHER! CHRISTOPHER TOOK THE KITTENS AWAY
SNIFF
DON'T WORRY... SHE'S AROUND SOMEWHERE... SHE FOUND A NEW HIDING PLACE BECAUSE YOU AND YOUR FRIENDS BOTHERED HER TOO MUCH
BUT SHE'LL GET HUNGRY!
WHEN SHE GETS HUNGRY SHE'LL COME OUT
OH, THEN I CAN FOLLOW HER AND SEE WHERE THE KITTENS ARE
LATER
MROWR!
IT'S CHRISTOPHER!
SO... MOTHER WAS RIGHT! YOU DID COME IN WHEN YOU WERE HUNGRY
MRRRR
WHEN YOU FINISH YOUR MILK I'M GOING TO FOLLOW YOU AN' FIND OUT WHERE YOUR KITTENS ARE
YA-A-AWN!
FINISHED?

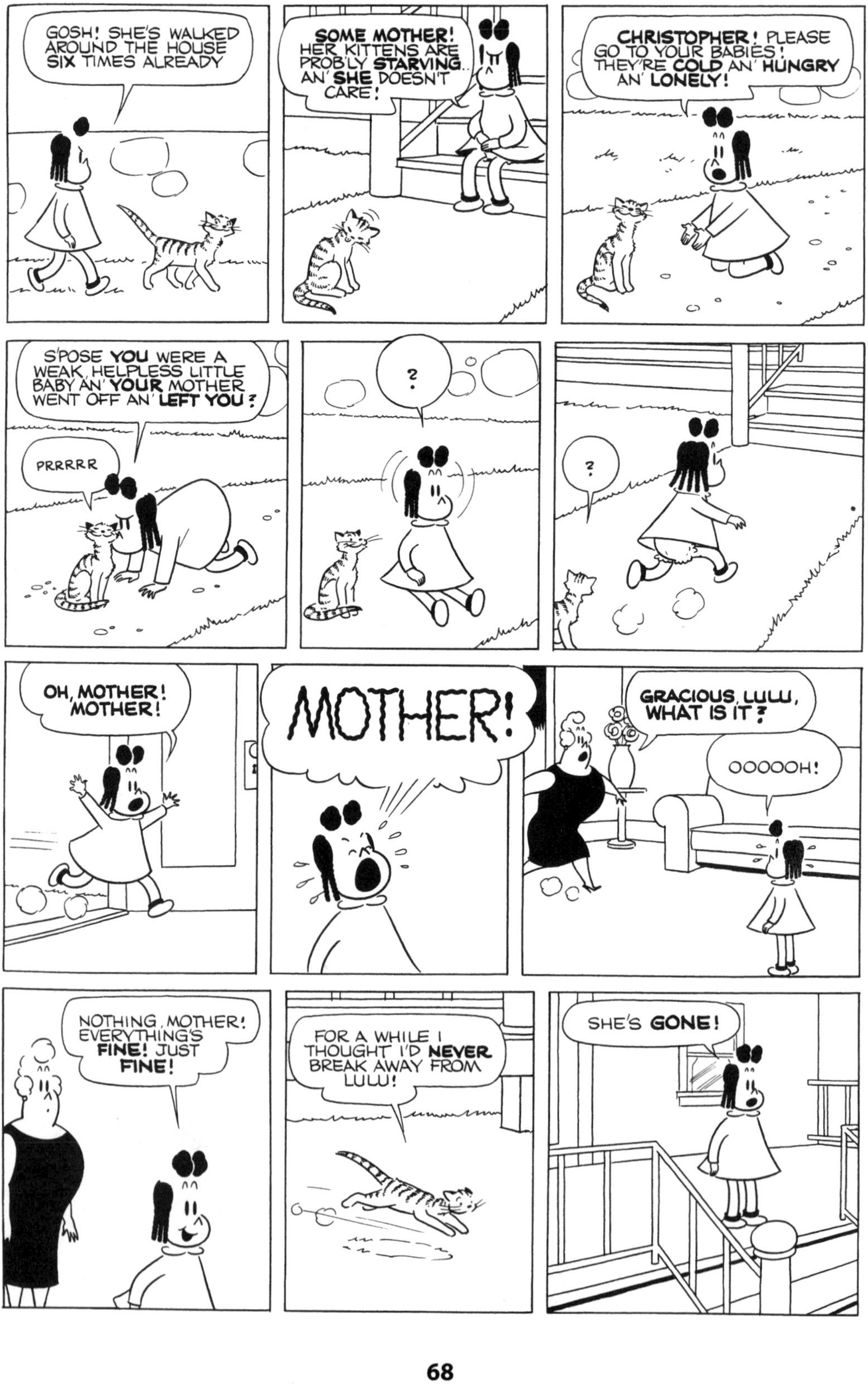
GOSH! SHE'S WALKED AROUND THE HOUSE SIX TIMES ALREADY
SOME MOTHER! HER KITTENS ARE PROB'LY STARVING... AN' SHE DOESN'T CARE!
CHRISTOPHER! PLEASE GO TO YOUR BABIES! THEY'RE COLD AN' HUNGRY AN' LONELY!
S'POSE YOU WERE A WEAK, HELPLESS LITTLE BABY AN' YOUR MOTHER WENT OFF AN' LEFT YOU?
PRRRRR
?
?
OH, MOTHER! MOTHER!
MOTHER!
GRACIOUS, LULU, WHAT IS IT?
OOOOOH!
NOTHING, MOTHER! EVERYTHING'S FINE! JUST FINE!
FOR A WHILE I THOUGHT I'D NEVER BREAK AWAY FROM LULU!
SHE'S GONE!

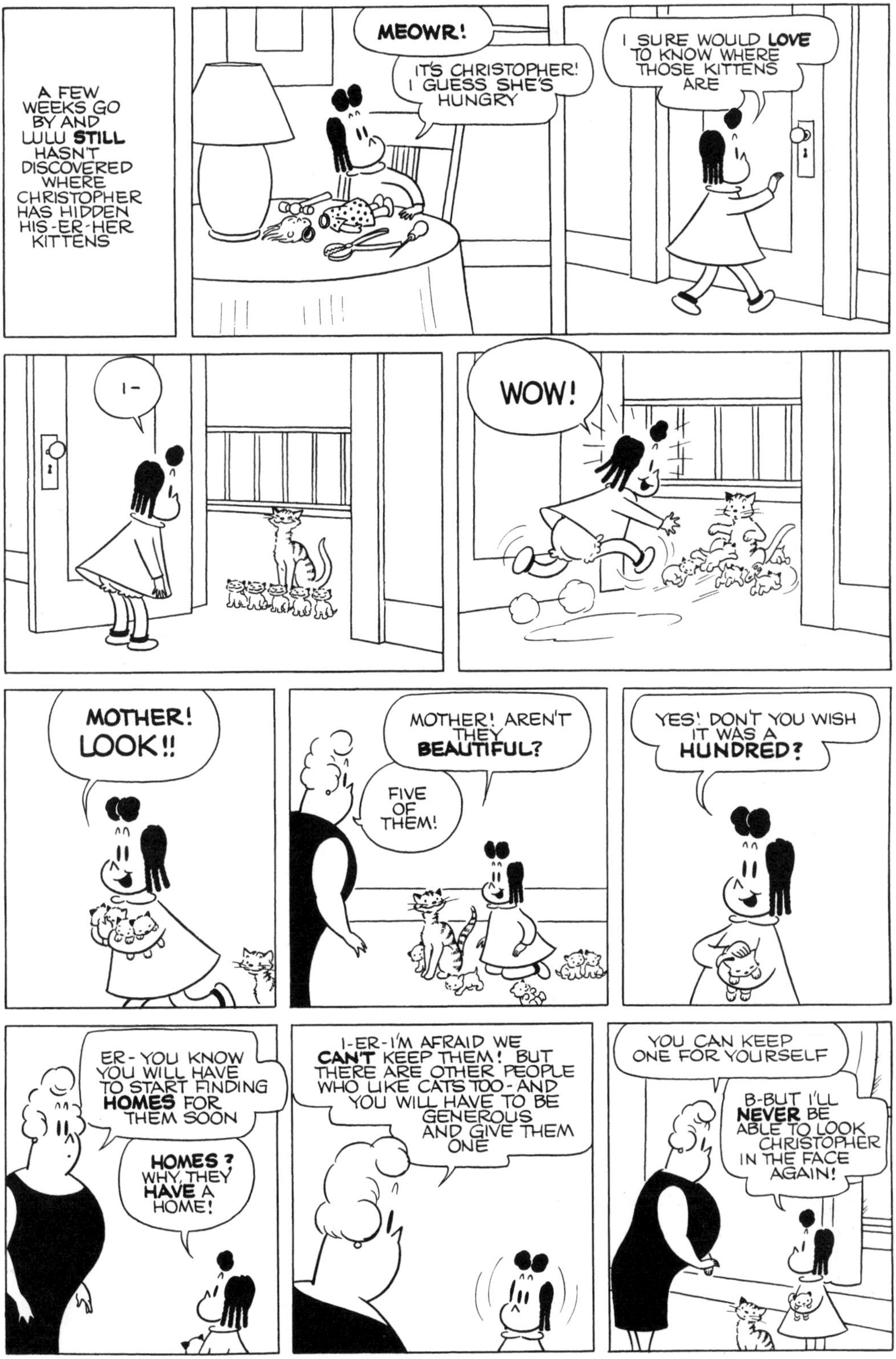
A FEW WEEKS GO BY AND LULU STILL HASN'T DISCOVERED WHERE CHRISTOPHER HAS HIDDEN HIS-ER-HER KITTENS
MEOWR!
IT'S CHRISTOPHER! I GUESS SHE'S HUNGRY
I SURE WOULD LOVE TO KNOW WHERE THOSE KITTENS ARE
I -
WOW!
MOTHER! LOOK!!
MOTHER! AREN'T THEY BEAUTIFUL?
FIVE OF THEM!
YES! DON'T YOU WISH IT WAS A HUNDRED?
ER- YOU KNOW YOU WILL HAVE TO START FINDING HOMES FOR THEM SOON
HOMES? WHY, THEY HAVE A HOME!
I-ER-I'M AFRAID WE CAN'T KEEP THEM! BUT THERE ARE OTHER PEOPLE WHO LIKE CATS TOO-AND YOU WILL HAVE TO BE GENEROUS AND GIVE THEM ONE
YOU CAN KEEP ONE FOR YOURSELF
B-BUT I'LL NEVER BE ABLE TO LOOK CHRISTOPHER IN THE FACE AGAIN!

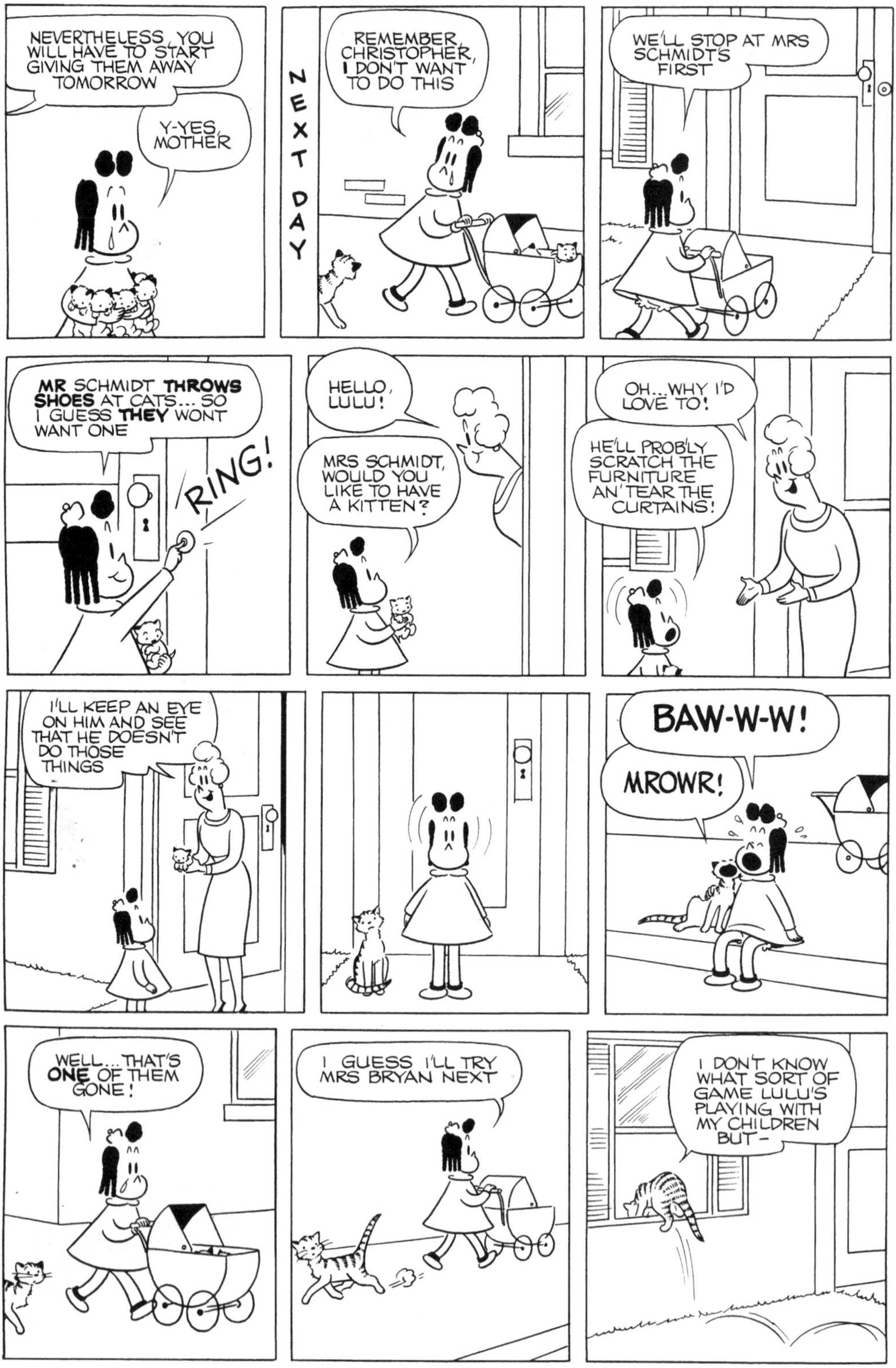
NEVERTHELESS, YOU WILL HAVE TO START GIVING THEM AWAY TOMORROW
Y-YES, MOTHER
NEXT DAY
REMEMBER, CHRISTOPHER, I DON'T WANT TO DO THIS
WE'LL STOP AT MRS SCHMIDT'S FIRST
MR SCHMIDT THROWS SHOES AT CATS... SO I GUESS THEY WONT WANT ONE
RING!
HELLO, LULU!
MRS SCHMIDT, WOULD YOU LIKE TO HAVE A KITTEN?
OH...WHY I'D LOVE TO!
HE'LL PROB'LY SCRATCH THE FURNITURE AN' TEAR THE CURTAINS!
I'LL KEEP AN EYE ON HIM AND SEE THAT HE DOESN'T DO THOSE THINGS
BAW-W-W!
MROWR!
WELL...THAT'S ONE OF THEM GONE!
I GUESS I'LL TRY MRS BRYAN NEXT
I DON'T KNOW WHAT SORT OF GAME LULU'S PLAYING WITH MY CHILDREN BUT-

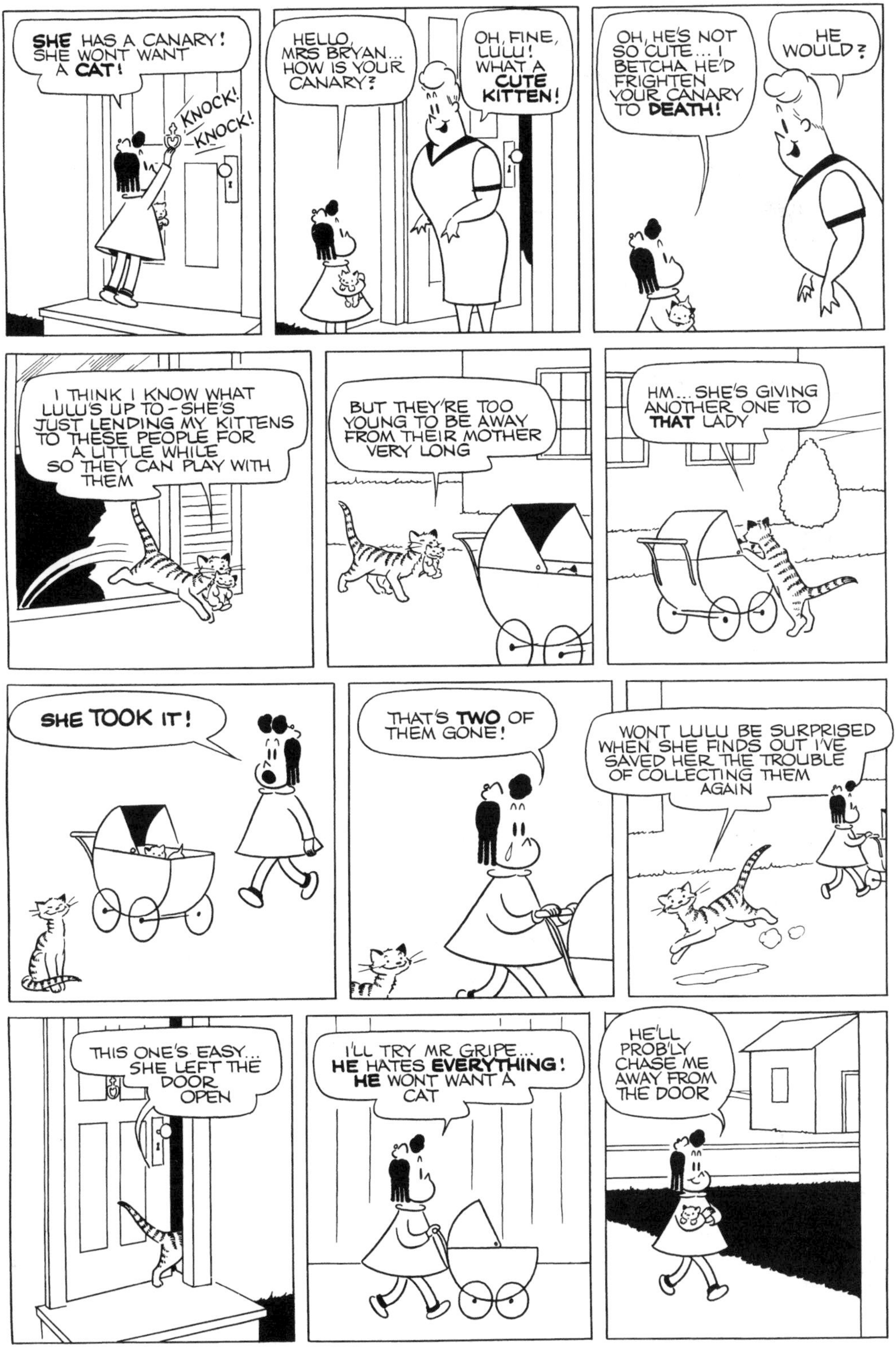
SHE HAS A CANARY! SHE WONT WANT A CAT!
KNOCK! KNOCK!
HELLO, MRS BRYAN... HOW IS YOUR CANARY?
OH, FINE, LULU! WHAT A CUTE KITTEN!
OH, HE'S NOT SO CUTE... I BETCHA HE'D FRIGHTEN YOUR CANARY TO DEATH!
HE WOULD?
I THINK I KNOW WHAT LULU'S UP TO - SHE'S JUST LENDING MY KITTENS TO THESE PEOPLE FOR A LITTLE WHILE SO THEY CAN PLAY WITH THEM
BUT THEY'RE TOO YOUNG TO BE AWAY FROM THEIR MOTHER VERY LONG
HM... SHE'S GIVING ANOTHER ONE TO THAT LADY
SHE TOOK IT!
THAT'S TWO OF THEM GONE!
WONT LULU BE SURPRISED WHEN SHE FINDS OUT I'VE SAVED HER THE TROUBLE OF COLLECTING THEM AGAIN
THIS ONE'S EASY... SHE LEFT THE DOOR OPEN
I'LL TRY MR GRIPE... HE HATES EVERYTHING! HE WONT WANT A CAT
HE'LL PROB'LY CHASE ME AWAY FROM THE DOOR

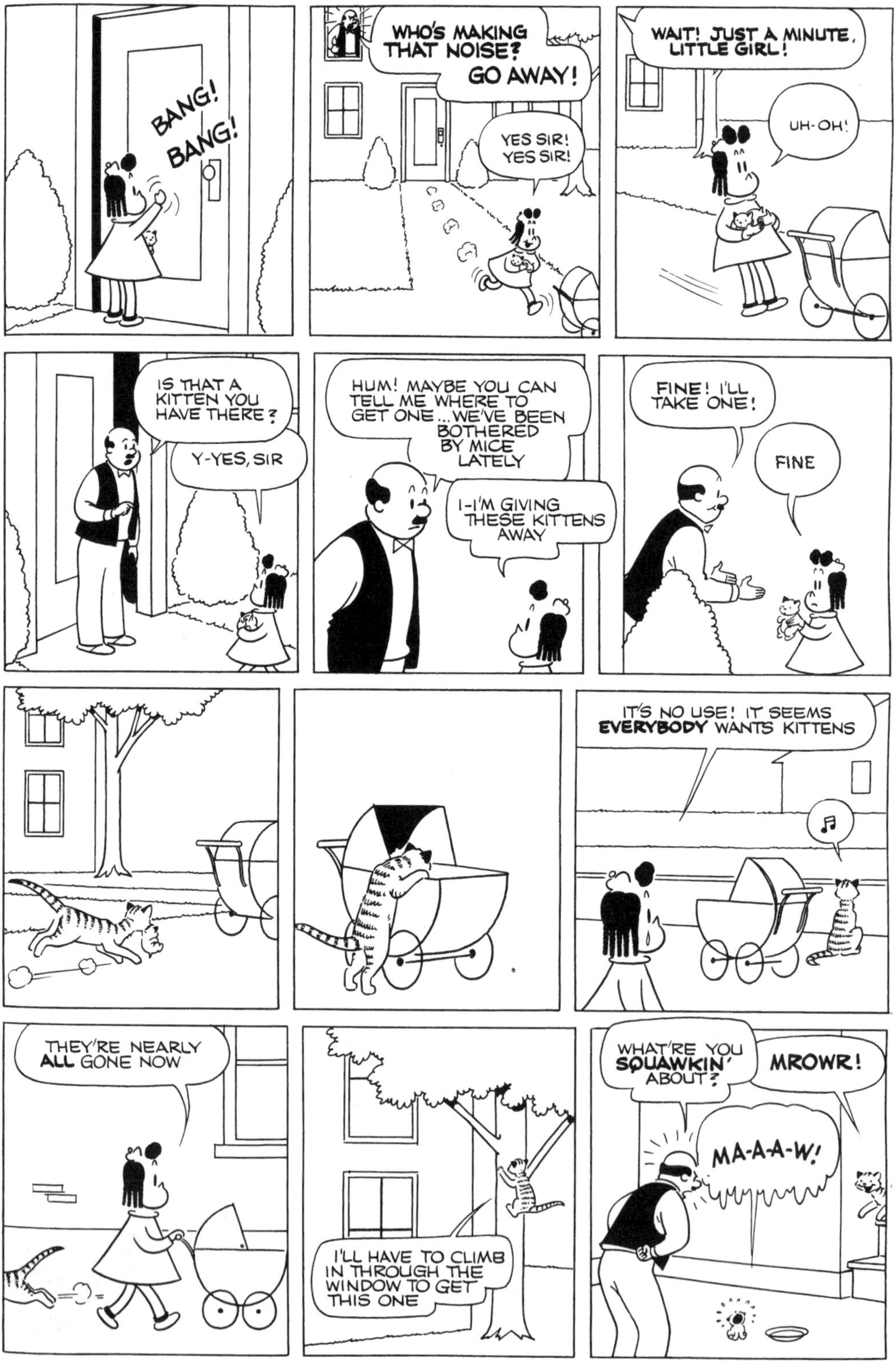
BANG! BANG!
WHO'S MAKING THAT NOISE? GO AWAY!
YES SIR! YES SIR!
WAIT! JUST A MINUTE, LITTLE GIRL!
UH-OH!
IS THAT A KITTEN YOU HAVE THERE?
Y-YES, SIR
HUM! MAYBE YOU CAN TELL ME WHERE TO GET ONE ... WE'VE BEEN BOTHERED BY MICE LATELY
I-I'M GIVING THESE KITTENS AWAY
FINE! I'LL TAKE ONE!
FINE
IT'S NO USE! IT SEEMS EVERYBODY WANTS KITTENS
THEY'RE NEARLY ALL GONE NOW
I'LL HAVE TO CLIMB IN THROUGH THE WINDOW TO GET THIS ONE
WHAT'RE YOU SQUAWKIN' ABOUT?
MROWR!
MA-A-A-W!

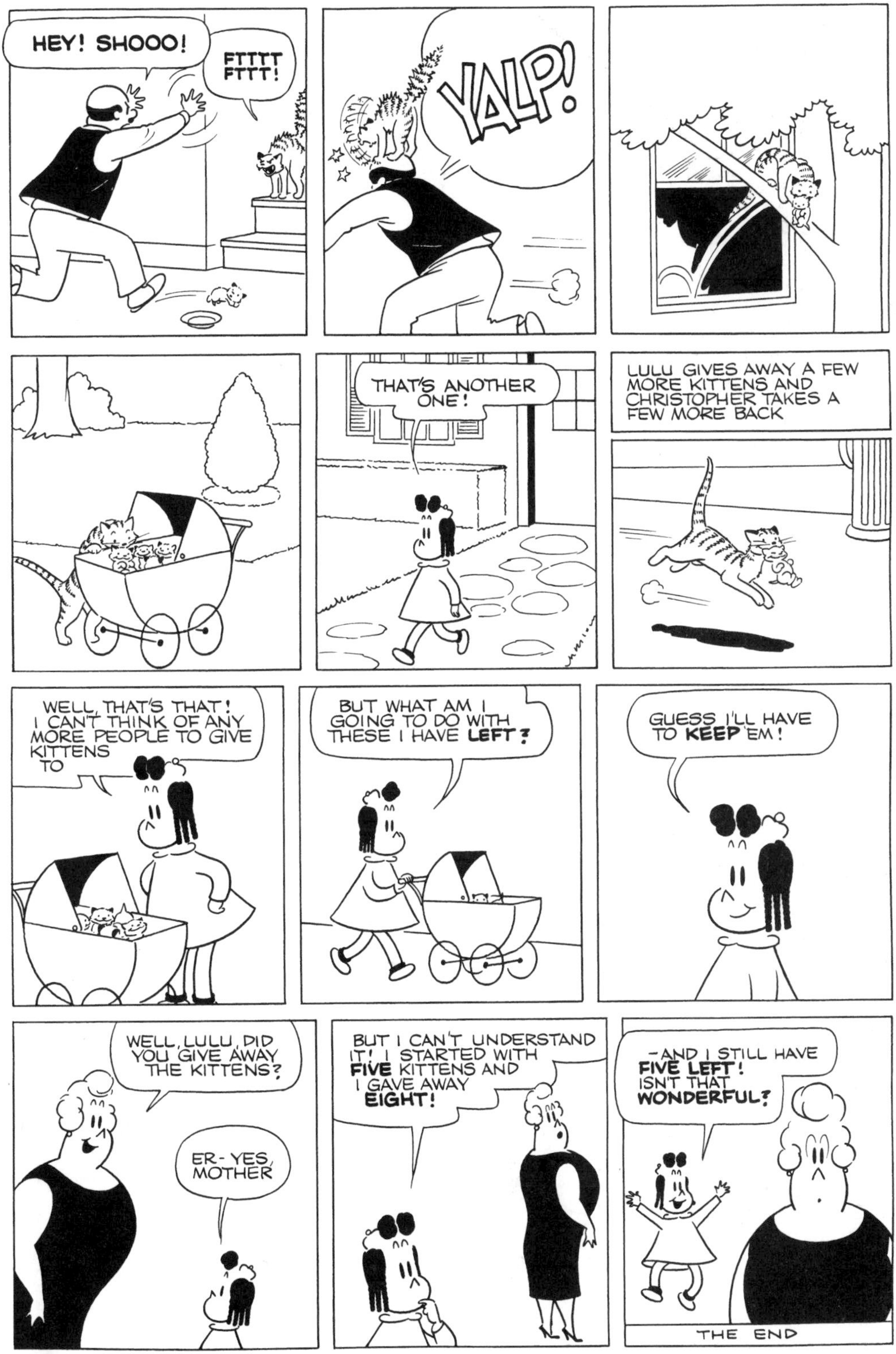
HEY! SHOOO!
FTTTT FTTT!
YALP!
THAT'S ANOTHER ONE!
LULU GIVES AWAY A FEW MORE KITTENS AND CHRISTOPHER TAKES A FEW MORE BACK
WELL, THAT'S THAT! I CAN'T THINK OF ANY MORE PEOPLE TO GIVE KITTENS TO
BUT WHAT AM I GOING TO DO WITH THESE I HAVE LEFT?
GUESS I'LL HAVE TO KEEP 'EM!
WELL, LULU, DID YOU GIVE AWAY THE KITTENS?
ER- YES, MOTHER
BUT I CAN'T UNDERSTAND IT! I STARTED WITH FIVE KITTENS AND I GAVE AWAY EIGHT!
-AND I STILL HAVE FIVE LEFT! ISN'T THAT WONDERFUL?
THE END

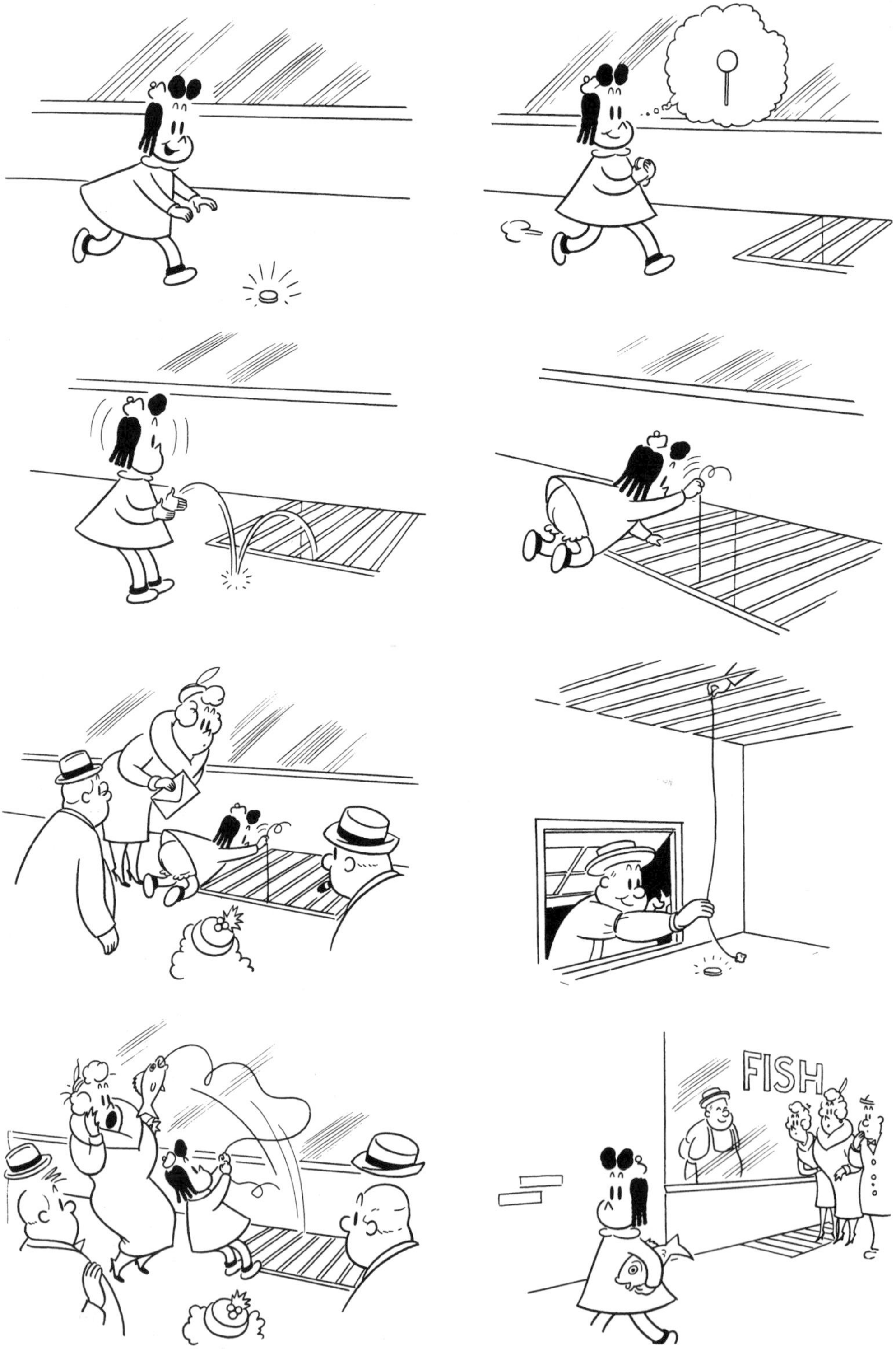
FISH

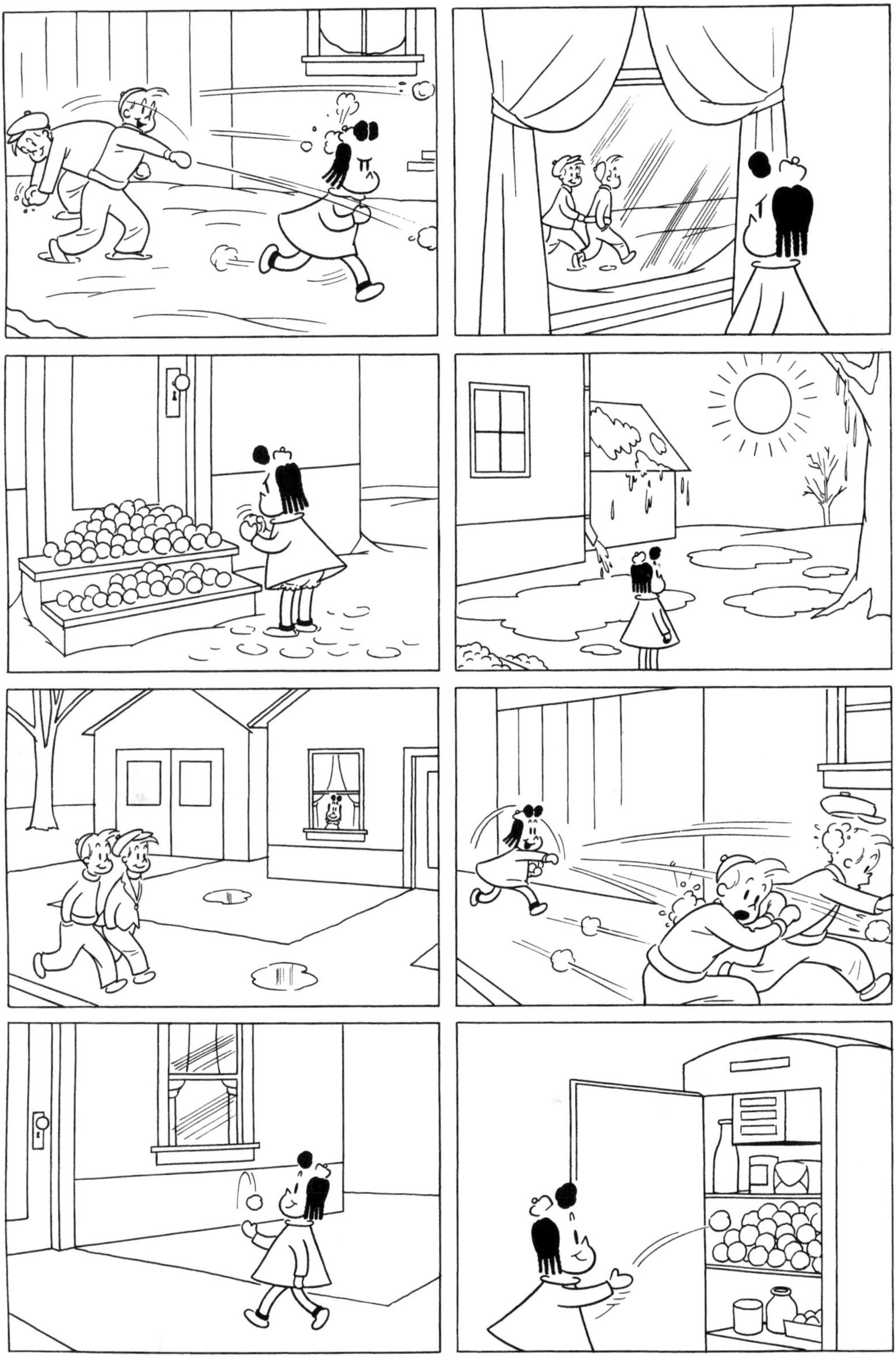

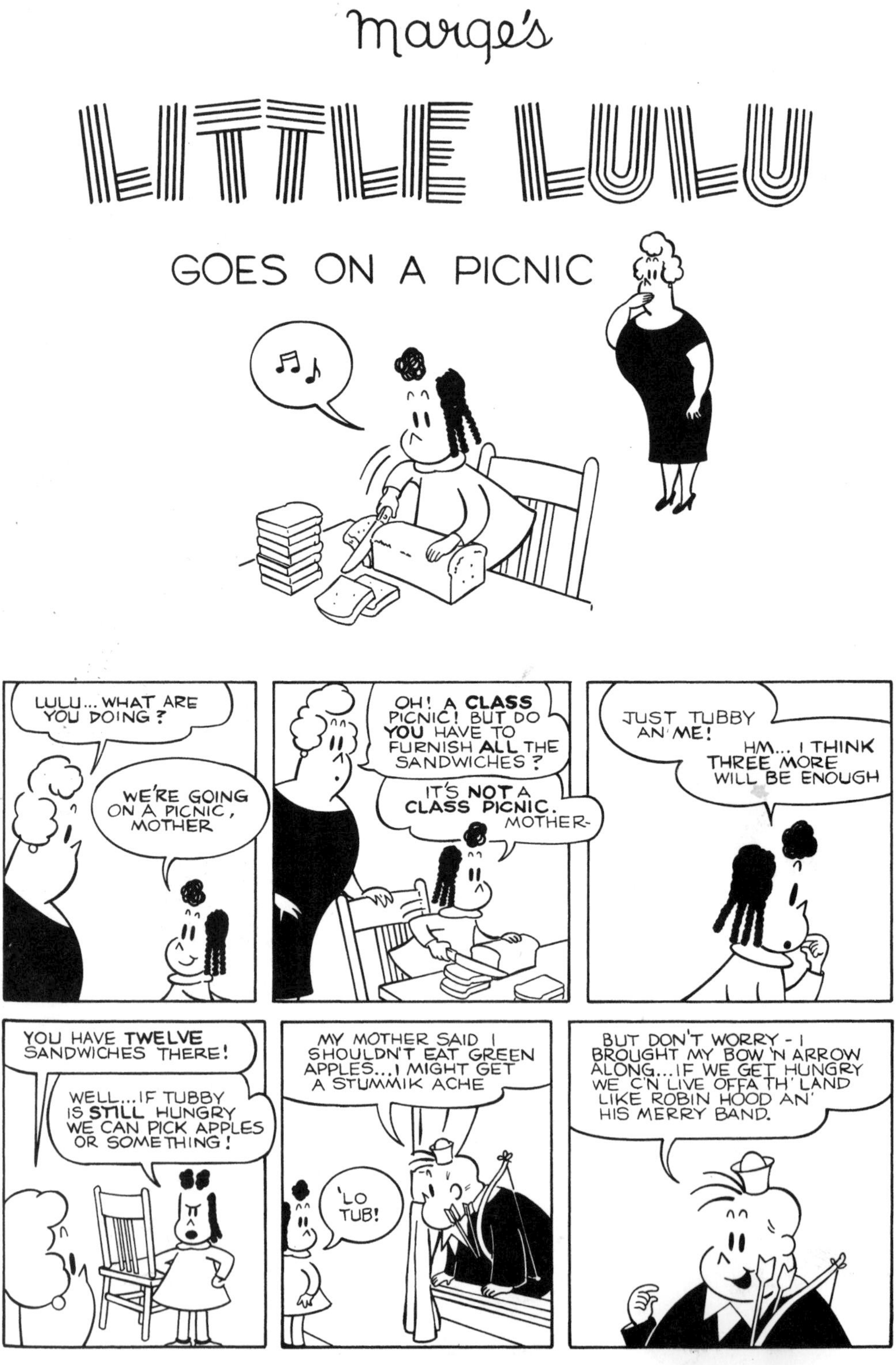
marge's
LITTLE LULU
GOES ON A PICNIC
LULU... WHAT ARE YOU DOING?
WE'RE GOING ON A PICNIC, MOTHER
OH! A CLASS PICNIC! BUT DO YOU HAVE TO FURNISH ALL THE SANDWICHES?
IT'S NOT A CLASS PICNIC. MOTHER-
JUST TUBBY AN' ME!
HM... I THINK THREE MORE WILL BE ENOUGH
YOU HAVE TWELVE SANDWICHES THERE!
WELL... IF TUBBY IS STILL HUNGRY WE CAN PICK APPLES OR SOMETHING!
MY MOTHER SAID I SHOULDN'T EAT GREEN APPLES... I MIGHT GET A STUMMIK ACHE
'LO TUB!
BUT DON'T WORRY - I BROUGHT MY BOW 'N ARROW ALONG... IF WE GET HUNGRY WE C'N LIVE OFFA TH' LAND LIKE ROBIN HOOD AN' HIS MERRY BAND.

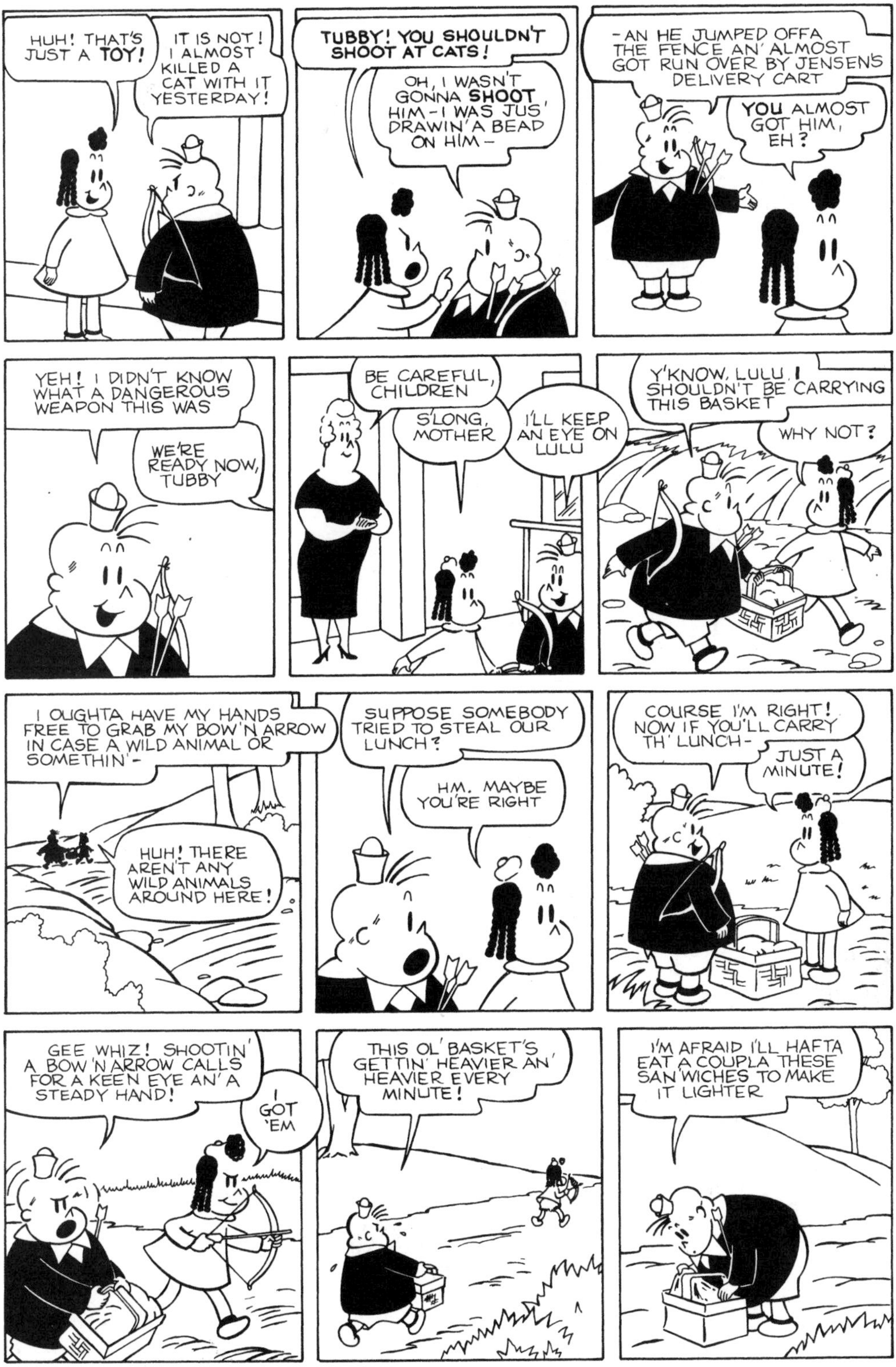
HUH! THAT'S JUST A **TOY!**
IT IS NOT! I ALMOST KILLED A CAT WITH IT YESTERDAY!
TUBBY! YOU SHOULDN'T SHOOT AT CATS!
OH, I WASN'T GONNA **SHOOT** HIM - I WAS JUS' DRAWIN' A BEAD ON HIM -
- AN HE JUMPED OFFA THE FENCE AN' ALMOST GOT RUN OVER BY JENSEN'S DELIVERY CART
YOU ALMOST GOT HIM, EH?
YEH! I DIDN'T KNOW WHAT A DANGEROUS WEAPON THIS WAS
WE'RE READY NOW, TUBBY
BE CAREFUL, CHILDREN
S'LONG, MOTHER
I'LL KEEP AN EYE ON LULU
Y'KNOW, LULU, I SHOULDN'T BE CARRYING THIS BASKET
WHY NOT?
I OUGHTA HAVE MY HANDS FREE TO GRAB MY BOW 'N ARROW IN CASE A WILD ANIMAL OR SOMETHIN' -
HUH! THERE AREN'T ANY WILD ANIMALS AROUND HERE!
SUPPOSE SOMEBODY TRIED TO STEAL OUR LUNCH?
HM. MAYBE YOU'RE RIGHT
COURSE I'M RIGHT! NOW IF YOU'LL CARRY TH' LUNCH -
JUST A MINUTE!
GEE WHIZ! SHOOTIN' A BOW 'N ARROW CALLS FOR A KEEN EYE AN' A STEADY HAND!
I GOT 'EM
THIS OL' BASKET'S GETTIN' HEAVIER AN' HEAVIER EVERY MINUTE!
I'M AFRAID I'LL HAFTA EAT A COUPLA THESE SAN'WICHES TO MAKE IT LIGHTER

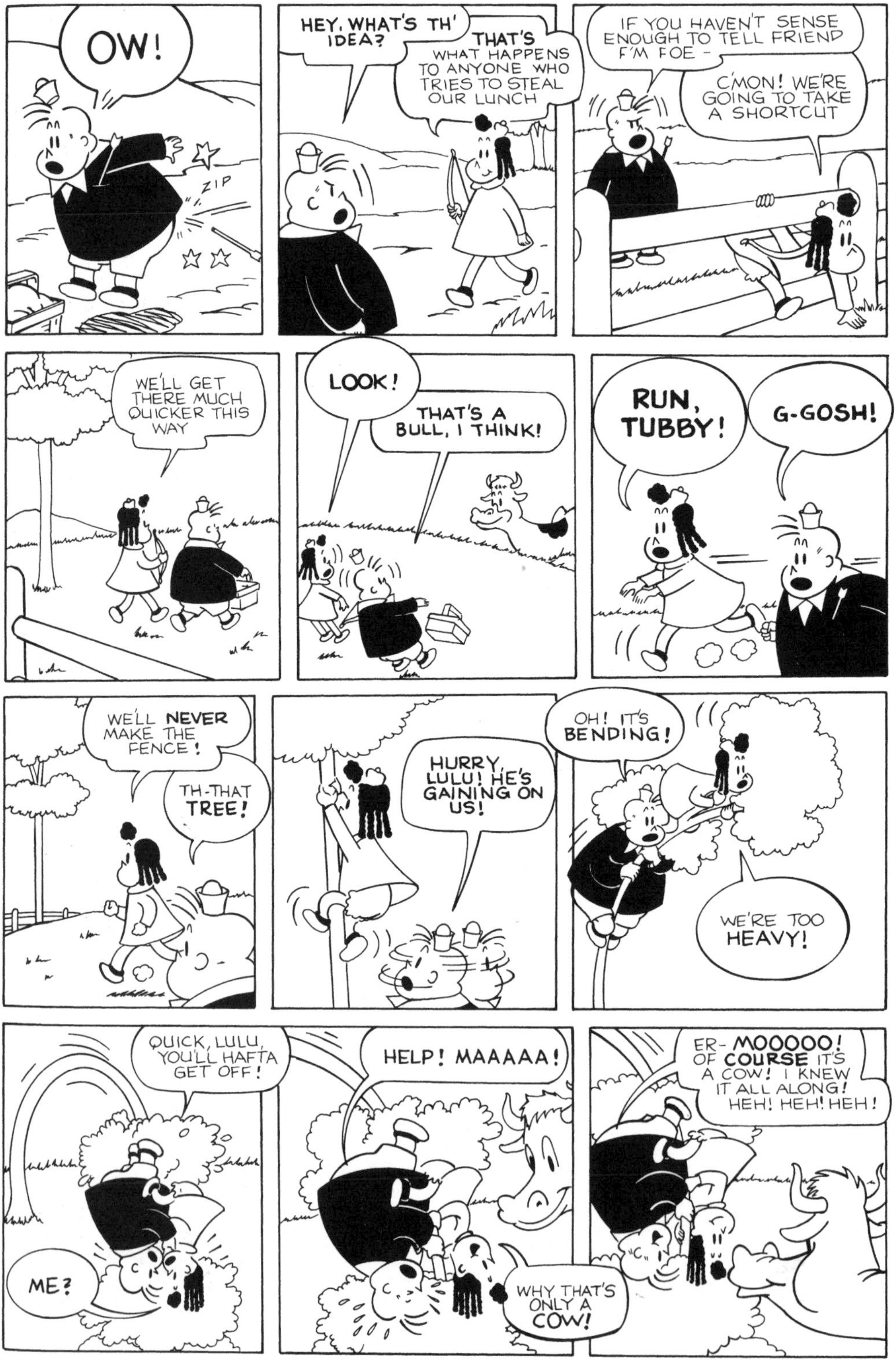

OW!
ZIP
HEY, WHAT'S TH' IDEA?
THAT'S WHAT HAPPENS TO ANYONE WHO TRIES TO STEAL OUR LUNCH
IF YOU HAVEN'T SENSE ENOUGH TO TELL FRIEND F'M FOE -
C'MON! WE'RE GOING TO TAKE A SHORTCUT
WE'LL GET THERE MUCH QUICKER THIS WAY
LOOK!
THAT'S A BULL, I THINK!
RUN, TUBBY!
G-GOSH!
WE'LL NEVER MAKE THE FENCE!
TH-THAT TREE!
HURRY, LULU! HE'S GAINING ON US!
OH! IT'S BENDING!
WE'RE TOO HEAVY!
QUICK, LULU, YOU'LL HAFTA GET OFF!
ME?
HELP! MAAAAA!
WHY THAT'S ONLY A COW!
ER- MOOOOO! OF COURSE IT'S A COW! I KNEW IT ALL ALONG! HEH! HEH! HEH!

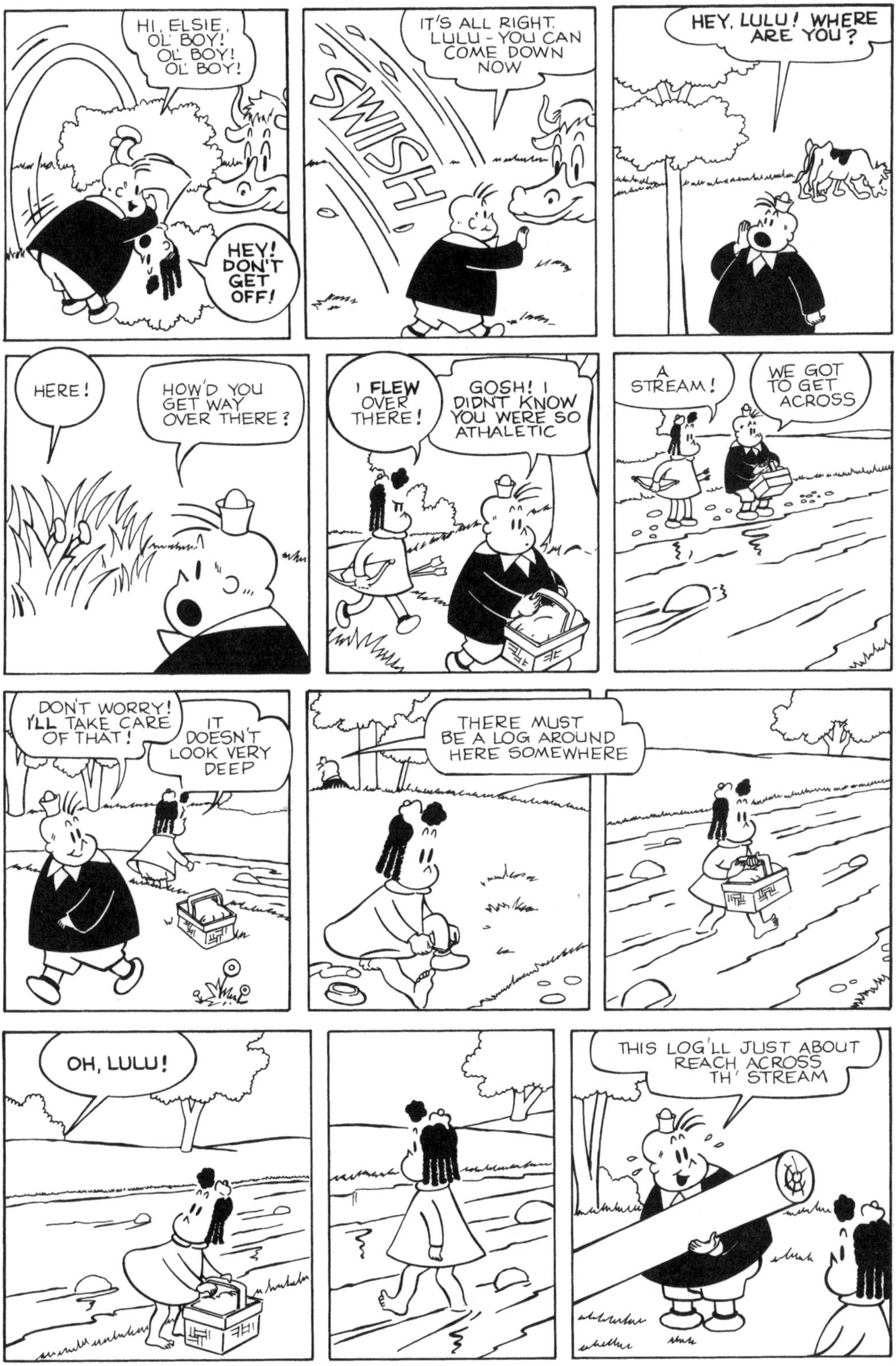

HI, ELSIE, OL' BOY! OL' BOY! OL' BOY!
HEY! DON'T GET OFF!
IT'S ALL RIGHT, LULU - YOU CAN COME DOWN NOW
SWISH
HEY, LULU! WHERE ARE YOU?
HERE!
HOW'D YOU GET WAY OVER THERE?
I FLEW OVER THERE!
GOSH! I DIDN'T KNOW YOU WERE SO ATHALETIC
A STREAM!
WE GOT TO GET ACROSS
DON'T WORRY! I'LL TAKE CARE OF THAT!
IT DOESN'T LOOK VERY DEEP
THERE MUST BE A LOG AROUND HERE SOMEWHERE
OH, LULU!
THIS LOG'LL JUST ABOUT REACH ACROSS TH' STREAM

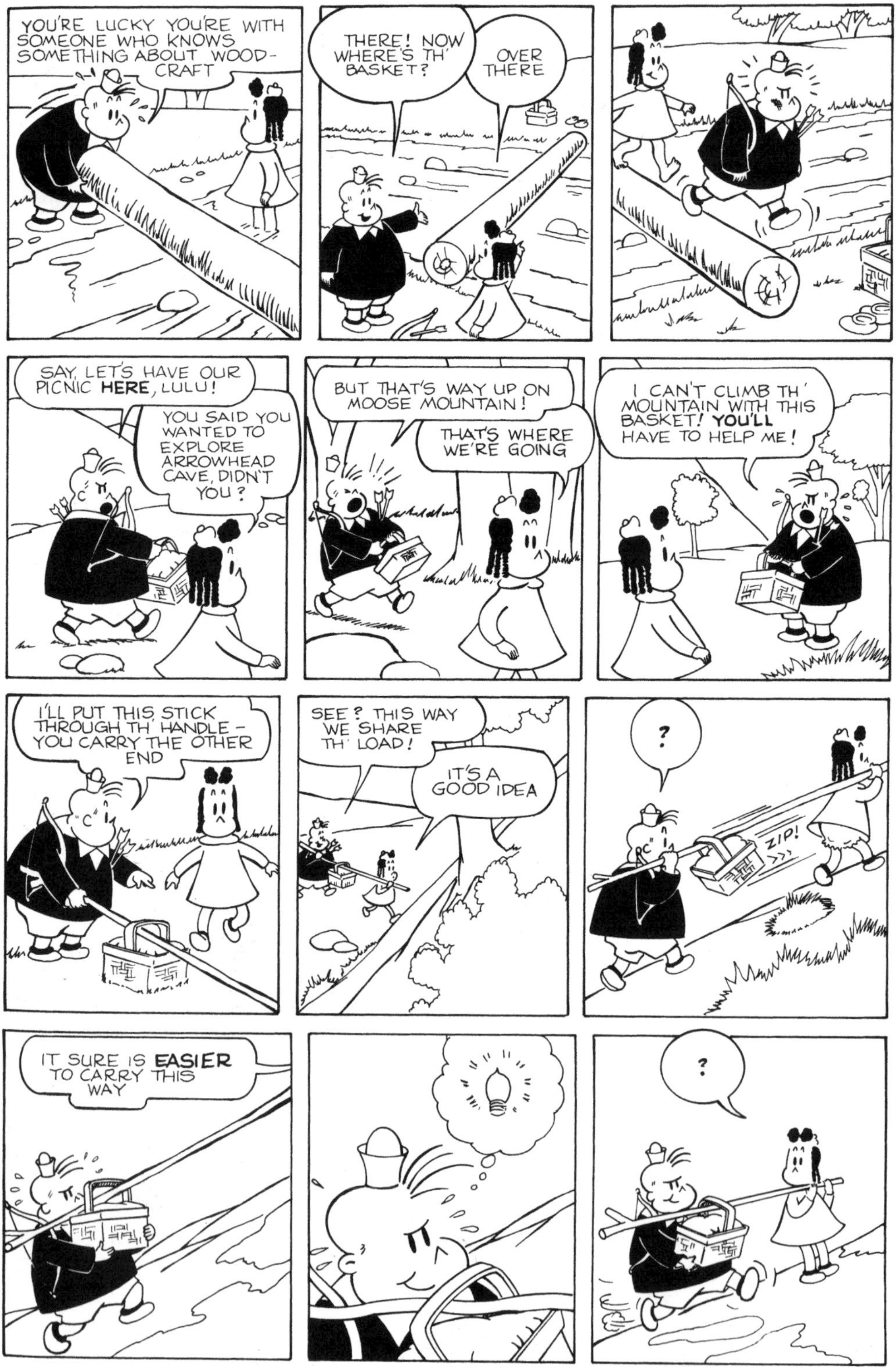
YOU'RE LUCKY YOU'RE WITH SOMEONE WHO KNOWS SOMETHING ABOUT WOOD-CRAFT
THERE! NOW WHERE'S TH' BASKET?
OVER THERE
SAY, LET'S HAVE OUR PICNIC HERE, LULU!
YOU SAID YOU WANTED TO EXPLORE ARROWHEAD CAVE, DIDN'T YOU?
BUT THAT'S WAY UP ON MOOSE MOUNTAIN!
THAT'S WHERE WE'RE GOING
I CAN'T CLIMB TH' MOUNTAIN WITH THIS BASKET! YOU'LL HAVE TO HELP ME!
I'LL PUT THIS STICK THROUGH TH' HANDLE - YOU CARRY THE OTHER END
SEE? THIS WAY WE SHARE TH' LOAD!
IT'S A GOOD IDEA
?
ZIP!
IT SURE IS EASIER TO CARRY THIS WAY
?

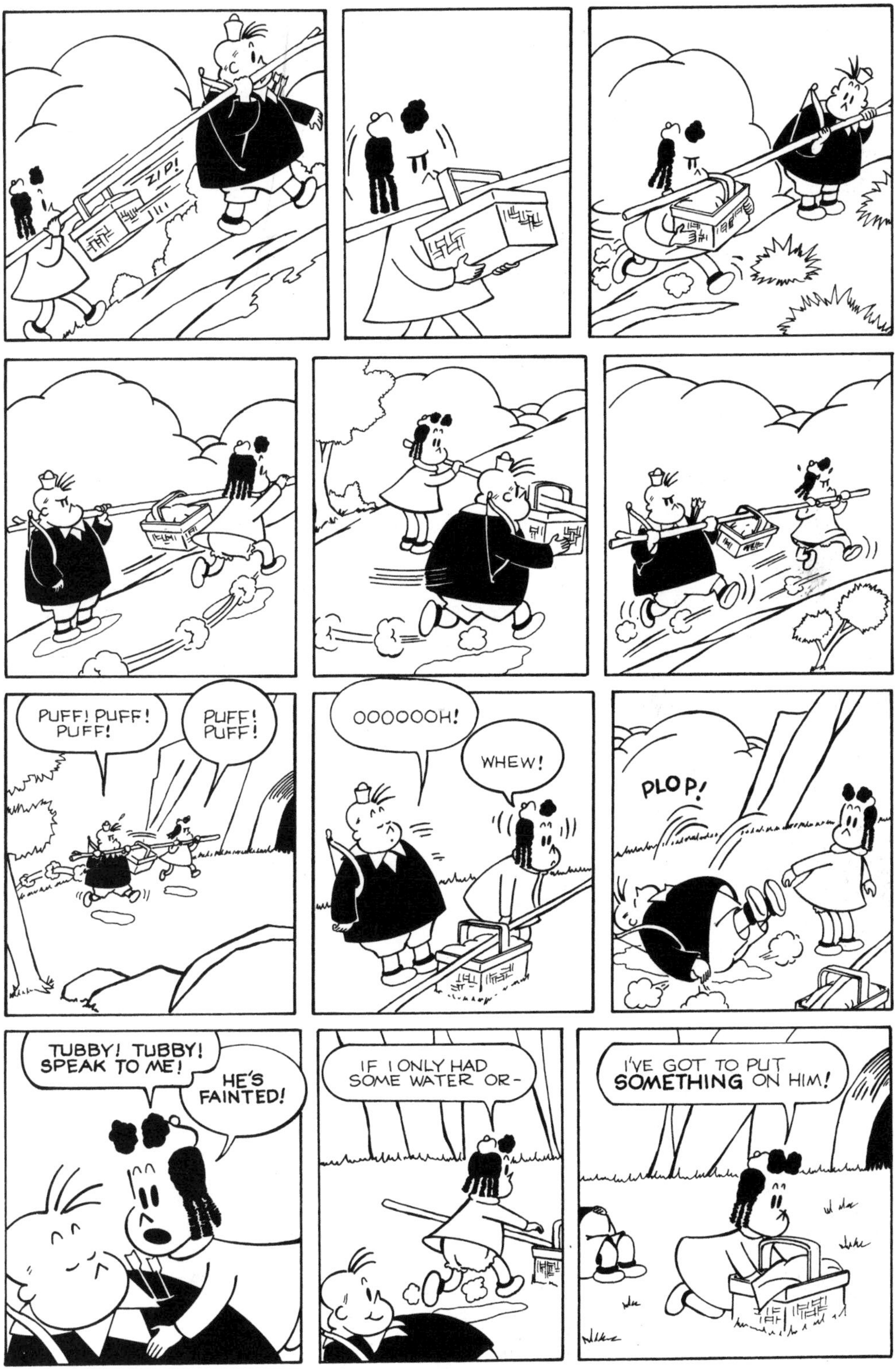
ZIP!
PUFF! PUFF! PUFF!
PUFF! PUFF!
OOOOOOH!
WHEW!
PLOP!
TUBBY! TUBBY! SPEAK TO ME!
HE'S FAINTED!
IF I ONLY HAD SOME WATER OR-
I'VE GOT TO PUT SOMETHING ON HIM!

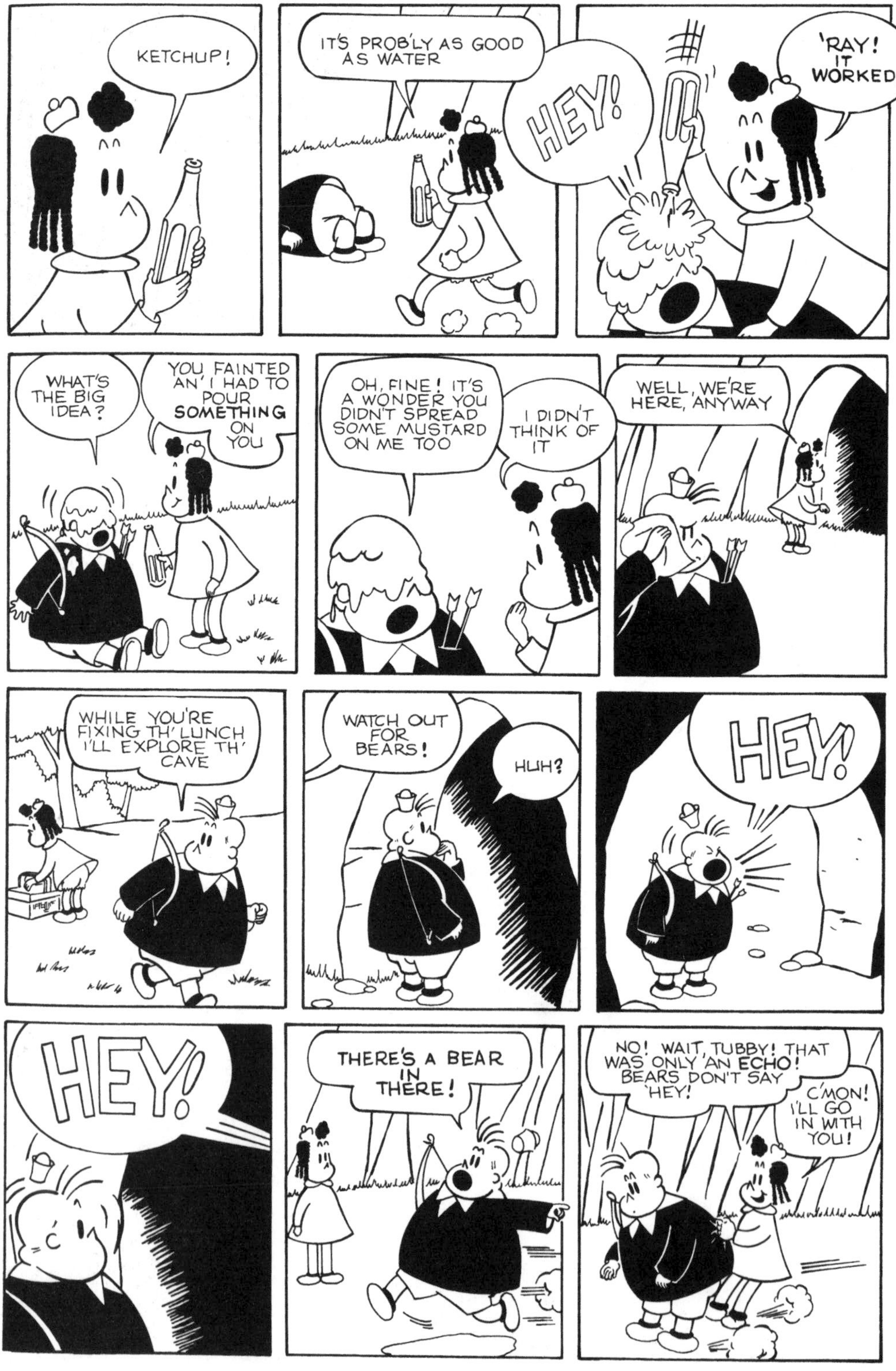

KETCHUP!
IT'S PROB'LY AS GOOD AS WATER
HEY!
'RAY! IT WORKED!
WHAT'S THE BIG IDEA?
YOU FAINTED AN' I HAD TO POUR SOMETHING ON YOU
OH, FINE! IT'S A WONDER YOU DIDN'T SPREAD SOME MUSTARD ON ME TOO
I DIDN'T THINK OF IT
WELL, WE'RE HERE, ANYWAY
WHILE YOU'RE FIXING TH' LUNCH I'LL EXPLORE TH' CAVE
WATCH OUT FOR BEARS!
HUH?
HEY!
HEY!
THERE'S A BEAR IN THERE!
NO! WAIT, TUBBY! THAT WAS ONLY AN ECHO! BEARS DON'T SAY 'HEY!
C'MON! I'LL GO IN WITH YOU!

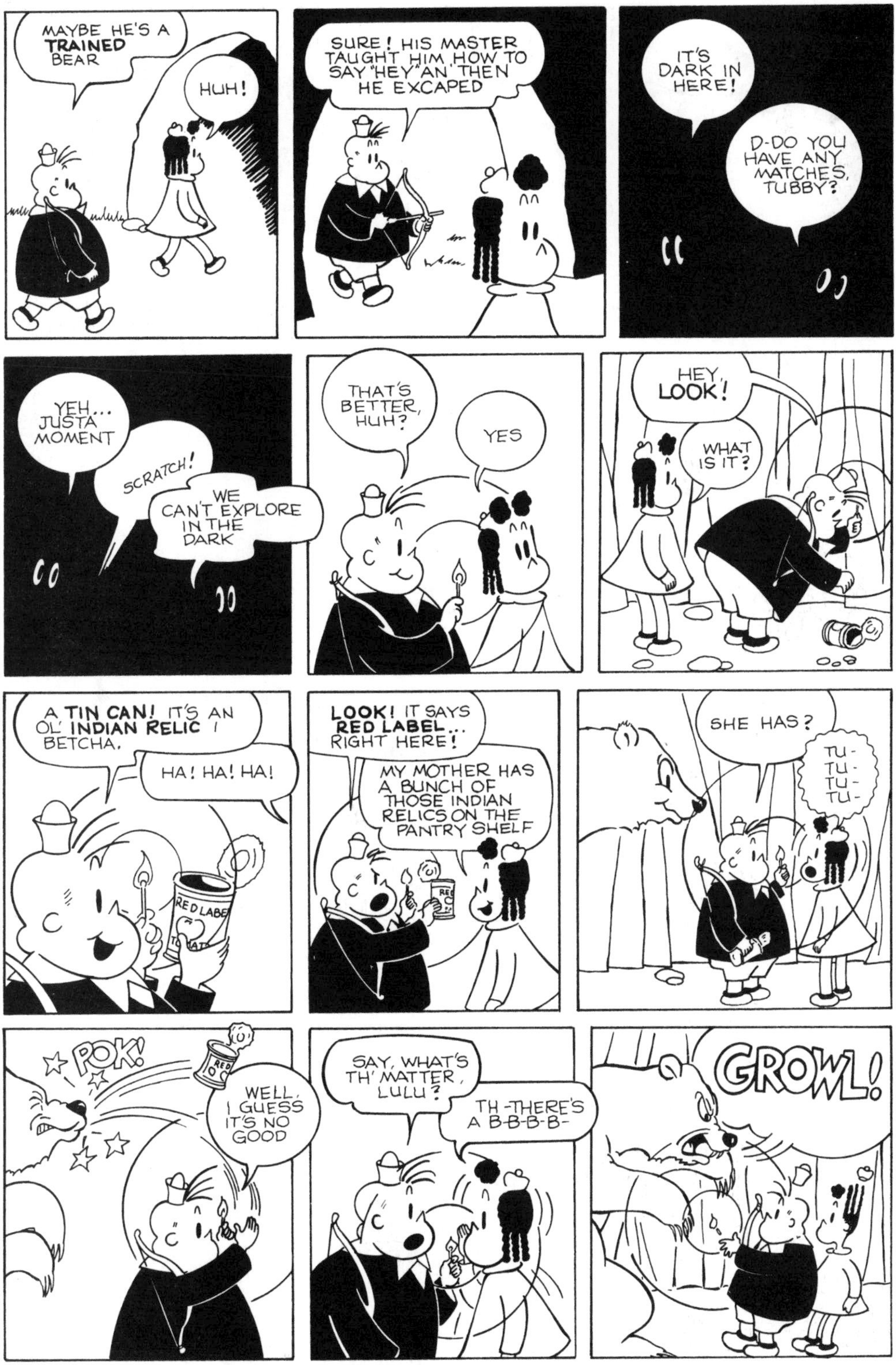
MAYBE HE'S A **TRAINED** BEAR
HUH!
SURE! HIS MASTER TAUGHT HIM HOW TO SAY "HEY" AN' THEN HE EXCAPED
IT'S DARK IN HERE!
D-DO YOU HAVE ANY MATCHES, TUBBY?
YEH... JUSTA MOMENT
SCRATCH!
WE CAN'T EXPLORE IN THE DARK
THAT'S BETTER, HUH?
YES
HEY, **LOOK!**
WHAT IS IT?
A **TIN CAN!** IT'S AN OL' **INDIAN RELIC** I BETCHA.
HA! HA! HA!
RED LABEL
LOOK! IT SAYS **RED LABEL...** RIGHT HERE!
MY MOTHER HAS A BUNCH OF THOSE INDIAN RELICS ON THE PANTRY SHELF
SHE HAS?
TU- TU- TU- TU-
POK!
WELL, I GUESS IT'S NO GOOD
SAY, WHAT'S TH' MATTER, LULU?
TH-THERE'S A B-B-B-B-
GROWL!

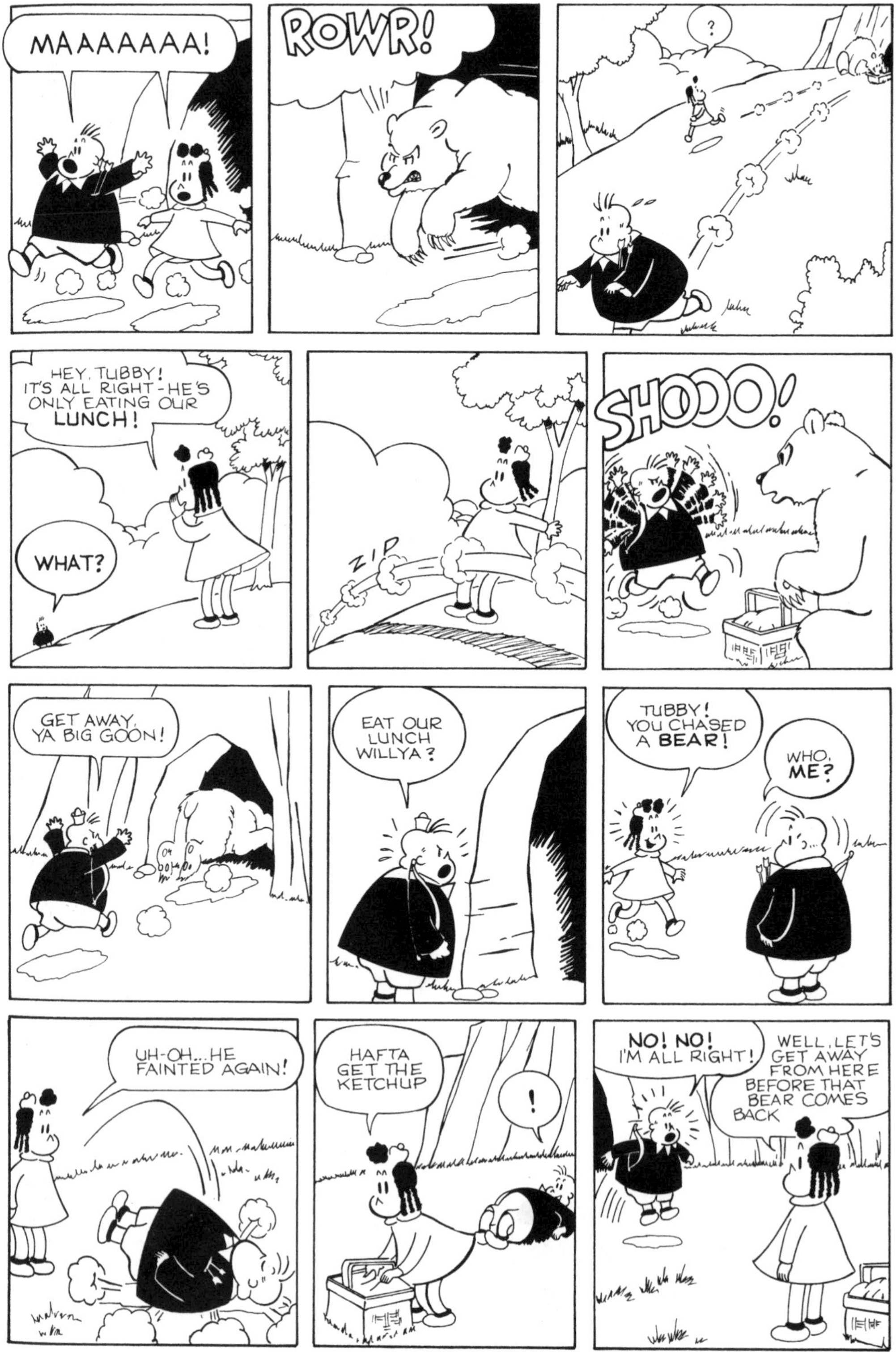
MAAAAAAA!
ROWR!
?
HEY, TUBBY! IT'S ALL RIGHT-HE'S ONLY EATING OUR LUNCH!
WHAT?
ZIP
SHOOO!
GET AWAY, YA BIG GOON!
EAT OUR LUNCH WILLYA?
TUBBY! YOU CHASED A BEAR!
WHO, ME?
UH-OH...HE FAINTED AGAIN!
HAFTA GET THE KETCHUP
!
NO! NO! I'M ALL RIGHT!
WELL, LET'S GET AWAY FROM HERE BEFORE THAT BEAR COMES BACK

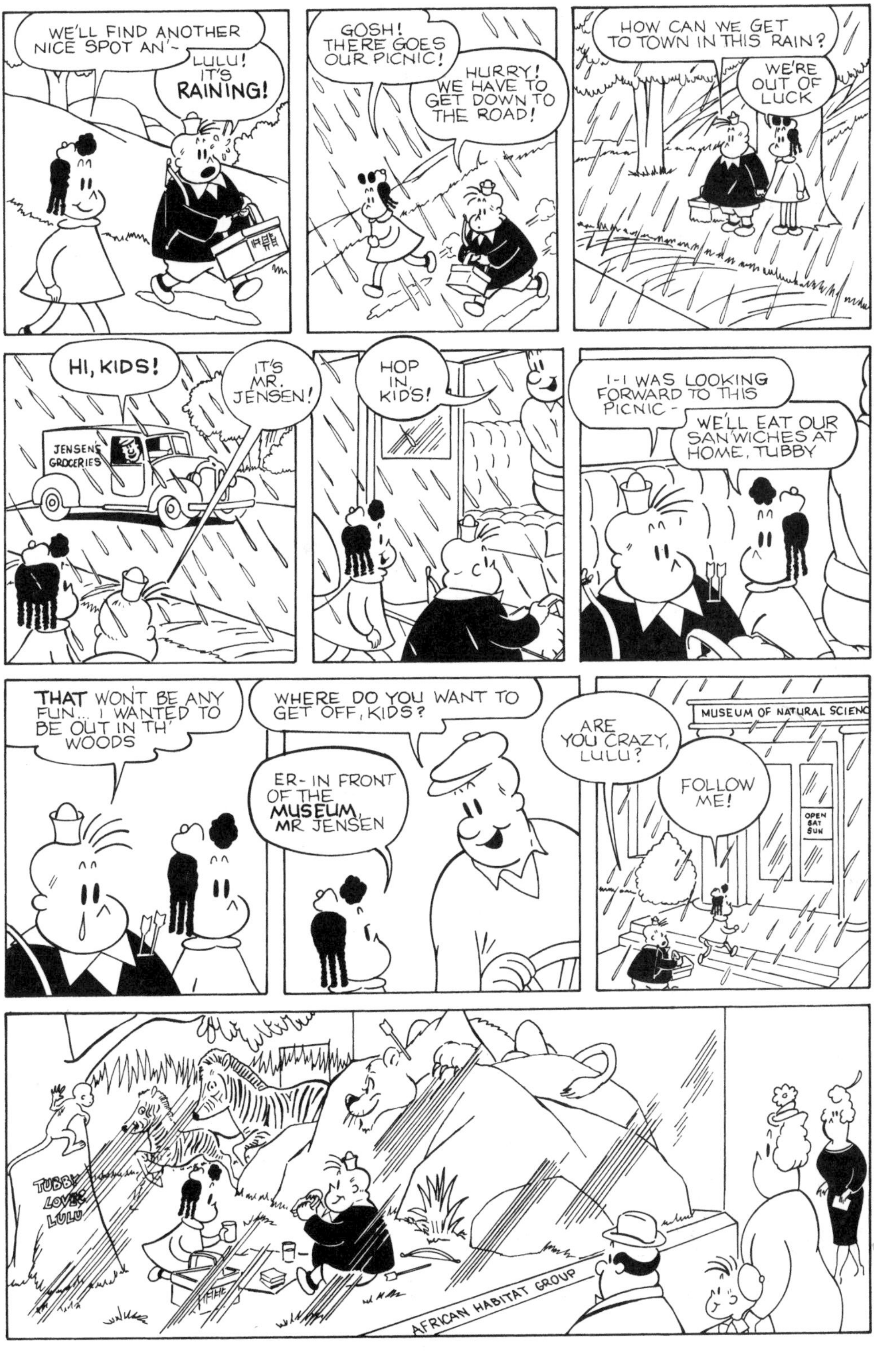
WE'LL FIND ANOTHER NICE SPOT AN'-
LULU! IT'S RAINING!
GOSH! THERE GOES OUR PICNIC!
HURRY! WE HAVE TO GET DOWN TO THE ROAD!
HOW CAN WE GET TO TOWN IN THIS RAIN?
WE'RE OUT OF LUCK
HI, KIDS!
JENSEN'S GROCERIES
IT'S MR. JENSEN!
HOP IN, KIDS!
I-I WAS LOOKING FORWARD TO THIS PICNIC-
WE'LL EAT OUR SAN'WICHES AT HOME, TUBBY
THAT WON'T BE ANY FUN... I WANTED TO BE OUT IN TH' WOODS
WHERE DO YOU WANT TO GET OFF, KIDS?
ER- IN FRONT OF THE MUSEUM, MR JENSEN
MUSEUM OF NATURAL SCIENC
ARE YOU CRAZY, LULU?
FOLLOW ME!
OPEN SAT SUN
TUBBY LOVES LULU
AFRICAN HABITAT GROUP

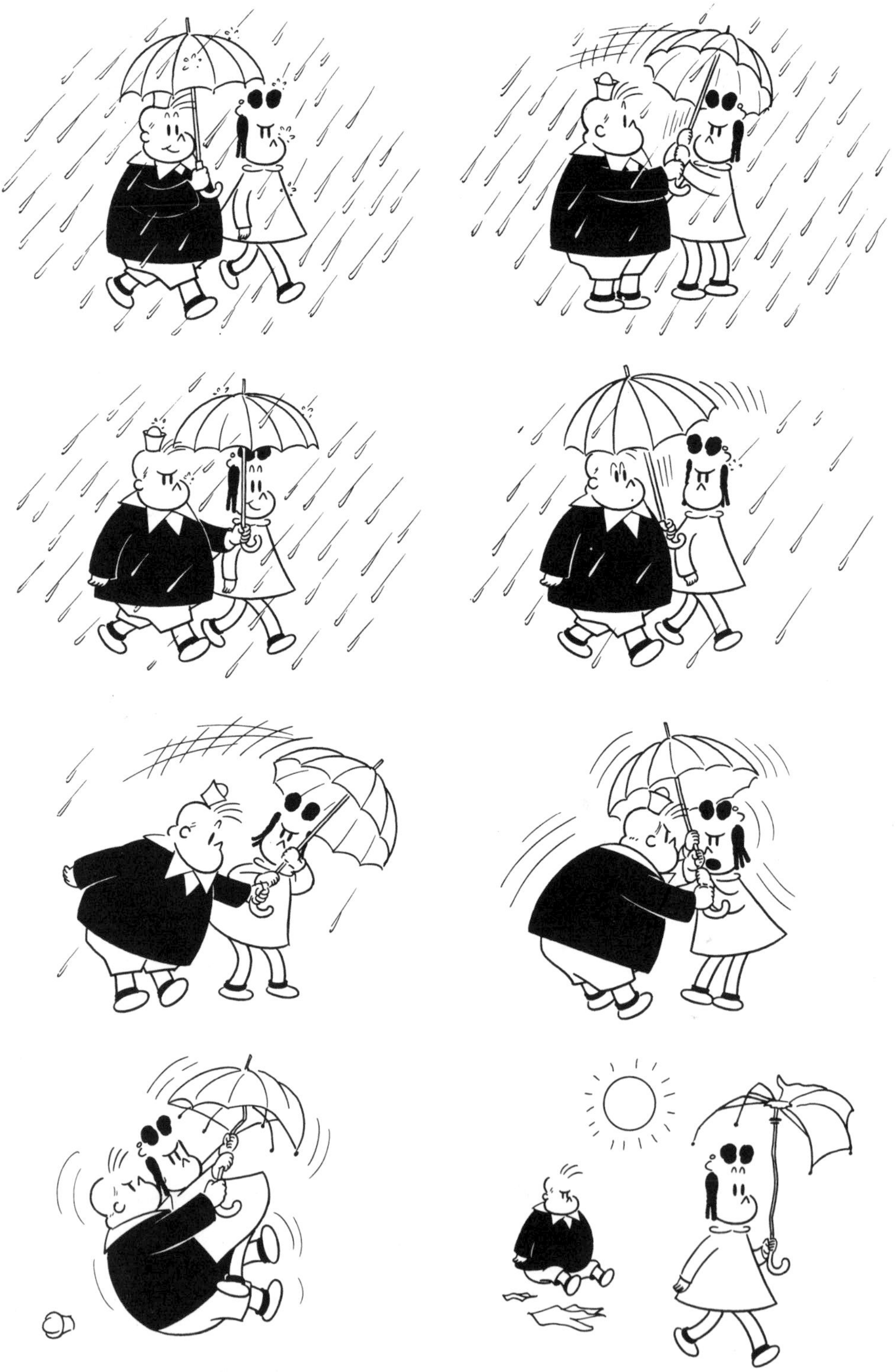

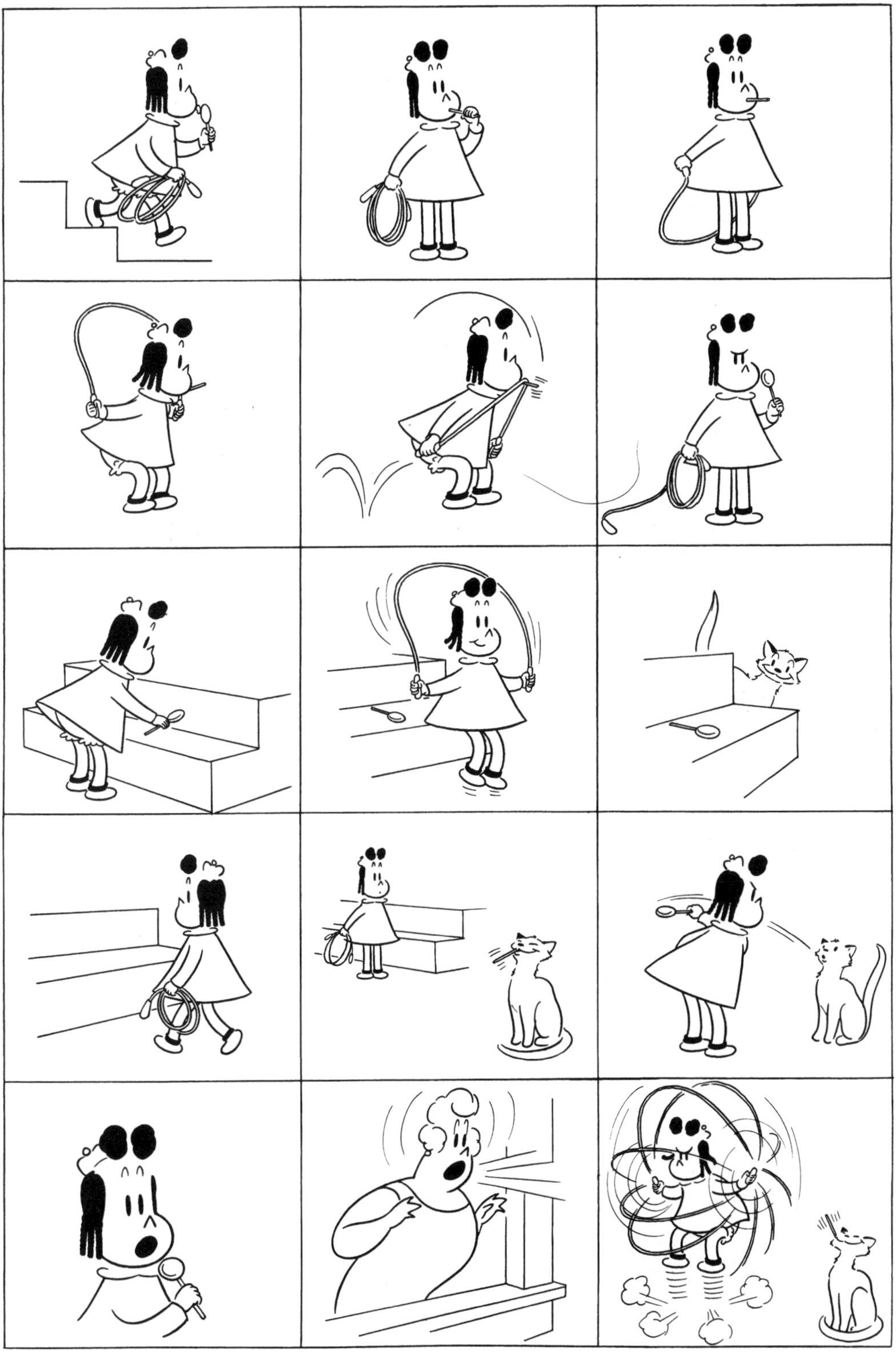

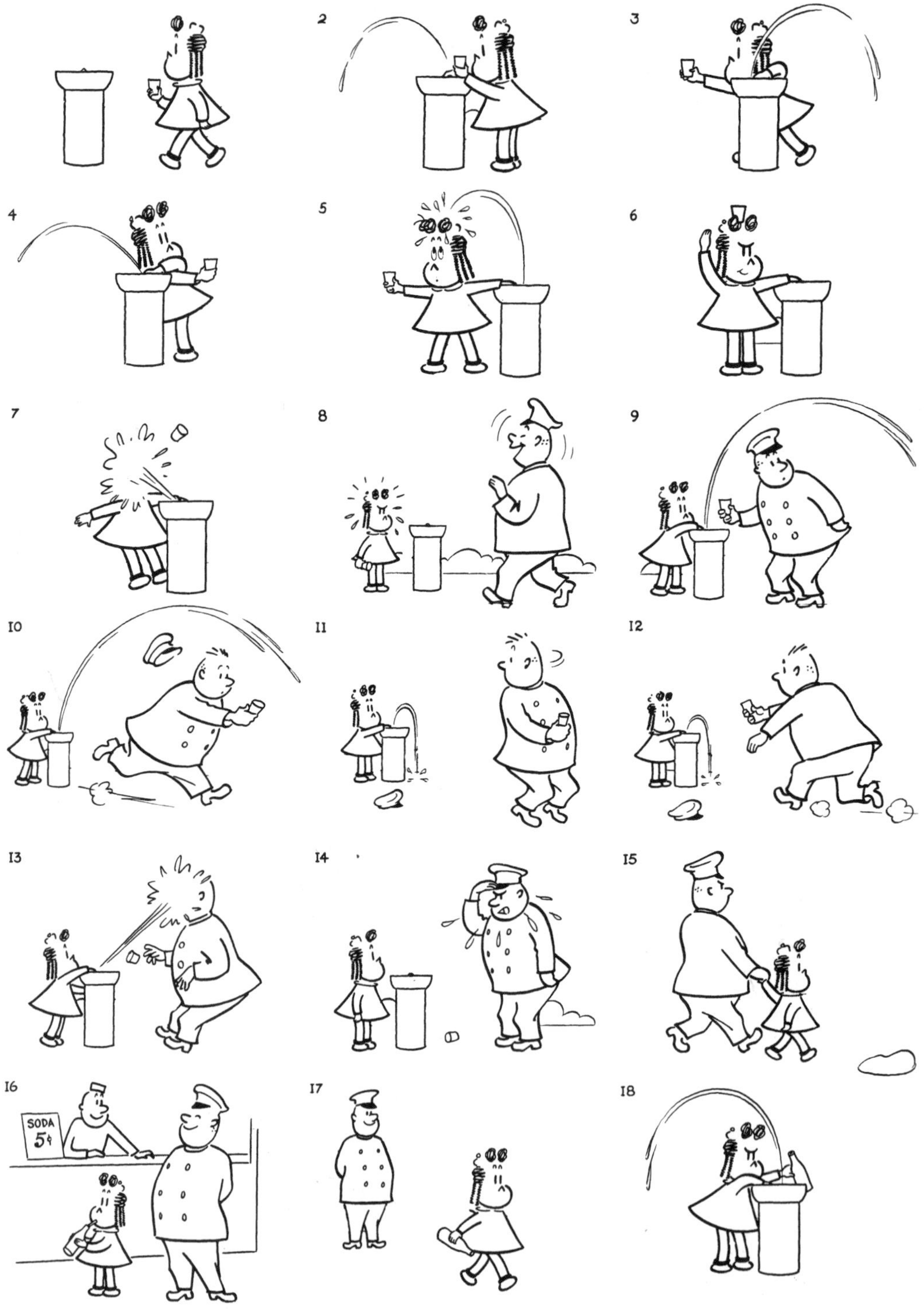
SODA
5¢

marge's LITTLE LULU

TREASURE HUNT

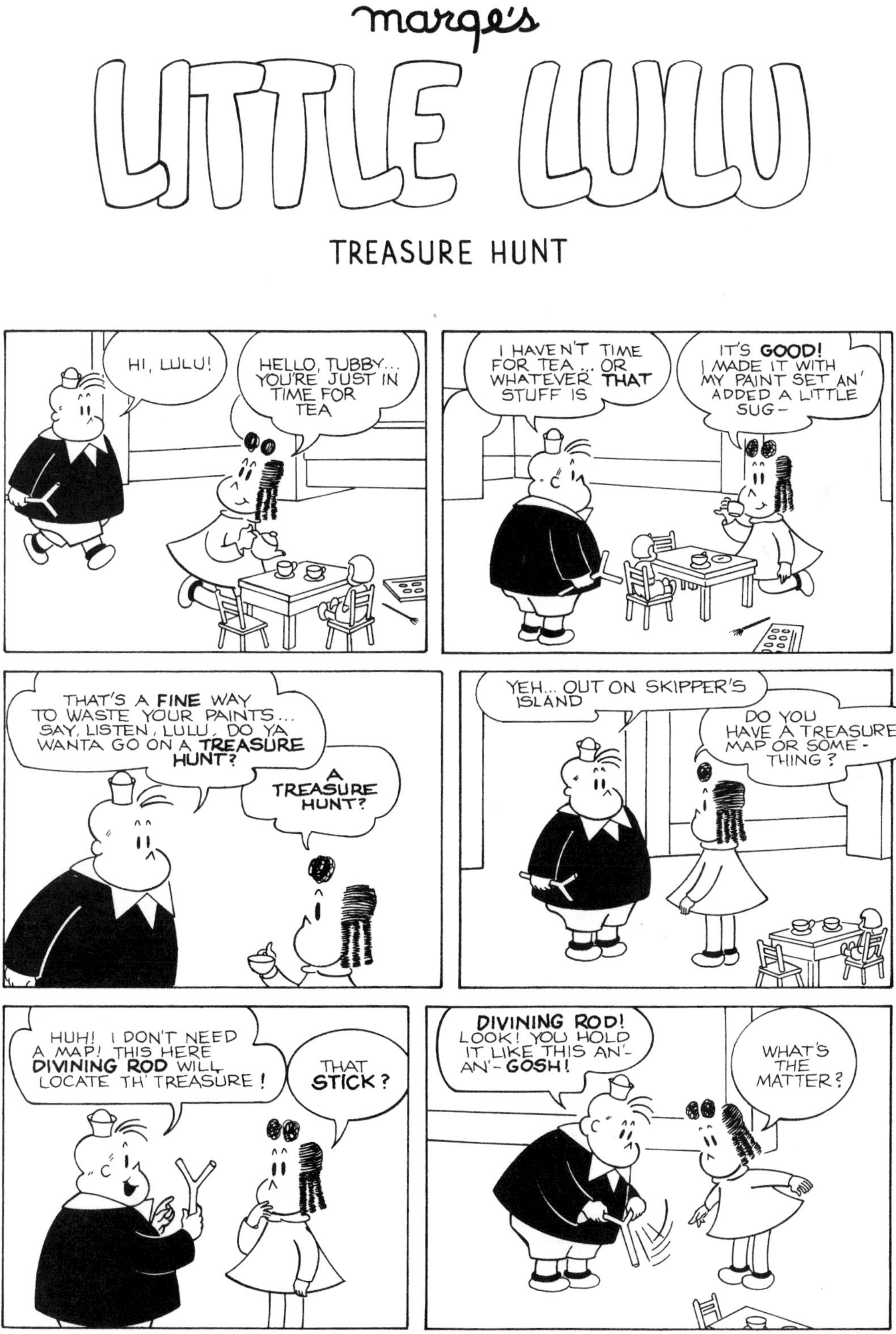

HI, LULU!
HELLO, TUBBY... YOU'RE JUST IN TIME FOR TEA
I HAVEN'T TIME FOR TEA... OR WHATEVER **THAT** STUFF IS
IT'S **GOOD!** I MADE IT WITH MY PAINT SET AN' ADDED A LITTLE SUG-
THAT'S A **FINE** WAY TO WASTE YOUR PAINTS... SAY, LISTEN, LULU, DO YA WANTA GO ON A **TREASURE HUNT?**
A **TREASURE HUNT?**
YEH... OUT ON SKIPPER'S ISLAND
DO YOU HAVE A TREASURE MAP OR SOME-THING?
HUH! I DON'T NEED A MAP! THIS HERE **DIVINING ROD** WILL LOCATE TH' TREASURE!
THAT **STICK?**
DIVINING ROD! LOOK! YOU HOLD IT LIKE THIS AN'- AN'-**GOSH!**
WHAT'S THE MATTER?

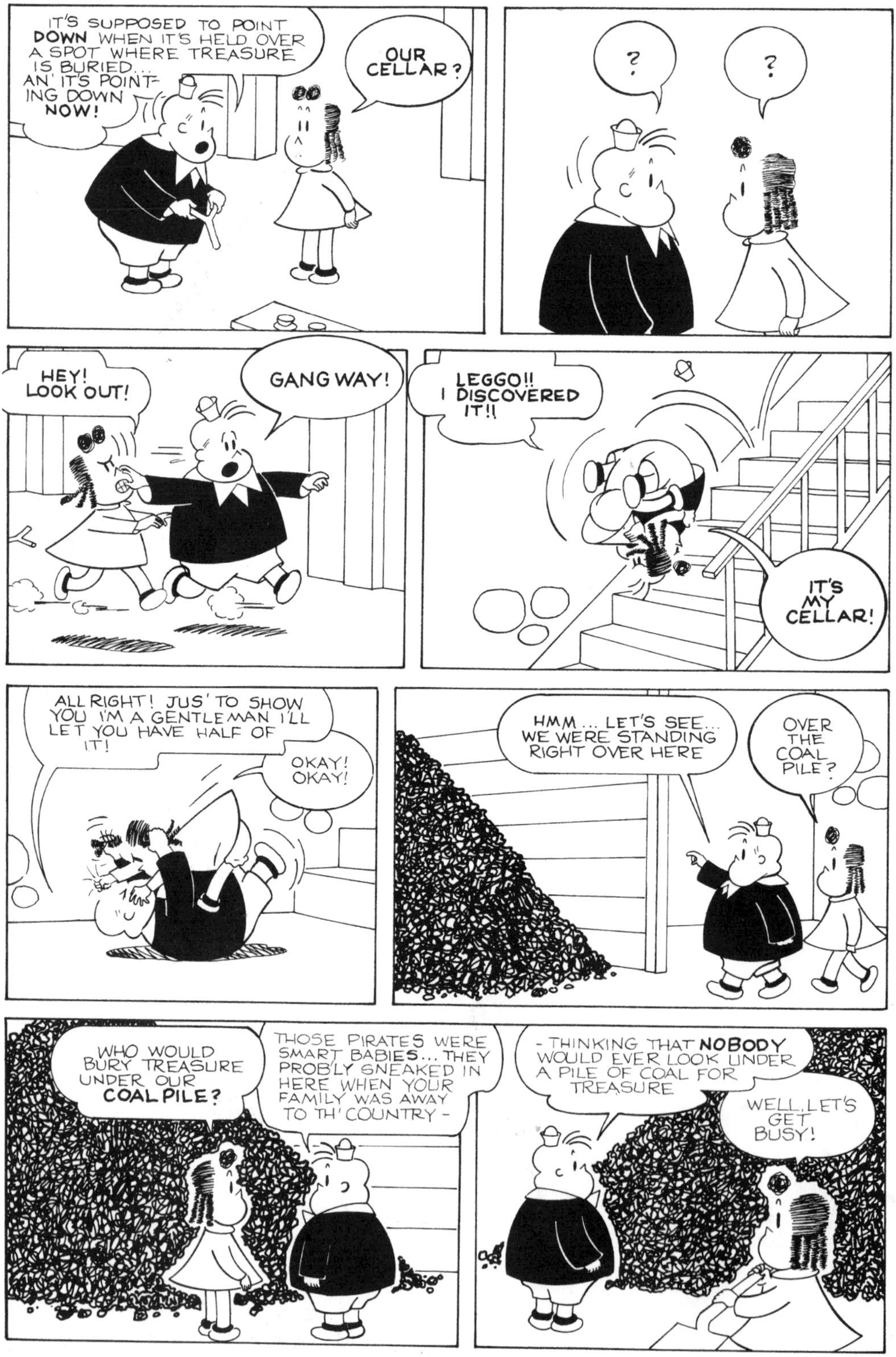
IT'S SUPPOSED TO POINT DOWN WHEN IT'S HELD OVER A SPOT WHERE TREASURE IS BURIED... AN' IT'S POINTING DOWN NOW!
OUR CELLAR?
?
?
HEY! LOOK OUT!
GANG WAY!
LEGGO!! I DISCOVERED IT!!
IT'S MY CELLAR!
ALL RIGHT! JUS' TO SHOW YOU I'M A GENTLEMAN I'LL LET YOU HAVE HALF OF IT!
OKAY! OKAY!
HMM... LET'S SEE... WE WERE STANDING RIGHT OVER HERE
OVER THE COAL PILE?
WHO WOULD BURY TREASURE UNDER OUR COAL PILE?
THOSE PIRATES WERE SMART BABIES... THEY PROB'LY SNEAKED IN HERE WHEN YOUR FAMILY WAS AWAY TO TH' COUNTRY -
- THINKING THAT NOBODY WOULD EVER LOOK UNDER A PILE OF COAL FOR TREASURE
WELL, LET'S GET BUSY!

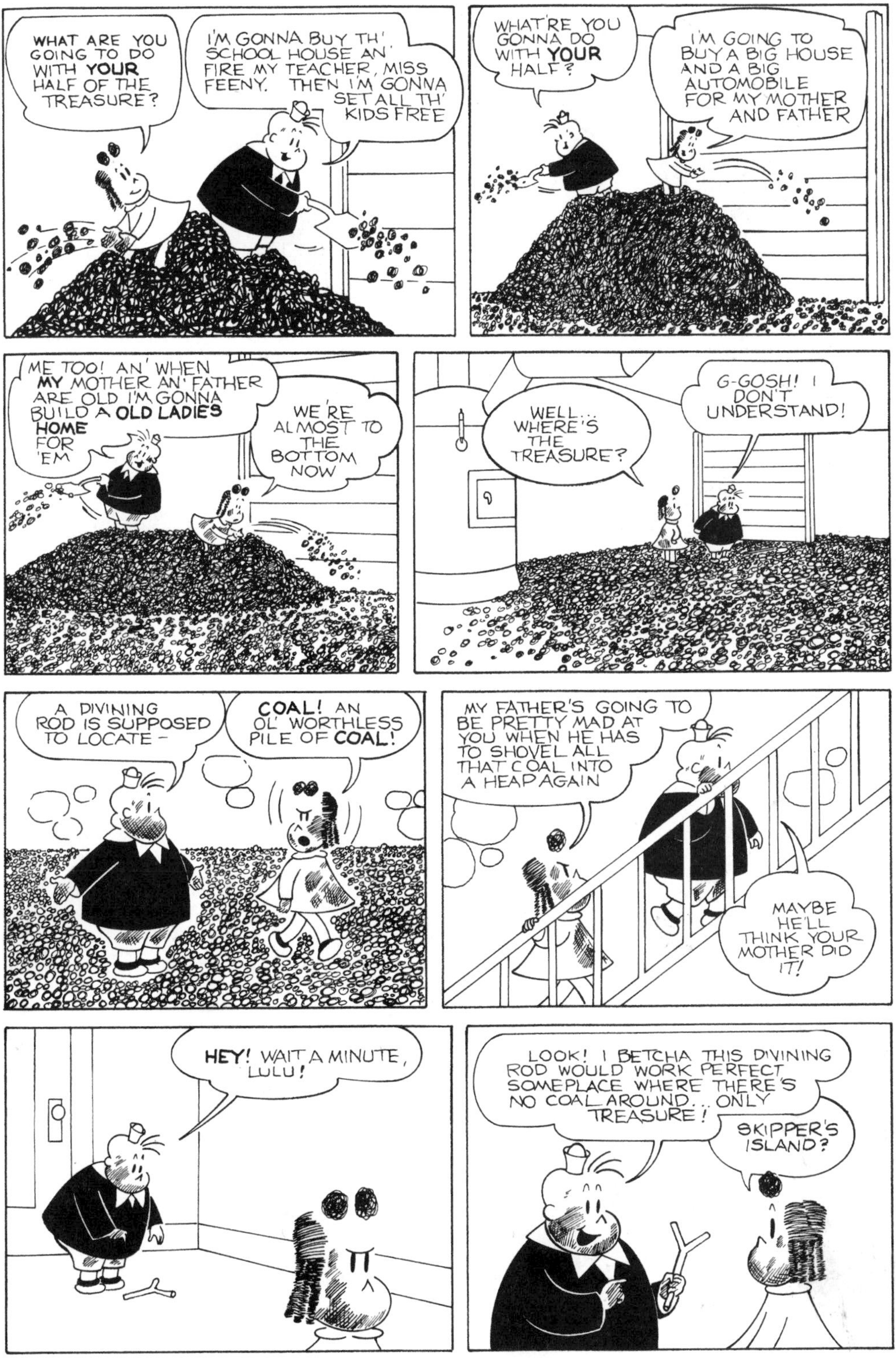
WHAT ARE YOU GOING TO DO WITH YOUR HALF OF THE TREASURE?
I'M GONNA BUY TH' SCHOOL HOUSE AN' FIRE MY TEACHER, MISS FEENY. THEN I'M GONNA SET ALL TH' KIDS FREE
WHAT'RE YOU GONNA DO WITH YOUR HALF?
I'M GOING TO BUY A BIG HOUSE AND A BIG AUTOMOBILE FOR MY MOTHER AND FATHER
ME TOO! AN' WHEN MY MOTHER AN' FATHER ARE OLD I'M GONNA BUILD A OLD LADIES HOME FOR 'EM
WE'RE ALMOST TO THE BOTTOM NOW
WELL... WHERE'S THE TREASURE?
G-GOSH! I DON'T UNDERSTAND!
A DIVINING ROD IS SUPPOSED TO LOCATE -
COAL! AN OL' WORTHLESS PILE OF COAL!
MY FATHER'S GOING TO BE PRETTY MAD AT YOU WHEN HE HAS TO SHOVEL ALL THAT COAL INTO A HEAP AGAIN
MAYBE HE'LL THINK YOUR MOTHER DID IT!
HEY! WAIT A MINUTE, LULU!
LOOK! I BETCHA THIS DIVINING ROD WOULD WORK PERFECT SOMEPLACE WHERE THERE'S NO COAL AROUND... ONLY TREASURE!
SKIPPER'S ISLAND?

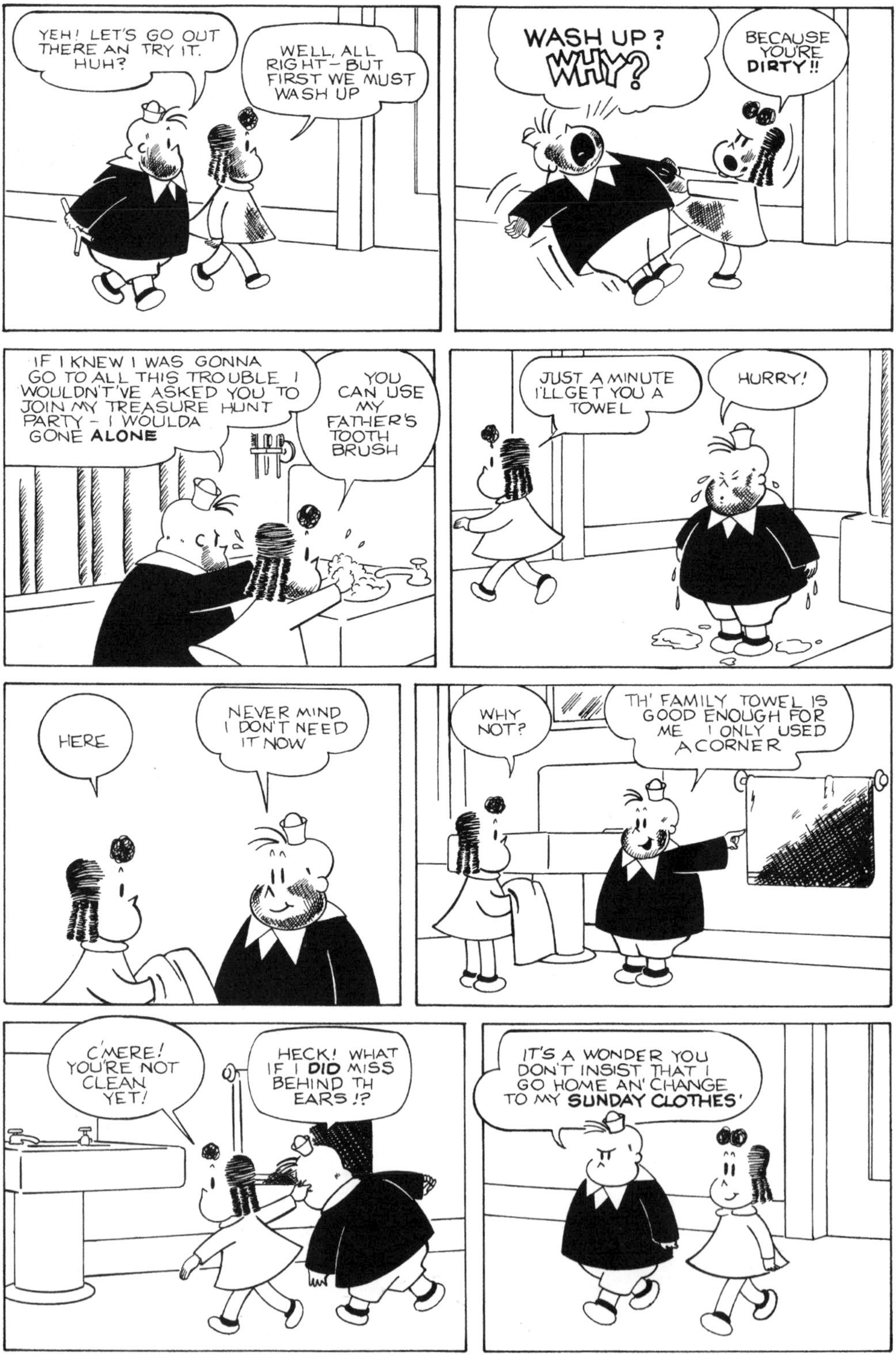

YEH! LET'S GO OUT THERE AN TRY IT. HUH?
WELL, ALL RIGHT— BUT FIRST WE MUST WASH UP
WASH UP? WHY?
BECAUSE YOU'RE DIRTY!!
IF I KNEW I WAS GONNA GO TO ALL THIS TROUBLE I WOULDN'T'VE ASKED YOU TO JOIN MY TREASURE HUNT PARTY — I WOULDA GONE ALONE
YOU CAN USE MY FATHER'S TOOTH BRUSH
JUST A MINUTE I'LL GET YOU A TOWEL
HURRY!
HERE
NEVER MIND I DON'T NEED IT NOW
WHY NOT?
TH' FAMILY TOWEL IS GOOD ENOUGH FOR ME I ONLY USED A CORNER
C'MERE! YOU'RE NOT CLEAN YET!
HECK! WHAT IF I DID MISS BEHIND TH EARS !?
IT'S A WONDER YOU DON'T INSIST THAT I GO HOME AN' CHANGE TO MY SUNDAY CLOTHES'

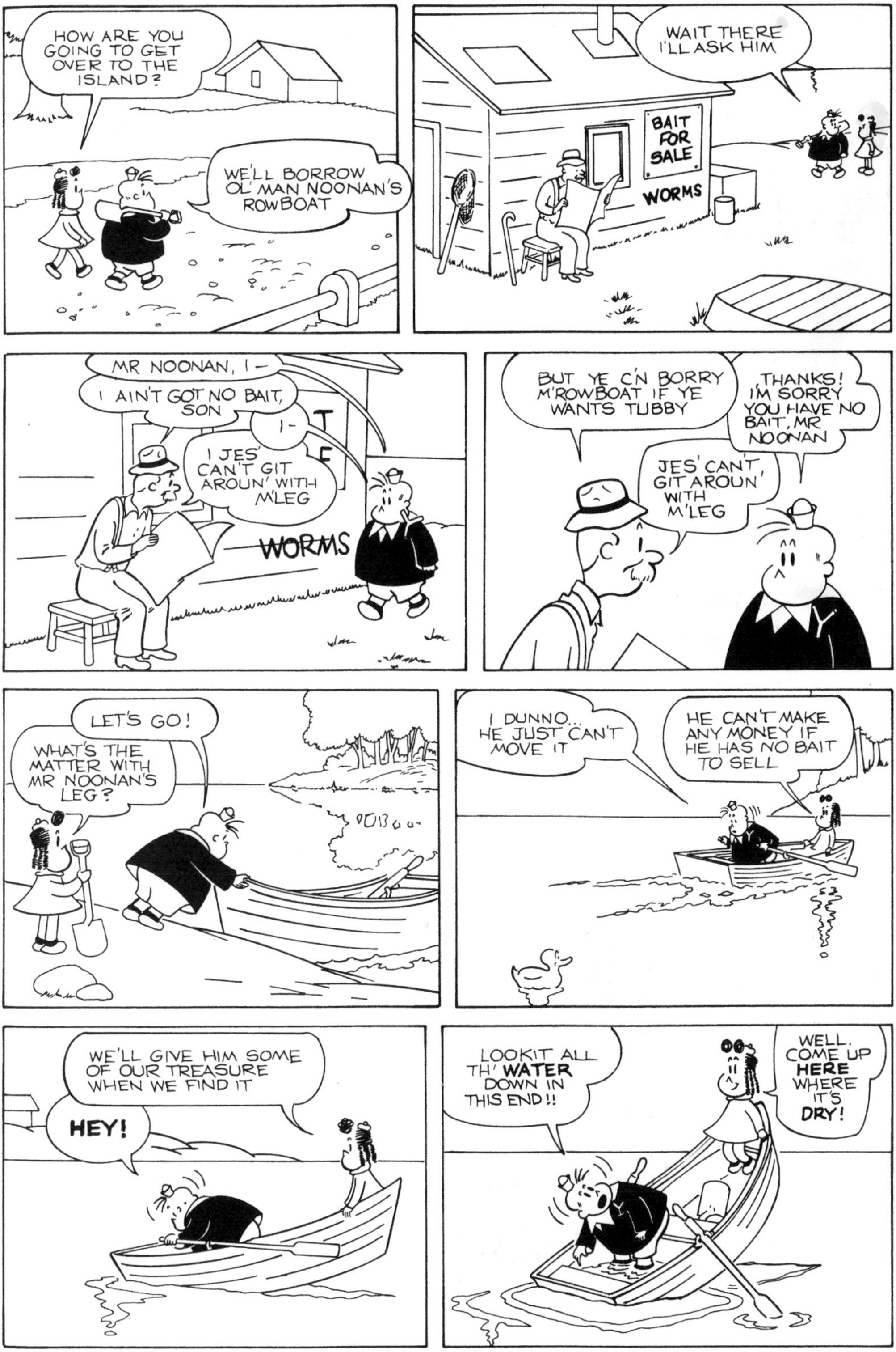

HOW ARE YOU GOING TO GET OVER TO THE ISLAND?
WE'LL BORROW OL' MAN NOONAN'S ROWBOAT
WAIT THERE I'LL ASK HIM
BAIT FOR SALE
WORMS
MR NOONAN, I —
I AIN'T GOT NO BAIT, SON
I —
I JES' CAN'T GIT AROUN' WITH M'LEG
WORMS
BUT YE C'N BORRY M'ROWBOAT IF YE WANTS TUBBY
THANKS! I'M SORRY YOU HAVE NO BAIT, MR NOONAN
JES' CAN'T GIT AROUN' WITH M'LEG
LET'S GO!
WHAT'S THE MATTER WITH MR NOONAN'S LEG?
I DUNNO... HE JUST CAN'T MOVE IT
HE CAN'T MAKE ANY MONEY IF HE HAS NO BAIT TO SELL
WE'LL GIVE HIM SOME OF OUR TREASURE WHEN WE FIND IT
HEY!
LOOKIT ALL TH' **WATER** DOWN IN THIS END!!
WELL, COME UP **HERE** WHERE IT'S **DRY**!

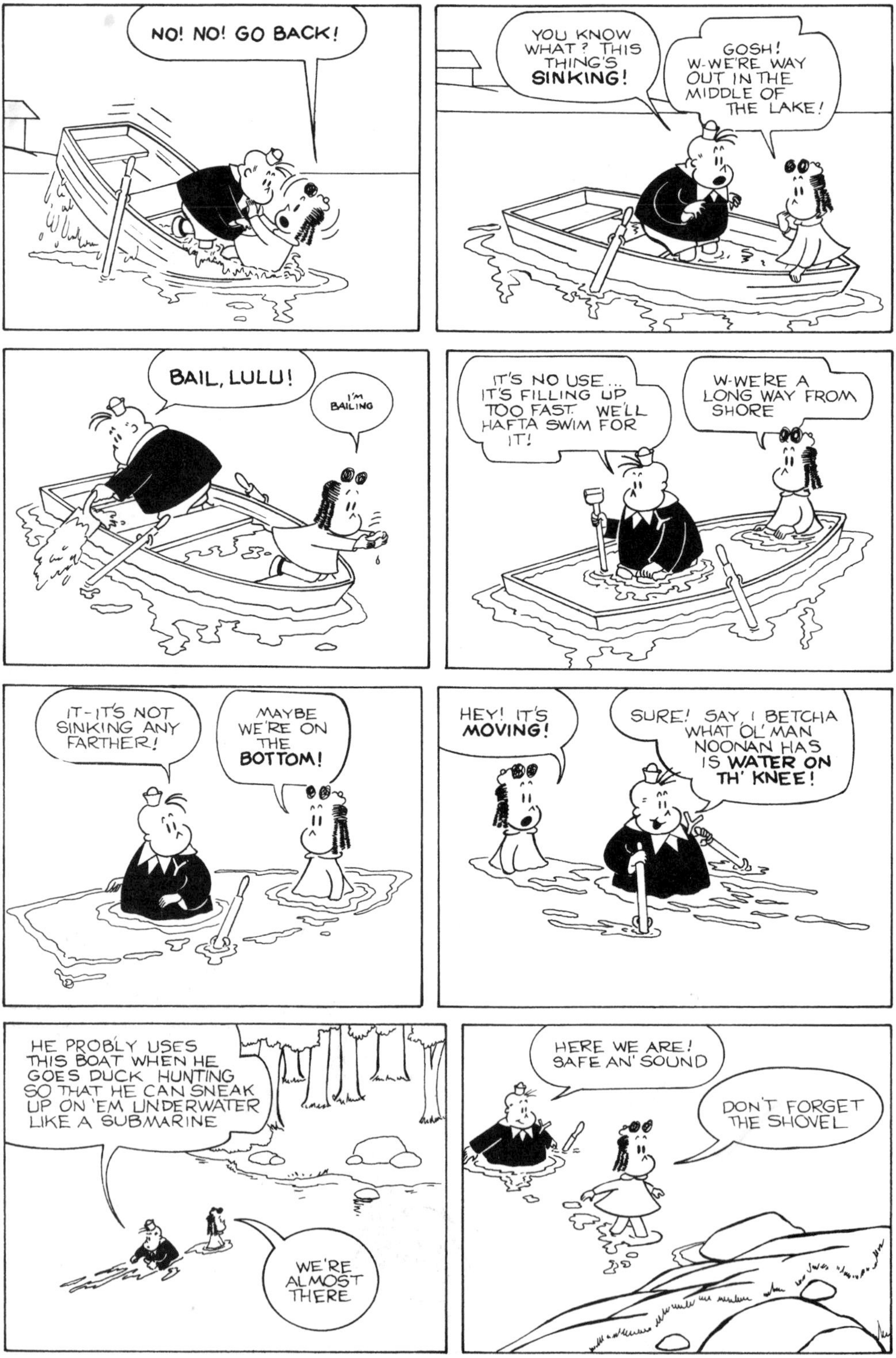
NO! NO! GO BACK!
YOU KNOW WHAT? THIS THING'S SINKING!
GOSH! W-WE'RE WAY OUT IN THE MIDDLE OF THE LAKE!
BAIL, LULU!
I'M BAILING
IT'S NO USE... IT'S FILLING UP TOO FAST. WE'LL HAFTA SWIM FOR IT!
W-WE'RE A LONG WAY FROM SHORE
IT-IT'S NOT SINKING ANY FARTHER!
MAYBE WE'RE ON THE BOTTOM!
HEY! IT'S MOVING!
SURE! SAY, I BETCHA WHAT OL' MAN NOONAN HAS IS WATER ON TH' KNEE!
HE PROB'LY USES THIS BOAT WHEN HE GOES DUCK HUNTING SO THAT HE CAN SNEAK UP ON 'EM UNDERWATER LIKE A SUBMARINE
WE'RE ALMOST THERE
HERE WE ARE! SAFE AN' SOUND
DON'T FORGET THE SHOVEL

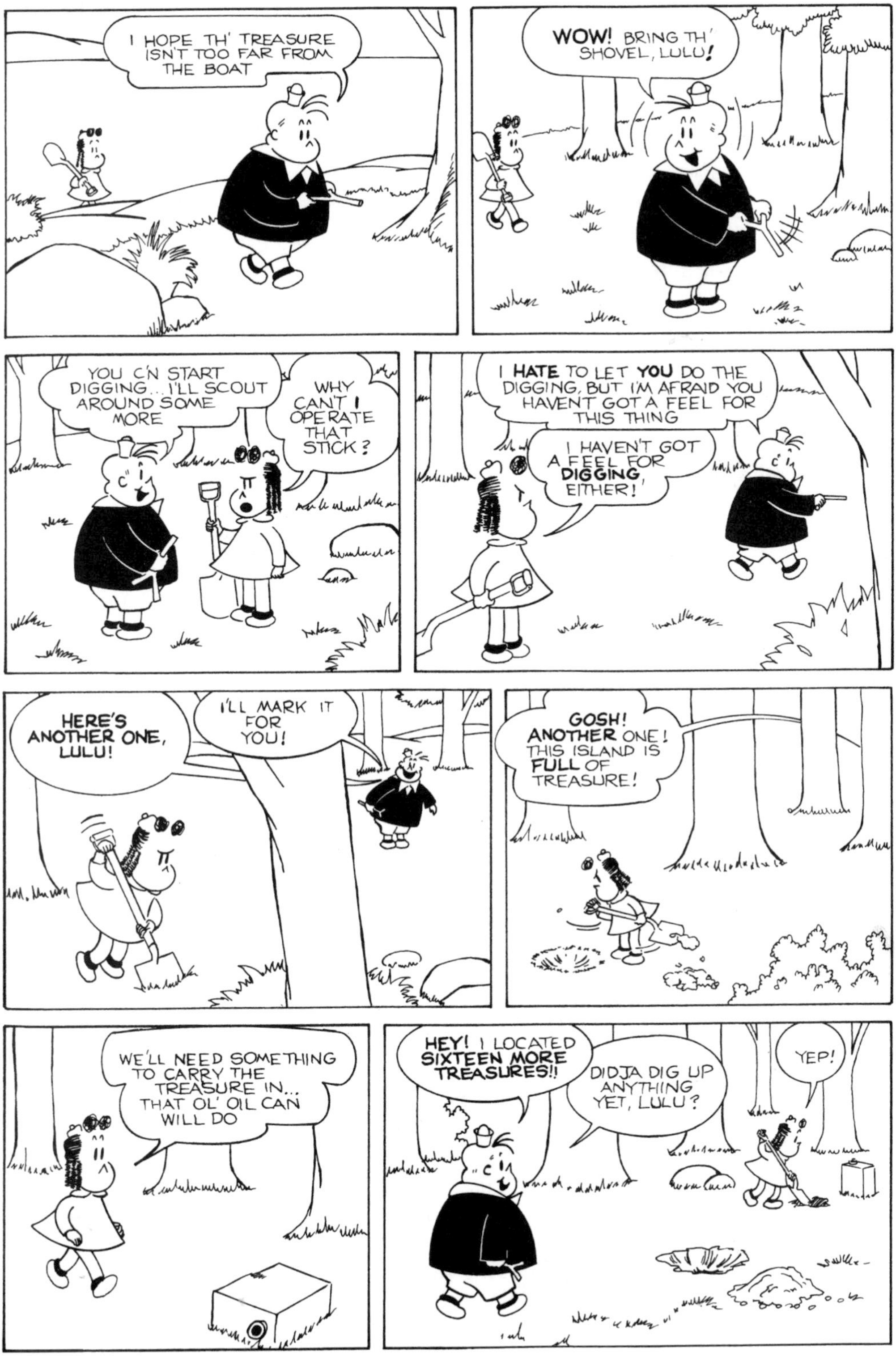
I HOPE TH' TREASURE ISN'T TOO FAR FROM THE BOAT
WOW! BRING TH' SHOVEL, LULU!
YOU C'N START DIGGING... I'LL SCOUT AROUND SOME MORE
WHY CAN'T I OPERATE THAT STICK?
I HATE TO LET YOU DO THE DIGGING, BUT I'M AFRAID YOU HAVEN'T GOT A FEEL FOR THIS THING
I HAVEN'T GOT A FEEL FOR DIGGING, EITHER!
HERE'S ANOTHER ONE, LULU!
I'LL MARK IT FOR YOU!
GOSH! ANOTHER ONE! THIS ISLAND IS FULL OF TREASURE!
WE'LL NEED SOMETHING TO CARRY THE TREASURE IN... THAT OL' OIL CAN WILL DO
HEY! I LOCATED SIXTEEN MORE TREASURES!!
DIDJA DIG UP ANYTHING YET, LULU?
YEP!

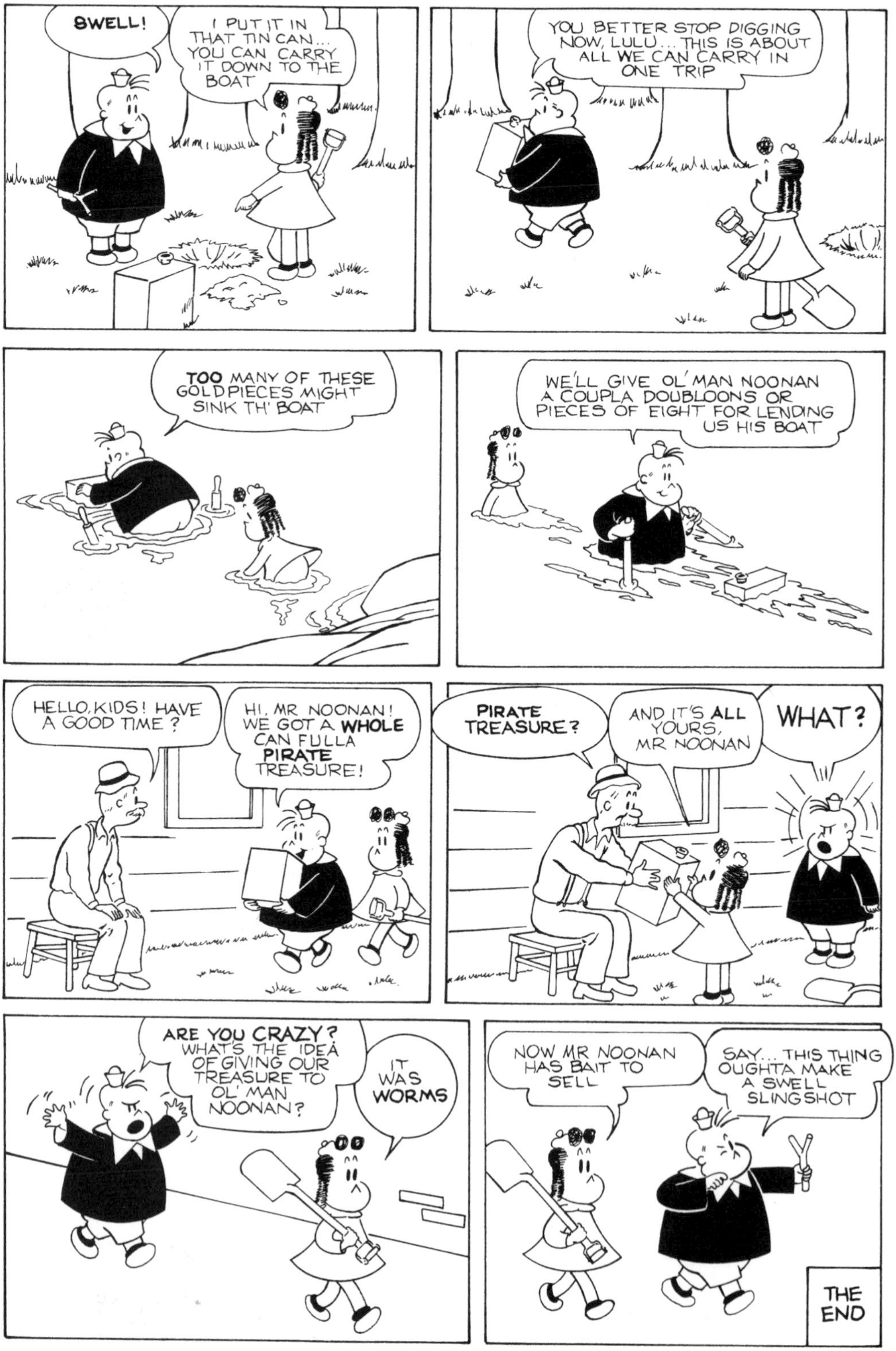
SWELL!
I PUT IT IN THAT TIN CAN... YOU CAN CARRY IT DOWN TO THE BOAT
YOU BETTER STOP DIGGING NOW, LULU... THIS IS ABOUT ALL WE CAN CARRY IN ONE TRIP
TOO MANY OF THESE GOLDPIECES MIGHT SINK TH' BOAT
WE'LL GIVE OL' MAN NOONAN A COUPLA DOUBLOONS OR PIECES OF EIGHT FOR LENDING US HIS BOAT
HELLO, KIDS! HAVE A GOOD TIME?
HI, MR NOONAN! WE GOT A WHOLE CAN FULLA PIRATE TREASURE!
PIRATE TREASURE?
AND IT'S ALL YOURS, MR NOONAN
WHAT?
ARE YOU CRAZY? WHAT'S THE IDEA OF GIVING OUR TREASURE TO OL' MAN NOONAN?
IT WAS WORMS
NOW MR NOONAN HAS BAIT TO SELL
SAY... THIS THING OUGHTA MAKE A SWELL SLINGSHOT
THE END

marge's

LITTLE LULU

"HE CAN'T HURT US"

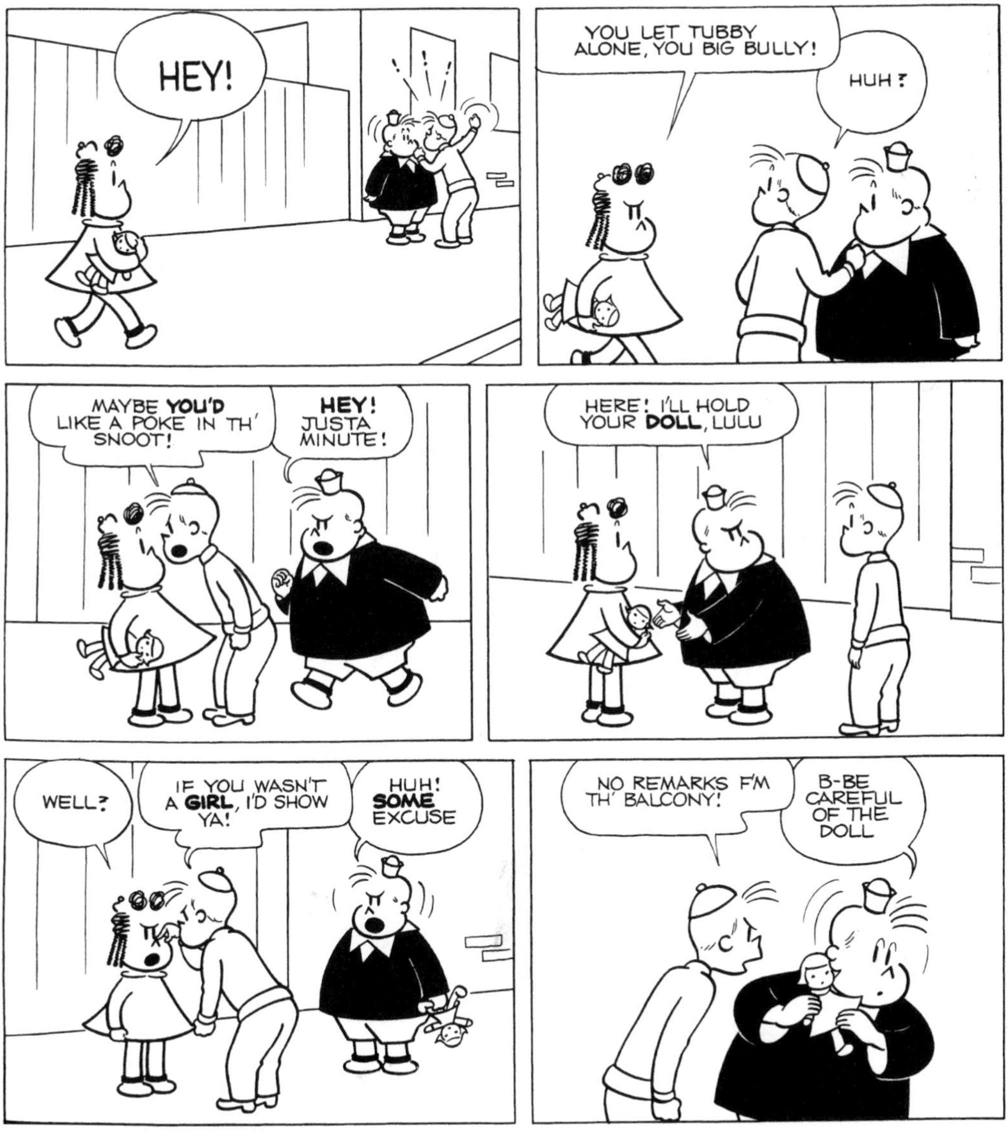
HEY!
YOU LET TUBBY ALONE, YOU BIG BULLY!
HUH?
MAYBE YOU'D LIKE A POKE IN TH' SNOOT!
HEY! JUSTA MINUTE!
HERE! I'LL HOLD YOUR DOLL, LULU
WELL?
IF YOU WASN'T A GIRL, I'D SHOW YA!
HUH! SOME EXCUSE
NO REMARKS F'M TH' BALCONY!
B-BE CAREFUL OF THE DOLL

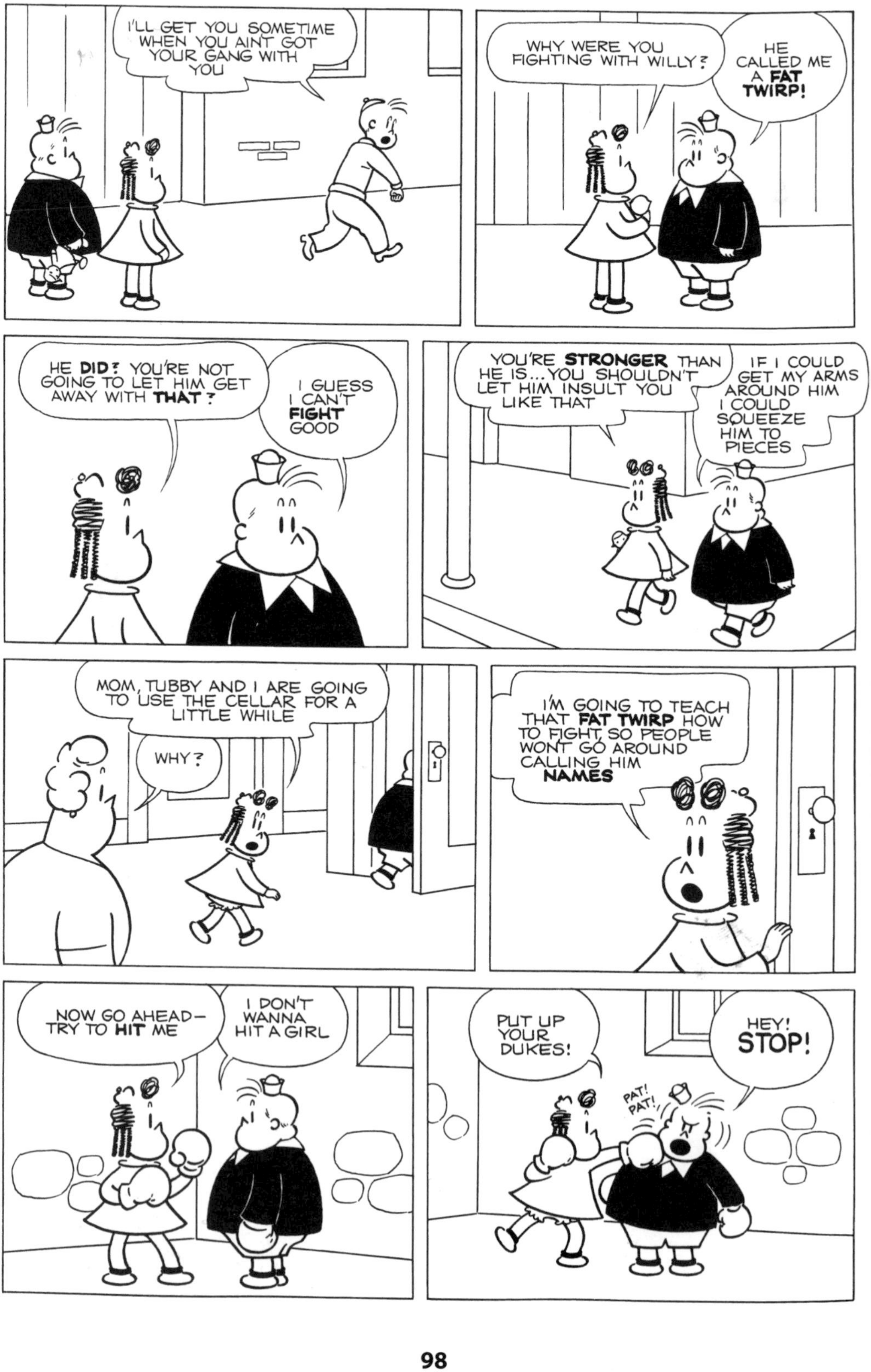
I'LL GET YOU SOMETIME WHEN YOU AIN'T GOT YOUR GANG WITH YOU
WHY WERE YOU FIGHTING WITH WILLY?
HE CALLED ME A **FAT TWIRP!**
HE **DID**? YOU'RE NOT GOING TO LET HIM GET AWAY WITH **THAT**?
I GUESS I CAN'T **FIGHT** GOOD
YOU'RE **STRONGER** THAN HE IS... YOU SHOULDN'T LET HIM INSULT YOU LIKE THAT
IF I COULD GET MY ARMS AROUND HIM I COULD SQUEEZE HIM TO PIECES
MOM, TUBBY AND I ARE GOING TO USE THE CELLAR FOR A LITTLE WHILE
WHY?
I'M GOING TO TEACH THAT **FAT TWIRP** HOW TO FIGHT, SO PEOPLE WON'T GO AROUND CALLING HIM **NAMES**
NOW GO AHEAD— TRY TO **HIT** ME
I DON'T WANNA HIT A GIRL
PUT UP YOUR DUKES!
PAT! PAT!
HEY! **STOP!**

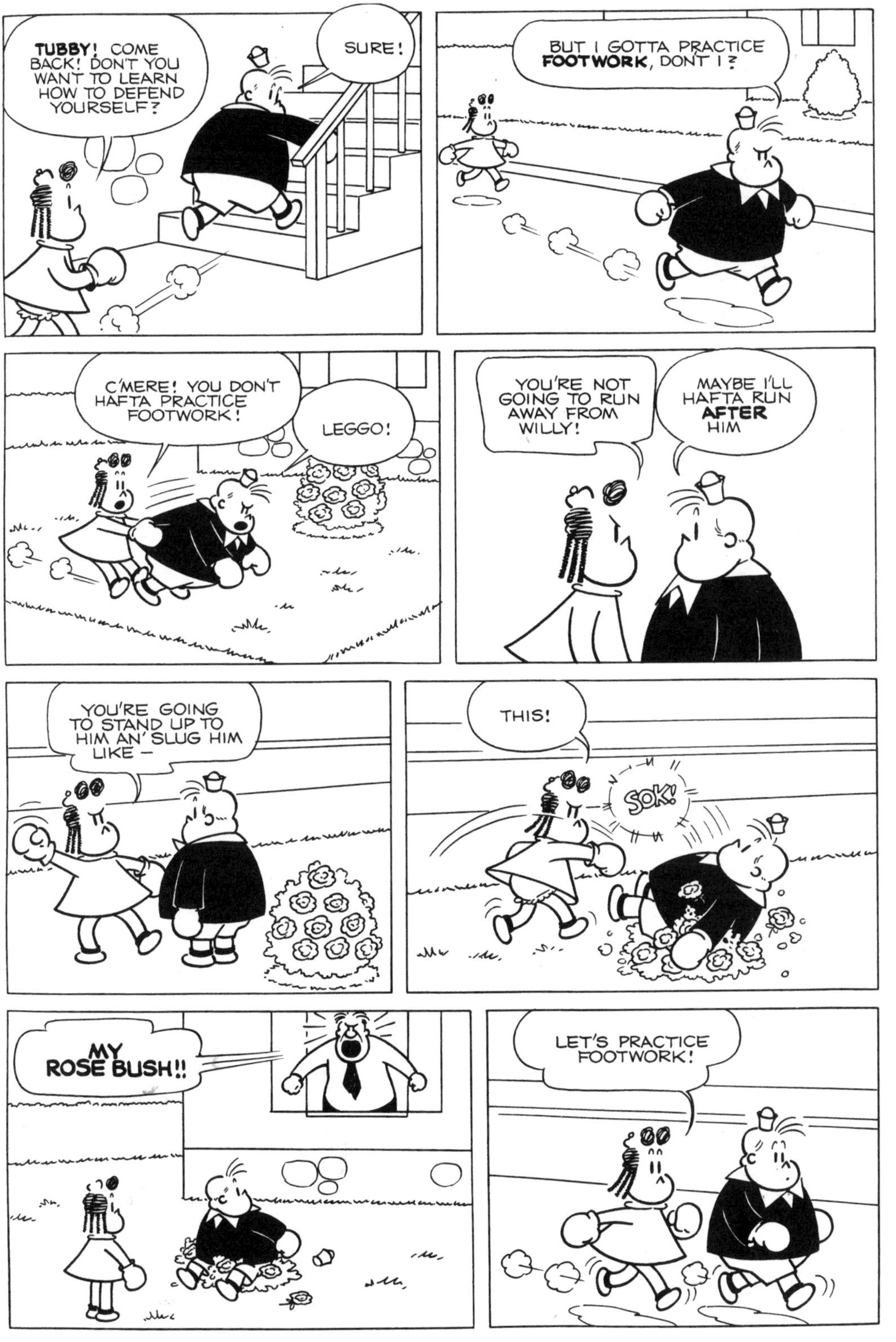
TUBBY! COME BACK! DON'T YOU WANT TO LEARN HOW TO DEFEND YOURSELF?
SURE!
BUT I GOTTA PRACTICE FOOTWORK, DON'T I?
C'MERE! YOU DON'T HAFTA PRACTICE FOOTWORK!
LEGGO!
YOU'RE NOT GOING TO RUN AWAY FROM WILLY!
MAYBE I'LL HAFTA RUN AFTER HIM
YOU'RE GOING TO STAND UP TO HIM AN' SLUG HIM LIKE —
THIS!
SOK!
MY ROSE BUSH!!
LET'S PRACTICE FOOTWORK!

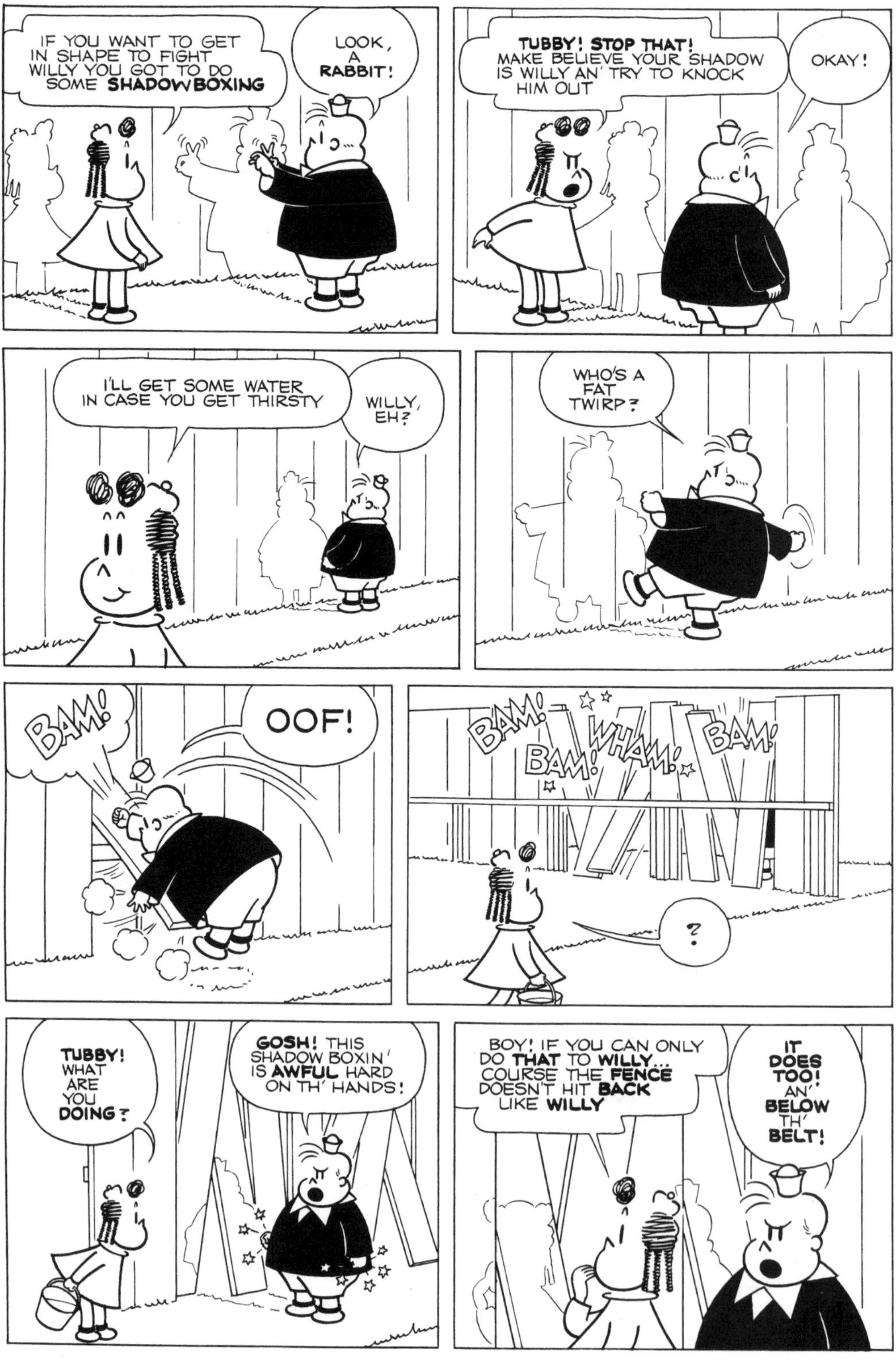
IF YOU WANT TO GET IN SHAPE TO FIGHT WILLY YOU GOT TO DO SOME SHADOWBOXING
LOOK, A RABBIT!
TUBBY! STOP THAT! MAKE BELIEVE YOUR SHADOW IS WILLY AN' TRY TO KNOCK HIM OUT
OKAY!
I'LL GET SOME WATER IN CASE YOU GET THIRSTY
WILLY, EH?
WHO'S A FAT TWIRP?
BAM!
OOF!
BAM!
BAM!
WHAM!
BAM!
?
TUBBY! WHAT ARE YOU DOING?
GOSH! THIS SHADOW BOXIN' IS AWFUL HARD ON TH' HANDS!
BOY! IF YOU CAN ONLY DO THAT TO WILLY... COURSE THE FENCE DOESN'T HIT BACK LIKE WILLY
IT DOES TOO! AN' BELOW TH' BELT!

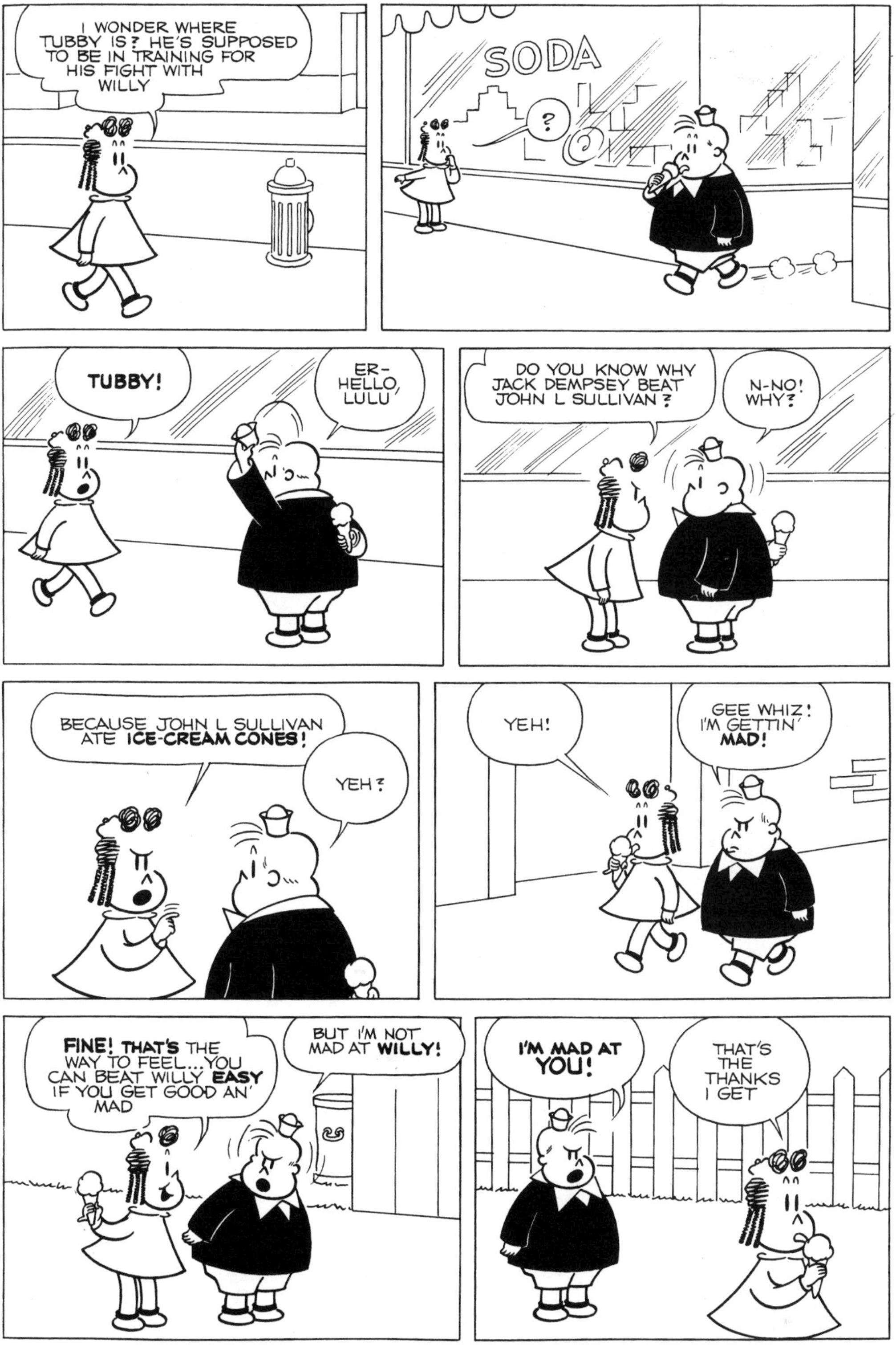
I WONDER WHERE TUBBY IS? HE'S SUPPOSED TO BE IN TRAINING FOR HIS FIGHT WITH WILLY
SODA
?
TUBBY!
ER-HELLO, LULU
DO YOU KNOW WHY JACK DEMPSEY BEAT JOHN L SULLIVAN?
N-NO! WHY?
BECAUSE JOHN L SULLIVAN ATE ICE-CREAM CONES!
YEH?
YEH!
GEE WHIZ! I'M GETTIN' MAD!
FINE! THAT'S THE WAY TO FEEL...YOU CAN BEAT WILLY EASY IF YOU GET GOOD AN' MAD
BUT I'M NOT MAD AT WILLY!
I'M MAD AT YOU!
THAT'S THE THANKS I GET

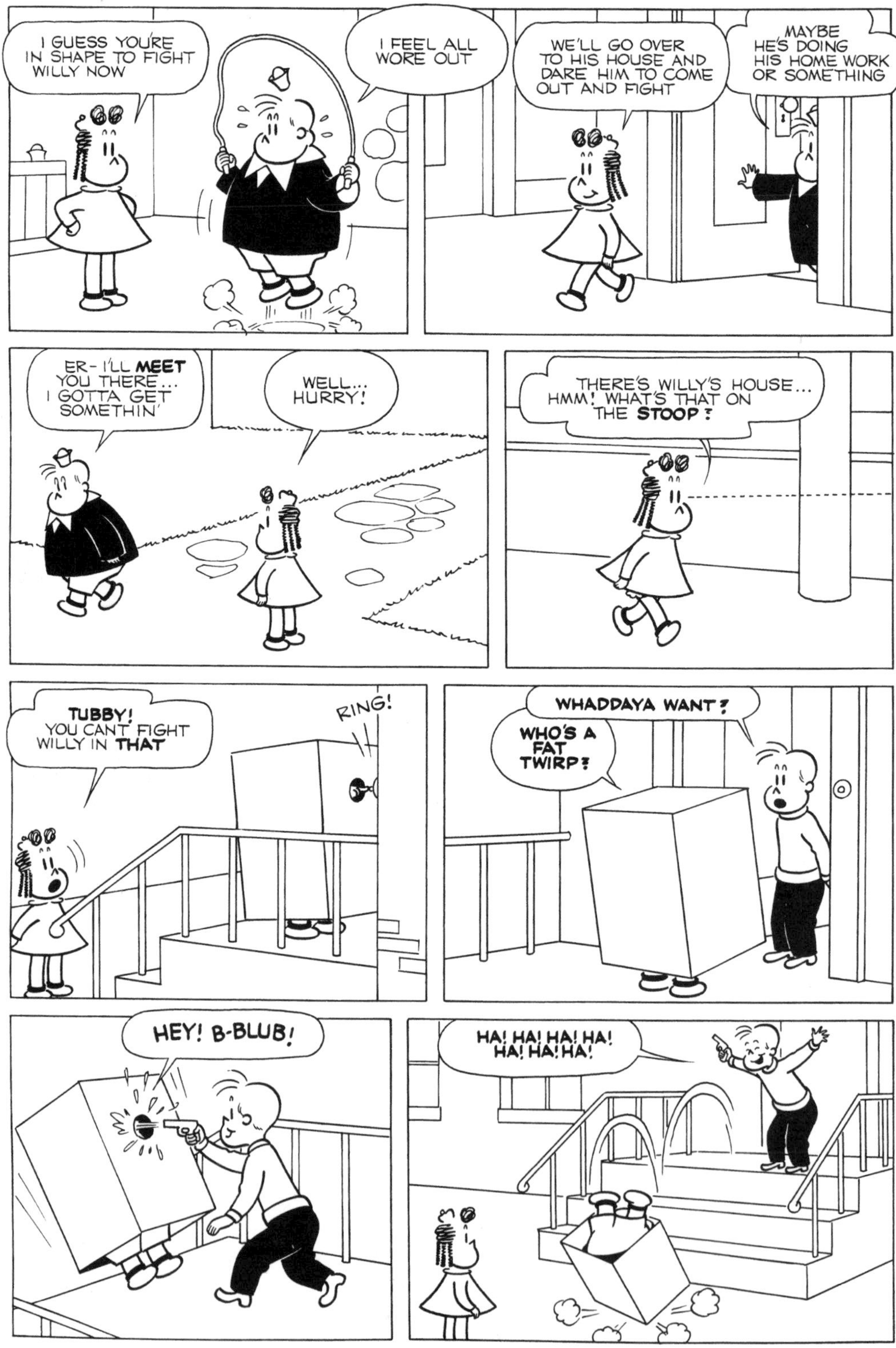
I GUESS YOU'RE IN SHAPE TO FIGHT WILLY NOW
I FEEL ALL WORE OUT
WE'LL GO OVER TO HIS HOUSE AND DARE HIM TO COME OUT AND FIGHT
MAYBE HE'S DOING HIS HOME WORK OR SOMETHING
ER- I'LL **MEET** YOU THERE... I GOTTA GET SOMETHIN'
WELL... HURRY!
THERE'S WILLY'S HOUSE... HMM! WHAT'S THAT ON THE **STOOP**?
TUBBY! YOU CAN'T FIGHT WILLY IN **THAT**
RING!
WHADDAYA WANT?
WHO'S A FAT TWIRP?
HEY! B-BLUB!
HA! HA! HA! HA! HA! HA! HA!

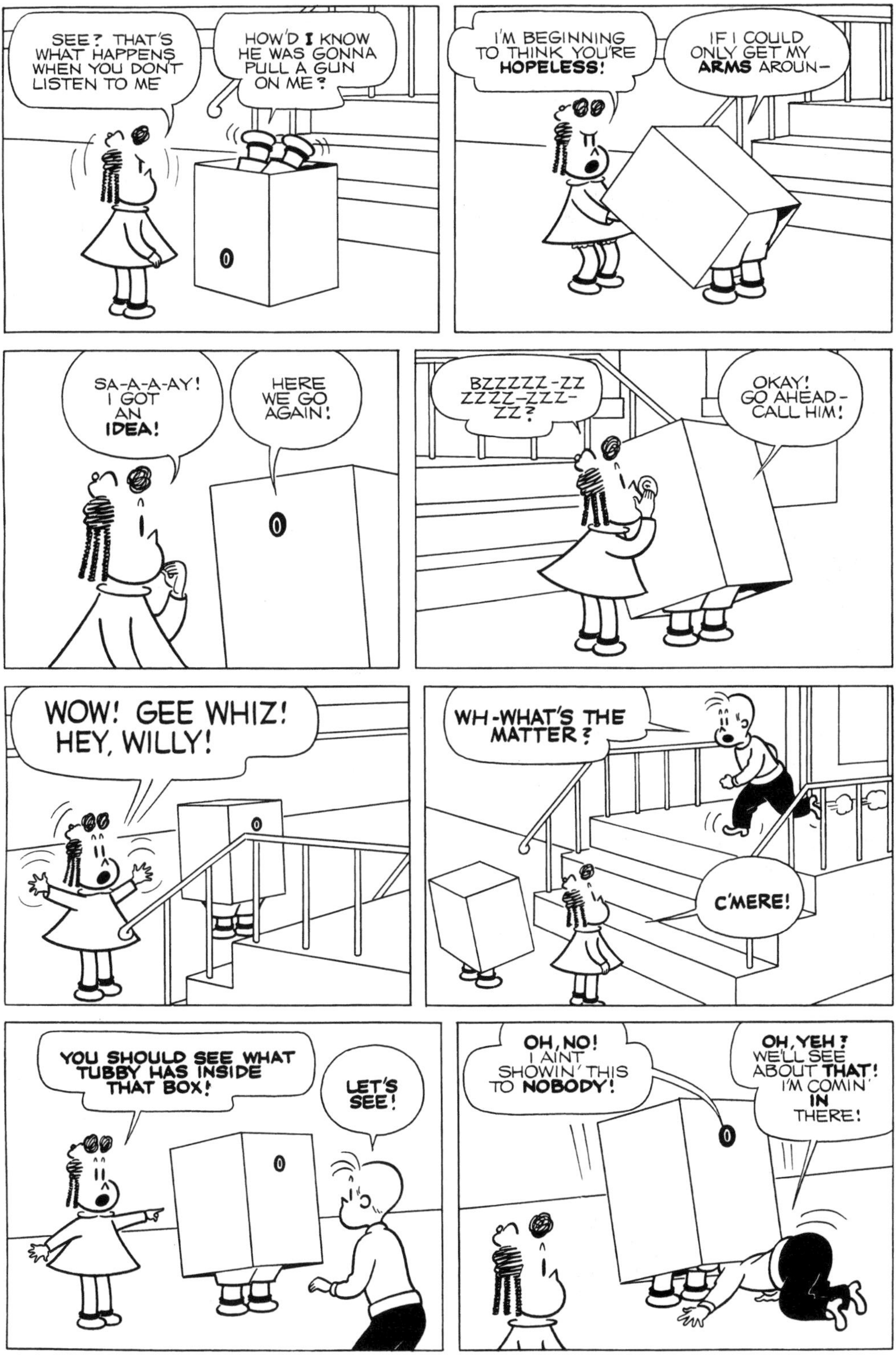
SEE? THAT'S WHAT HAPPENS WHEN YOU DON'T LISTEN TO ME
HOW'D **I** KNOW HE WAS GONNA PULL A GUN ON ME?
I'M BEGINNING TO THINK YOU'RE **HOPELESS**!
IF I COULD ONLY GET MY **ARMS** AROUN–
SA-A-A-AY! I GOT AN **IDEA**!
HERE WE GO AGAIN!
BZZZZZ-ZZ ZZZZ-ZZZ-ZZ?
OKAY! GO AHEAD-CALL HIM!
WOW! GEE WHIZ! HEY, WILLY!
WH-WHAT'S THE MATTER?
C'MERE!
YOU SHOULD SEE WHAT TUBBY HAS INSIDE THAT BOX!
LET'S SEE!
OH, NO! I AINT SHOWIN' THIS TO **NOBODY**!
OH, YEH? WE'LL SEE ABOUT **THAT**! I'M COMIN' **IN** THERE!

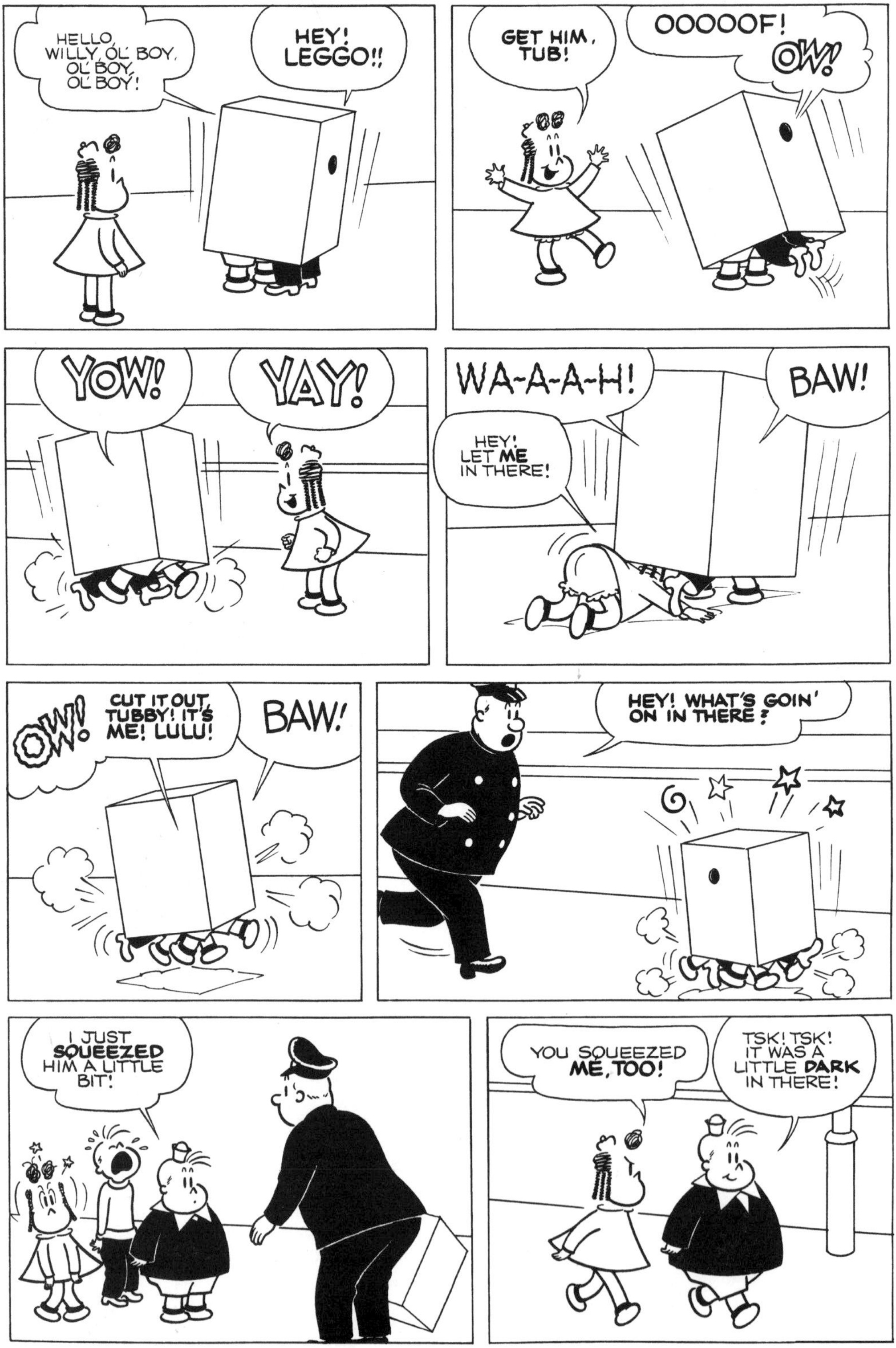
HELLO, WILLY, OL' BOY, OL' BOY, OL' BOY!
HEY! LEGGO!!
GET HIM, TUB!
OOOOOF!
OW!
YOW!
YAY!
WA-A-A-H!
BAW!
HEY! LET ME IN THERE!
OW!
CUT IT OUT, TUBBY! IT'S ME! LULU!
BAW!
HEY! WHAT'S GOIN' ON IN THERE?
I JUST SQUEEZED HIM A LITTLE BIT!
YOU SQUEEZED ME, TOO!
TSK! TSK! IT WAS A LITTLE DARK IN THERE!

marge's

LITTLE LULU

STUFF AN' NONSENSE

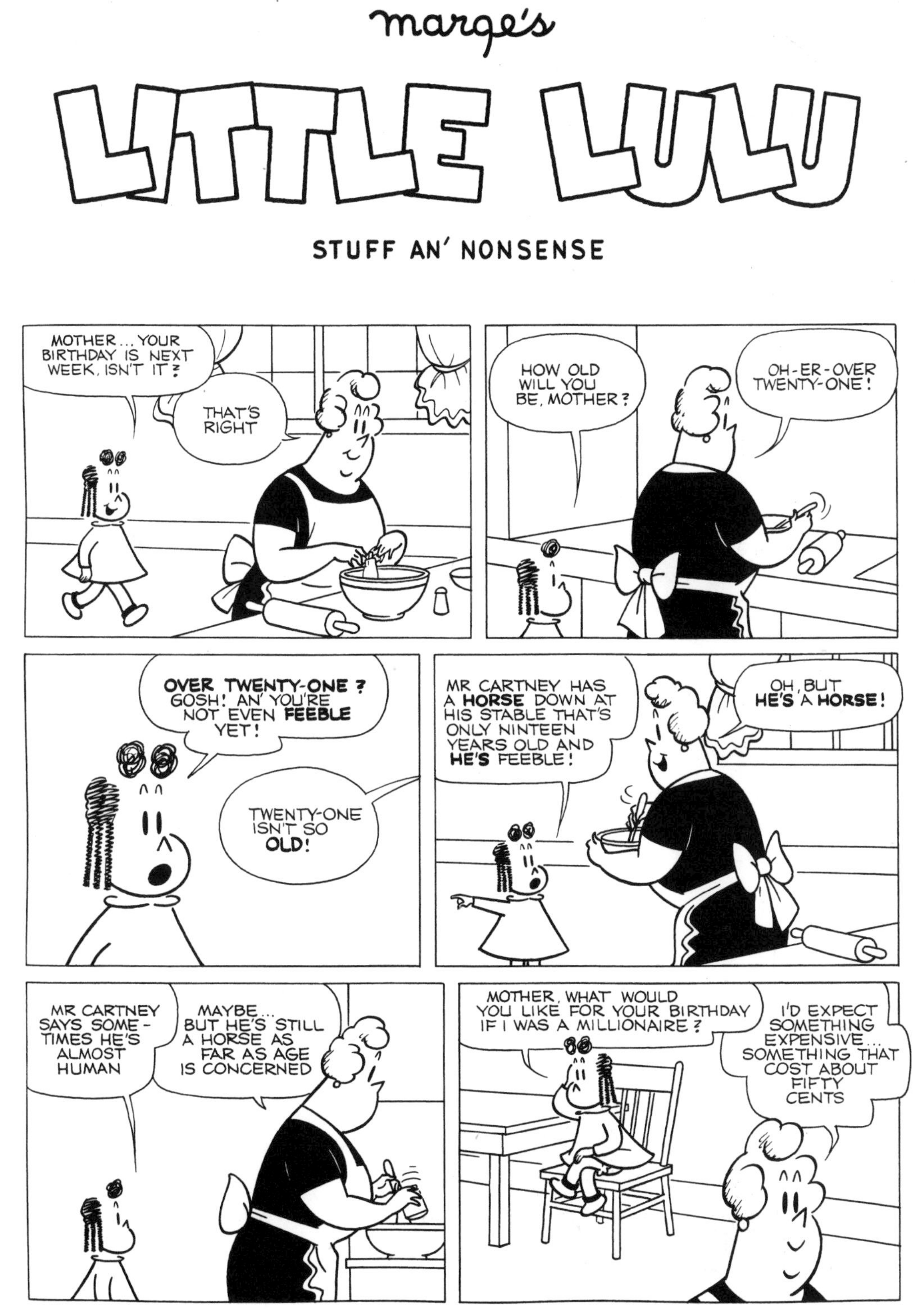
MOTHER... YOUR BIRTHDAY IS NEXT WEEK, ISN'T IT?
THAT'S RIGHT
HOW OLD WILL YOU BE, MOTHER?
OH-ER-OVER TWENTY-ONE!
OVER TWENTY-ONE? GOSH! AN' YOU'RE NOT EVEN **FEEBLE** YET!
TWENTY-ONE ISN'T SO **OLD!**
MR CARTNEY HAS A **HORSE** DOWN AT HIS STABLE THAT'S ONLY NINTEEN YEARS OLD AND **HE'S** FEEBLE!
OH, BUT **HE'S** A **HORSE!**
MR CARTNEY SAYS SOME-TIMES HE'S ALMOST HUMAN
MAYBE... BUT HE'S STILL A HORSE AS FAR AS AGE IS CONCERNED
MOTHER, WHAT WOULD YOU LIKE FOR YOUR BIRTHDAY IF I WAS A MILLIONAIRE?
I'D EXPECT SOMETHING EXPENSIVE... SOMETHING THAT COST ABOUT FIFTY CENTS

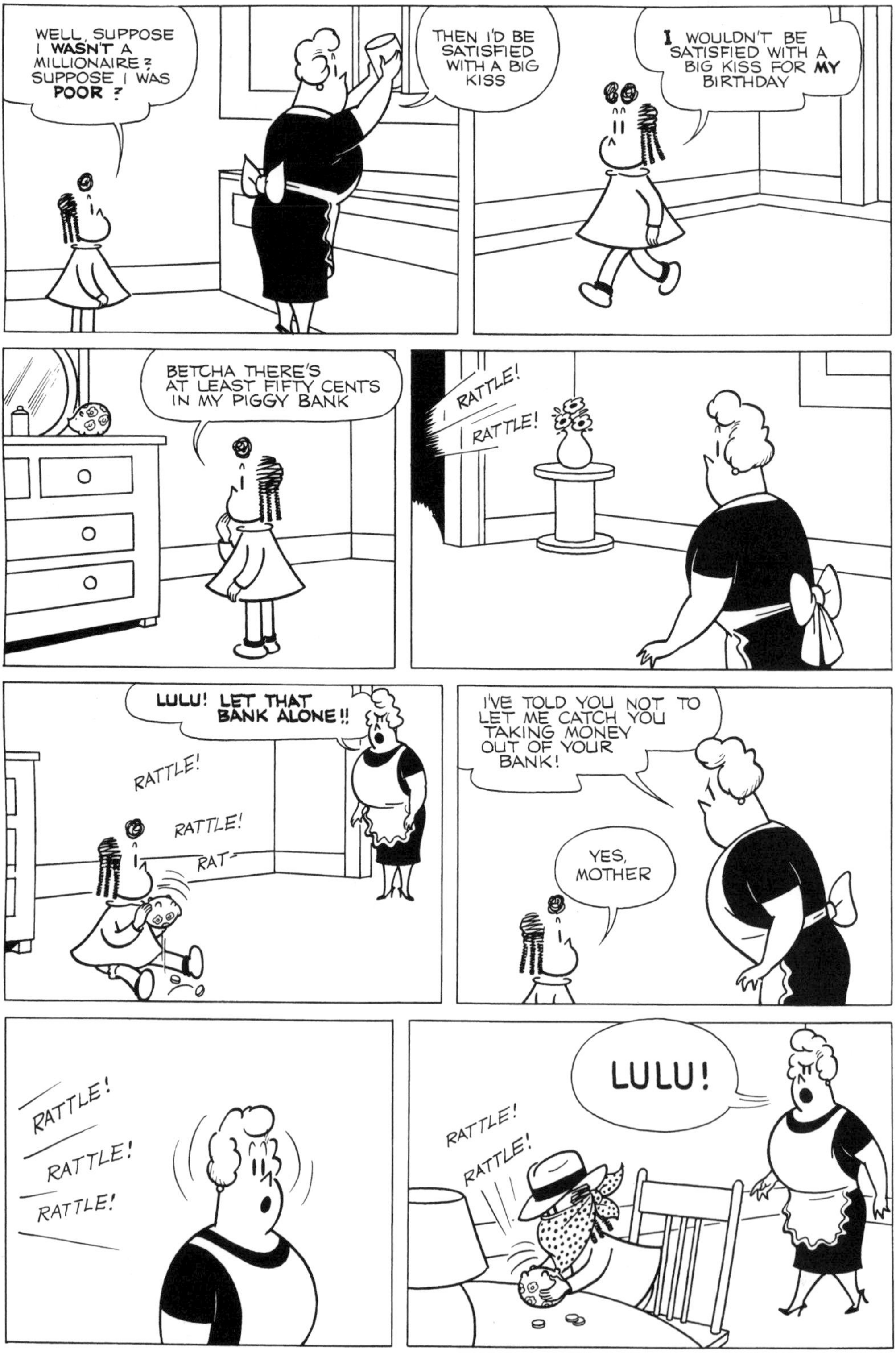
WELL, SUPPOSE I **WASN'T** A MILLIONAIRE? SUPPOSE I WAS **POOR**?
THEN I'D BE SATISFIED WITH A BIG KISS
I WOULDN'T BE SATISFIED WITH A BIG KISS FOR **MY** BIRTHDAY
BETCHA THERE'S AT LEAST FIFTY CENTS IN MY PIGGY BANK
RATTLE!
RATTLE!
LULU! LET THAT BANK ALONE!!
RATTLE!
RATTLE!
RAT-
I'VE TOLD YOU NOT TO LET ME CATCH YOU TAKING MONEY OUT OF YOUR BANK!
YES, MOTHER
RATTLE!
RATTLE!
RATTLE!
LULU!
RATTLE!
RATTLE!

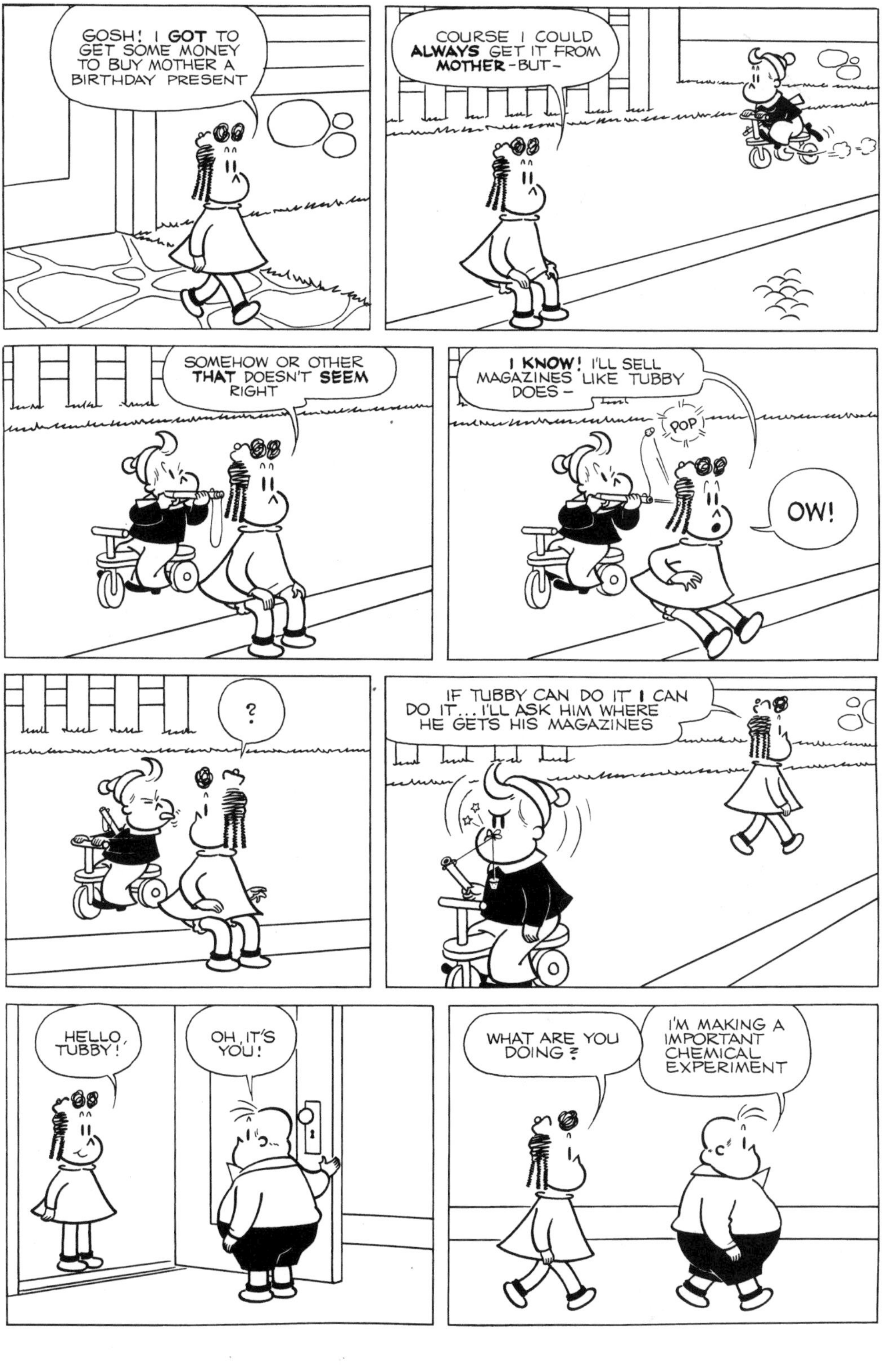
GOSH! I GOT TO GET SOME MONEY TO BUY MOTHER A BIRTHDAY PRESENT
COURSE I COULD ALWAYS GET IT FROM MOTHER-BUT-
SOMEHOW OR OTHER THAT DOESN'T SEEM RIGHT
I KNOW! I'LL SELL MAGAZINES LIKE TUBBY DOES-
POP
OW!
?
IF TUBBY CAN DO IT I CAN DO IT... I'LL ASK HIM WHERE HE GETS HIS MAGAZINES
HELLO TUBBY!
OH, IT'S YOU!
WHAT ARE YOU DOING?
I'M MAKING A IMPORTANT CHEMICAL EXPERIMENT

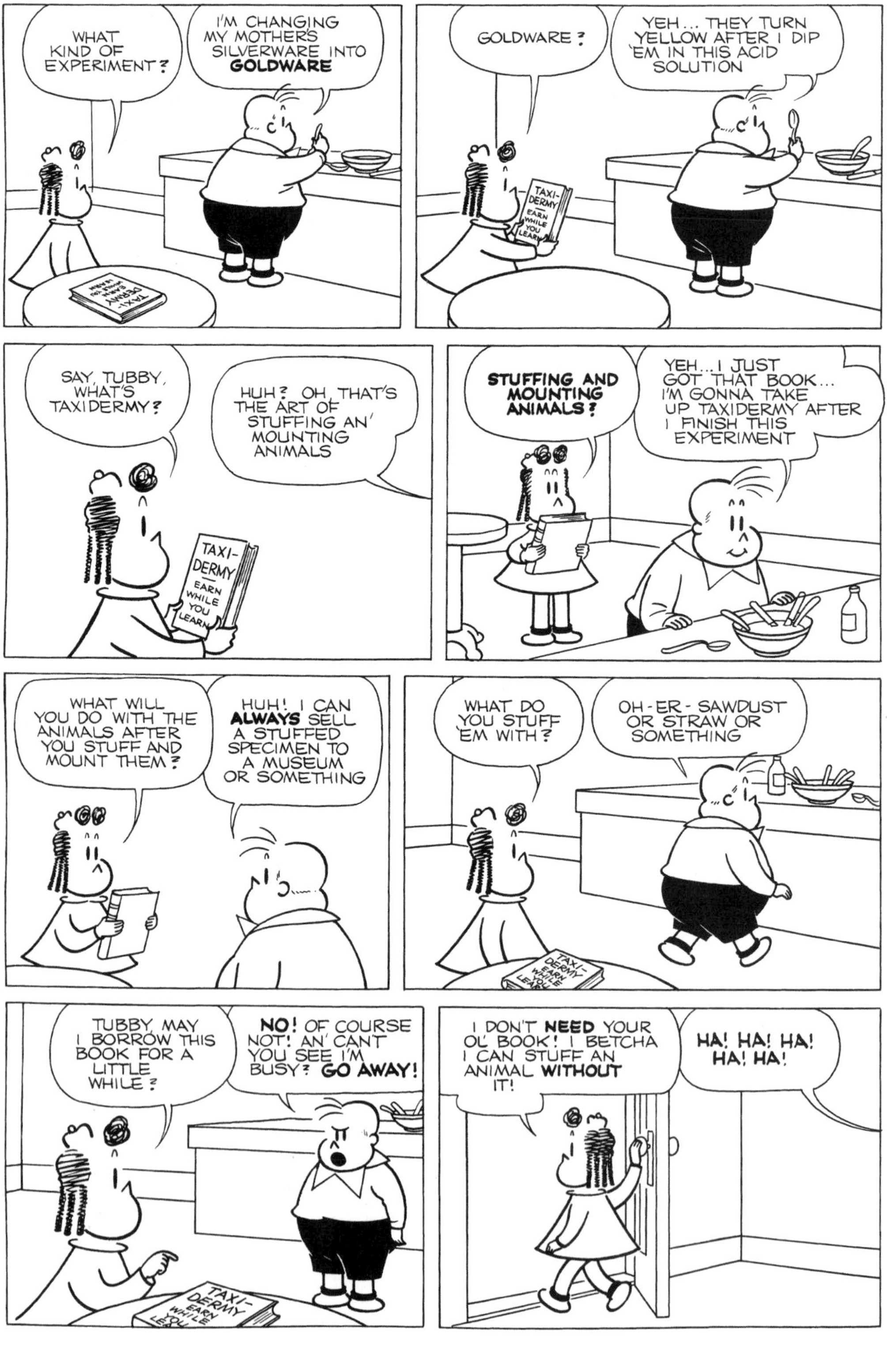
WHAT KIND OF EXPERIMENT?
I'M CHANGING MY MOTHER'S SILVERWARE INTO **GOLDWARE**
GOLDWARE?
YEH... THEY TURN YELLOW AFTER I DIP 'EM IN THIS ACID SOLUTION
TAXI-DERMY EARN WHILE YOU LEARN
SAY, TUBBY, WHAT'S TAXIDERMY?
HUH? OH, THAT'S THE ART OF STUFFING AN' MOUNTING ANIMALS
STUFFING AND MOUNTING ANIMALS?
YEH... I JUST GOT THAT BOOK... I'M GONNA TAKE UP TAXIDERMY AFTER I FINISH THIS EXPERIMENT
WHAT WILL YOU DO WITH THE ANIMALS AFTER YOU STUFF AND MOUNT THEM?
HUH! I CAN **ALWAYS** SELL A STUFFED SPECIMEN TO A MUSEUM OR SOMETHING
WHAT DO YOU STUFF 'EM WITH?
OH-ER-SAWDUST OR STRAW OR SOMETHING
TUBBY, MAY I BORROW THIS BOOK FOR A LITTLE WHILE?
NO! OF COURSE NOT! AN' CAN'T YOU SEE I'M BUSY? **GO AWAY!**
I DON'T **NEED** YOUR OL' BOOK! I BETCHA I CAN STUFF AN ANIMAL **WITHOUT** IT!
HA! HA! HA! HA! HA!

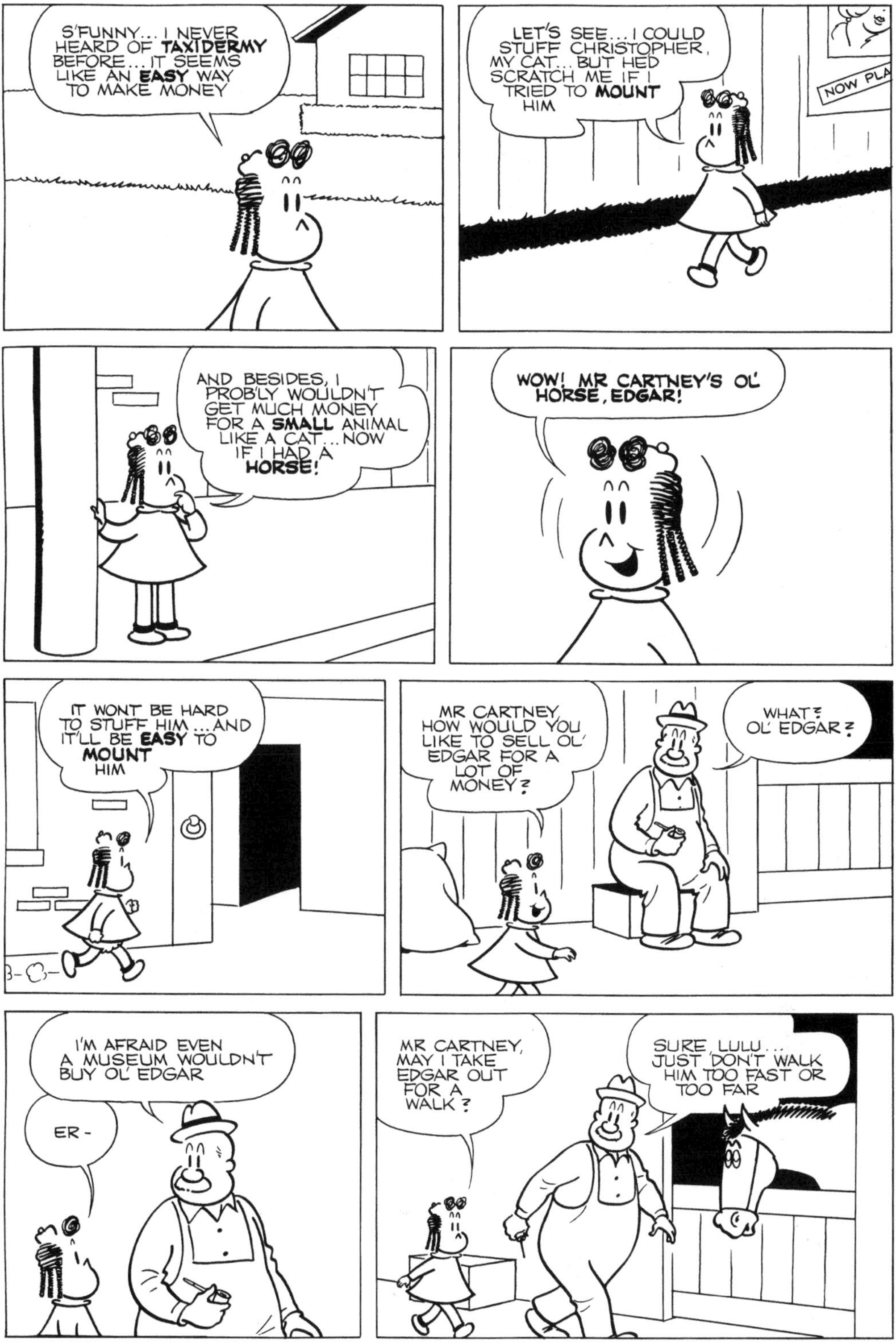
S'FUNNY... I NEVER HEARD OF TAXIDERMY BEFORE... IT SEEMS LIKE AN EASY WAY TO MAKE MONEY
LET'S SEE... I COULD STUFF CHRISTOPHER, MY CAT... BUT HED SCRATCH ME IF I TRIED TO MOUNT HIM
NOW PLA
AND BESIDES, I PROB'LY WOULDN'T GET MUCH MONEY FOR A SMALL ANIMAL LIKE A CAT... NOW IF I HAD A HORSE!
WOW! MR CARTNEY'S OL' HORSE, EDGAR!
IT WONT BE HARD TO STUFF HIM ...AND IT'LL BE EASY TO MOUNT HIM
MR CARTNEY, HOW WOULD YOU LIKE TO SELL OL' EDGAR FOR A LOT OF MONEY?
WHAT? OL' EDGAR?
I'M AFRAID EVEN A MUSEUM WOULDN'T BUY OL' EDGAR
ER -
MR CARTNEY, MAY I TAKE EDGAR OUT FOR A WALK?
SURE, LULU... JUST DON'T WALK HIM TOO FAST OR TOO FAR

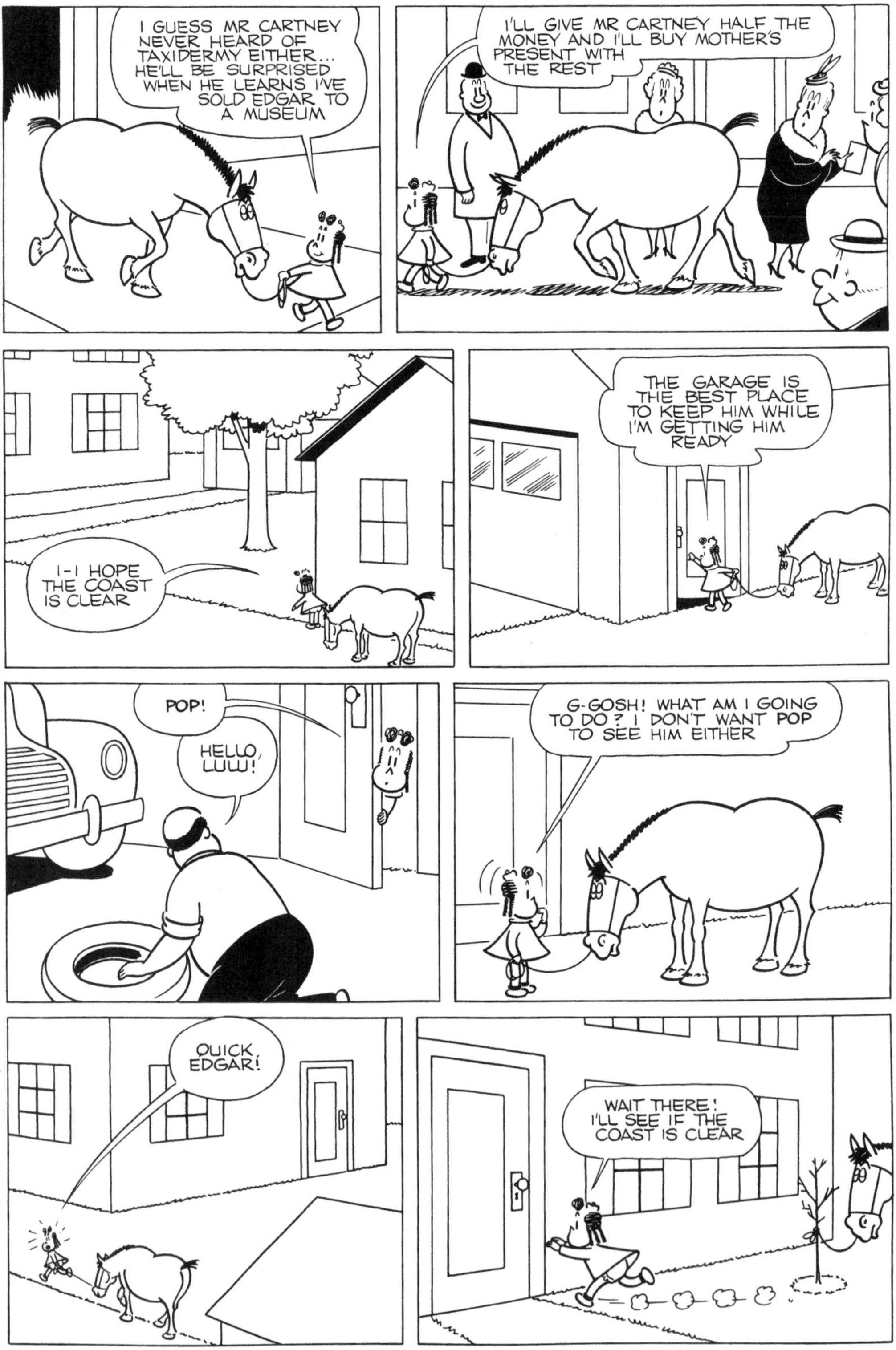
I GUESS MR CARTNEY NEVER HEARD OF TAXIDERMY EITHER... HE'LL BE SURPRISED WHEN HE LEARNS I'VE SOLD EDGAR TO A MUSEUM
I'LL GIVE MR CARTNEY HALF THE MONEY AND I'LL BUY MOTHER'S PRESENT WITH THE REST
I-I HOPE THE COAST IS CLEAR
THE GARAGE IS THE BEST PLACE TO KEEP HIM WHILE I'M GETTING HIM READY
POP!
HELLO, LULU!
G-GOSH! WHAT AM I GOING TO DO? I DON'T WANT POP TO SEE HIM EITHER
QUICK, EDGAR!
WAIT THERE! I'LL SEE IF THE COAST IS CLEAR

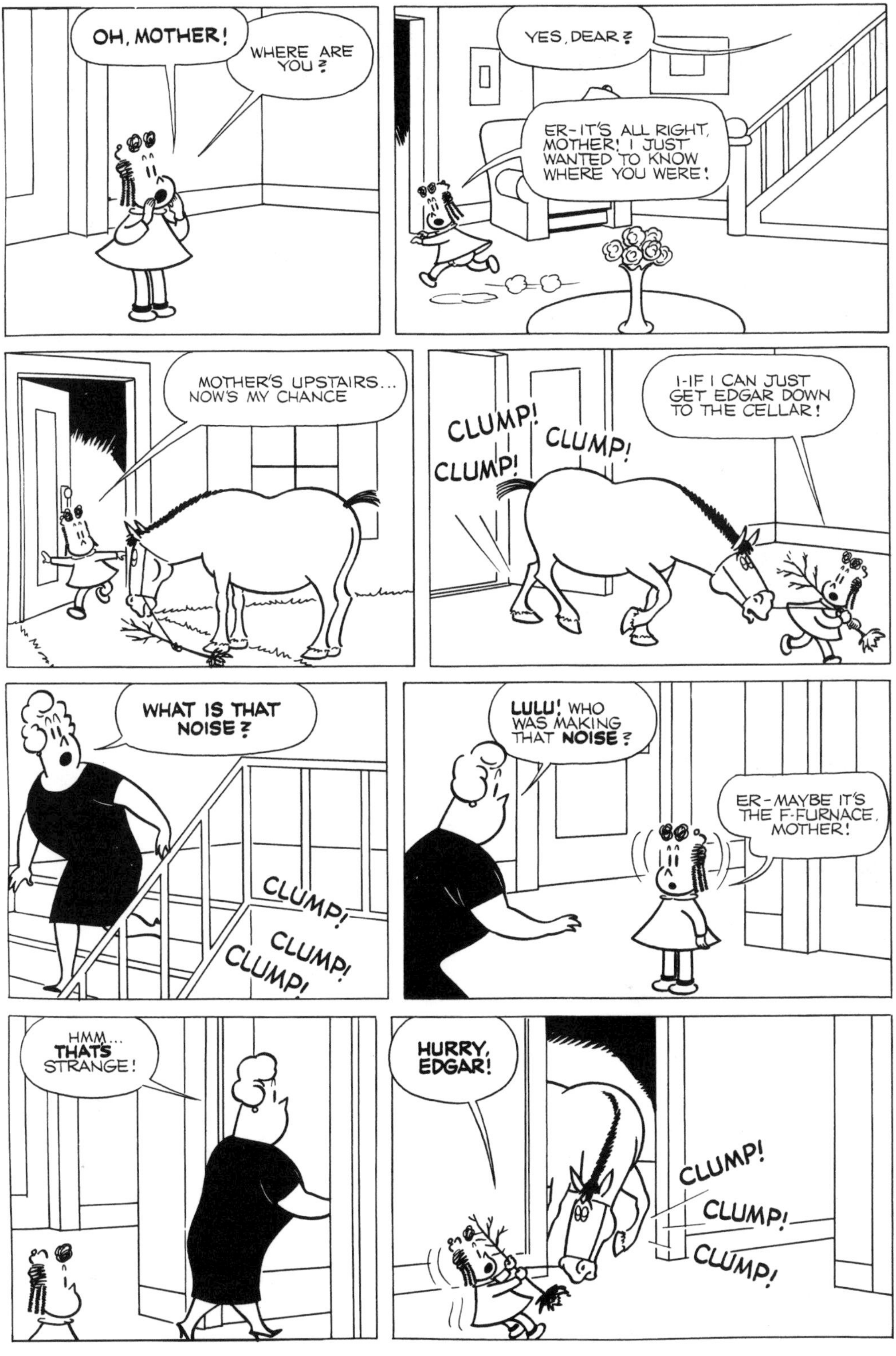
OH, MOTHER!
WHERE ARE YOU?
YES, DEAR?
ER-IT'S ALL RIGHT, MOTHER! I JUST WANTED TO KNOW WHERE YOU WERE!
MOTHER'S UPSTAIRS... NOW'S MY CHANCE
CLUMP! CLUMP! CLUMP!
I-IF I CAN JUST GET EDGAR DOWN TO THE CELLAR!
WHAT IS THAT NOISE?
CLUMP! CLUMP! CLUMP!
LULU! WHO WAS MAKING THAT NOISE?
ER-MAYBE IT'S THE F-FURNACE, MOTHER!
HMM... THAT'S STRANGE!
HURRY, EDGAR!
CLUMP! CLUMP! CLUMP!

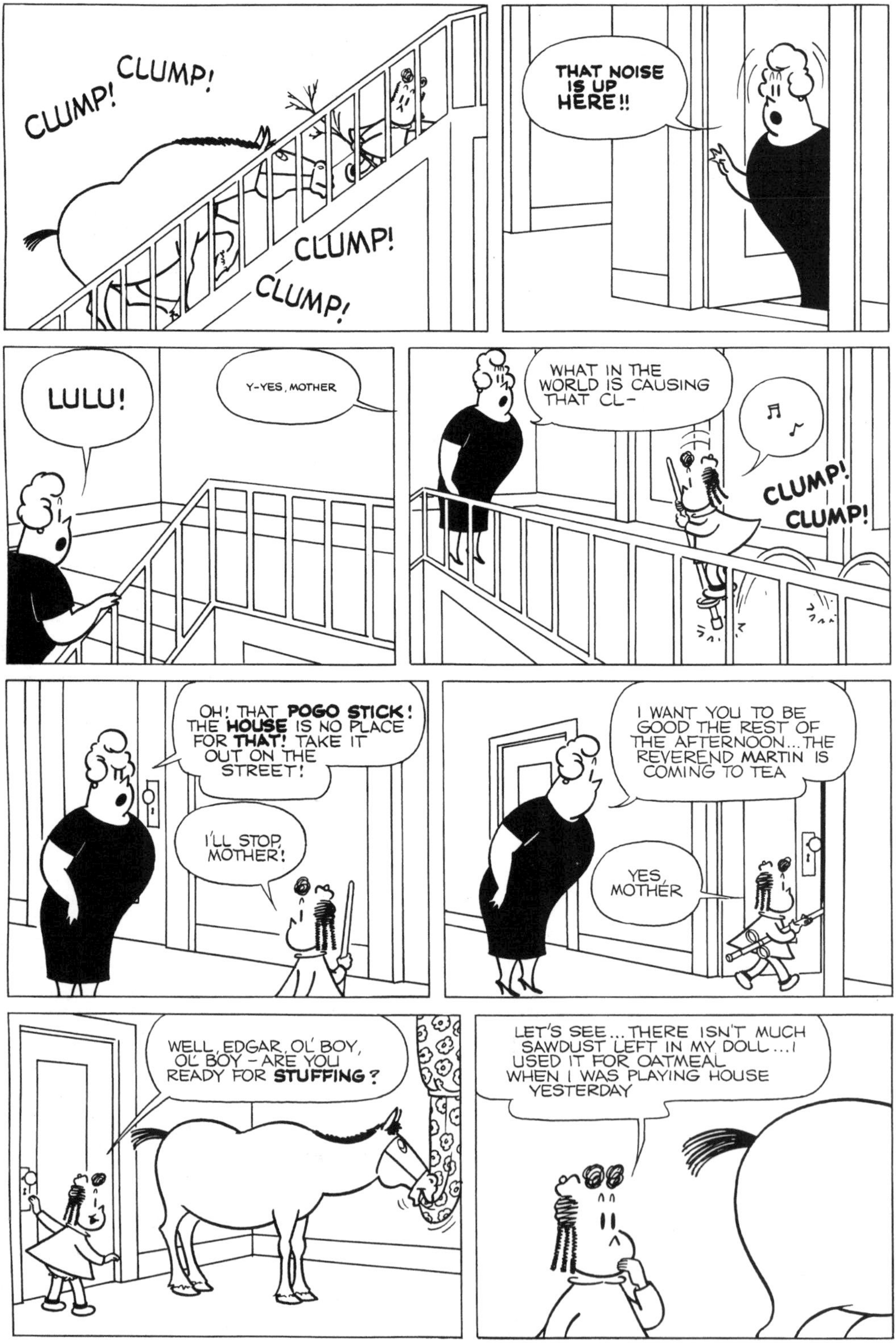
CLUMP! CLUMP!
CLUMP!
CLUMP!
THAT NOISE IS UP HERE!!
LULU!
Y-YES, MOTHER
WHAT IN THE WORLD IS CAUSING THAT CL-
CLUMP! CLUMP!
OH! THAT POGO STICK! THE HOUSE IS NO PLACE FOR THAT! TAKE IT OUT ON THE STREET!
I'LL STOP, MOTHER!
I WANT YOU TO BE GOOD THE REST OF THE AFTERNOON... THE REVEREND MARTIN IS COMING TO TEA
YES, MOTHER
WELL, EDGAR, OL' BOY, OL' BOY - ARE YOU READY FOR STUFFING?
LET'S SEE... THERE ISN'T MUCH SAWDUST LEFT IN MY DOLL... I USED IT FOR OATMEAL WHEN I WAS PLAYING HOUSE YESTERDAY

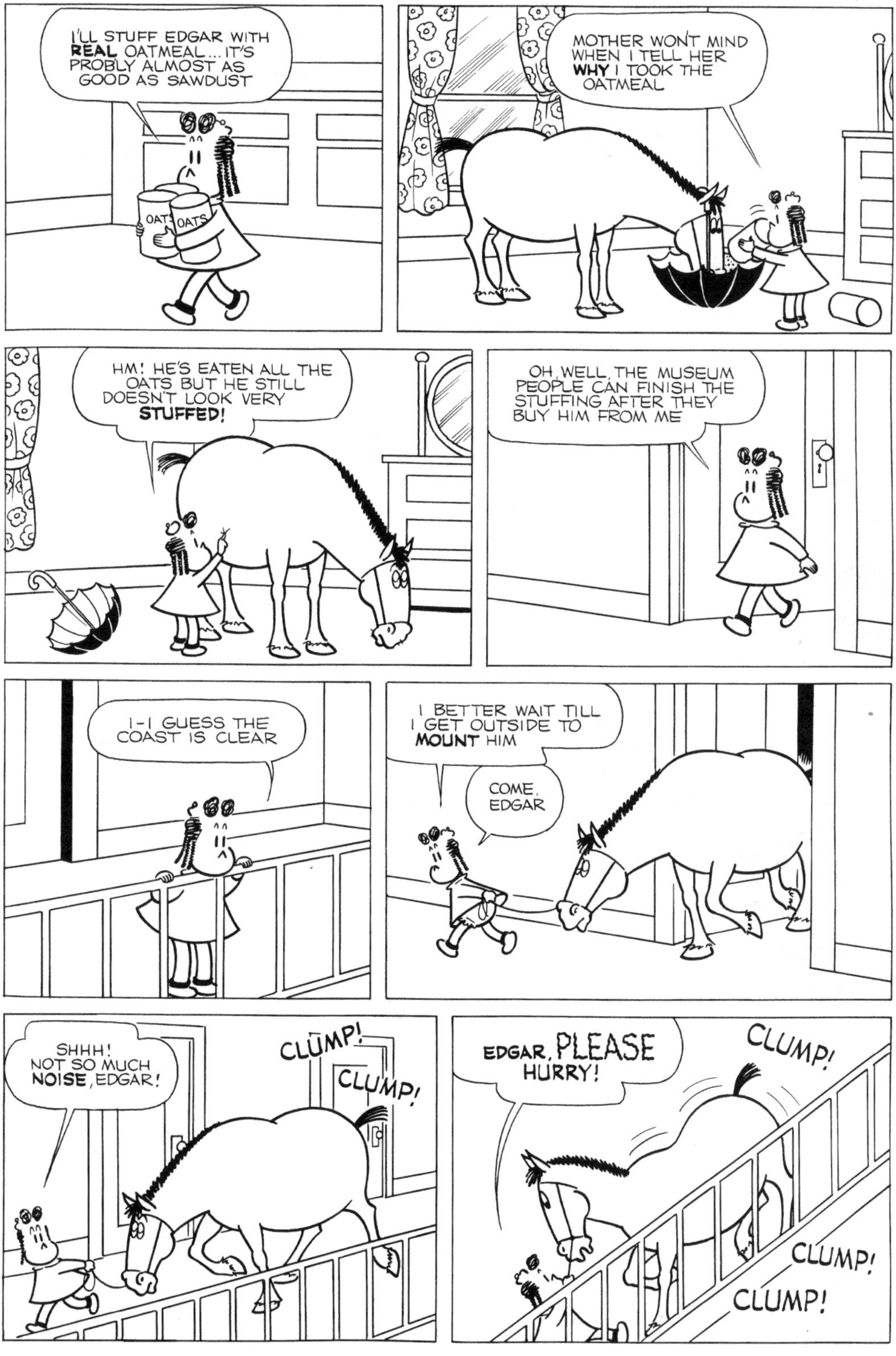
I'LL STUFF EDGAR WITH REAL OATMEAL... IT'S PROBLY ALMOST AS GOOD AS SAWDUST
OATS
OATS
MOTHER WON'T MIND WHEN I TELL HER WHY I TOOK THE OATMEAL
HM! HE'S EATEN ALL THE OATS BUT HE STILL DOESN'T LOOK VERY STUFFED!
OH, WELL, THE MUSEUM PEOPLE CAN FINISH THE STUFFING AFTER THEY BUY HIM FROM ME
I-I GUESS THE COAST IS CLEAR
I BETTER WAIT TILL I GET OUTSIDE TO MOUNT HIM
COME, EDGAR
SHHH! NOT SO MUCH NOISE, EDGAR!
CLUMP!
CLUMP!
EDGAR, PLEASE HURRY!
CLUMP!
CLUMP!
CLUMP!

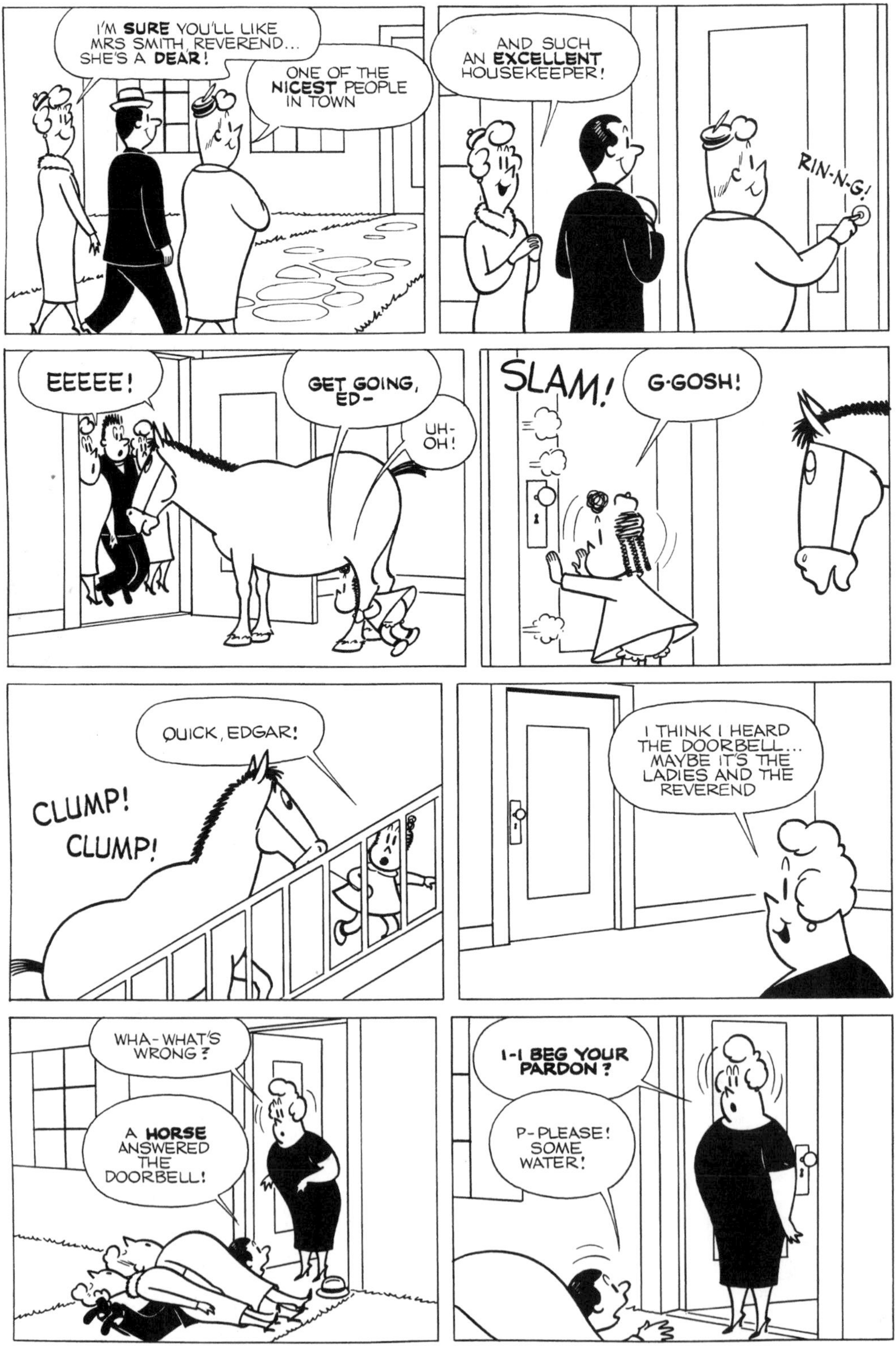

I'M SURE YOU'LL LIKE MRS SMITH, REVEREND... SHE'S A DEAR!
ONE OF THE NICEST PEOPLE IN TOWN
AND SUCH AN EXCELLENT HOUSEKEEPER!
RIN-N-G!
EEEEE!
GET GOING, ED–
UH-OH!
SLAM!
G-GOSH!
QUICK, EDGAR!
CLUMP! CLUMP!
I THINK I HEARD THE DOORBELL... MAYBE IT'S THE LADIES AND THE REVEREND
WHA-WHAT'S WRONG?
A HORSE ANSWERED THE DOORBELL!
I-I BEG YOUR PARDON?
P-PLEASE! SOME WATER!

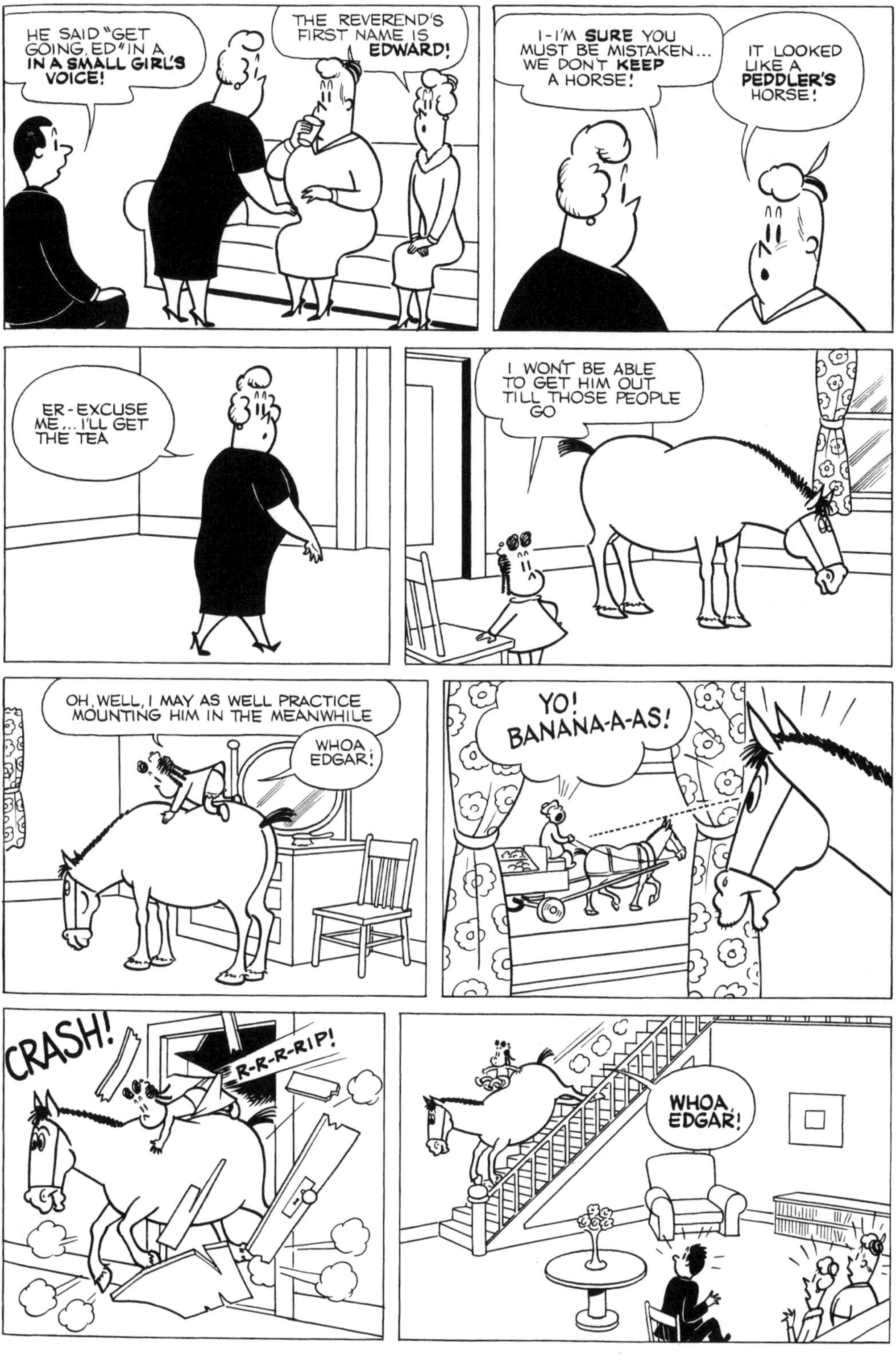
HE SAID "GET GOING, ED" IN A IN A SMALL GIRL'S VOICE!
THE REVEREND'S FIRST NAME IS EDWARD!
I-I'M SURE YOU MUST BE MISTAKEN... WE DON'T KEEP A HORSE!
IT LOOKED LIKE A PEDDLER'S HORSE!
ER-EXCUSE ME... I'LL GET THE TEA
I WON'T BE ABLE TO GET HIM OUT TILL THOSE PEOPLE GO
OH, WELL, I MAY AS WELL PRACTICE MOUNTING HIM IN THE MEANWHILE
WHOA EDGAR!
YO! BANANA-A-AS!
CRASH!
R-R-R-RIP!
WHOA, EDGAR!

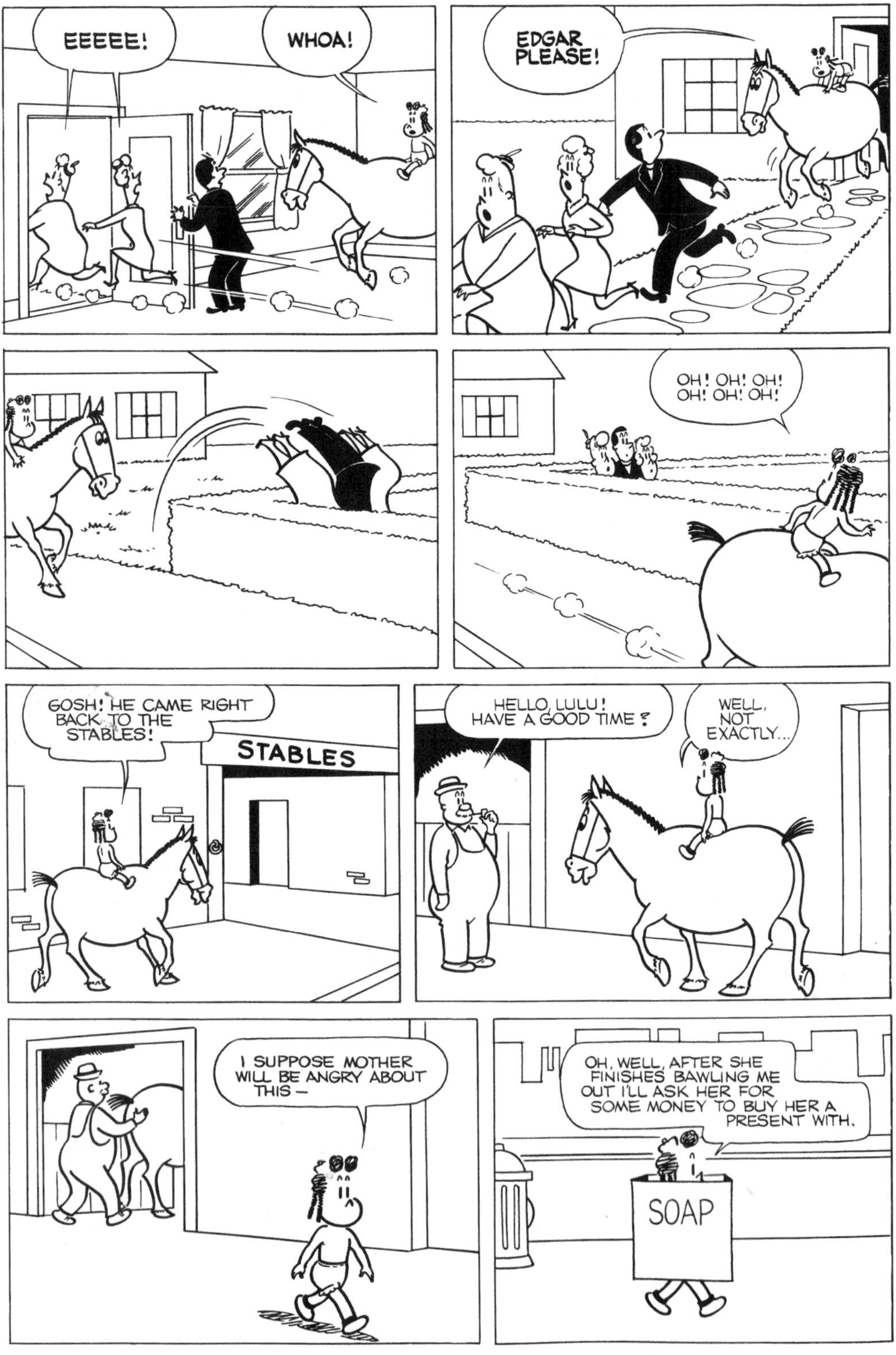
EEEEE!
WHOA!
EDGAR PLEASE!
OH! OH! OH! OH! OH! OH!
GOSH! HE CAME RIGHT BACK TO THE STABLES!
STABLES
HELLO, LULU! HAVE A GOOD TIME?
WELL, NOT EXACTLY...
I SUPPOSE MOTHER WILL BE ANGRY ABOUT THIS —
OH, WELL, AFTER SHE FINISHES BAWLING ME OUT I'LL ASK HER FOR SOME MONEY TO BUY HER A PRESENT WITH.
SOAP

marge's

Little Lulu

THE WORKING GIRL

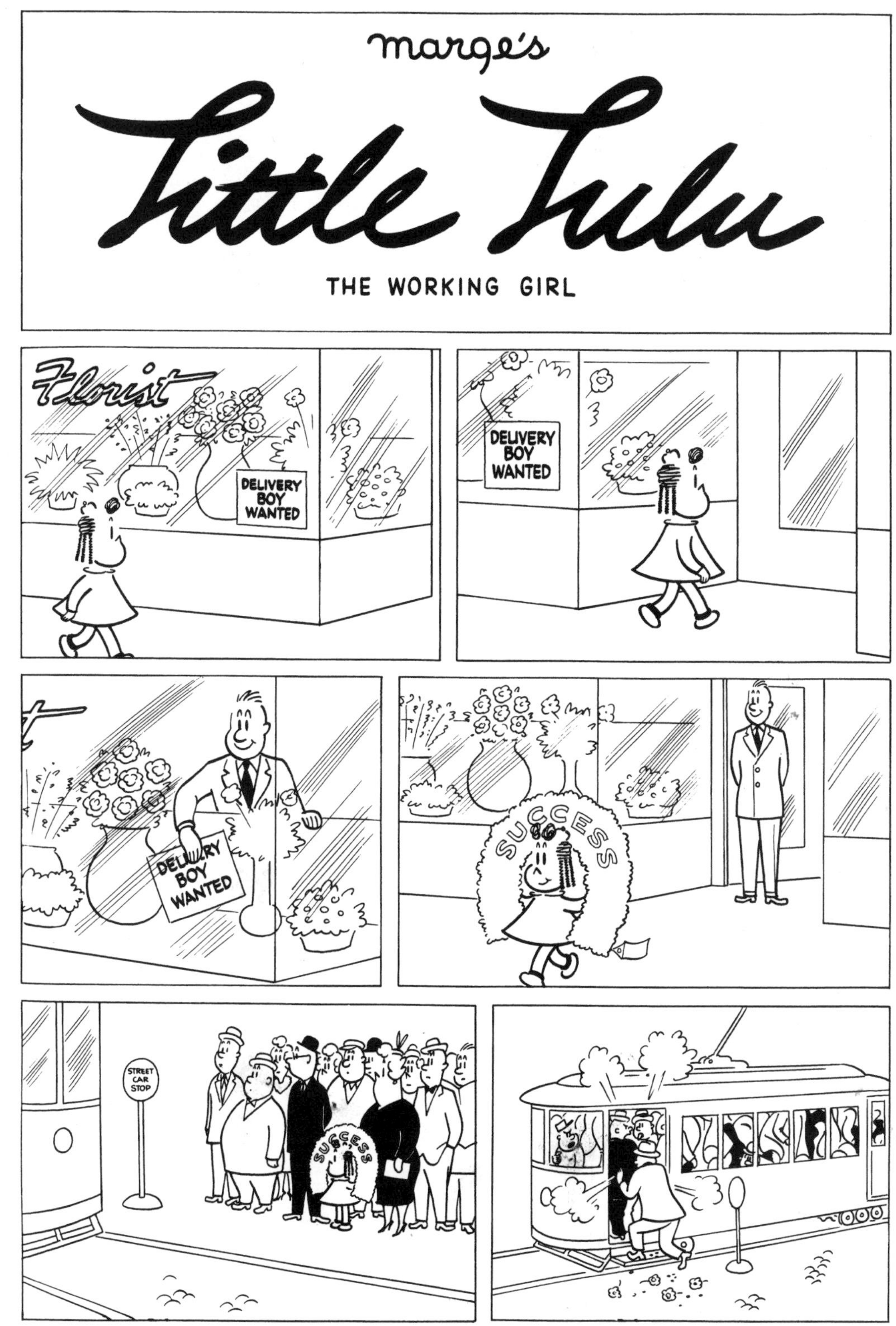
Florist
DELIVERY BOY WANTED
DELIVERY BOY WANTED
BOY WANTED
SUCCESS
STREET CAR STOP
SUCCESS

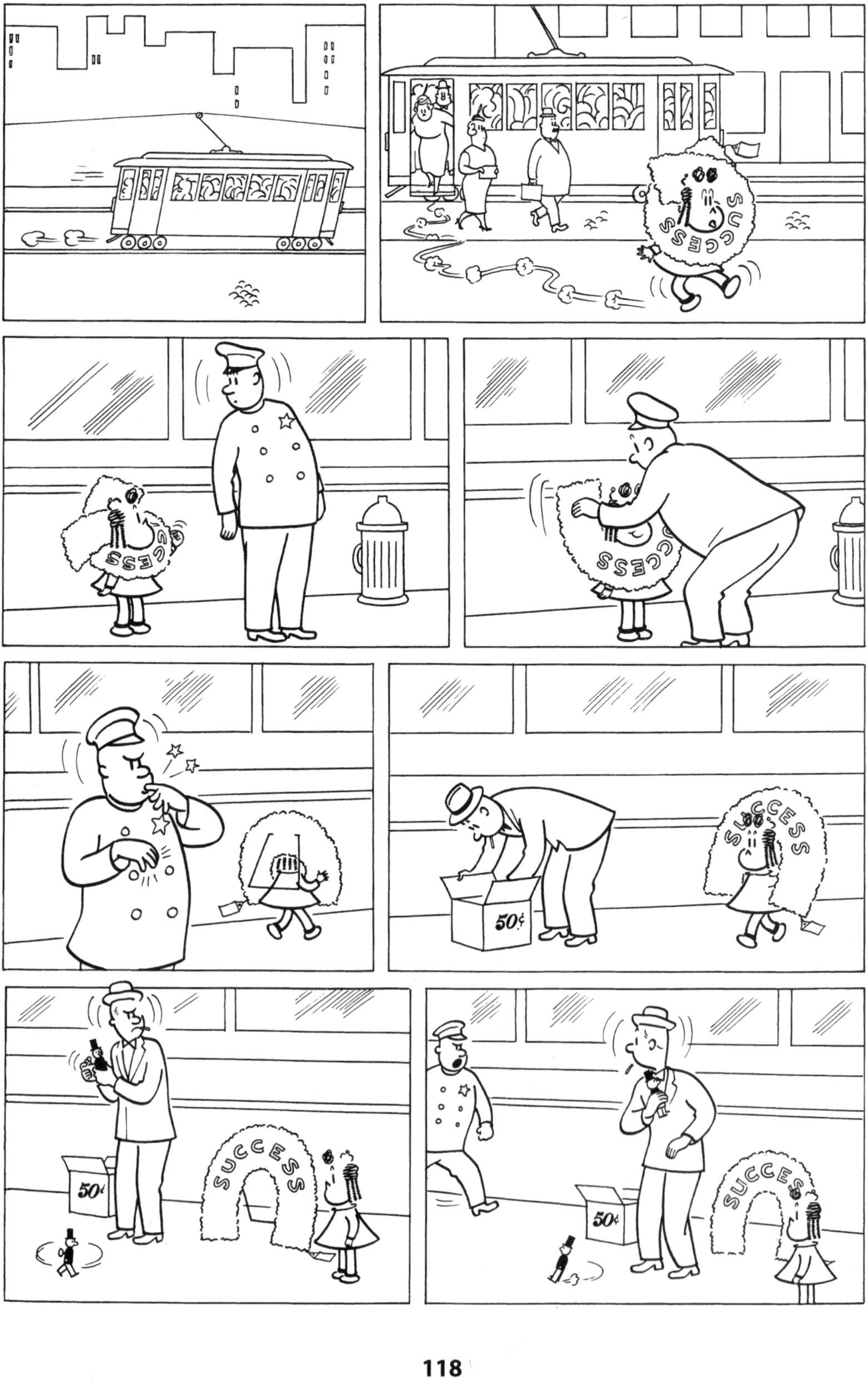
SUCCESS
SUCCESS
SUCCESS
SUCCESS
50¢
SUCCESS
50¢
SUCCES
50¢

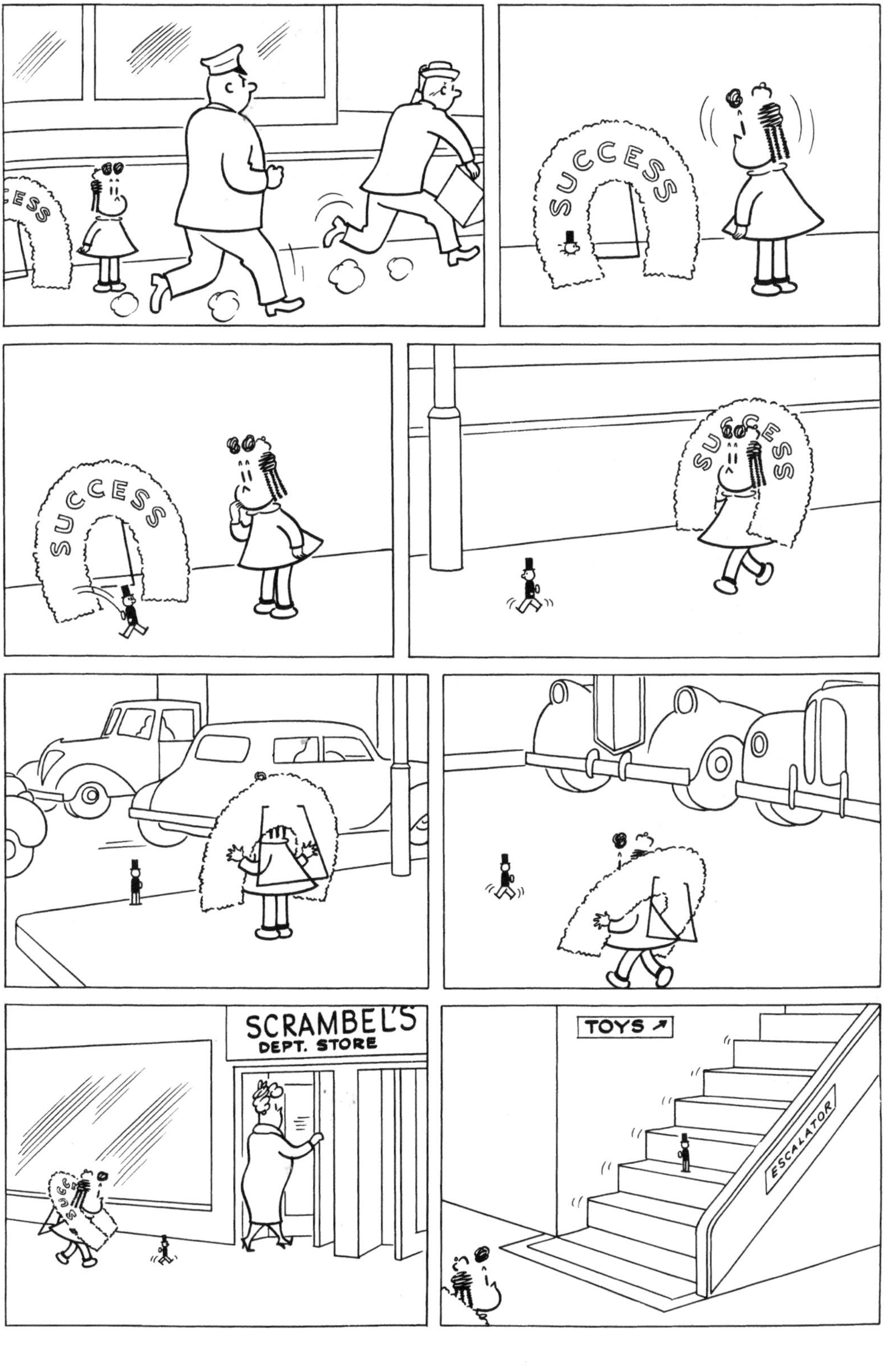
SUCCESS
SUCCESS
SUCCESS
SUCCESS
SCRAMBEL'S
DEPT. STORE
TOYS ↗
ESCALATOR

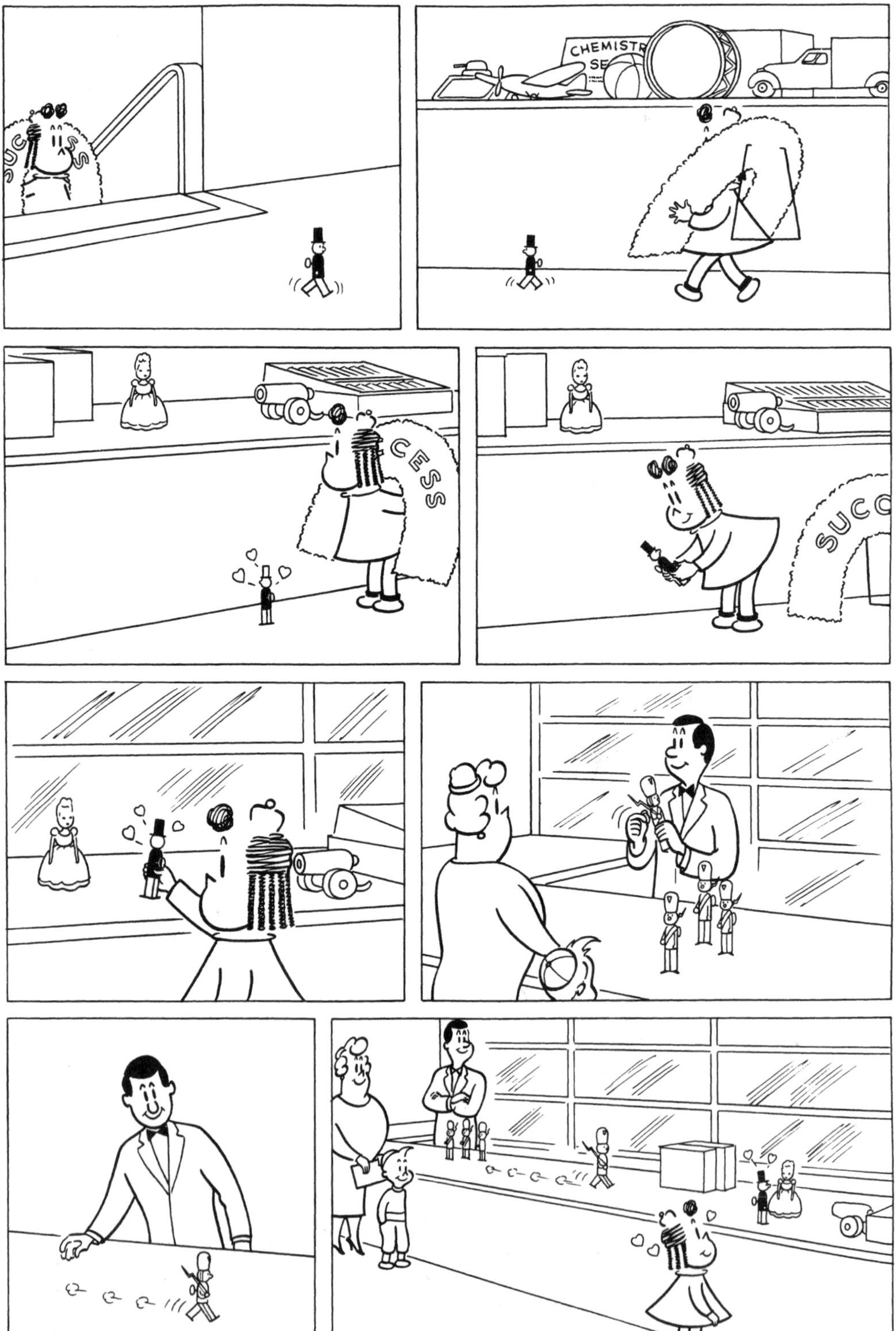
CHEMISTR
SE
CESS

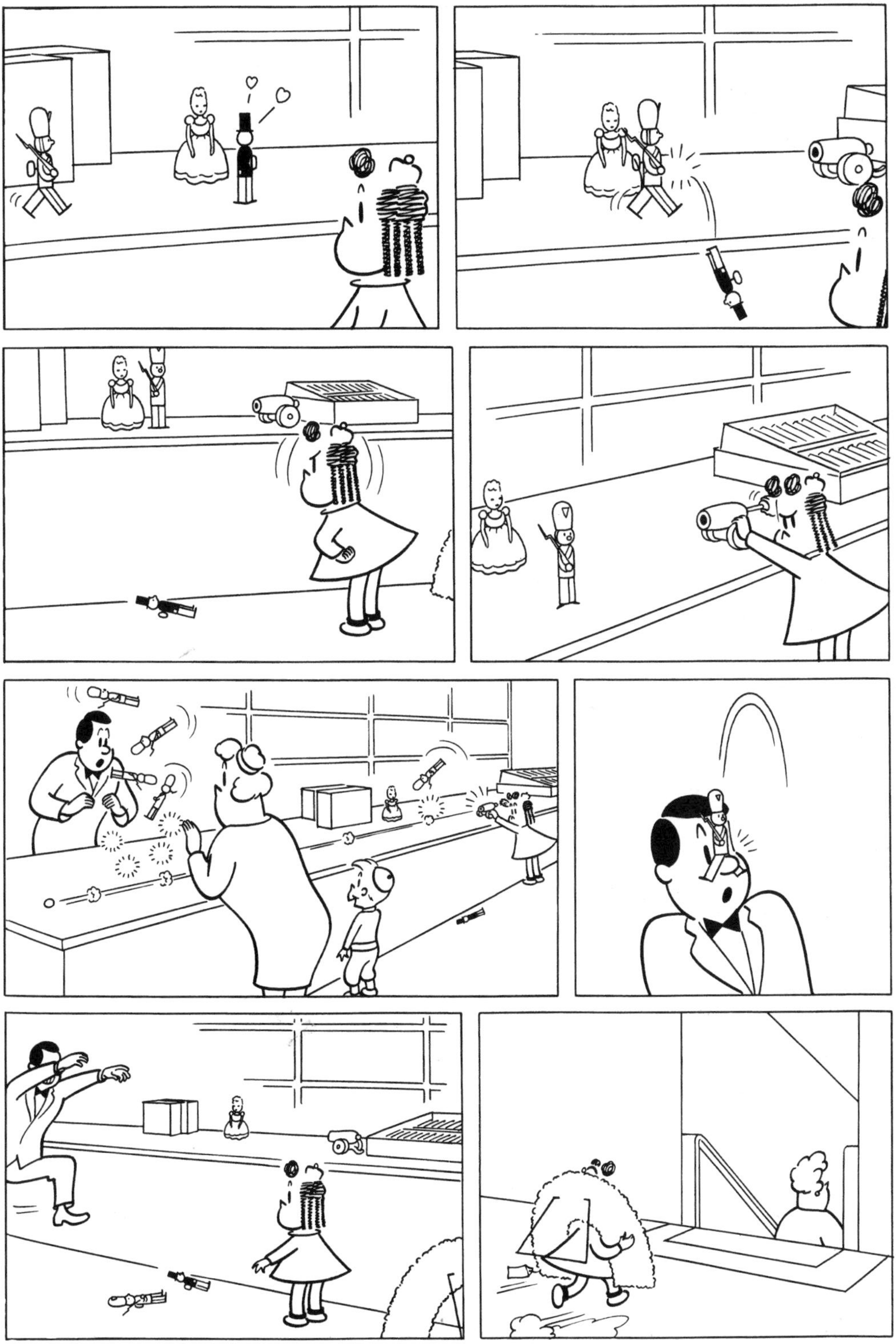

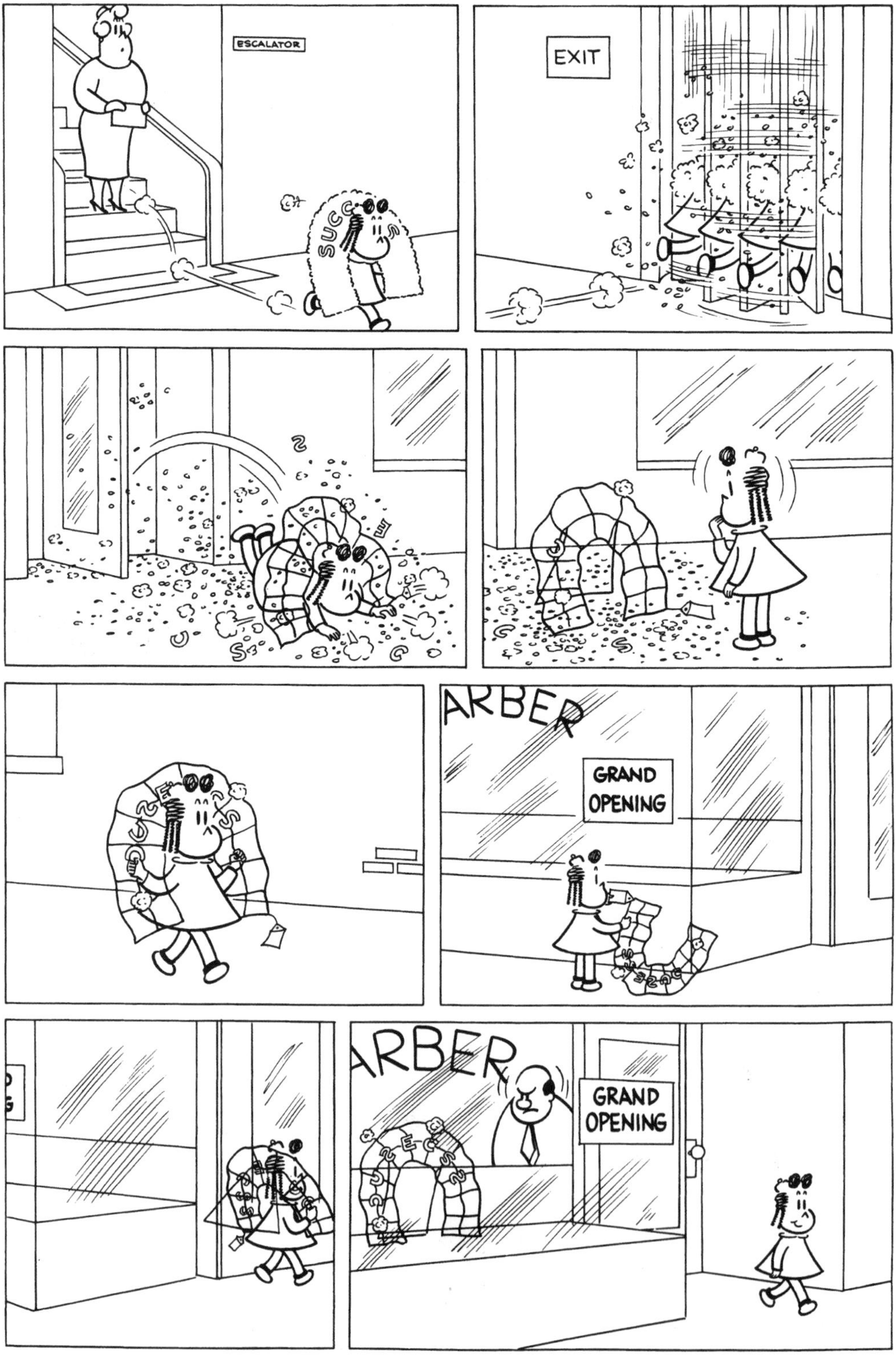
ESCALATOR
EXIT
GRAND OPENING
GRAND OPENING

marge's

LITTLE LULU

lulu in distress

A Tragedy

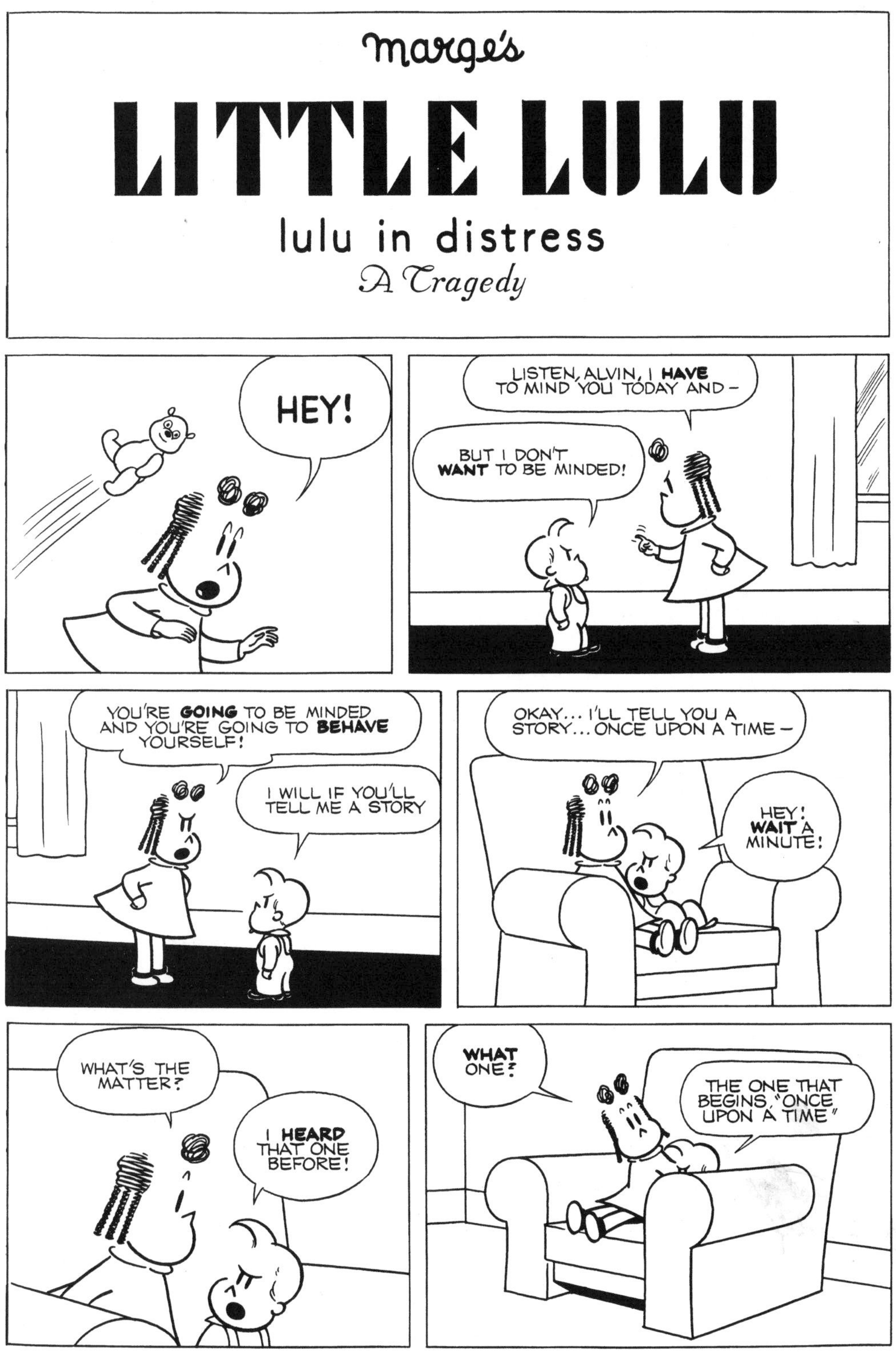
HEY!
LISTEN, ALVIN, I **HAVE** TO MIND YOU TODAY AND —
BUT I DON'T **WANT** TO BE MINDED!
YOU'RE **GOING** TO BE MINDED AND YOU'RE GOING TO **BEHAVE** YOURSELF!
I WILL IF YOU'LL TELL ME A STORY
OKAY... I'LL TELL YOU A STORY... ONCE UPON A TIME —
HEY! **WAIT** A MINUTE!
WHAT'S THE MATTER?
I **HEARD** THAT ONE BEFORE!
WHAT ONE?
THE ONE THAT BEGINS "ONCE UPON A TIME"

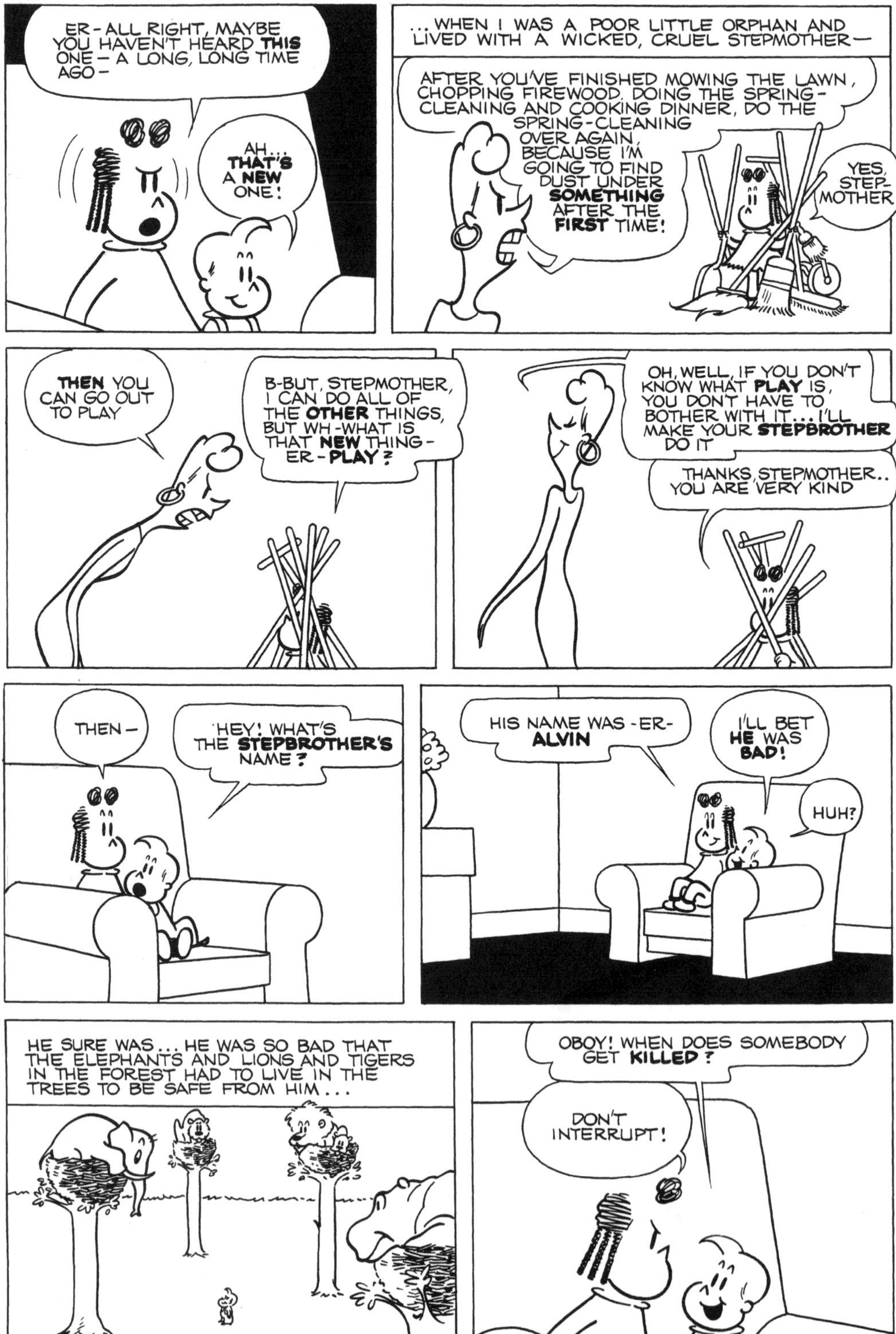
ER-ALL RIGHT, MAYBE YOU HAVEN'T HEARD THIS ONE – A LONG, LONG TIME AGO –
AH... THAT'S A NEW ONE!
...WHEN I WAS A POOR LITTLE ORPHAN AND LIVED WITH A WICKED, CRUEL STEPMOTHER—
AFTER YOU'VE FINISHED MOWING THE LAWN, CHOPPING FIREWOOD, DOING THE SPRING-CLEANING AND COOKING DINNER, DO THE SPRING-CLEANING OVER AGAIN, BECAUSE I'M GOING TO FIND DUST UNDER SOMETHING AFTER THE FIRST TIME!
YES, STEP-MOTHER
THEN YOU CAN GO OUT TO PLAY
B-BUT, STEPMOTHER, I CAN DO ALL OF THE OTHER THINGS, BUT WH-WHAT IS THAT NEW THING-ER-PLAY?
OH, WELL, IF YOU DON'T KNOW WHAT PLAY IS, YOU DON'T HAVE TO BOTHER WITH IT... I'LL MAKE YOUR STEPBROTHER DO IT
THANKS, STEPMOTHER.. YOU ARE VERY KIND
THEN –
HEY! WHAT'S THE STEPBROTHER'S NAME?
HIS NAME WAS-ER-ALVIN
I'LL BET HE WAS BAD!
HUH?
HE SURE WAS... HE WAS SO BAD THAT THE ELEPHANTS AND LIONS AND TIGERS IN THE FOREST HAD TO LIVE IN THE TREES TO BE SAFE FROM HIM...
OBOY! WHEN DOES SOMEBODY GET KILLED?
DON'T INTERRUPT!

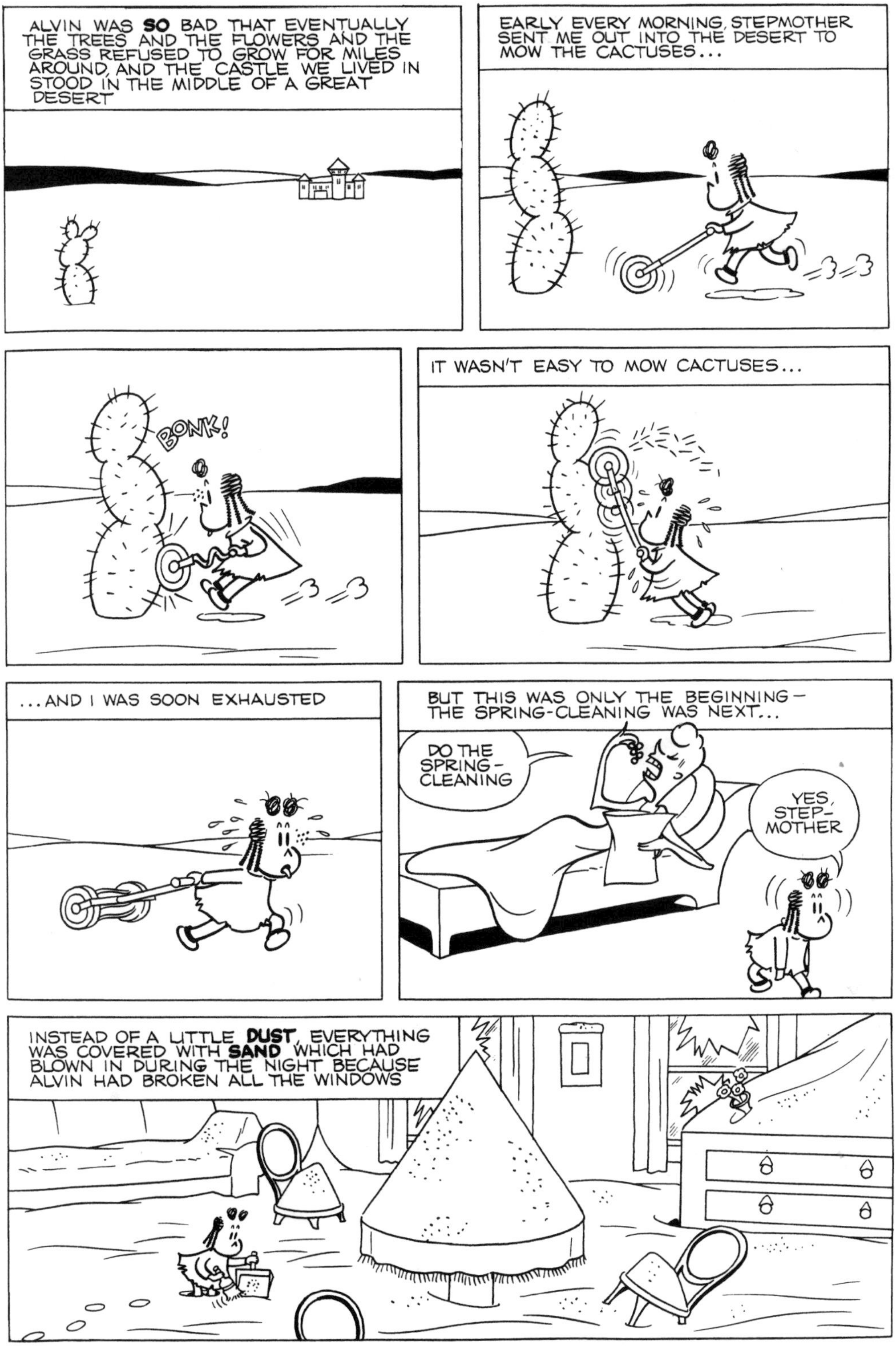

ALVIN WAS **SO** BAD THAT EVENTUALLY THE TREES AND THE FLOWERS AND THE GRASS REFUSED TO GROW FOR MILES AROUND, AND THE CASTLE WE LIVED IN STOOD IN THE MIDDLE OF A GREAT DESERT
EARLY EVERY MORNING, STEPMOTHER SENT ME OUT INTO THE DESERT TO MOW THE CACTUSES...
BONK!
IT WASN'T EASY TO MOW CACTUSES...
...AND I WAS SOON EXHAUSTED
BUT THIS WAS ONLY THE BEGINNING— THE SPRING-CLEANING WAS NEXT...
DO THE SPRING-CLEANING
YES, STEPMOTHER
INSTEAD OF A LITTLE **DUST**, EVERYTHING WAS COVERED WITH **SAND** WHICH HAD BLOWN IN DURING THE NIGHT BECAUSE ALVIN HAD BROKEN ALL THE WINDOWS

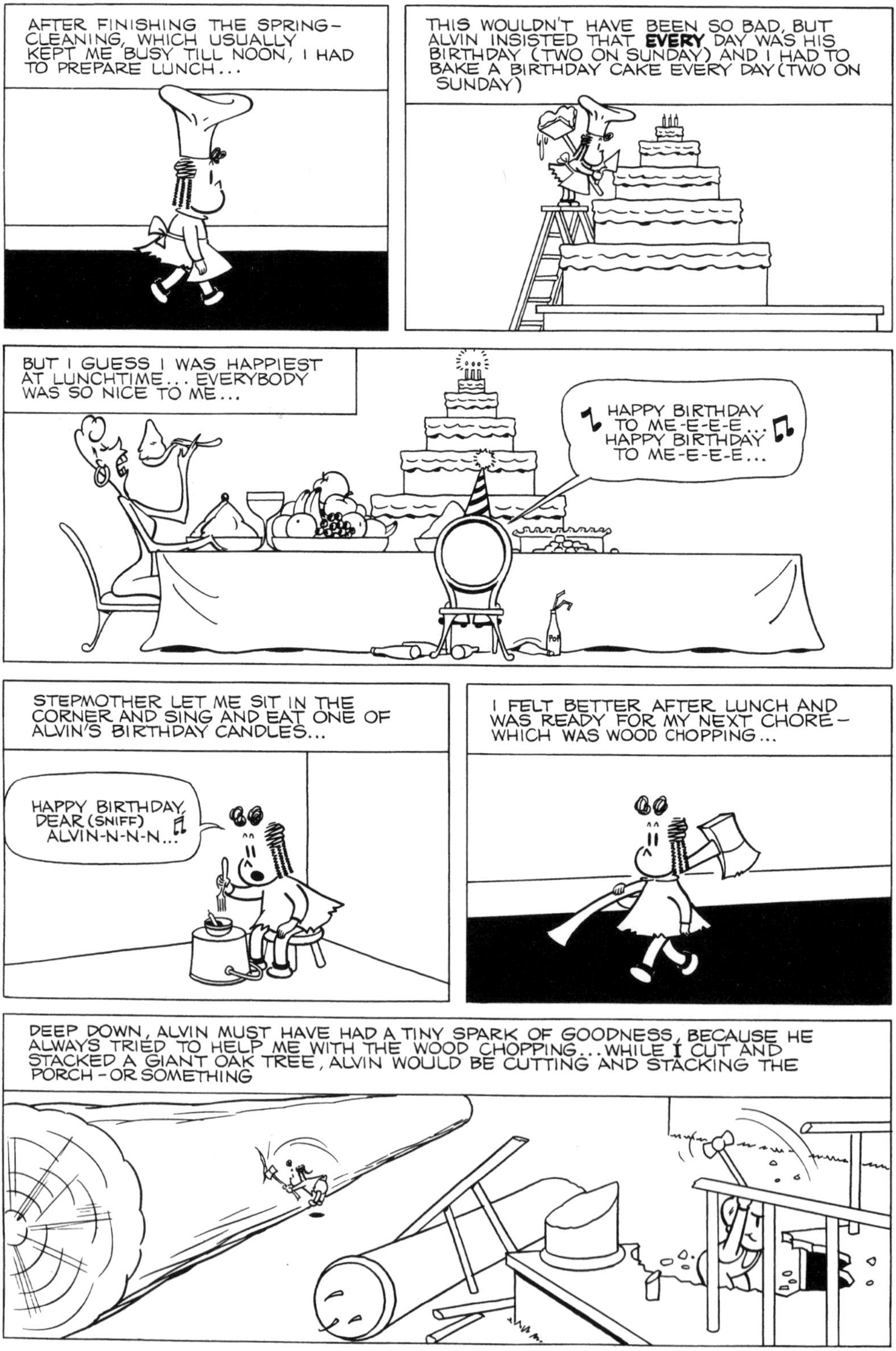
AFTER FINISHING THE SPRING-CLEANING, WHICH USUALLY KEPT ME BUSY TILL NOON, I HAD TO PREPARE LUNCH...
THIS WOULDN'T HAVE BEEN SO BAD, BUT ALVIN INSISTED THAT **EVERY** DAY WAS HIS BIRTHDAY (TWO ON SUNDAY) AND I HAD TO BAKE A BIRTHDAY CAKE EVERY DAY (TWO ON SUNDAY)
BUT I GUESS I WAS HAPPIEST AT LUNCHTIME... EVERYBODY WAS SO NICE TO ME...
HAPPY BIRTHDAY TO ME-E-E-E... HAPPY BIRTHDAY TO ME-E-E-E...
STEPMOTHER LET ME SIT IN THE CORNER AND SING AND EAT ONE OF ALVIN'S BIRTHDAY CANDLES...
HAPPY BIRTHDAY, DEAR (SNIFF) ALVIN-N-N-N...
I FELT BETTER AFTER LUNCH AND WAS READY FOR MY NEXT CHORE — WHICH WAS WOOD CHOPPING...
DEEP DOWN, ALVIN MUST HAVE HAD A TINY SPARK OF GOODNESS, BECAUSE HE ALWAYS TRIED TO HELP ME WITH THE WOOD CHOPPING... WHILE I CUT AND STACKED A GIANT OAK TREE, ALVIN WOULD BE CUTTING AND STACKING THE PORCH - OR SOMETHING

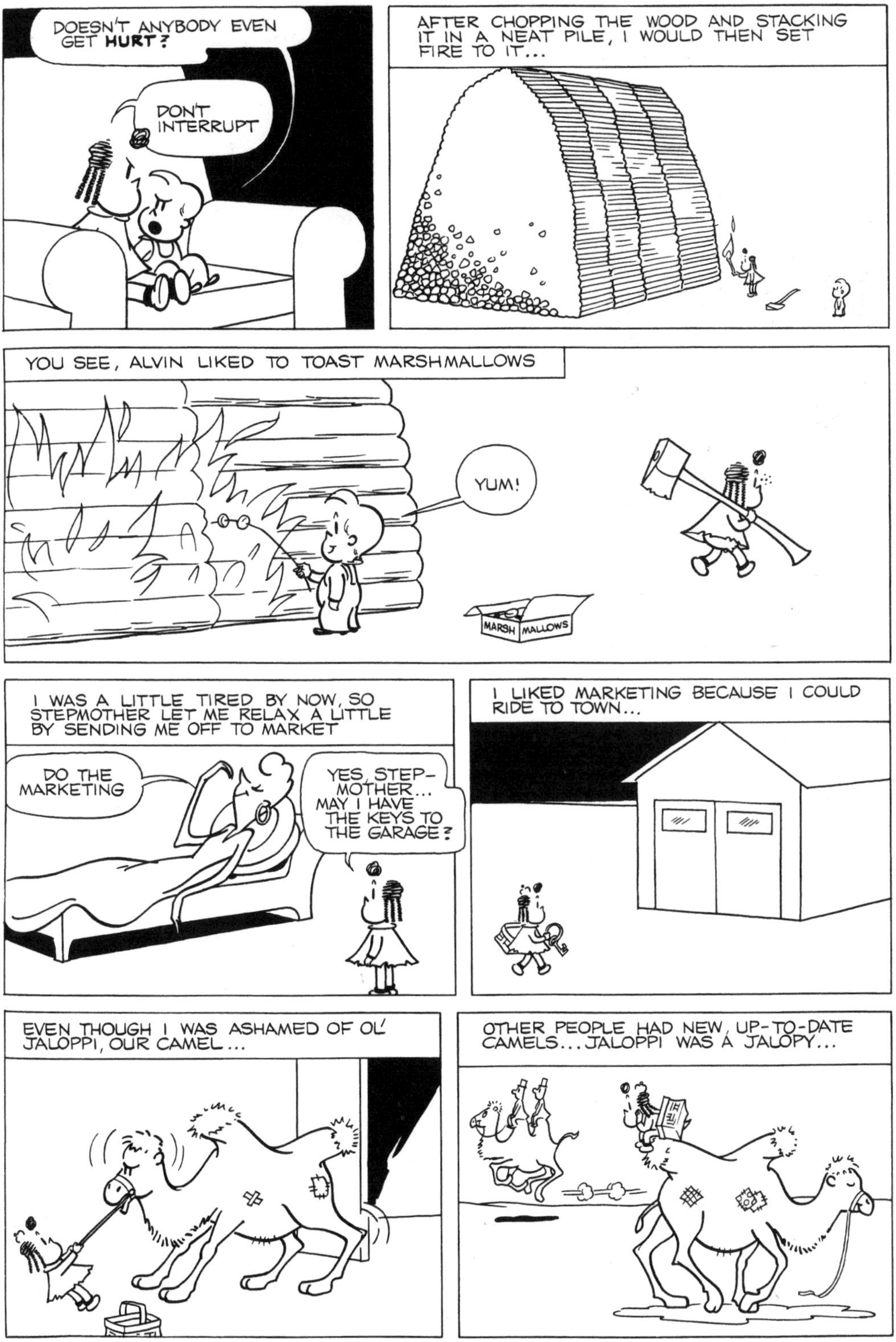
DOESN'T ANYBODY EVEN GET **HURT?**
DON'T INTERRUPT
AFTER CHOPPING THE WOOD AND STACKING IT IN A NEAT PILE, I WOULD THEN SET FIRE TO IT...
YOU SEE, ALVIN LIKED TO TOAST MARSHMALLOWS
YUM!
MARSH MALLOWS
I WAS A LITTLE TIRED BY NOW, SO STEPMOTHER LET ME RELAX A LITTLE BY SENDING ME OFF TO MARKET
DO THE MARKETING
YES, STEP-MOTHER... MAY I HAVE THE KEYS TO THE GARAGE?
I LIKED MARKETING BECAUSE I COULD RIDE TO TOWN...
EVEN THOUGH I WAS ASHAMED OF OL' JALOPPI, OUR CAMEL...
OTHER PEOPLE HAD NEW, UP-TO-DATE CAMELS... JALOPPI WAS A JALOPY...

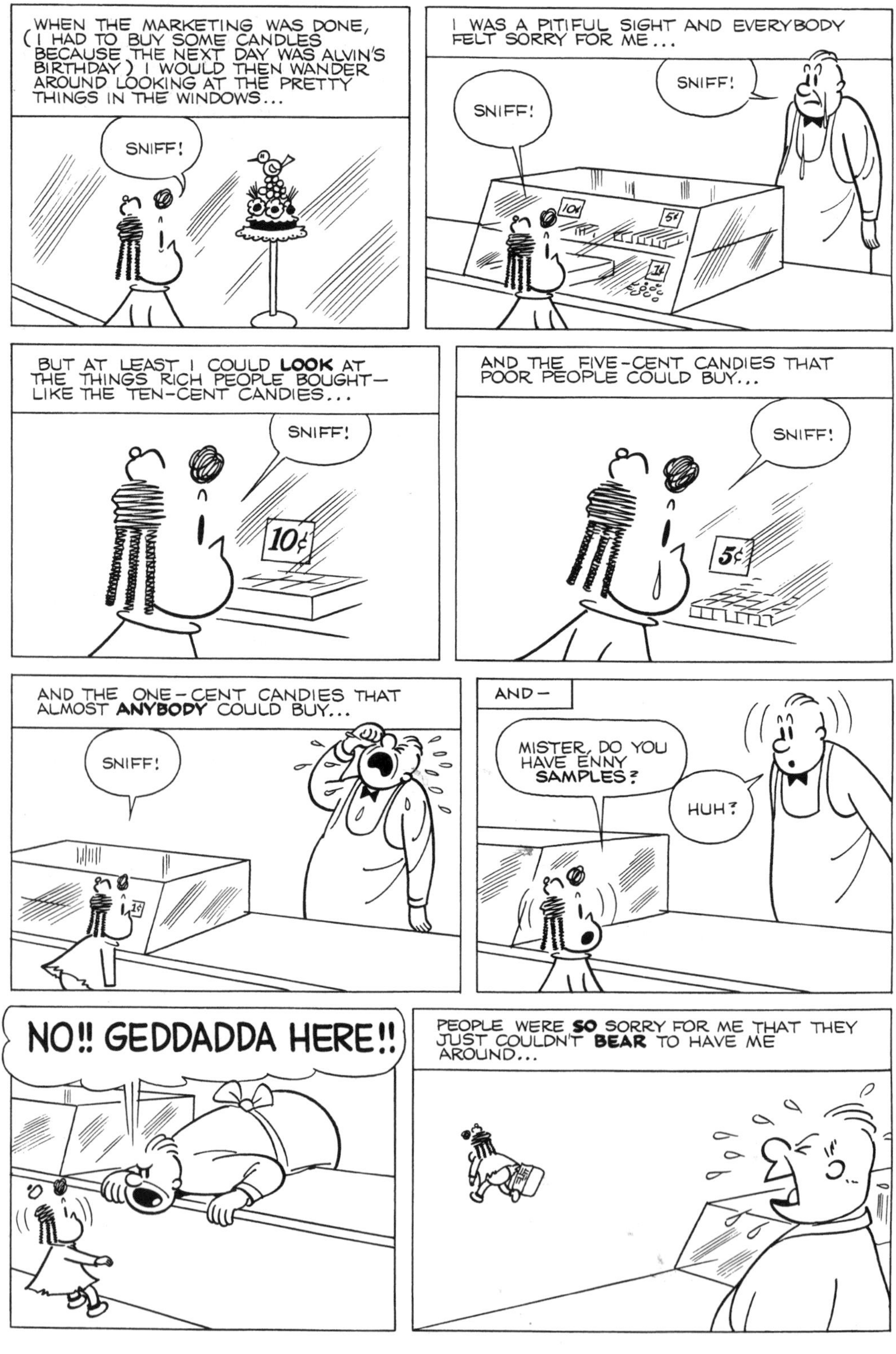
WHEN THE MARKETING WAS DONE, (I HAD TO BUY SOME CANDLES BECAUSE THE NEXT DAY WAS ALVIN'S BIRTHDAY) I WOULD THEN WANDER AROUND LOOKING AT THE PRETTY THINGS IN THE WINDOWS...
SNIFF!
I WAS A PITIFUL SIGHT AND EVERYBODY FELT SORRY FOR ME...
SNIFF!
SNIFF!
BUT AT LEAST I COULD **LOOK** AT THE THINGS RICH PEOPLE BOUGHT— LIKE THE TEN-CENT CANDIES...
SNIFF!
10¢
AND THE FIVE-CENT CANDIES THAT POOR PEOPLE COULD BUY...
SNIFF!
5¢
AND THE ONE-CENT CANDIES THAT ALMOST **ANYBODY** COULD BUY...
SNIFF!
AND—
MISTER, DO YOU HAVE ENNY **SAMPLES**?
HUH?
NO!! GEDDADDA HERE!!
PEOPLE WERE **SO** SORRY FOR ME THAT THEY JUST COULDN'T **BEAR** TO HAVE ME AROUND...

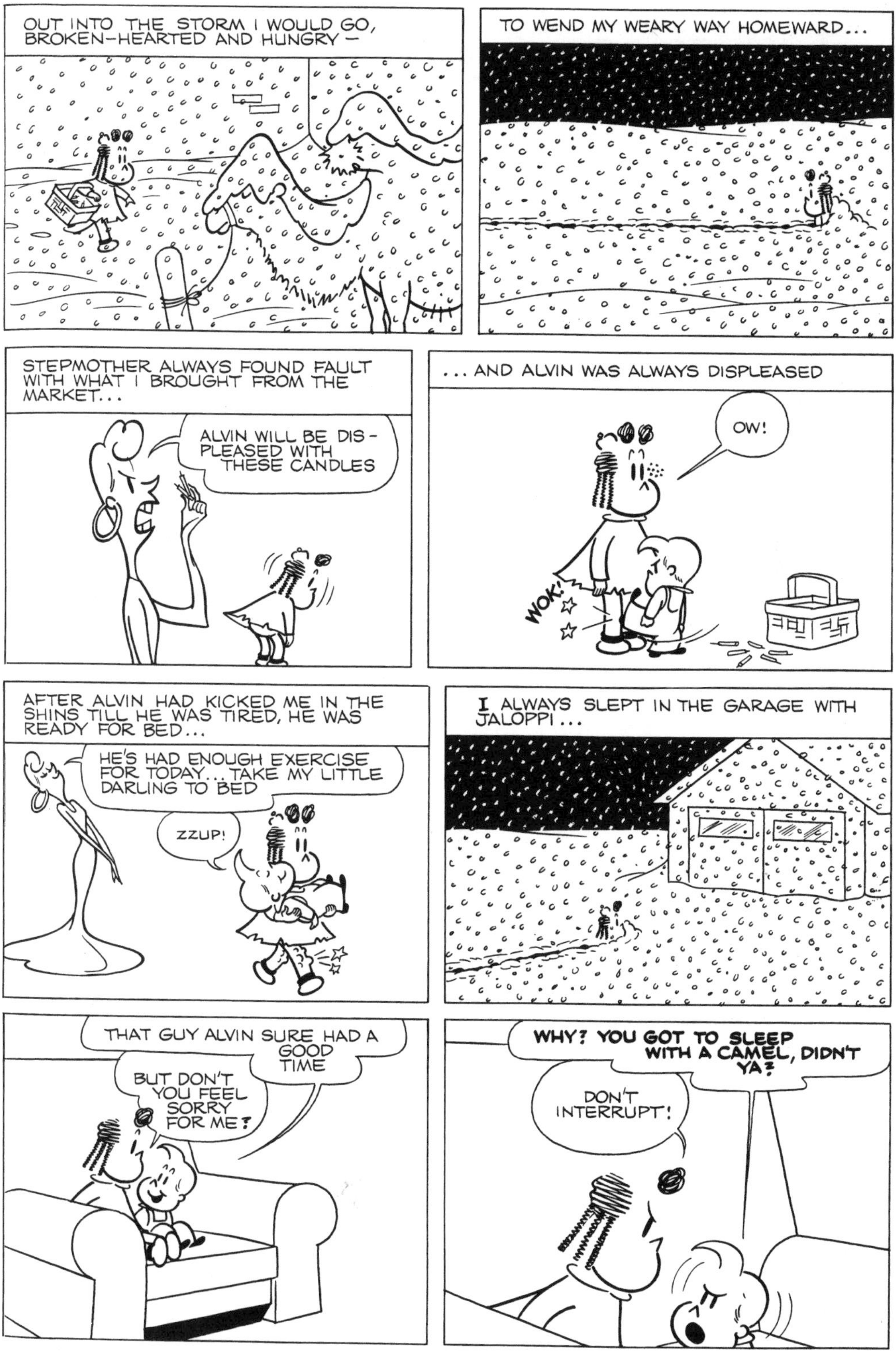
OUT INTO THE STORM I WOULD GO, BROKEN-HEARTED AND HUNGRY —
TO WEND MY WEARY WAY HOMEWARD...
STEPMOTHER ALWAYS FOUND FAULT WITH WHAT I BROUGHT FROM THE MARKET...
ALVIN WILL BE DIS-PLEASED WITH THESE CANDLES
... AND ALVIN WAS ALWAYS DISPLEASED
OW!
WOK!
AFTER ALVIN HAD KICKED ME IN THE SHINS TILL HE WAS TIRED, HE WAS READY FOR BED...
HE'S HAD ENOUGH EXERCISE FOR TODAY... TAKE MY LITTLE DARLING TO BED
ZZUP!
I ALWAYS SLEPT IN THE GARAGE WITH JALOPPI...
THAT GUY ALVIN SURE HAD A GOOD TIME
BUT DON'T YOU FEEL SORRY FOR ME?
WHY? YOU GOT TO SLEEP WITH A CAMEL, DIDN'T YA?
DON'T INTERRUPT!

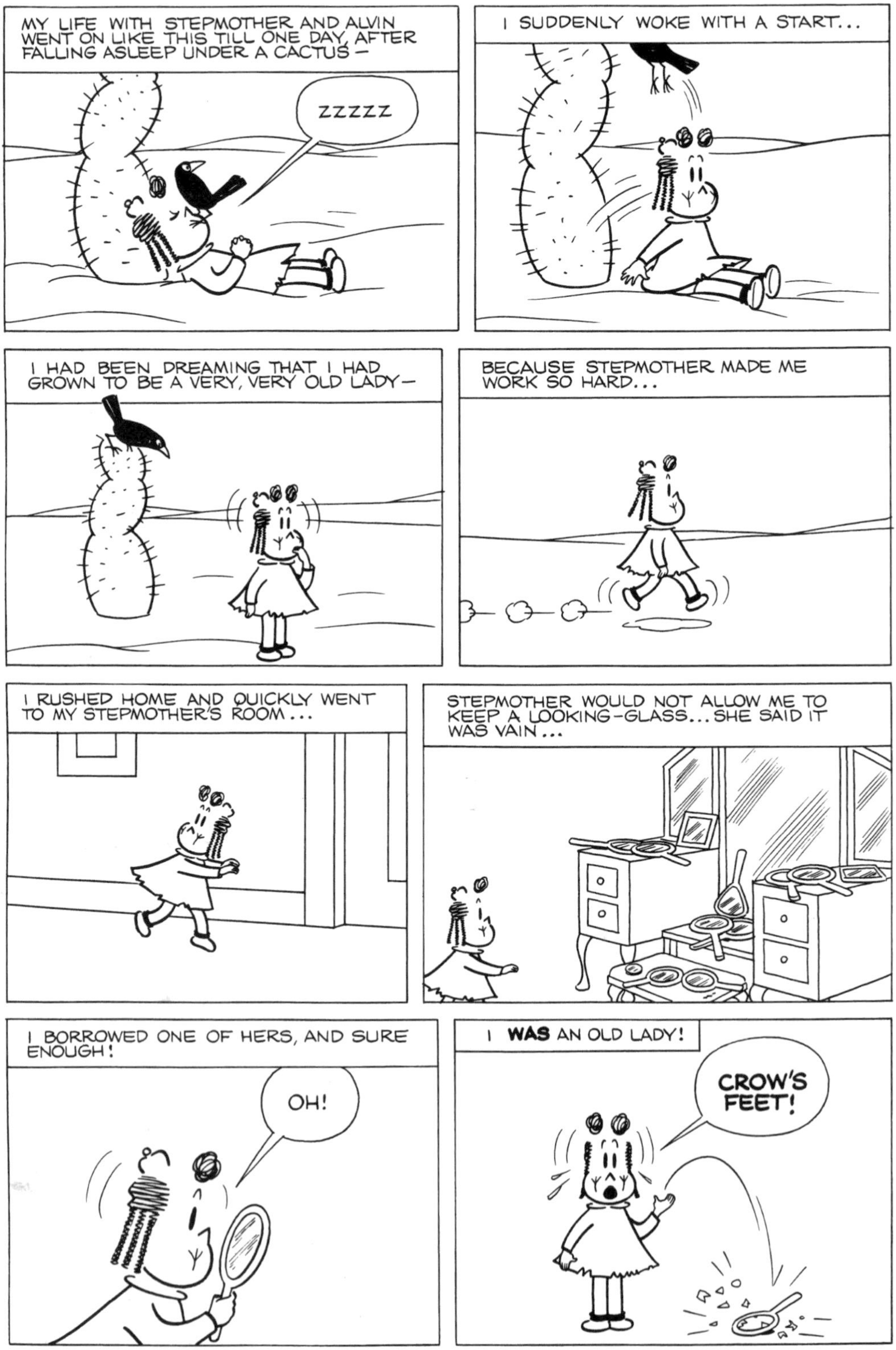
MY LIFE WITH STEPMOTHER AND ALVIN WENT ON LIKE THIS TILL ONE DAY, AFTER FALLING ASLEEP UNDER A CACTUS –
ZZZZZ
I SUDDENLY WOKE WITH A START...
I HAD BEEN DREAMING THAT I HAD GROWN TO BE A VERY, VERY OLD LADY –
BECAUSE STEPMOTHER MADE ME WORK SO HARD...
I RUSHED HOME AND QUICKLY WENT TO MY STEPMOTHER'S ROOM...
STEPMOTHER WOULD NOT ALLOW ME TO KEEP A LOOKING-GLASS... SHE SAID IT WAS VAIN...
I BORROWED ONE OF HERS, AND SURE ENOUGH!
OH!
I **WAS** AN OLD LADY!
CROW'S FEET!

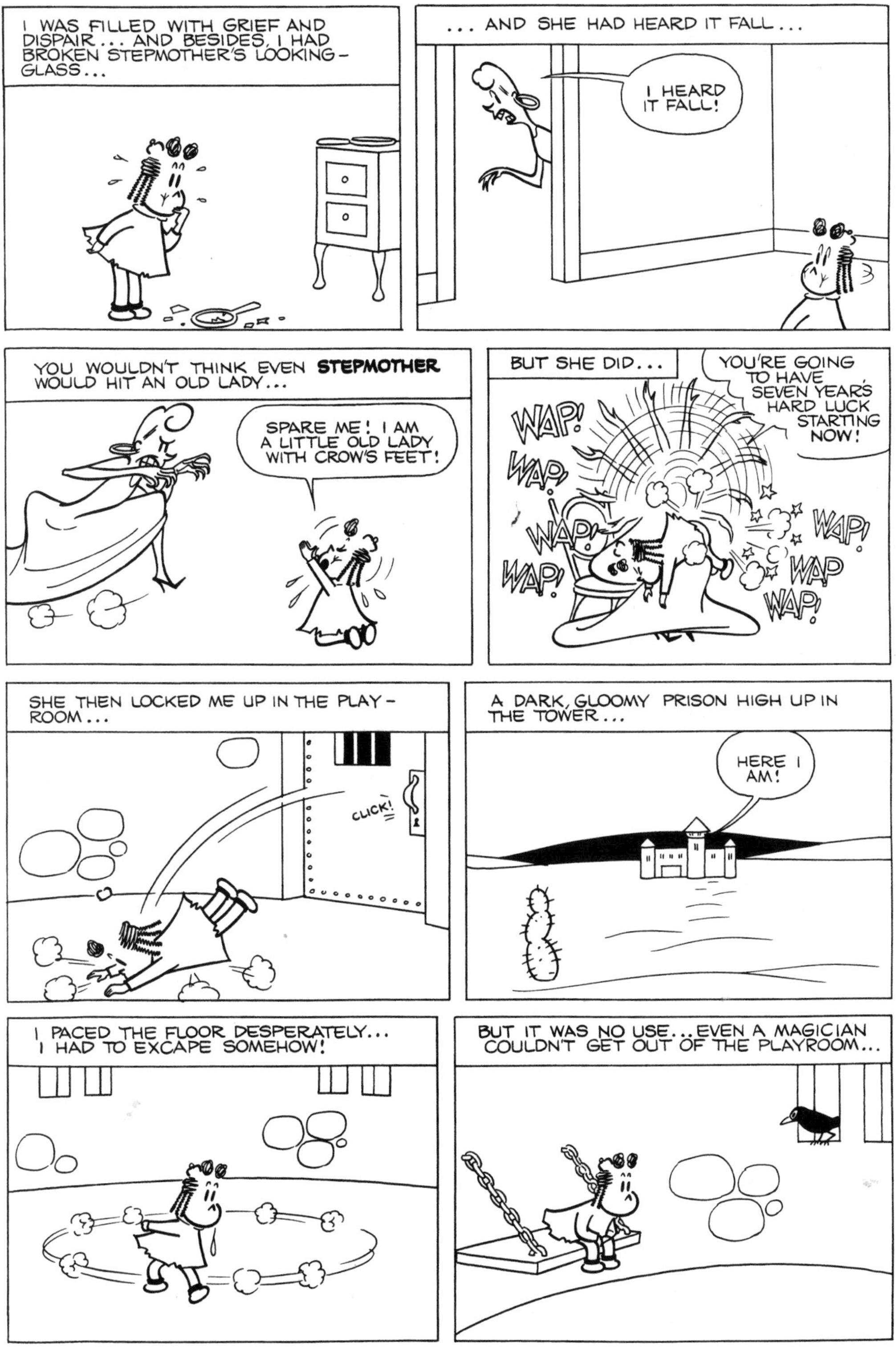
I WAS FILLED WITH GRIEF AND DISPAIR... AND BESIDES, I HAD BROKEN STEPMOTHER'S LOOKING-GLASS...
... AND SHE HAD HEARD IT FALL...
I HEARD IT FALL!
YOU WOULDN'T THINK EVEN **STEPMOTHER** WOULD HIT AN OLD LADY...
SPARE ME! I AM A LITTLE OLD LADY WITH CROW'S FEET!
BUT SHE DID...
YOU'RE GOING TO HAVE SEVEN YEAR'S HARD LUCK STARTING NOW!
WAP! WAP! WAP! WAP! WAP! WAP WAP!
SHE THEN LOCKED ME UP IN THE PLAY-ROOM...
CLICK!
A DARK, GLOOMY PRISON HIGH UP IN THE TOWER...
HERE I AM!
I PACED THE FLOOR DESPERATELY... I HAD TO EXCAPE SOMEHOW!
BUT IT WAS NO USE... EVEN A MAGICIAN COULDN'T GET OUT OF THE PLAYROOM...

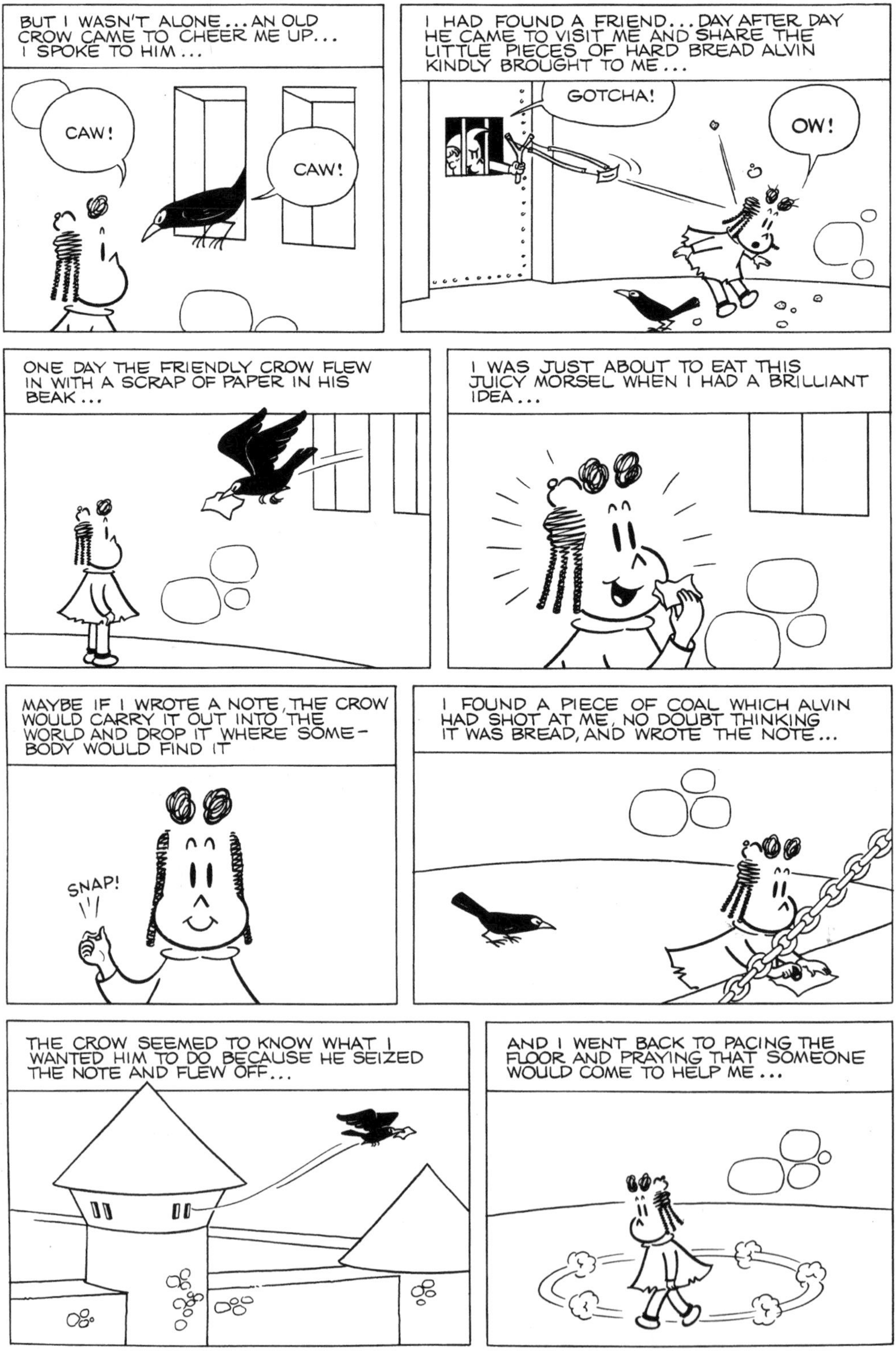
BUT I WASN'T ALONE... AN OLD CROW CAME TO CHEER ME UP... I SPOKE TO HIM...
CAW!
CAW!
I HAD FOUND A FRIEND... DAY AFTER DAY HE CAME TO VISIT ME AND SHARE THE LITTLE PIECES OF HARD BREAD ALVIN KINDLY BROUGHT TO ME...
GOTCHA!
OW!
ONE DAY THE FRIENDLY CROW FLEW IN WITH A SCRAP OF PAPER IN HIS BEAK...
I WAS JUST ABOUT TO EAT THIS JUICY MORSEL WHEN I HAD A BRILLIANT IDEA...
MAYBE IF I WROTE A NOTE, THE CROW WOULD CARRY IT OUT INTO THE WORLD AND DROP IT WHERE SOME-BODY WOULD FIND IT
SNAP!
I FOUND A PIECE OF COAL WHICH ALVIN HAD SHOT AT ME, NO DOUBT THINKING IT WAS BREAD, AND WROTE THE NOTE...
THE CROW SEEMED TO KNOW WHAT I WANTED HIM TO DO BECAUSE HE SEIZED THE NOTE AND FLEW OFF...
AND I WENT BACK TO PACING THE FLOOR AND PRAYING THAT SOMEONE WOULD COME TO HELP ME...

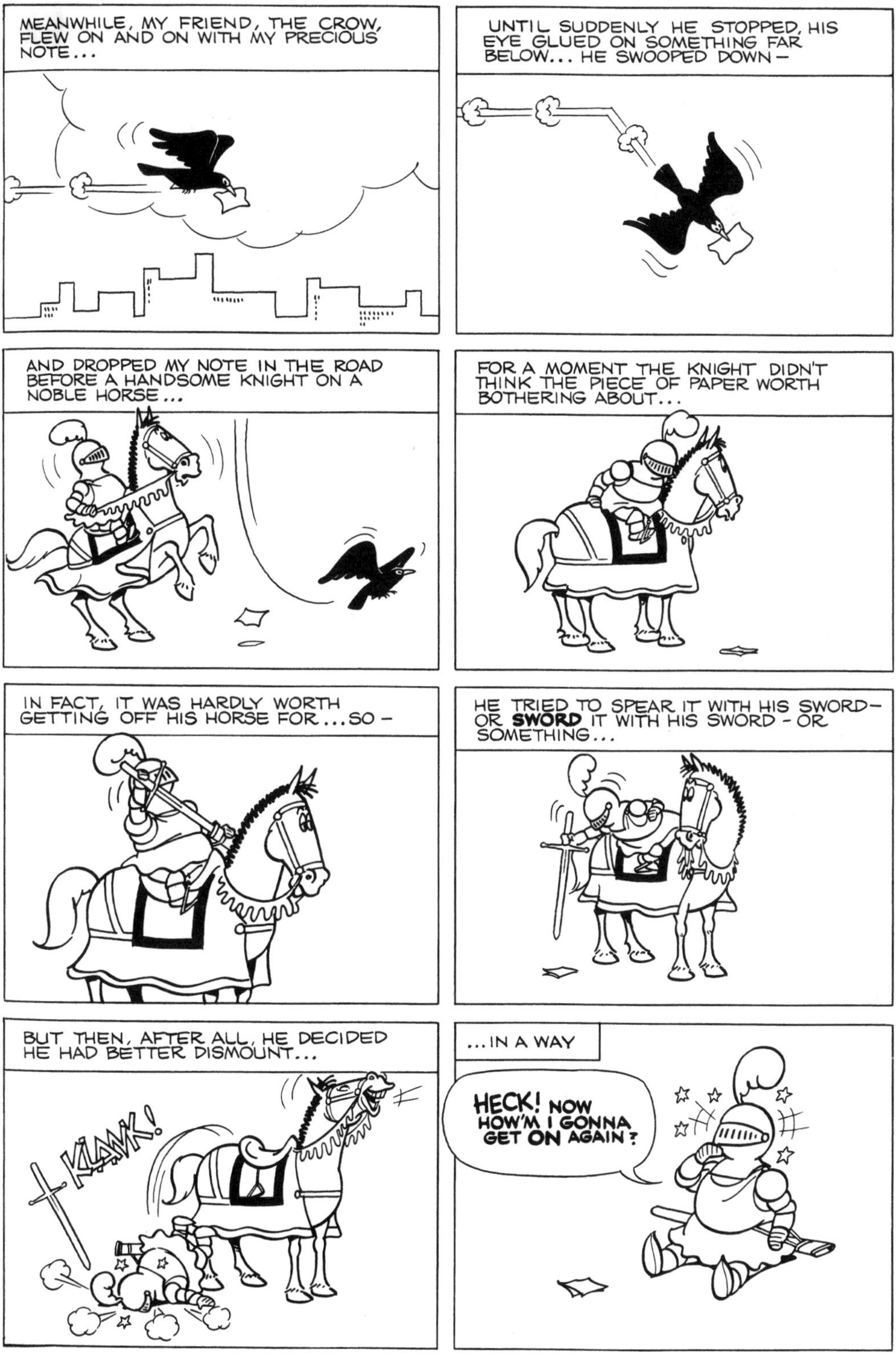
MEANWHILE, MY FRIEND, THE CROW, FLEW ON AND ON WITH MY PRECIOUS NOTE...
UNTIL SUDDENLY HE STOPPED, HIS EYE GLUED ON SOMETHING FAR BELOW... HE SWOOPED DOWN –
AND DROPPED MY NOTE IN THE ROAD BEFORE A HANDSOME KNIGHT ON A NOBLE HORSE...
FOR A MOMENT THE KNIGHT DIDN'T THINK THE PIECE OF PAPER WORTH BOTHERING ABOUT...
IN FACT, IT WAS HARDLY WORTH GETTING OFF HIS HORSE FOR...SO –
HE TRIED TO SPEAR IT WITH HIS SWORD– OR SWORD IT WITH HIS SWORD – OR SOMETHING...
BUT THEN, AFTER ALL, HE DECIDED HE HAD BETTER DISMOUNT...
KLANK!
...IN A WAY
HECK! NOW HOW'M I GONNA GET ON AGAIN?

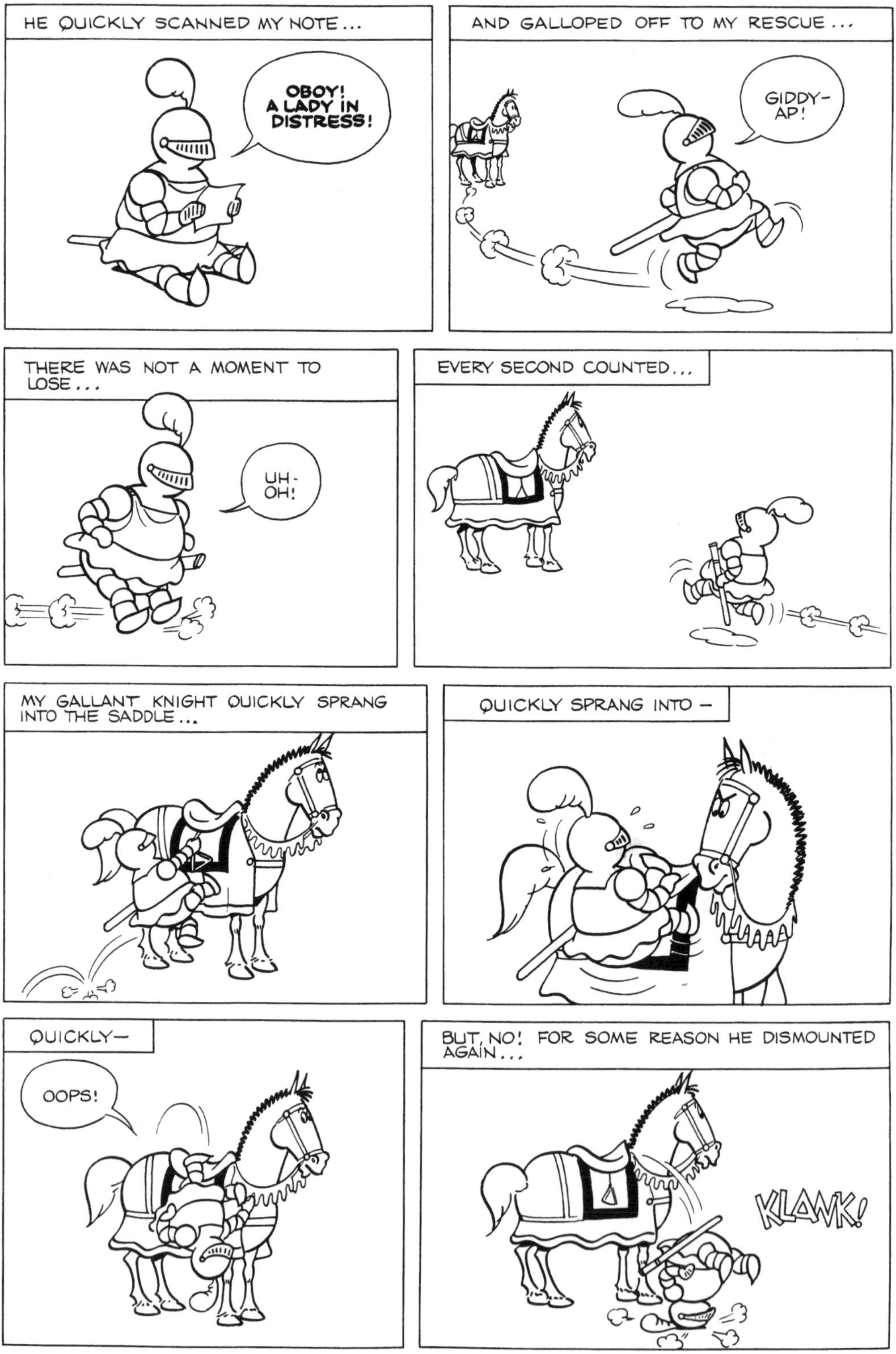
HE QUICKLY SCANNED MY NOTE...
OBOY! A LADY IN DISTRESS!
AND GALLOPED OFF TO MY RESCUE...
GIDDY-AP!
THERE WAS NOT A MOMENT TO LOSE...
UH-OH!
EVERY SECOND COUNTED...
MY GALLANT KNIGHT QUICKLY SPRANG INTO THE SADDLE...
QUICKLY SPRANG INTO—
QUICKLY—
OOPS!
BUT, NO! FOR SOME REASON HE DISMOUNTED AGAIN...
KLANK!

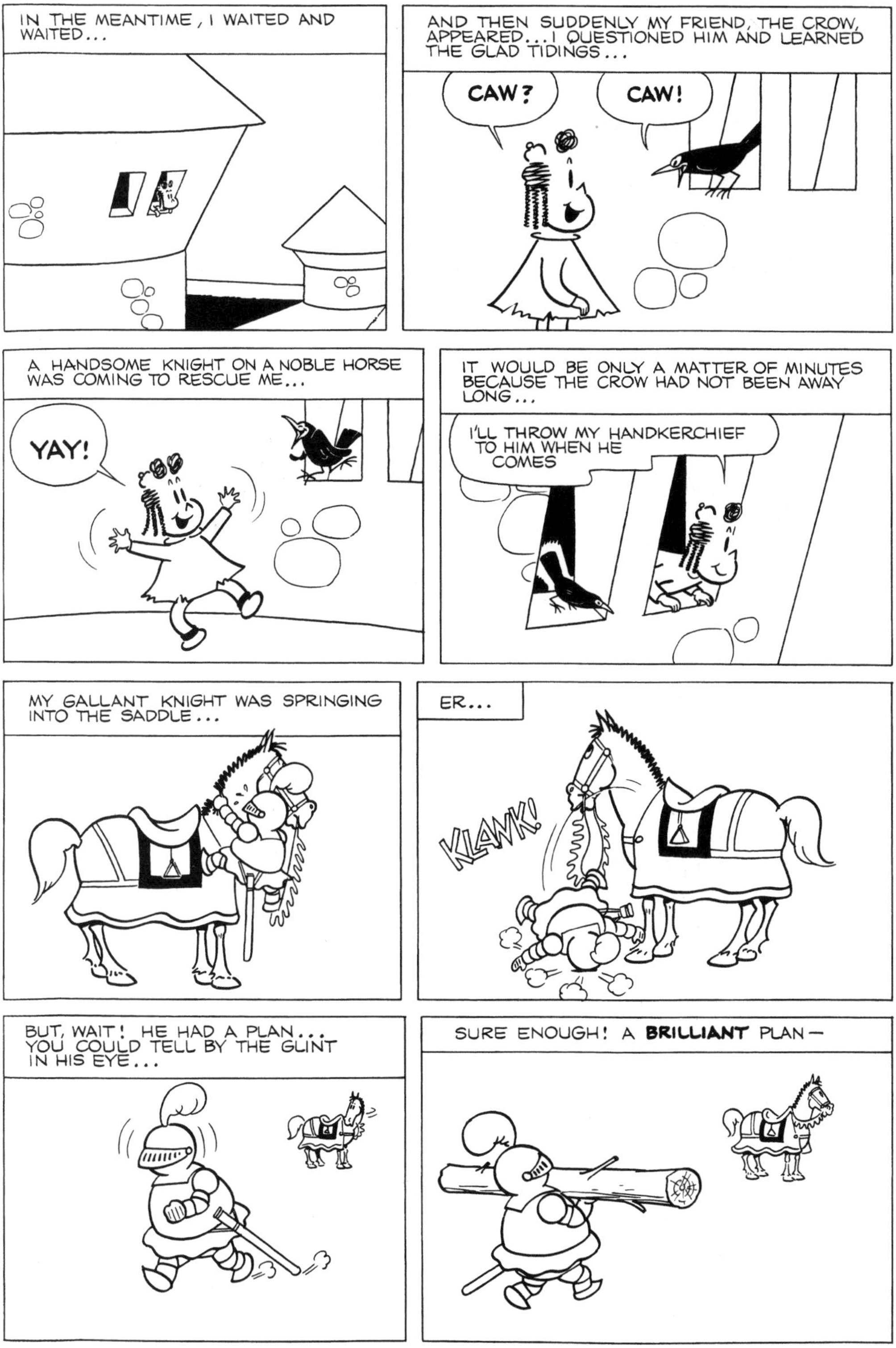
IN THE MEANTIME, I WAITED AND WAITED...
AND THEN SUDDENLY MY FRIEND, THE CROW, APPEARED... I QUESTIONED HIM AND LEARNED THE GLAD TIDINGS...
CAW?
CAW!
A HANDSOME KNIGHT ON A NOBLE HORSE WAS COMING TO RESCUE ME...
YAY!
IT WOULD BE ONLY A MATTER OF MINUTES BECAUSE THE CROW HAD NOT BEEN AWAY LONG...
I'LL THROW MY HANDKERCHIEF TO HIM WHEN HE COMES
MY GALLANT KNIGHT WAS SPRINGING INTO THE SADDLE...
ER...
KLANK!
BUT, WAIT! HE HAD A PLAN... YOU COULD TELL BY THE GLINT IN HIS EYE...
SURE ENOUGH! A BRILLIANT PLAN—

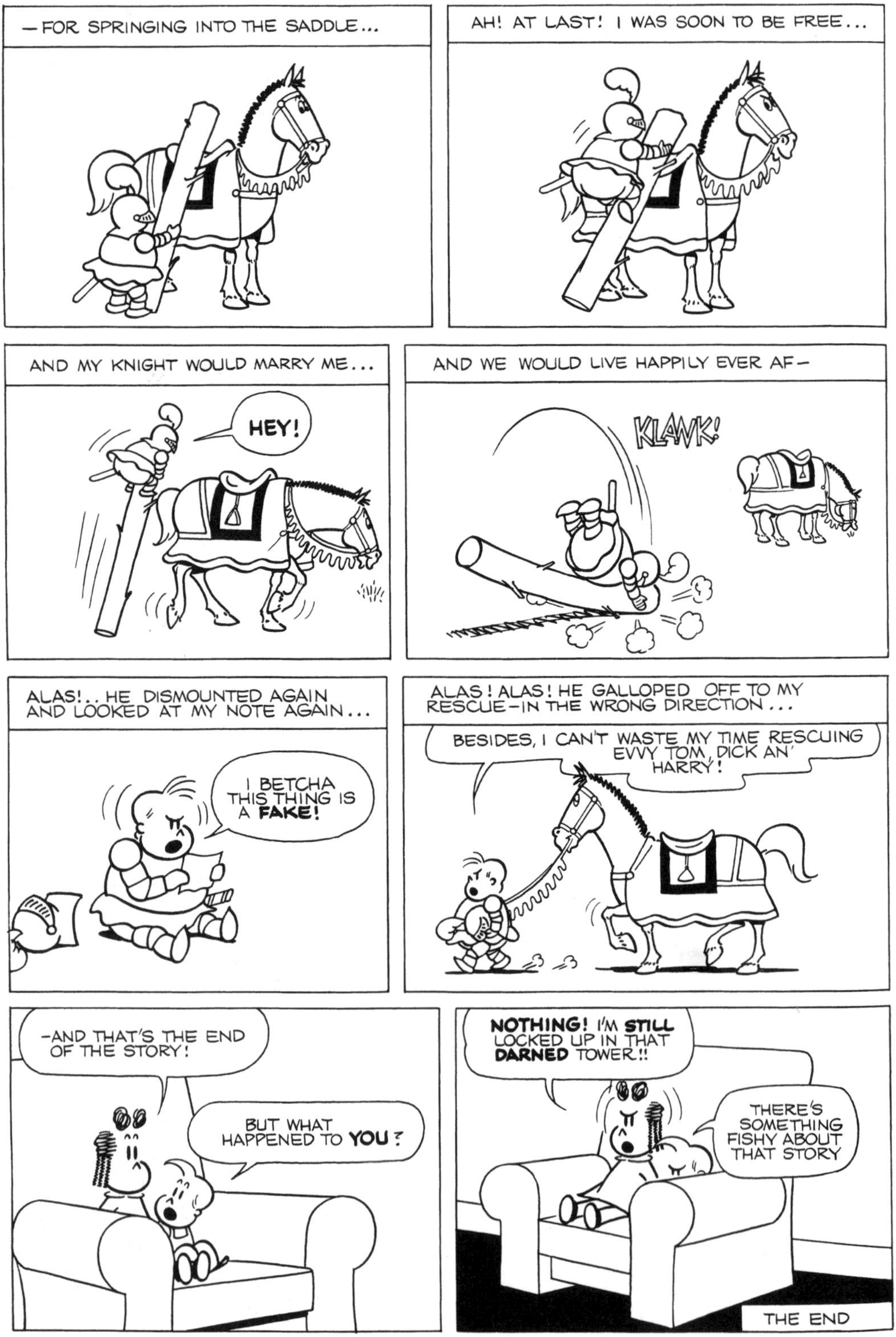

—FOR SPRINGING INTO THE SADDLE...
AH! AT LAST! I WAS SOON TO BE FREE...
AND MY KNIGHT WOULD MARRY ME...
HEY!
AND WE WOULD LIVE HAPPILY EVER AF—
KLANK!
ALAS!.. HE DISMOUNTED AGAIN AND LOOKED AT MY NOTE AGAIN...
I BETCHA THIS THING IS A FAKE!
ALAS! ALAS! HE GALLOPED OFF TO MY RESCUE—IN THE WRONG DIRECTION...
BESIDES, I CAN'T WASTE MY TIME RESCUING EVVY TOM, DICK AN' HARRY!
—AND THAT'S THE END OF THE STORY!
BUT WHAT HAPPENED TO YOU?
NOTHING! I'M STILL LOCKED UP IN THAT DARNED TOWER!!
THERE'S SOMETHING FISHY ABOUT THAT STORY
THE END

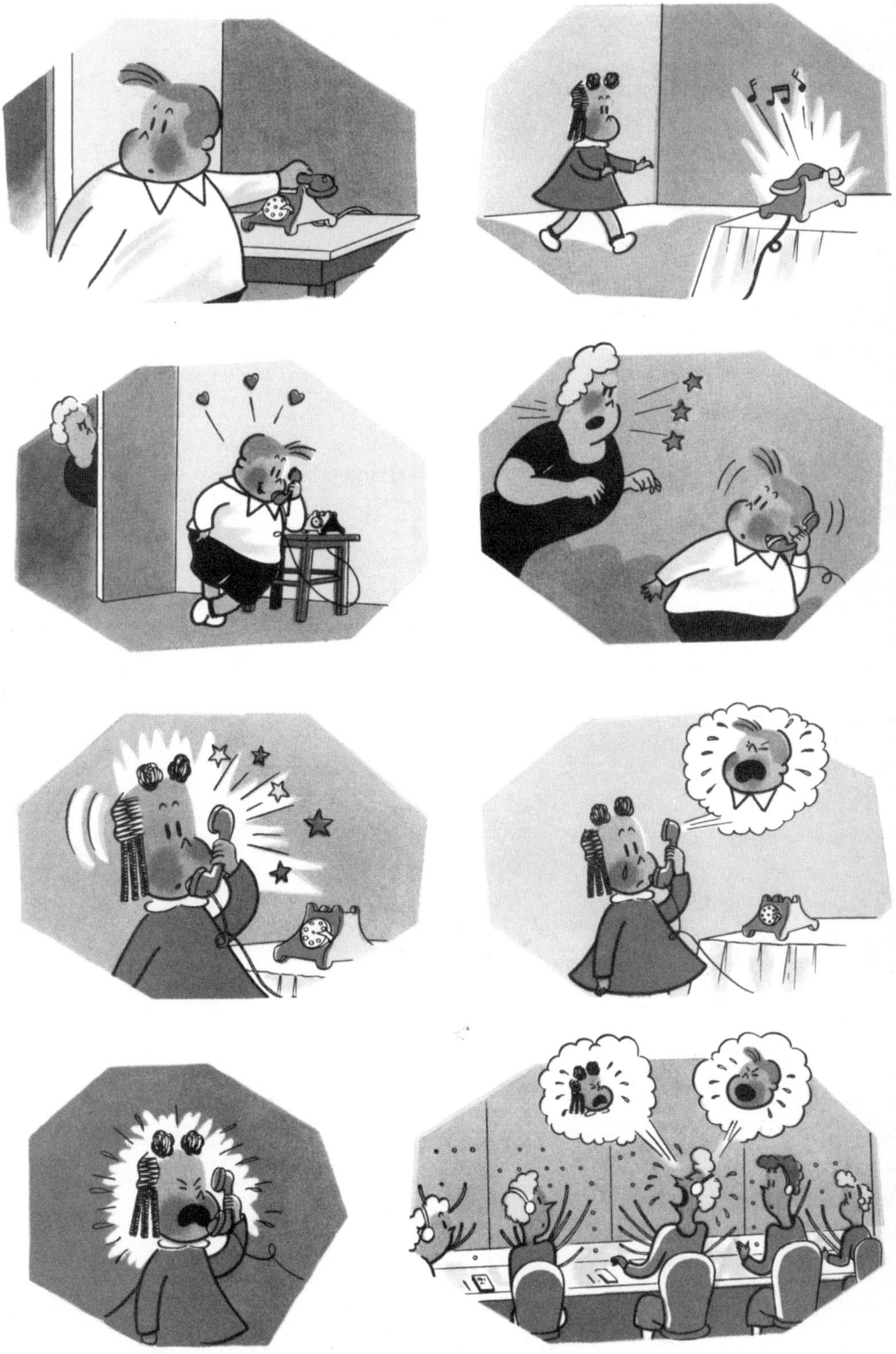

marge's

LITTLE LULU

FIGHTS BACK WITH A CLUB

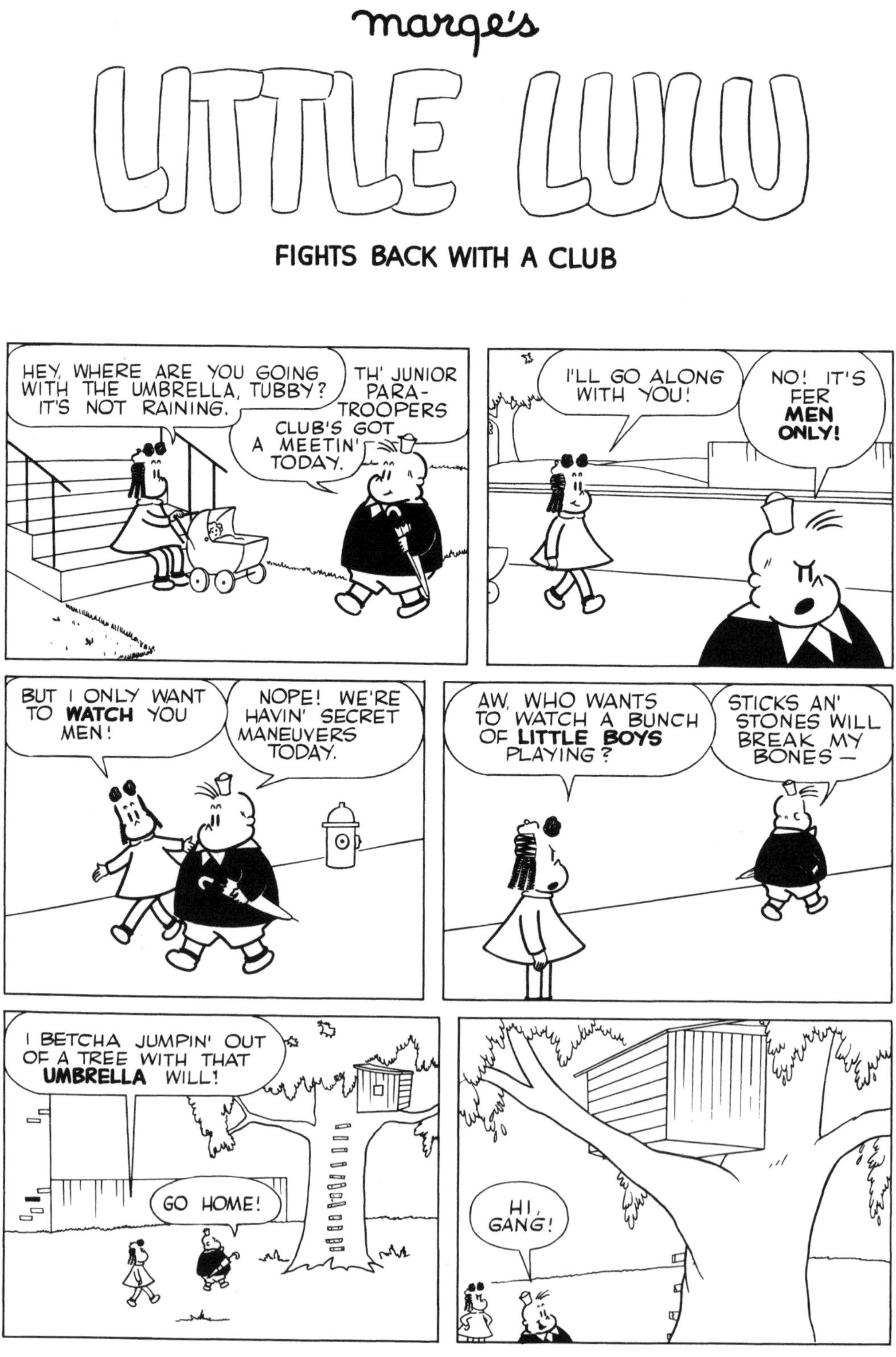
HEY, WHERE ARE YOU GOING WITH THE UMBRELLA, TUBBY? IT'S NOT RAINING.
TH' JUNIOR PARA-TROOPERS CLUB'S GOT A MEETIN' TODAY.
I'LL GO ALONG WITH YOU!
NO! IT'S FER **MEN ONLY!**
BUT I ONLY WANT TO **WATCH** YOU MEN!
NOPE! WE'RE HAVIN' SECRET MANEUVERS TODAY.
AW, WHO WANTS TO WATCH A BUNCH OF **LITTLE BOYS** PLAYING?
STICKS AN' STONES WILL BREAK MY BONES —
I BETCHA JUMPIN' OUT OF A TREE WITH THAT **UMBRELLA** WILL!
GO HOME!
HI, GANG!

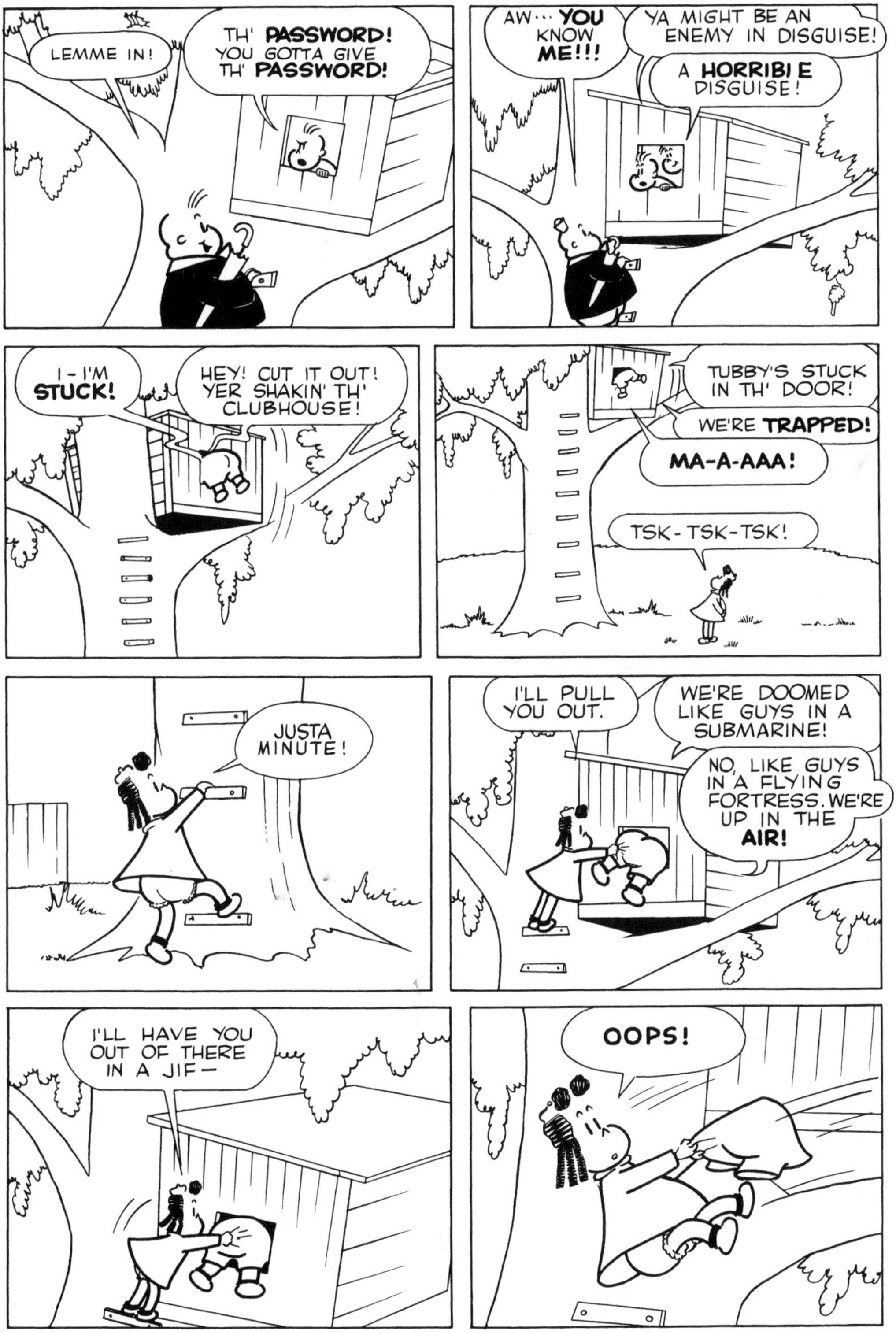
LEMME IN!
TH' PASSWORD! YOU GOTTA GIVE TH' PASSWORD!
AW... YOU KNOW ME!!!
YA MIGHT BE AN ENEMY IN DISGUISE!
A HORRIBLE DISGUISE!
I-I'M STUCK!
HEY! CUT IT OUT! YER SHAKIN' TH' CLUBHOUSE!
TUBBY'S STUCK IN TH' DOOR!
WE'RE TRAPPED!
MA-A-AAA!
TSK-TSK-TSK!
JUSTA MINUTE!
I'LL PULL YOU OUT.
WE'RE DOOMED LIKE GUYS IN A SUBMARINE!
NO, LIKE GUYS IN A FLYING FORTRESS. WE'RE UP IN THE AIR!
I'LL HAVE YOU OUT OF THERE IN A JIF—
OOPS!

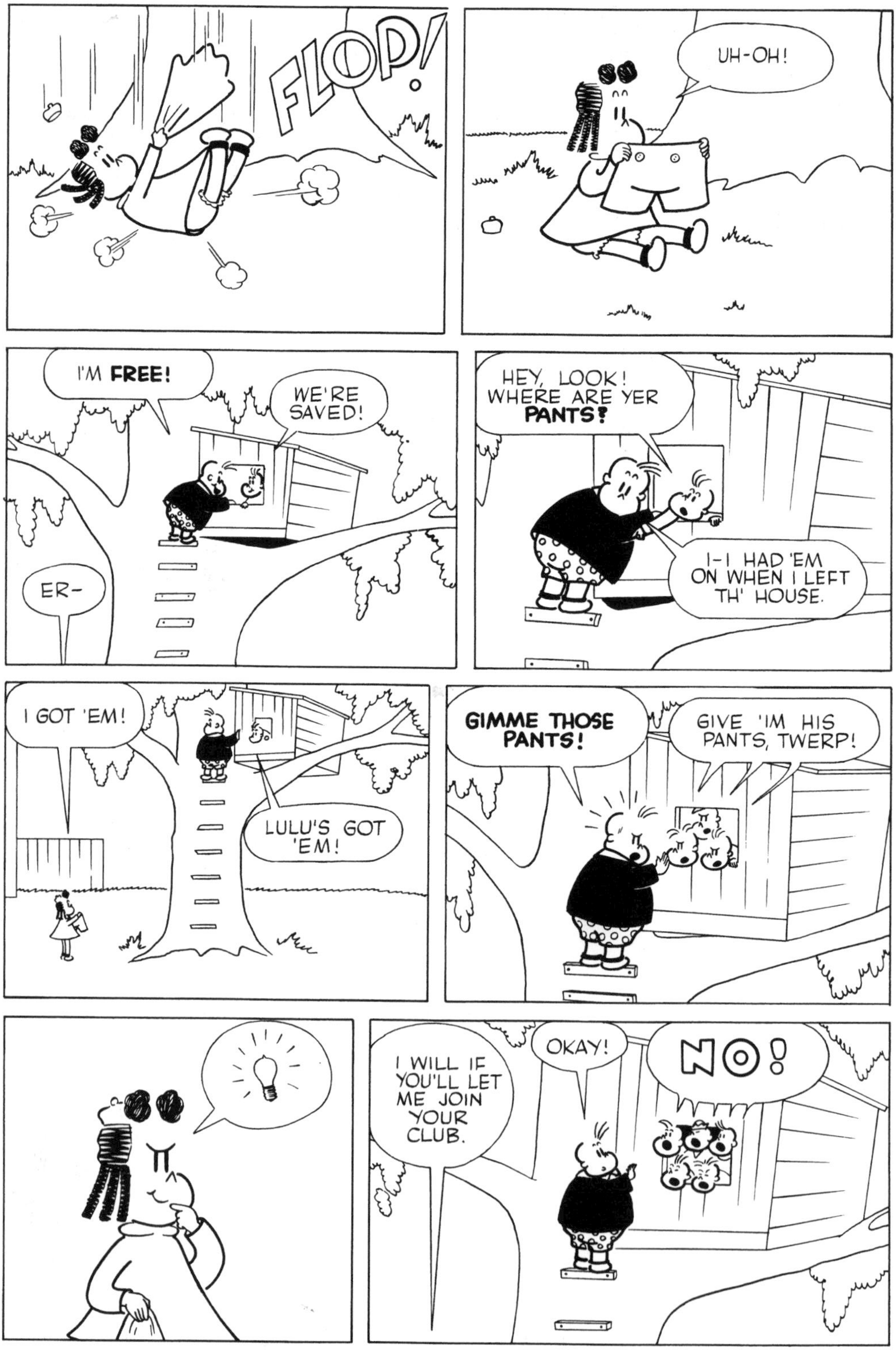
FLOP!
UH-OH!
I'M FREE!
WE'RE SAVED!
ER-
HEY, LOOK! WHERE ARE YER PANTS?
I-I HAD 'EM ON WHEN I LEFT TH' HOUSE.
I GOT 'EM!
LULU'S GOT 'EM!
GIMME THOSE PANTS!
GIVE 'IM HIS PANTS, TWERP!
I WILL IF YOU'LL LET ME JOIN YOUR CLUB.
OKAY!
NO!

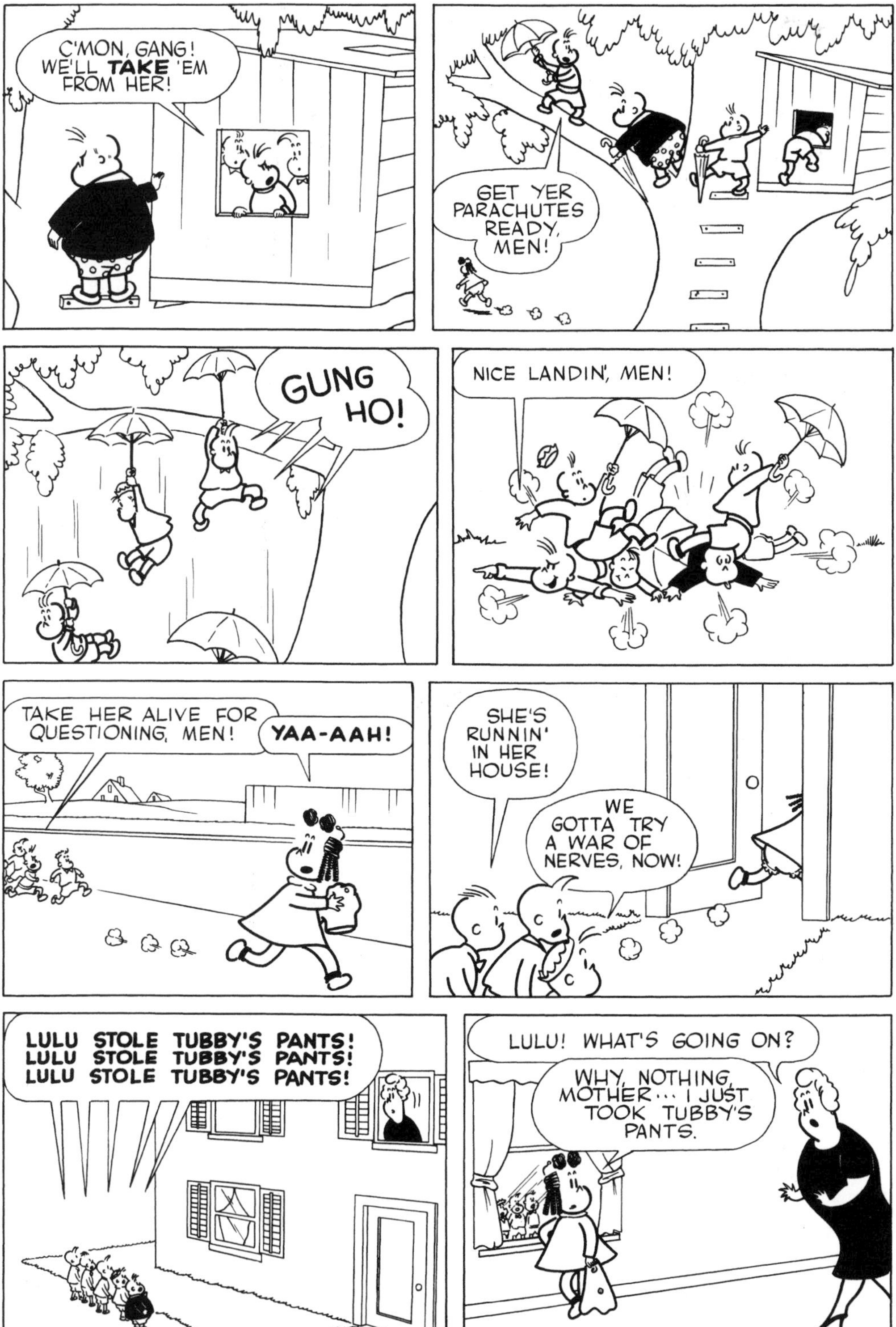
C'MON, GANG! WE'LL **TAKE** 'EM FROM HER!
GET YER PARACHUTES READY, MEN!
GUNG HO!
NICE LANDIN', MEN!
TAKE HER ALIVE FOR QUESTIONING, MEN!
YAA-AAH!
SHE'S RUNNIN' IN HER HOUSE!
WE GOTTA TRY A WAR OF NERVES, NOW!
LULU STOLE TUBBY'S PANTS! LULU STOLE TUBBY'S PANTS! LULU STOLE TUBBY'S PANTS!
LULU! WHAT'S GOING ON?
WHY, NOTHING, MOTHER... I JUST TOOK TUBBY'S PANTS.

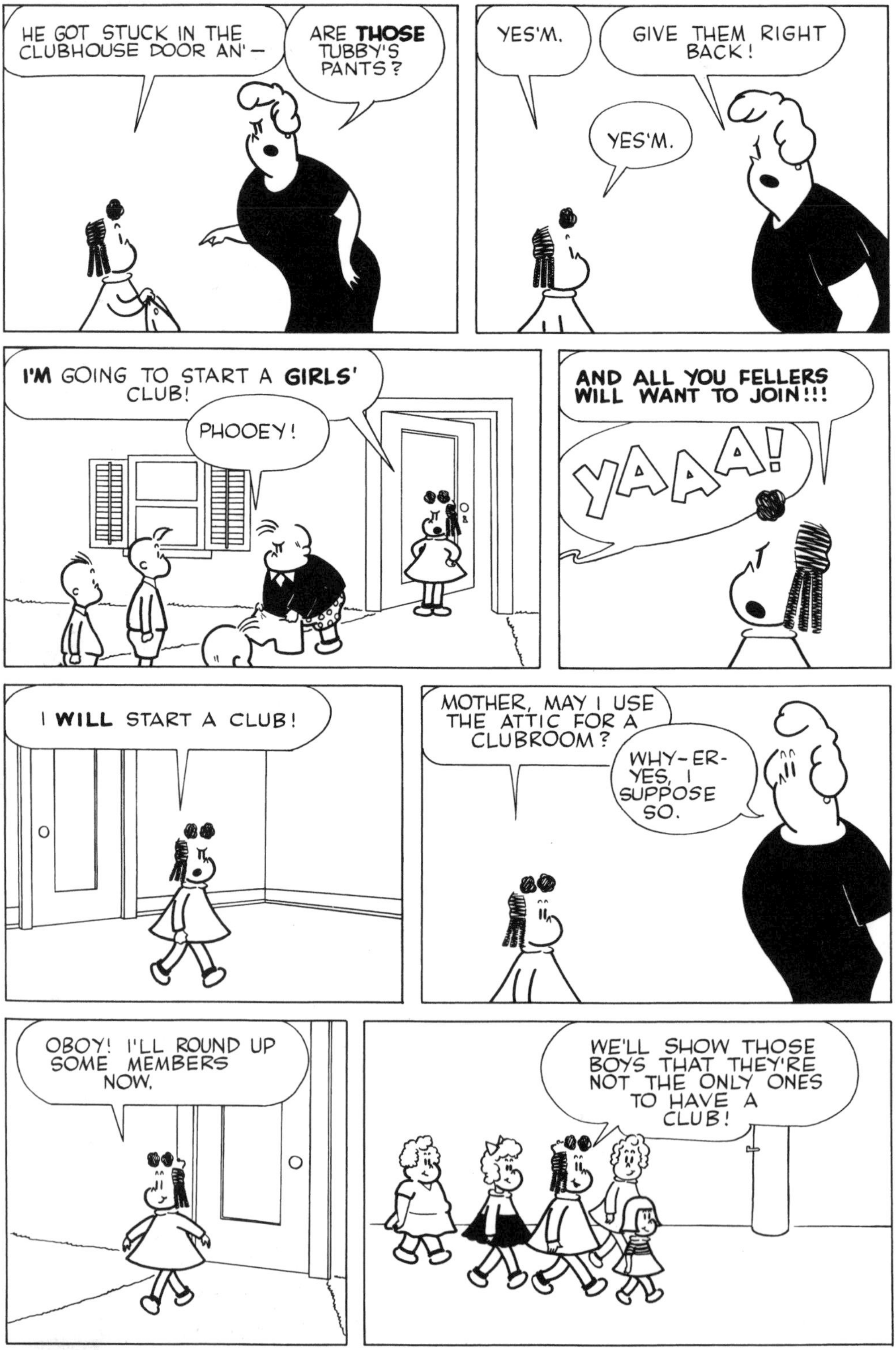
HE GOT STUCK IN THE CLUBHOUSE DOOR AN'—
ARE **THOSE** TUBBY'S PANTS?
YES'M.
GIVE THEM RIGHT BACK!
YES'M.
I'M GOING TO START A **GIRLS'** CLUB!
PHOOEY!
AND ALL YOU FELLERS WILL WANT TO JOIN!!!
YAAA!
I **WILL** START A CLUB!
MOTHER, MAY I USE THE ATTIC FOR A CLUBROOM?
WHY-ER-YES, I SUPPOSE SO.
OBOY! I'LL ROUND UP SOME MEMBERS NOW.
WE'LL SHOW THOSE BOYS THAT THEY'RE NOT THE ONLY ONES TO HAVE A CLUB!

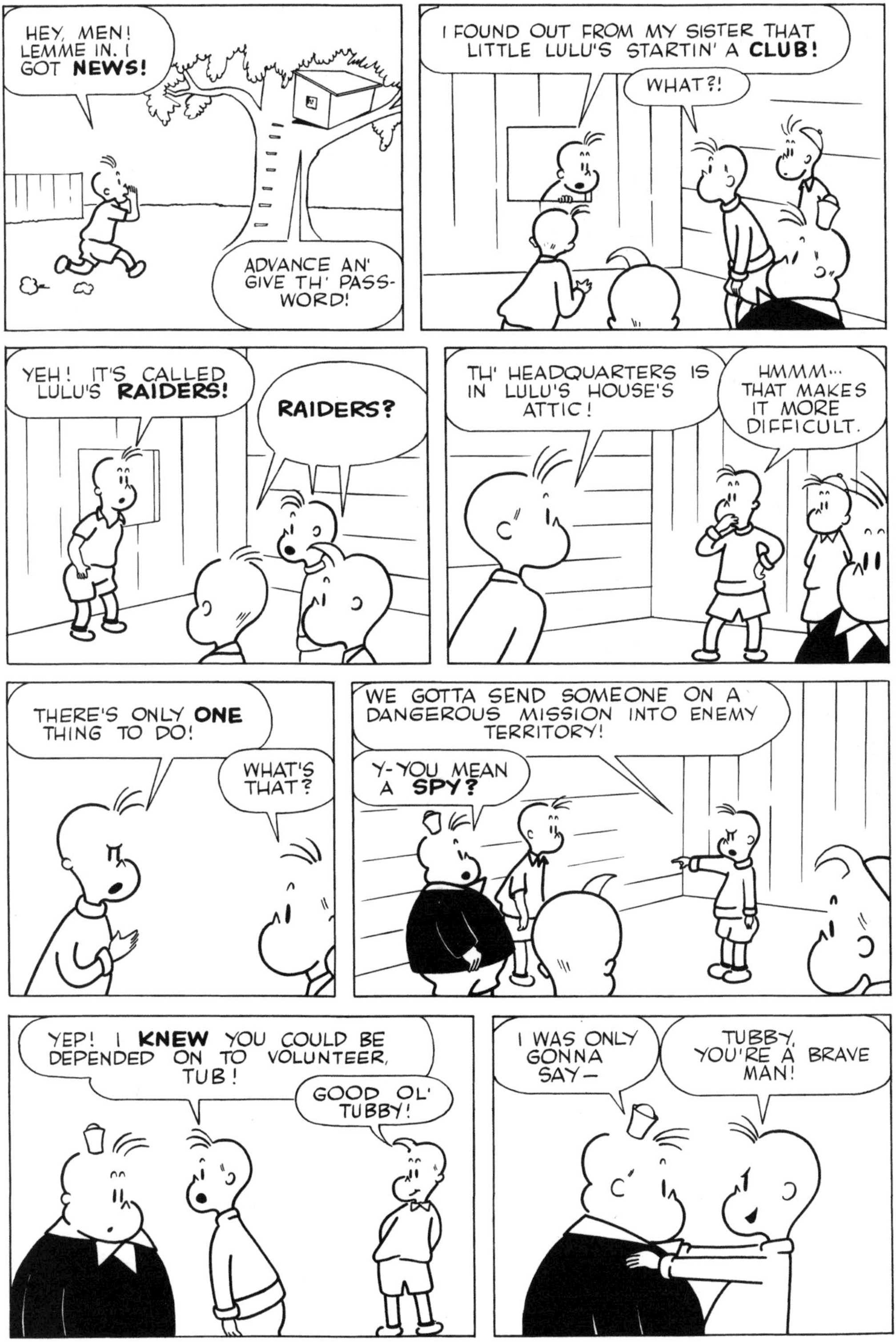
HEY, MEN! LEMME IN. I GOT NEWS!
ADVANCE AN' GIVE TH' PASS-WORD!
I FOUND OUT FROM MY SISTER THAT LITTLE LULU'S STARTIN' A CLUB!
WHAT?!
YEH! IT'S CALLED LULU'S RAIDERS!
RAIDERS?
TH' HEADQUARTERS IS IN LULU'S HOUSE'S ATTIC!
HMMM... THAT MAKES IT MORE DIFFICULT.
THERE'S ONLY ONE THING TO DO!
WHAT'S THAT?
WE GOTTA SEND SOMEONE ON A DANGEROUS MISSION INTO ENEMY TERRITORY!
Y-YOU MEAN A SPY?
YEP! I KNEW YOU COULD BE DEPENDED ON TO VOLUNTEER, TUB!
GOOD OL' TUBBY!
I WAS ONLY GONNA SAY—
TUBBY, YOU'RE A BRAVE MAN!

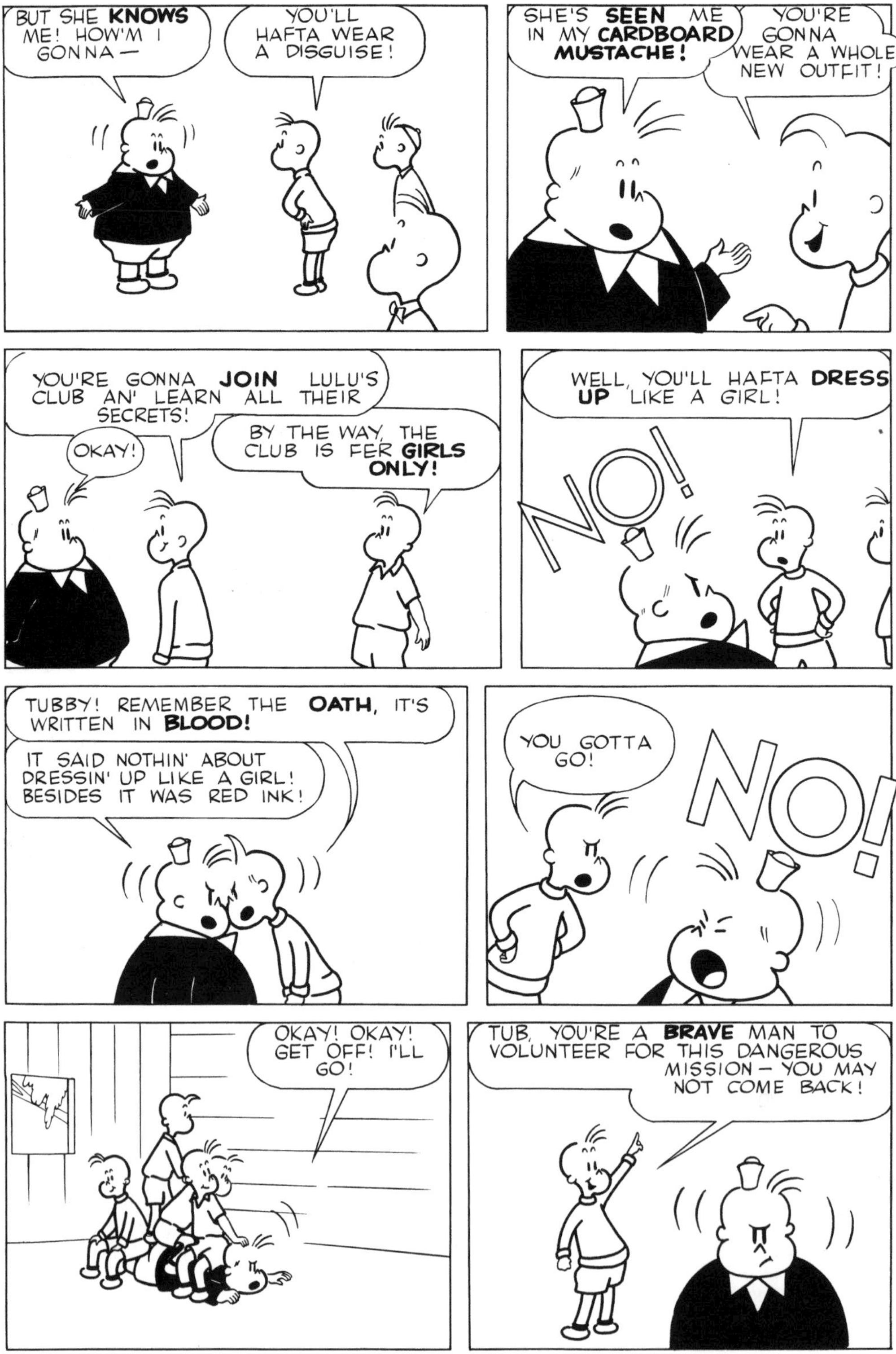

BUT SHE **KNOWS** ME! HOW'M I GONNA—
YOU'LL HAFTA WEAR A DISGUISE!
SHE'S **SEEN** ME IN MY **CARDBOARD MUSTACHE!**
YOU'RE GONNA WEAR A WHOLE NEW OUTFIT!
YOU'RE GONNA **JOIN** LULU'S CLUB AN' LEARN ALL THEIR SECRETS!
OKAY!
BY THE WAY, THE CLUB IS FER **GIRLS ONLY!**
WELL, YOU'LL HAFTA **DRESS UP** LIKE A GIRL!
NO!
TUBBY! REMEMBER THE **OATH**, IT'S WRITTEN IN **BLOOD!**
IT SAID NOTHIN' ABOUT DRESSIN' UP LIKE A GIRL! BESIDES IT WAS RED INK!
YOU GOTTA GO!
NO!
OKAY! OKAY! GET OFF! I'LL GO!
TUB, YOU'RE A **BRAVE** MAN TO VOLUNTEER FOR THIS DANGEROUS MISSION — YOU MAY NOT COME BACK!

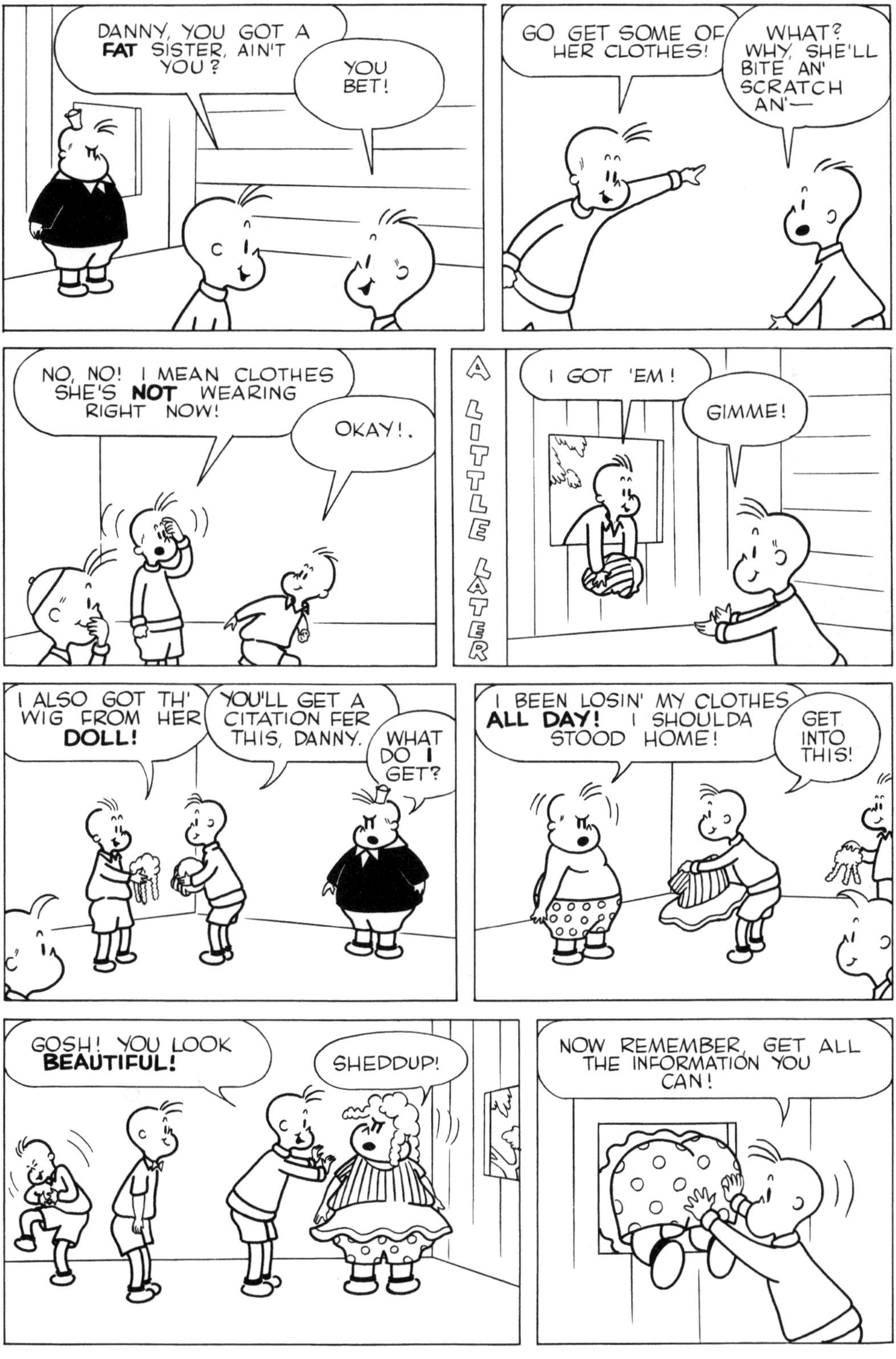
DANNY, YOU GOT A FAT SISTER, AIN'T YOU?
YOU BET!
GO GET SOME OF HER CLOTHES!
WHAT? WHY, SHE'LL BITE AN' SCRATCH AN'—
NO, NO! I MEAN CLOTHES SHE'S NOT WEARING RIGHT NOW!
OKAY!.
A LITTLE LATER
I GOT 'EM!
GIMME!
I ALSO GOT TH' WIG FROM HER DOLL!
YOU'LL GET A CITATION FER THIS, DANNY.
WHAT DO I GET?
I BEEN LOSIN' MY CLOTHES ALL DAY! I SHOULDA STOOD HOME!
GET INTO THIS!
GOSH! YOU LOOK BEAUTIFUL!
SHEDDUP!
NOW REMEMBER, GET ALL THE INFORMATION YOU CAN!

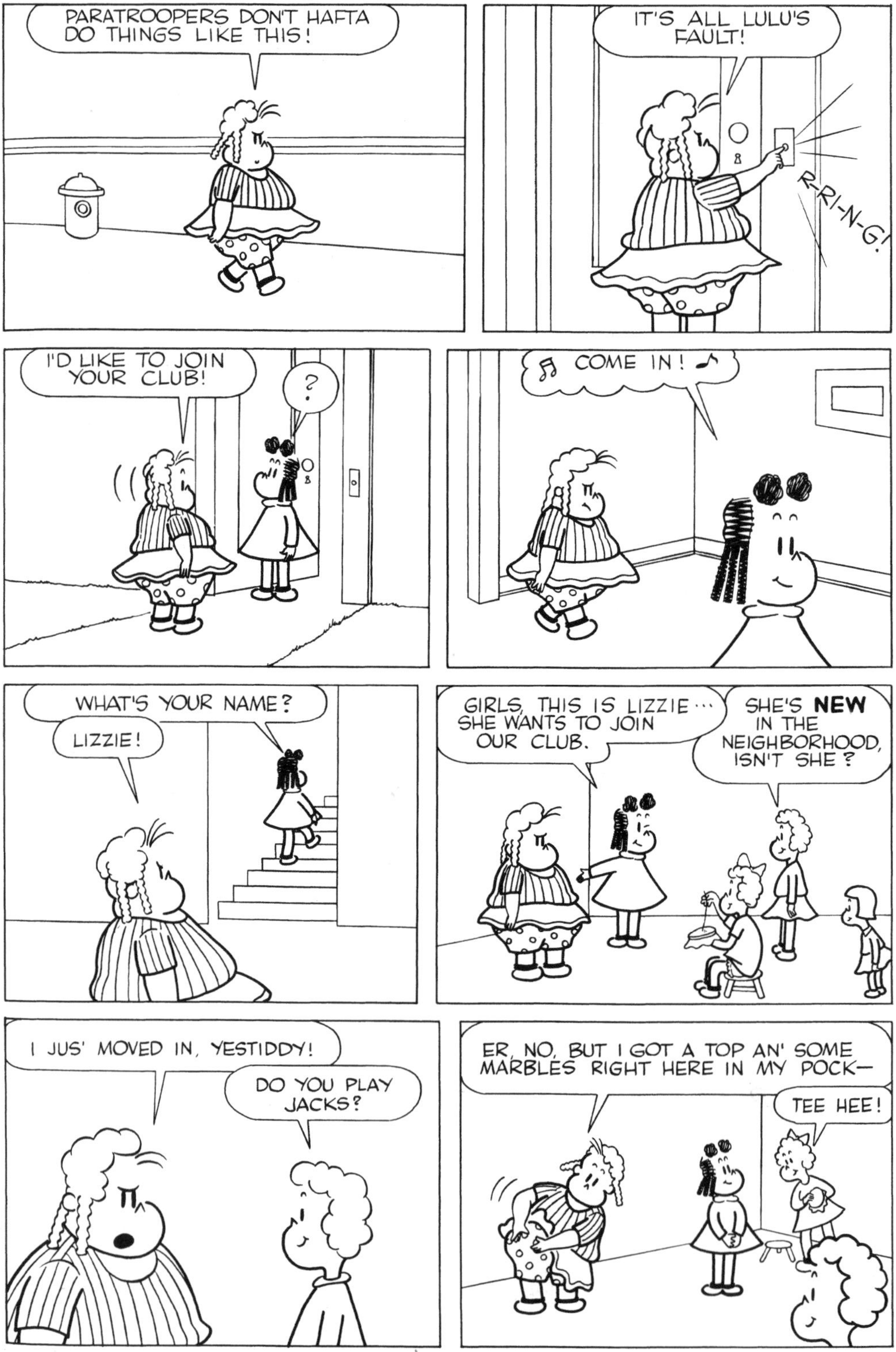
PARATROOPERS DON'T HAFTA DO THINGS LIKE THIS!
IT'S ALL LULU'S FAULT!
R-R-I-N-G!
I'D LIKE TO JOIN YOUR CLUB!
?
♫ COME IN! ♪
WHAT'S YOUR NAME?
LIZZIE!
GIRLS, THIS IS LIZZIE... SHE WANTS TO JOIN OUR CLUB.
SHE'S **NEW** IN THE NEIGHBORHOOD, ISN'T SHE?
I JUS' MOVED IN, YESTIDDY!
DO YOU PLAY JACKS?
ER, NO, BUT I GOT A TOP AN' SOME MARBLES RIGHT HERE IN MY POCK—
TEE HEE!

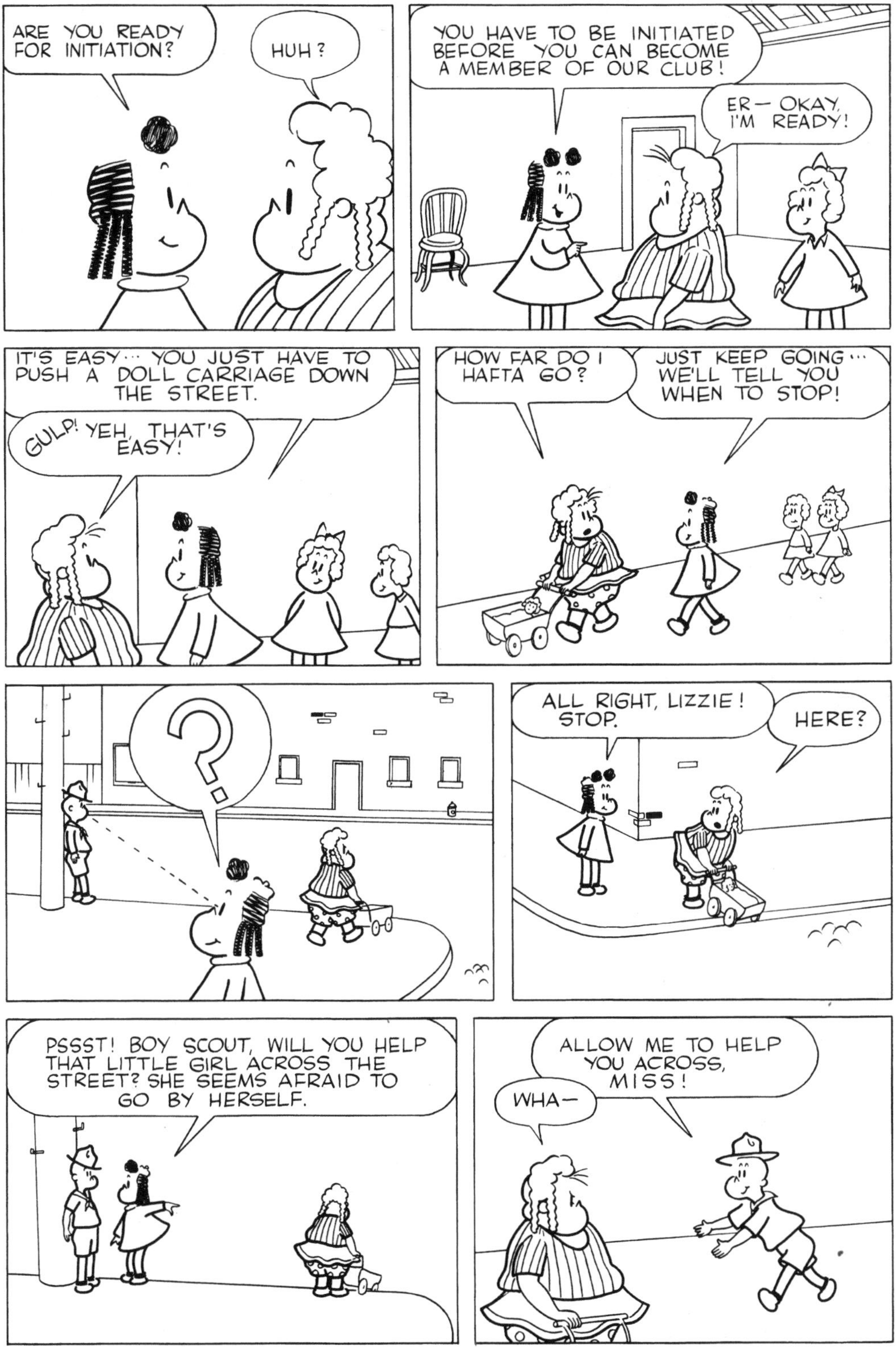
ARE YOU READY FOR INITIATION?
HUH?
YOU HAVE TO BE INITIATED BEFORE YOU CAN BECOME A MEMBER OF OUR CLUB!
ER— OKAY, I'M READY!
IT'S EASY... YOU JUST HAVE TO PUSH A DOLL CARRIAGE DOWN THE STREET.
GULP! YEH, THAT'S EASY!
HOW FAR DO I HAFTA GO?
JUST KEEP GOING... WE'LL TELL YOU WHEN TO STOP!
?
ALL RIGHT, LIZZIE! STOP.
HERE?
PSSST! BOY SCOUT, WILL YOU HELP THAT LITTLE GIRL ACROSS THE STREET? SHE SEEMS AFRAID TO GO BY HERSELF.
ALLOW ME TO HELP YOU ACROSS, MISS!
WHA—

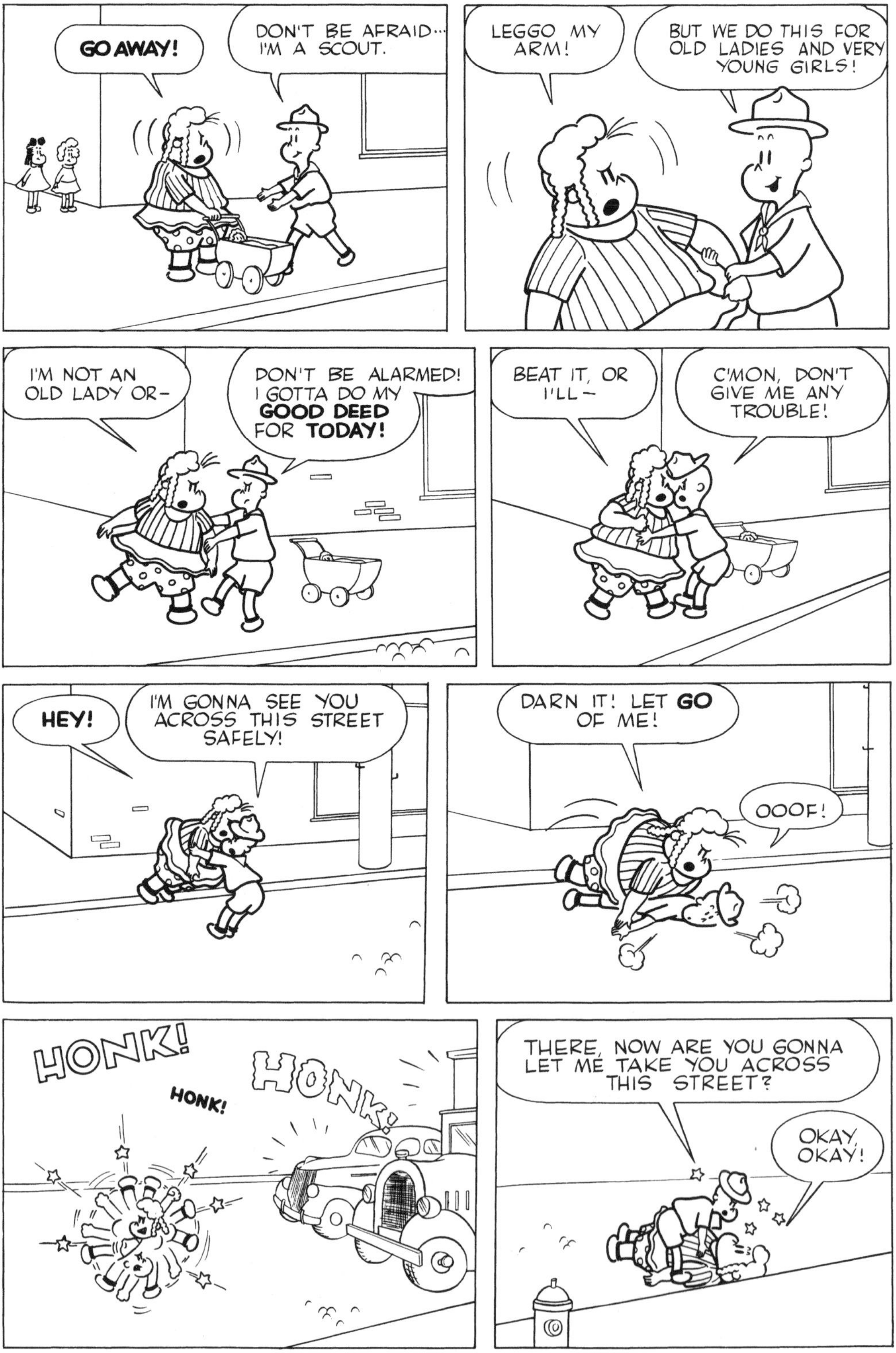
GO AWAY!
DON'T BE AFRAID... I'M A SCOUT.
LEGGO MY ARM!
BUT WE DO THIS FOR OLD LADIES AND VERY YOUNG GIRLS!
I'M NOT AN OLD LADY OR–
DON'T BE ALARMED! I GOTTA DO MY GOOD DEED FOR TODAY!
BEAT IT, OR I'LL–
C'MON, DON'T GIVE ME ANY TROUBLE!
HEY!
I'M GONNA SEE YOU ACROSS THIS STREET SAFELY!
DARN IT! LET GO OF ME!
OOOF!
HONK!
HONK!
HONK!
THERE, NOW ARE YOU GONNA LET ME TAKE YOU ACROSS THIS STREET?
OKAY, OKAY!

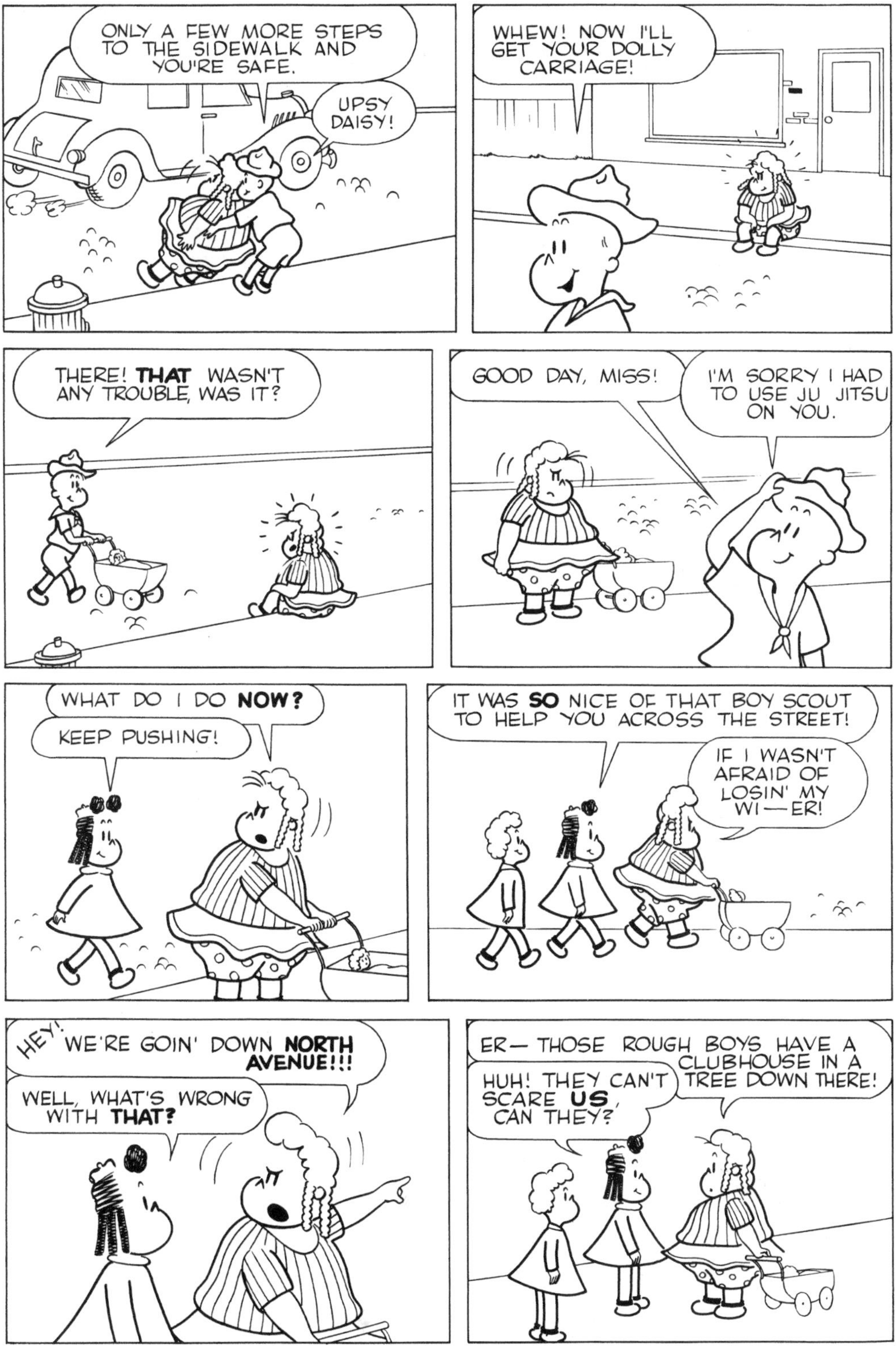
ONLY A FEW MORE STEPS TO THE SIDEWALK AND YOU'RE SAFE.
UPSY DAISY!
WHEW! NOW I'LL GET YOUR DOLLY CARRIAGE!
THERE! THAT WASN'T ANY TROUBLE, WAS IT?
GOOD DAY, MISS!
I'M SORRY I HAD TO USE JU JITSU ON YOU.
WHAT DO I DO NOW?
KEEP PUSHING!
IT WAS SO NICE OF THAT BOY SCOUT TO HELP YOU ACROSS THE STREET!
IF I WASN'T AFRAID OF LOSIN' MY WI—ER!
HEY! WE'RE GOIN' DOWN NORTH AVENUE!!!
WELL, WHAT'S WRONG WITH THAT?
ER— THOSE ROUGH BOYS HAVE A CLUBHOUSE IN A TREE DOWN THERE!
HUH! THEY CAN'T SCARE US, CAN THEY?

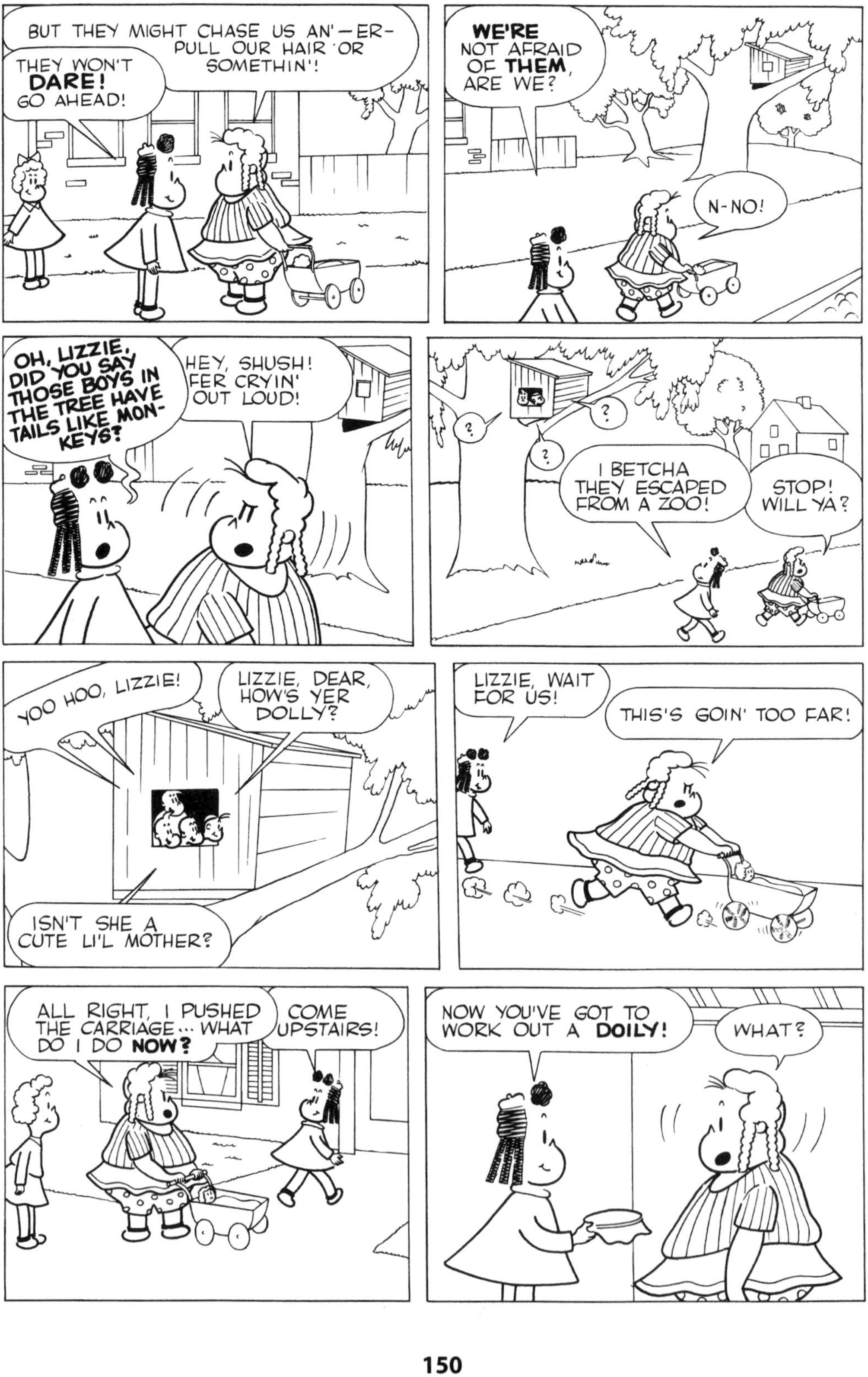

BUT THEY MIGHT CHASE US AN'—ER— PULL OUR HAIR OR SOMETHIN'!
THEY WON'T DARE! GO AHEAD!
WE'RE NOT AFRAID OF THEM, ARE WE?
N-NO!
OH, LIZZIE, DID YOU SAY THOSE BOYS IN THE TREE HAVE TAILS LIKE MON-KEYS?
HEY, SHUSH! FER CRYIN' OUT LOUD!
?
?
?
I BETCHA THEY ESCAPED FROM A ZOO!
STOP! WILL YA?
YOO HOO, LIZZIE!
LIZZIE, DEAR, HOW'S YER DOLLY?
ISN'T SHE A CUTE LI'L MOTHER?
LIZZIE, WAIT FOR US!
THIS'S GOIN' TOO FAR!
ALL RIGHT, I PUSHED THE CARRIAGE... WHAT DO I DO NOW?
COME UPSTAIRS!
NOW YOU'VE GOT TO WORK OUT A DOILY!
WHAT?

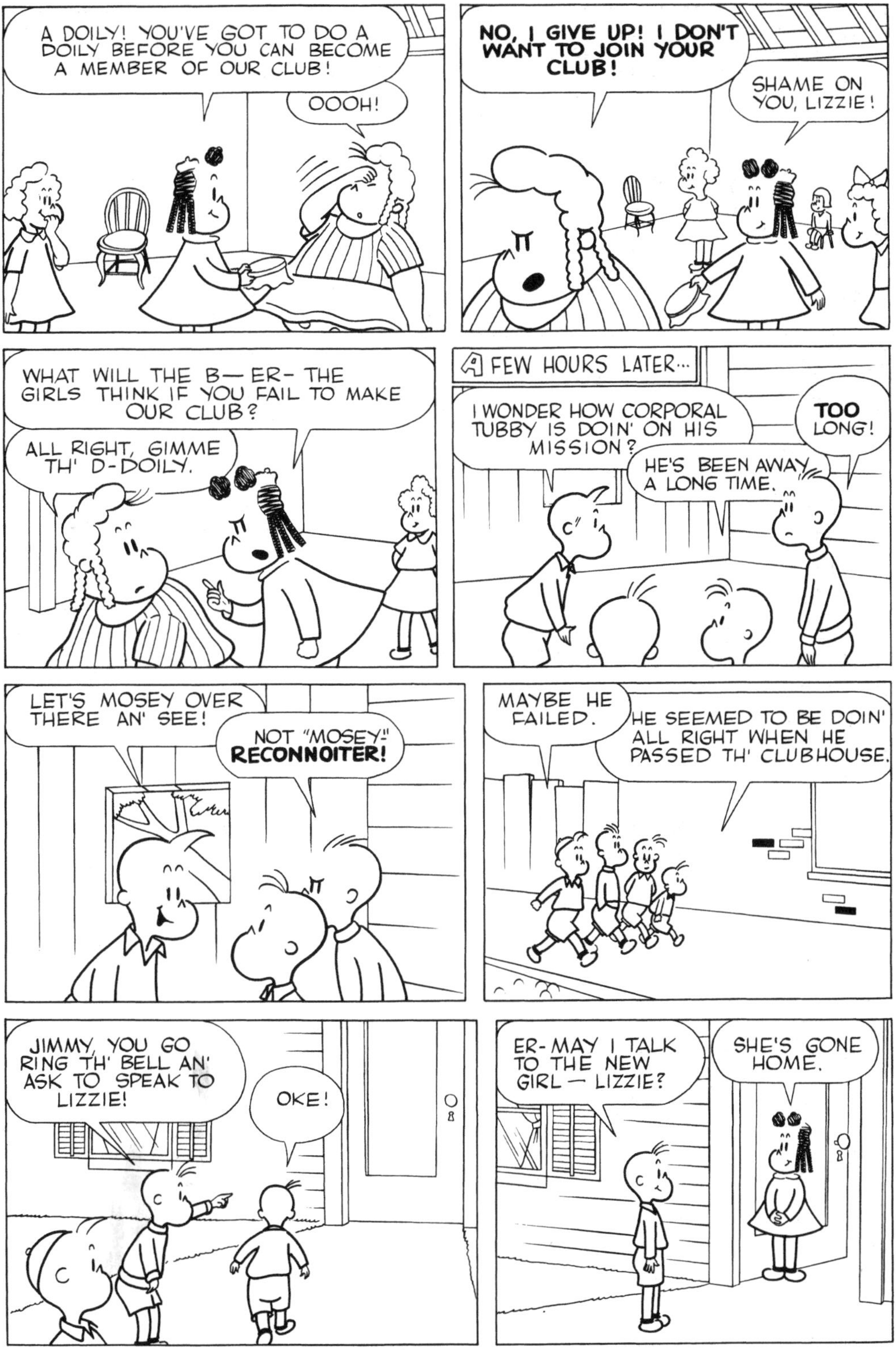
A DOILY! YOU'VE GOT TO DO A DOILY BEFORE YOU CAN BECOME A MEMBER OF OUR CLUB!
OOOH!
NO, I GIVE UP! I DON'T WANT TO JOIN YOUR CLUB!
SHAME ON YOU, LIZZIE!
WHAT WILL THE B— ER— THE GIRLS THINK IF YOU FAIL TO MAKE OUR CLUB?
ALL RIGHT, GIMME TH' D-DOILY.
A FEW HOURS LATER...
I WONDER HOW CORPORAL TUBBY IS DOIN' ON HIS MISSION?
HE'S BEEN AWAY A LONG TIME.
TOO LONG!
LET'S MOSEY OVER THERE AN' SEE!
NOT "MOSEY!" RECONNOITER!
MAYBE HE FAILED.
HE SEEMED TO BE DOIN' ALL RIGHT WHEN HE PASSED TH' CLUBHOUSE.
JIMMY, YOU GO RING TH' BELL AN' ASK TO SPEAK TO LIZZIE!
OKE!
ER-MAY I TALK TO THE NEW GIRL — LIZZIE?
SHE'S GONE HOME.

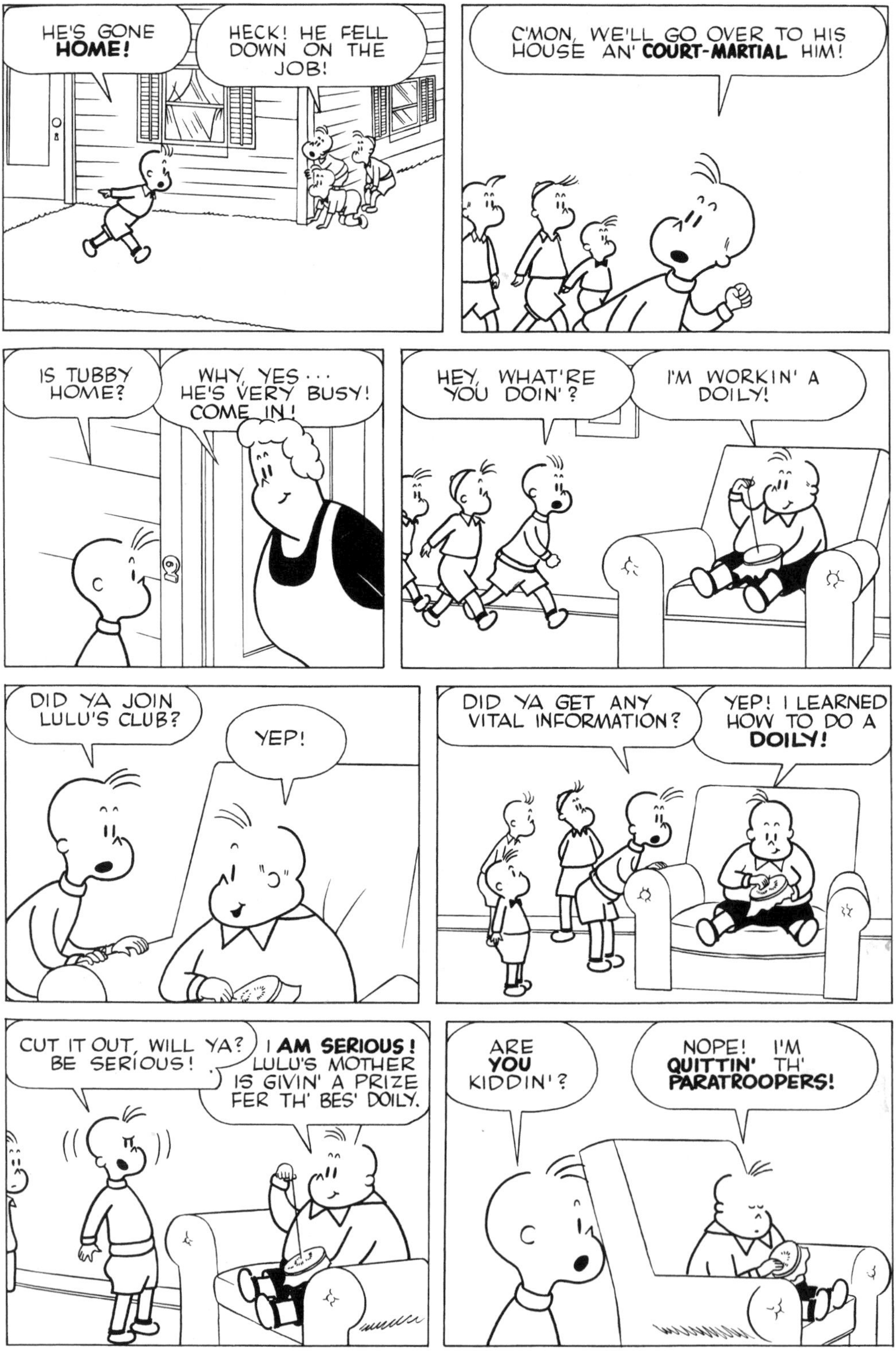
HE'S GONE **HOME!**
HECK! HE FELL DOWN ON THE JOB!
C'MON, WE'LL GO OVER TO HIS HOUSE AN' **COURT-MARTIAL** HIM!
IS TUBBY HOME?
WHY, YES... HE'S VERY BUSY! COME IN!
HEY, WHAT'RE YOU DOIN'?
I'M WORKIN' A DOILY!
DID YA JOIN LULU'S CLUB?
YEP!
DID YA GET ANY VITAL INFORMATION?
YEP! I LEARNED HOW TO DO A **DOILY!**
CUT IT OUT, WILL YA? BE SERIOUS!
I **AM SERIOUS!** LULU'S MOTHER IS GIVIN' A PRIZE FER TH' BES' DOILY.
ARE **YOU** KIDDIN'?
NOPE! I'M **QUITTIN'** TH' **PARATROOPERS!**

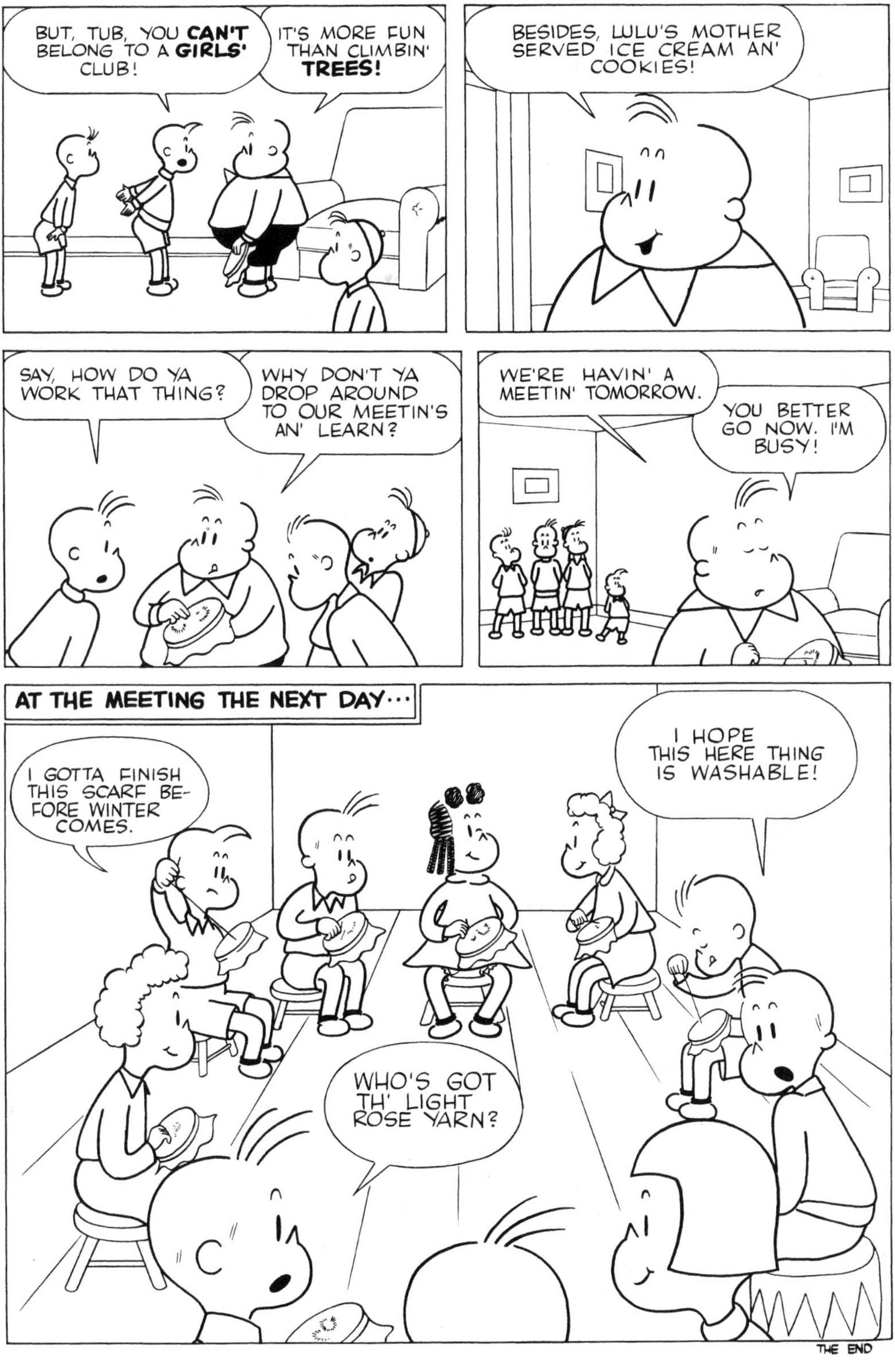
BUT, TUB, YOU **CAN'T** BELONG TO A **GIRLS'** CLUB!
IT'S MORE FUN THAN CLIMBIN' **TREES!**
BESIDES, LULU'S MOTHER SERVED ICE CREAM AN' COOKIES!
SAY, HOW DO YA WORK THAT THING?
WHY DON'T YA DROP AROUND TO OUR MEETIN'S AN' LEARN?
WE'RE HAVIN' A MEETIN' TOMORROW.
YOU BETTER GO NOW. I'M BUSY!
AT THE MEETING THE NEXT DAY···
I GOTTA FINISH THIS SCARF BE-FORE WINTER COMES.
I HOPE THIS HERE THING IS WASHABLE!
WHO'S GOT TH' LIGHT ROSE YARN?
THE END

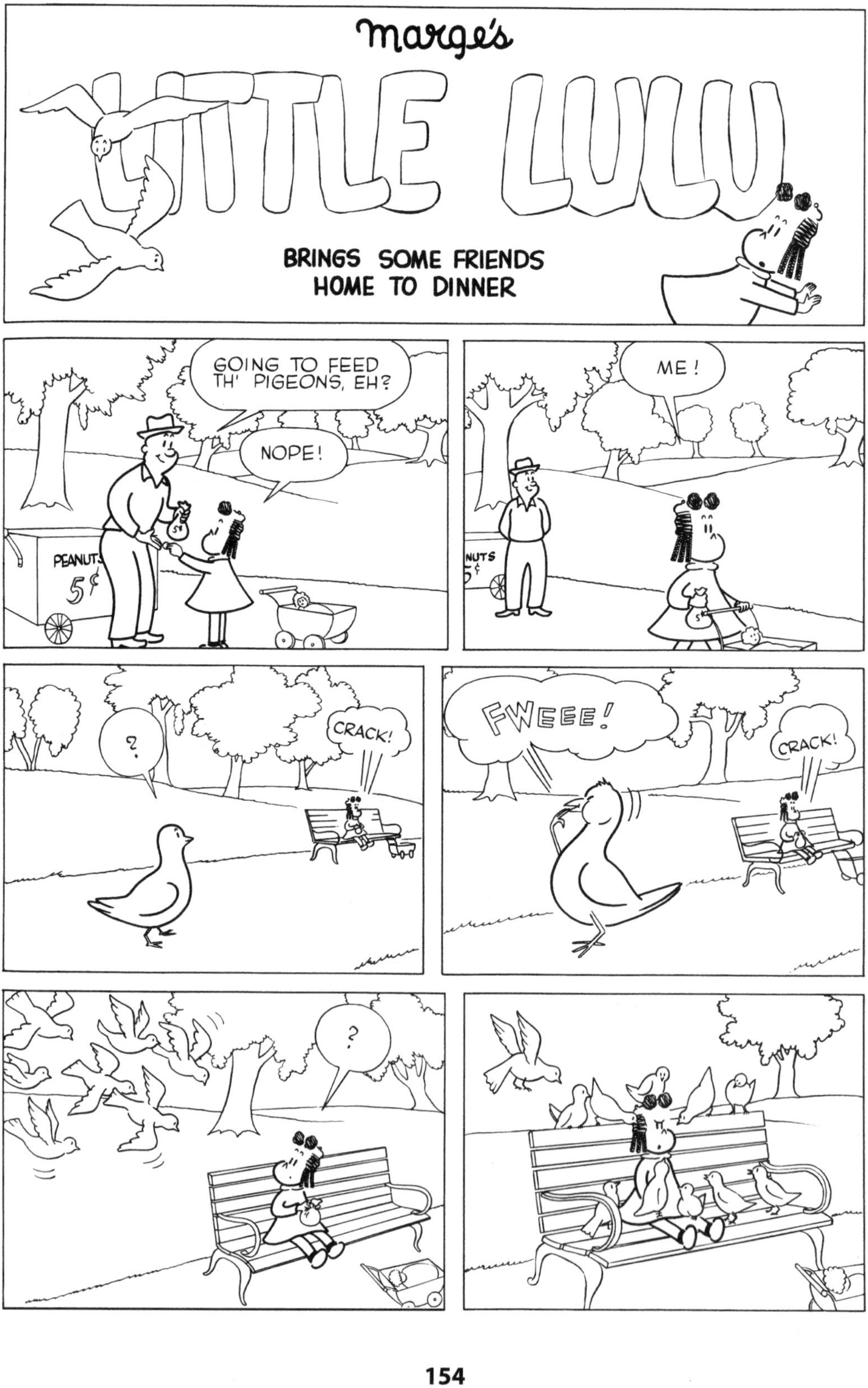
marge's
LITTLE LULU
BRINGS SOME FRIENDS
HOME TO DINNER
GOING TO FEED
TH' PIGEONS, EH?
NOPE!
PEANUTS
5¢
ME!
?
CRACK!
FWEEE!
CRACK!
?

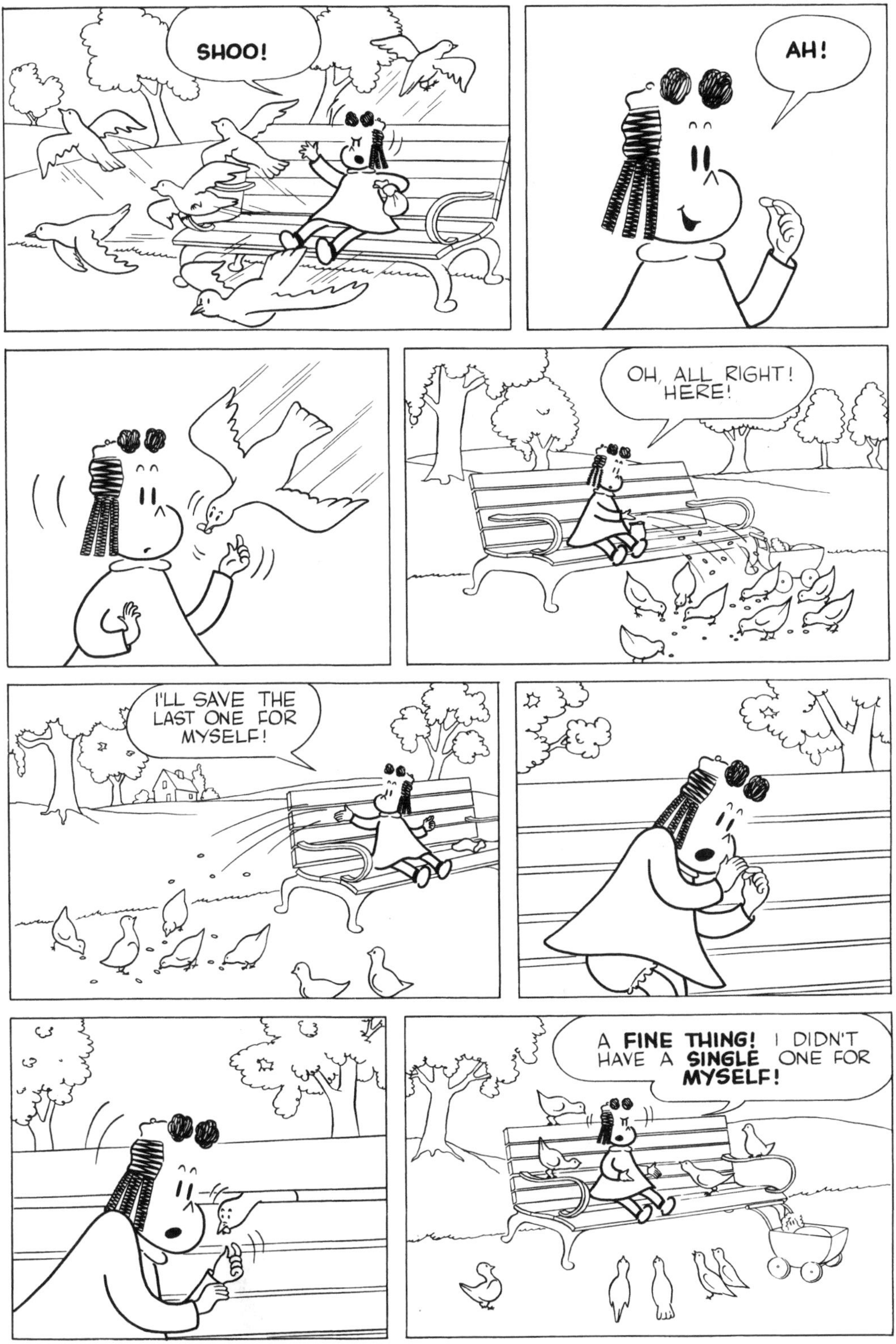
SHOO!
AH!
OH, ALL RIGHT! HERE!
I'LL SAVE THE LAST ONE FOR MYSELF!
A **FINE THING!** I DIDN'T HAVE A **SINGLE** ONE FOR **MYSELF!**

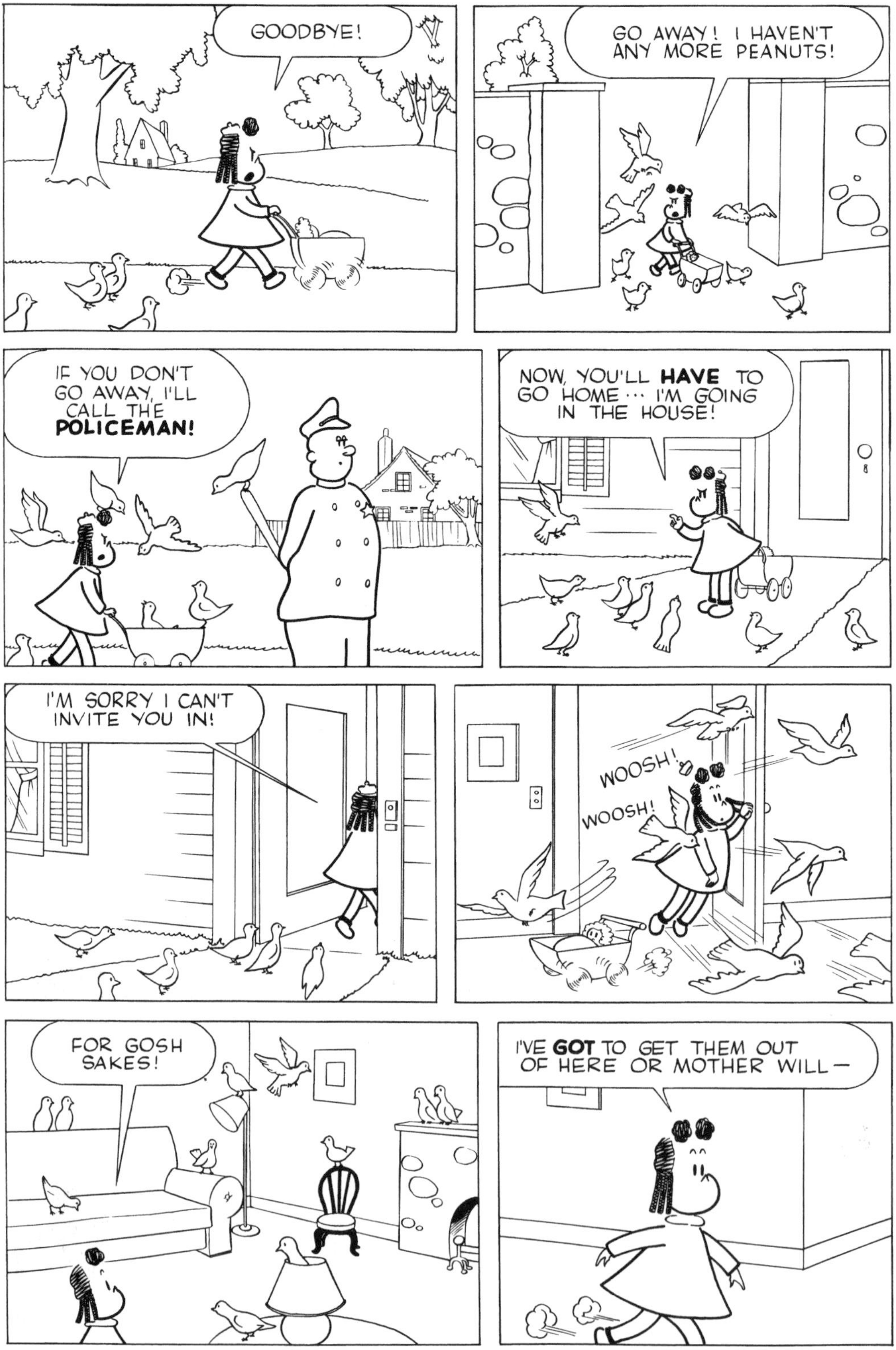
GOODBYE!
GO AWAY! I HAVEN'T ANY MORE PEANUTS!
IF YOU DON'T GO AWAY, I'LL CALL THE **POLICEMAN!**
NOW, YOU'LL **HAVE** TO GO HOME ··· I'M GOING IN THE HOUSE!
I'M SORRY I CAN'T INVITE YOU IN!
WOOSH!
WOOSH!
FOR GOSH SAKES!
I'VE **GOT** TO GET THEM OUT OF HERE OR MOTHER WILL—

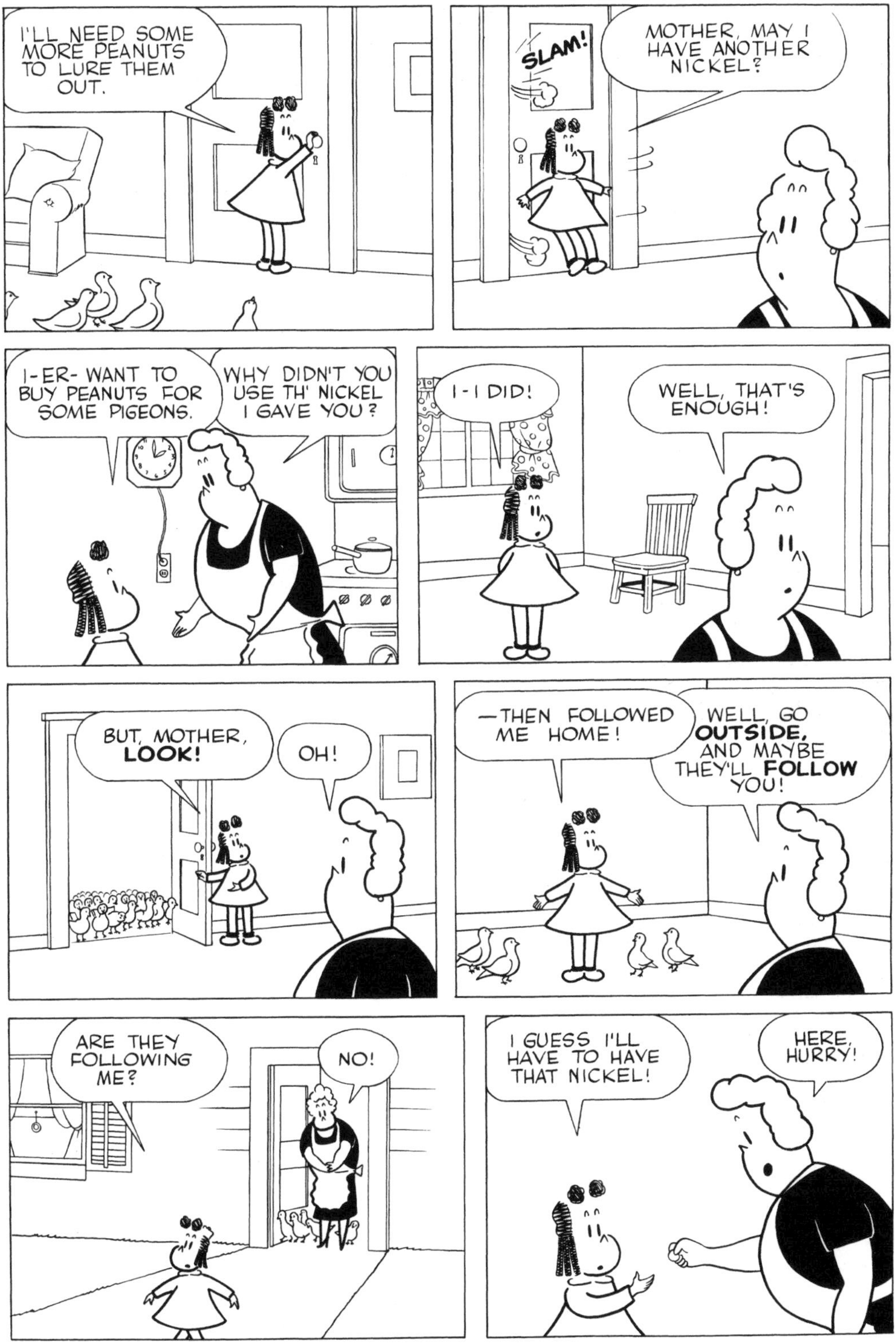
I'LL NEED SOME MORE PEANUTS TO LURE THEM OUT.
SLAM!
MOTHER, MAY I HAVE ANOTHER NICKEL?
I-ER- WANT TO BUY PEANUTS FOR SOME PIGEONS.
WHY DIDN'T YOU USE TH' NICKEL I GAVE YOU?
I-I DID!
WELL, THAT'S ENOUGH!
BUT, MOTHER, LOOK!
OH!
—THEN FOLLOWED ME HOME!
WELL, GO OUTSIDE, AND MAYBE THEY'LL FOLLOW YOU!
ARE THEY FOLLOWING ME?
NO!
I GUESS I'LL HAVE TO HAVE THAT NICKEL!
HERE, HURRY!

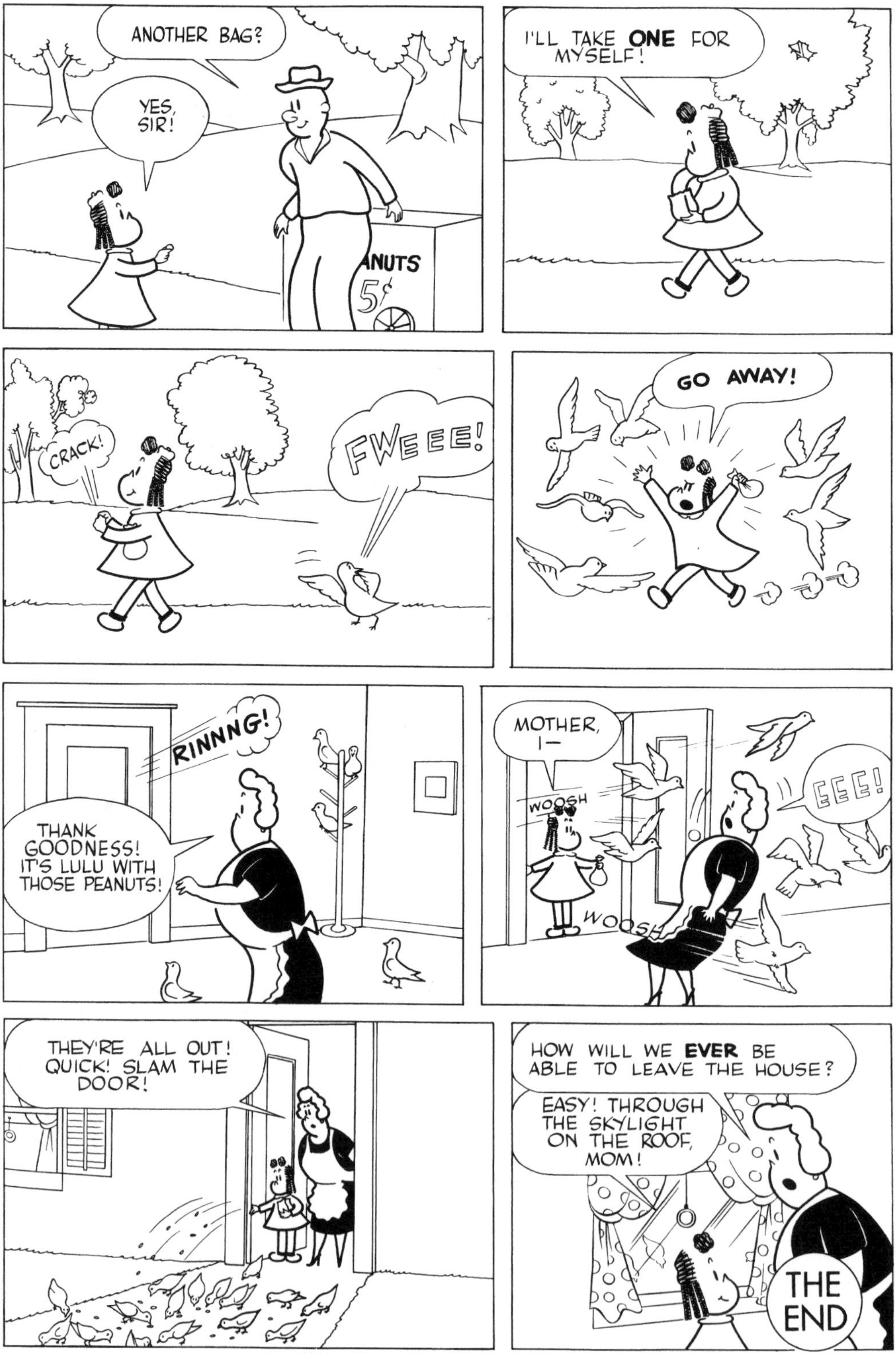
ANOTHER BAG?
YES, SIR!
ANUTS 5¢
I'LL TAKE ONE FOR MYSELF!
CRACK!
FWEEE!
GO AWAY!
RINNNG!
THANK GOODNESS! IT'S LULU WITH THOSE PEANUTS!
MOTHER, I—
WOOSH
EEE!
WOOSH
THEY'RE ALL OUT! QUICK! SLAM THE DOOR!
HOW WILL WE EVER BE ABLE TO LEAVE THE HOUSE?
EASY! THROUGH THE SKYLIGHT ON THE ROOF, MOM!
THE END

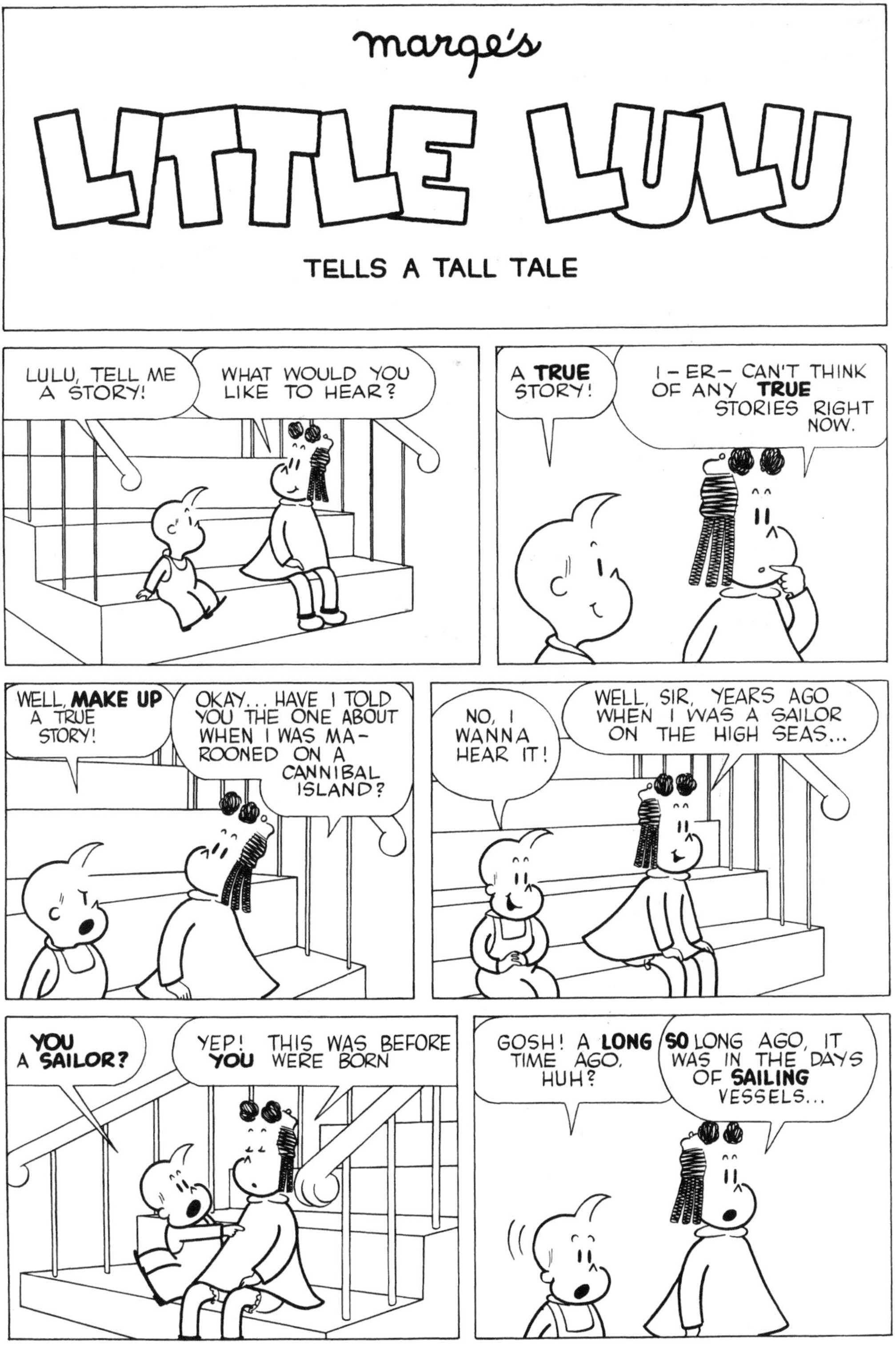
marge's
LITTLE LULU
TELLS A TALL TALE
LULU, TELL ME A STORY!
WHAT WOULD YOU LIKE TO HEAR?
A TRUE STORY!
I—ER— CAN'T THINK OF ANY TRUE STORIES RIGHT NOW.
WELL, MAKE UP A TRUE STORY!
OKAY... HAVE I TOLD YOU THE ONE ABOUT WHEN I WAS MA-ROONED ON A CANNIBAL ISLAND?
NO, I WANNA HEAR IT!
WELL, SIR, YEARS AGO WHEN I WAS A SAILOR ON THE HIGH SEAS...
YOU A SAILOR?
YEP! THIS WAS BEFORE YOU WERE BORN
GOSH! A LONG TIME AGO, HUH?
SO LONG AGO, IT WAS IN THE DAYS OF SAILING VESSELS...

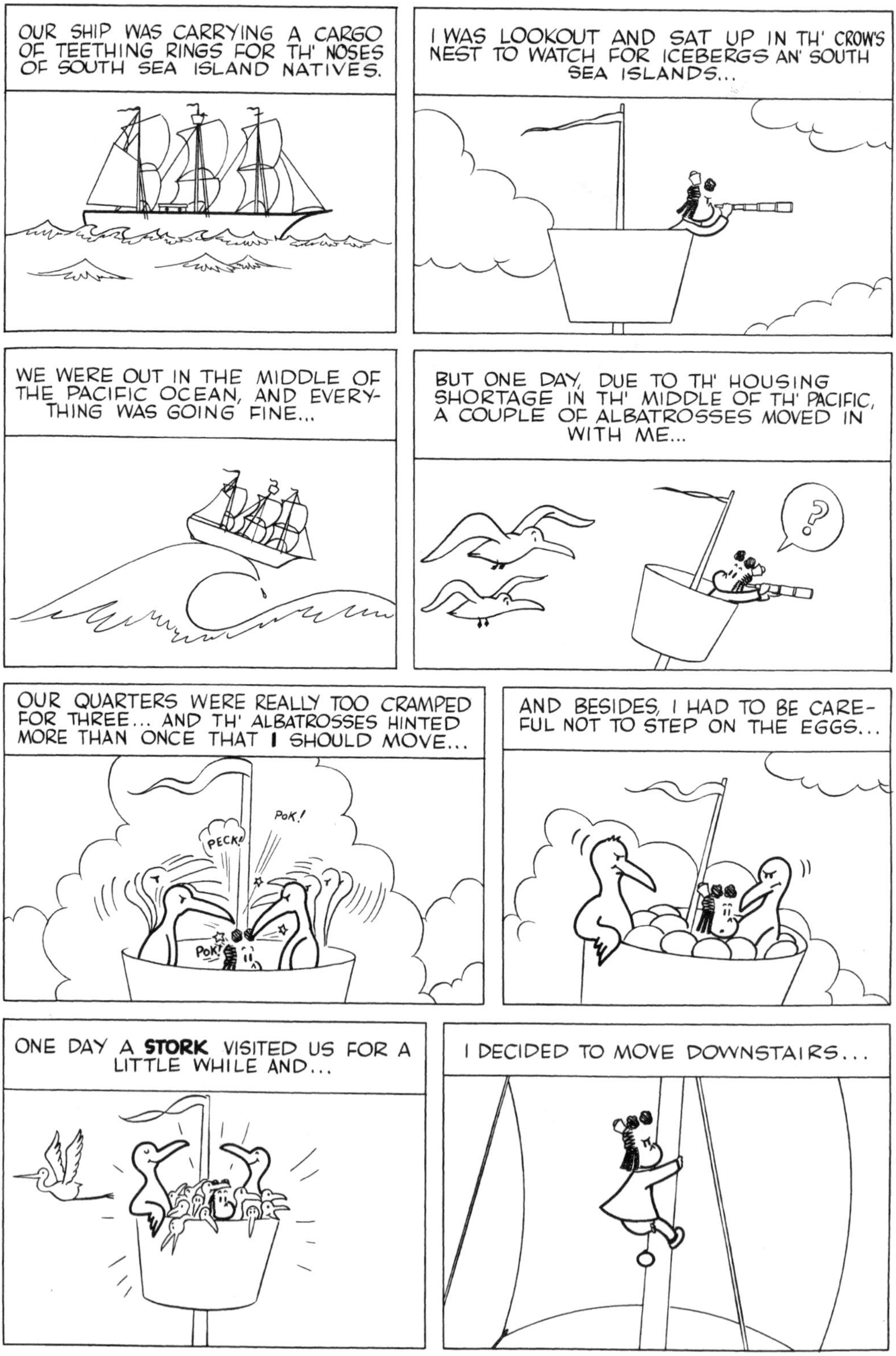

OUR SHIP WAS CARRYING A CARGO OF TEETHING RINGS FOR TH' NOSES OF SOUTH SEA ISLAND NATIVES.
I WAS LOOKOUT AND SAT UP IN TH' CROW'S NEST TO WATCH FOR ICEBERGS AN' SOUTH SEA ISLANDS...
WE WERE OUT IN THE MIDDLE OF THE PACIFIC OCEAN, AND EVERY-THING WAS GOING FINE...
BUT ONE DAY, DUE TO TH' HOUSING SHORTAGE IN TH' MIDDLE OF TH' PACIFIC, A COUPLE OF ALBATROSSES MOVED IN WITH ME...
?
OUR QUARTERS WERE REALLY TOO CRAMPED FOR THREE... AND TH' ALBATROSSES HINTED MORE THAN ONCE THAT I SHOULD MOVE...
POK!
PECK!
POK!
AND BESIDES, I HAD TO BE CARE-FUL NOT TO STEP ON THE EGGS...
ONE DAY A **STORK** VISITED US FOR A LITTLE WHILE AND...
I DECIDED TO MOVE DOWNSTAIRS...

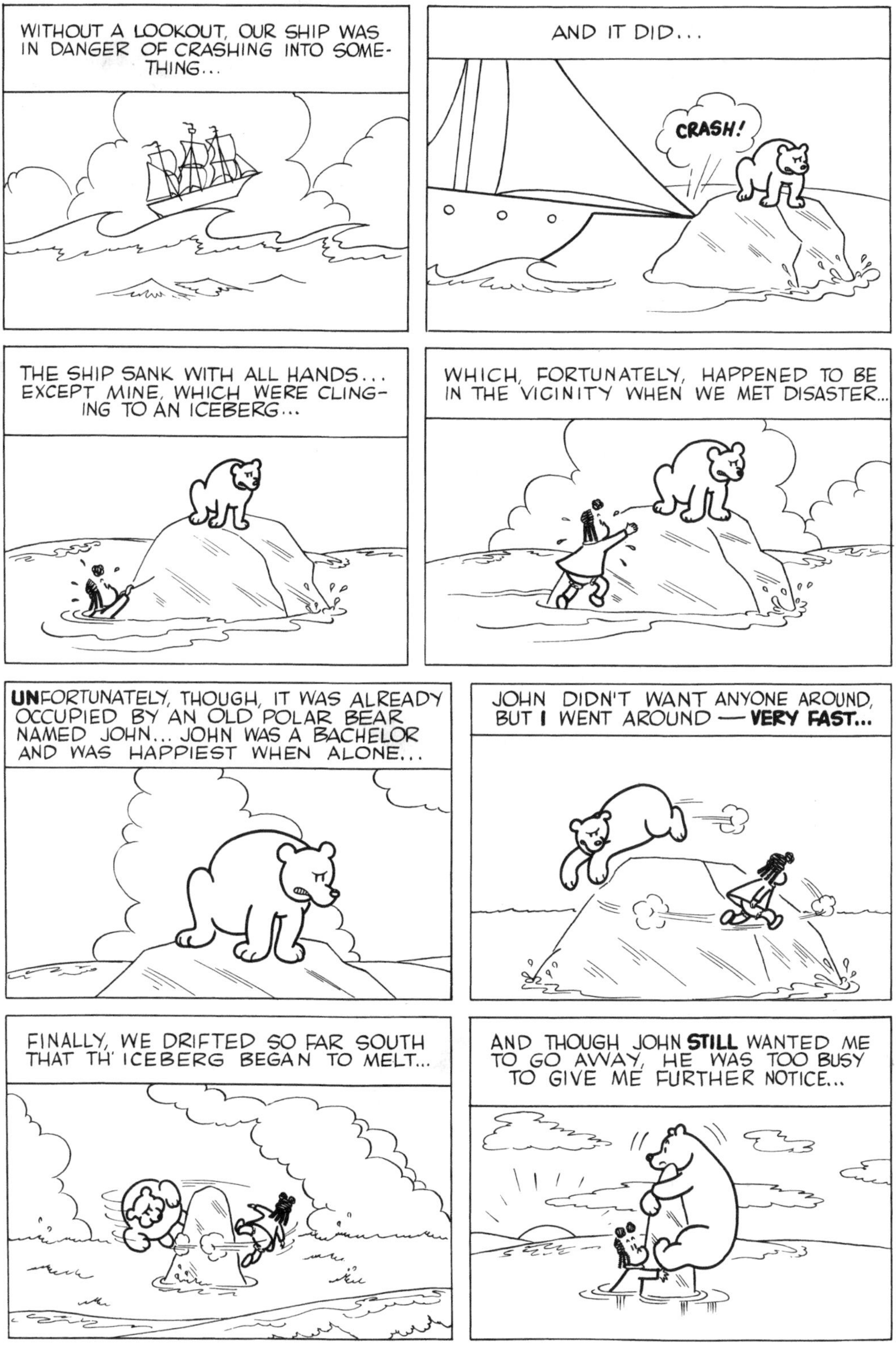
WITHOUT A LOOKOUT, OUR SHIP WAS IN DANGER OF CRASHING INTO SOMETHING...
AND IT DID...
CRASH!
THE SHIP SANK WITH ALL HANDS... EXCEPT MINE, WHICH WERE CLINGING TO AN ICEBERG...
WHICH, FORTUNATELY, HAPPENED TO BE IN THE VICINITY WHEN WE MET DISASTER...
UNFORTUNATELY, THOUGH, IT WAS ALREADY OCCUPIED BY AN OLD POLAR BEAR NAMED JOHN... JOHN WAS A BACHELOR AND WAS HAPPIEST WHEN ALONE...
JOHN DIDN'T WANT ANYONE AROUND, BUT I WENT AROUND — VERY FAST...
FINALLY, WE DRIFTED SO FAR SOUTH THAT TH' ICEBERG BEGAN TO MELT...
AND THOUGH JOHN STILL WANTED ME TO GO AWAY, HE WAS TOO BUSY TO GIVE ME FURTHER NOTICE...

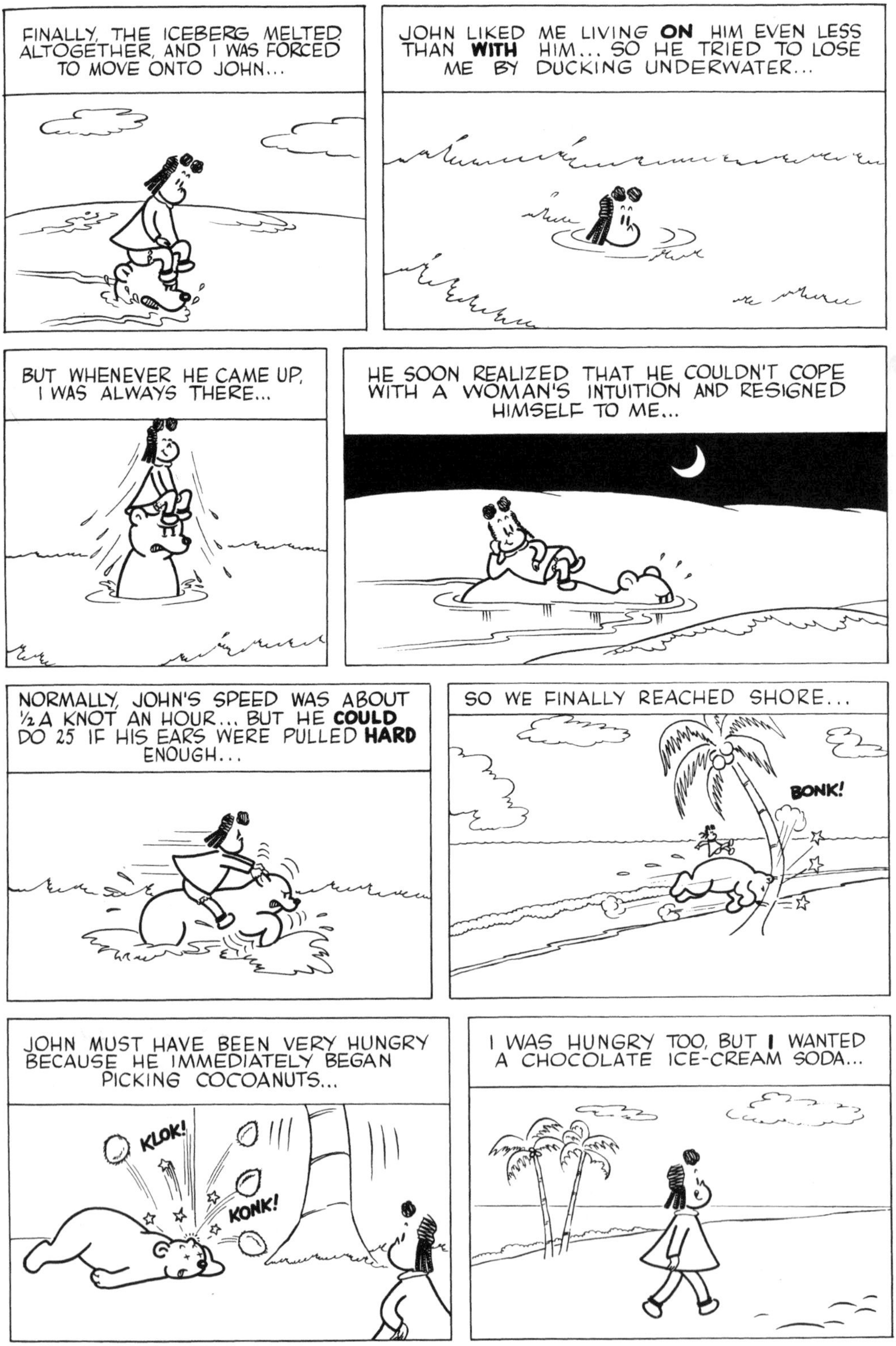
FINALLY, THE ICEBERG MELTED ALTOGETHER, AND I WAS FORCED TO MOVE ONTO JOHN...
JOHN LIKED ME LIVING **ON** HIM EVEN LESS THAN **WITH** HIM... SO HE TRIED TO LOSE ME BY DUCKING UNDERWATER...
BUT WHENEVER HE CAME UP, I WAS ALWAYS THERE...
HE SOON REALIZED THAT HE COULDN'T COPE WITH A WOMAN'S INTUITION AND RESIGNED HIMSELF TO ME...
NORMALLY, JOHN'S SPEED WAS ABOUT ½ A KNOT AN HOUR... BUT HE **COULD** DO 25 IF HIS EARS WERE PULLED **HARD** ENOUGH...
SO WE FINALLY REACHED SHORE...
BONK!
JOHN MUST HAVE BEEN VERY HUNGRY BECAUSE HE IMMEDIATELY BEGAN PICKING COCOANUTS...
KLOK!
KONK!
I WAS HUNGRY TOO, BUT **I** WANTED A CHOCOLATE ICE-CREAM SODA...

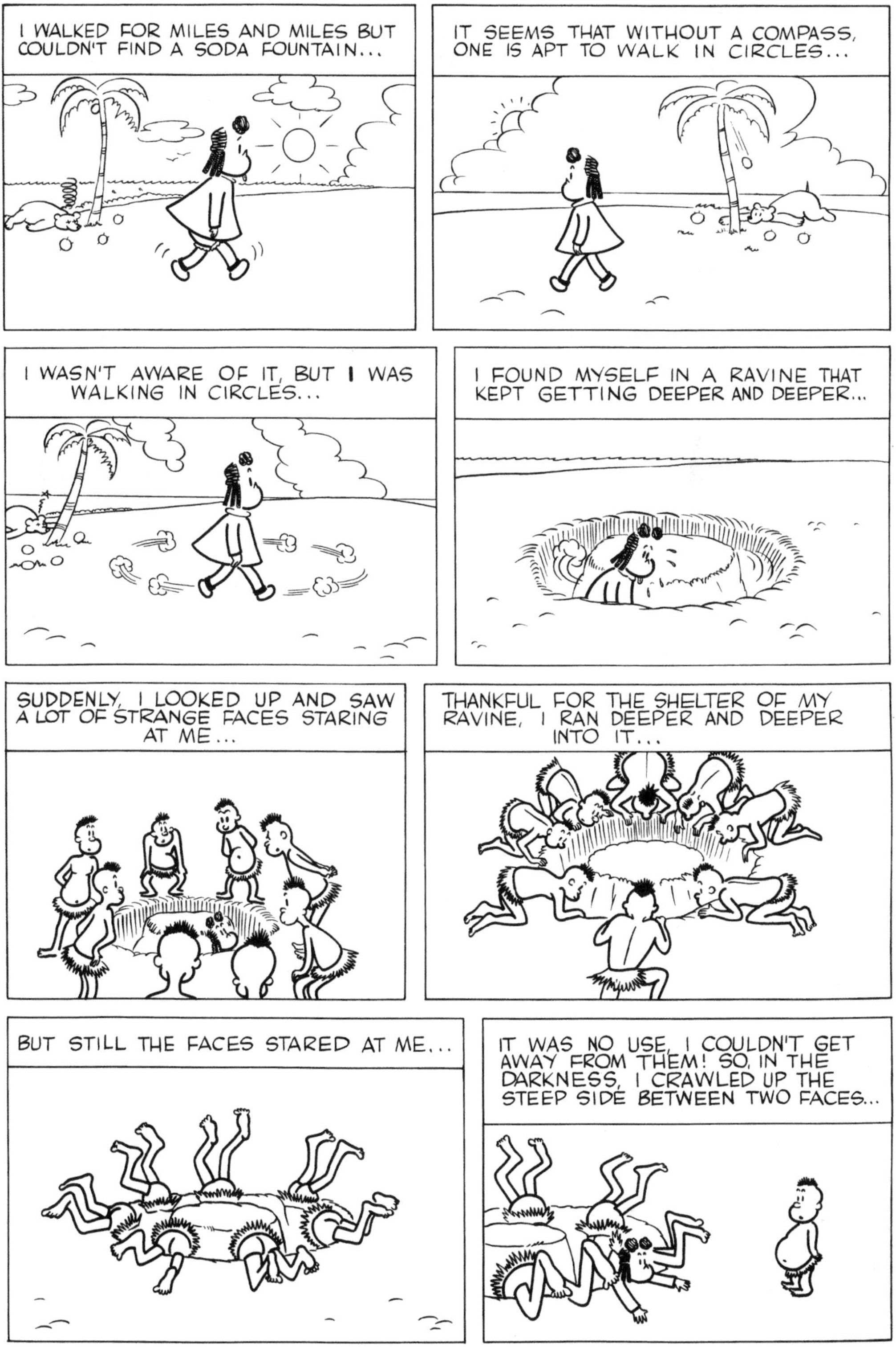
I WALKED FOR MILES AND MILES BUT COULDN'T FIND A SODA FOUNTAIN...
IT SEEMS THAT WITHOUT A COMPASS, ONE IS APT TO WALK IN CIRCLES...
I WASN'T AWARE OF IT, BUT I WAS WALKING IN CIRCLES...
I FOUND MYSELF IN A RAVINE THAT KEPT GETTING DEEPER AND DEEPER...
SUDDENLY, I LOOKED UP AND SAW A LOT OF STRANGE FACES STARING AT ME...
THANKFUL FOR THE SHELTER OF MY RAVINE, I RAN DEEPER AND DEEPER INTO IT...
BUT STILL THE FACES STARED AT ME...
IT WAS NO USE, I COULDN'T GET AWAY FROM THEM! SO, IN THE DARKNESS, I CRAWLED UP THE STEEP SIDE BETWEEN TWO FACES...

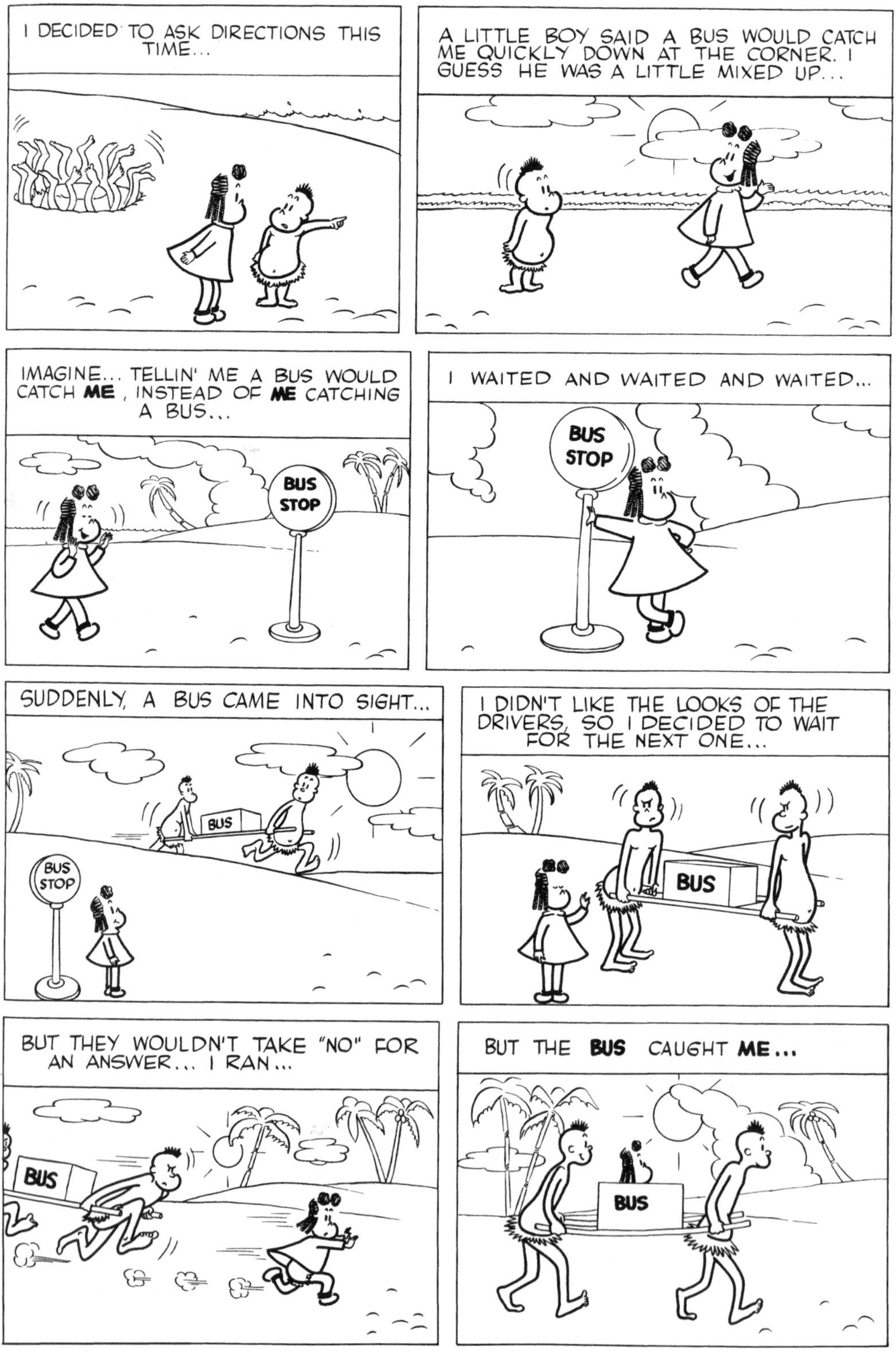
I DECIDED TO ASK DIRECTIONS THIS TIME...
A LITTLE BOY SAID A BUS WOULD CATCH ME QUICKLY DOWN AT THE CORNER. I GUESS HE WAS A LITTLE MIXED UP...
IMAGINE... TELLIN' ME A BUS WOULD CATCH **ME**, INSTEAD OF **ME** CATCHING A BUS...
BUS STOP
I WAITED AND WAITED AND WAITED...
BUS STOP
SUDDENLY, A BUS CAME INTO SIGHT...
BUS
BUS STOP
I DIDN'T LIKE THE LOOKS OF THE DRIVERS, SO I DECIDED TO WAIT FOR THE NEXT ONE...
BUS
BUT THEY WOULDN'T TAKE "NO" FOR AN ANSWER... I RAN...
BUS
BUT THE **BUS** CAUGHT **ME**...
BUS

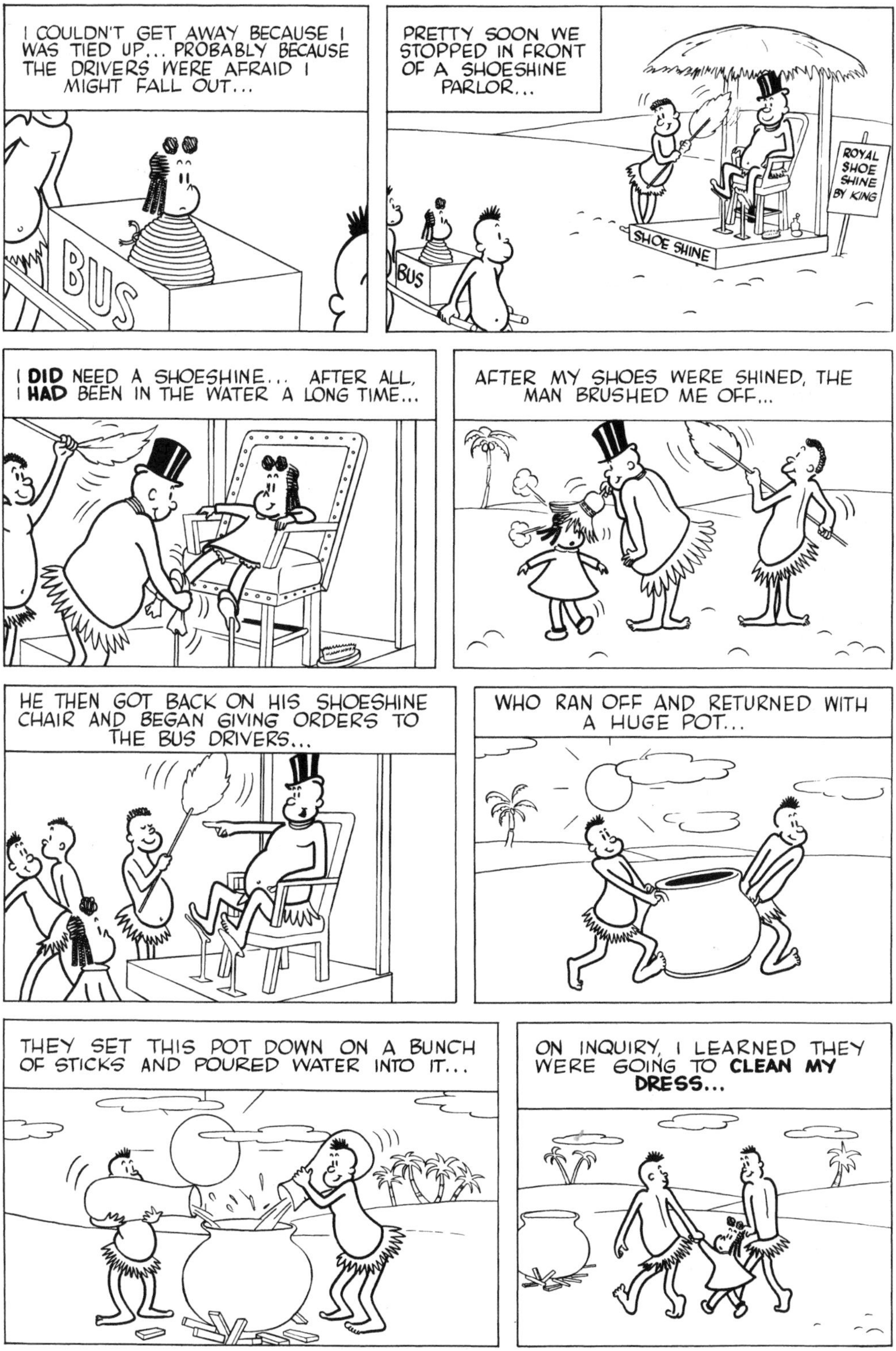
I COULDN'T GET AWAY BECAUSE I WAS TIED UP... PROBABLY BECAUSE THE DRIVERS WERE AFRAID I MIGHT FALL OUT...
BUS
PRETTY SOON WE STOPPED IN FRONT OF A SHOESHINE PARLOR...
BUS
SHOE SHINE
ROYAL SHOE SHINE BY KING
I DID NEED A SHOESHINE... AFTER ALL, I HAD BEEN IN THE WATER A LONG TIME...
AFTER MY SHOES WERE SHINED, THE MAN BRUSHED ME OFF...
HE THEN GOT BACK ON HIS SHOESHINE CHAIR AND BEGAN GIVING ORDERS TO THE BUS DRIVERS...
WHO RAN OFF AND RETURNED WITH A HUGE POT...
THEY SET THIS POT DOWN ON A BUNCH OF STICKS AND POURED WATER INTO IT...
ON INQUIRY, I LEARNED THEY WERE GOING TO CLEAN MY DRESS...

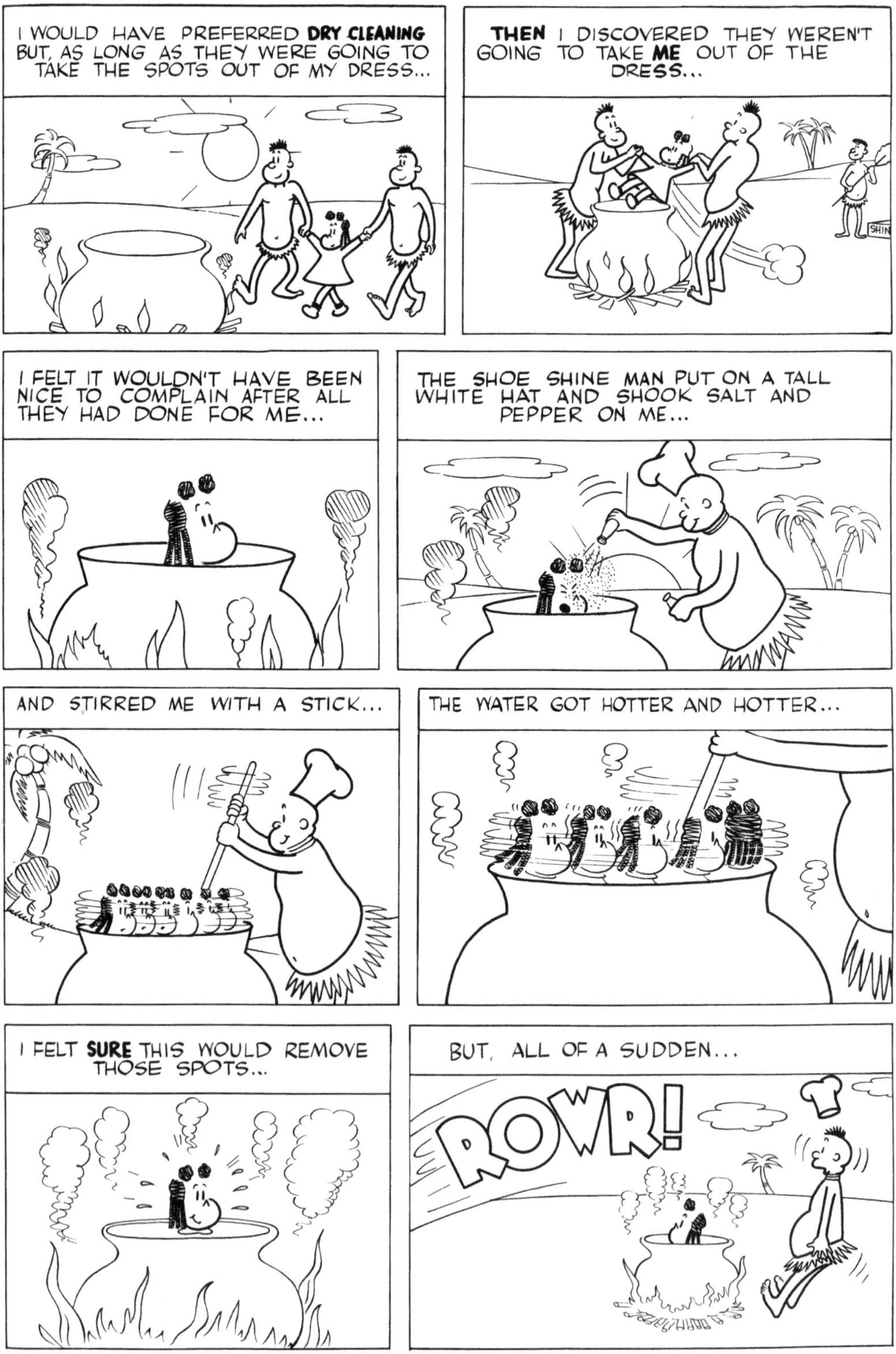
I WOULD HAVE PREFERRED **DRY CLEANING** BUT, AS LONG AS THEY WERE GOING TO TAKE THE SPOTS OUT OF MY DRESS...
THEN I DISCOVERED THEY WEREN'T GOING TO TAKE **ME** OUT OF THE DRESS...
SHIN
I FELT IT WOULDN'T HAVE BEEN NICE TO COMPLAIN AFTER ALL THEY HAD DONE FOR ME...
THE SHOE SHINE MAN PUT ON A TALL WHITE HAT AND SHOOK SALT AND PEPPER ON ME...
AND STIRRED ME WITH A STICK...
THE WATER GOT HOTTER AND HOTTER...
I FELT **SURE** THIS WOULD REMOVE THOSE SPOTS...
BUT, ALL OF A SUDDEN...
ROWR!

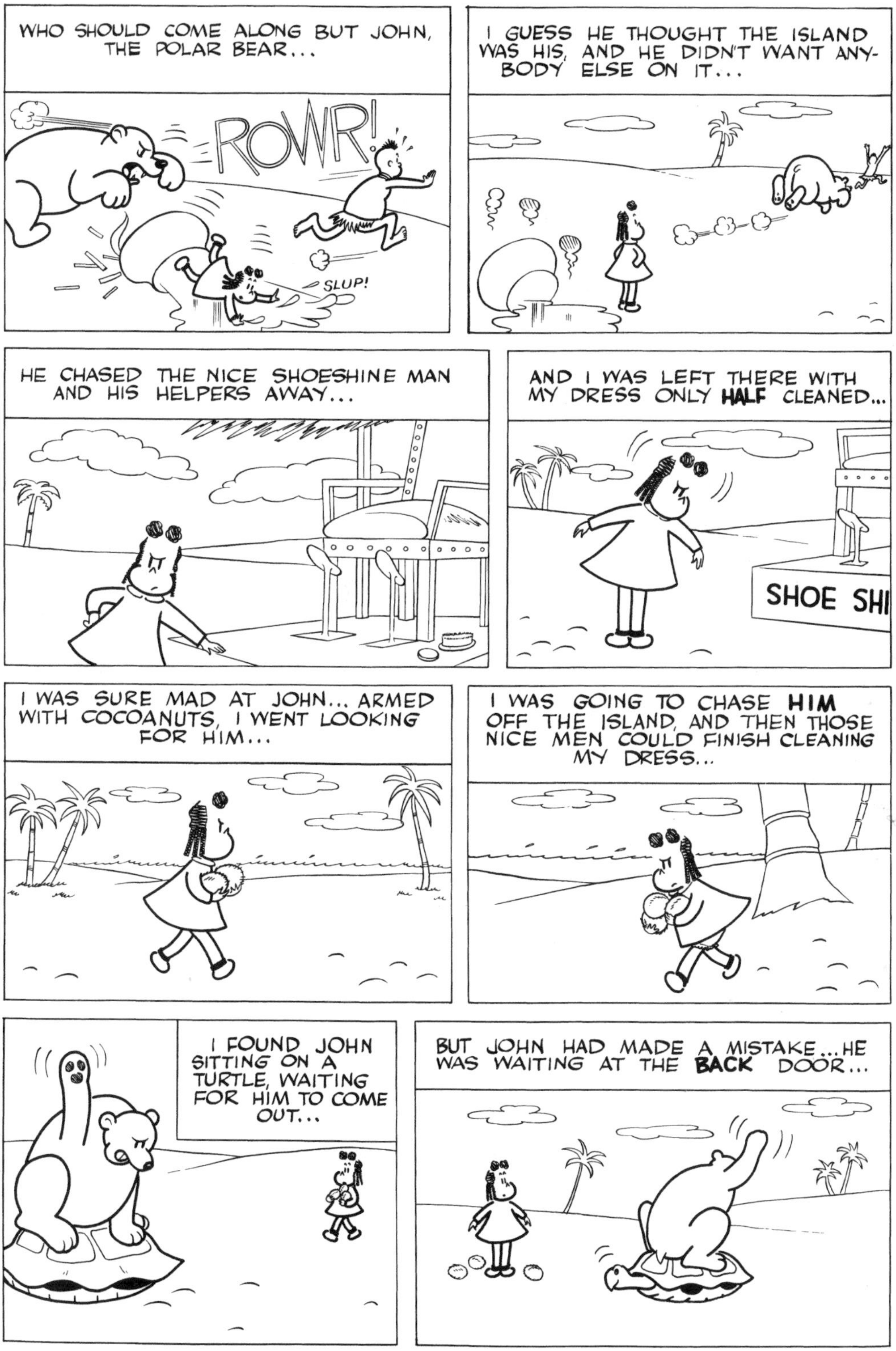
WHO SHOULD COME ALONG BUT JOHN, THE POLAR BEAR...
ROWR!
SLUP!
I GUESS HE THOUGHT THE ISLAND WAS HIS, AND HE DIDN'T WANT ANY-BODY ELSE ON IT...
HE CHASED THE NICE SHOESHINE MAN AND HIS HELPERS AWAY...
AND I WAS LEFT THERE WITH MY DRESS ONLY HALF CLEANED...
SHOE SHI
I WAS SURE MAD AT JOHN... ARMED WITH COCOANUTS, I WENT LOOKING FOR HIM...
I WAS GOING TO CHASE HIM OFF THE ISLAND, AND THEN THOSE NICE MEN COULD FINISH CLEANING MY DRESS...
I FOUND JOHN SITTING ON A TURTLE, WAITING FOR HIM TO COME OUT...
BUT JOHN HAD MADE A MISTAKE...HE WAS WAITING AT THE BACK DOOR...

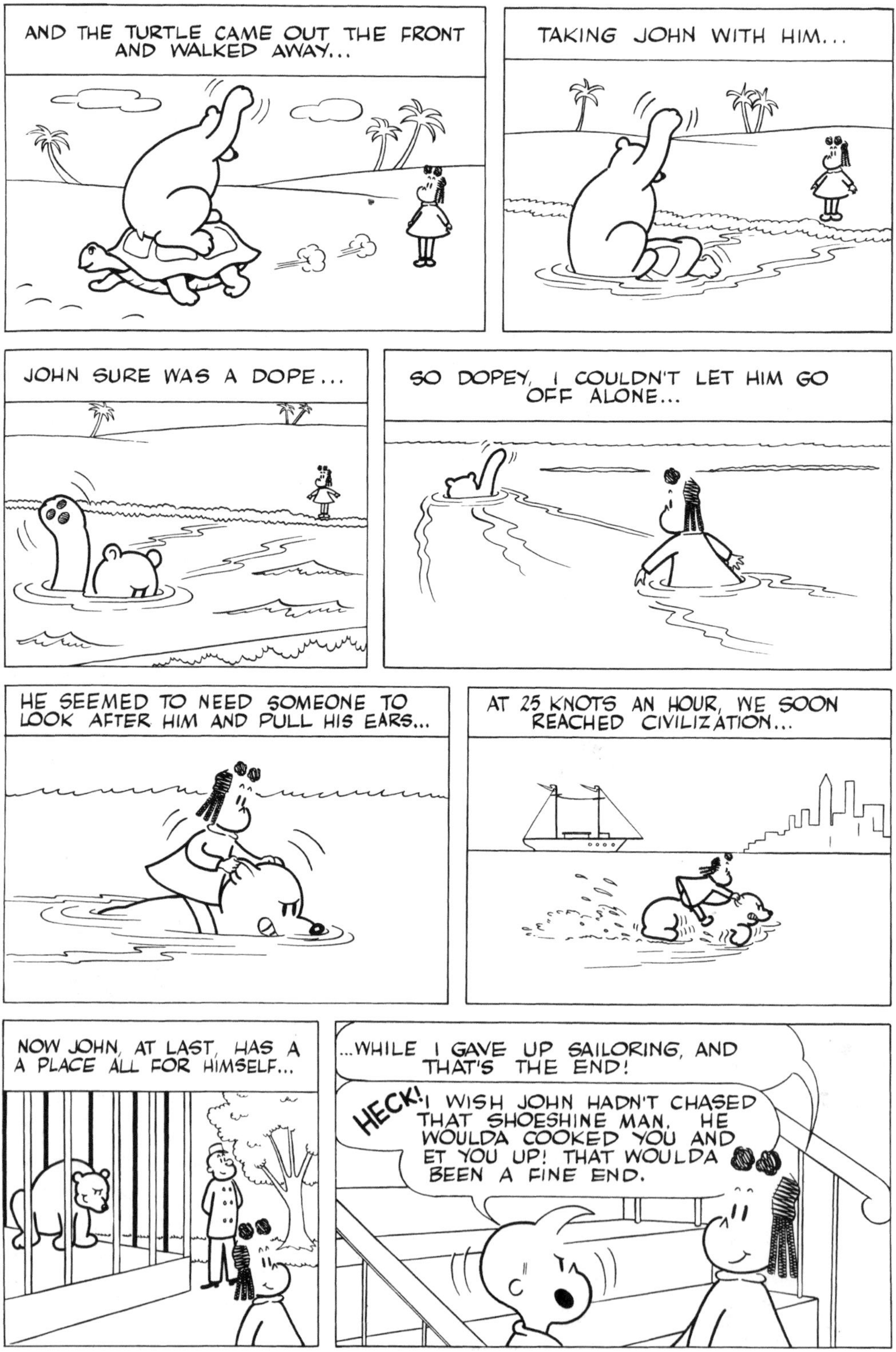
AND THE TURTLE CAME OUT THE FRONT AND WALKED AWAY...
TAKING JOHN WITH HIM...
JOHN SURE WAS A DOPE...
SO DOPEY, I COULDN'T LET HIM GO OFF ALONE...
HE SEEMED TO NEED SOMEONE TO LOOK AFTER HIM AND PULL HIS EARS...
AT 25 KNOTS AN HOUR, WE SOON REACHED CIVILIZATION...
NOW JOHN, AT LAST, HAS A A PLACE ALL FOR HIMSELF...
...WHILE I GAVE UP SAILORING, AND THAT'S THE END!
HECK! I WISH JOHN HADN'T CHASED THAT SHOESHINE MAN. HE WOULDA COOKED YOU AND ET YOU UP! THAT WOULDA BEEN A FINE END.

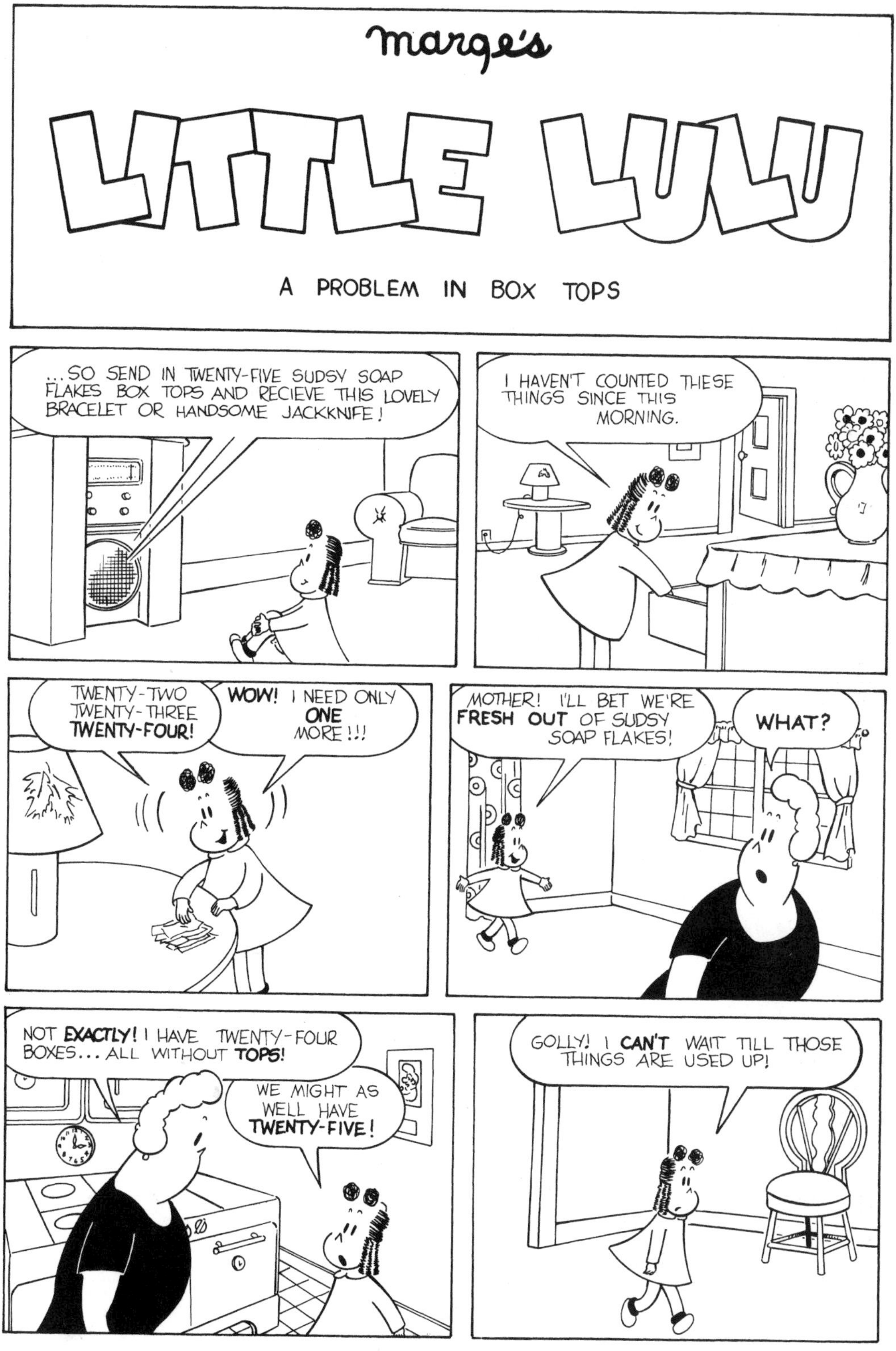
marge's
LITTLE LULU
A PROBLEM IN BOX TOPS
...SO SEND IN TWENTY-FIVE SUDSY SOAP FLAKES BOX TOPS AND RECIEVE THIS LOVELY BRACELET OR HANDSOME JACKKNIFE!
I HAVEN'T COUNTED THESE THINGS SINCE THIS MORNING.
TWENTY-TWO TWENTY-THREE TWENTY-FOUR!
WOW! I NEED ONLY ONE MORE!!!
MOTHER! I'LL BET WE'RE FRESH OUT OF SUDSY SOAP FLAKES!
WHAT?
NOT EXACTLY! I HAVE TWENTY-FOUR BOXES... ALL WITHOUT TOPS!
WE MIGHT AS WELL HAVE TWENTY-FIVE!
GOLLY! I CAN'T WAIT TILL THOSE THINGS ARE USED UP!

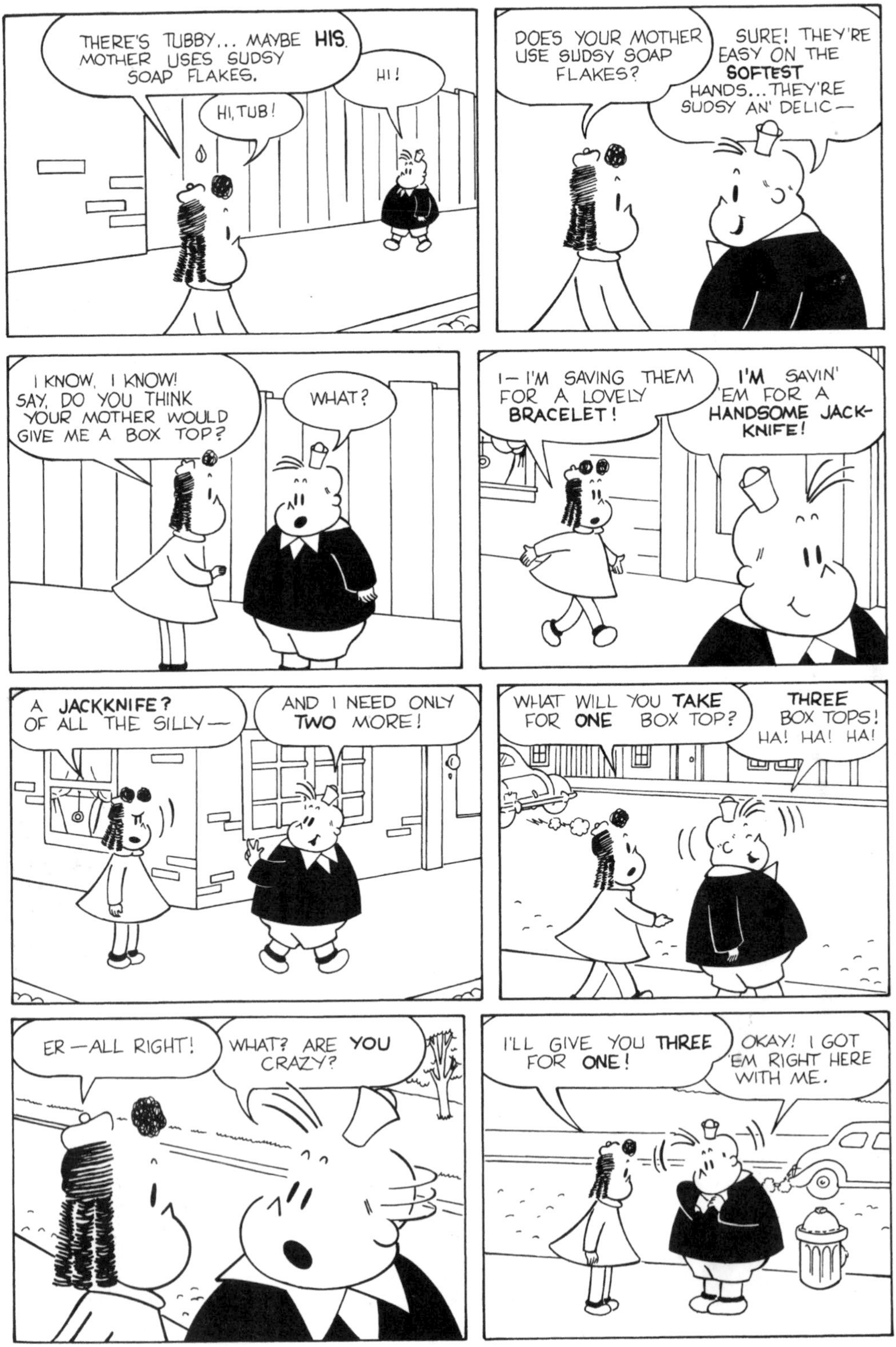
THERE'S TUBBY... MAYBE HIS MOTHER USES SUDSY SOAP FLAKES.
HI!
HI, TUB!
DOES YOUR MOTHER USE SUDSY SOAP FLAKES?
SURE! THEY'RE EASY ON THE SOFTEST HANDS... THEY'RE SUDSY AN' DELIC—
I KNOW, I KNOW! SAY, DO YOU THINK YOUR MOTHER WOULD GIVE ME A BOX TOP?
WHAT?
I— I'M SAVING THEM FOR A LOVELY BRACELET!
I'M SAVIN' 'EM FOR A HANDSOME JACK-KNIFE!
A JACKKNIFE? OF ALL THE SILLY—
AND I NEED ONLY TWO MORE!
WHAT WILL YOU TAKE FOR ONE BOX TOP?
THREE BOX TOPS! HA! HA! HA!
ER—ALL RIGHT!
WHAT? ARE YOU CRAZY?
I'LL GIVE YOU THREE FOR ONE!
OKAY! I GOT 'EM RIGHT HERE WITH ME.

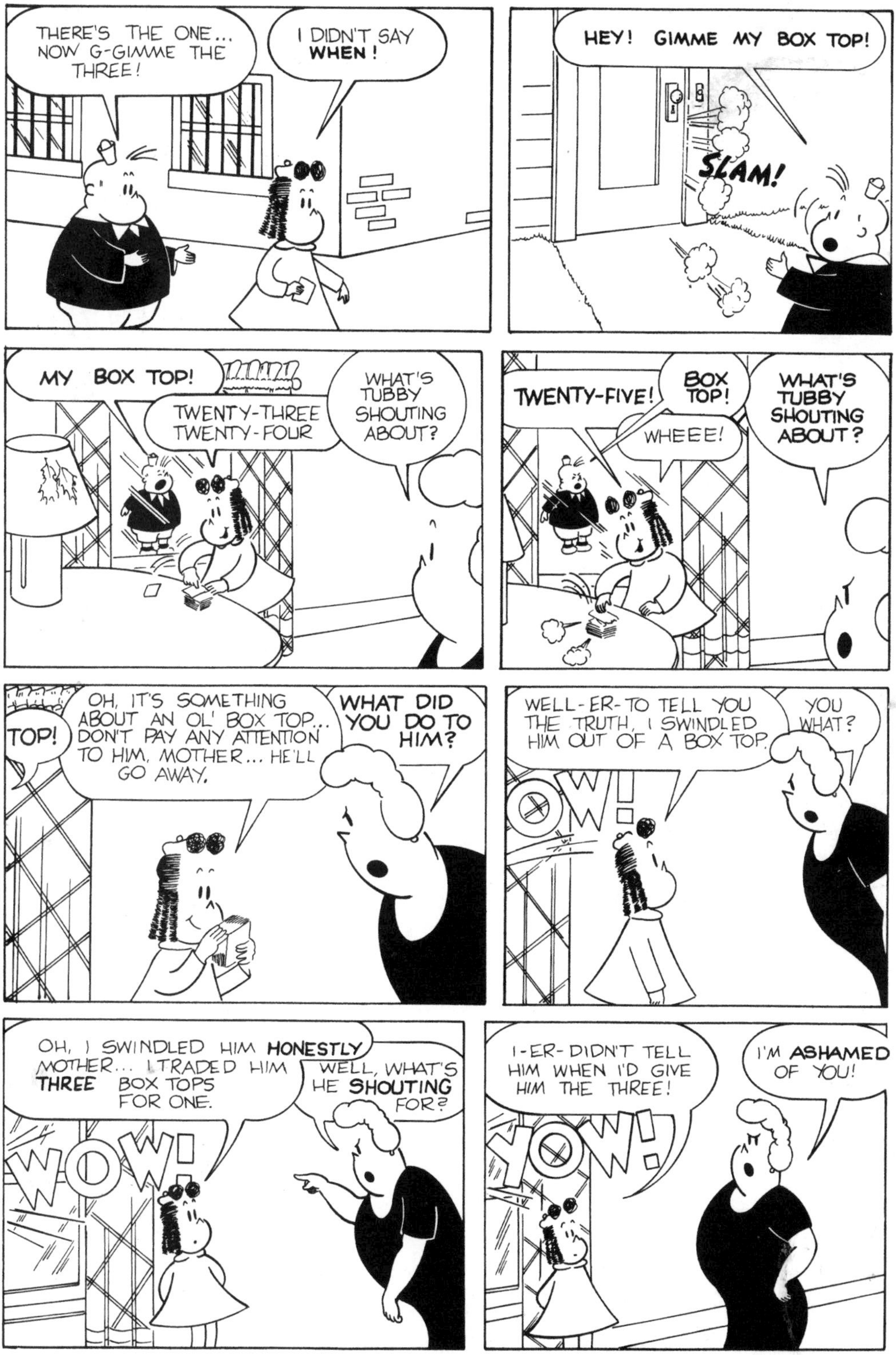
THERE'S THE ONE... NOW G-GIMME THE THREE!
I DIDN'T SAY WHEN!
HEY! GIMME MY BOX TOP!
SLAM!
MY BOX TOP!
TWENTY-THREE TWENTY-FOUR
WHAT'S TUBBY SHOUTING ABOUT?
TWENTY-FIVE!
BOX TOP!
WHEEE!
WHAT'S TUBBY SHOUTING ABOUT?
TOP!
OH, IT'S SOMETHING ABOUT AN OL' BOX TOP... DON'T PAY ANY ATTENTION TO HIM, MOTHER... HE'LL GO AWAY.
WHAT DID YOU DO TO HIM?
WELL-ER-TO TELL YOU THE TRUTH, I SWINDLED HIM OUT OF A BOX TOP.
YOU WHAT?
OW!
OH, I SWINDLED HIM HONESTLY MOTHER... I TRADED HIM THREE BOX TOPS FOR ONE.
WELL, WHAT'S HE SHOUTING FOR?
WOW!
I-ER-DIDN'T TELL HIM WHEN I'D GIVE HIM THE THREE!
I'M ASHAMED OF YOU!
YOW!

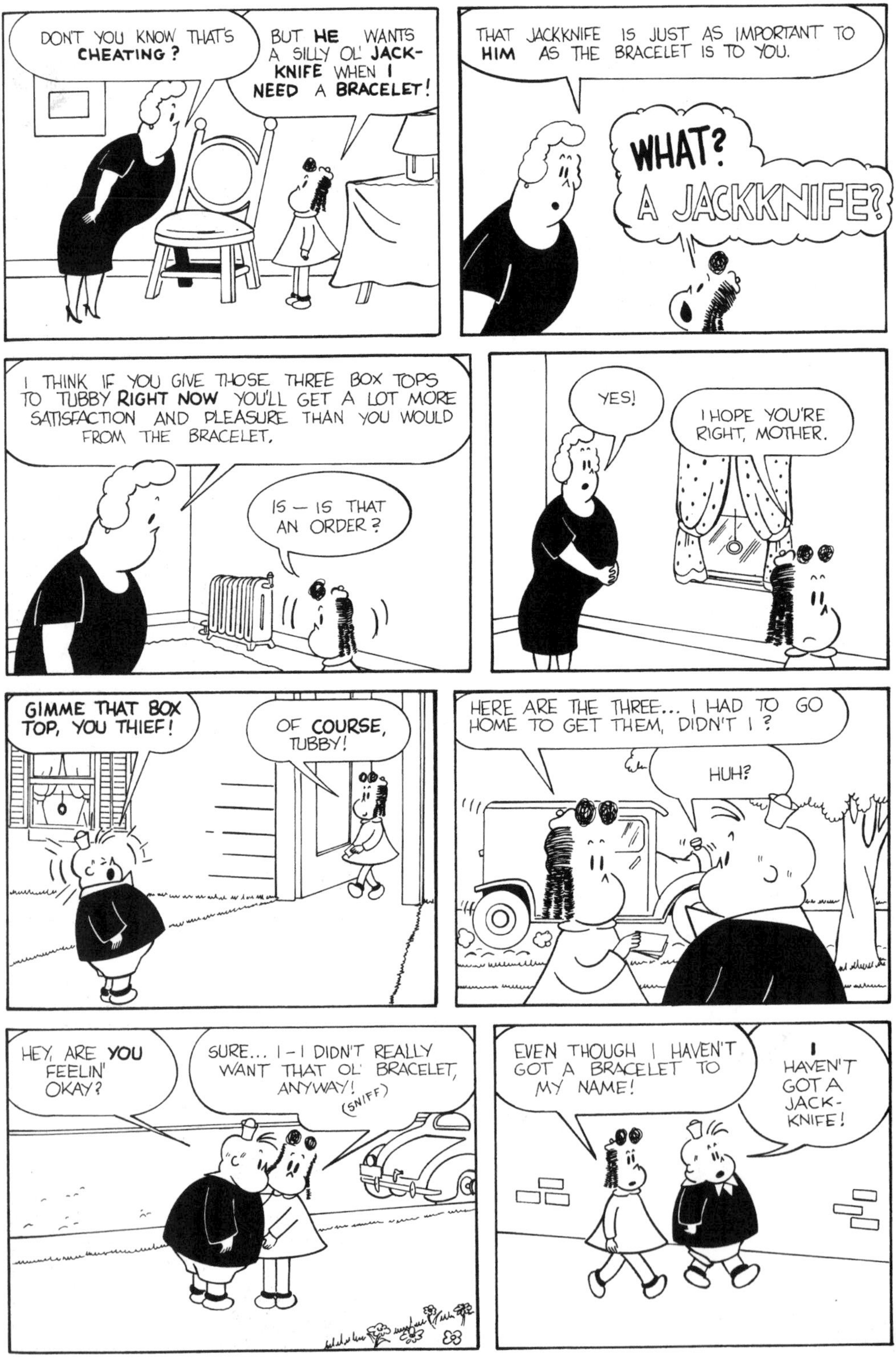
DON'T YOU KNOW THAT'S **CHEATING?**
BUT **HE** WANTS A SILLY OL' **JACK-KNIFE** WHEN **I NEED** A **BRACELET!**
THAT JACKKNIFE IS JUST AS IMPORTANT TO **HIM** AS THE BRACELET IS TO YOU.
WHAT? A JACKKNIFE?
I THINK IF YOU GIVE THOSE THREE BOX TOPS TO TUBBY **RIGHT NOW** YOU'LL GET A LOT MORE SATISFACTION AND PLEASURE THAN YOU WOULD FROM THE BRACELET.
IS — IS THAT AN ORDER?
YES!
I HOPE YOU'RE RIGHT, MOTHER.
GIMME THAT BOX TOP, YOU THIEF!
OF **COURSE**, TUBBY!
HERE ARE THE THREE... I HAD TO GO HOME TO GET THEM, DIDN'T I?
HUH?
HEY, ARE **YOU** FEELIN' OKAY?
SURE... I-I DIDN'T REALLY WANT THAT OL' BRACELET, ANYWAY!
(SNIFF)
EVEN THOUGH I HAVEN'T GOT A BRACELET TO MY NAME!
I HAVEN'T GOT A JACK-KNIFE!

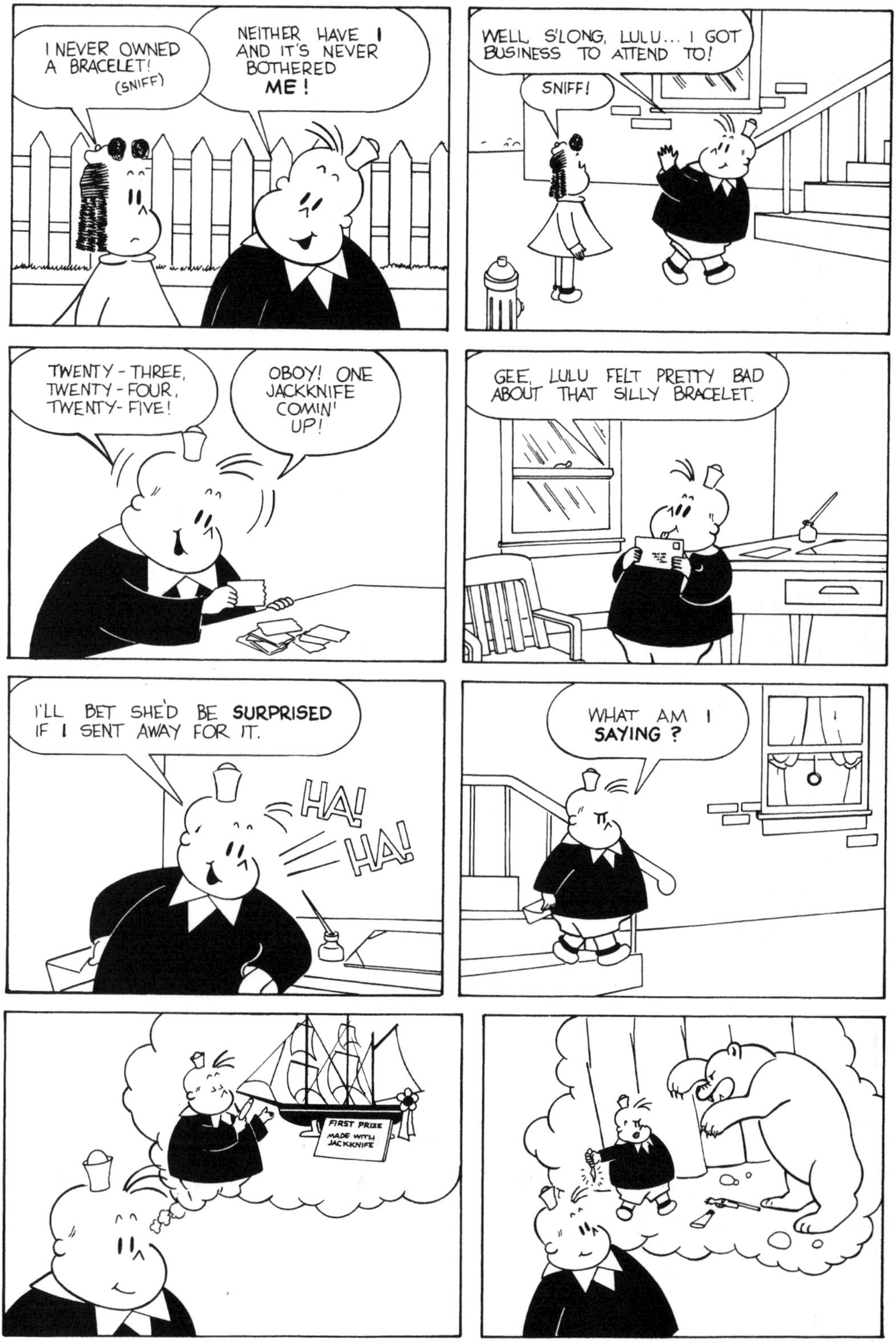
I NEVER OWNED A BRACELET! (SNIFF)
NEITHER HAVE I AND IT'S NEVER BOTHERED ME!
WELL, S'LONG, LULU... I GOT BUSINESS TO ATTEND TO!
SNIFF!
TWENTY-THREE, TWENTY-FOUR, TWENTY-FIVE!
OBOY! ONE JACKKNIFE COMIN' UP!
GEE, LULU FELT PRETTY BAD ABOUT THAT SILLY BRACELET.
I'LL BET SHE'D BE SURPRISED IF I SENT AWAY FOR IT.
HA! HA!
WHAT AM I SAYING?
FIRST PRIZE
MADE WITH JACKKNIFE

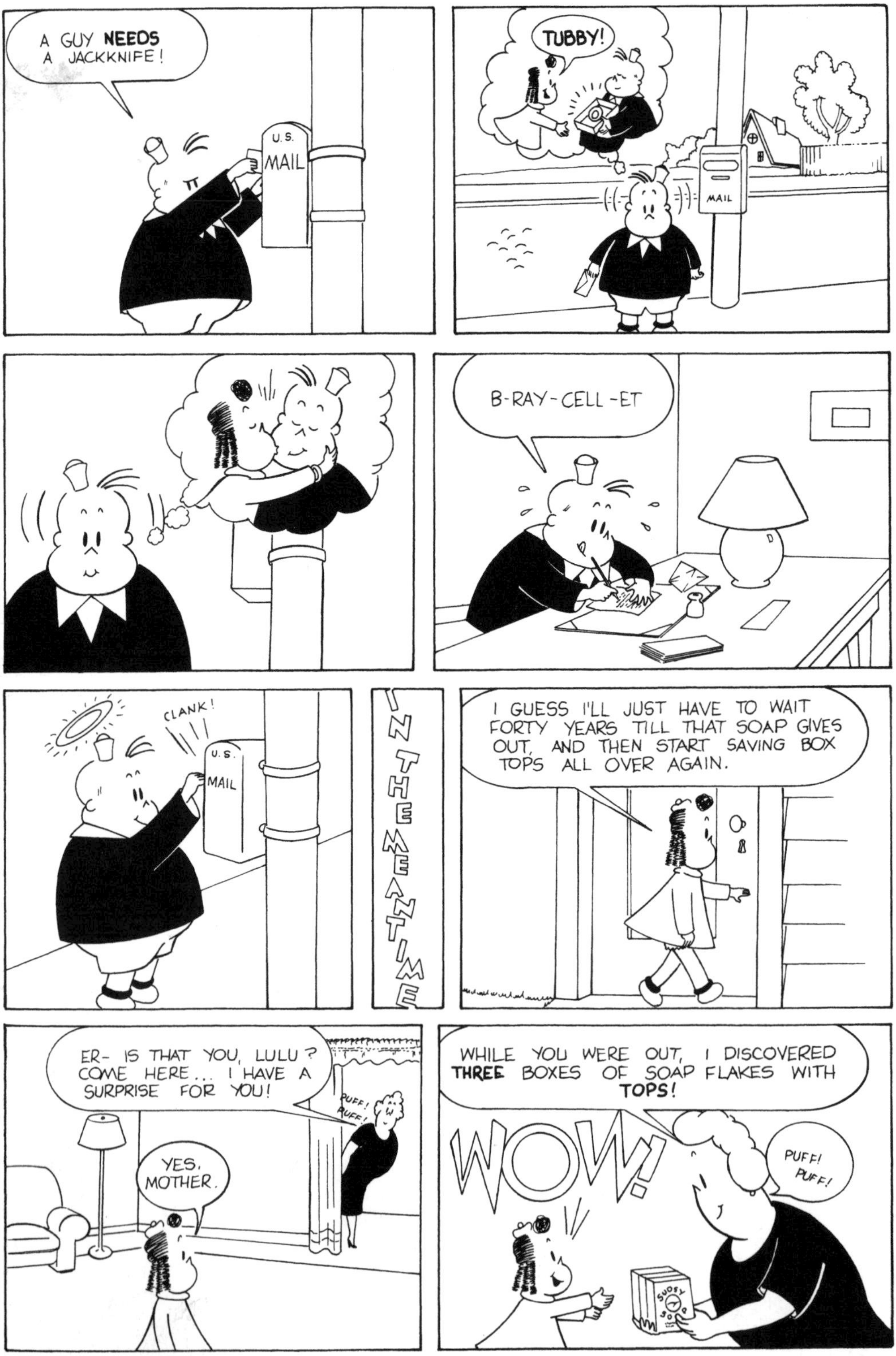
A GUY NEEDS A JACKKNIFE!
U.S. MAIL
TUBBY!
MAIL
B-RAY-CELL-ET
CLANK!
U.S. MAIL
IN THE MEANTIME
I GUESS I'LL JUST HAVE TO WAIT FORTY YEARS TILL THAT SOAP GIVES OUT, AND THEN START SAVING BOX TOPS ALL OVER AGAIN.
ER- IS THAT YOU, LULU? COME HERE... I HAVE A SURPRISE FOR YOU!
PUFF! PUFF!
YES, MOTHER.
WHILE YOU WERE OUT, I DISCOVERED THREE BOXES OF SOAP FLAKES WITH TOPS!
WOW!
PUFF! PUFF!
SUDSY SOAP

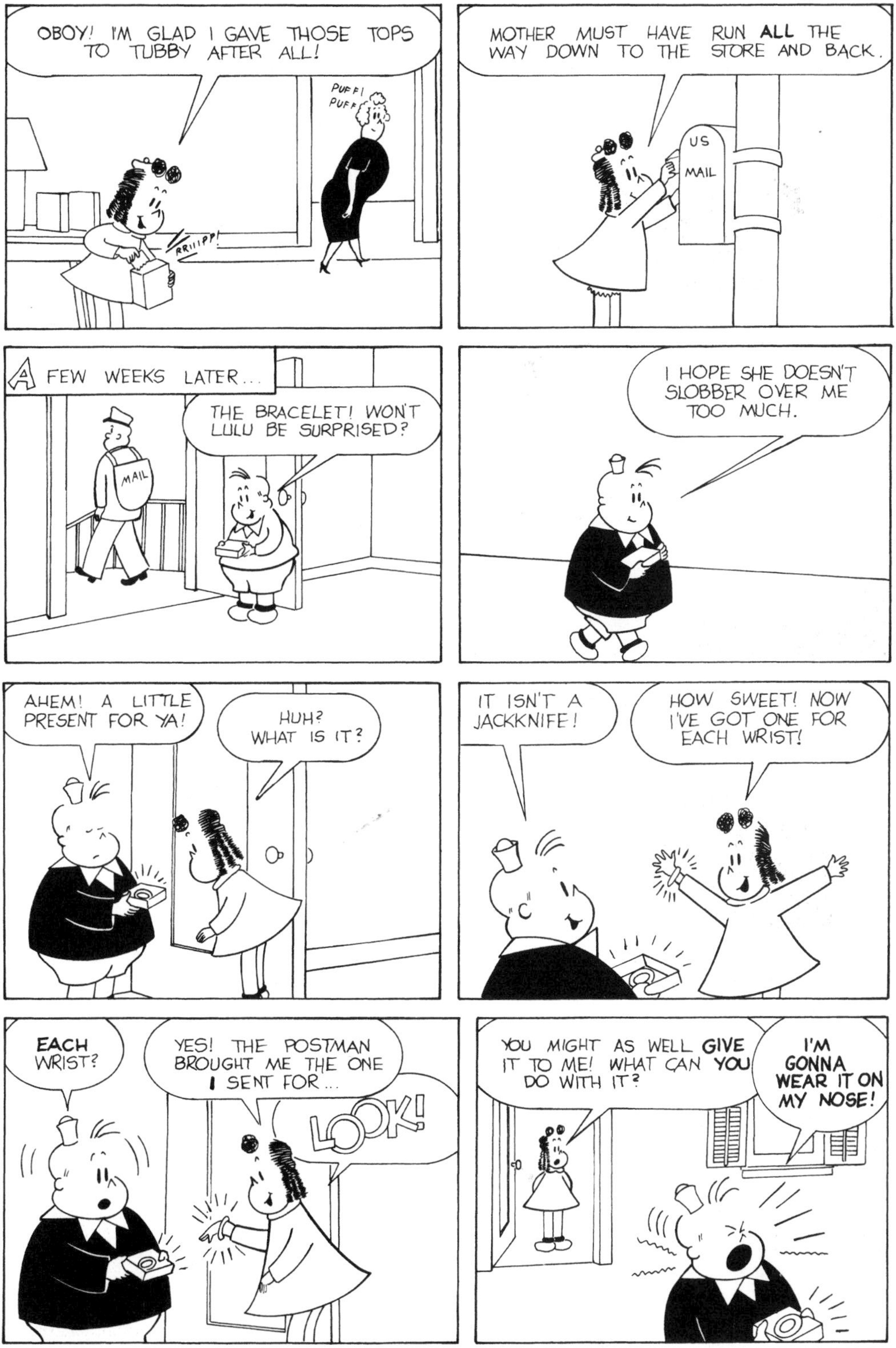
OBOY! I'M GLAD I GAVE THOSE TOPS TO TUBBY AFTER ALL!
PUFF! PUFF!
RRIIIPP!
MOTHER MUST HAVE RUN **ALL** THE WAY DOWN TO THE STORE AND BACK.
US MAIL
A FEW WEEKS LATER...
MAIL
THE BRACELET! WON'T LULU BE SURPRISED?
I HOPE SHE DOESN'T SLOBBER OVER ME TOO MUCH.
AHEM! A LITTLE PRESENT FOR YA!
HUH? WHAT IS IT?
IT ISN'T A JACKKNIFE!
HOW SWEET! NOW I'VE GOT ONE FOR EACH WRIST!
EACH WRIST?
YES! THE POSTMAN BROUGHT ME THE ONE **I** SENT FOR...
LOOK!
YOU MIGHT AS WELL **GIVE** IT TO ME! WHAT CAN **YOU** DO WITH IT?
I'M GONNA WEAR IT ON MY NOSE!

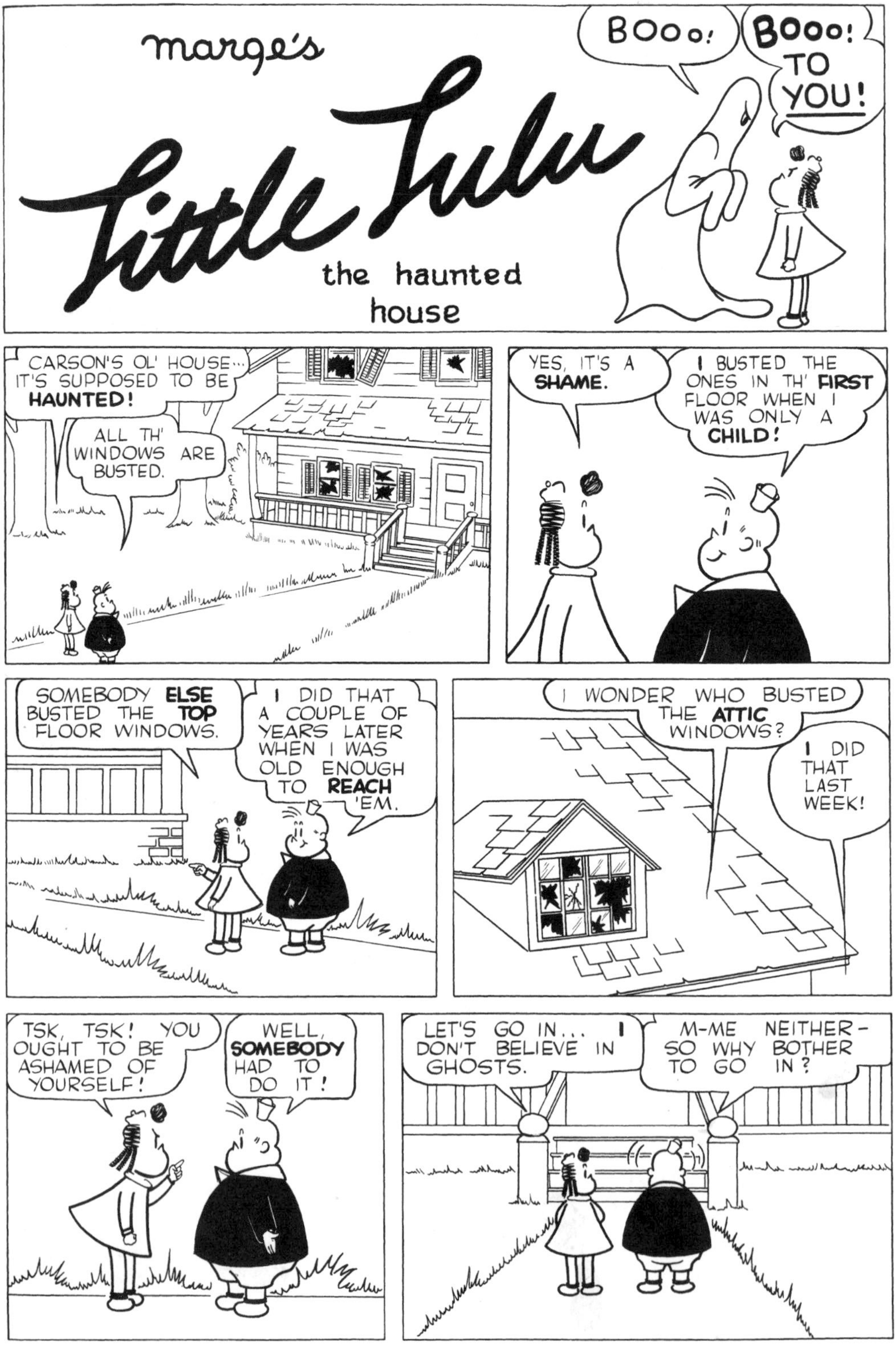
marge's
Little Lulu
the haunted house
BOOo!
BOOo! TO YOU!
CARSON'S OL' HOUSE... IT'S SUPPOSED TO BE HAUNTED!
ALL TH' WINDOWS ARE BUSTED.
YES, IT'S A SHAME.
I BUSTED THE ONES IN TH' FIRST FLOOR WHEN I WAS ONLY A CHILD!
SOMEBODY ELSE BUSTED THE TOP FLOOR WINDOWS.
I DID THAT A COUPLE OF YEARS LATER WHEN I WAS OLD ENOUGH TO REACH 'EM.
I WONDER WHO BUSTED THE ATTIC WINDOWS?
I DID THAT LAST WEEK!
TSK, TSK! YOU OUGHT TO BE ASHAMED OF YOURSELF!
WELL, SOMEBODY HAD TO DO IT!
LET'S GO IN... I DON'T BELIEVE IN GHOSTS.
M-ME NEITHER- SO WHY BOTHER TO GO IN?

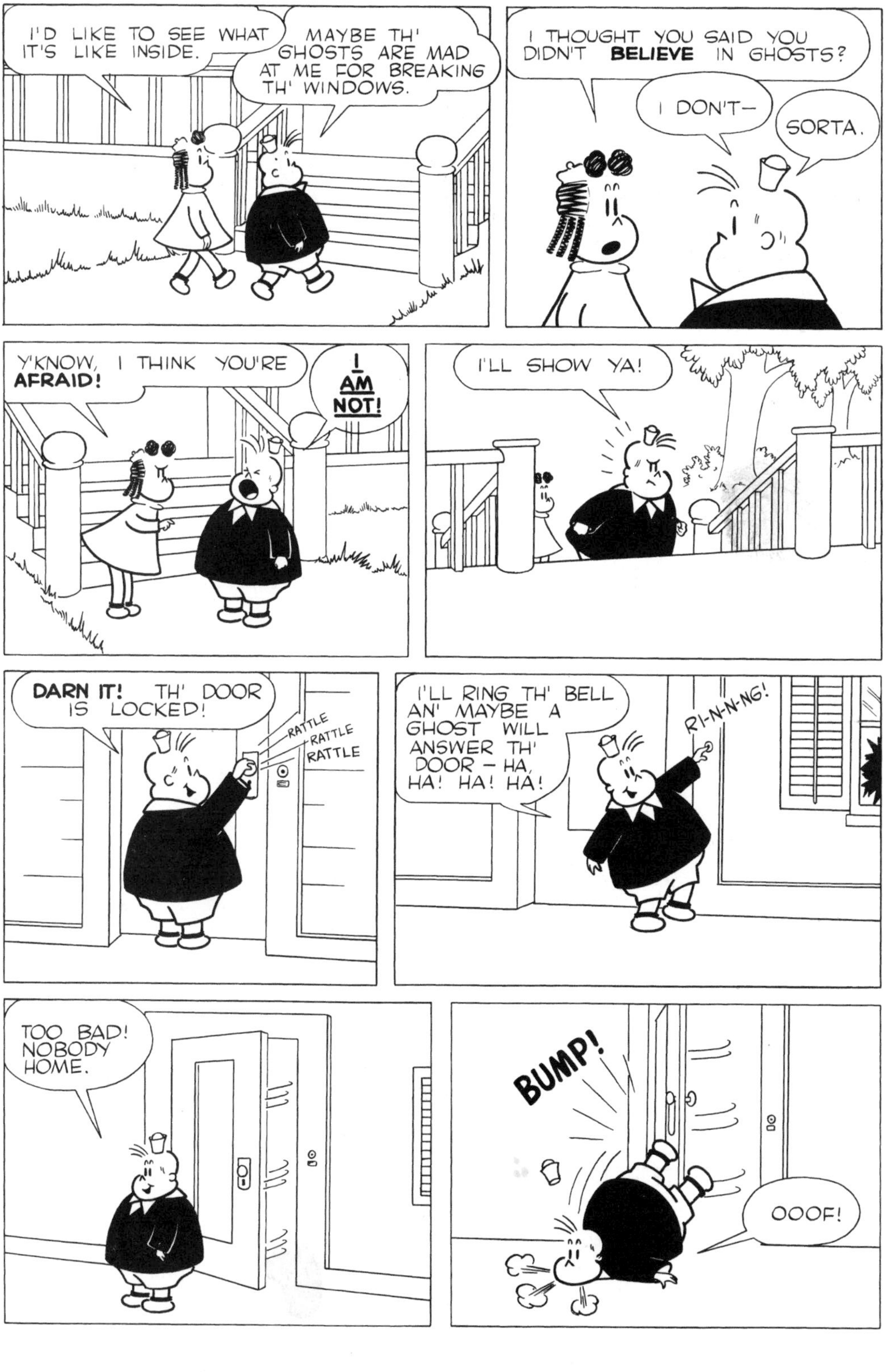
I'D LIKE TO SEE WHAT IT'S LIKE INSIDE.
MAYBE TH' GHOSTS ARE MAD AT ME FOR BREAKING TH' WINDOWS.
I THOUGHT YOU SAID YOU DIDN'T **BELIEVE** IN GHOSTS?
I DON'T—
SORTA.
Y'KNOW, I THINK YOU'RE **AFRAID!**
I AM NOT!
I'LL SHOW YA!
DARN IT! TH' DOOR IS LOCKED!
RATTLE RATTLE RATTLE
I'LL RING TH' BELL AN' MAYBE A GHOST WILL ANSWER TH' DOOR – HA, HA! HA! HA!
RI-N-N-NG!
TOO BAD! NOBODY HOME.
BUMP!
OOOF!

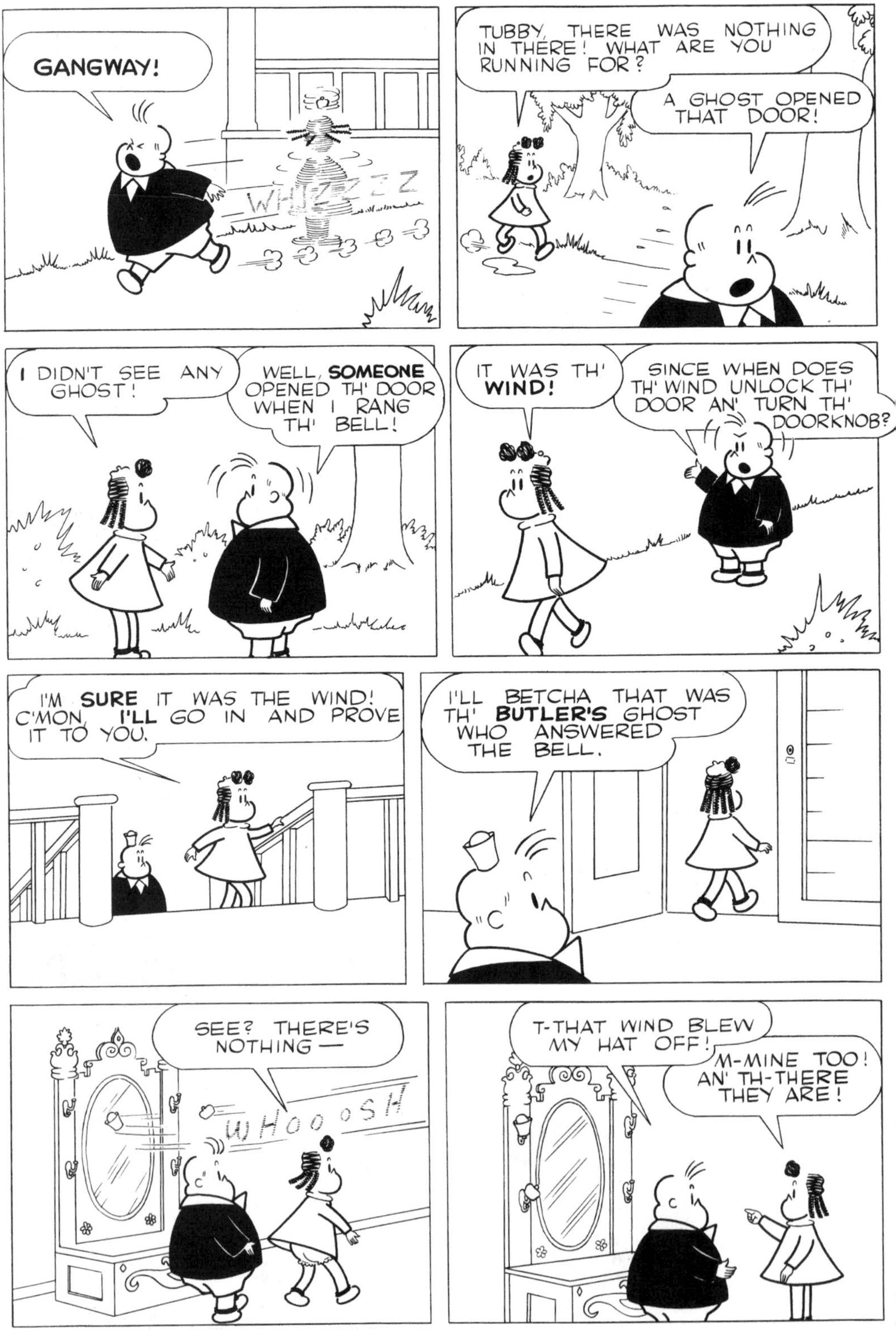

GANGWAY!
WHIZZZZ
TUBBY, THERE WAS NOTHING IN THERE! WHAT ARE YOU RUNNING FOR?
A GHOST OPENED THAT DOOR!
I DIDN'T SEE ANY GHOST!
WELL, SOMEONE OPENED TH' DOOR WHEN I RANG TH' BELL!
IT WAS TH' WIND!
SINCE WHEN DOES TH' WIND UNLOCK TH' DOOR AN' TURN TH' DOORKNOB?
I'M SURE IT WAS THE WIND! C'MON, I'LL GO IN AND PROVE IT TO YOU.
I'LL BETCHA THAT WAS TH' BUTLER'S GHOST WHO ANSWERED THE BELL.
SEE? THERE'S NOTHING—
WHOOOSH!
T-THAT WIND BLEW MY HAT OFF!
M-MINE TOO! AN' TH-THERE THEY ARE!

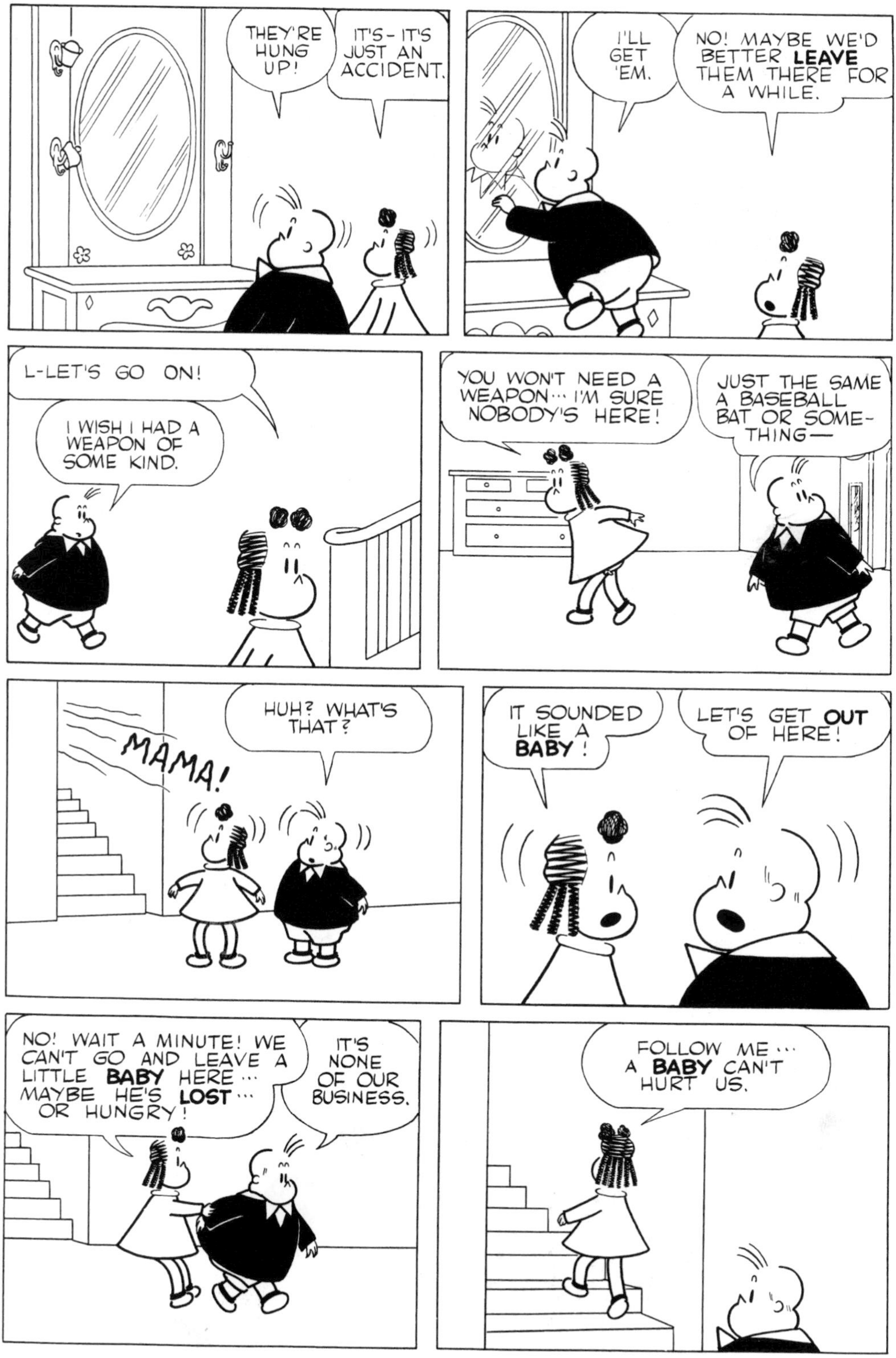
THEY'RE HUNG UP!
IT'S- IT'S JUST AN ACCIDENT.
I'LL GET 'EM.
NO! MAYBE WE'D BETTER **LEAVE** THEM THERE FOR A WHILE.
L-LET'S GO ON!
I WISH I HAD A WEAPON OF SOME KIND.
YOU WON'T NEED A WEAPON... I'M SURE NOBODY'S HERE!
JUST THE SAME A BASEBALL BAT OR SOME-THING—
MAMA!
HUH? WHAT'S THAT?
IT SOUNDED LIKE A **BABY**!
LET'S GET **OUT** OF HERE!
NO! WAIT A MINUTE! WE CAN'T GO AND LEAVE A LITTLE **BABY** HERE... MAYBE HE'S **LOST**... OR HUNGRY!
IT'S NONE OF OUR BUSINESS.
FOLLOW ME... A **BABY** CAN'T HURT US.

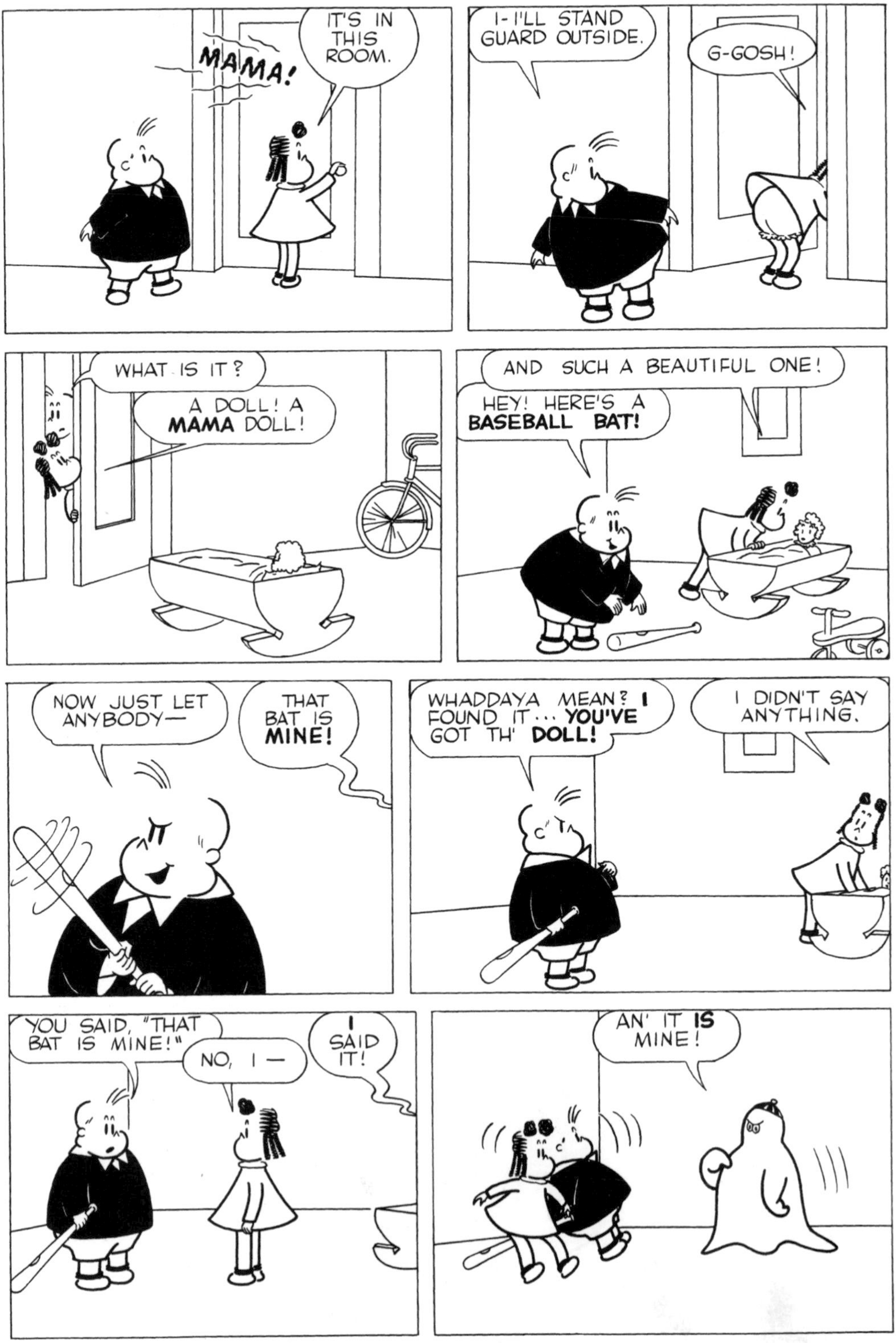
MAMA!
IT'S IN THIS ROOM.
I-I'LL STAND GUARD OUTSIDE.
G-GOSH!
WHAT IS IT?
A DOLL! A MAMA DOLL!
AND SUCH A BEAUTIFUL ONE!
HEY! HERE'S A BASEBALL BAT!
NOW JUST LET ANYBODY—
THAT BAT IS MINE!
WHADDAYA MEAN? I FOUND IT... YOU'VE GOT TH' DOLL!
I DIDN'T SAY ANYTHING.
YOU SAID, "THAT BAT IS MINE!"
NO, I —
I SAID IT!
AN' IT IS MINE!

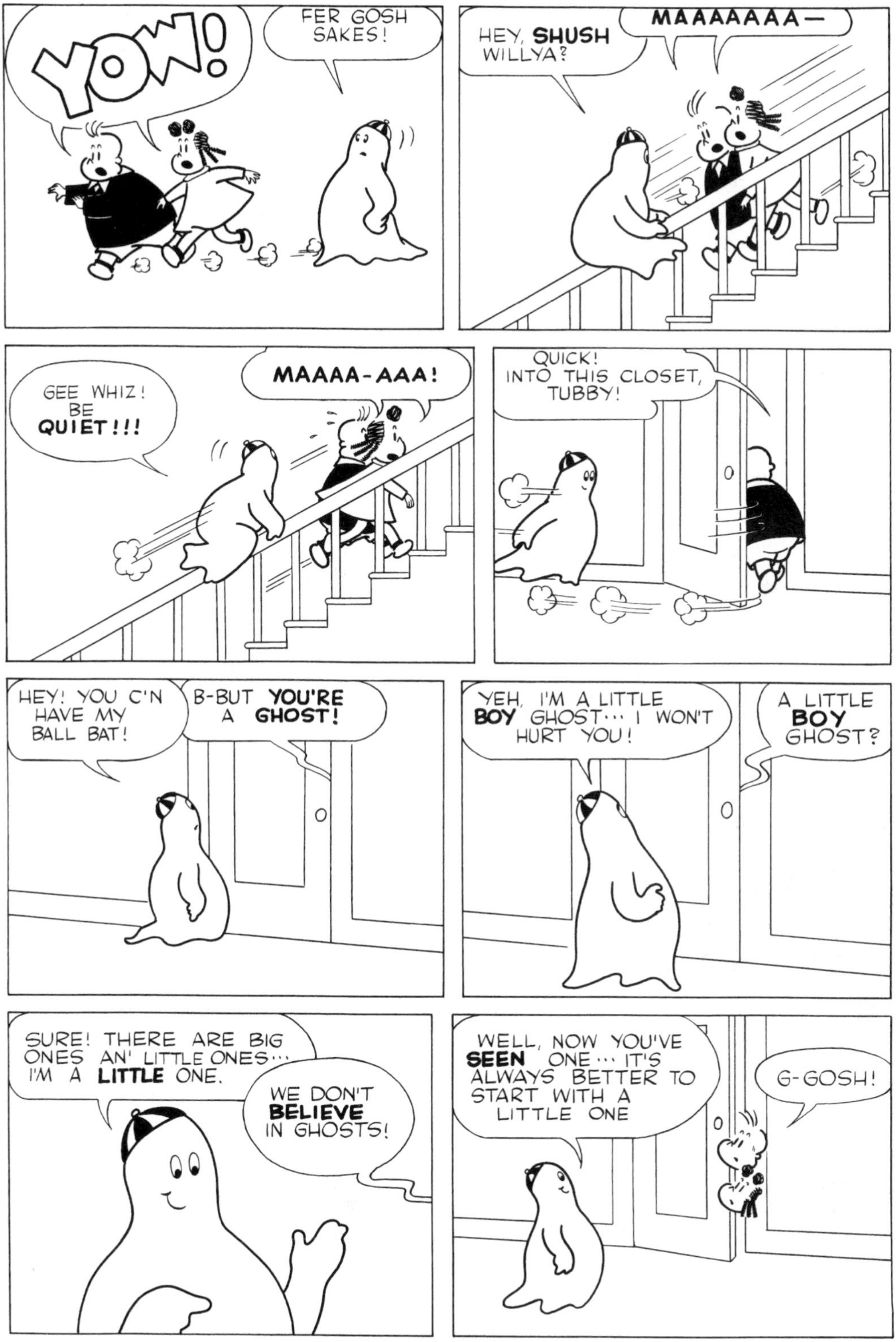
YOW!
FER GOSH SAKES!
HEY, SHUSH WILLYA?
MAAAAAAA—
GEE WHIZ! BE QUIET!!!
MAAAA-AAA!
QUICK! INTO THIS CLOSET, TUBBY!
HEY! YOU C'N HAVE MY BALL BAT!
B-BUT YOU'RE A GHOST!
YEH, I'M A LITTLE BOY GHOST··· I WON'T HURT YOU!
A LITTLE BOY GHOST?
SURE! THERE ARE BIG ONES AN' LITTLE ONES··· I'M A LITTLE ONE.
WE DON'T BELIEVE IN GHOSTS!
WELL, NOW YOU'VE SEEN ONE··· IT'S ALWAYS BETTER TO START WITH A LITTLE ONE
G-GOSH!

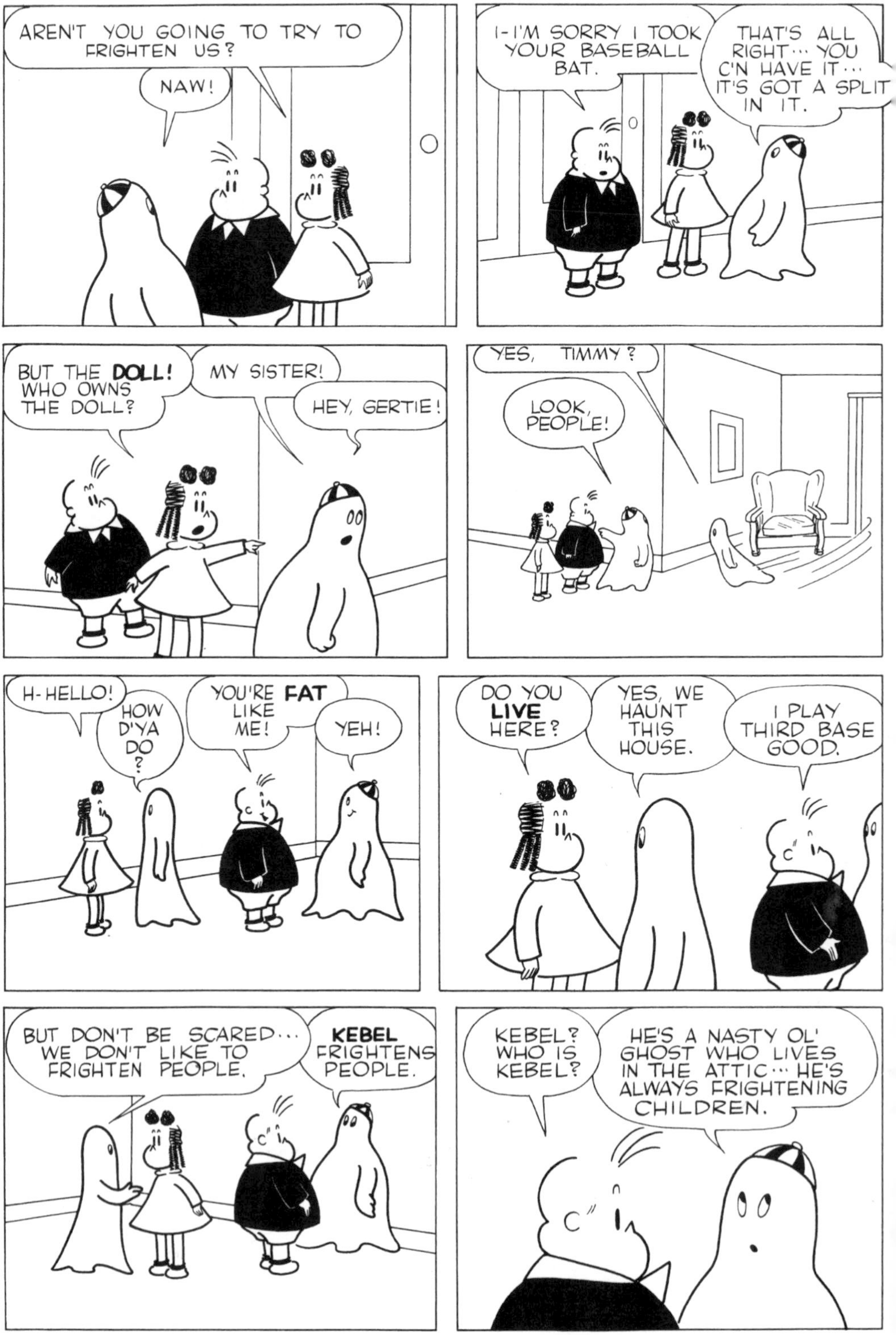
AREN'T YOU GOING TO TRY TO FRIGHTEN US?
NAW!
I-I'M SORRY I TOOK YOUR BASEBALL BAT.
THAT'S ALL RIGHT··· YOU C'N HAVE IT··· IT'S GOT A SPLIT IN IT.
BUT THE **DOLL!** WHO OWNS THE DOLL?
MY SISTER!
HEY, GERTIE!
YES, TIMMY?
LOOK, PEOPLE!
H-HELLO!
HOW D'YA DO?
YOU'RE **FAT** LIKE ME!
YEH!
DO YOU **LIVE** HERE?
YES, WE HAUNT THIS HOUSE.
I PLAY THIRD BASE GOOD.
BUT DON'T BE SCARED··· WE DON'T LIKE TO FRIGHTEN PEOPLE.
KEBEL FRIGHTENS PEOPLE.
KEBEL? WHO IS KEBEL?
HE'S A NASTY OL' GHOST WHO LIVES IN THE ATTIC··· HE'S ALWAYS FRIGHTENING CHILDREN.

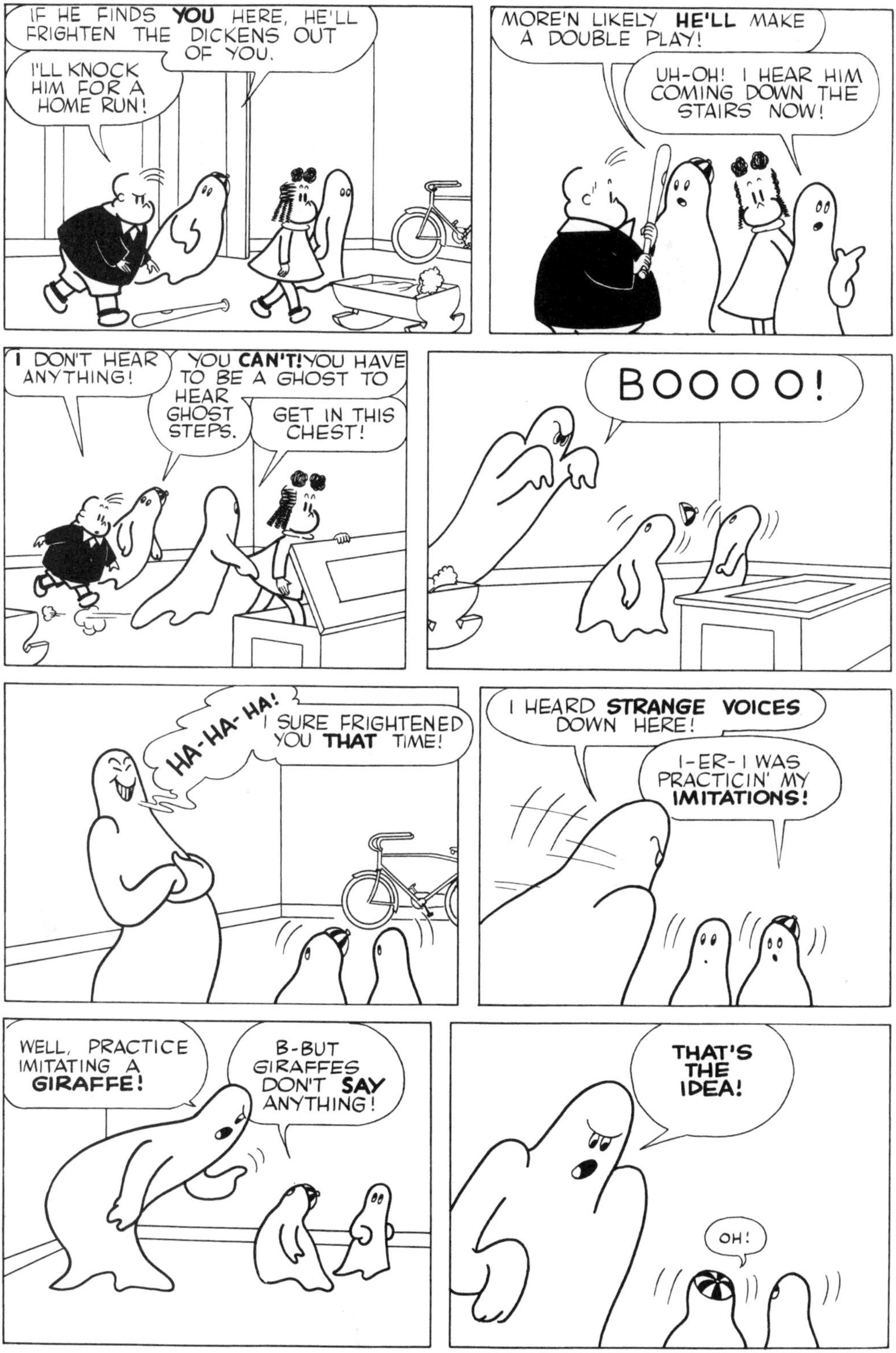
IF HE FINDS YOU HERE, HE'LL FRIGHTEN THE DICKENS OUT OF YOU.
I'LL KNOCK HIM FOR A HOME RUN!
MORE'N LIKELY HE'LL MAKE A DOUBLE PLAY!
UH-OH! I HEAR HIM COMING DOWN THE STAIRS NOW!
I DON'T HEAR ANYTHING!
YOU CAN'T! YOU HAVE TO BE A GHOST TO HEAR GHOST STEPS.
GET IN THIS CHEST!
BOOOO!
HA-HA-HA!
I SURE FRIGHTENED YOU THAT TIME!
I HEARD STRANGE VOICES DOWN HERE!
I-ER-I WAS PRACTICIN' MY IMITATIONS!
WELL, PRACTICE IMITATING A GIRAFFE!
B-BUT GIRAFFES DON'T SAY ANYTHING!
THAT'S THE IDEA!
OH!

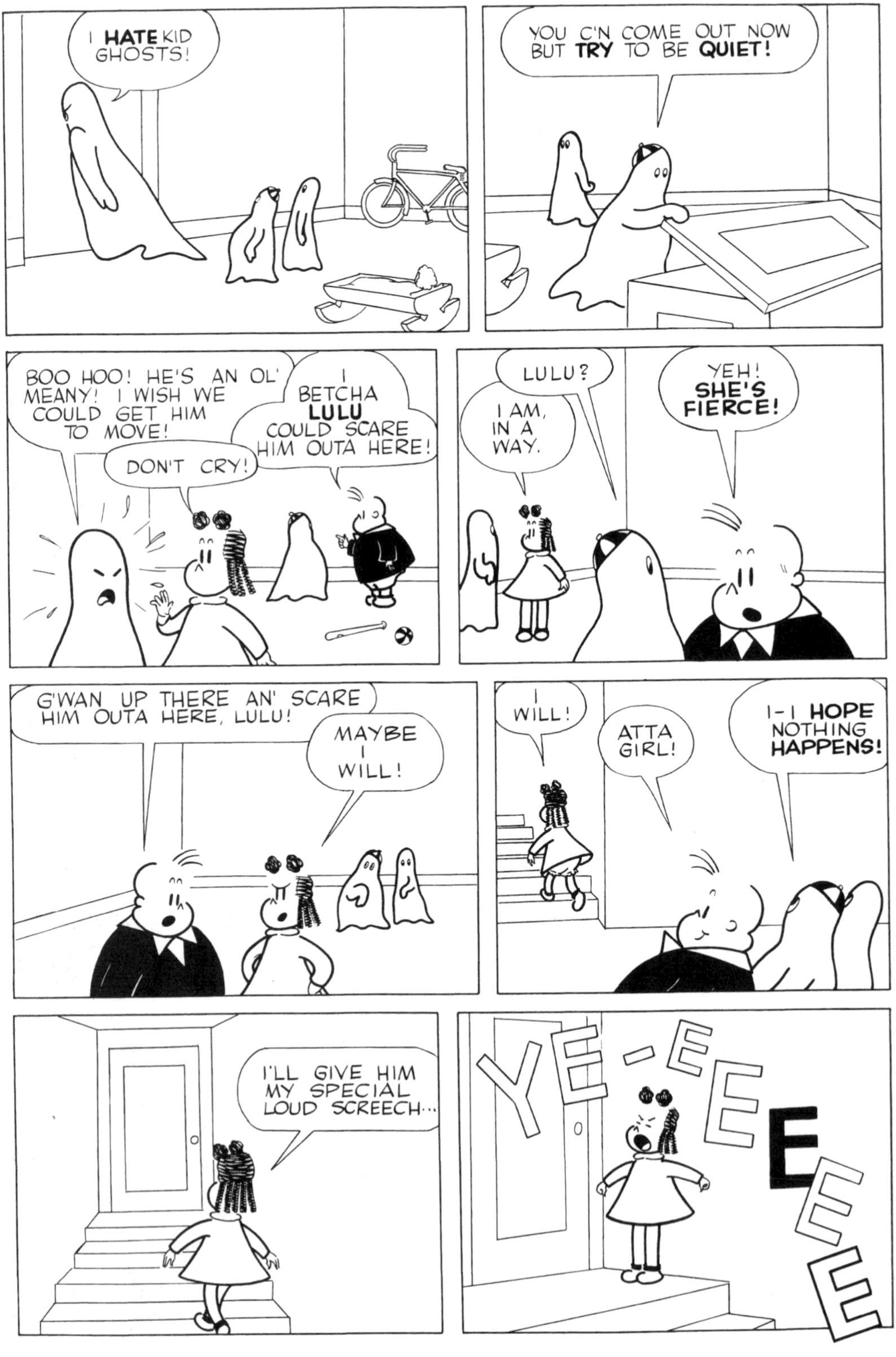
I **HATE** KID GHOSTS!
YOU C'N COME OUT NOW BUT **TRY** TO BE **QUIET**!
BOO HOO! HE'S AN OL' MEANY! I WISH WE COULD GET HIM TO MOVE!
DON'T CRY!
I BETCHA **LULU** COULD SCARE HIM OUTA HERE!
I AM, IN A WAY.
LULU?
YEH! **SHE'S FIERCE!**
G'WAN UP THERE AN' SCARE HIM OUTA HERE, LULU!
MAYBE I WILL!
I WILL!
ATTA GIRL!
I-I **HOPE** NOTHING **HAPPENS!**
I'LL GIVE HIM MY SPECIAL LOUD SCREECH...
YE-EEEEEE

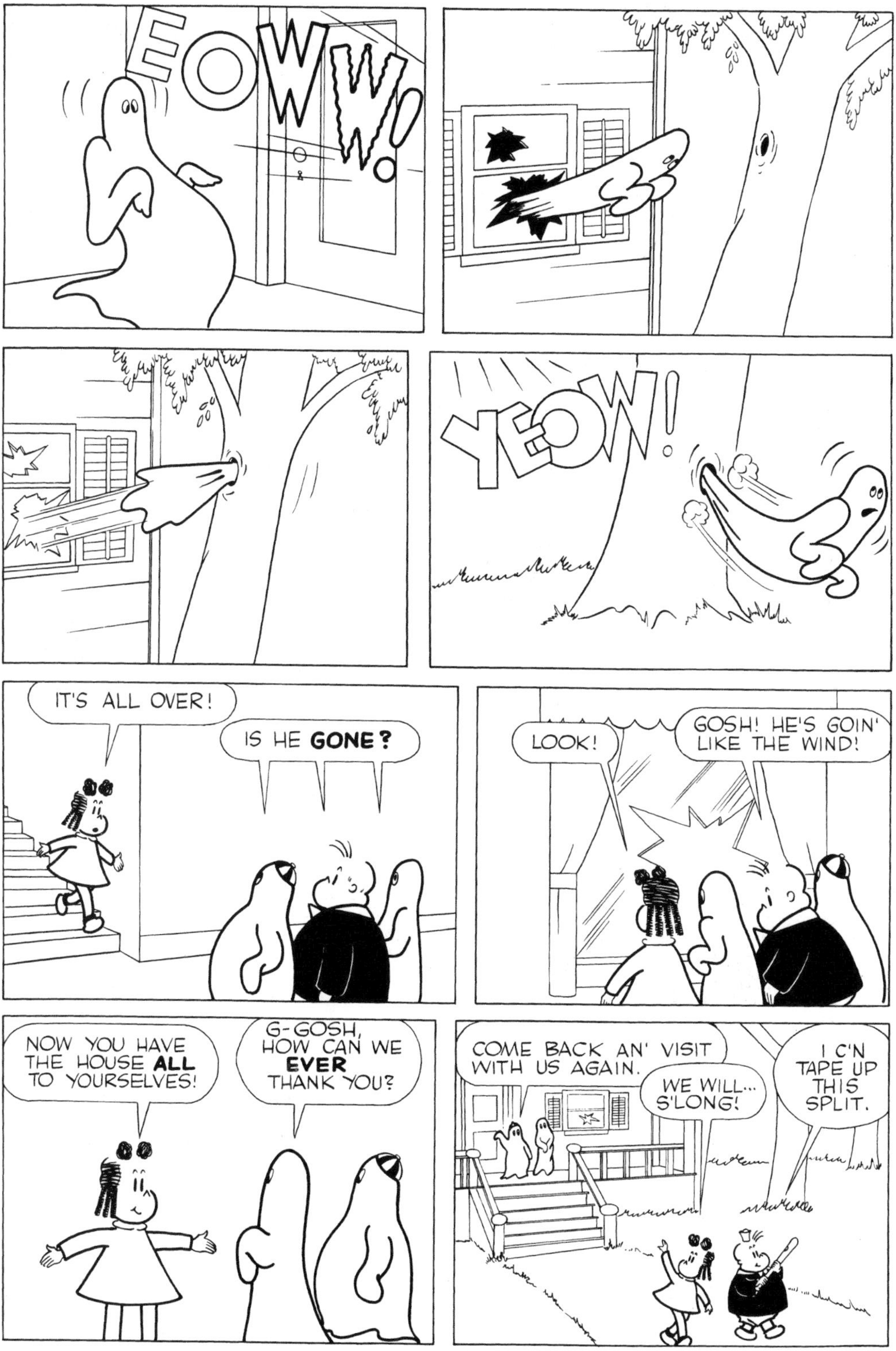
EOWW!
YEOW!
IT'S ALL OVER!
IS HE GONE?
LOOK!
GOSH! HE'S GOIN' LIKE THE WIND!
NOW YOU HAVE THE HOUSE ALL TO YOURSELVES!
G-GOSH, HOW CAN WE EVER THANK YOU?
COME BACK AN' VISIT WITH US AGAIN.
WE WILL... S'LONG!
I C'N TAPE UP THIS SPLIT.

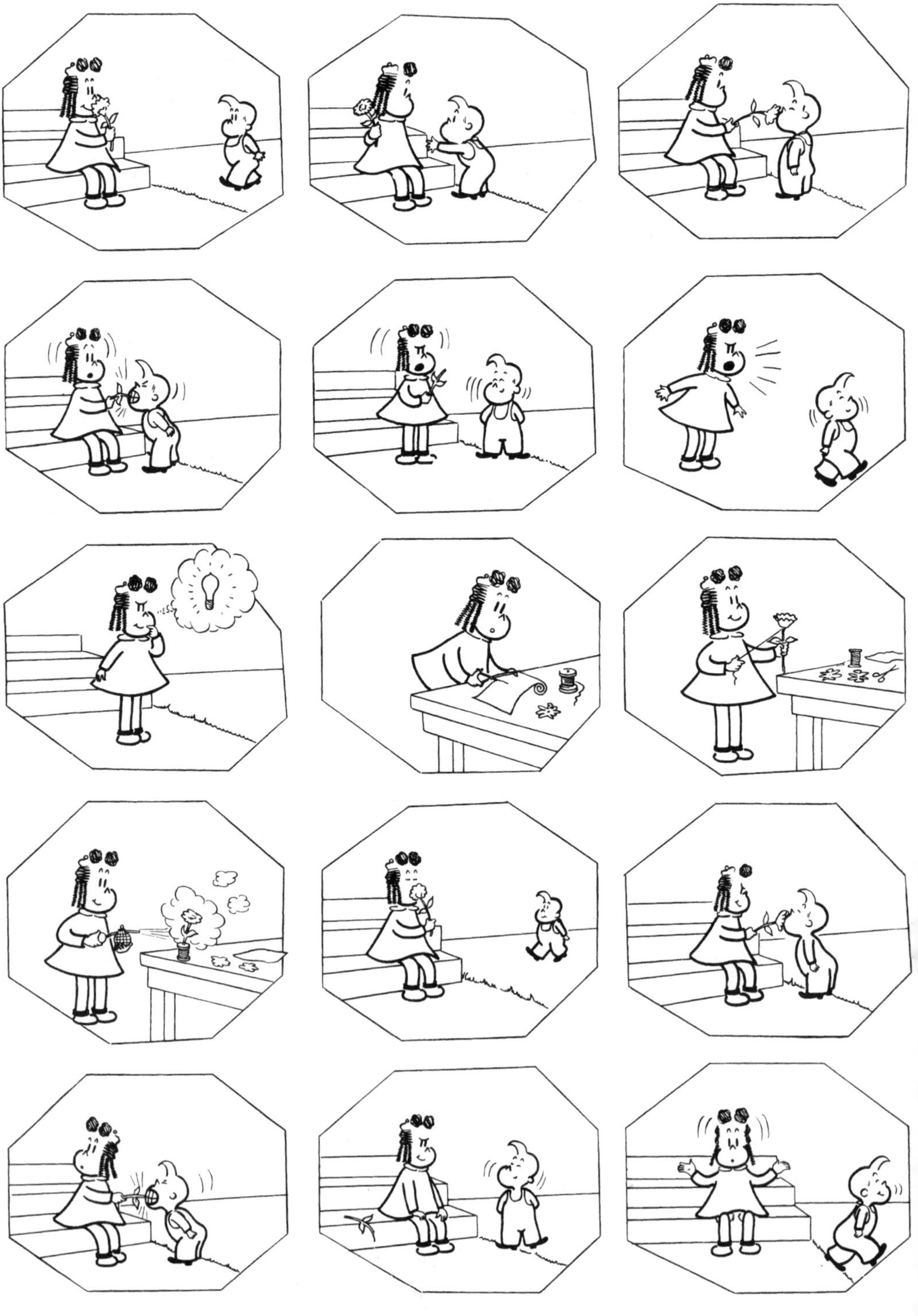

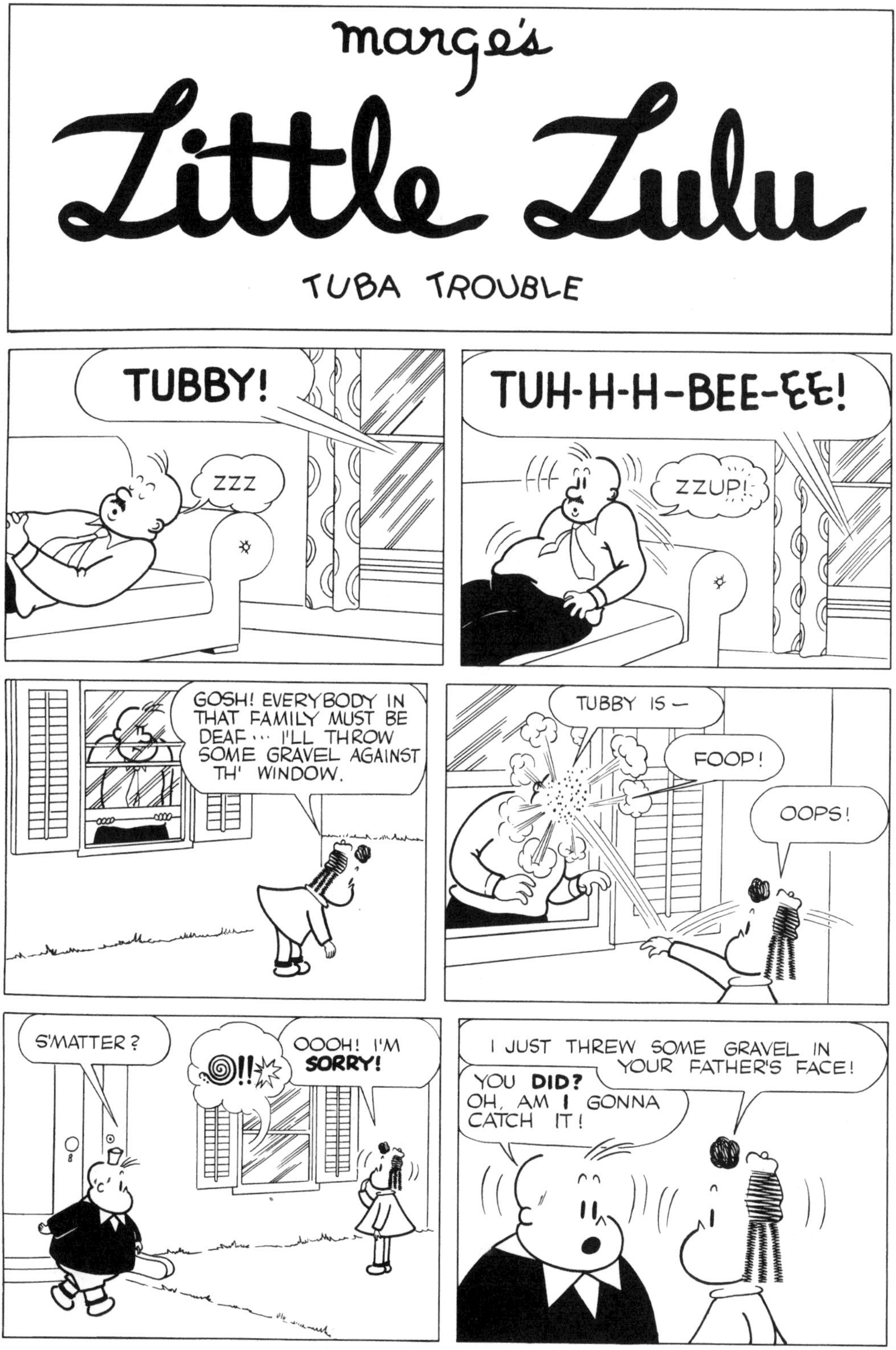
marge's
Little Lulu
TUBA TROUBLE
TUBBY!
ZZZ
TUH-H-H-BEE-EE!
ZZUP!
GOSH! EVERYBODY IN THAT FAMILY MUST BE DEAF... I'LL THROW SOME GRAVEL AGAINST TH' WINDOW.
TUBBY IS —
FOOP!
OOPS!
S'MATTER?
!!
OOOH! I'M SORRY!
I JUST THREW SOME GRAVEL IN YOUR FATHER'S FACE!
YOU DID? OH, AM I GONNA CATCH IT!

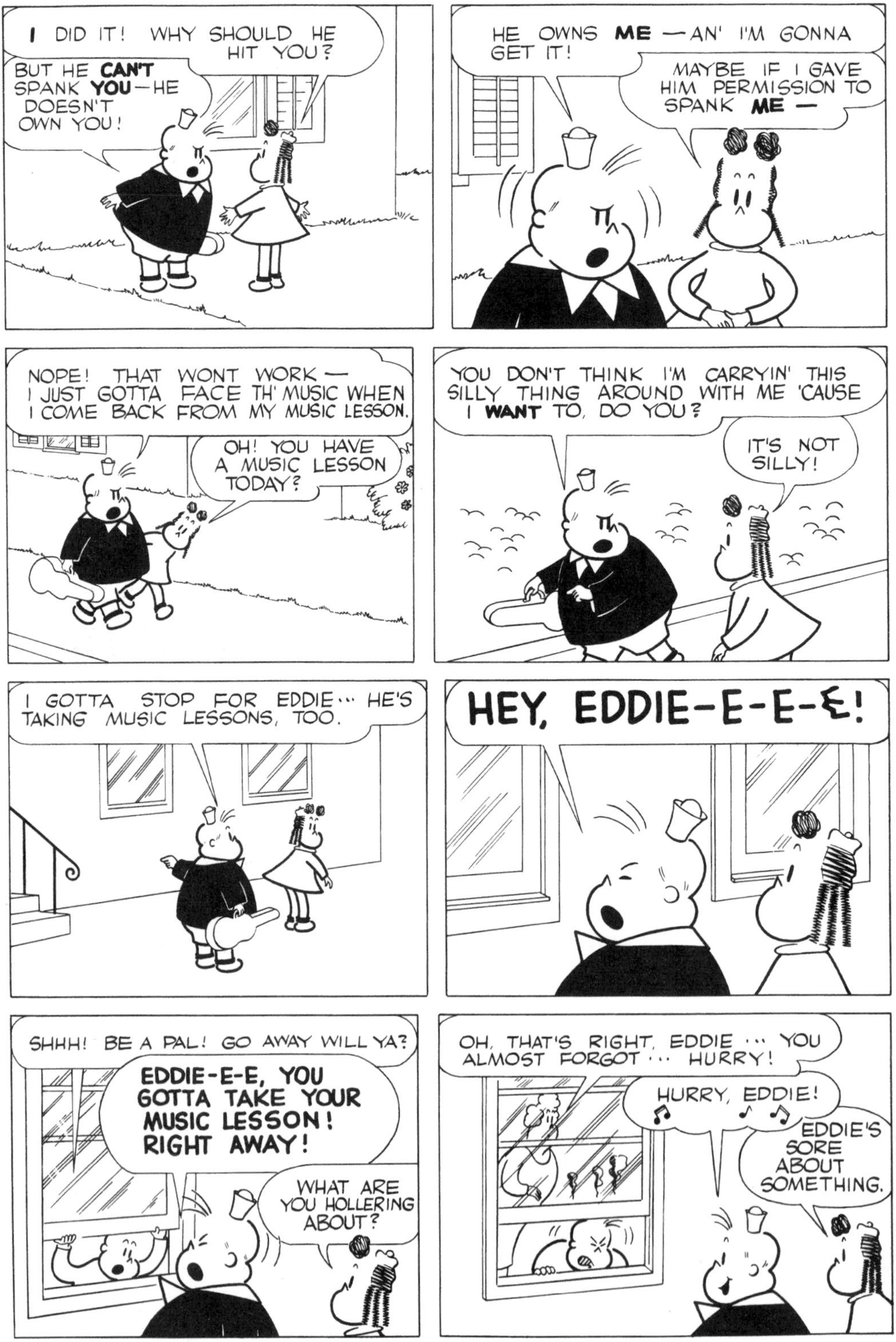
I DID IT! WHY SHOULD HE HIT YOU?
BUT HE CAN'T SPANK YOU—HE DOESN'T OWN YOU!
HE OWNS ME —AN' I'M GONNA GET IT!
MAYBE IF I GAVE HIM PERMISSION TO SPANK ME —
NOPE! THAT WONT WORK— I JUST GOTTA FACE TH' MUSIC WHEN I COME BACK FROM MY MUSIC LESSON.
OH! YOU HAVE A MUSIC LESSON TODAY?
YOU DON'T THINK I'M CARRYIN' THIS SILLY THING AROUND WITH ME 'CAUSE I WANT TO, DO YOU?
IT'S NOT SILLY!
I GOTTA STOP FOR EDDIE··· HE'S TAKING MUSIC LESSONS, TOO.
HEY, EDDIE-E-E-E!
SHHH! BE A PAL! GO AWAY WILL YA?
EDDIE-E-E, YOU GOTTA TAKE YOUR MUSIC LESSON! RIGHT AWAY!
WHAT ARE YOU HOLLERING ABOUT?
OH, THAT'S RIGHT, EDDIE ··· YOU ALMOST FORGOT ··· HURRY!
HURRY, EDDIE!
EDDIE'S SORE ABOUT SOMETHING.

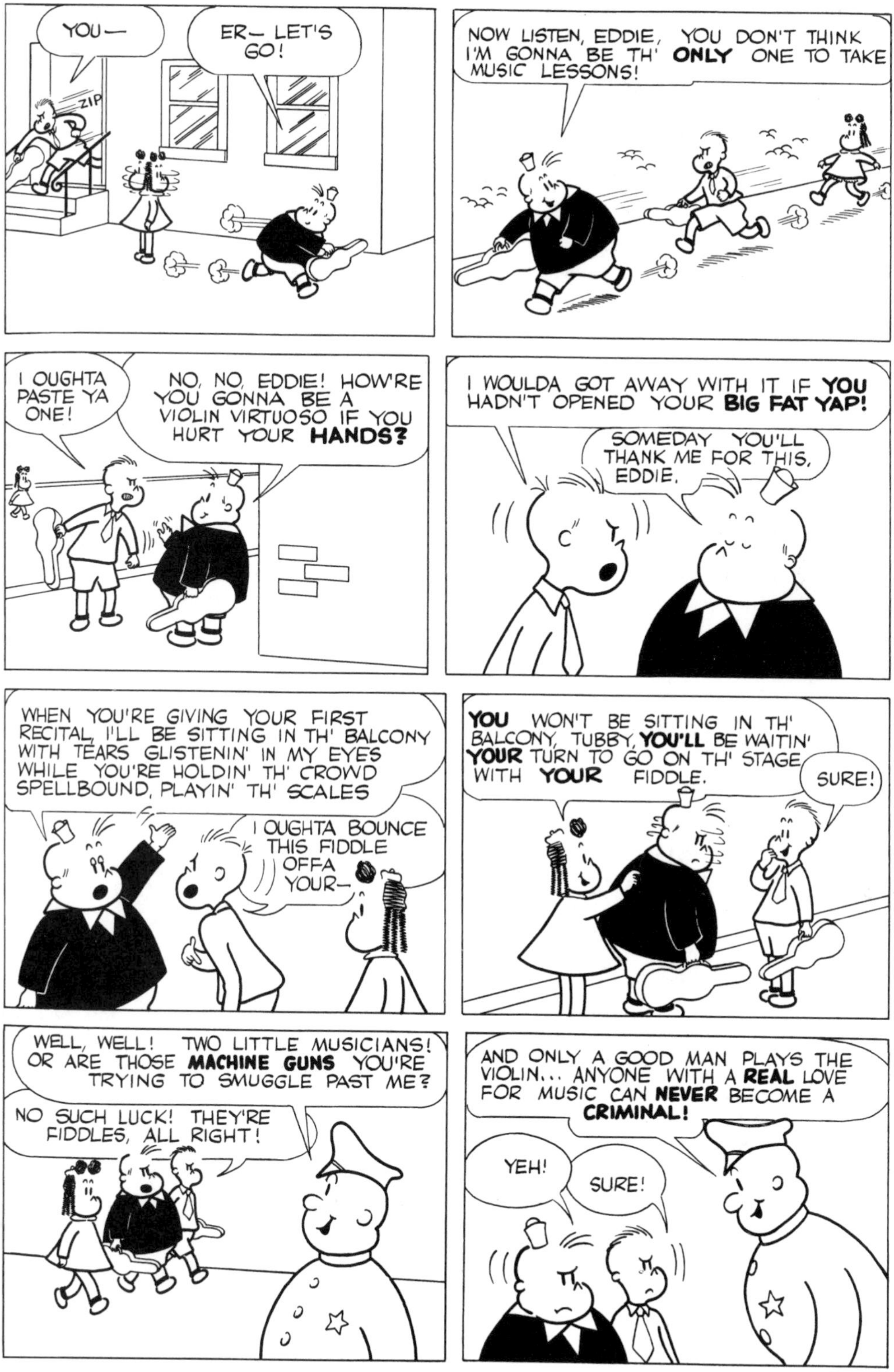
YOU—
ZIP
ER— LET'S GO!
NOW LISTEN, EDDIE, YOU DON'T THINK I'M GONNA BE TH' ONLY ONE TO TAKE MUSIC LESSONS!
I OUGHTA PASTE YA ONE!
NO, NO, EDDIE! HOW'RE YOU GONNA BE A VIOLIN VIRTUOSO IF YOU HURT YOUR HANDS?
I WOULDA GOT AWAY WITH IT IF YOU HADN'T OPENED YOUR BIG FAT YAP!
SOMEDAY YOU'LL THANK ME FOR THIS, EDDIE.
WHEN YOU'RE GIVING YOUR FIRST RECITAL, I'LL BE SITTING IN TH' BALCONY WITH TEARS GLISTENIN' IN MY EYES WHILE YOU'RE HOLDIN' TH' CROWD SPELLBOUND, PLAYIN' TH' SCALES
I OUGHTA BOUNCE THIS FIDDLE OFFA YOUR—
YOU WON'T BE SITTING IN TH' BALCONY, TUBBY, YOU'LL BE WAITIN' YOUR TURN TO GO ON TH' STAGE WITH YOUR FIDDLE.
SURE!
WELL, WELL! TWO LITTLE MUSICIANS! OR ARE THOSE MACHINE GUNS YOU'RE TRYING TO SMUGGLE PAST ME?
NO SUCH LUCK! THEY'RE FIDDLES, ALL RIGHT!
AND ONLY A GOOD MAN PLAYS THE VIOLIN... ANYONE WITH A REAL LOVE FOR MUSIC CAN NEVER BECOME A CRIMINAL!
YEH!
SURE!

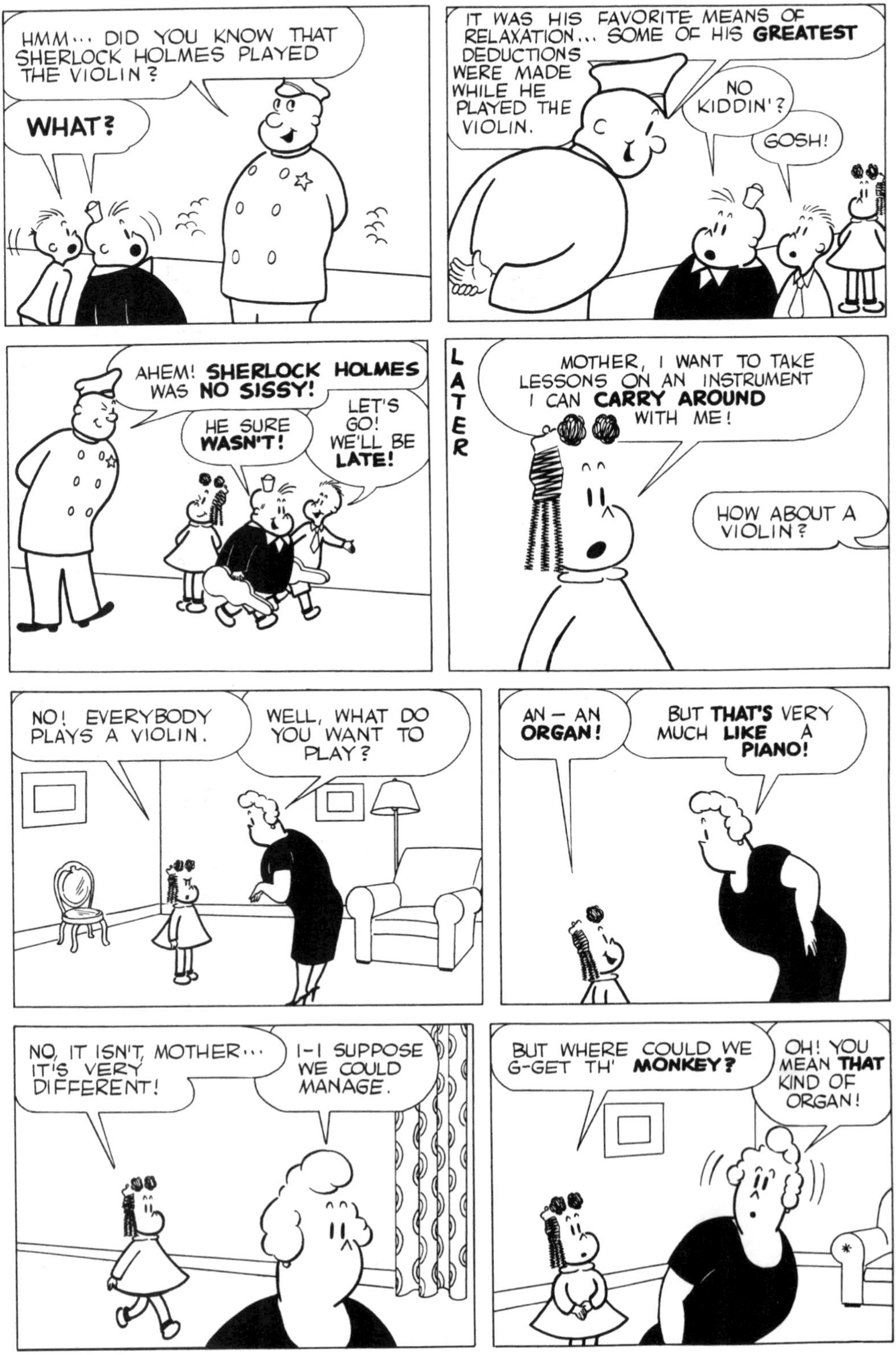
HMM... DID YOU KNOW THAT SHERLOCK HOLMES PLAYED THE VIOLIN?
WHAT?
IT WAS HIS FAVORITE MEANS OF RELAXATION... SOME OF HIS GREATEST DEDUCTIONS WERE MADE WHILE HE PLAYED THE VIOLIN.
NO KIDDIN'?
GOSH!
AHEM! SHERLOCK HOLMES WAS NO SISSY!
HE SURE WASN'T!
LET'S GO! WE'LL BE LATE!
LATER
MOTHER, I WANT TO TAKE LESSONS ON AN INSTRUMENT I CAN CARRY AROUND WITH ME!
HOW ABOUT A VIOLIN?
NO! EVERYBODY PLAYS A VIOLIN.
WELL, WHAT DO YOU WANT TO PLAY?
AN — AN ORGAN!
BUT THAT'S VERY MUCH LIKE A PIANO!
NO, IT ISN'T, MOTHER... IT'S VERY DIFFERENT!
I-I SUPPOSE WE COULD MANAGE.
BUT WHERE COULD WE G-GET TH' MONKEY?
OH! YOU MEAN THAT KIND OF ORGAN!

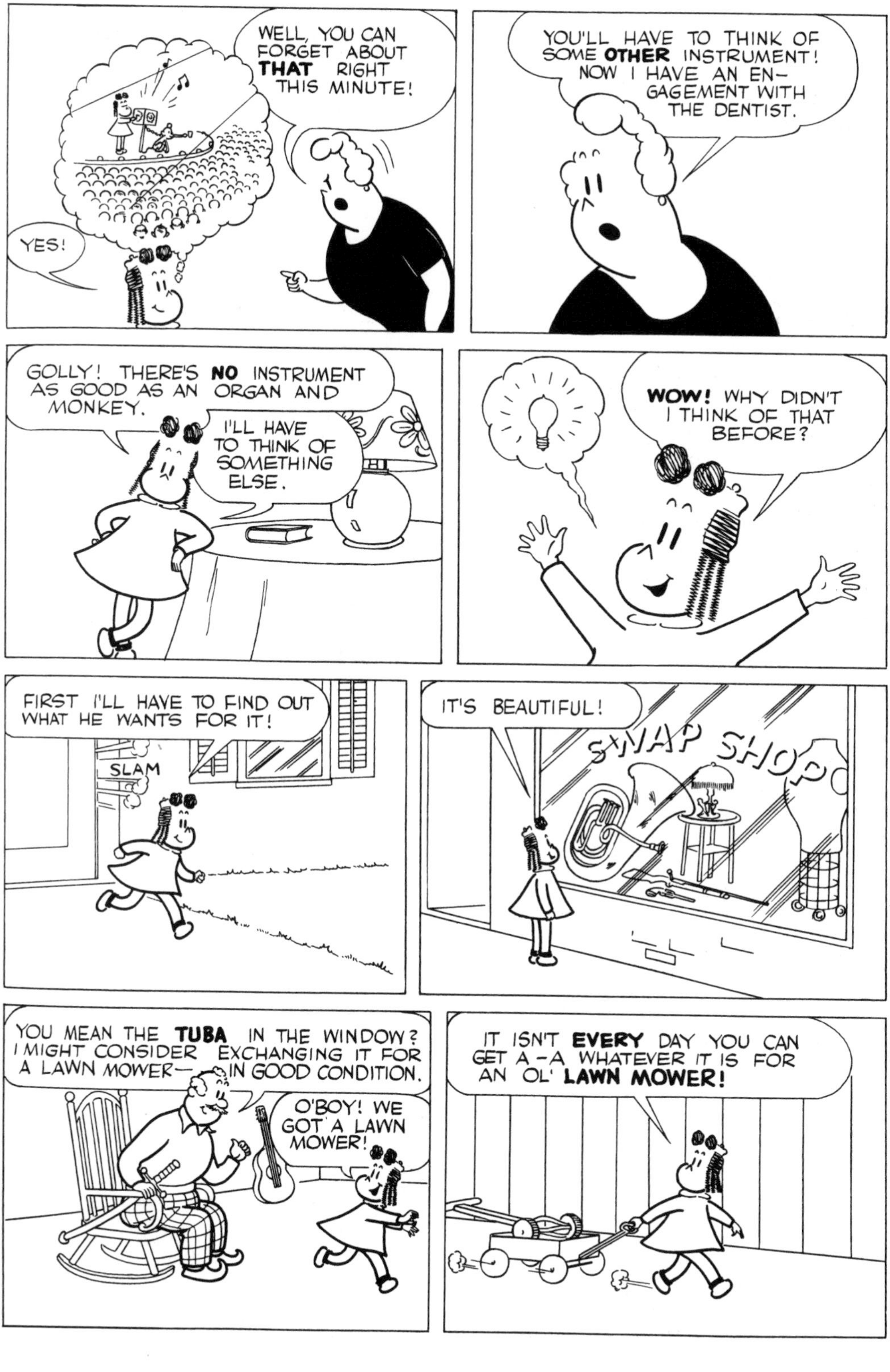
WELL, YOU CAN FORGET ABOUT THAT RIGHT THIS MINUTE!
YES!
YOU'LL HAVE TO THINK OF SOME OTHER INSTRUMENT! NOW I HAVE AN EN-GAGEMENT WITH THE DENTIST.
GOLLY! THERE'S NO INSTRUMENT AS GOOD AS AN ORGAN AND MONKEY.
I'LL HAVE TO THINK OF SOMETHING ELSE.
WOW! WHY DIDN'T I THINK OF THAT BEFORE?
FIRST I'LL HAVE TO FIND OUT WHAT HE WANTS FOR IT!
SLAM
IT'S BEAUTIFUL!
SWAP SHOP
YOU MEAN THE TUBA IN THE WINDOW? I MIGHT CONSIDER EXCHANGING IT FOR A LAWN MOWER— IN GOOD CONDITION.
O'BOY! WE GOT A LAWN MOWER!
IT ISN'T EVERY DAY YOU CAN GET A-A WHATEVER IT IS FOR AN OL' LAWN MOWER!

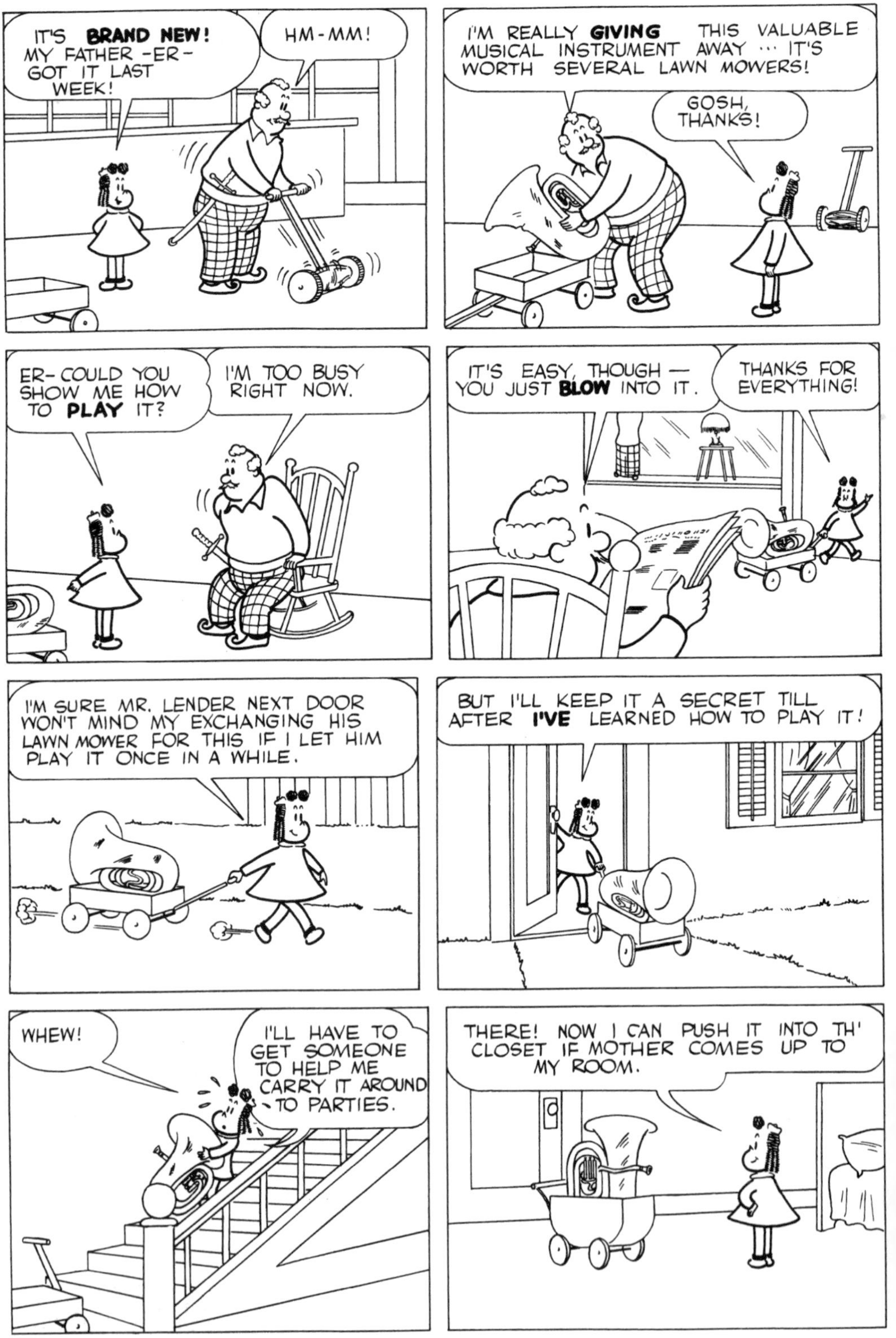
IT'S **BRAND NEW!** MY FATHER -ER- GOT IT LAST WEEK!
HM-MM!
I'M REALLY **GIVING** THIS VALUABLE MUSICAL INSTRUMENT AWAY ... IT'S WORTH SEVERAL LAWN MOWERS!
GOSH, THANKS!
ER- COULD YOU SHOW ME HOW TO **PLAY** IT?
I'M TOO BUSY RIGHT NOW.
IT'S EASY, THOUGH — YOU JUST **BLOW** INTO IT.
THANKS FOR EVERYTHING!
I'M SURE MR. LENDER NEXT DOOR WON'T MIND MY EXCHANGING HIS LAWN MOWER FOR THIS IF I LET HIM PLAY IT ONCE IN A WHILE.
BUT I'LL KEEP IT A SECRET TILL AFTER **I'VE** LEARNED HOW TO PLAY IT!
WHEW!
I'LL HAVE TO GET SOMEONE TO HELP ME CARRY IT AROUND TO PARTIES.
THERE! NOW I CAN PUSH IT INTO TH' CLOSET IF MOTHER COMES UP TO MY ROOM.

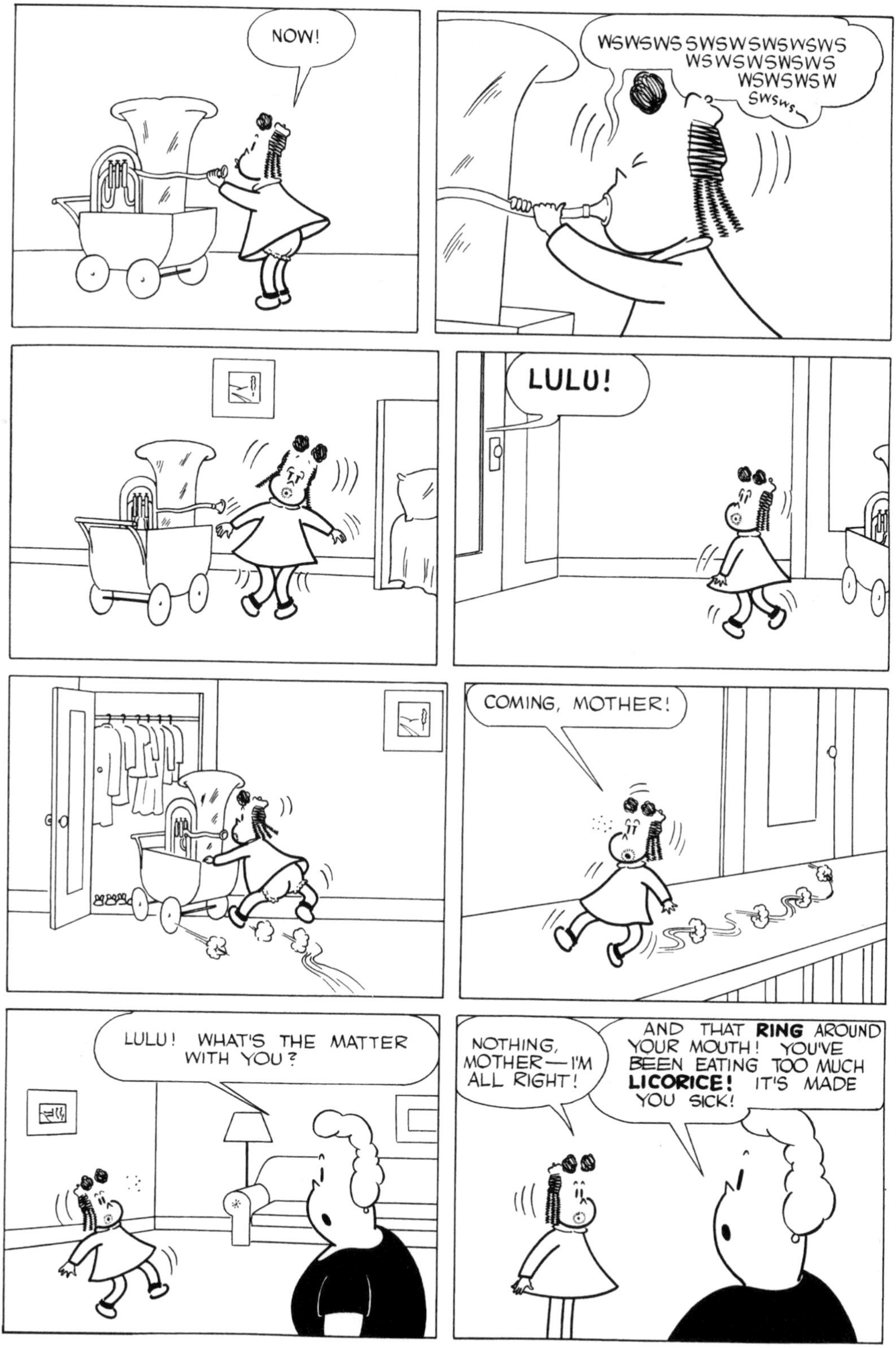
NOW!
WSWSWS SWSWSWSWSWS WSWSWSWSWS WSWSWSW SWSWS
LULU!
COMING, MOTHER!
LULU! WHAT'S THE MATTER WITH YOU?
NOTHING, MOTHER—I'M ALL RIGHT!
AND THAT RING AROUND YOUR MOUTH! YOU'VE BEEN EATING TOO MUCH LICORICE! IT'S MADE YOU SICK!

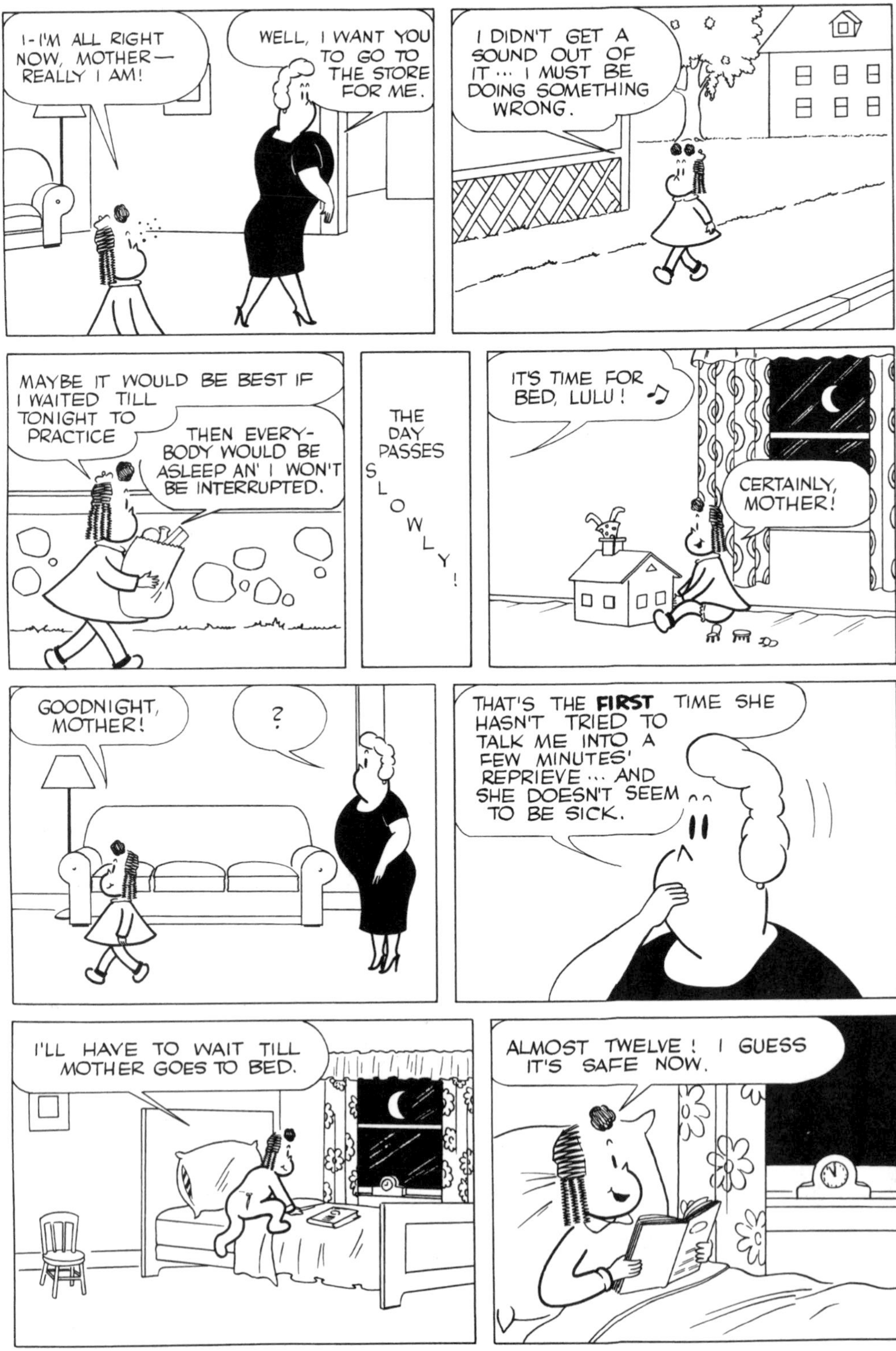
I-I'M ALL RIGHT NOW, MOTHER— REALLY I AM!
WELL, I WANT YOU TO GO TO THE STORE FOR ME.
I DIDN'T GET A SOUND OUT OF IT ... I MUST BE DOING SOMETHING WRONG.
MAYBE IT WOULD BE BEST IF I WAITED TILL TONIGHT TO PRACTICE
THEN EVERY-BODY WOULD BE ASLEEP AN' I WON'T BE INTERRUPTED.
THE DAY PASSES SLOWLY!
IT'S TIME FOR BED, LULU!
CERTAINLY, MOTHER!
GOODNIGHT, MOTHER!
?
THAT'S THE FIRST TIME SHE HASN'T TRIED TO TALK ME INTO A FEW MINUTES' REPRIEVE ... AND SHE DOESN'T SEEM TO BE SICK.
I'LL HAVE TO WAIT TILL MOTHER GOES TO BED.
ALMOST TWELVE! I GUESS IT'S SAFE NOW.

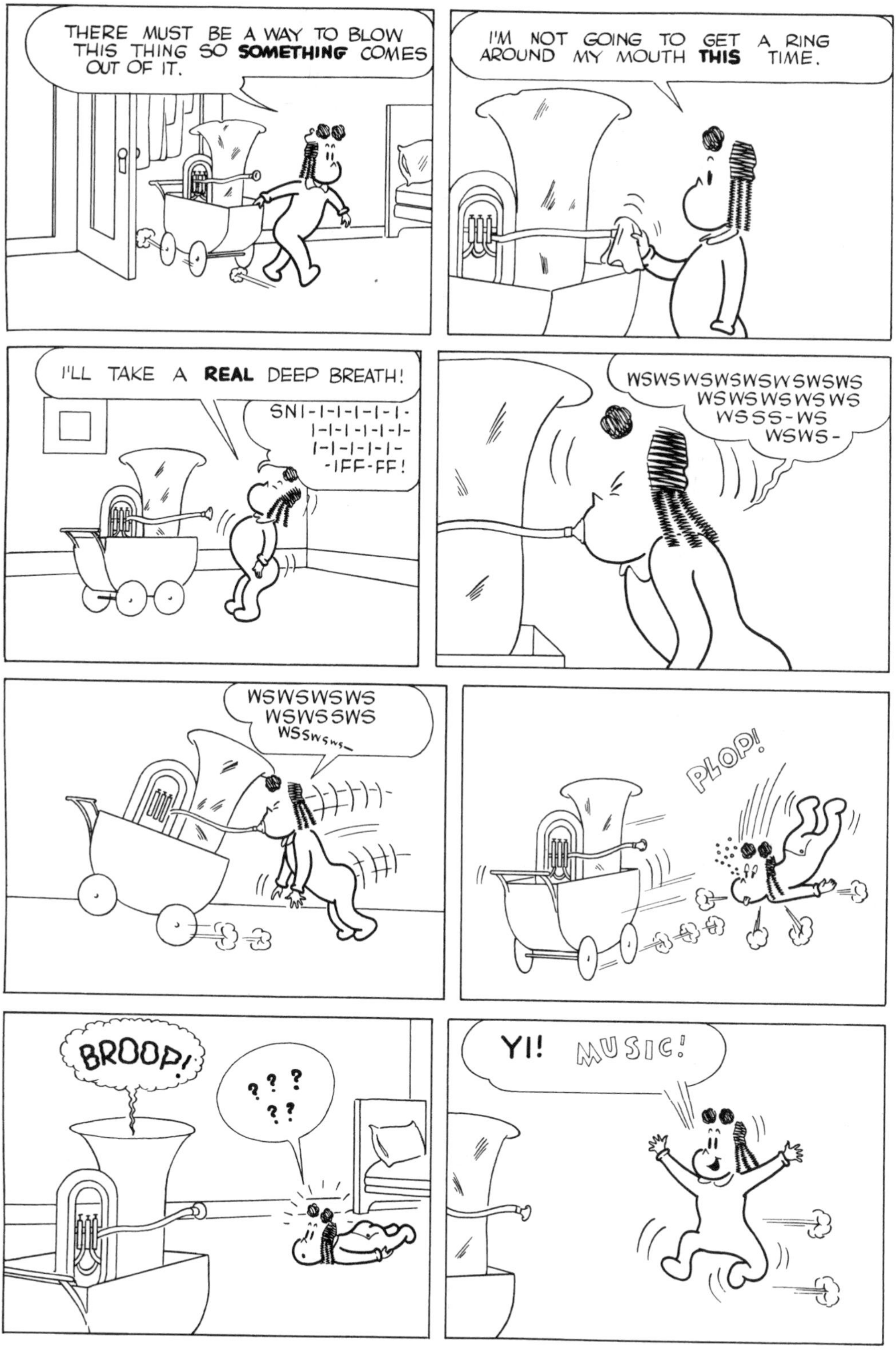

THERE MUST BE A WAY TO BLOW THIS THING SO **SOMETHING** COMES OUT OF IT.
I'M NOT GOING TO GET A RING AROUND MY MOUTH **THIS** TIME.
I'LL TAKE A **REAL** DEEP BREATH!
SNI-I-I-I-I-I-I-I-I-I-I-I-I-I-I-I-I-I-I-I-IFF-FF!
WSWSWSWSWSWSWSWS WSWSWSWSWS WSSS-WS WSWS-
WSWSWSWS WSWSSWS WSSwsws-
PLOP!
BROOP!
? ? ? ? ?
YI! MUSIC!

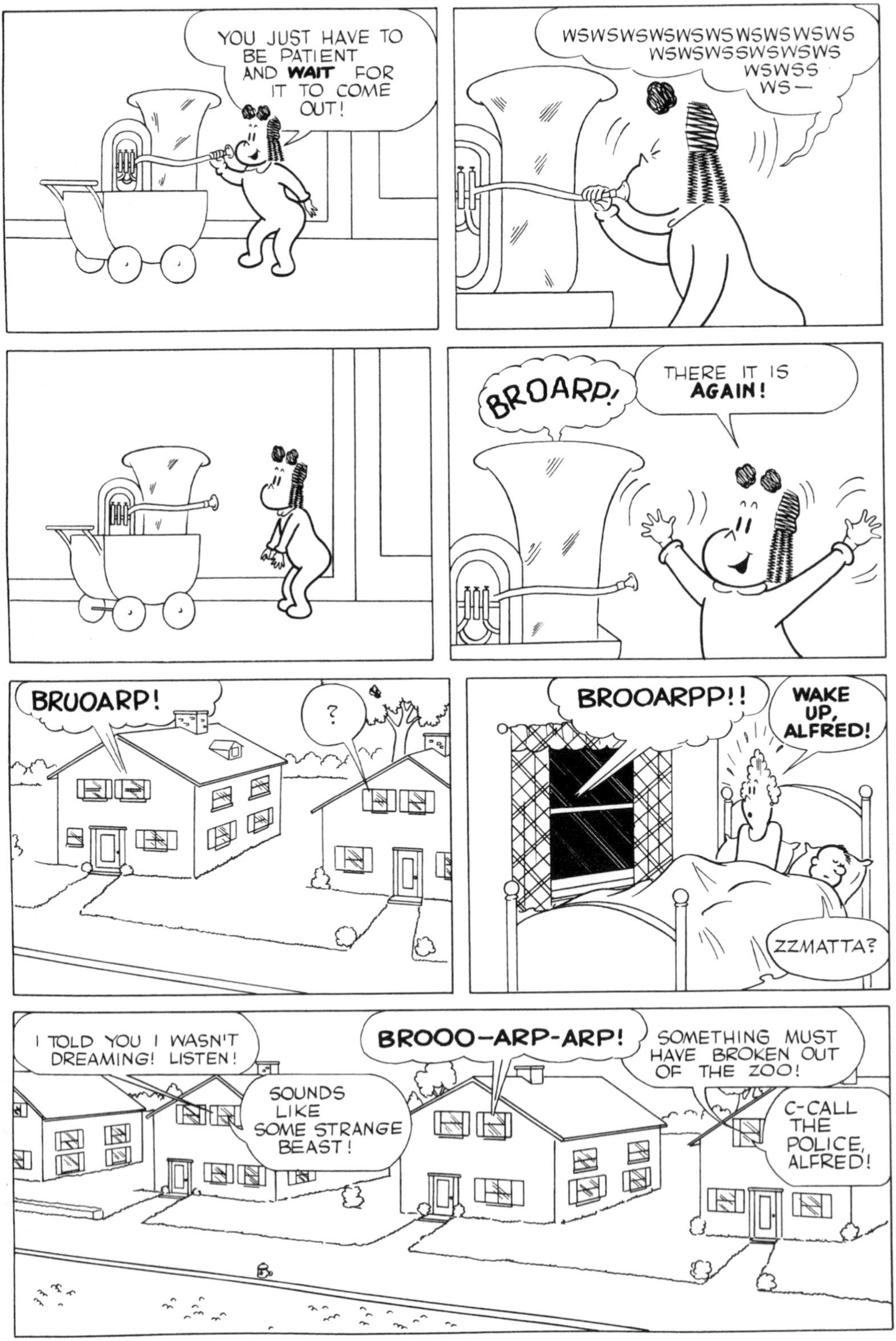
YOU JUST HAVE TO BE PATIENT AND **WAIT** FOR IT TO COME OUT!
WSWSWSWSWSWSWSWSWSWS WSWSWSSWSWSWS WSWSS WS—
BROARP!
THERE IT IS **AGAIN!**
BRUOARP!
?
BROOARPP!!
WAKE UP, ALFRED!
ZZMATTA?
I TOLD YOU I WASN'T DREAMING! LISTEN!
SOUNDS LIKE SOME STRANGE BEAST!
BROOO-ARP-ARP!
SOMETHING MUST HAVE BROKEN OUT OF THE ZOO!
C-CALL THE POLICE, ALFRED!

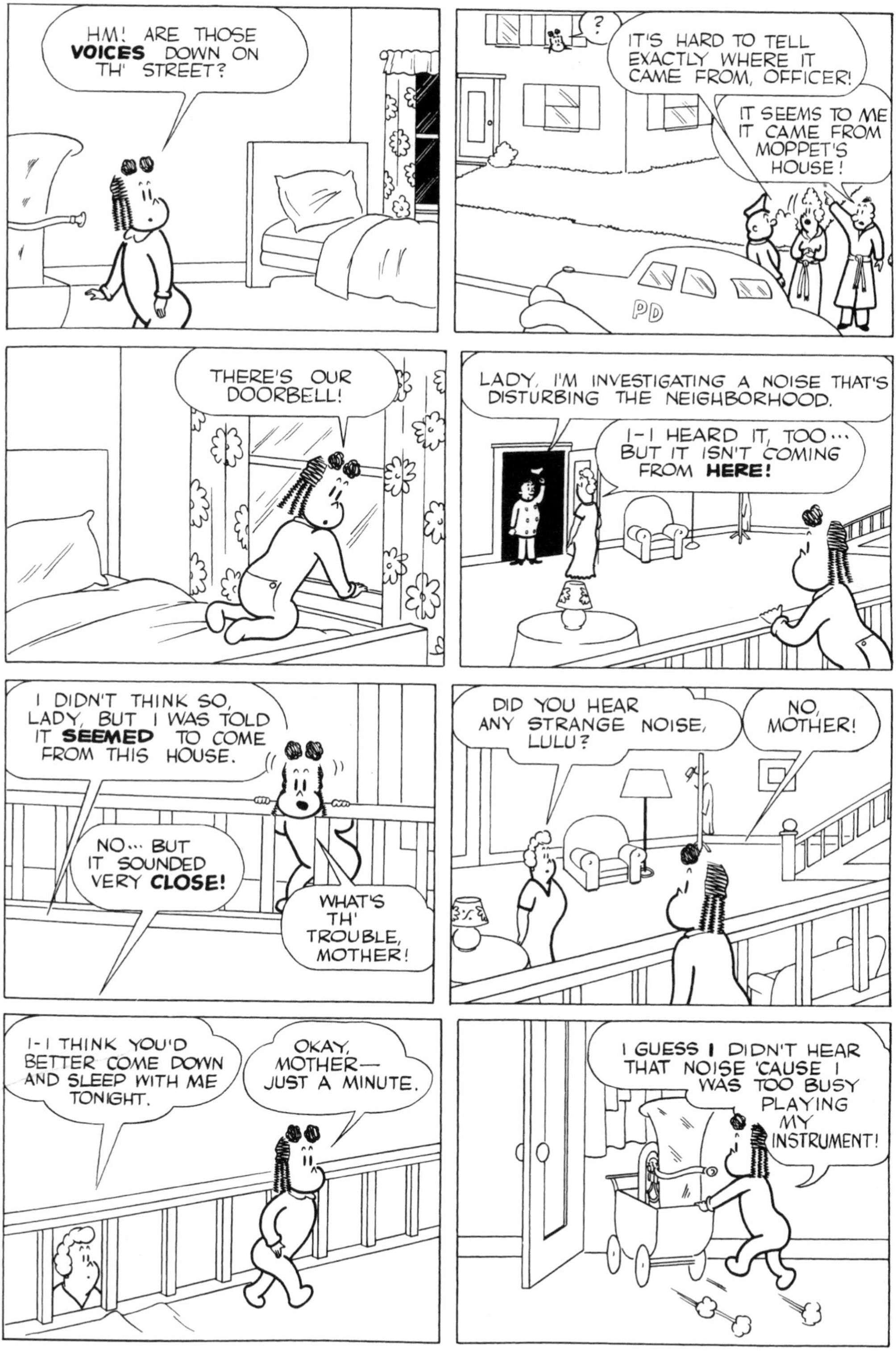
HM! ARE THOSE **VOICES** DOWN ON TH' STREET?
IT'S HARD TO TELL EXACTLY WHERE IT CAME FROM, OFFICER!
IT SEEMS TO ME IT CAME FROM MOPPET'S HOUSE!
?
PD
THERE'S OUR DOORBELL!
LADY, I'M INVESTIGATING A NOISE THAT'S DISTURBING THE NEIGHBORHOOD.
I-I HEARD IT, TOO... BUT IT ISN'T COMING FROM **HERE!**
I DIDN'T THINK SO, LADY, BUT I WAS TOLD IT **SEEMED** TO COME FROM THIS HOUSE.
NO... BUT IT SOUNDED VERY **CLOSE!**
WHAT'S TH' TROUBLE, MOTHER!
DID YOU HEAR ANY STRANGE NOISE, LULU?
NO, MOTHER!
I-I THINK YOU'D BETTER COME DOWN AND SLEEP WITH ME TONIGHT.
OKAY, MOTHER— JUST A MINUTE.
I GUESS **I** DIDN'T HEAR THAT NOISE 'CAUSE I WAS TOO BUSY PLAYING MY INSTRUMENT!

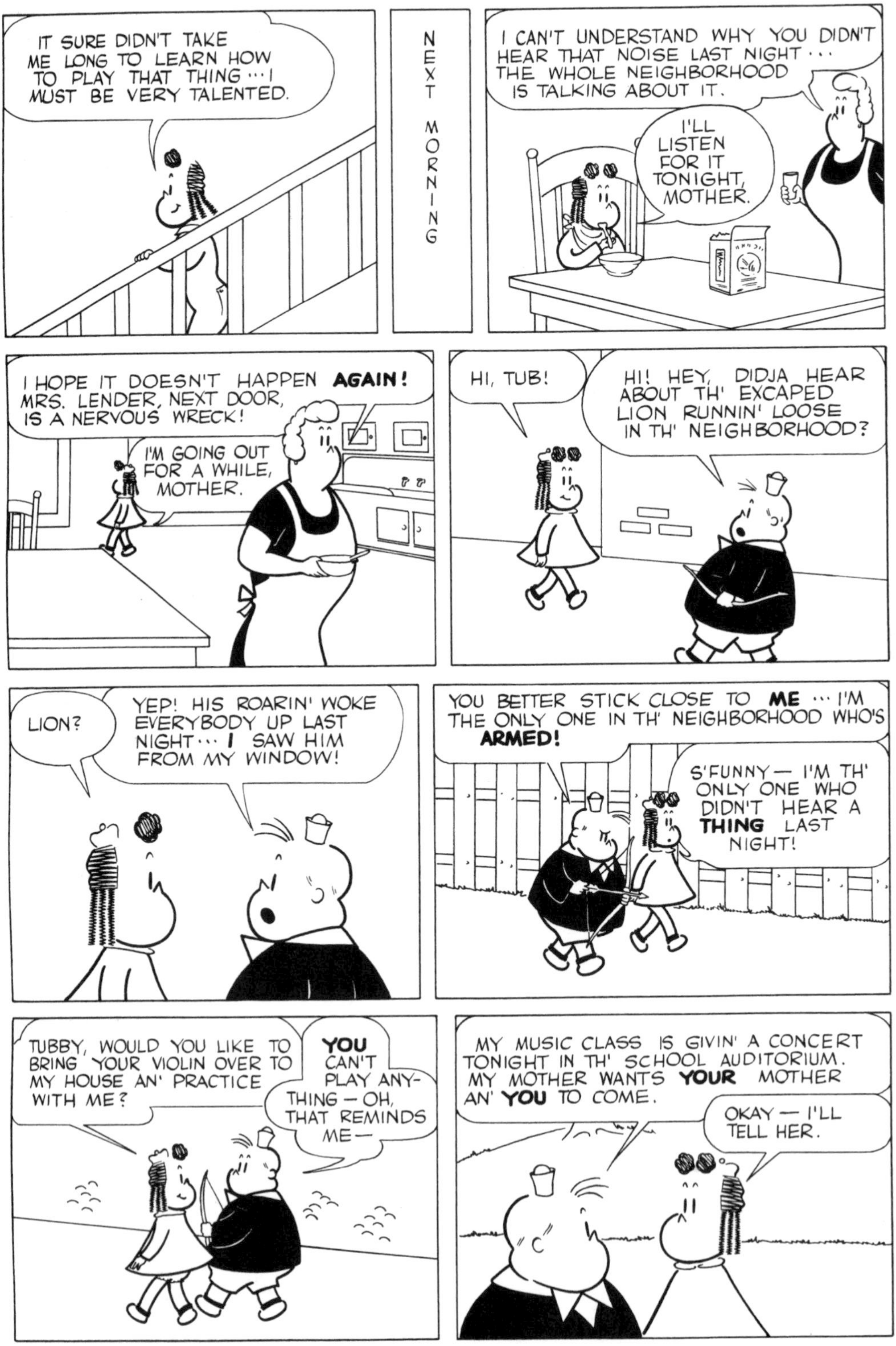

IT SURE DIDN'T TAKE ME LONG TO LEARN HOW TO PLAY THAT THING ··· I MUST BE VERY TALENTED.
NEXT MORNING
I CAN'T UNDERSTAND WHY YOU DIDN'T HEAR THAT NOISE LAST NIGHT ··· THE WHOLE NEIGHBORHOOD IS TALKING ABOUT IT.
I'LL LISTEN FOR IT TONIGHT, MOTHER.
I HOPE IT DOESN'T HAPPEN **AGAIN!** MRS. LENDER, NEXT DOOR, IS A NERVOUS WRECK!
I'M GOING OUT FOR A WHILE, MOTHER.
HI, TUB!
HI! HEY, DIDJA HEAR ABOUT TH' EXCAPED LION RUNNIN' LOOSE IN TH' NEIGHBORHOOD?
LION?
YEP! HIS ROARIN' WOKE EVERYBODY UP LAST NIGHT ··· **I** SAW HIM FROM MY WINDOW!
YOU BETTER STICK CLOSE TO **ME** ··· I'M THE ONLY ONE IN TH' NEIGHBORHOOD WHO'S **ARMED!**
S'FUNNY— I'M TH' ONLY ONE WHO DIDN'T HEAR A **THING** LAST NIGHT!
TUBBY, WOULD YOU LIKE TO BRING YOUR VIOLIN OVER TO MY HOUSE AN' PRACTICE WITH ME?
YOU CAN'T PLAY ANYTHING—OH, THAT REMINDS ME—
MY MUSIC CLASS IS GIVIN' A CONCERT TONIGHT IN TH' SCHOOL AUDITORIUM. MY MOTHER WANTS **YOUR** MOTHER AN' **YOU** TO COME.
OKAY— I'LL TELL HER.

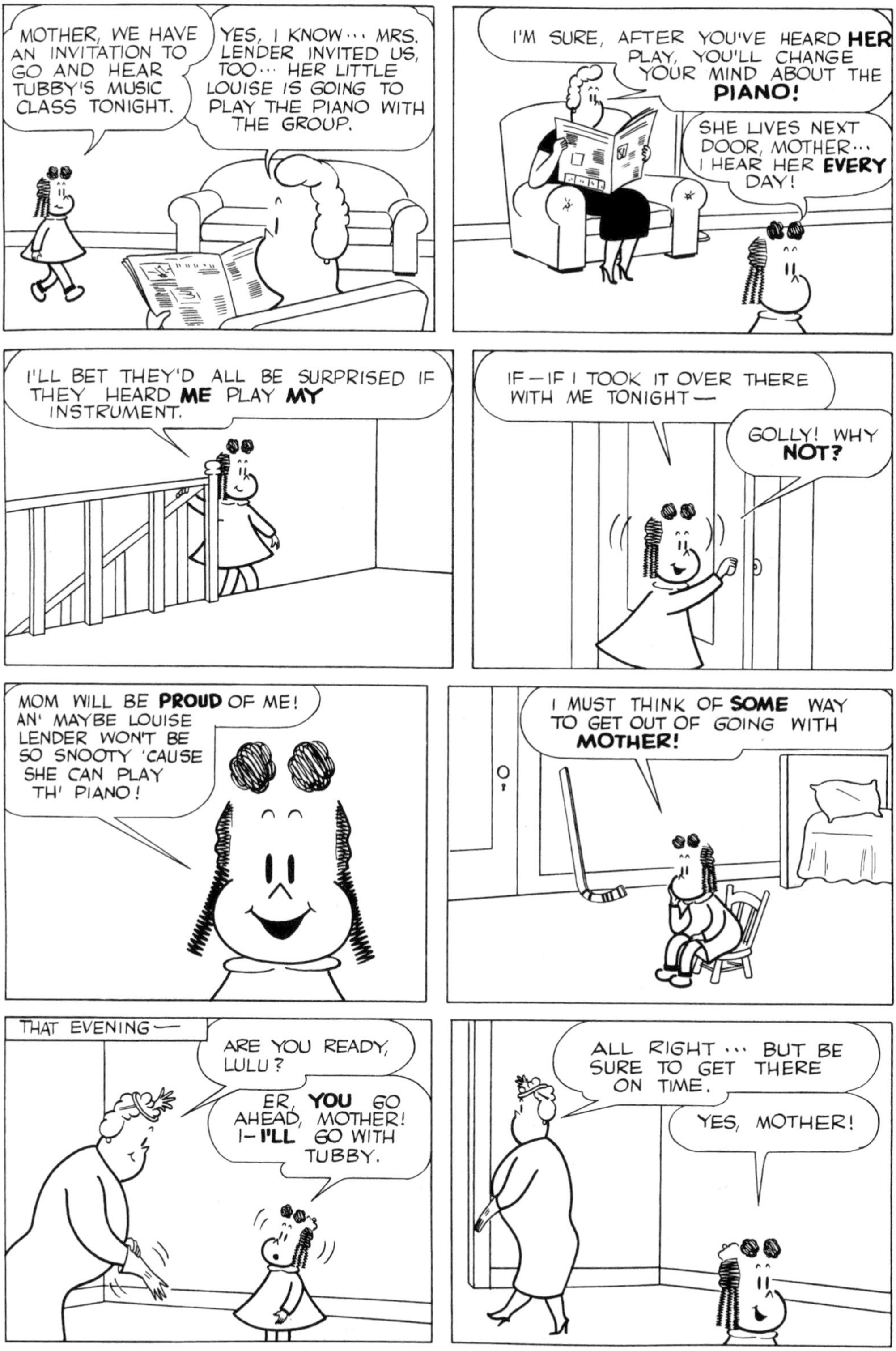
MOTHER, WE HAVE AN INVITATION TO GO AND HEAR TUBBY'S MUSIC CLASS TONIGHT.
YES, I KNOW··· MRS. LENDER INVITED US, TOO··· HER LITTLE LOUISE IS GOING TO PLAY THE PIANO WITH THE GROUP.
I'M SURE, AFTER YOU'VE HEARD **HER** PLAY, YOU'LL CHANGE YOUR MIND ABOUT THE **PIANO!**
SHE LIVES NEXT DOOR, MOTHER··· I HEAR HER **EVERY** DAY!
I'LL BET THEY'D ALL BE SURPRISED IF THEY HEARD **ME** PLAY **MY** INSTRUMENT.
IF—IF I TOOK IT OVER THERE WITH ME TONIGHT—
GOLLY! WHY **NOT?**
MOM WILL BE **PROUD** OF ME! AN' MAYBE LOUISE LENDER WON'T BE SO SNOOTY 'CAUSE SHE CAN PLAY TH' PIANO!
I MUST THINK OF **SOME** WAY TO GET OUT OF GOING WITH **MOTHER!**
THAT EVENING—
ARE YOU READY, LULU?
ER, **YOU** GO AHEAD, MOTHER! I—**I'LL** GO WITH TUBBY.
ALL RIGHT··· BUT BE SURE TO GET THERE ON TIME.
YES, MOTHER!

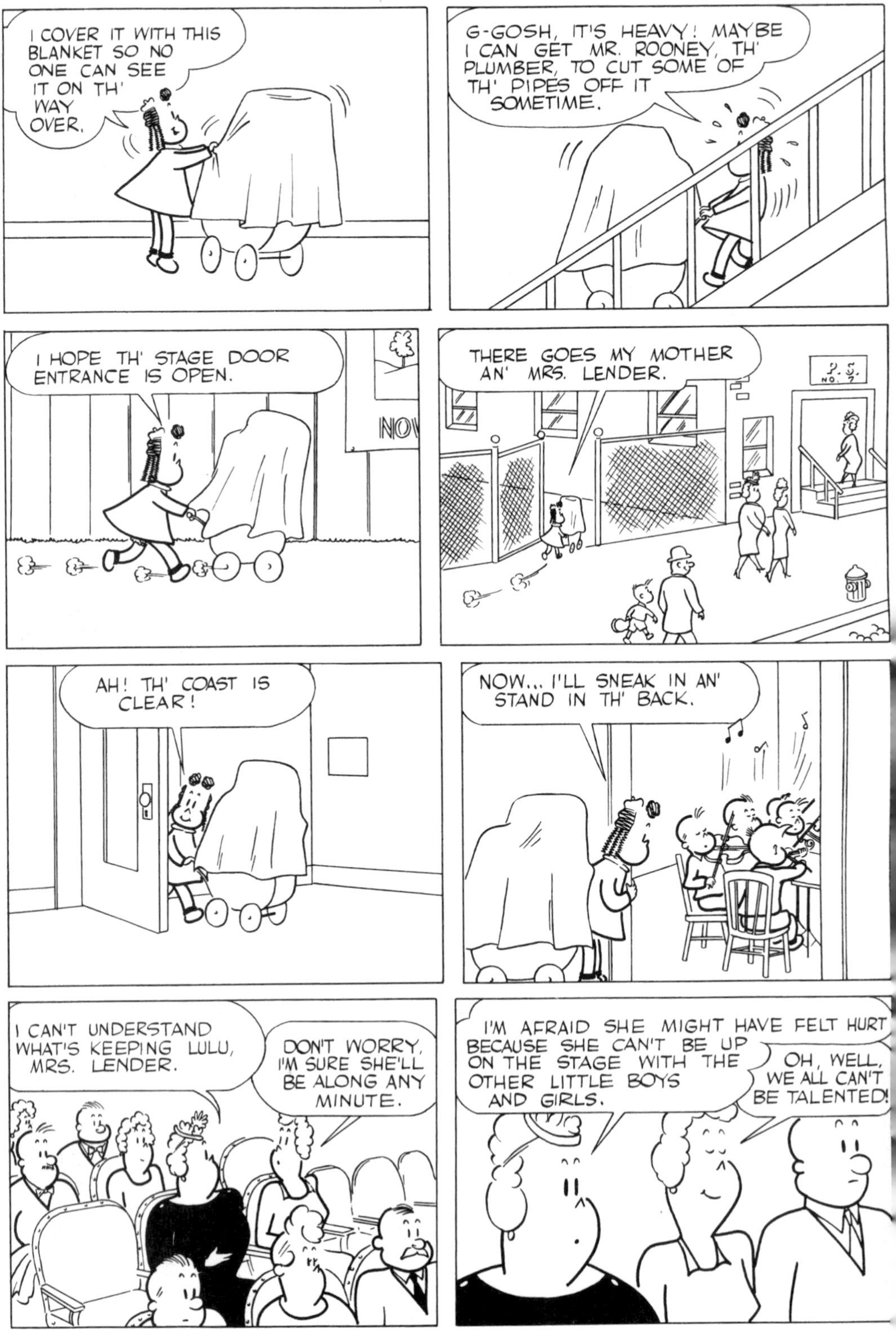

I COVER IT WITH THIS BLANKET SO NO ONE CAN SEE IT ON TH' WAY OVER.
G-GOSH, IT'S HEAVY! MAYBE I CAN GET MR. ROONEY, TH' PLUMBER, TO CUT SOME OF TH' PIPES OFF IT SOMETIME.
I HOPE TH' STAGE DOOR ENTRANCE IS OPEN.
NOW
THERE GOES MY MOTHER AN' MRS. LENDER.
P. S. NO. 7
AH! TH' COAST IS CLEAR!
NOW... I'LL SNEAK IN AN' STAND IN TH' BACK.
I CAN'T UNDERSTAND WHAT'S KEEPING LULU, MRS. LENDER.
DON'T WORRY, I'M SURE SHE'LL BE ALONG ANY MINUTE.
I'M AFRAID SHE MIGHT HAVE FELT HURT BECAUSE SHE CAN'T BE UP ON THE STAGE WITH THE OTHER LITTLE BOYS AND GIRLS.
OH, WELL, WE ALL CAN'T BE TALENTED!

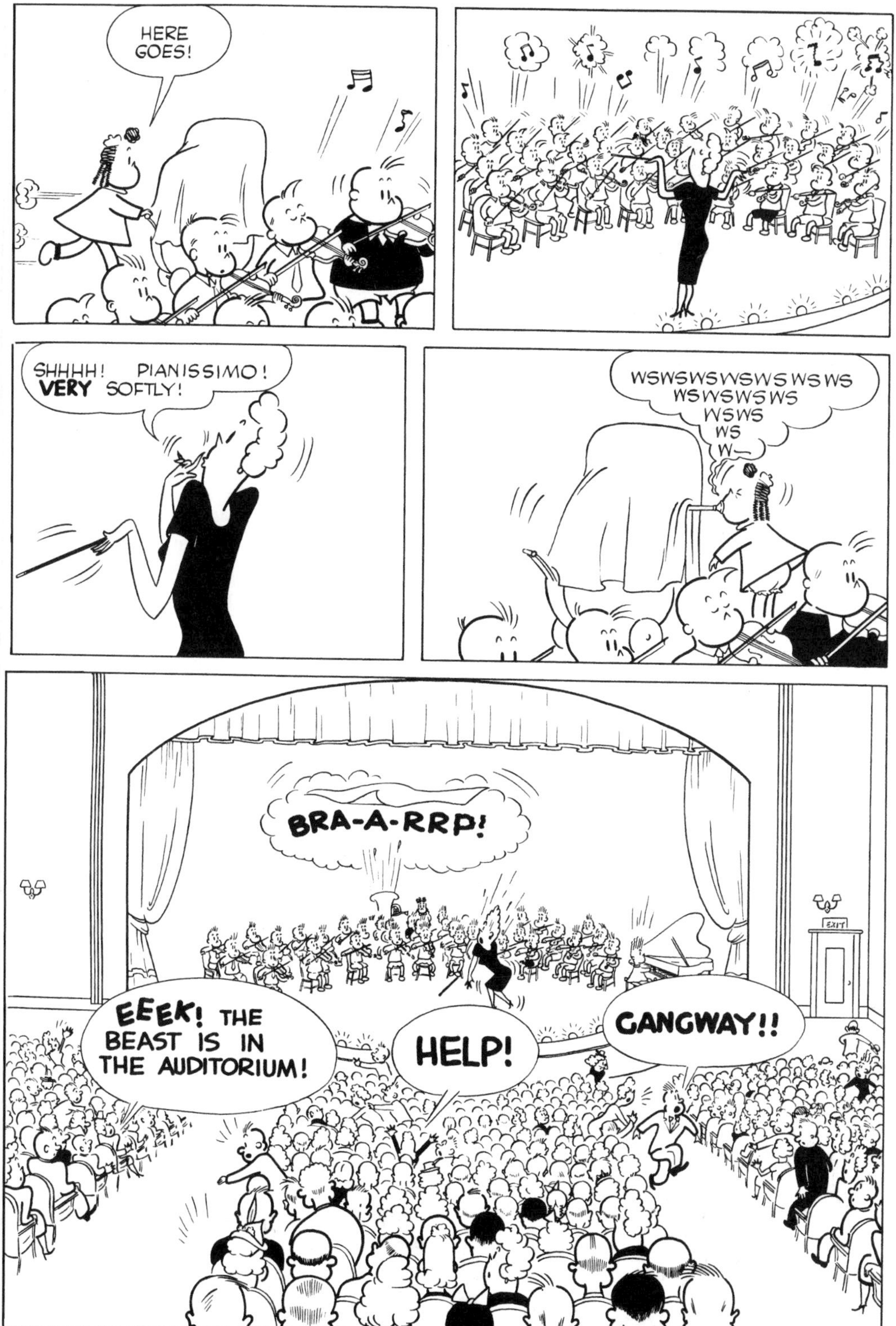
HERE GOES!
SHHHH! PIANISSIMO! VERY SOFTLY!
WSWSWSWSWSWSWS WSWSWSWS WSWS WS W—
BRA-A-RRP!
EXIT
EEEK! THE BEAST IS IN THE AUDITORIUM!
HELP!
GANGWAY!!

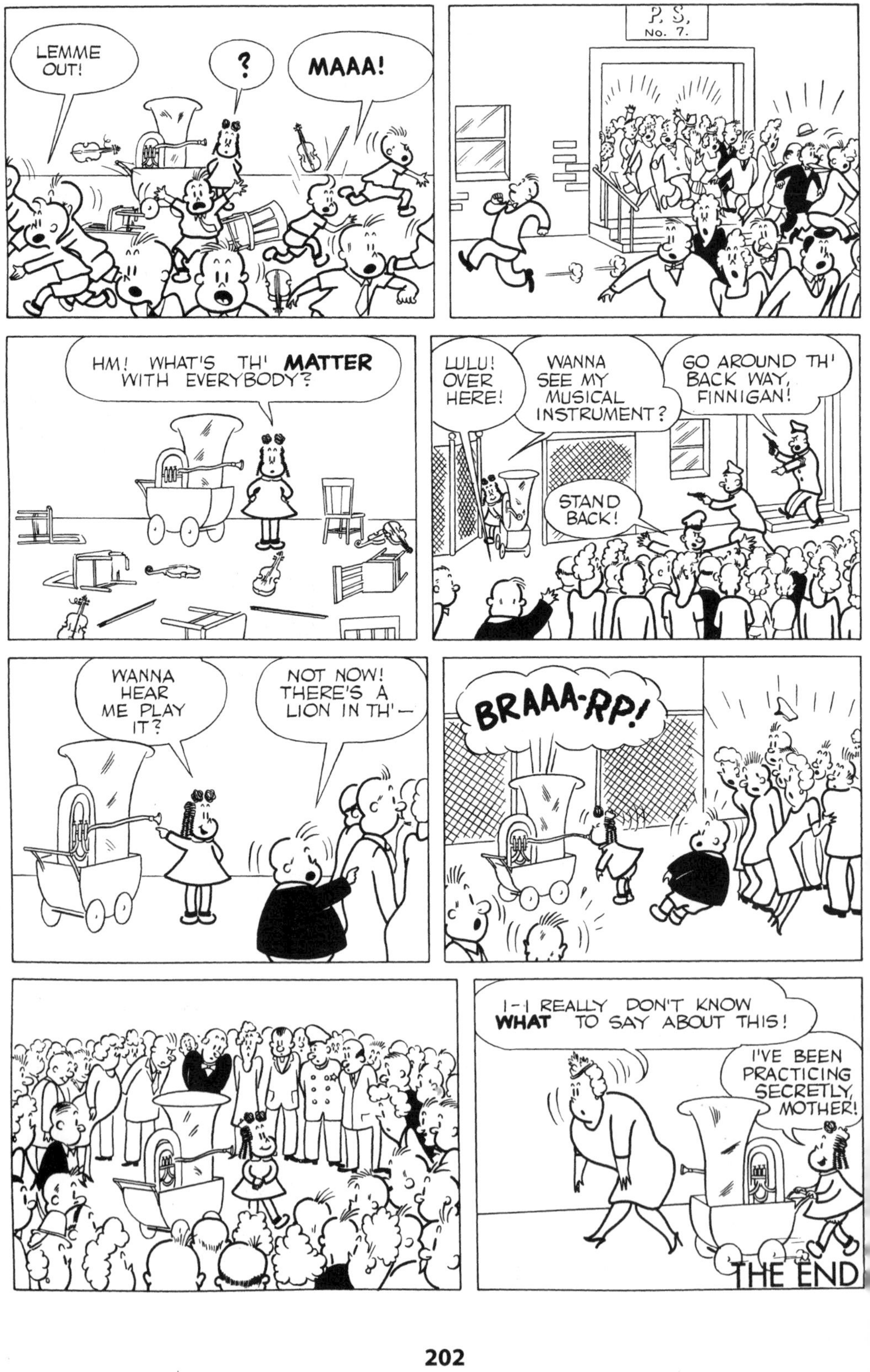
LEMME OUT!
?
MAAA!
P. S, No. 7.
HM! WHAT'S TH' MATTER WITH EVERYBODY?
LULU! OVER HERE!
WANNA SEE MY MUSICAL INSTRUMENT?
GO AROUND TH' BACK WAY, FINNIGAN!
STAND BACK!
WANNA HEAR ME PLAY IT?
NOT NOW! THERE'S A LION IN TH'—
BRAAA-RP!
I-I REALLY DON'T KNOW WHAT TO SAY ABOUT THIS!
I'VE BEEN PRACTICING SECRETLY, MOTHER!
THE END

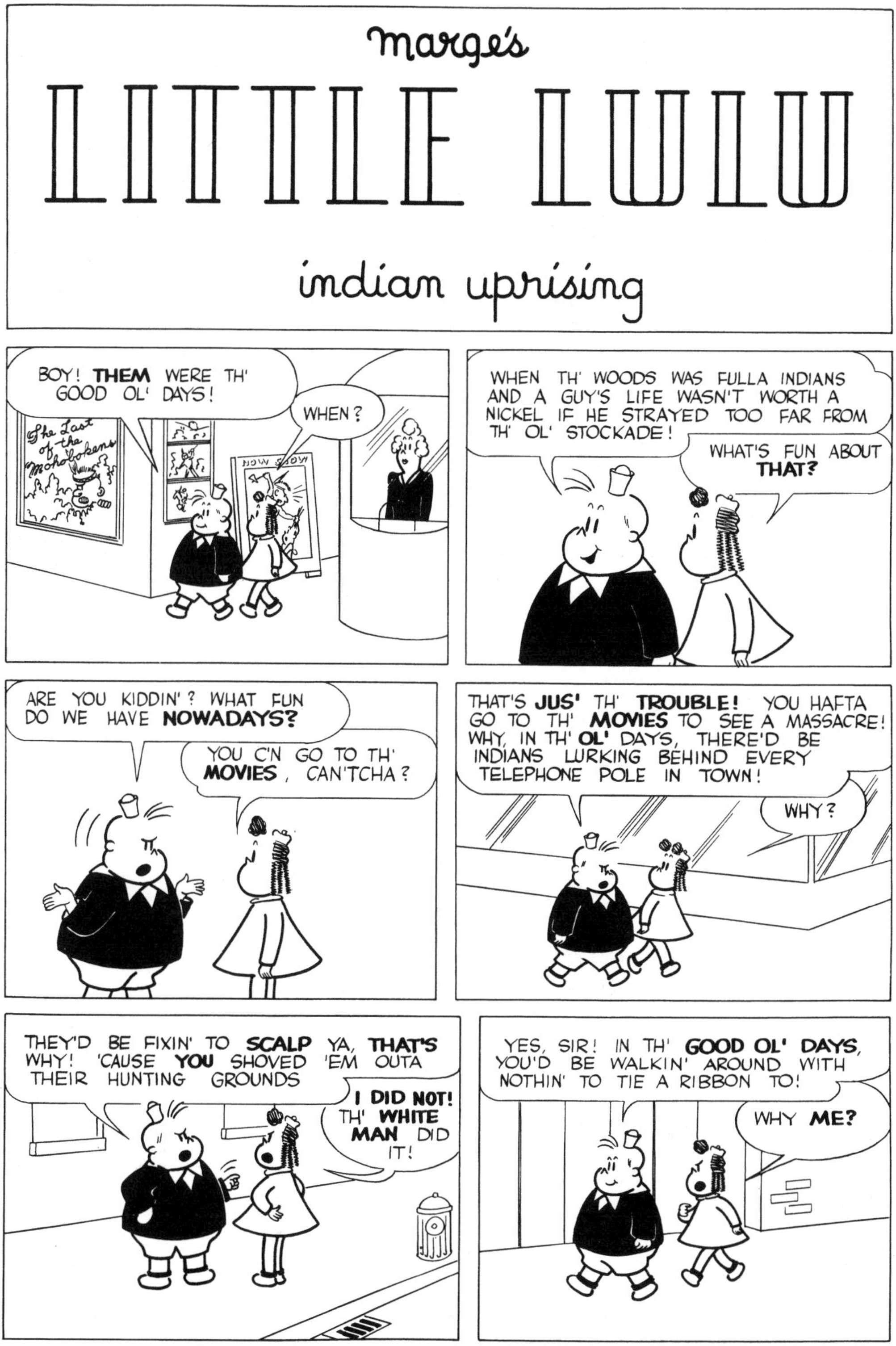
marge's
LITTLE LULU
indian uprising
The Last of the Mohobokens
NOW SHOWING
BOY! THEM WERE TH' GOOD OL' DAYS!
WHEN?
WHEN TH' WOODS WAS FULLA INDIANS AND A GUY'S LIFE WASN'T WORTH A NICKEL IF HE STRAYED TOO FAR FROM TH' OL' STOCKADE!
WHAT'S FUN ABOUT THAT?
ARE YOU KIDDIN'? WHAT FUN DO WE HAVE NOWADAYS?
YOU C'N GO TO TH' MOVIES, CAN'TCHA?
THAT'S JUS' TH' TROUBLE! YOU HAFTA GO TO TH' MOVIES TO SEE A MASSACRE! WHY, IN TH' OL' DAYS, THERE'D BE INDIANS LURKING BEHIND EVERY TELEPHONE POLE IN TOWN!
WHY?
THEY'D BE FIXIN' TO SCALP YA, THAT'S WHY! 'CAUSE YOU SHOVED 'EM OUTA THEIR HUNTING GROUNDS
I DID NOT! TH' WHITE MAN DID IT!
YES, SIR! IN TH' GOOD OL' DAYS, YOU'D BE WALKIN' AROUND WITH NOTHIN' TO TIE A RIBBON TO!
WHY ME?

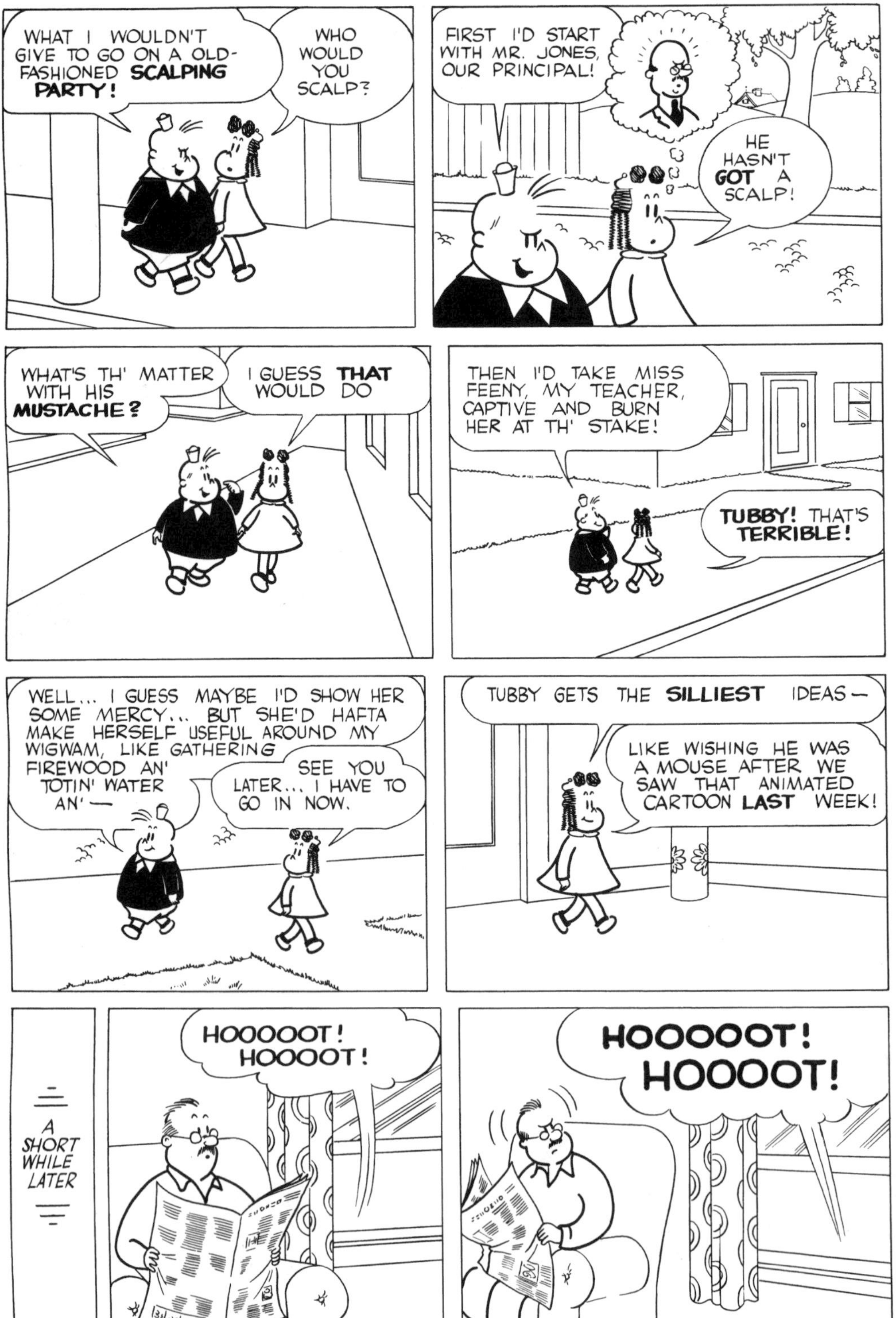
WHAT I WOULDN'T GIVE TO GO ON A OLD-FASHIONED SCALPING PARTY!
WHO WOULD YOU SCALP?
FIRST I'D START WITH MR. JONES, OUR PRINCIPAL!
HE HASN'T GOT A SCALP!
WHAT'S TH' MATTER WITH HIS MUSTACHE?
I GUESS THAT WOULD DO
THEN I'D TAKE MISS FEENY, MY TEACHER, CAPTIVE AND BURN HER AT TH' STAKE!
TUBBY! THAT'S TERRIBLE!
WELL... I GUESS MAYBE I'D SHOW HER SOME MERCY... BUT SHE'D HAFTA MAKE HERSELF USEFUL AROUND MY WIGWAM, LIKE GATHERING FIREWOOD AN' TOTIN' WATER AN'—
SEE YOU LATER... I HAVE TO GO IN NOW.
TUBBY GETS THE SILLIEST IDEAS—
LIKE WISHING HE WAS A MOUSE AFTER WE SAW THAT ANIMATED CARTOON LAST WEEK!
A SHORT WHILE LATER
HOOOOOT! HOOOOT!
HOOOOOT! HOOOOT!

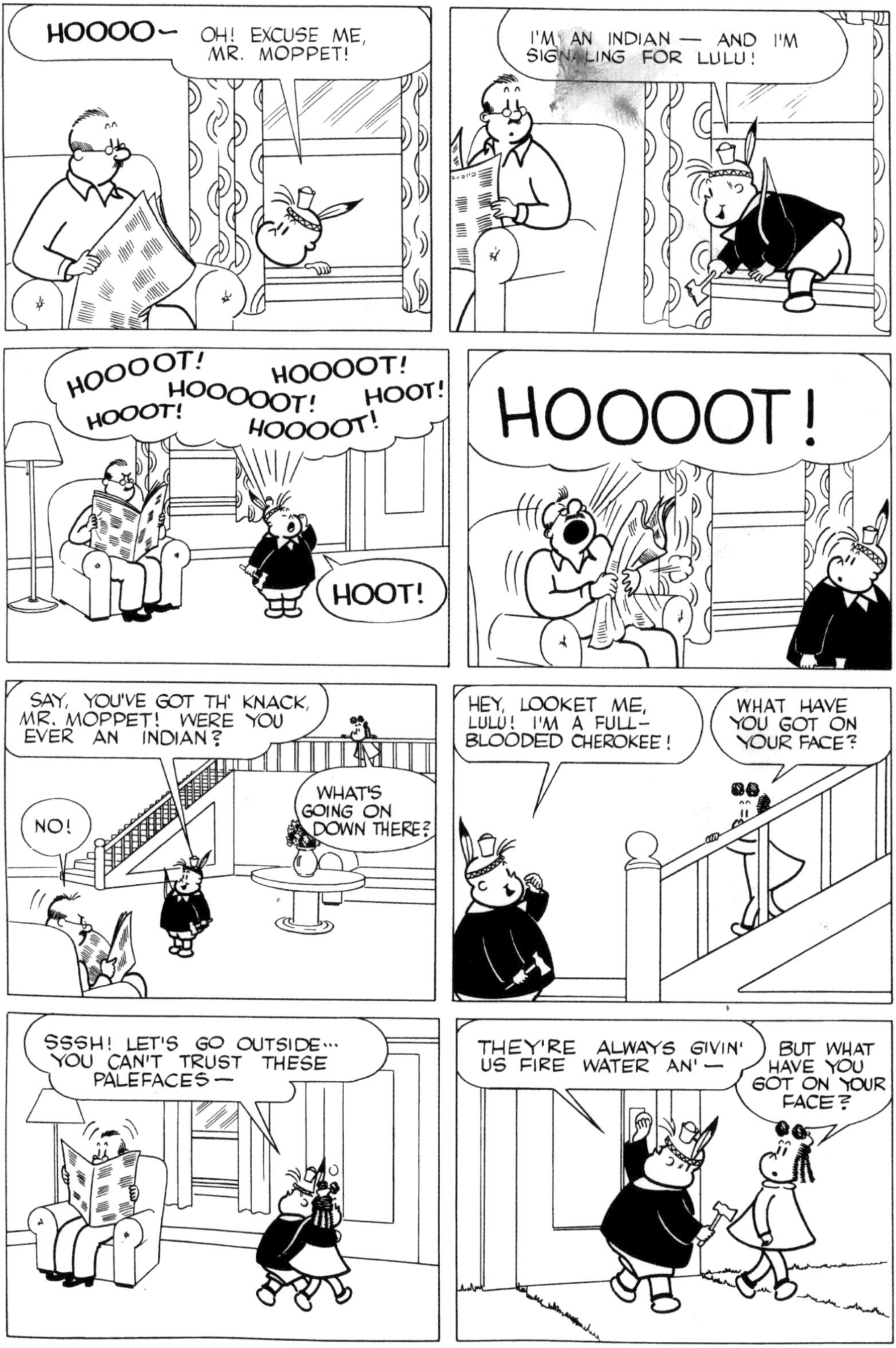
HOOOO—
OH! EXCUSE ME, MR. MOPPET!
I'M AN INDIAN — AND I'M SIGNALING FOR LULU!
HOOOOT! HOOOOT! HOOOOOT! HOOOT! HOOT! HOOOOT!
HOOT!
HOOOOT!
SAY, YOU'VE GOT TH' KNACK, MR. MOPPET! WERE YOU EVER AN INDIAN?
NO!
WHAT'S GOING ON DOWN THERE?
HEY, LOOKET ME, LULU! I'M A FULL-BLOODED CHEROKEE!
WHAT HAVE YOU GOT ON YOUR FACE?
SSSH! LET'S GO OUTSIDE... YOU CAN'T TRUST THESE PALEFACES—
THEY'RE ALWAYS GIVIN' US FIRE WATER AN'—
BUT WHAT HAVE YOU GOT ON YOUR FACE?

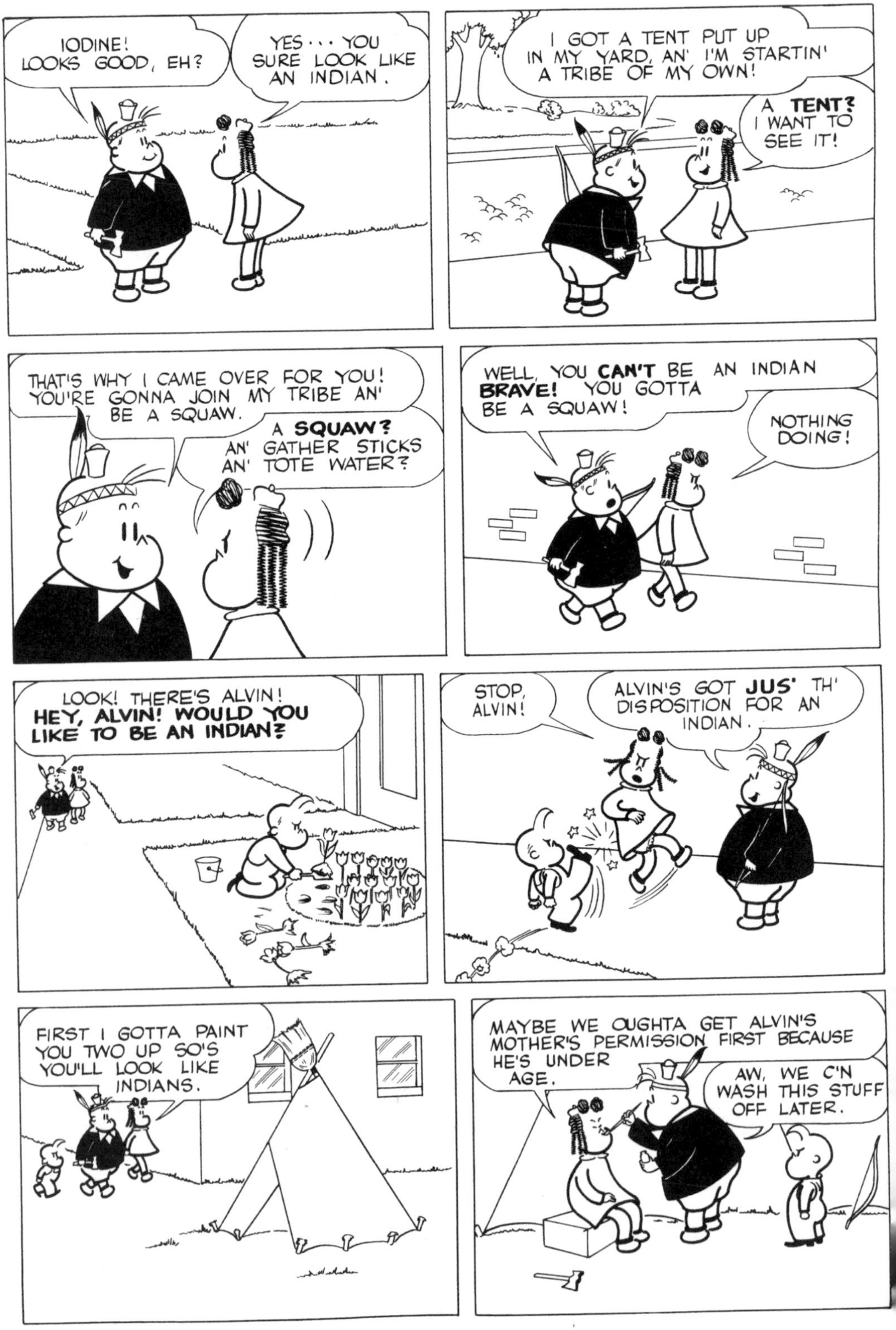
IODINE! LOOKS GOOD, EH?
YES... YOU SURE LOOK LIKE AN INDIAN.
I GOT A TENT PUT UP IN MY YARD, AN' I'M STARTIN' A TRIBE OF MY OWN!
A TENT? I WANT TO SEE IT!
THAT'S WHY I CAME OVER FOR YOU! YOU'RE GONNA JOIN MY TRIBE AN' BE A SQUAW.
A SQUAW? AN' GATHER STICKS AN' TOTE WATER?
WELL, YOU CAN'T BE AN INDIAN BRAVE! YOU GOTTA BE A SQUAW!
NOTHING DOING!
LOOK! THERE'S ALVIN! HEY, ALVIN! WOULD YOU LIKE TO BE AN INDIAN?
STOP, ALVIN!
ALVIN'S GOT JUS' TH' DISPOSITION FOR AN INDIAN.
FIRST I GOTTA PAINT YOU TWO UP SO'S YOU'LL LOOK LIKE INDIANS.
MAYBE WE OUGHTA GET ALVIN'S MOTHER'S PERMISSION FIRST BECAUSE HE'S UNDER AGE.
AW, WE C'N WASH THIS STUFF OFF LATER.

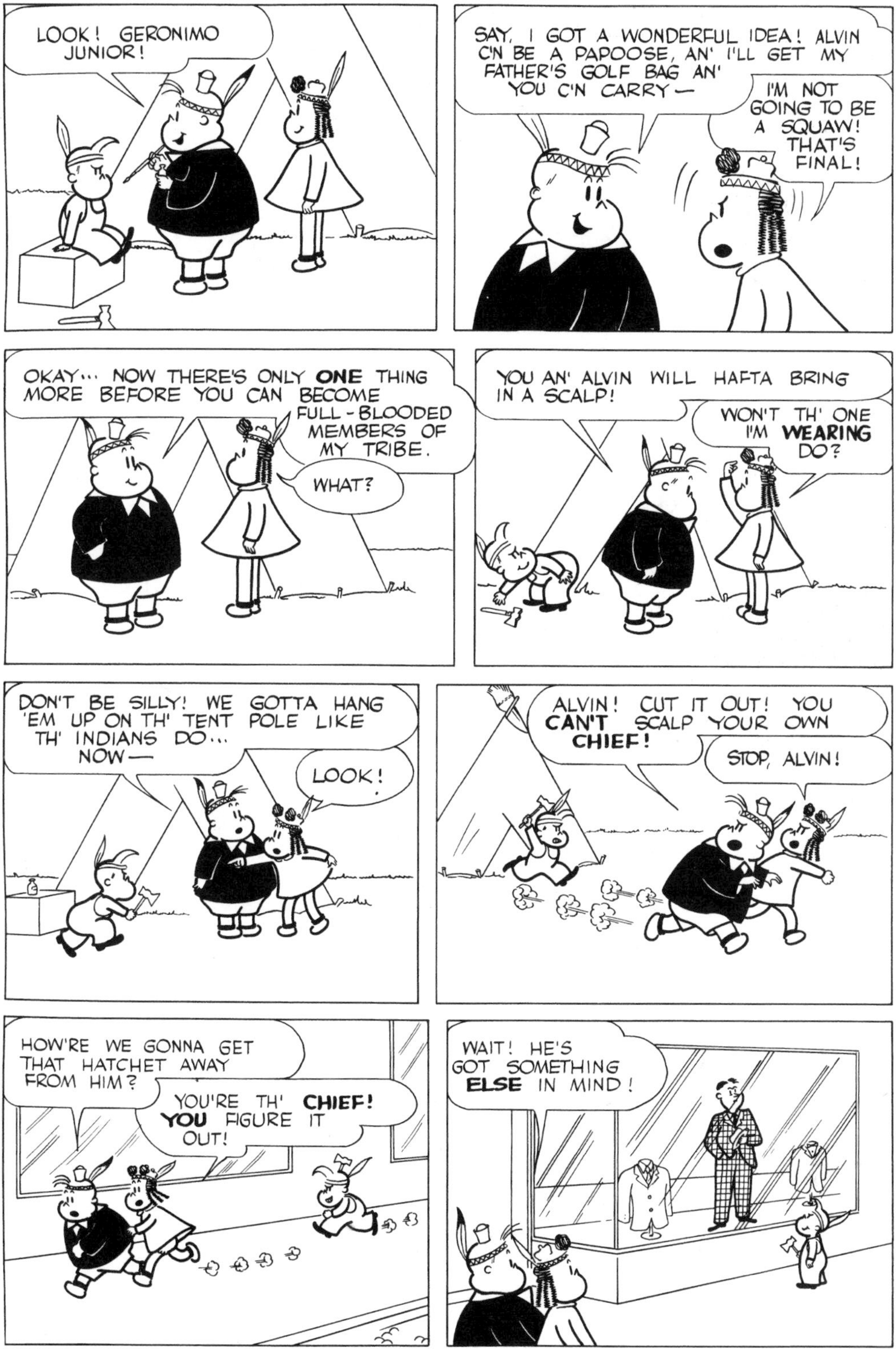
LOOK! GERONIMO JUNIOR!
SAY, I GOT A WONDERFUL IDEA! ALVIN C'N BE A PAPOOSE, AN' I'LL GET MY FATHER'S GOLF BAG AN' YOU C'N CARRY—
I'M NOT GOING TO BE A SQUAW! THAT'S FINAL!
OKAY... NOW THERE'S ONLY **ONE** THING MORE BEFORE YOU CAN BECOME FULL-BLOODED MEMBERS OF MY TRIBE.
WHAT?
YOU AN' ALVIN WILL HAFTA BRING IN A SCALP!
WON'T TH' ONE I'M **WEARING** DO?
DON'T BE SILLY! WE GOTTA HANG 'EM UP ON TH' TENT POLE LIKE TH' INDIANS DO... NOW—
LOOK!
ALVIN! CUT IT OUT! YOU **CAN'T** SCALP YOUR OWN **CHIEF!**
STOP, ALVIN!
HOW'RE WE GONNA GET THAT HATCHET AWAY FROM HIM?
YOU'RE TH' **CHIEF! YOU** FIGURE IT OUT!
WAIT! HE'S GOT SOMETHING **ELSE** IN MIND!

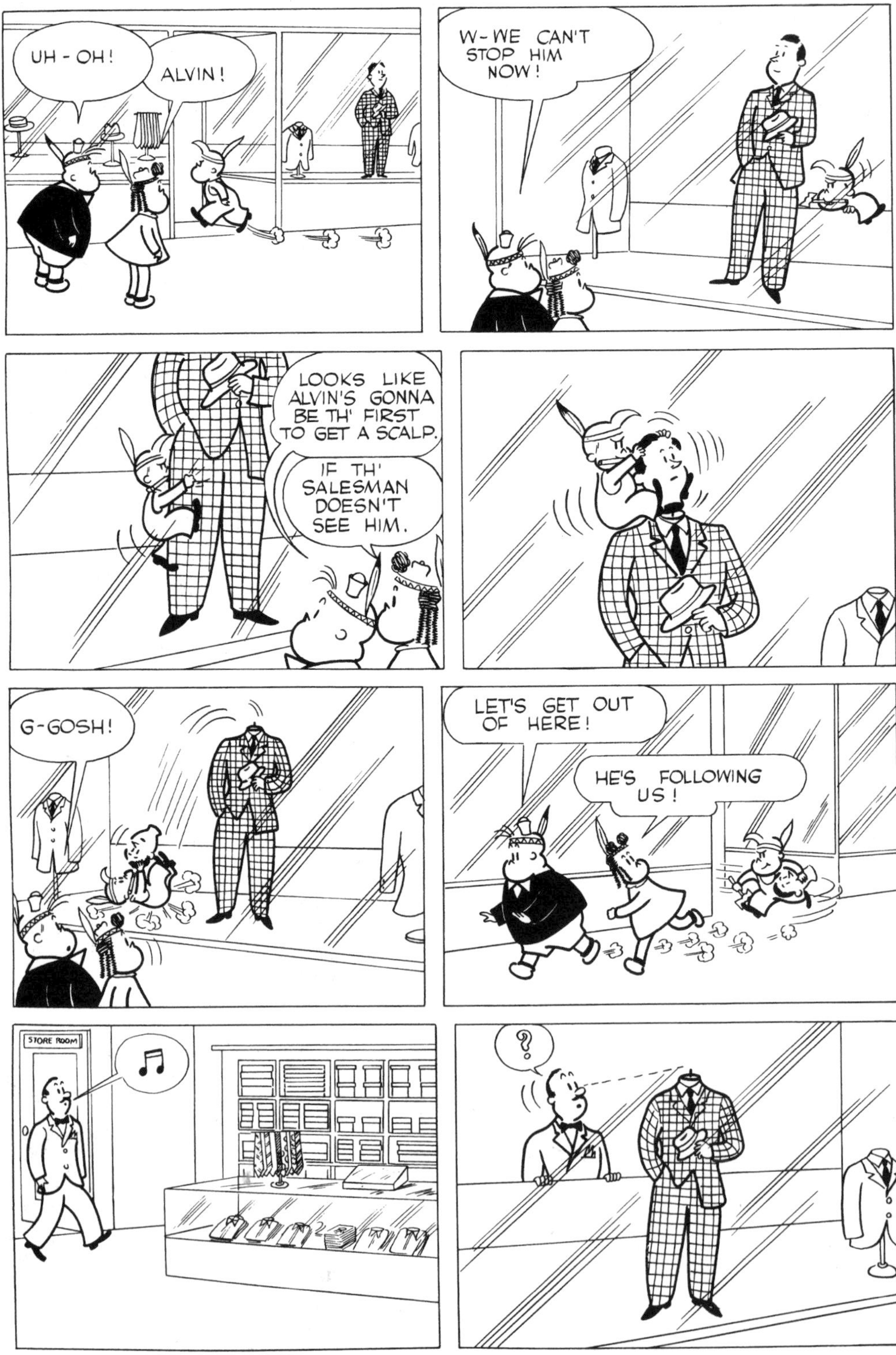
UH-OH!
ALVIN!
W-WE CAN'T STOP HIM NOW!
LOOKS LIKE ALVIN'S GONNA BE TH' FIRST TO GET A SCALP.
IF TH' SALESMAN DOESN'T SEE HIM.
G-GOSH!
LET'S GET OUT OF HERE!
HE'S FOLLOWING US!
STORE ROOM
?

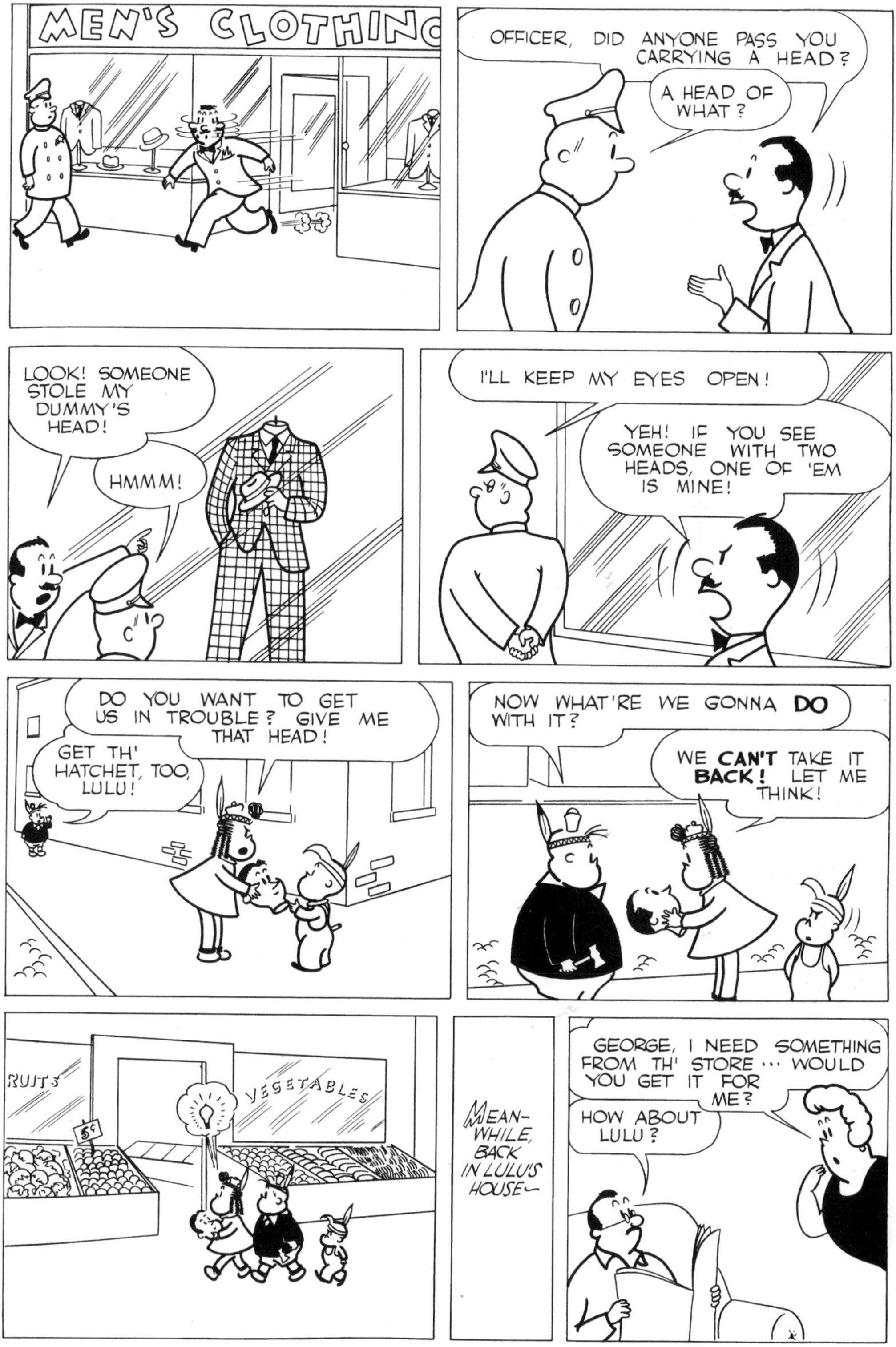
MEN'S CLOTHING
OFFICER, DID ANYONE PASS YOU CARRYING A HEAD?
A HEAD OF WHAT?
LOOK! SOMEONE STOLE MY DUMMY'S HEAD!
HMMM!
I'LL KEEP MY EYES OPEN!
YEH! IF YOU SEE SOMEONE WITH TWO HEADS, ONE OF 'EM IS MINE!
DO YOU WANT TO GET US IN TROUBLE? GIVE ME THAT HEAD!
GET TH' HATCHET, TOO, LULU!
NOW WHAT'RE WE GONNA **DO** WITH IT?
WE **CAN'T** TAKE IT **BACK!** LET ME THINK!
VEGETABLES
5¢
MEANWHILE, BACK IN LULU'S HOUSE—
GEORGE, I NEED SOMETHING FROM TH' STORE... WOULD YOU GET IT FOR ME?
HOW ABOUT LULU?

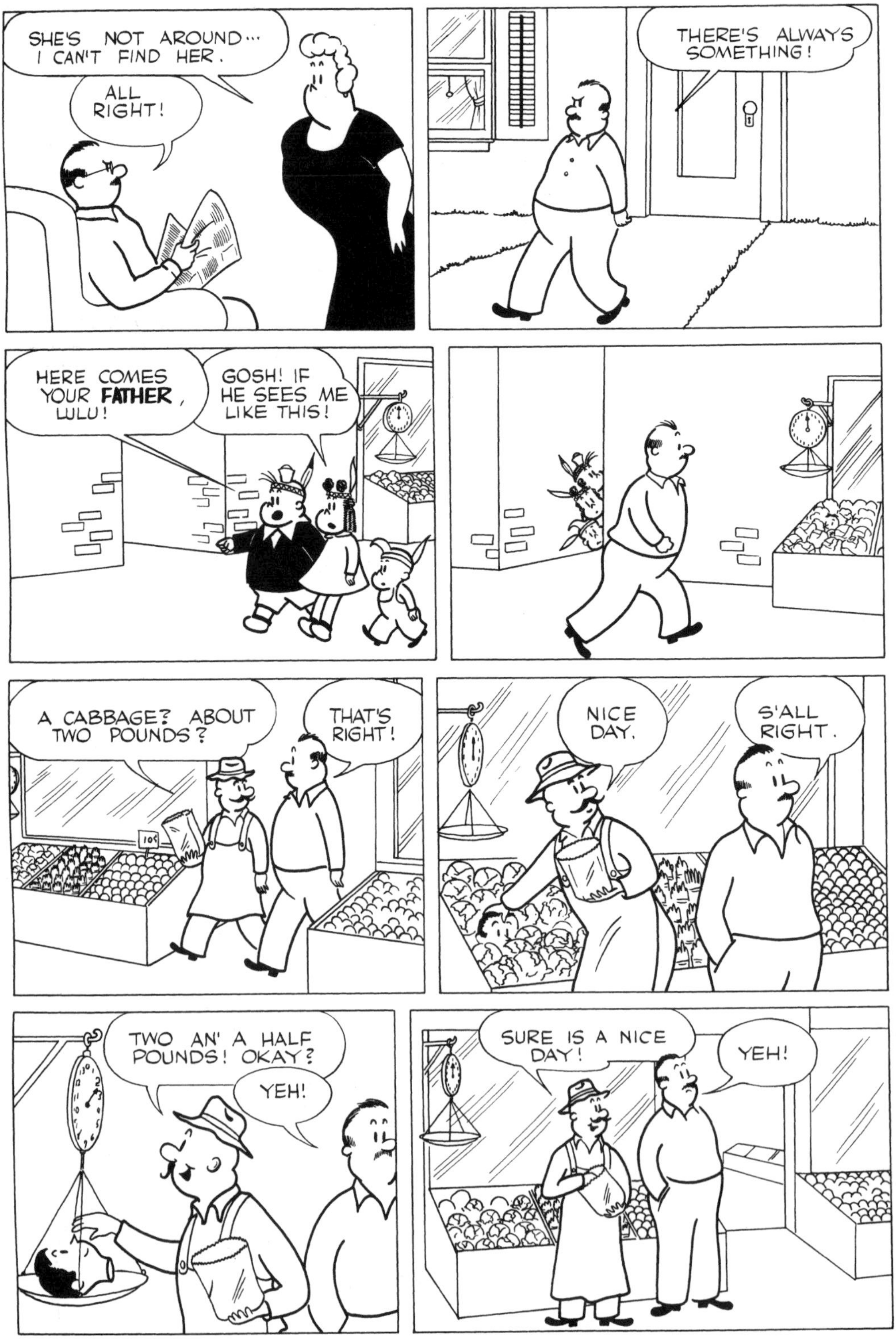
SHE'S NOT AROUND... I CAN'T FIND HER.
ALL RIGHT!
THERE'S ALWAYS SOMETHING!
HERE COMES YOUR **FATHER**, LULU!
GOSH! IF HE SEES ME LIKE THIS!
A CABBAGE? ABOUT TWO POUNDS?
THAT'S RIGHT!
NICE DAY.
S'ALL RIGHT.
TWO AN' A HALF POUNDS! OKAY?
YEH!
SURE IS A NICE DAY!
YEH!

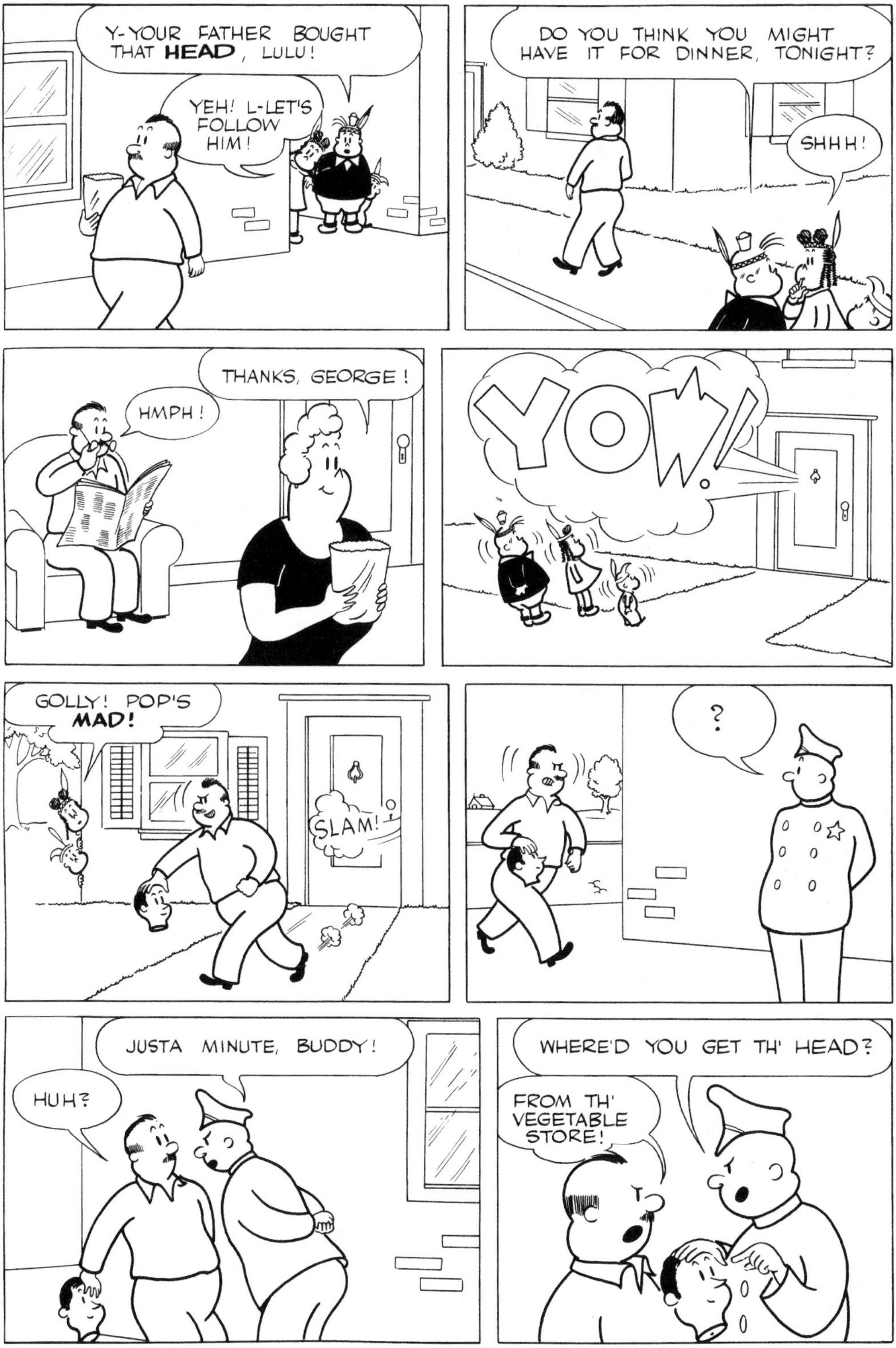
Y-YOUR FATHER BOUGHT THAT **HEAD**, LULU!
YEH! L-LET'S FOLLOW HIM!
DO YOU THINK YOU MIGHT HAVE IT FOR DINNER, TONIGHT?
SHHH!
THANKS, GEORGE!
HMPH!
YOW!
GOLLY! POP'S **MAD!**
SLAM!
?
JUSTA MINUTE, BUDDY!
HUH?
WHERE'D YOU GET TH' HEAD?
FROM TH' VEGETABLE STORE!

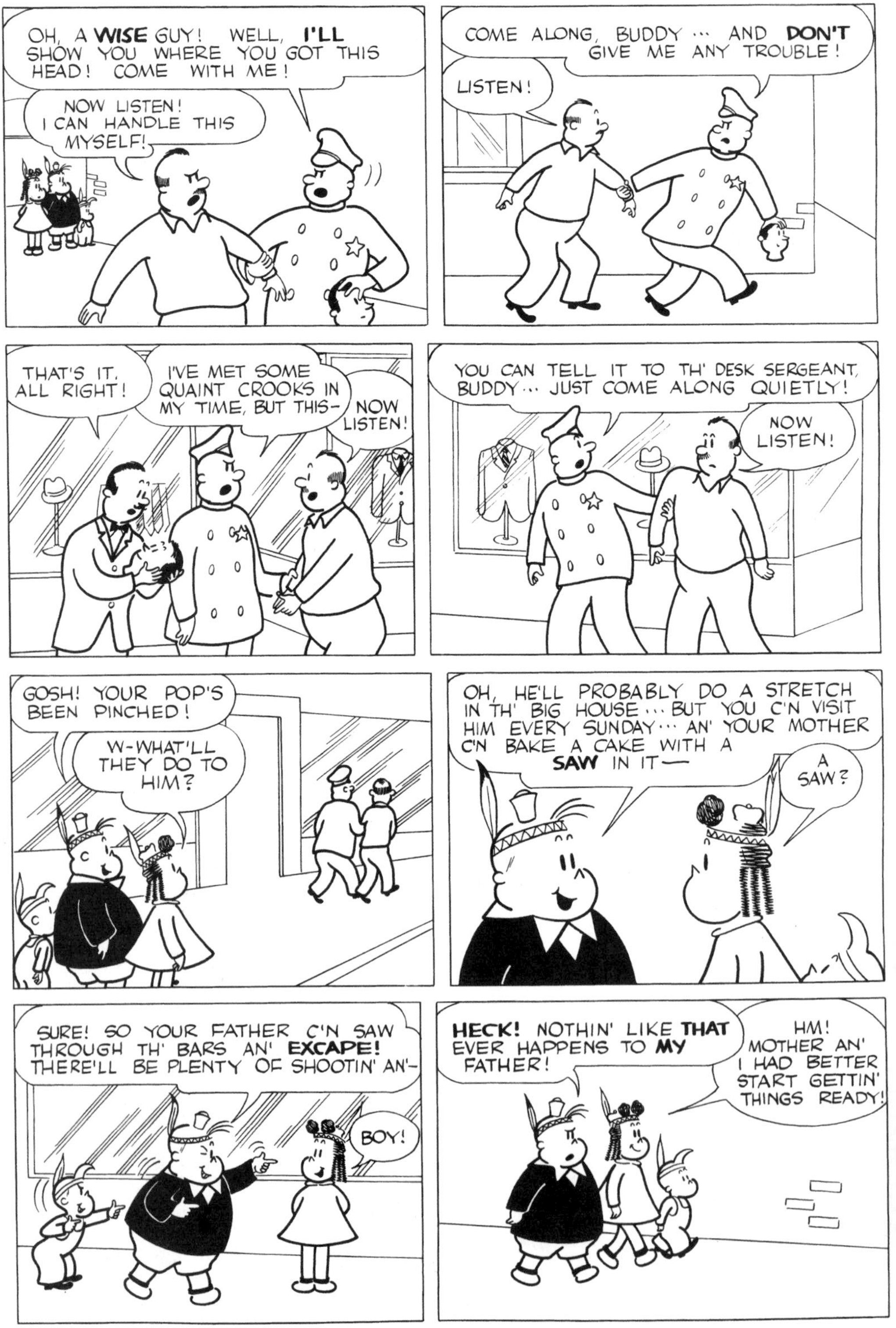
OH, A WISE GUY! WELL, I'LL SHOW YOU WHERE YOU GOT THIS HEAD! COME WITH ME!
NOW LISTEN! I CAN HANDLE THIS MYSELF!
COME ALONG, BUDDY ... AND DON'T GIVE ME ANY TROUBLE!
LISTEN!
THAT'S IT, ALL RIGHT!
I'VE MET SOME QUAINT CROOKS IN MY TIME, BUT THIS-
NOW LISTEN!
YOU CAN TELL IT TO TH' DESK SERGEANT, BUDDY ... JUST COME ALONG QUIETLY!
NOW LISTEN!
GOSH! YOUR POP'S BEEN PINCHED!
W-WHAT'LL THEY DO TO HIM?
OH, HE'LL PROBABLY DO A STRETCH IN TH' BIG HOUSE ... BUT YOU C'N VISIT HIM EVERY SUNDAY ... AN' YOUR MOTHER C'N BAKE A CAKE WITH A SAW IN IT—
A SAW?
SURE! SO YOUR FATHER C'N SAW THROUGH TH' BARS AN' EXCAPE! THERE'LL BE PLENTY OF SHOOTIN' AN'-
BOY!
HECK! NOTHIN' LIKE THAT EVER HAPPENS TO MY FATHER!
HM! MOTHER AN' I HAD BETTER START GETTIN' THINGS READY!

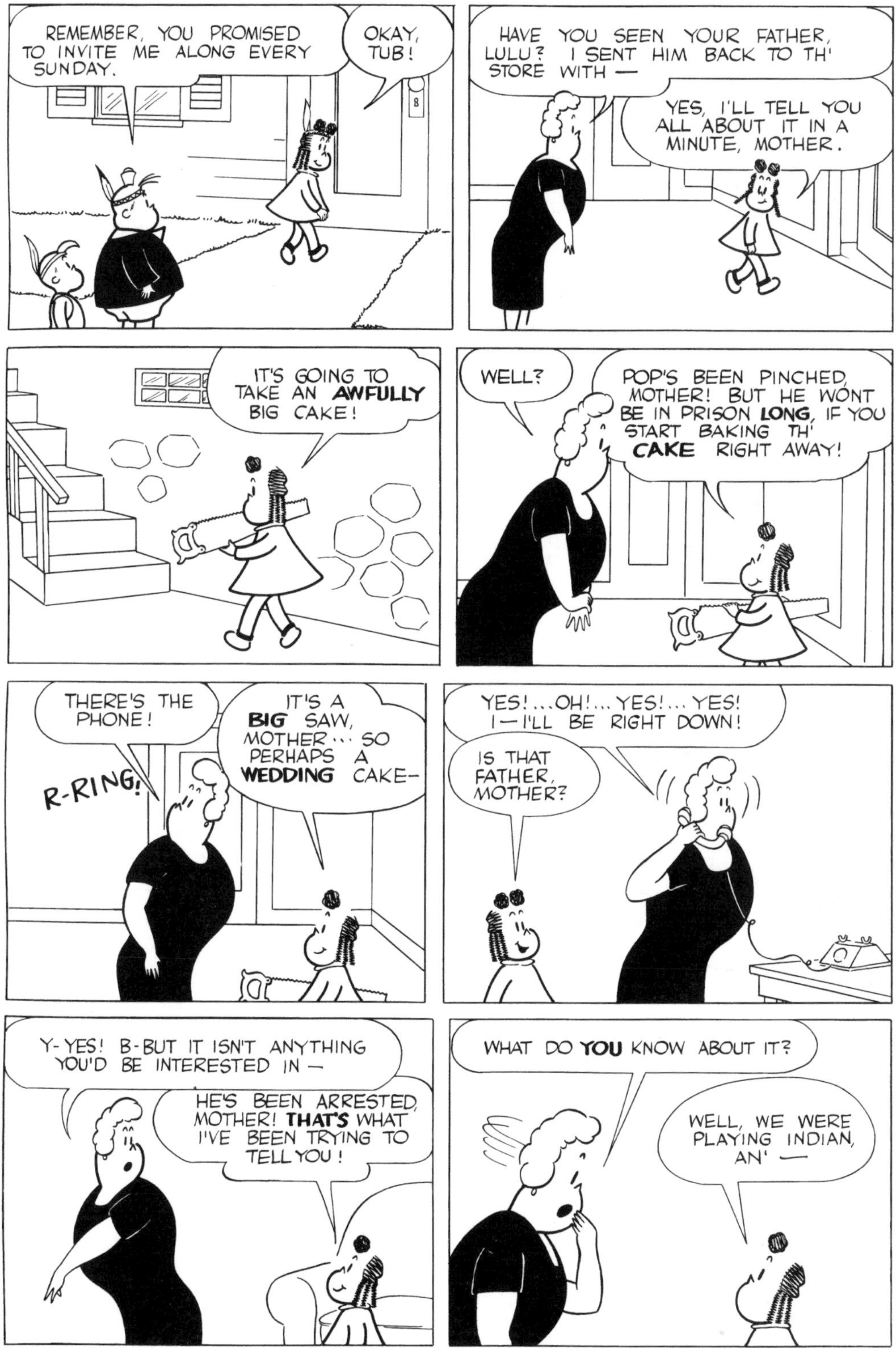
REMEMBER, YOU PROMISED TO INVITE ME ALONG EVERY SUNDAY.
OKAY, TUB!
HAVE YOU SEEN YOUR FATHER, LULU? I SENT HIM BACK TO TH' STORE WITH —
YES, I'LL TELL YOU ALL ABOUT IT IN A MINUTE, MOTHER.
IT'S GOING TO TAKE AN AWFULLY BIG CAKE!
WELL?
POP'S BEEN PINCHED, MOTHER! BUT HE WONT BE IN PRISON LONG, IF YOU START BAKING TH' CAKE RIGHT AWAY!
THERE'S THE PHONE!
R-RING!
IT'S A BIG SAW, MOTHER... SO PERHAPS A WEDDING CAKE—
YES!...OH!...YES!...YES! I—I'LL BE RIGHT DOWN!
IS THAT FATHER, MOTHER?
Y-YES! B-BUT IT ISN'T ANYTHING YOU'D BE INTERESTED IN —
HE'S BEEN ARRESTED, MOTHER! THAT'S WHAT I'VE BEEN TRYING TO TELL YOU!
WHAT DO YOU KNOW ABOUT IT?
WELL, WE WERE PLAYING INDIAN, AN' —

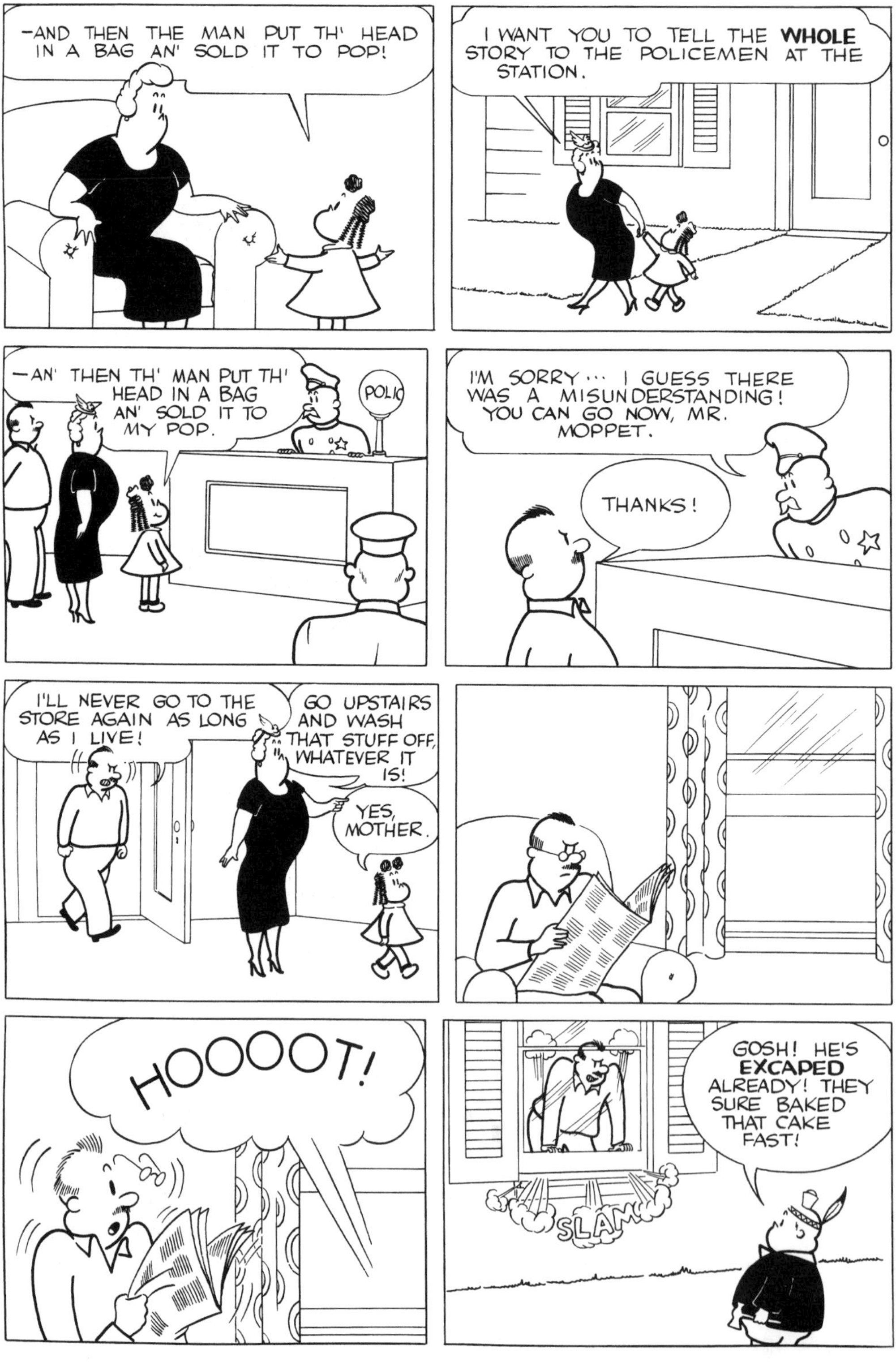
-AND THEN THE MAN PUT TH' HEAD IN A BAG AN' SOLD IT TO POP!
I WANT YOU TO TELL THE **WHOLE** STORY TO THE POLICEMEN AT THE STATION.
-AN' THEN TH' MAN PUT TH' HEAD IN A BAG AN' SOLD IT TO MY POP.
POLIC
I'M SORRY... I GUESS THERE WAS A MISUNDERSTANDING! YOU CAN GO NOW, MR. MOPPET.
THANKS!
I'LL NEVER GO TO THE STORE AGAIN AS LONG AS I LIVE!
GO UPSTAIRS AND WASH THAT STUFF OFF, WHATEVER IT IS!
YES, MOTHER.
HOOOOT!
SLAM
GOSH! HE'S **EXCAPED** ALREADY! THEY SURE BAKED THAT CAKE FAST!

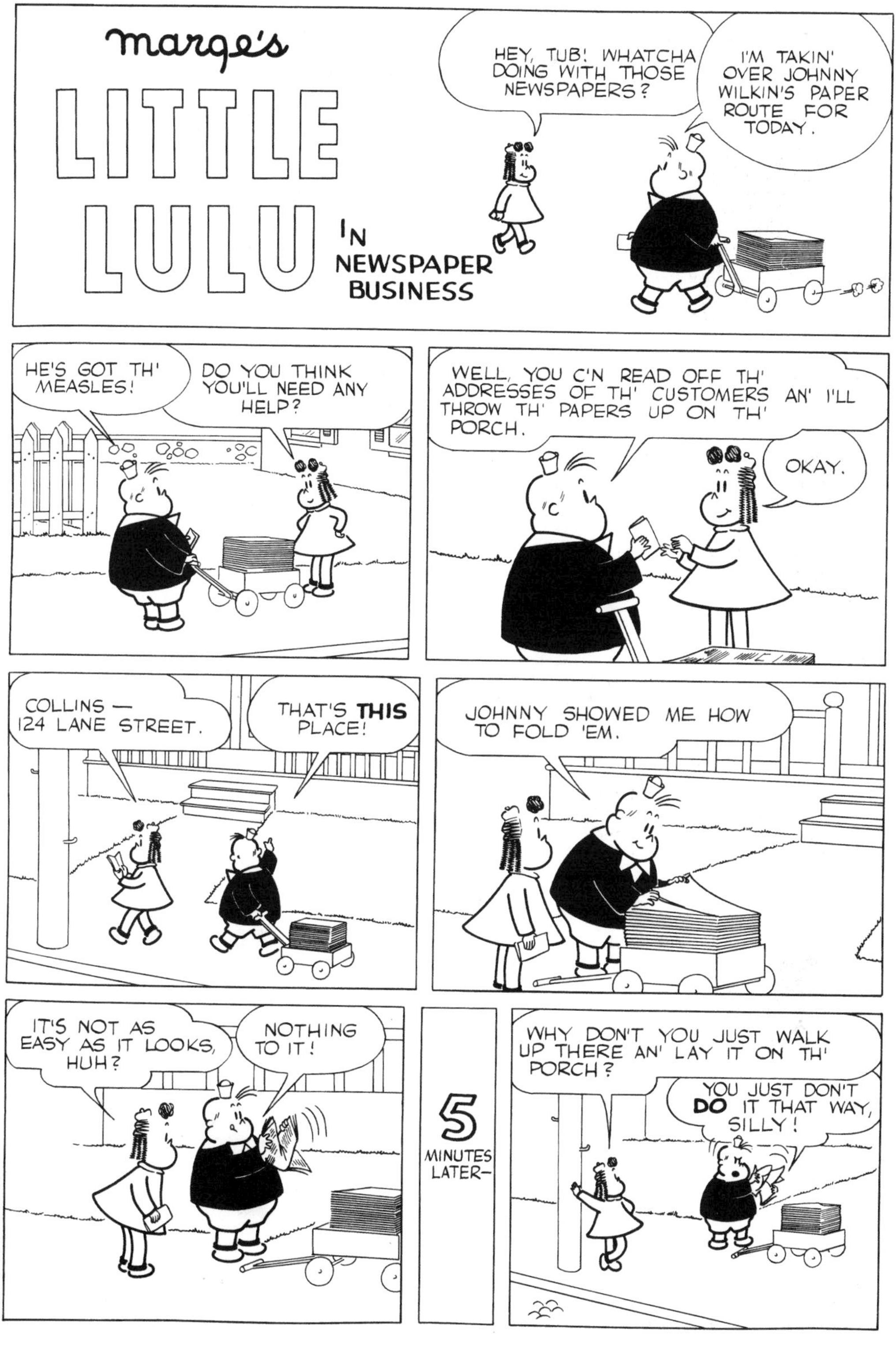
marge's
LITTLE LULU
IN NEWSPAPER BUSINESS
HEY, TUB! WHATCHA DOING WITH THOSE NEWSPAPERS?
I'M TAKIN' OVER JOHNNY WILKIN'S PAPER ROUTE FOR TODAY.
HE'S GOT TH' MEASLES!
DO YOU THINK YOU'LL NEED ANY HELP?
WELL, YOU C'N READ OFF TH' ADDRESSES OF TH' CUSTOMERS AN' I'LL THROW TH' PAPERS UP ON TH' PORCH.
OKAY.
COLLINS — 124 LANE STREET.
THAT'S **THIS** PLACE!
JOHNNY SHOWED ME HOW TO FOLD 'EM.
IT'S NOT AS EASY AS IT LOOKS, HUH?
NOTHING TO IT!
5 MINUTES LATER—
WHY DON'T YOU JUST WALK UP THERE AN' LAY IT ON TH' PORCH?
YOU JUST DON'T **DO** IT THAT WAY, SILLY!

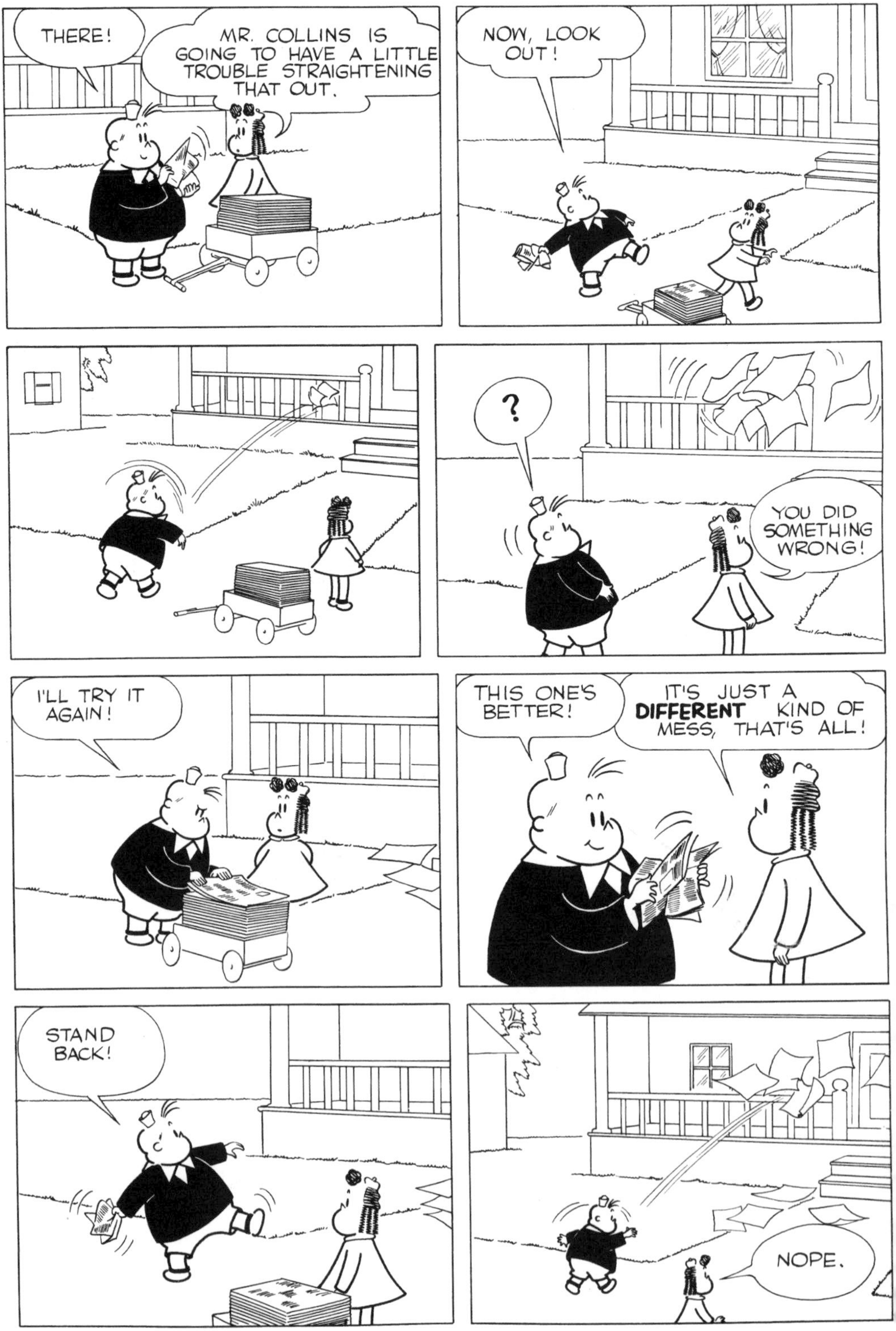
THERE!
MR. COLLINS IS GOING TO HAVE A LITTLE TROUBLE STRAIGHTENING THAT OUT.
NOW, LOOK OUT!
?
YOU DID SOMETHING WRONG!
I'LL TRY IT AGAIN!
THIS ONE'S BETTER!
IT'S JUST A DIFFERENT KIND OF MESS, THAT'S ALL!
STAND BACK!
NOPE.

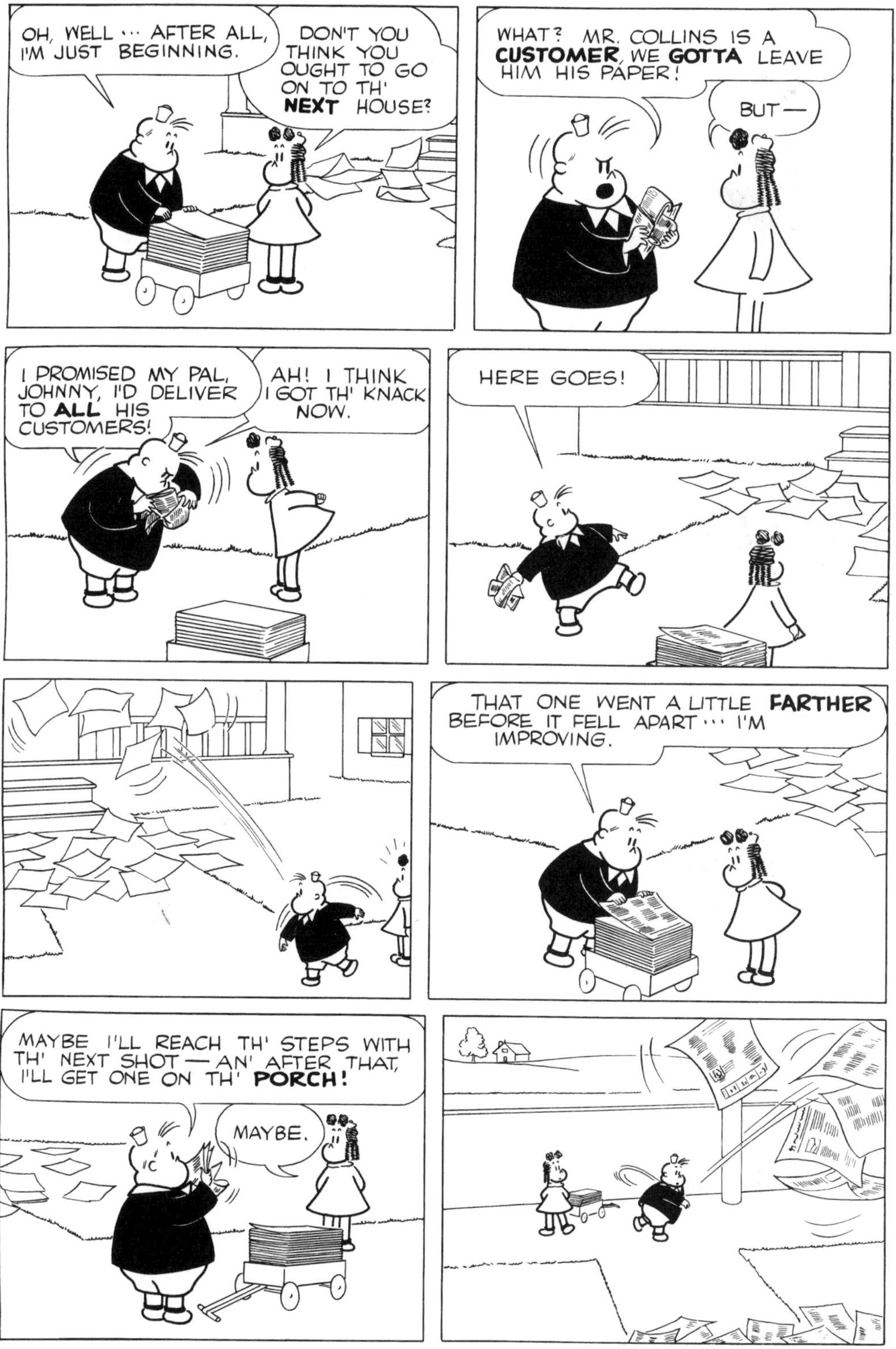
OH, WELL ··· AFTER ALL, I'M JUST BEGINNING.
DON'T YOU THINK YOU OUGHT TO GO ON TO TH' NEXT HOUSE?
WHAT? MR. COLLINS IS A CUSTOMER, WE GOTTA LEAVE HIM HIS PAPER!
BUT—
I PROMISED MY PAL, JOHNNY, I'D DELIVER TO ALL HIS CUSTOMERS!
AH! I THINK I GOT TH' KNACK NOW.
HERE GOES!
THAT ONE WENT A LITTLE FARTHER BEFORE IT FELL APART ··· I'M IMPROVING.
MAYBE I'LL REACH TH' STEPS WITH TH' NEXT SHOT—AN' AFTER THAT, I'LL GET ONE ON TH' PORCH!
MAYBE.

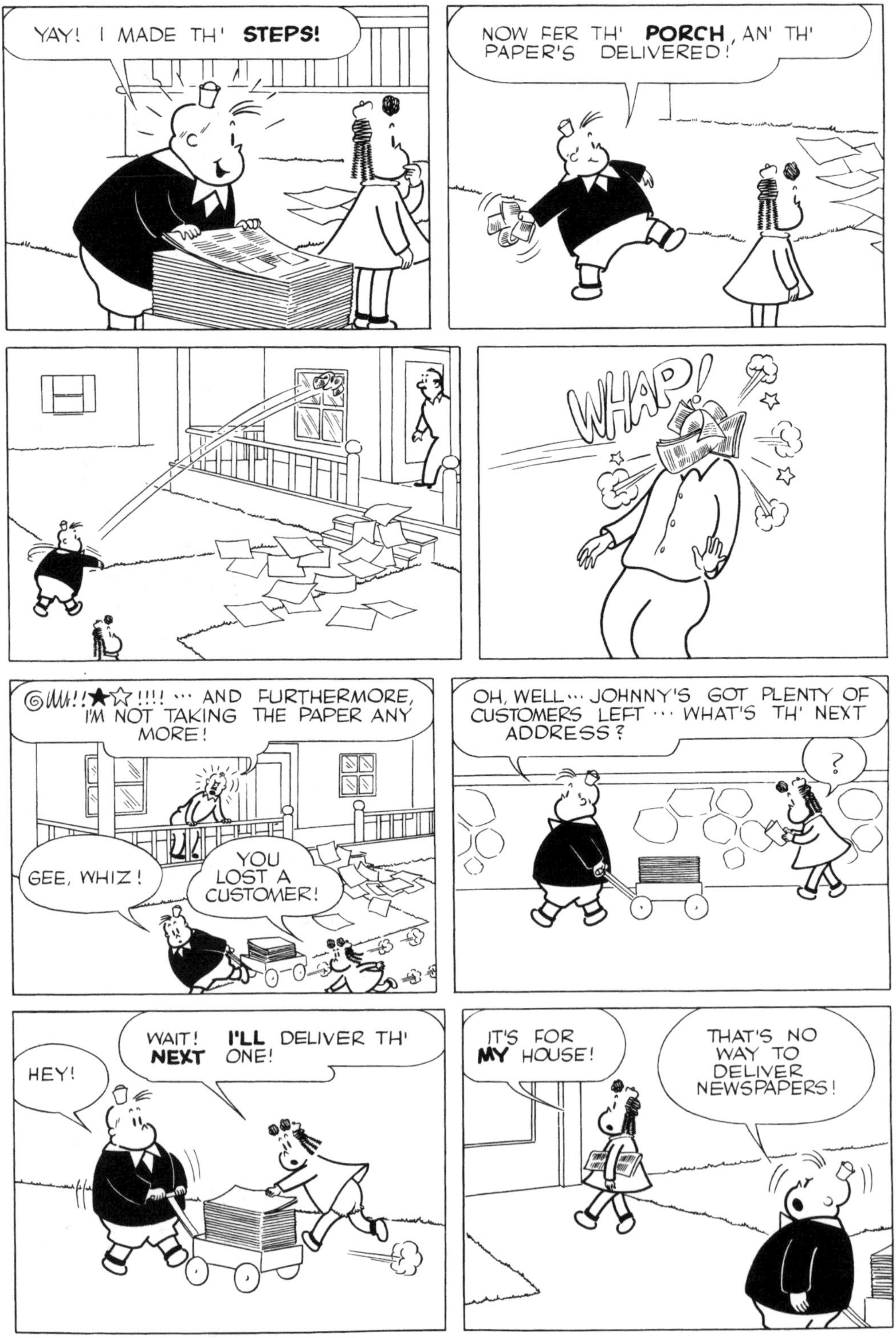
YAY! I MADE TH' **STEPS!**
NOW FER TH' **PORCH**, AN' TH' PAPER'S DELIVERED!
WHAP!
★☆!!!! ··· AND FURTHERMORE, I'M NOT TAKING THE PAPER ANY MORE!
GEE, WHIZ!
YOU LOST A CUSTOMER!
OH, WELL··· JOHNNY'S GOT PLENTY OF CUSTOMERS LEFT ··· WHAT'S TH' NEXT ADDRESS?
?
HEY!
WAIT! **I'LL** DELIVER TH' **NEXT** ONE!
IT'S FOR **MY** HOUSE!
THAT'S NO WAY TO DELIVER NEWSPAPERS!

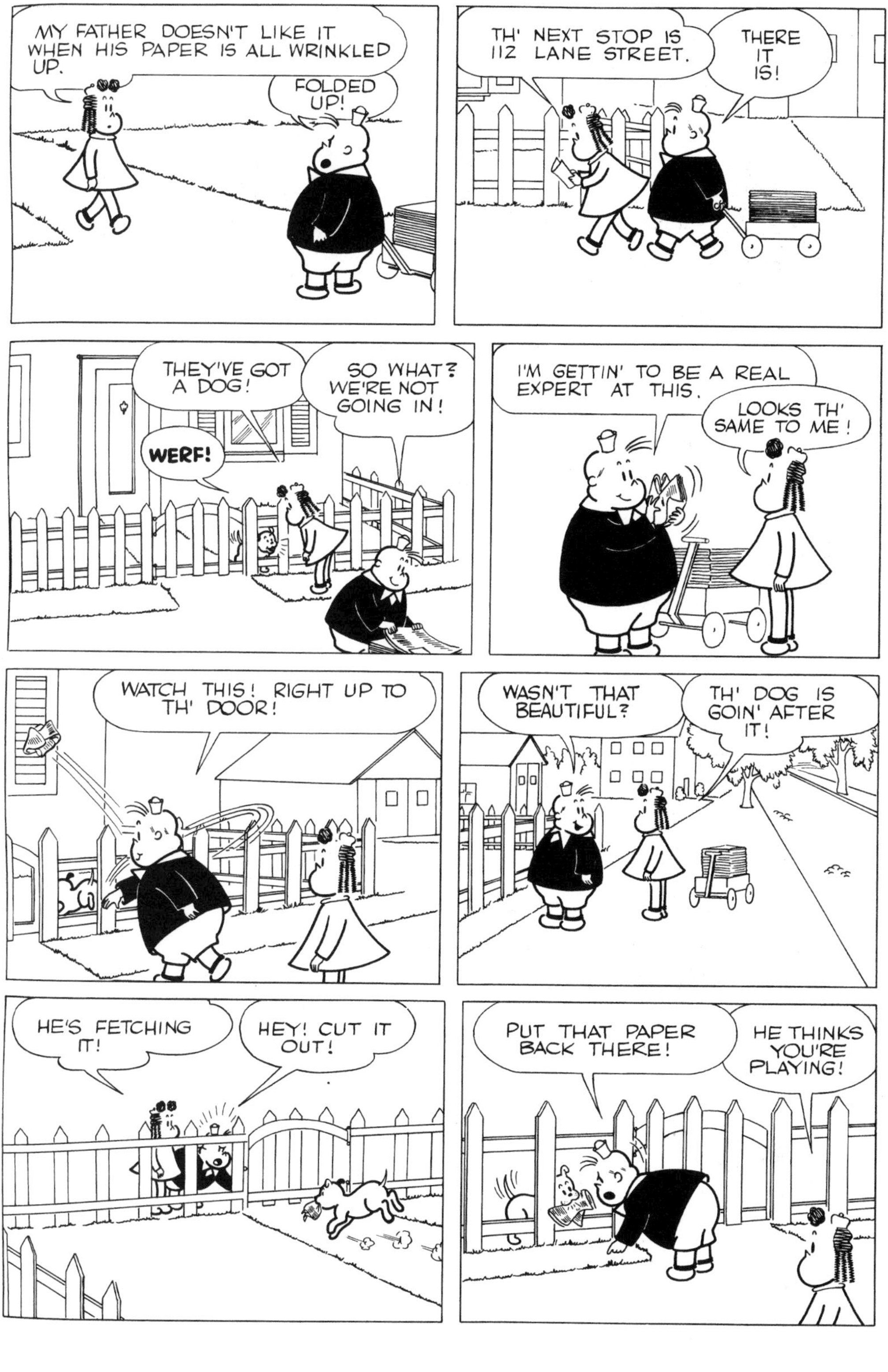
MY FATHER DOESN'T LIKE IT WHEN HIS PAPER IS ALL WRINKLED UP.
FOLDED UP!
TH' NEXT STOP IS 112 LANE STREET.
THERE IT IS!
THEY'VE GOT A DOG!
SO WHAT? WE'RE NOT GOING IN!
WERF!
I'M GETTIN' TO BE A REAL EXPERT AT THIS.
LOOKS TH' SAME TO ME!
WATCH THIS! RIGHT UP TO TH' DOOR!
WASN'T THAT BEAUTIFUL?
TH' DOG IS GOIN' AFTER IT!
HE'S FETCHING IT!
HEY! CUT IT OUT!
PUT THAT PAPER BACK THERE!
HE THINKS YOU'RE PLAYING!

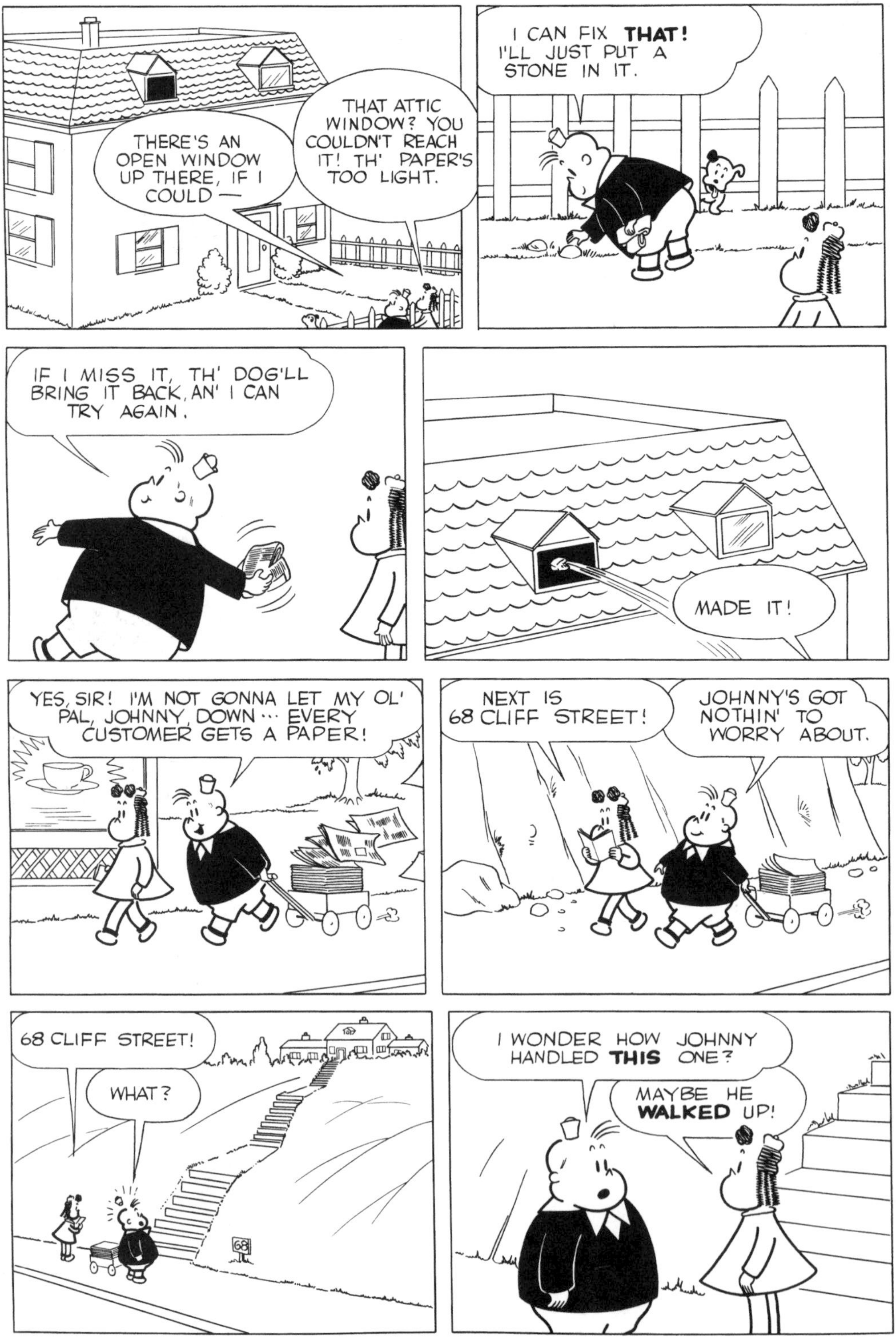
THERE'S AN OPEN WINDOW UP THERE, IF I COULD —
THAT ATTIC WINDOW? YOU COULDN'T REACH IT! TH' PAPER'S TOO LIGHT.
I CAN FIX THAT! I'LL JUST PUT A STONE IN IT.
IF I MISS IT, TH' DOG'LL BRING IT BACK, AN' I CAN TRY AGAIN.
MADE IT!
YES, SIR! I'M NOT GONNA LET MY OL' PAL, JOHNNY, DOWN ··· EVERY CUSTOMER GETS A PAPER!
NEXT IS 68 CLIFF STREET!
JOHNNY'S GOT NOTHIN' TO WORRY ABOUT.
68 CLIFF STREET!
WHAT?
68
I WONDER HOW JOHNNY HANDLED THIS ONE?
MAYBE HE WALKED UP!

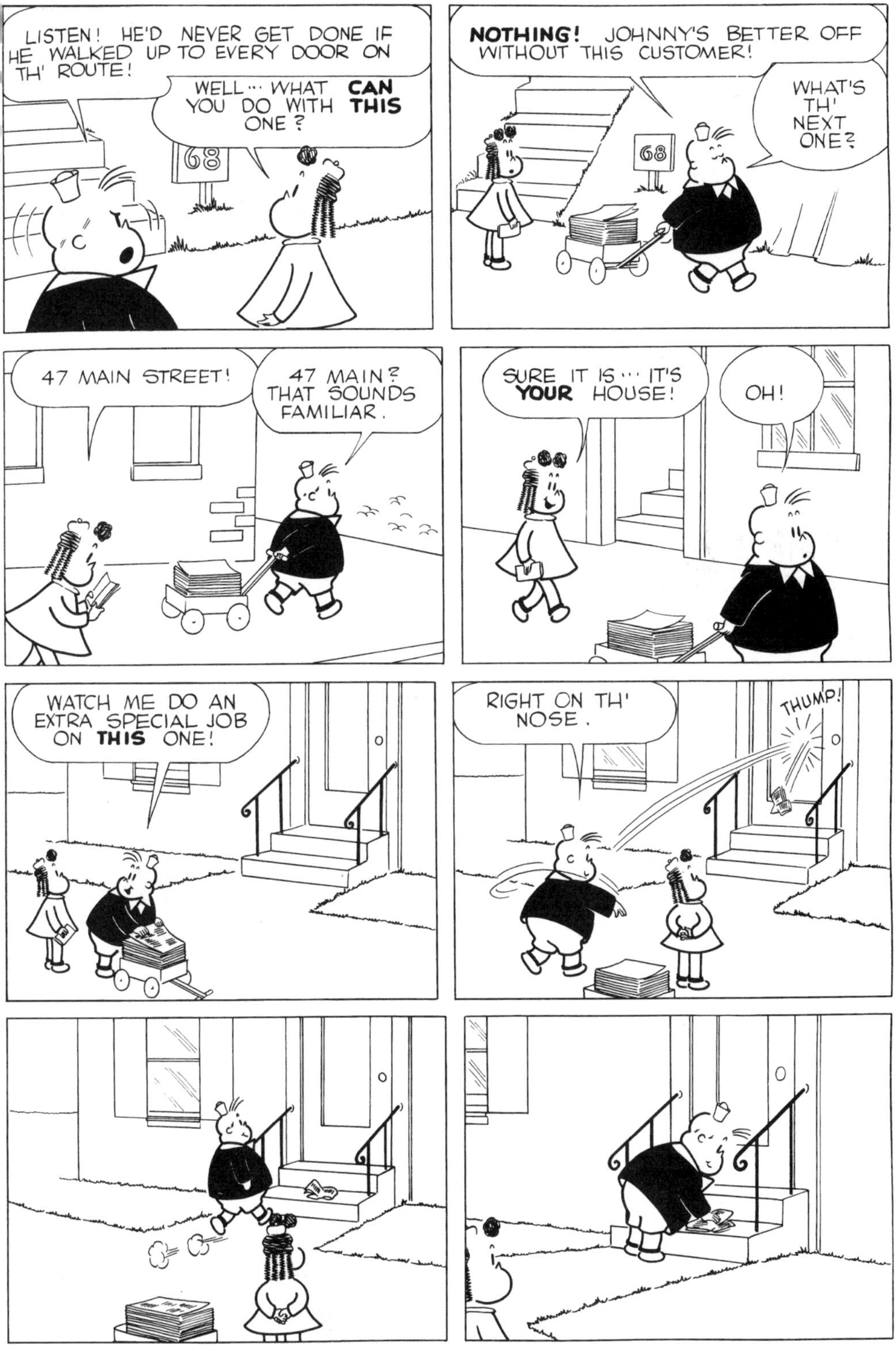
LISTEN! HE'D NEVER GET DONE IF HE WALKED UP TO EVERY DOOR ON TH' ROUTE!
WELL... WHAT **CAN** YOU DO WITH **THIS** ONE?
68
NOTHING! JOHNNY'S BETTER OFF WITHOUT THIS CUSTOMER!
WHAT'S TH' NEXT ONE?
68
47 MAIN STREET!
47 MAIN? THAT SOUNDS FAMILIAR.
SURE IT IS... IT'S **YOUR** HOUSE!
OH!
WATCH ME DO AN EXTRA SPECIAL JOB ON **THIS** ONE!
RIGHT ON TH' NOSE.
THUMP!

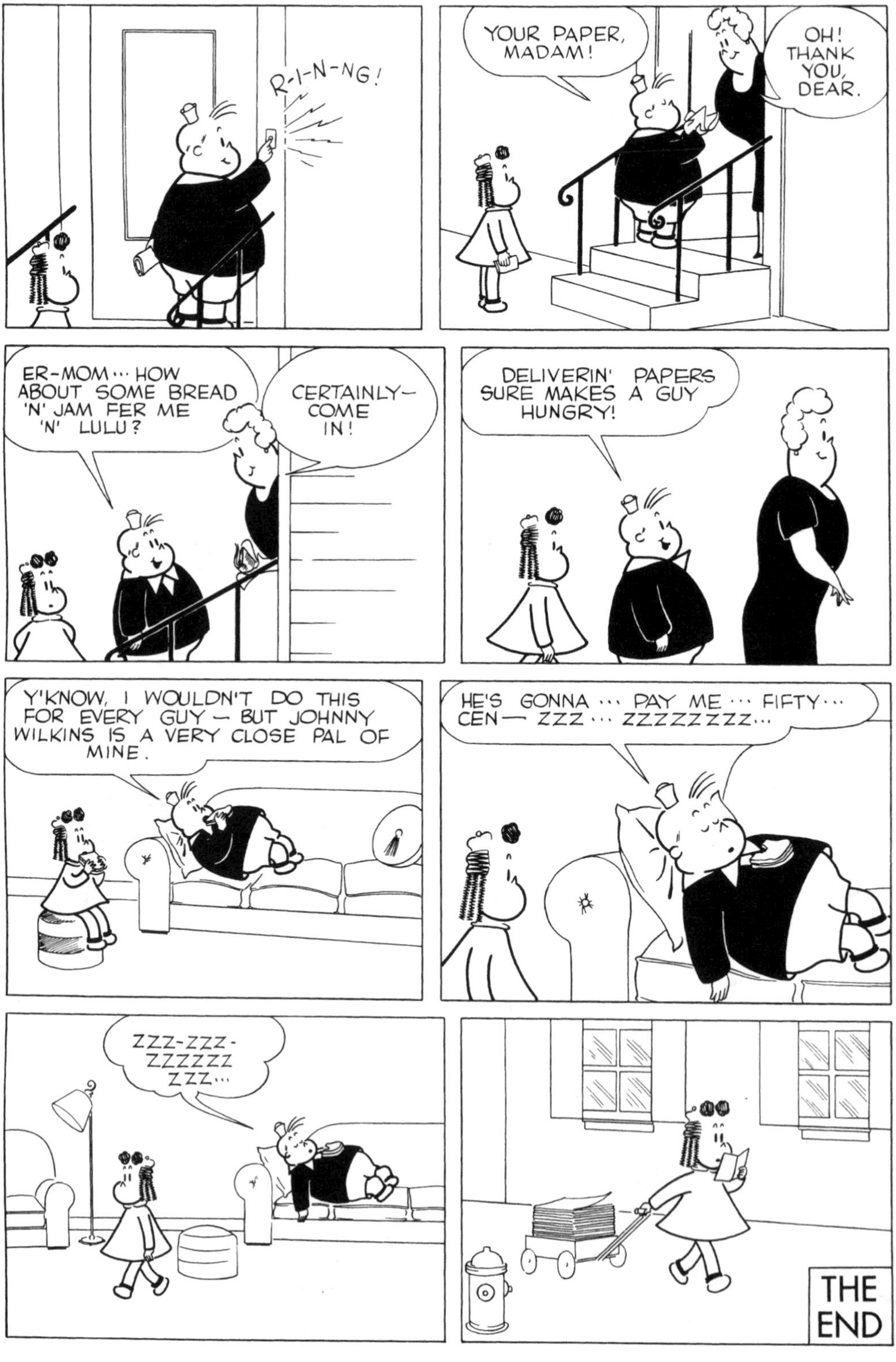
R-I-N-NG!
YOUR PAPER, MADAM!
OH! THANK YOU, DEAR.
ER-MOM... HOW ABOUT SOME BREAD 'N' JAM FER ME 'N' LULU?
CERTAINLY—COME IN!
DELIVERIN' PAPERS SURE MAKES A GUY HUNGRY!
Y'KNOW, I WOULDN'T DO THIS FOR EVERY GUY — BUT JOHNNY WILKINS IS A VERY CLOSE PAL OF MINE.
HE'S GONNA ... PAY ME ... FIFTY... CEN— ZZZ ... ZZZZZZZZ...
ZZZ-ZZZ-ZZZZZZ ZZZ...
THE END

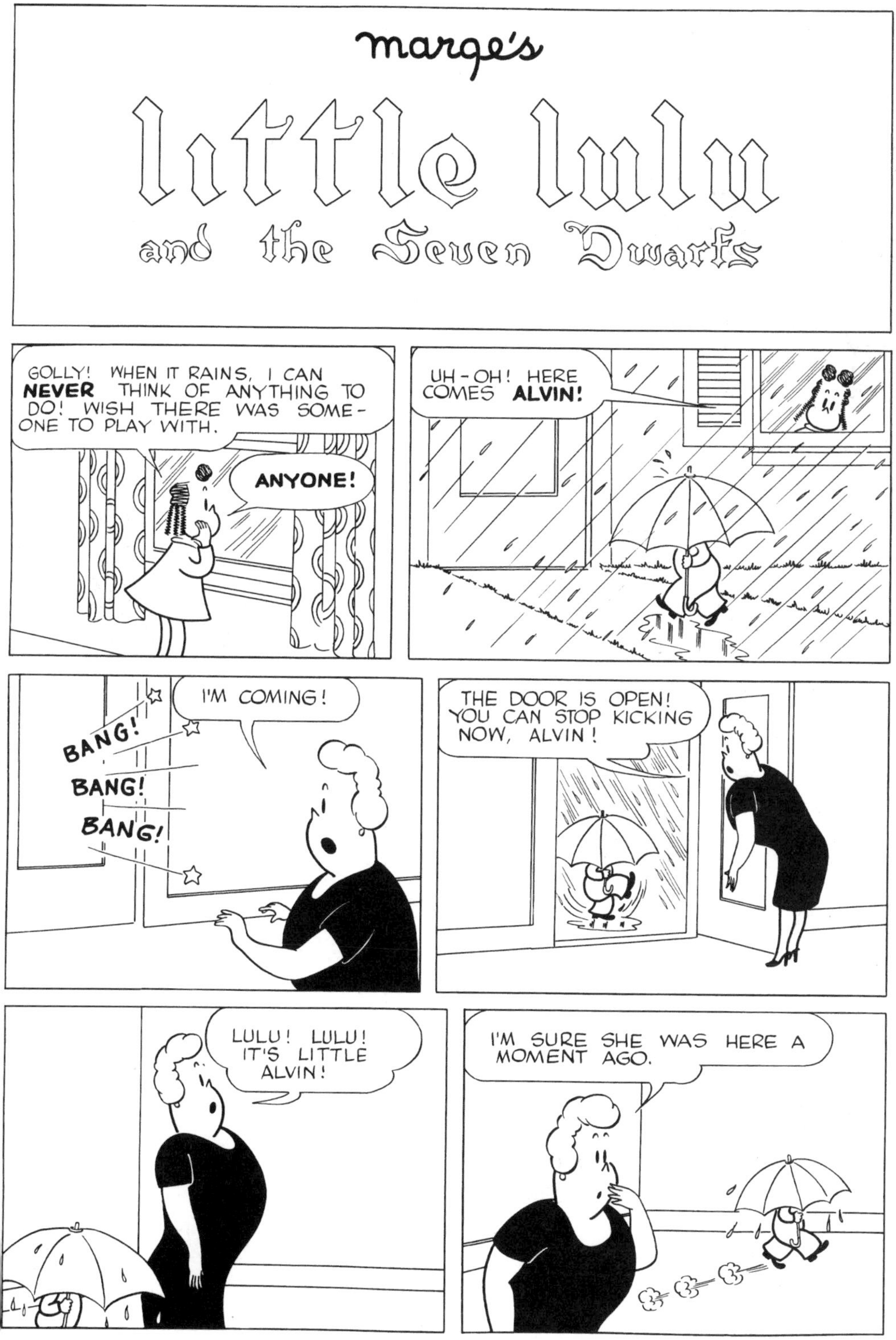
marge's
little lulu
and the Seven Dwarfs
GOLLY! WHEN IT RAINS, I CAN NEVER THINK OF ANYTHING TO DO! WISH THERE WAS SOMEONE TO PLAY WITH.
ANYONE!
UH-OH! HERE COMES ALVIN!
BANG! BANG! BANG!
I'M COMING!
THE DOOR IS OPEN! YOU CAN STOP KICKING NOW, ALVIN!
LULU! LULU! IT'S LITTLE ALVIN!
I'M SURE SHE WAS HERE A MOMENT AGO.

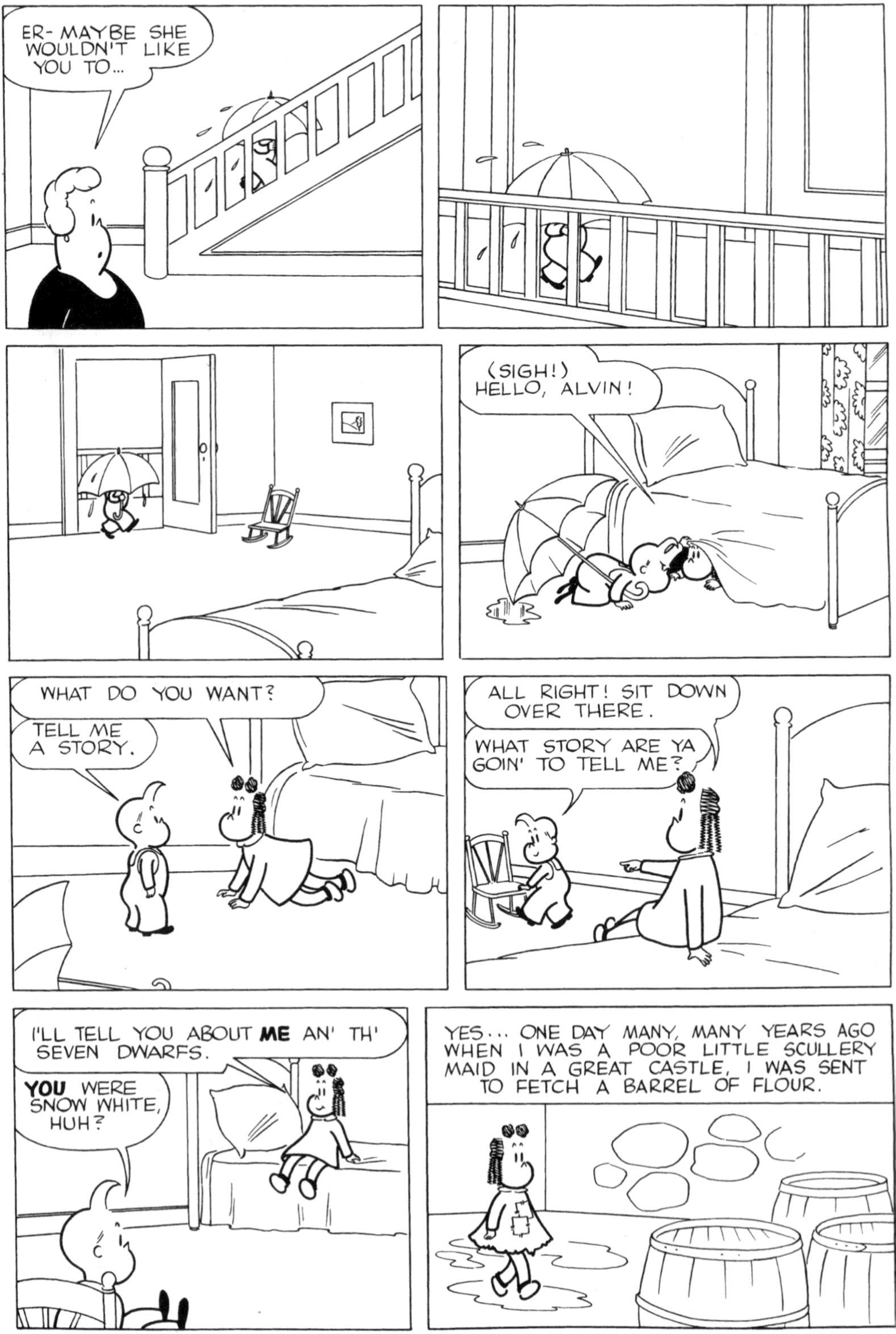
ER- MAYBE SHE WOULDN'T LIKE YOU TO...
(SIGH!) HELLO, ALVIN!
WHAT DO YOU WANT?
TELL ME A STORY.
ALL RIGHT! SIT DOWN OVER THERE.
WHAT STORY ARE YA GOIN' TO TELL ME?
I'LL TELL YOU ABOUT **ME** AN' TH' SEVEN DWARFS.
YOU WERE SNOW WHITE, HUH?
YES... ONE DAY MANY, MANY YEARS AGO WHEN I WAS A POOR LITTLE SCULLERY MAID IN A GREAT CASTLE, I WAS SENT TO FETCH A BARREL OF FLOUR.

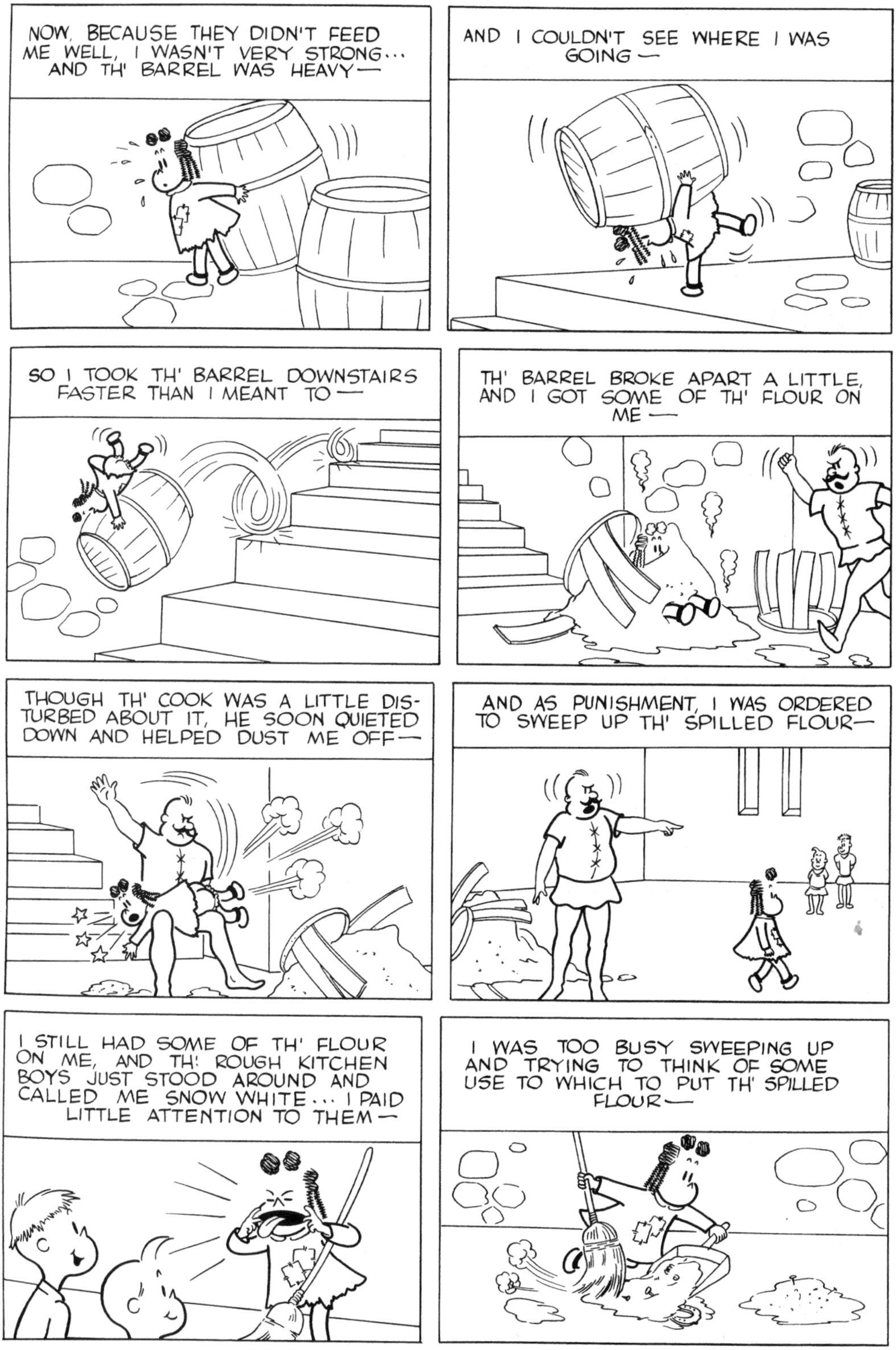
NOW, BECAUSE THEY DIDN'T FEED ME WELL, I WASN'T VERY STRONG... AND TH' BARREL WAS HEAVY—
AND I COULDN'T SEE WHERE I WAS GOING—
SO I TOOK TH' BARREL DOWNSTAIRS FASTER THAN I MEANT TO—
TH' BARREL BROKE APART A LITTLE, AND I GOT SOME OF TH' FLOUR ON ME—
THOUGH TH' COOK WAS A LITTLE DISTURBED ABOUT IT, HE SOON QUIETED DOWN AND HELPED DUST ME OFF—
AND AS PUNISHMENT, I WAS ORDERED TO SWEEP UP TH' SPILLED FLOUR—
I STILL HAD SOME OF TH' FLOUR ON ME, AND TH' ROUGH KITCHEN BOYS JUST STOOD AROUND AND CALLED ME SNOW WHITE... I PAID LITTLE ATTENTION TO THEM—
I WAS TOO BUSY SWEEPING UP AND TRYING TO THINK OF SOME USE TO WHICH TO PUT TH' SPILLED FLOUR—

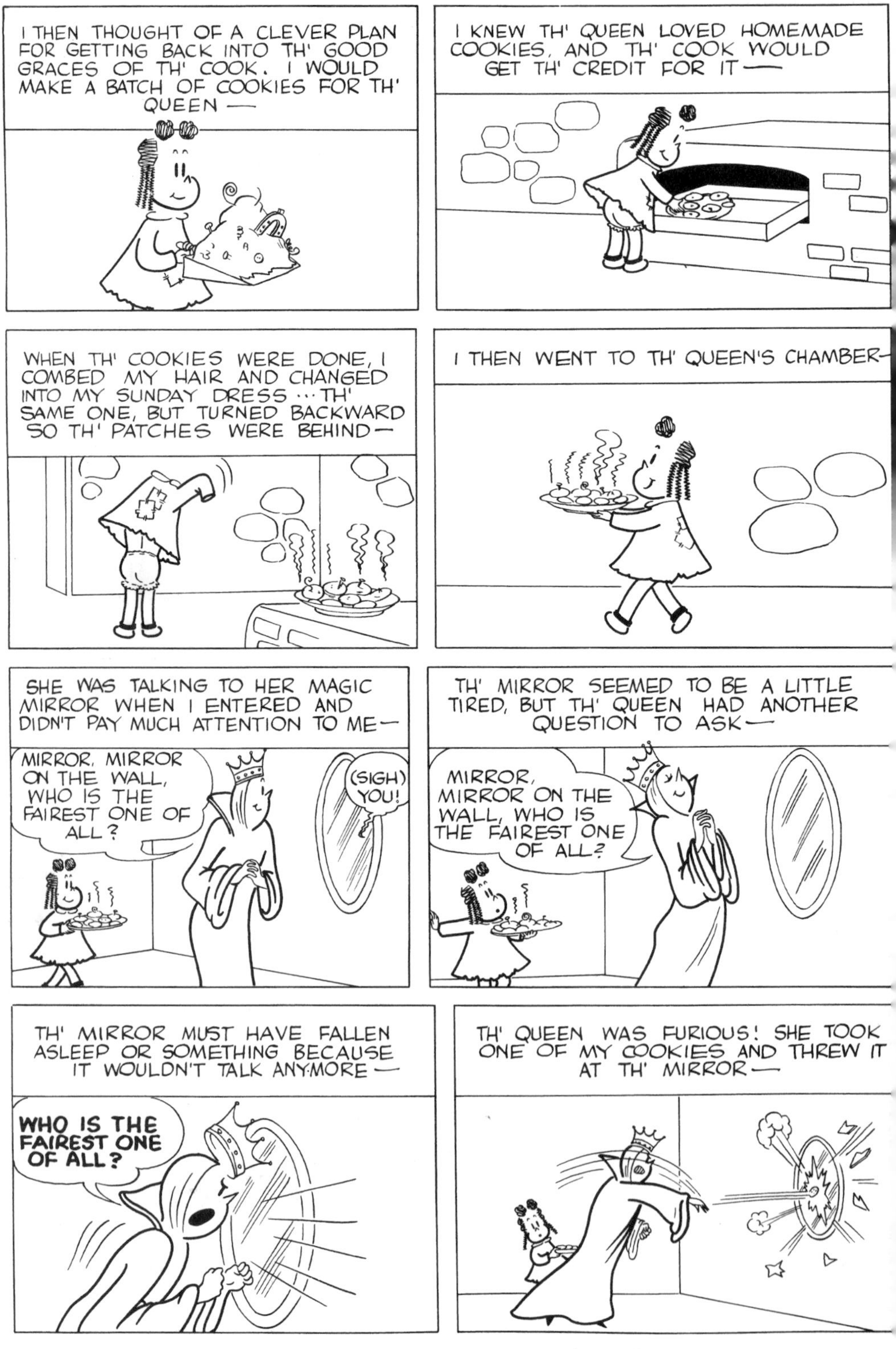
I THEN THOUGHT OF A CLEVER PLAN FOR GETTING BACK INTO TH' GOOD GRACES OF TH' COOK. I WOULD MAKE A BATCH OF COOKIES FOR TH' QUEEN —
I KNEW TH' QUEEN LOVED HOMEMADE COOKIES, AND TH' COOK WOULD GET TH' CREDIT FOR IT —
WHEN TH' COOKIES WERE DONE, I COMBED MY HAIR AND CHANGED INTO MY SUNDAY DRESS ··· TH' SAME ONE, BUT TURNED BACKWARD SO TH' PATCHES WERE BEHIND —
I THEN WENT TO TH' QUEEN'S CHAMBER —
SHE WAS TALKING TO HER MAGIC MIRROR WHEN I ENTERED AND DIDN'T PAY MUCH ATTENTION TO ME —
MIRROR, MIRROR ON THE WALL, WHO IS THE FAIREST ONE OF ALL?
(SIGH) YOU!
TH' MIRROR SEEMED TO BE A LITTLE TIRED, BUT TH' QUEEN HAD ANOTHER QUESTION TO ASK —
MIRROR, MIRROR ON THE WALL, WHO IS THE FAIREST ONE OF ALL?
TH' MIRROR MUST HAVE FALLEN ASLEEP OR SOMETHING BECAUSE IT WOULDN'T TALK ANYMORE —
WHO IS THE FAIREST ONE OF ALL?
TH' QUEEN WAS FURIOUS! SHE TOOK ONE OF MY COOKIES AND THREW IT AT TH' MIRROR —

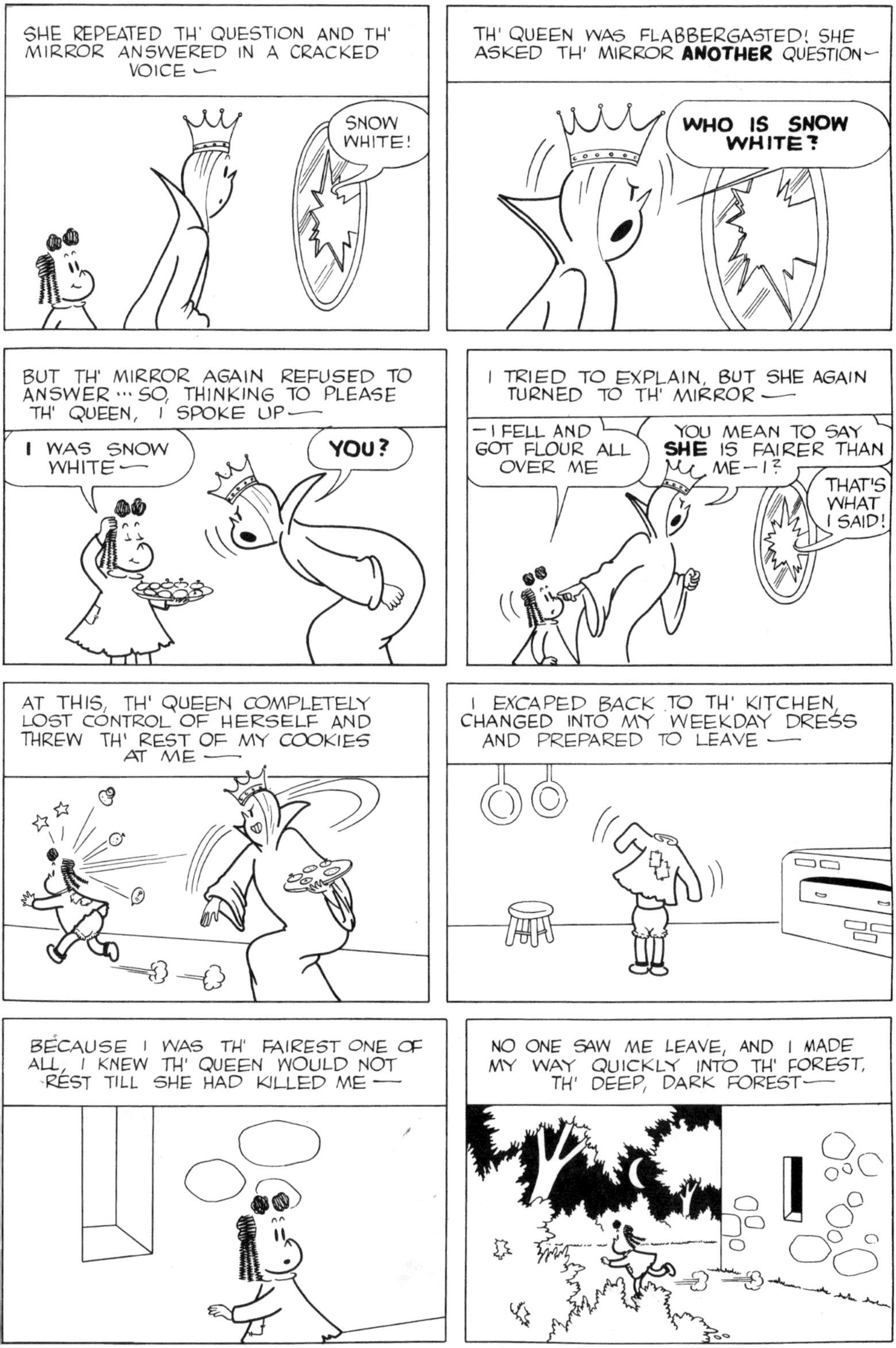

SHE REPEATED TH' QUESTION AND TH' MIRROR ANSWERED IN A CRACKED VOICE —
SNOW WHITE!
TH' QUEEN WAS FLABBERGASTED! SHE ASKED TH' MIRROR ANOTHER QUESTION —
WHO IS SNOW WHITE?
BUT TH' MIRROR AGAIN REFUSED TO ANSWER ··· SO, THINKING TO PLEASE TH' QUEEN, I SPOKE UP —
I WAS SNOW WHITE —
YOU?
I TRIED TO EXPLAIN, BUT SHE AGAIN TURNED TO TH' MIRROR —
— I FELL AND GOT FLOUR ALL OVER ME
YOU MEAN TO SAY SHE IS FAIRER THAN ME — I?
THAT'S WHAT I SAID!
AT THIS, TH' QUEEN COMPLETELY LOST CONTROL OF HERSELF AND THREW TH' REST OF MY COOKIES AT ME —
I EXCAPED BACK TO TH' KITCHEN, CHANGED INTO MY WEEKDAY DRESS AND PREPARED TO LEAVE —
BECAUSE I WAS TH' FAIREST ONE OF ALL, I KNEW TH' QUEEN WOULD NOT REST TILL SHE HAD KILLED ME —
NO ONE SAW ME LEAVE, AND I MADE MY WAY QUICKLY INTO TH' FOREST, TH' DEEP, DARK FOREST —

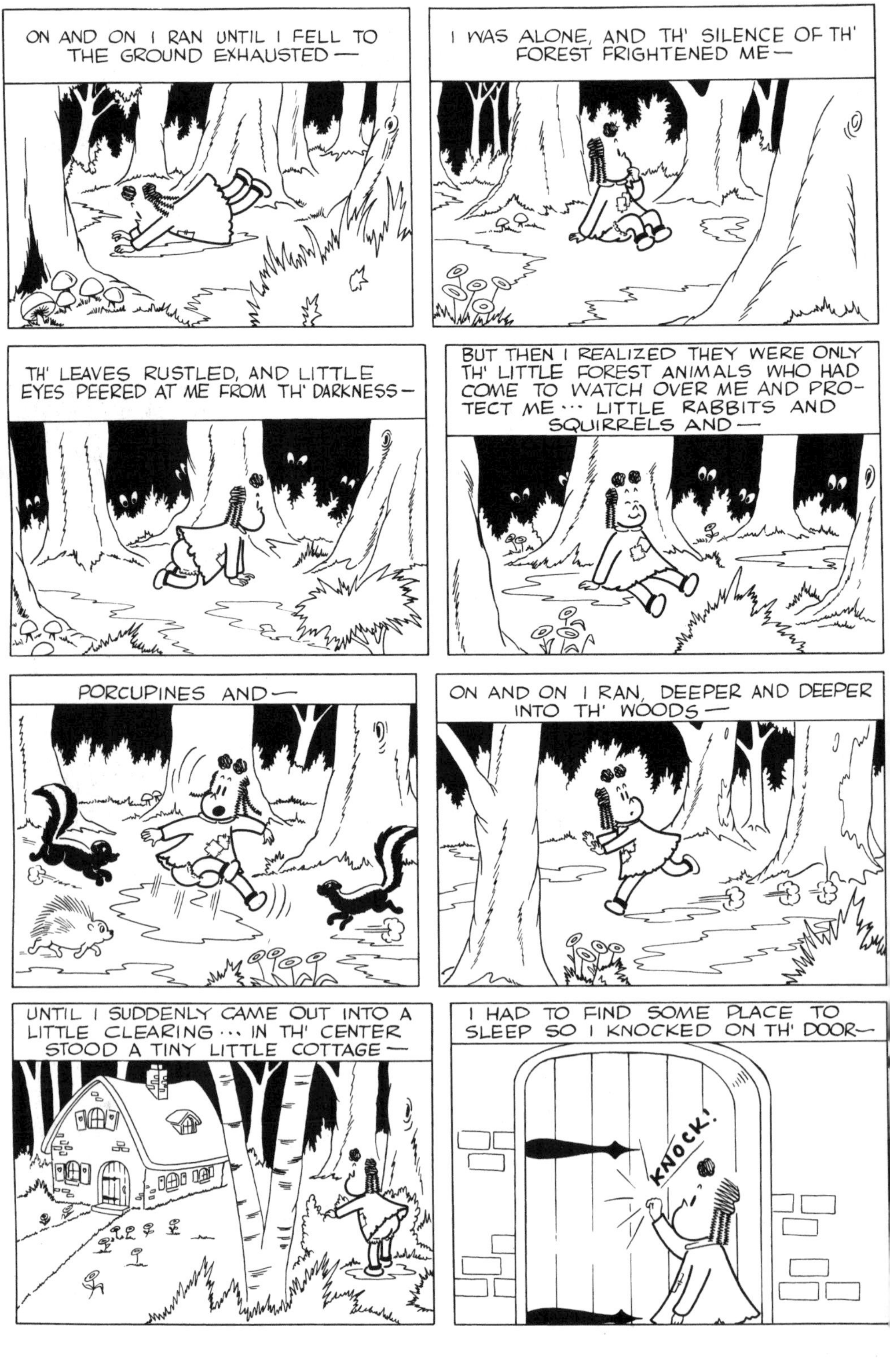
ON AND ON I RAN UNTIL I FELL TO THE GROUND EXHAUSTED—
I WAS ALONE, AND TH' SILENCE OF TH' FOREST FRIGHTENED ME—
TH' LEAVES RUSTLED, AND LITTLE EYES PEERED AT ME FROM TH' DARKNESS—
BUT THEN I REALIZED THEY WERE ONLY TH' LITTLE FOREST ANIMALS WHO HAD COME TO WATCH OVER ME AND PROTECT ME... LITTLE RABBITS AND SQUIRRELS AND—
PORCUPINES AND—
ON AND ON I RAN, DEEPER AND DEEPER INTO TH' WOODS—
UNTIL I SUDDENLY CAME OUT INTO A LITTLE CLEARING... IN TH' CENTER STOOD A TINY LITTLE COTTAGE—
I HAD TO FIND SOME PLACE TO SLEEP SO I KNOCKED ON TH' DOOR—
KNOCK!

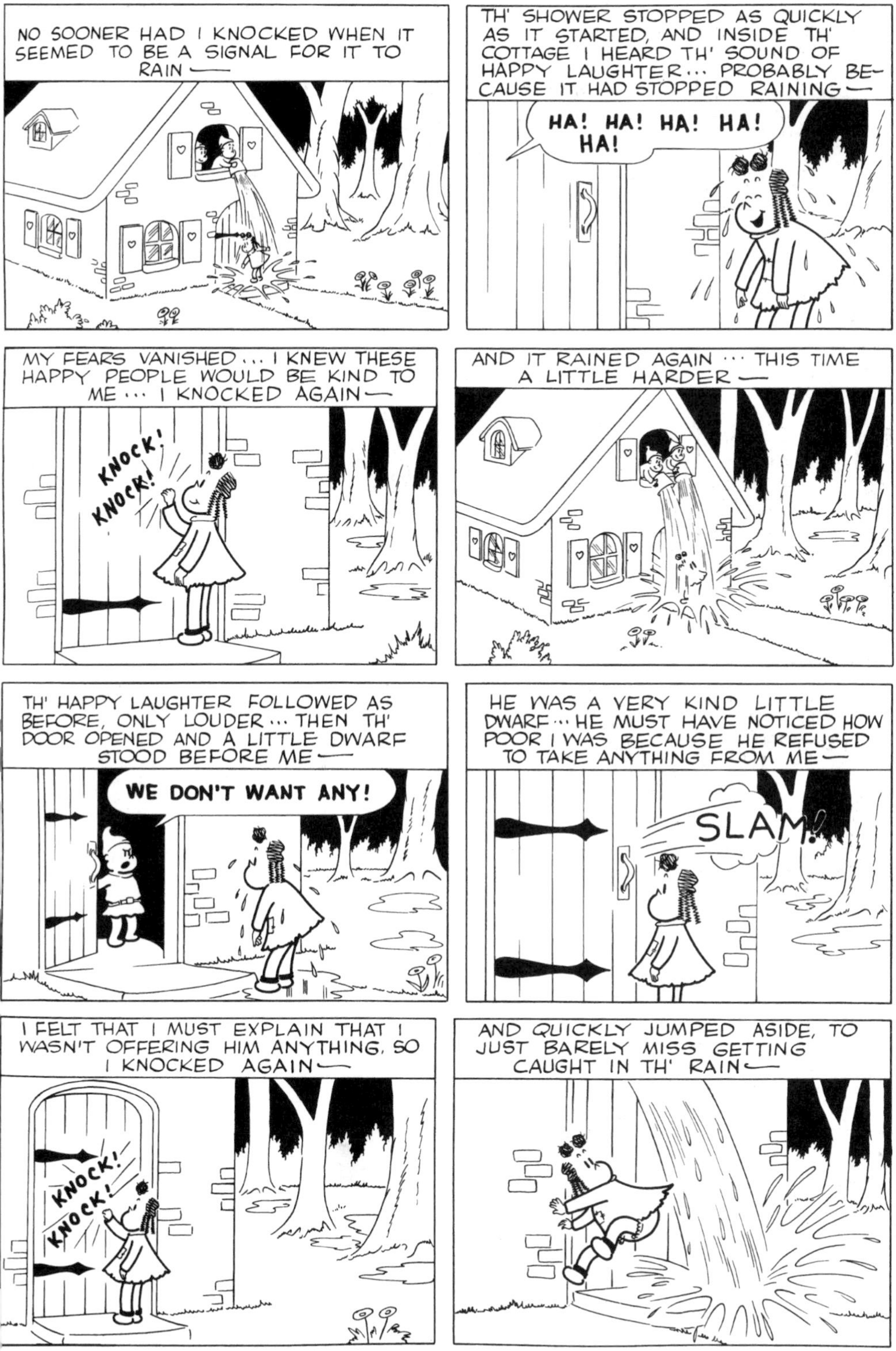

NO SOONER HAD I KNOCKED WHEN IT SEEMED TO BE A SIGNAL FOR IT TO RAIN—
TH' SHOWER STOPPED AS QUICKLY AS IT STARTED, AND INSIDE TH' COTTAGE I HEARD TH' SOUND OF HAPPY LAUGHTER... PROBABLY BE-CAUSE IT HAD STOPPED RAINING—
HA! HA! HA! HA! HA!
MY FEARS VANISHED... I KNEW THESE HAPPY PEOPLE WOULD BE KIND TO ME... I KNOCKED AGAIN—
KNOCK! KNOCK!
AND IT RAINED AGAIN ··· THIS TIME A LITTLE HARDER—
TH' HAPPY LAUGHTER FOLLOWED AS BEFORE, ONLY LOUDER... THEN TH' DOOR OPENED AND A LITTLE DWARF STOOD BEFORE ME—
WE DON'T WANT ANY!
HE WAS A VERY KIND LITTLE DWARF... HE MUST HAVE NOTICED HOW POOR I WAS BECAUSE HE REFUSED TO TAKE ANYTHING FROM ME—
SLAM!
I FELT THAT I MUST EXPLAIN THAT I WASN'T OFFERING HIM ANYTHING, SO I KNOCKED AGAIN—
KNOCK! KNOCK!
AND QUICKLY JUMPED ASIDE, TO JUST BARELY MISS GETTING CAUGHT IN TH' RAIN—

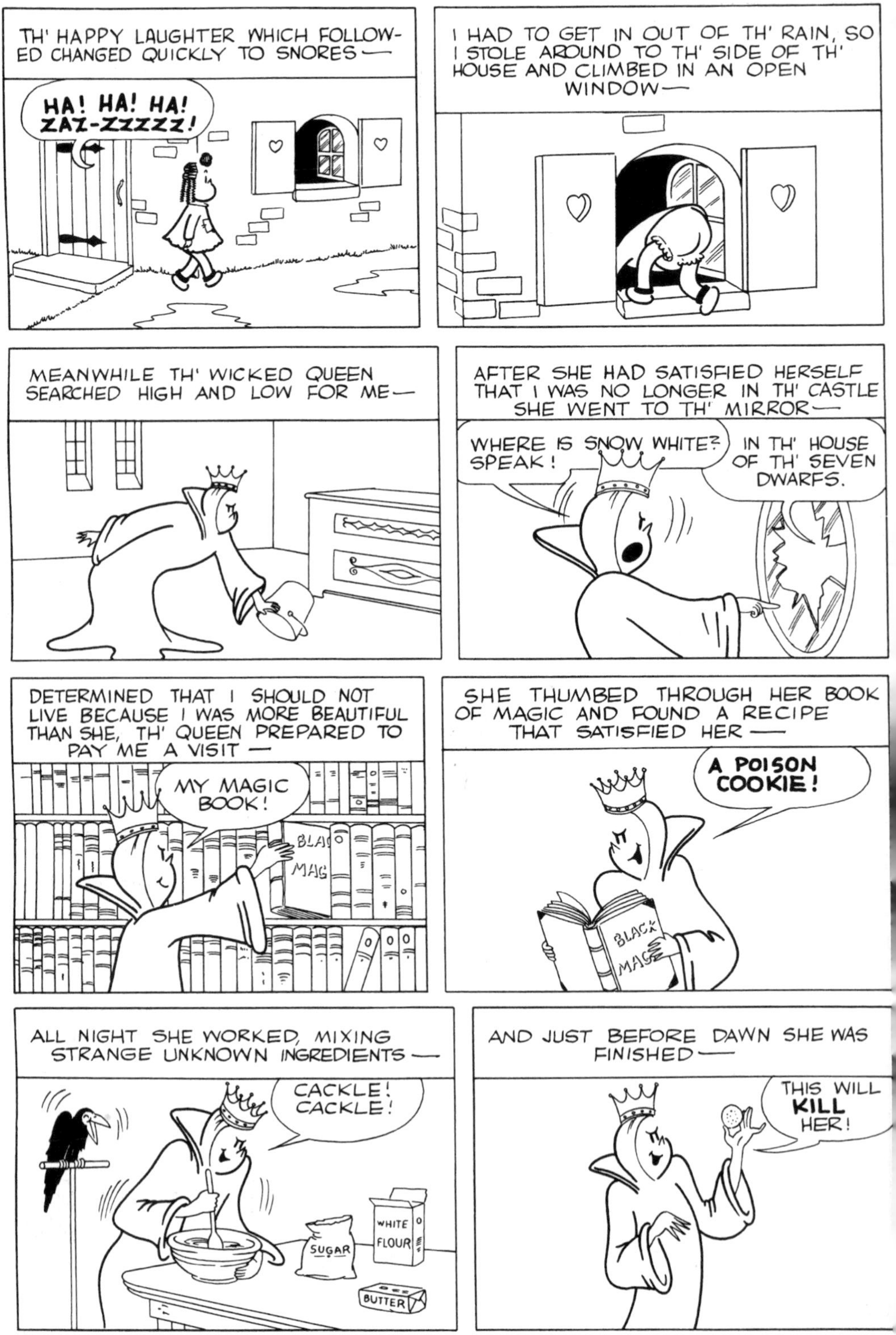
TH' HAPPY LAUGHTER WHICH FOLLOWED CHANGED QUICKLY TO SNORES —
HA! HA! HA! ZAZ-ZZZZZ!
I HAD TO GET IN OUT OF TH' RAIN, SO I STOLE AROUND TO TH' SIDE OF TH' HOUSE AND CLIMBED IN AN OPEN WINDOW —
MEANWHILE TH' WICKED QUEEN SEARCHED HIGH AND LOW FOR ME —
AFTER SHE HAD SATISFIED HERSELF THAT I WAS NO LONGER IN TH' CASTLE SHE WENT TO TH' MIRROR —
WHERE IS SNOW WHITE? SPEAK!
IN TH' HOUSE OF TH' SEVEN DWARFS.
DETERMINED THAT I SHOULD NOT LIVE BECAUSE I WAS MORE BEAUTIFUL THAN SHE, TH' QUEEN PREPARED TO PAY ME A VISIT —
MY MAGIC BOOK!
BLAC
MAG
SHE THUMBED THROUGH HER BOOK OF MAGIC AND FOUND A RECIPE THAT SATISFIED HER —
A POISON COOKIE!
BLACK
MAG
ALL NIGHT SHE WORKED, MIXING STRANGE UNKNOWN INGREDIENTS —
CACKLE! CACKLE!
SUGAR
WHITE FLOUR
BUTTER
AND JUST BEFORE DAWN SHE WAS FINISHED —
THIS WILL **KILL** HER!

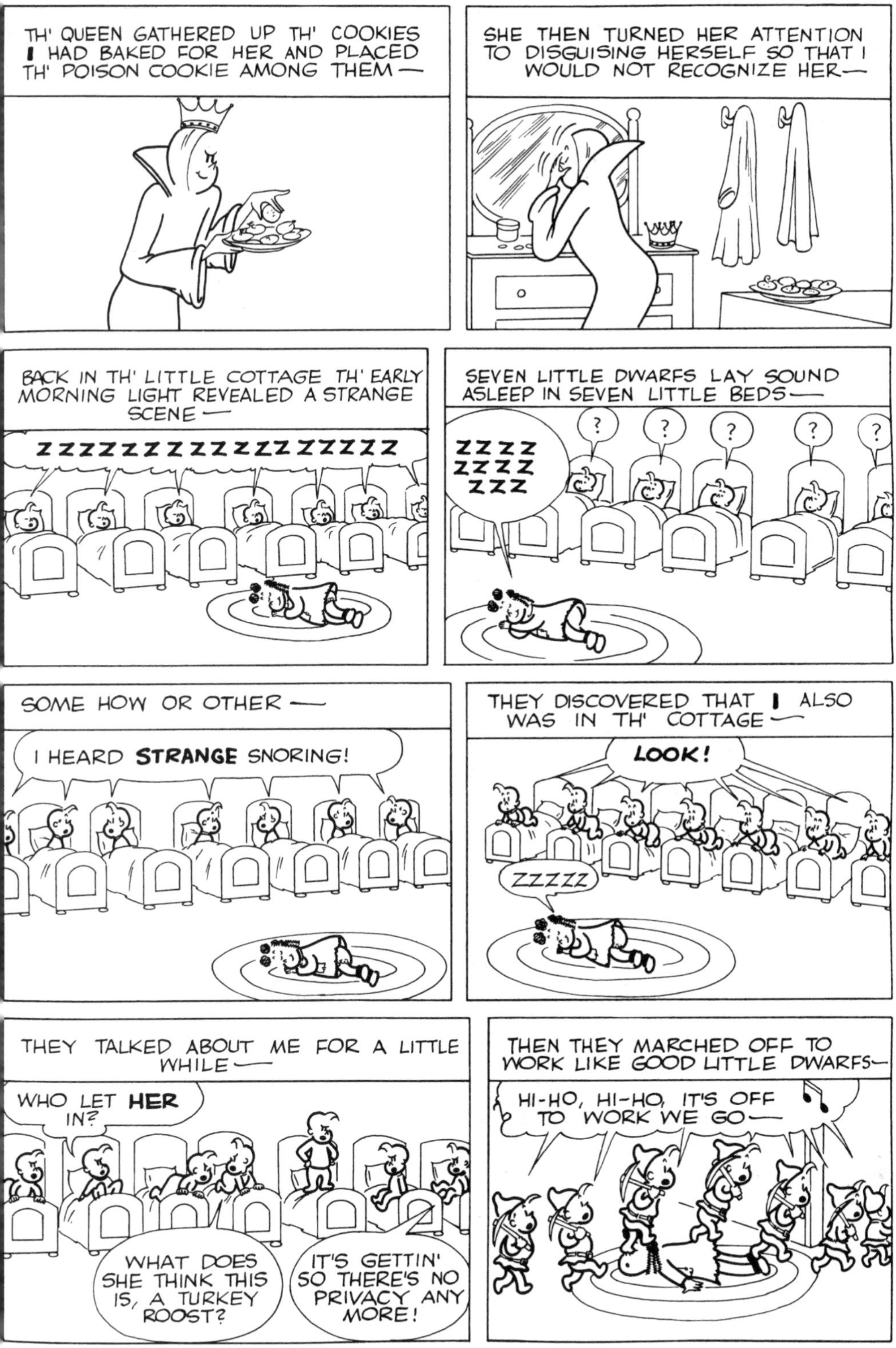
TH' QUEEN GATHERED UP TH' COOKIES I HAD BAKED FOR HER AND PLACED TH' POISON COOKIE AMONG THEM—
SHE THEN TURNED HER ATTENTION TO DISGUISING HERSELF SO THAT I WOULD NOT RECOGNIZE HER—
BACK IN TH' LITTLE COTTAGE TH' EARLY MORNING LIGHT REVEALED A STRANGE SCENE—
ZZZZZZZZZZZZZZZZZZZ
SEVEN LITTLE DWARFS LAY SOUND ASLEEP IN SEVEN LITTLE BEDS—
ZZZZ ZZZZ ZZZ
?
?
?
?
?
SOME HOW OR OTHER—
I HEARD STRANGE SNORING!
THEY DISCOVERED THAT I ALSO WAS IN TH' COTTAGE—
LOOK!
ZZZZZ
THEY TALKED ABOUT ME FOR A LITTLE WHILE—
WHO LET HER IN?
WHAT DOES SHE THINK THIS IS, A TURKEY ROOST?
IT'S GETTIN' SO THERE'S NO PRIVACY ANY MORE!
THEN THEY MARCHED OFF TO WORK LIKE GOOD LITTLE DWARFS—
HI-HO, HI-HO, IT'S OFF TO WORK WE GO—

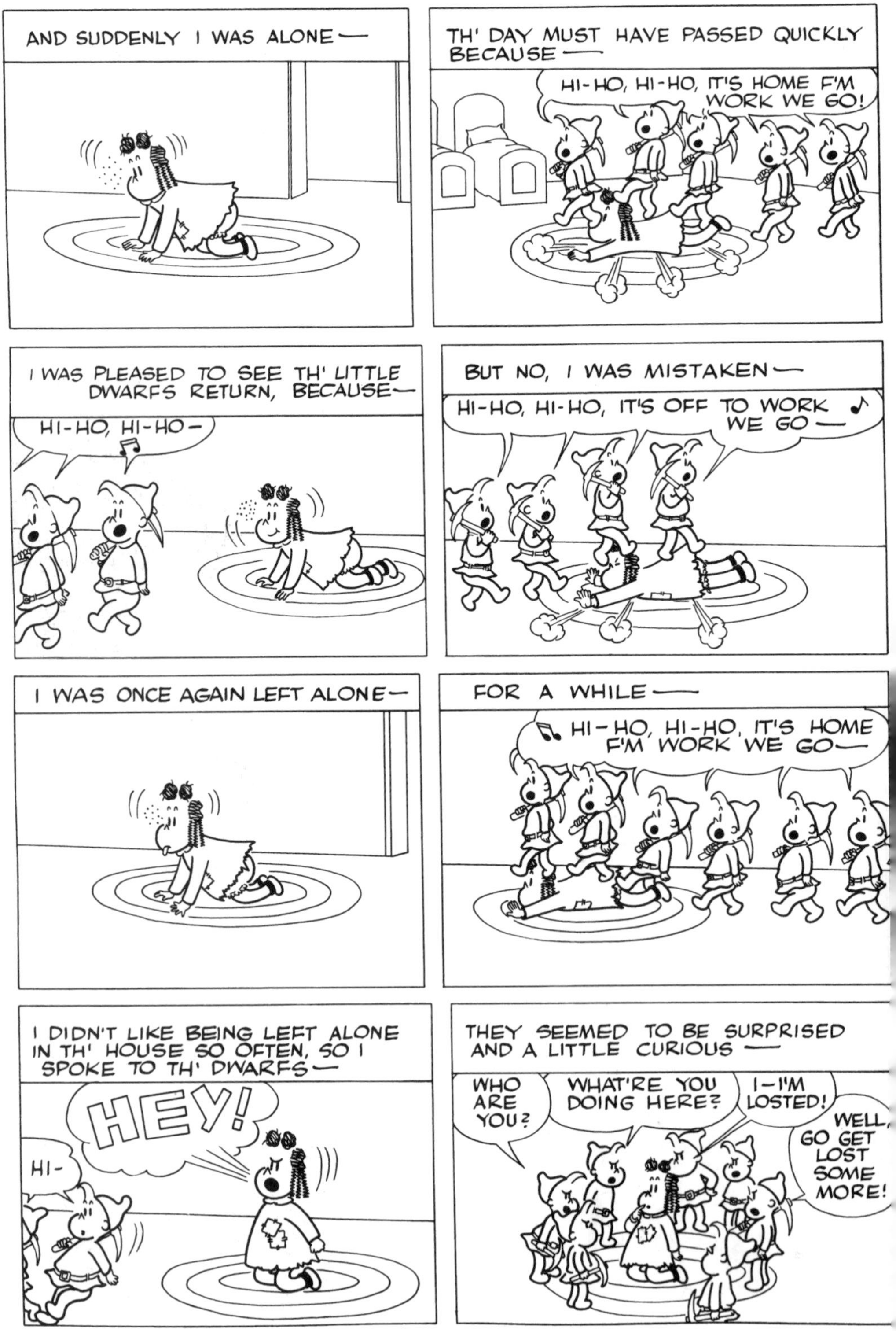
AND SUDDENLY I WAS ALONE—
TH' DAY MUST HAVE PASSED QUICKLY BECAUSE—
HI-HO, HI-HO, IT'S HOME F'M WORK WE GO!
I WAS PLEASED TO SEE TH' LITTLE DWARFS RETURN, BECAUSE—
HI-HO, HI-HO—
BUT NO, I WAS MISTAKEN—
HI-HO, HI-HO, IT'S OFF TO WORK WE GO—
I WAS ONCE AGAIN LEFT ALONE—
FOR A WHILE—
HI-HO, HI-HO, IT'S HOME F'M WORK WE GO—
I DIDN'T LIKE BEING LEFT ALONE IN TH' HOUSE SO OFTEN, SO I SPOKE TO TH' DWARFS—
HEY!
HI-
THEY SEEMED TO BE SURPRISED AND A LITTLE CURIOUS—
WHO ARE YOU?
WHAT'RE YOU DOING HERE?
I—I'M LOSTED!
WELL, GO GET LOST SOME MORE!

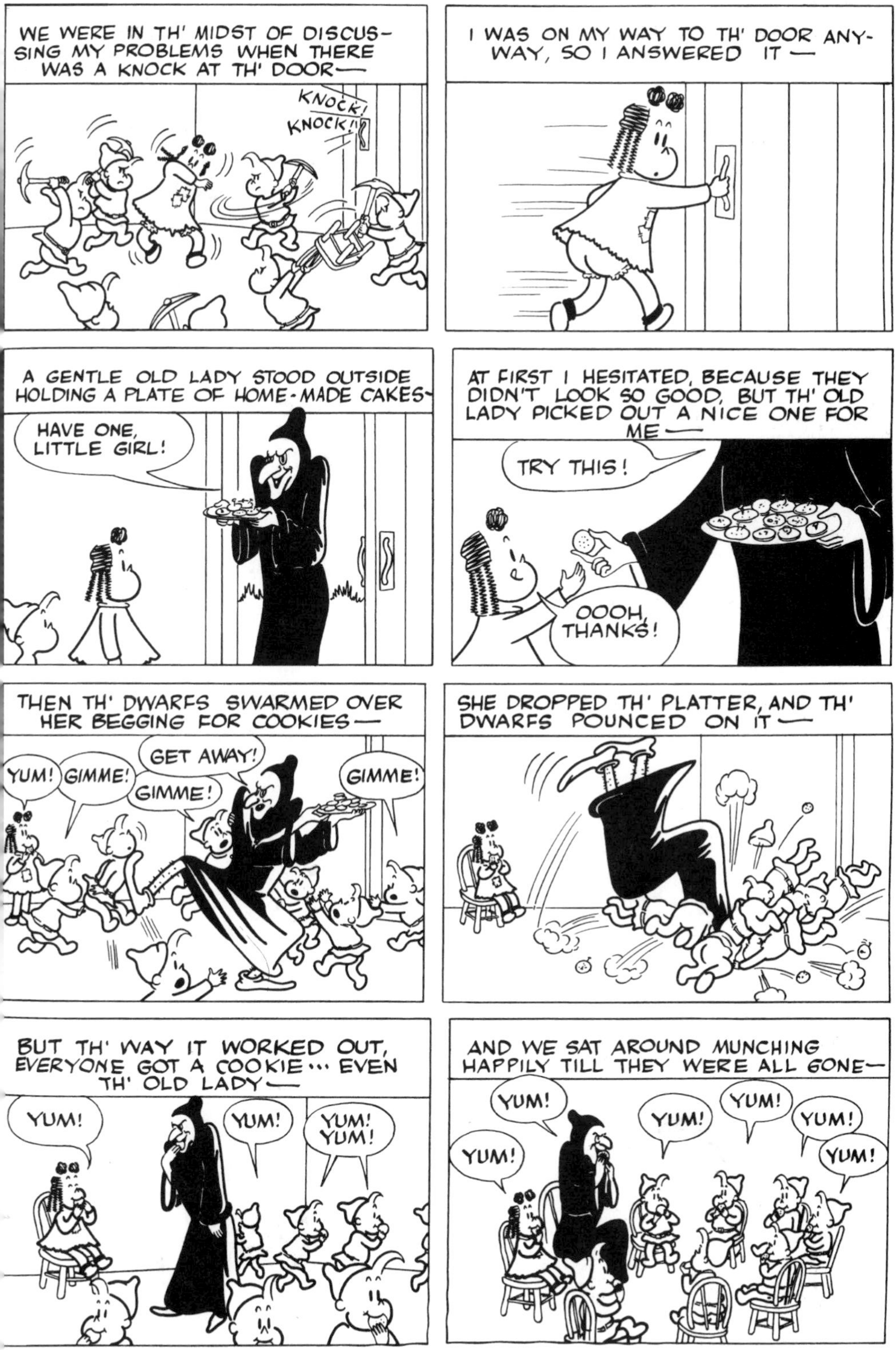
WE WERE IN TH' MIDST OF DISCUSSING MY PROBLEMS WHEN THERE WAS A KNOCK AT TH' DOOR—
KNOCK! KNOCK!
I WAS ON MY WAY TO TH' DOOR ANYWAY, SO I ANSWERED IT—
A GENTLE OLD LADY STOOD OUTSIDE HOLDING A PLATE OF HOME-MADE CAKES—
HAVE ONE, LITTLE GIRL!
AT FIRST I HESITATED, BECAUSE THEY DIDN'T LOOK SO GOOD, BUT TH' OLD LADY PICKED OUT A NICE ONE FOR ME—
TRY THIS!
OOOH, THANKS!
THEN TH' DWARFS SWARMED OVER HER BEGGING FOR COOKIES—
YUM!
GIMME!
GET AWAY!
GIMME!
GIMME!
SHE DROPPED TH' PLATTER, AND TH' DWARFS POUNCED ON IT—
BUT TH' WAY IT WORKED OUT, EVERYONE GOT A COOKIE··· EVEN TH' OLD LADY—
YUM!
YUM!
YUM! YUM!
AND WE SAT AROUND MUNCHING HAPPILY TILL THEY WERE ALL GONE—
YUM!
YUM!
YUM!
YUM!
YUM!
YUM!

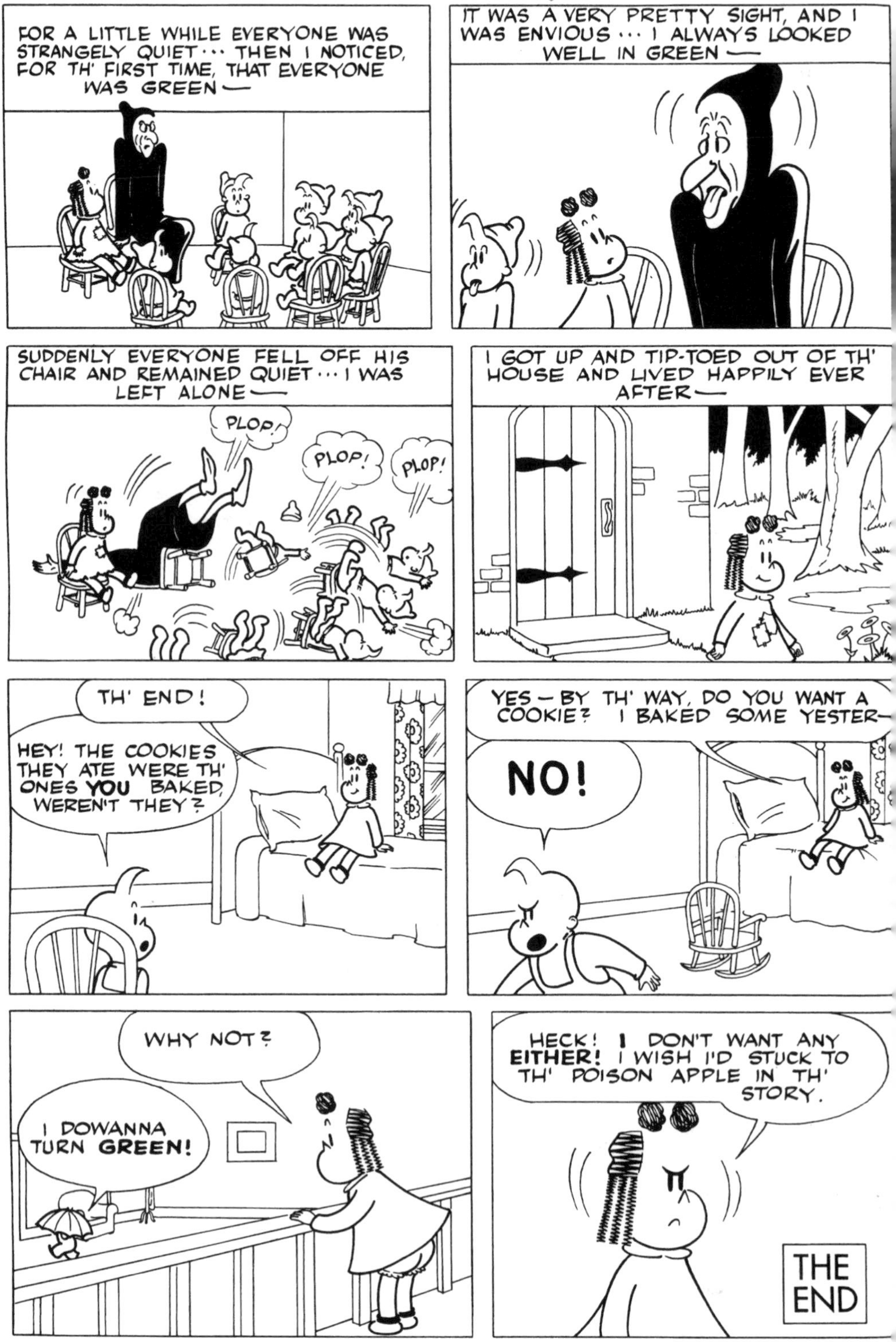
FOR A LITTLE WHILE EVERYONE WAS STRANGELY QUIET··· THEN I NOTICED, FOR TH' FIRST TIME, THAT EVERYONE WAS GREEN—
IT WAS A VERY PRETTY SIGHT, AND I WAS ENVIOUS··· I ALWAYS LOOKED WELL IN GREEN—
SUDDENLY EVERYONE FELL OFF HIS CHAIR AND REMAINED QUIET··· I WAS LEFT ALONE—
PLOP!
PLOP!
PLOP!
I GOT UP AND TIP-TOED OUT OF TH' HOUSE AND LIVED HAPPILY EVER AFTER—
TH' END!
HEY! THE COOKIES THEY ATE WERE TH' ONES **YOU** BAKED, WEREN'T THEY?
YES—BY TH' WAY, DO YOU WANT A COOKIE? I BAKED SOME YESTER—
NO!
WHY NOT?
I DOWANNA TURN **GREEN**!
HECK! **I** DON'T WANT ANY **EITHER**! I WISH I'D STUCK TO TH' POISON APPLE IN TH' STORY.
THE END

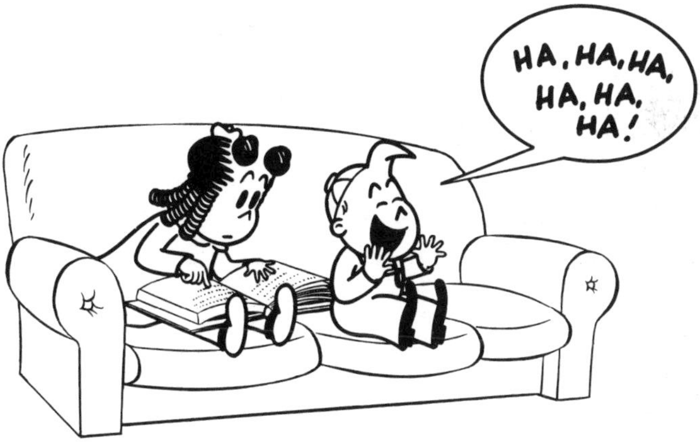
HA, HA, HA, HA, HA, HA!

ALSO AVAILABLE FROM DARK HORSE BOOKS

FROM WALLY WOOD

M.A.R.S. Patrol Total War
Soft cover, 112 pages, Full color
ISBN: 1-59307-262-7 $12.95

FROM RUSS MANNING

Magnus, Robot Fighter Volume 1
Hardcover, 200 pages, Full color
ISBN: 1-59307-269-4 $49.95

Magnus, Robot Fighter Volume 2
Hardcover, 200 pages, Full color
ISBN: 1-59307-290-2 $49.95

Magnus, Robot Fighter Volume 3
Hardcover, 176 pages, Full color
ISBN: 1-59307-339-9 $49.95

Edgar Rice Burroughs' Tarzan of the Apes
Soft cover, 104 pages, Full color
ISBN: 1-56971-416-9 $12.95

Edgar Rice Burroughs' Tarzan and The Jewels of Opar
Soft cover, 80 pages, Full color
ISBN: 1-56971-417-7 $10.95

Edgar Rice Burroughs' Tarzan The Untamed
Soft cover, 96 pageas, Full color
ISBN: 1-56971-418-5 $11.95

Edgar Rice Burroughs' Tarzan in The Land That Time Forgot and The Pool of Time
Soft cover, 104 pages, Full color
ISBN: 1-56971-151-8 $12.95

Classic Star Wars: The Early Adventures TPB
Soft cover, Full color
ISBN: 1-56971-178-X $19.95

FROM FRANK FRAZETTA

Al Capp's Li'l Abner: The Frazetta Years Volume 1 (1954-55) HC
Hard cover, 128 pages, Full color
ISBN: 1-56971-959-4 $18.95

Al Capp's Li'l Abner: The Frazetta Years Volume 2 (1956-57) HC
Hard cover, 128 pages, Full color
ISBN: 1-56971-976-4 $18.95

Al Capp's Li'l Abner: The Frazetta Years Volume 3 (1958-59) HC
Hard cover, 128 pages, Full color
ISBN: 1-56971-977-2 $18.95

Al Capp's Li'l Abner: The Frazetta Years Volume 4 (1960-61) HC
Hard cover, 120 pages, Full color
ISBN: 1-59307-133-7 $18.95

FROM MAC RABOY

Mac Raboy's Flash Gordon Volume 1 TPB
Soft cover, 256 pages, b&w
ISBN: 1-56971-882-2 $19.95

Mac Raboy's Flash Gordon Volume 2 TPB
Soft cover, 256 pages, b&w
ISBN: 1-56971-911-X $19.95

Mac Raboy's Flash Gordon Volume 3 TPB
Soft cover, 256 pages, b&w
ISBN: 1-56971-978-0 $19.95

Mac Raboy's Flash Gordon Volume 4 TPB
Format: Soft cover, 256 pages, b&w
ISBN: 1-56971-979-9 $19.95

Little Lulu ®

Lulu Goes Shopping
ISBN: 1-59307-270-8 / $9.95

Lulu Takes a Trip
ISBN: 1-59307-317-8 / $9.95

My Dinner with Lulu
ISBN: 1-59307-318-6 / $9.95

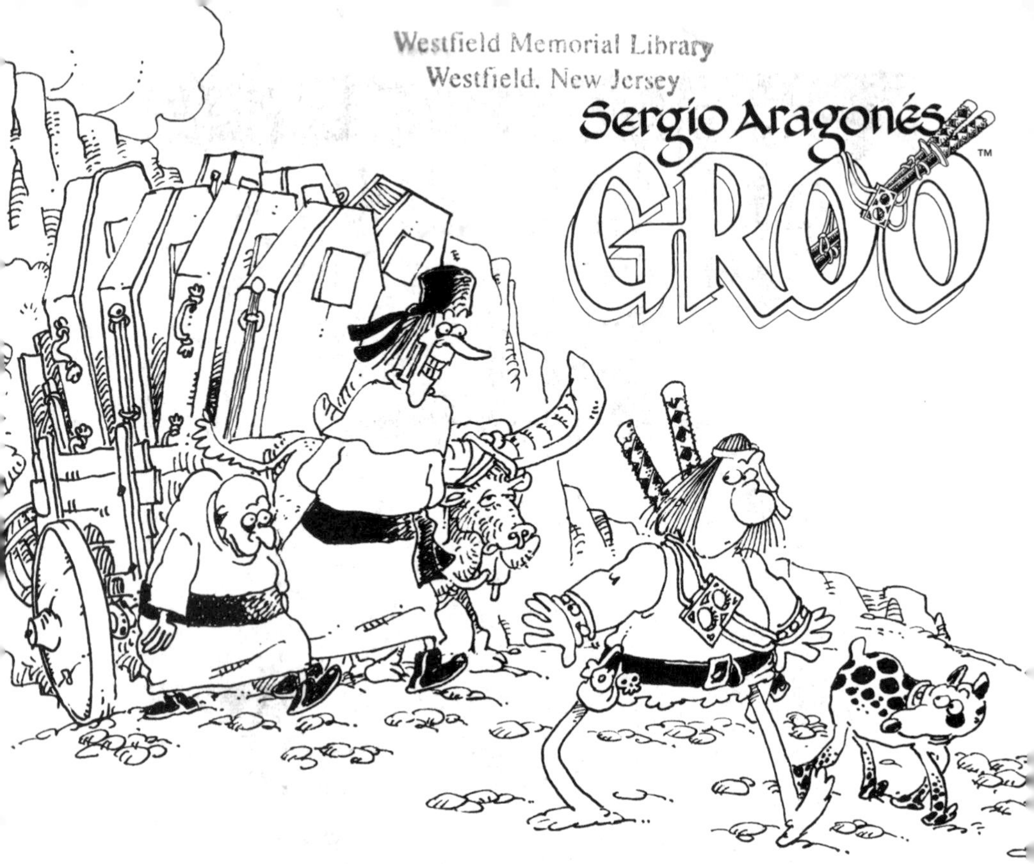
Sergio Aragonés
GROO™

The Groo Houndbook
ISBN: 1-56971-385-5 / $9.95

The Groo Inferno
ISBN: 1-56971-430-4 / $9.95

The Groo Jamboree
ISBN: 1-56971-462-2 / $9.95

The Groo Kingdom
ISBN: 1-56971-478-9 / $9.95

The Groo Library
ISBN: 1-56971-571-8 / $12.95

The Groo Maiden
ISBN: 1-56971-756-7 / $12.95

The Groo Nursery
ISBN: 156971-794-X / $11.95

The Groo Odyssey
ISBN: 1-56971-858-X / $12.95

The Most Intelligent Man in the World
ISBN: 1-56971-294-8 / $9.95

Groo and Rufferto
ISBN: 1-56971-447-9 / $9.95

Mightier than the Sword
ISBN: 1-56971-612-9 / $13.95

Death and Taxes
ISBN: 1-56971-797-4 / $12.95

AVAILABLE AT YOUR LOCAL COMICS SHOP OR BOOKSTORE!

To find a comics shop in your area, call 1-888-266-4226.
For more information or to order direct visit Darkhorse.com or
call 1-800-862-0052 Mon.-Sat. 9 A.M. to 5 P.M. Pacific Time

*Prices and availability subject to change without notice

DARK HORSE BOOKS

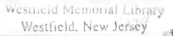

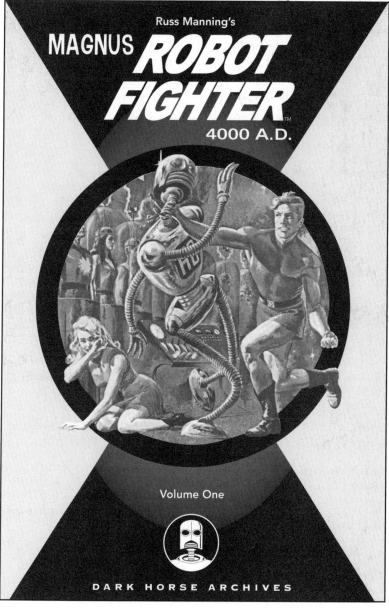

Magnus, Robot Fighter Volume One
ISBN: 1-59307-269-4 / $49.95

Magnus, Robot Fighter Volume Three
ISBN: 1-59307-339-9 / $49.95

Magnus, Robot Fighter Volume Two
ISBN: 1-59307-290-2 / $49.95

TONY MILLIONAIRE'S
SOCK MONKEY™ COLLECTION

Westfield Memorial Library
Westfield, New Jersey

JUL 05

BOOKS

The Adventures of Tony Millionaire's Sock Monkey
1-56971-490-8 $9.95

Tony Millionaire's Sock Monkey A Children's Book
1-56971-549-1 $9.95

The Collected Works of Tony Millionaire's Sock Monkey Volumes 3 and 4
1-59307-098-5 $12.95

Tony Millionaire's Sock Monkey The Glass Doorknob
1-56971-782-6 $14.95

Tony Millionaire's Sock Monkey Uncle Gabby
1-59307-026-8 $14.95

Tony Millionaire's Sock Monkey That Darn Yarn
1-59582-009-4 $7.95

MERCHANDISE

Tony Millionaire's Sock Monkey Journal
1-56971-856-3 $9.99

Tony Millionaire's Sock Monkey Stationery
1-56971-875-X $4.99

Sock Monkey Bendy Toy
1-56971-705-2 $9.99

Sock Monkey Plush
1-56971-708-7 $19.99

Sock Monkey Statue
statue stands 8" tall
item #10-279 $75.00

Sock Monkey Lunch Box (& Postcard)
1-56971-706-0 $14.99

Sock Monkey Zippo® Lighter
item #10-149 $29.99

Sock Monkey Magnet Set
1-56971-707-9 $9.99

Sock Monkey Shot Glass
item #10-134 $6.99

Mr. Crow Shot Glass
item #10-137 $6.99

Sock Monkey T-Shirt
youth tee, white
Small   item #11-191
Medium   item #11-196
Large   item #11-200
X-Large   item #11-203
S-XL $17.99

Sock Monkey T-Shirt
adult tee, white
Medium   item #11-207
Large   item #11-212
X-Large   item #11-216
XX-Large   item #11-220
M-XL $17.99
XXL $19.99

Mr. Crow T-Shirt
youth tee, white
Small   item #11-224
Medium   item #11-228
Large   item #11-231
X-Large   Item #11-234
S-XL $17.99

Mr. Crow T-Shirt
adult tee, white
Medium   item #11-236
Large   item #11-239
X-Large   item #11-242
XX-Large   Item #11-244
M-XL $17.99
XXL $19.99

Sock Monkey Stickers
Sticker #1   item #11-360
Sticker #2   item #11-363
Sticker #3   item #11-366
Sticker #4   item #11-368
all stickers are each $1.99

Tony Millionaire's Maakies: Drinky Crow
comes with interchangeable eyes and a bottle of booze!
1-56971-809-1 $19.99

Uncle Gabby
comes with removable hat and brain!
1-56971-041-1 $24.99

Drinky Crow Coaster Set
item #12-240 $9.99

Tony Millionaire's Sock Monkey™ & © 2005 Tony Millionaire